ENCYCLOPEDIA OF AMERICAN NATIONAL PARKS

EDITED BY HAL K. ROTHMAN AND SARA DANT EWERT

VOLUME TWO

SHARPE REFERENCE

an imprint of M.E. Sharpe, Inc.

SHARPE REFERENCE

Sharpe Reference is an imprint of M.E. Sharpe, Inc.

M.E. Sharpe, Inc.
80 Business Park Drive
Armonk, NY 10504

© 2004 by Hal K. Rothman

Library of Congress Cataloging-in-Publication Data

Rothman, Hal, 1958-
    Encyclopedia of American national parks/Hal K. Rothman, Sara Dant Ewert.
        p. cm.
    Includes bibliographical references and index.
    ISBN 0-7656-8057-2 (cloth : alk. paper)
    1. National parks and reserves—United States—Encyclopedias. 2. Historic sites—United States—Encyclopedias. 3. United States—History, Local—Encyclopedias. 4. United States—Biography. I. Ewert, Sara Dant. II. Title.

E160.R54 2004
973'.03—dc21

2003053985

Printed and bound in the United States

MV (c) 10 9 8 7 6 5 4 3 2 1

Publisher: Myron E. Sharpe
Vice President and Editorial Director: Patricia Kolb
Vice President and Production Director: Carmen Chetti
Executive Editor and Manager of Reference: Todd Hallman
Project Editor: Laura Brengelman
Editorial Assistant: Cathleen Prisco
Cover and Text Design: Jesse Sanchez

CONTENTS

VOLUME 2

PARKS BY STATE AND TERRITORY

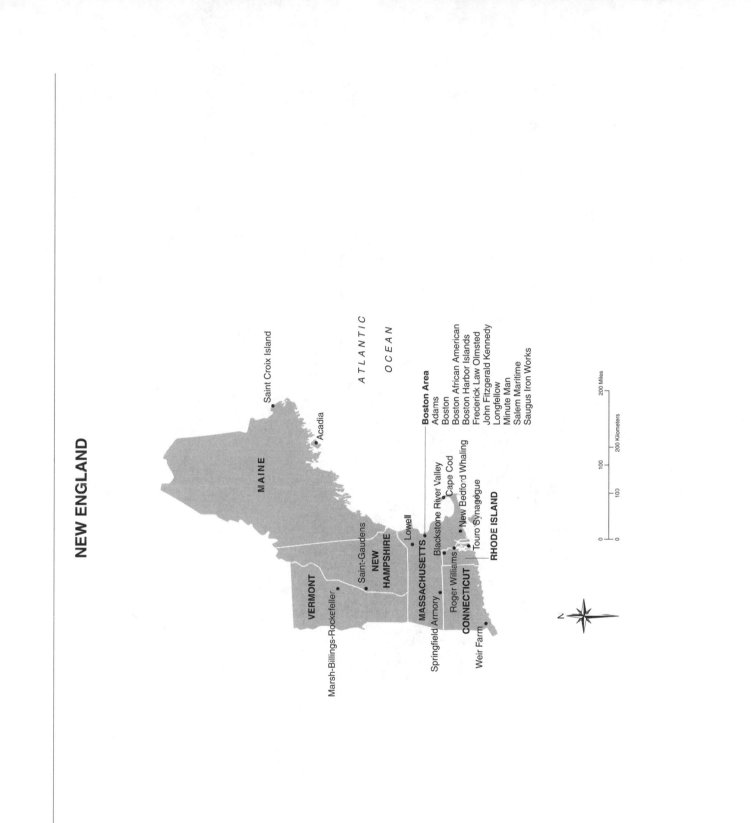

NEW ENGLAND

Saint Croix Island

Acadia

MAINE

ATLANTIC
OCEAN

Marsh-Billings-Rockefeller

VERMONT

Saint-Gaudens

NEW
HAMPSHIRE

Lowell

Springfield Armory

MASSACHUSETTS

Blackstone River Valley

Cape Cod

Roger Williams

New Bedford Whaling

CONNECTICUT

Touro Synagogue

RHODE ISLAND

Weir Farm

Boston Area
Adams
Boston
Boston African American
Boston Harbor Islands
Frederick Law Olmsted
John Fitzgerald Kennedy
Longfellow
Minute Man
Salem Maritime
Saugus Iron Works

N

0   100   200 Miles

0   100   200 Kilometers

MID-ATLANTIC

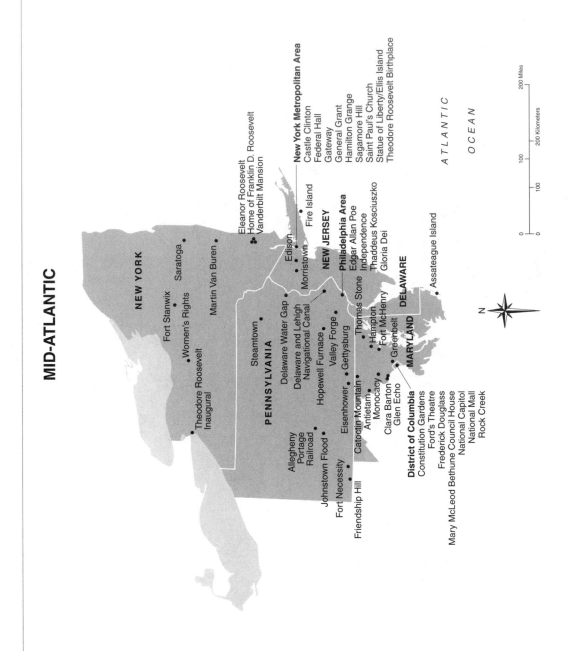

NEW YORK

Fort Stanwix
Saratoga
Women's Rights
Martin Van Buren
Theodore Roosevelt Inaugural

Eleanor Roosevelt
Home of Franklin D. Roosevelt
Vanderbilt Mansion

Edison
Fire Island

NEW JERSEY

Morristown

New York Metropolitan Area
Castle Clinton
Federal Hall
Gateway
General Grant
Hamilton Grange
Sagamore Hill
Saint Paul's Church
Statue of Liberty/Ellis Island
Theodore Roosevelt Birthplace

Philadelphia Area
Edgar Allan Poe
Independence
Thaddeus Kosciuszko
Gloria Dei

PENNSYLVANIA

Steamtown
Delaware Water Gap
Delaware and Lehigh Navigational Canal
Hopewell Furnace
Valley Forge
Gettysburg

Allegheny Portage Railroad
Johnstown Flood
Fort Necessity
Friendship Hill
Eisenhower
Catoctin Mountain
Antietam
Monocacy
Clara Barton
Glen Echo

Thomas Stone
Hampton
Fort McHenry
Greenbelt

DELAWARE

MARYLAND

District of Columbia
Constitution Gardens
Ford's Theatre
Frederick Douglass
Mary McLeod Bethune Council House
National Capitol
National Mall
Rock Creek

Assateague Island

ATLANTIC

OCEAN

N

200 Miles

200 Kilometers

100

100

0

0

THE SOUTH

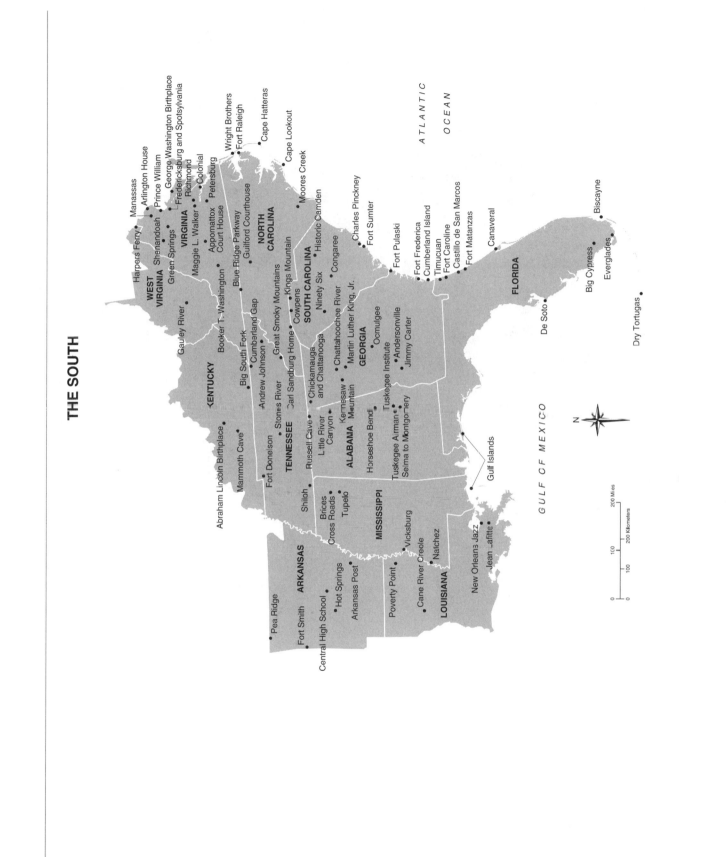

ATLANTIC OCEAN

GULF OF MEXICO

WEST VIRGINIA
Harpers Ferry
Manassas
Arlington House
Prince William
George Washington Birthplace
Fredericksburg and Spotsylvania
Richmond
Colonial
Petersburg
Wright Brothers
Fort Raleigh
Cape Hatteras
Cape Lookout

VIRGINIA
Shenandoah
Green Springs
Maggie L. Walker
Appomattox Court House
Blue Ridge Parkway
Guilford Courthouse
Moores Creek

NORTH CAROLINA

Gauley River
Booker T. Washington
Cumberland Gap
Great Smoky Mountains
Kings Mountain
Ninety Six
Historic Camden
Congaree
Charles Pinckney
Fort Sumter

KENTUCKY
Big South Fork
Andrew Johnson
Stones River
Carl Sandburg Home
Cowpens

SOUTH CAROLINA

Abraham Lincoln Birthplace
Mammoth Cave
Fort Donelson
Little River Canyon
Russell Cave
Chickamauga and Chattanooga
Chattahoochee River
Martin Luther King, Jr.

TENNESSEE

Shiloh
Brices Cross Roads
Tupelo

Kennesaw Mountain
Horseshoe Bend
Tuskegee Institute
Ocmulgee
Andersonville
Jimmy Carter

GEORGIA

ALABAMA
Tuskegee Airmen
Selma to Montgomery

Fort Pulaski
Fort Frederica
Cumberland Island
Timucuan
Fort Caroline
Castillo de San Marcos
Fort Matanzas
Canaveral

FLORIDA
Biscayne
Big Cypress
Everglades
De Soto
Dry Tortugas

Pea Ridge
Fort Smith
Central High School
Hot Springs
Arkansas Post

ARKANSAS

Poverty Point
Cane River Creole
Natchez
Vicksburg

MISSISSIPPI

LOUISIANA
New Orleans Jazz
Jean Lafitte
Gulf Islands

N

Miles
200
100
0

200 Kilometers
100
0

xxi

THE SOUTHWEST

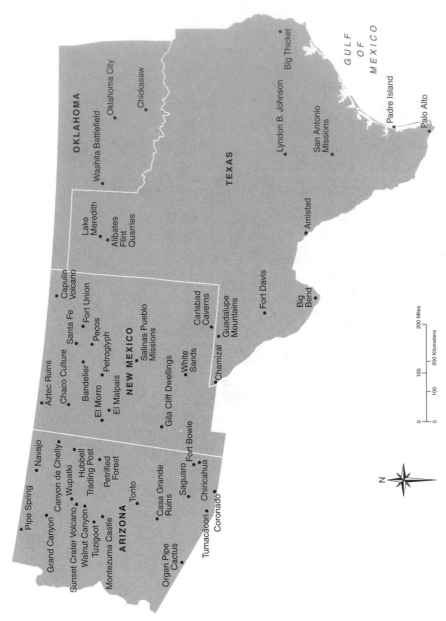

ARIZONA

Pipe Spring
Grand Canyon
Navajo
Canyon de Chelly
Sunset Crater Volcano
Wupatki
Walnut Canyon
Hubbell Trading Post
Tuzigoot
Petrified Forest
Montezuma Castle
Tonto
Casa Grande Ruins
Saguaro
Fort Bowie
Chiricahua
Organ Pipe Cactus
Tumacácori
Coronado

NEW MEXICO

Aztec Ruins
Chaco Culture
Santa Fe
Capulin Volcano
Bandelier
Fort Union
El Morro
Petroglyph
Pecos
El Malpais
Salinas Pueblo Missions
Gila Cliff Dwellings
White Sands
Chamizal
Carlsbad Caverns
Guadalupe Mountains

OKLAHOMA

Washita Battlefield
Oklahoma City
Chickasaw

Lake Meredith
Alibates Flint Quarries

TEXAS

Fort Davis
Big Bend
Amistad
Lyndon B. Johnson
San Antonio Missions
Big Thicket
Padre Island
Palo Alto

GULF OF MEXICO

N

0   100   200 Miles
0   100   200 Kilometers

THE MIDWEST

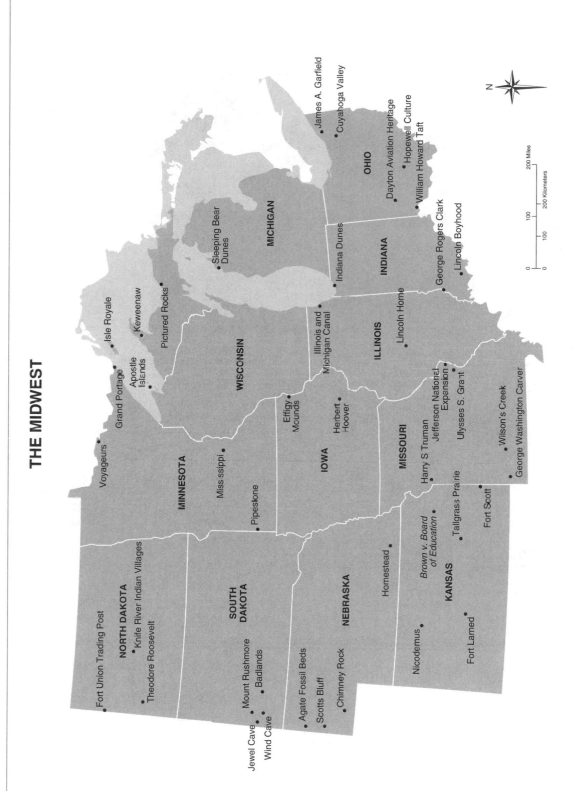

NORTH DAKOTA
- Fort Union Trading Post
- Knife River Indian Villages
- Theodore Roosevelt

SOUTH DAKOTA
- Mount Rushmore
- Badlands
- Jewel Cave
- Wind Cave

MINNESOTA
- Voyageurs
- Grand Portage
- Mississippi
- Pipestone

WISCONSIN
- Apostle Islands
- Isle Royale
- Keweenaw
- Pictured Rocks

MICHIGAN
- Sleeping Bear Dunes

OHIO
- James A. Garfield
- Cuyahoga Valley
- Dayton Aviation Heritage
- Hopewell Culture
- William Howard Taft

INDIANA
- Indiana Dunes
- George Rogers Clark
- Lincoln Boyhood

ILLINOIS
- Illinois and Michigan Canal
- Lincoln Home

IOWA
- Effigy Mounds
- Herbert Hoover

MISSOURI
- Jefferson National Expansion
- Ulysses S. Grant
- Harry S Truman
- Wilson's Creek
- George Washington Carver

NEBRASKA
- Agate Fossil Beds
- Scotts Bluff
- Chimney Rock
- Homestead

KANSAS
- Nicodemus
- Brown v. Board of Education
- Tallgrass Prairie
- Fort Scott
- Fort Larned

N

200 Miles
100   200 Kilometers
0   100   200

xxiii

THE WEST

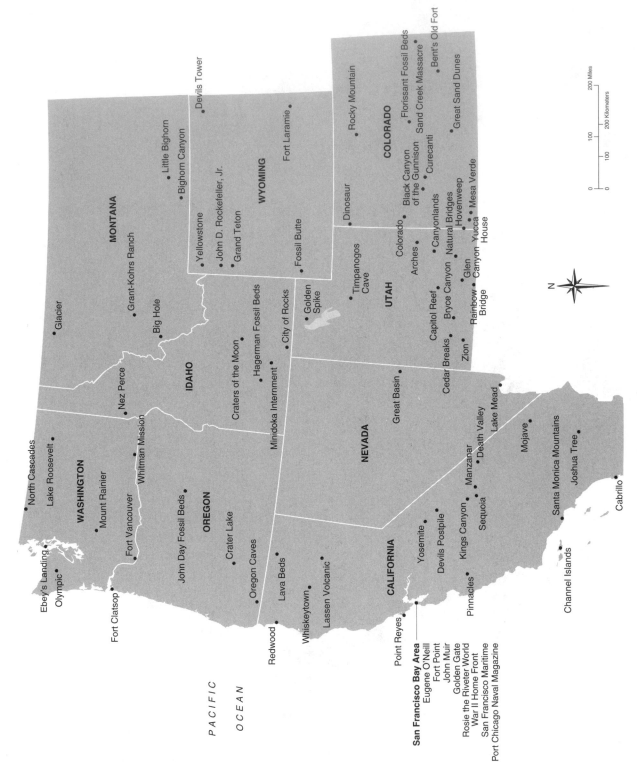

PACIFIC

OCEAN

WASHINGTON

Ebey's Landing
Olympic
North Cascades
Lake Roosevelt
Mount Rainier
Fort Vancouver
Fort Clatsop

OREGON

John Day Fossil Beds
Crater Lake
Oregon Caves
Whitman Mission

CALIFORNIA

Redwood
Whiskeytown
Lava Beds
Lassen Volcanic
Point Reyes
Yosemite
Devils Postpile
Kings Canyon
Sequoia
Pinnacles
Manzanar
Death Valley
Mojave
Santa Monica Mountains
Joshua Tree
Channel Islands
Cabrillo

San Francisco Bay Area
Eugene O'Neill
Fort Point
John Muir
Golden Gate
Rosie the Riveter World
War II Home Front
San Francisco Maritime
Port Chicago Naval Magazine

NEVADA

Great Basin
Lake Mead

IDAHO

Nez Perce
Craters of the Moon
Hagerman Fossil Beds
Minidoka Internment
City of Rocks

MONTANA

Glacier
Grant-Kohrs Ranch
Big Hole
Little Bighorn
Bighorn Canyon

WYOMING

Devils Tower
Yellowstone
John D. Rockefeller, Jr.
Grand Teton
Fort Laramie
Fossil Butte

UTAH

Golden Spike
Timpanogos Cave
Capitol Reef
Cedar Breaks
Zion
Bryce Canyon
Arches
Canyonlands
Natural Bridges
Glen Canyon
Rainbow Bridge
Hovenweep

COLORADO

Dinosaur
Rocky Mountain
Florissant Fossil Beds
Sand Creek Massacre
Bent's Old Fort
Great Sand Dunes
Curecanti
Colorado
Black Canyon of the Gunnison
Yucca House
Mesa Verde

N

0   100   200 Miles

0   100   200 Kilometers

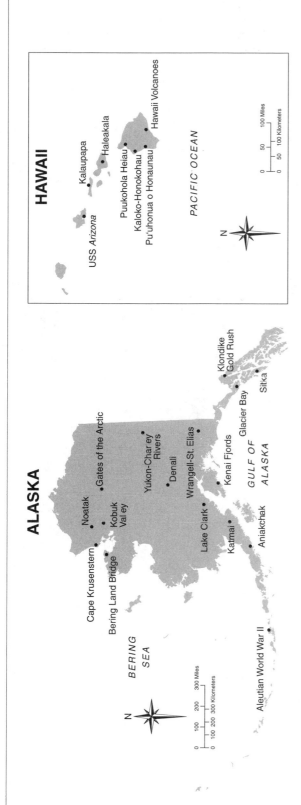

HAWAII

Kalaupapa

Haleakala

Puukohola Heiau
Kaloko-Honokohau
Pu'uhonua o Honaunau

Hawaii Volcanoes

USS *Arizona*

PACIFIC OCEAN

N

| 0 | 50 | 100 Miles |

| 0 | 50 | 100 Kilometers |

ALASKA

Gates of the Arctic

Yukon-Charley
Rivers

Denali

Noatak

Kobuk
Valley

Wrangell-St. Elias

Cape Krusenstern

Lake Clark

Kenai Fjords

Glacier Bay

Klondike
Gold Rush

Sitka

Katmai

Aniakchak

*GULF OF
ALASKA*

Bering Land Bridge

*BERING
SEA*

N

| 0 | 100 | 200 | 300 Miles |

| 0 | 100 | 200 | 300 Kilometers |

Aleutian World War II

UNITED STATES TERRITORIES

NORTHERN MARIANA ISLANDS

FARALLON DE PAJAROS

MAUG ISLANDS

ASUNCION ISLAND

AGRIHAN

PAGAN

ALAMAGAN

GUGUAN

SARIGAN

ANATAHAN

FARALLON DE MEDINILLA

PHILIPPINE SEA

NORTH PACIFIC OCEAN

See inset at right.

SAIPAN

TINIAN

AGUIJAN

ROTA

GUAM

War in the Pacific

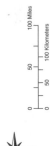

PHILIPPINE SEA

NORTH PACIFIC OCEAN

American Memorial

SAIPAN

0   50   100 Miles

0   50   100 Kilometers

N

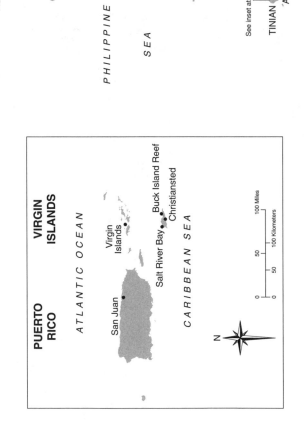

PUERTO RICO   VIRGIN ISLANDS

ATLANTIC OCEAN

Virgin Islands

Buck Island Reef

Salt River Bay

Christiansted

San Juan

CARIBBEAN SEA

0   50   100 Miles

0   50   100 Kilometers

N

ENCYCLOPEDIA OF AMERICAN NATIONAL PARKS

VOLUME TWO

I

ILLINOIS AND MICHIGAN CANAL NATIONAL HERITAGE CORRIDOR

Location: Lockport, Illinois
Acreage: not applicable
Established: August 24, 1984

When completed in 1848, the Illinois and Michigan Canal joined Lake Michigan with the Illinois River at La Salle, forming the final transportation link between the Atlantic Ocean and the Gulf of Mexico. As it penetrated northern Illinois, the 97-mile canal not only played an important role in America's westward expansion, but played a crucial role in the transformation of Chicago from a small settlement into a critical transportation hub between the East and the developing Midwest.

Regional American Indian tribes such as the Miami and Potawatomi had used the area around the canal for a portage to Lake Michigan centuries before French explorers Louis Jolliet and Father Jacques Marquette arrived in 1673. By the late 1700s, trade and commerce over this portage had increased so much that a shipping canal was deemed necessary. Although construction on the canal began in 1836, financial difficulties delayed its completion until 1848. Roughly following the Des Plaines and Illinois rivers, engineers designed the canal to be 6 feet deep and 60 feet wide along a 97-mile right-of-way. Fifteen locks allowed the lifting or lowering of boats and barges. After its completion, increased commerce sparked the growth of Chicago and by the 1850s, it surpassed St. Louis as the Midwest's largest center of population and commerce. Other communities located adjacent to or near the canal, including Joliet, La Salle, and Peru, also prospered.

After the Civil War, the canal's importance diminished. The expansion of efficient, faster railroad networks captured most of the commercial and passenger traffic that had once relied on the slower canal. Although the surrounding area continued to develop, by 1900, the canal had been abandoned. In 1984, as a result of an active citizenry that sought its preservation, Congress designated this region as the Illinois and Michigan Canal National Heritage Corridor. The first national heritage corridor and the first in a series of "partnership parks," the Corridor incorporates state and local parks, historic sites (including the Chicago Portage National Historic Site), museums, and a wide variety of recreational facilities. While it encompasses a large segment of the state's industrial heartland, much of the corridor's landscape is rural and wooded. The National Park Service does not operate any facilities within the Corridor. Hours and days of operation at the numerous parks, historic sites, and other visitor attractions remain fairly constant year-round, and they are set by each managing entity.

There are no admission fees to the Corridor nor to most of the parks and historic sites contained within. The main Illinois and Michigan (I&M) Canal Visitor Center in Lockport is open all year from 10 A.M. until 5 P.M., but is closed on Mondays. The center has a Hands-On History gallery on the second floor where students, families, and researchers can explore the connections between the I&M Canal and local, regional, and national history. The "Illinois Passageway" gallery on the ground floor introduces the

Corridor to visitors, and various exhibits focus on historical topics. The Illinois Waterway Visitor Center, just outside of Utica across from Starved Rock State Park, is open all year from 9 A.M. until 5 P.M., and it offers guided tours of the Starved Rock Lock and Dam on summer weekends. From January to March, visitors can participate in an area-wide "Flock to the Rock" program, which encourages people to watch the bald eagles that come to spend the winter near the dam. There are five other small visitor centers/museums located within the Corridor: Isle a la Cache in Romeoville, Will County Historical Society Museum in Lockport, Will-Joliet Bicentennial Park in Joliet, Little Red Schoolhouse Nature Center in Willow Springs, and the Goose Lake Prairie State Natural Area in Morris.

Hiking and biking opportunities abound within the Corridor. The I&M Canal State Trail is a 61-mile trail from Rockdale (on Joliet's southwest side) to Peru. Hiking trails are also available at Matthiessen, Starved Rock, Buffalo Rock, Illini, and Goose Lake Prairie State Parks. The Forest Preserve Districts of Cook, DuPage, and Will counties have hiking trails of varying lengths as well. Canoeing is also a popular Corridor activity. A 23-mile canoe trail exists on the Des Plaines River between Lyons and Lockport, and there is a 15-mile trail on the I&M Canal between Channahon and Morris. Visitors can also canoe the 5 miles on the I&M Canal between Utica and Peru.

Towns and cities in or near the Corridor offer all traveler services. The historic Starved Rock Lodge (800-868-ROCK) is a full resort facility, which also has a handful of cabins available for overnight stays. Developed campgrounds are available at Starved Rock State Park southwest of LaSalle, Illini State Park near Marseilles, and Des Plaines Conservation Area south of Channahon. Limited walk-in or backpack tent-camping sites are also available along the Illinois and Michigan Canal State Trail. All camping facilities charge fees.

For more information, write Illinois and Michigan Canal National Heritage Corridor, 15701 South Independence Boulevard, Lockport, IL 60441, or telephone (815) 588-6040. The park's informative Web site is www.nps.gov/ilmi.

FURTHER READING

Conzen, Michael P., and Kay J. Carr, eds. *The Illinois and Michigan Canal National Heritage Corridor: A Guide to Its History and Sources.* DeKalb: Northern Illinois University Press, 1988.

Ranney, Edward. *Prairie Passage: The Illinois and Michigan Canal Corridor.* Urbana: University of Illinois Press, 1998.

Redd, Jim. *The Illinois and Michigan Canal: A Contemporary Perspective in Essays and Photographs.* Carbondale: Southern Illinois University Press, 1993.

INDEPENDENCE NATIONAL HISTORICAL PARK

Location: Philadelphia, Pennsylvania
Acreage: 45
Established: June 28, 1948

Philadelphia was the birthplace of the American nation, the crucible in which its people honed, shaped, and formed the loose set of ideas, derived from Enlightenment thinking, into the documents that defined and later redefined the United States. The country's founding fathers signed the Declaration of Independence here, and more than a decade later, the closed-door negotiations that led to the U.S. Constitution also took place here. The symbol of American freedom, the Liberty Bell, graces this park, which contains much of the fabric of the eighteenth-century nation.

In the 1770s, Philadelphia was the principal city in the American colonies. It was the leading commercial center, home to inspirational intellects and entrepreneurs such as Benjamin Franklin, and was centrally located and easily accessible to delegates from the

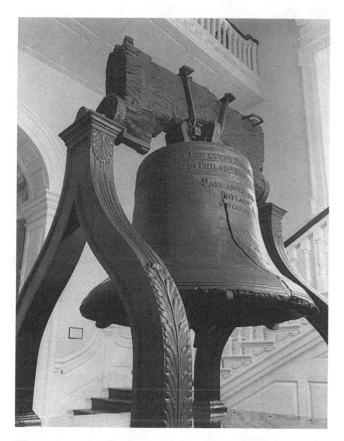

The Liberty Bell at Independence National Historical Park. *(Library of Congress)*

North and South. When colonists decided to form the First Continental Congress in September 1774, there was no better location than Philadelphia. When they met in Carpenter's Hall, at Fourth and Chestnut streets in center city Philadelphia, the colonial delegates determined that the situation they faced with Great Britain was no longer tolerable. The First Continental Congress addressed a declaration of rights and grievances to King George III, agreed to boycott English goods, and determined that they would reassemble the following spring if their demands were not met. The British ignored the demands, but in the ensuing months, the situation changed greatly. By May 10, 1775, when the Continental Congress reconvened, armed conflict had broken out along the road to Lexington and Concord, and the resolution of colonial grievances seemed farther away.

Reluctantly, the delegates moved from protest to resistance, assuming authority over continental troops at Boston and appointing George Washington as commander in chief. While the battles at Lexington and Concord began the fighting, the Second Continental Congress affirmed the direction the Minutemen took. The American Revolution was under way.

During the following year, fighting continued as the Continental Congress searched for a solution to the conflict. Throughout the rest of 1775 and into 1776, the colonists did not cry for independence; instead they sought a place within the British system under more favorable terms. The British rejected all entreaties, forcing the delegates to reassess their stance. The move toward independence rather than reconciliation came slowly. Only in June 1776 did Richard Henry Lee, a Virginia delegate, offer a resolution advocating that the colonies be seen as "United States" that were entitled to freedom as their right. Another Virginian, the lanky, young, and red-haired Thomas Jefferson took on the burden of drafting what became the Declaration of Independence. Two days after the Continental Congress passed Lee's resolution, on July 4, 1776, delegates approved the Declaration of Independence, and the colonists declared themselves a new and independent nation.

Among the provisions of Lee's resolution was the call for a plan of confederation, a way to link the independent colonies together in some form of federated government that would maintain their independence but allow great cooperation and interaction between them. A committee offered the "Articles of Confederation and Perpetual Union" in 1776. Congress debated for an entire year and finally passed the articles on November 15, 1777, as the first constitution of the United States. The Articles of Confederation were ratified March 1, 1781, but they were insufficient to the needs of the new nation. They created not a country, but a league of states. Particularly noteworthy was the document's inability to provide for a strong central government, the absence of which led to the calling of a Grand Convention in 1787 in Philadelphia to revise the document. When they could not reach a consensus, the delegates set out a new charter to replace the Articles of Confederation. On September 15, 1787, the constitutional convention adopted the Constitution of the United States. American voters ratified the document in 1788 and the new national government began March 4, 1789.

The creation of the Constitution also returned the capital of the nation to Philadelphia. After 1783, it had been moved, first to Trenton, New Jersey, then to Annapolis, Maryland. It ended up in New York City before Pennsylvania's delegates brought it back to Philadelphia in 1790 as part of a compromise that assured the construction of a federal city to become the nation's permanent capital. As a result, Philadelphia was only a temporary capital, but events of great significance occurred during the decade it served as the center for the nation's government. George Washington's second inauguration in 1793 took place there, as did the formal addition of the Bill of Rights to the Constitution, the admission of the first three new states to the Union—Vermont, Kentucky, and Tennessee—and the establishment of the Mint and the First Bank of the United States. By 1800, when the capital moved to the new city of Washington in the District of Columbia, Philadelphia had been imprinted on the nation's consciousness as the place where the nation, and the principles that drove its founding, came together.

Independence National Historical Park reveals all of this and much more. The fabric of eighteenth-century North America and the intellectual and social genesis of the idea of an American nation became clear here. The park includes many of the structures of American government, such as Independence Hall, where delegates approved the Declaration of Independence in 1776, where the Second Continental Congress met from 1775 to 1783—except for a brief British occupation in 1777–1778, and where Congress appointed Washington commander in chief of the Continental Army. Next to it stands Congress Hall, completed in 1789 to serve as the Philadelphia County Courthouse but which served as the seat of the U.S. Congress from 1790 to 1800. Nearby are the First Bank of the United States building and the Old City Hall, which housed the U.S. Supreme Court from 1791 to 1800. Other nearby structures add to the setting and give the feel of an earlier time. Some attest to religious freedom and tolerance. These include Christ Church, with its 200-foot spire completed in 1754, the home congregation for Benjamin Franklin and Thomas Jefferson; the cemetery for Congregation Mikveh Israel, the only synagogue that functioned in the United States during the Revolutionary War; the Free Quaker Meeting House; St. George's Church, the oldest United Methodist Church building in continuous use in North America and the place where the first African American licensed to preach in a Methodist Church spoke from the pulpit late in the eighteenth century; and St. Joseph's Church, the first Roman Catholic Church in Philadelphia. Other buildings show the broader dimensions of eighteenth-century culture. These include Library Hall, founded in 1789, the oldest subscription library in the United States, and Philosophical Hall.

Perhaps the most symbolically important place in Independence National Historical Park is the Liberty Bell Center, on Market Street. Cast in England in 1751 to commemorate the fiftieth anniversary of the Pennsylvania colony's democratic constitution, the

Charter of Privileges, the bell cracked beyond repair at its first ringing. A second Liberty Bell was cast from the first, but it too cracked, finally beyond repair in 1846. The crack in the Liberty Bell became a symbol, first of the American desire for freedom and the colonists' feelings that they were oppressed and, later in the nineteenth century, for the abolition movement, which saw the crack in the Liberty Bell as the symbol of a flawed nation, one that spoke of all men being created equal, but that practiced an entirely different conception of rights. The symbols of independence took on new and different meanings as the issues that confronted the American nation changed.

The park's spacious and inviting visitor center, located at Sixth and Market streets, is open daily from 8:30 A.M. until 5 P.M., and admission is free. However, a fee of $3 per person is charged for visitors seventeen years and over for the tour of the Bishop White and Todd Houses and for entrance to the Second Bank of the United States Portrait Gallery. Donations are also accepted through donation boxes available in some park buildings. Lodging is available in the historic park at the Thomas Bond House (129 South Second Street), a restored colonial-period guesthouse operated under a historic lease program with the National Park Service, and listed on the National Register of Historic Places. There are also several hotels, bed-and-breakfast facilities, and a youth hostel within walking distance, and all traveler services can be found in the Philadelphia area.

For more information, write Independence National Historical Park, 143 South Third Street, Philadelphia, PA 19106, or telephone (215) 597-8974. The park's Web site is www.nps.gov/inde.

FURTHER READING

Bailyn, Bernard. *The Ideological Origins of the American Revolution.* Cambridge, MA: Belknap, 1992.

Brands, H.W. *The First American: The Life and Times of Benjamin Franklin.* New York: Doubleday, 2000.

Ellis, Joseph J. *Founding Brothers: The Revolutionary Generation.* New York: Alfred A. Knopf, 2000.

Jensen, Merrill. *The Articles of Confederation: An Interpretation of the Social-Constitutional History of the American Revolution, 1774–1781.* Madison: University of Wisconsin Press, 1970.

Morgan, Edmund S. *Benjamin Franklin.* New Haven, CT: Yale University Press, 2002.

INDIANA DUNES NATIONAL LAKESHORE

Location: Porter, Indiana
Acreage: 15,060
Established: November 5, 1966

Located 50 miles southeast of Chicago along Lake Michigan's south shore, Indiana Dunes National Lakeshore preserves more than 15,000 acres of magnificent dunes, beaches, bogs, marshes, woodlands, and prairie remnants for recreation and education purposes. Authorized by Congress in 1966 as America's second national lakeshore, it is a fine example of how natural and human history have helped shape this unique landscape.

The dunes' history began tens of thousands of years ago, when the massive glaciers that formed Lake Michigan retreated and left in their wake pristine sand dunes along the lake's southern tip. Over the millennia, the prevailing southerly winds molded, shaped, and moved the dunes inland as much as 60 feet a year. As the dunes shifted away from the lakeshore, they stabilized through the accumulation of plant-producing soils. These dunes also blocked the normal course of streams and drainages, creating bogs, marshy sinks, and ponds that supported a broad range of vegetation. Within the confines of 2 miles, the dunes ecosystem contains, from inland to lake, swamps and bogs, hardwood forests, and other vegetation half-buried under a carpet of sand, the "blowouts" (amphitheaters) of the active dunes, then the storm

Playing in the sand at Indiana Dunes National Lakeshore. *(National Park Service)*

beaches adjoining the lake itself. Time is also a good indicator of the ecosystem's age, for the closer to the lake, the younger the natural feature, be it dune, forest, or wetland.

Humans have long valued the dunes country. Native Americans traversed the region in their journeys between the Great Lakes and the Mississippi River, while the French and British traded for furs. In 1822, French-Canadian fur trader Joseph Bailly started a trading post and homestead. In 1872, Swedish immigrants Anders and Joanna Chellberg established their farm. The government has restored both. At the turn of the century, University of Chicago professor Henry Cowles performed his pioneering studies on plant ecology in the dunes' ecosystem. To counter increasing encroachment from steel and utility industries, after World War I, the first director of the National Park Service,

Stephen T. Mather, tried—and failed—to turn the area into a national park. The Park Service realized partial success in 1923 with the creation of Indiana Dunes State Park. In the 1950 and 1960s, as the local steel industries expanded, local preservationist Dorothy Buell and Illinois Senator Paul H. Douglas worked together to help save what little dunes land remained. They benefited from the rise of environmental sentiment that made lakeshores such as Indiana Dunes into national symbols and from a pervasive sense that dated from the 1950s that industrial development and privatization were combining to deprive Americans of access to their coasts. These efforts culminated in the lakeshore's establishment.

Because of the dunes' varied landscape and history, there are many activities for visitors. With the exception of a parking fee at

West Beach, there is no admission charge to the lakeshore itself. An extensive trail system through the dunes and wetlands allows hikers to view varied plant, animal, and bird species. A short climb to the summit of Mount Baldy, a huge, moving sand dune on the lakeshore's northeastern tip near Michigan City, demonstrates just how much these "shifting sands" can alter a landscape. The lakeshore's beaches—West, Porter, Kemil, Lake View, Central, and Mount Baldy—although crowded during the summer weekends, are excellent. Boating and fishing are also welcome. Boaters must stay 500 feet from marked swimming areas and the park requires an Indiana fishing license.

For human and natural history buffs, the Park Service has restored the Bailly Homestead and Chellberg Farm to provide a window into the region's past. The Paul II. Douglas Center for Environmental Education, at the park's western end near Gary, educates students on ecology and the environmental sciences through multimedia means, while the Dorothy Buell Memorial Visitor Center is a good introductory location for new visitors, as well as to buy books and souvenirs and watch dunes-oriented films. The park is open year-round; cross-country skiing, hiking, and snowshoeing are popular winter activities, but the park prohibits snowmobiling.

The lakeshore's weather is unpredictable and greatly affected by Lake Michigan. Summers are generally warm and humid, with highs in the mid-80s and lows in the mid-60s. On the average, there are about fifteen days over 90 degrees. Frontal systems descending from Canada, which can bring days of pleasant, dry weather, occasionally interrupt these warm spells. Winters are generally cold, with high temperatures ranging from the low 20s to mid-30s, and lows in the single digits to the teens. There are about fifteen days per year below 0 degrees. Winters also tend to be cloudy, except for periods of extreme cold.

Visitors can get to the national lakeshore via I-94 (the Indiana Toll Road), I-80/90, U.S. Highway 20, U.S. Highway 12, and other state highways. The Gary Regional Airport, South Bend Airport, and Chicago's Midway and O'Hare airports service the surrounding communities. The Chicago South Shore and South Bend Railroad stops at several stations throughout the park.

In the park, visitors can travel in personal vehicles. Regulations permit bicycles on the main roads, but prohibit them on all trails except Calumet Bike Trail between Mineral Springs Road and U.S. Highway 12 at the Porter/LaPorte county line; Long Lake Trail between Ogden Dunes and West Beach; Marquette Trail between West Beach and Grand Boulevard in Gary; and Lake Front Drive to Central Avenue, only on the beach's flat portion.

There is no lodging within the park. Hotels and motels in nearby communities, including Gary, Portage, Chesterton, Porter, and Michigan City, provide varied accommodations suitable for any budget, as well as other travel services. Although numerous commercial campgrounds exist in the area, the only campground within the park is Dunewood, near the Buell Visitor Center. For a small fee, campers can choose from 54 drive-in and 25 walk-in sites. There are showers and rest rooms, but no electrical hookups. All facilities are accessible to people with disabilities. A campground exists in the state park, but it is administered separately.

For more information, write to the superintendent, Indiana Dunes National Lakeshore, 1100 North Mineral Springs Road, Porter, IN 46304, or telephone (219) 926-7651. The park's Web site is www.nps.gov/indu.

FURTHER READING
Engel, J. Ronald. *Sacred Sands: The Struggle for Community in the Indiana Dunes.* Middletown, CT: Wesleyan University Press. Distributed by Harper & Row, 1983.

Engel, Joan G., ed. *The Indiana Dunes Story: How Nature and People Made a Park.* Michigan City, IN: Shirley Heinze Environmental Fund, 1997.

Franklin, Kay, and Norma Schaeffer. *Duel for the Dunes: Land Use Conflict on the Shores of Lake Michigan.* Urbana: University of Illinois Press, 1983.

ISLE ROYALE NATIONAL PARK

Location: Houghton, Michigan
Acreage: 571,790
Established: March 3, 1931

Any visit to wet, wild, and isolated Isle Royale National Park requires substantial preparation and planning. Located in far northwestern Lake Superior, 16 miles from the Canadian mainland, this wilderness archipelago of more than 200 islands is accessible only by private or commercial boat, ferry, or floatplane. Named by French trappers, the 45-mile-long Isle Royale island chain was created by volcanic lava flows later carved and shaped by glaciers. The island's interior contains more than 30 lakes, surrounded by dense hardwood, conifer, and evergreen forests.

Human use of the island dates back more than four thousand years. Around 2000 B.C.E., prehistoric tribes started to mine the rich copper deposits on Isle Royale, and they continued to do so until first contact with French explorers in the seventeenth century. By 1840, white copper miners had begun large-scale extractive activities that continued until the resource was exhausted around 1900. Many ruins of these mines are visible today.

Established by Congress in March 1931, Isle Royale National Park encompasses a total area of 850 square miles, including submerged lands, and has 165 miles of scenic hiking trails and 36 campgrounds for backpackers and recreational boaters. Cultural resources include historic lighthouses, shipwrecks, and ancient copper-mining sites. In all, more than 200 bird species nest here, and visitors may spy timber wolves, moose, beaver, red fox, and squirrels in the park.

Isle Royale is located about 20 miles southeast of Grand Portage, Minnesota, and about 53 miles north of Copper Harbor, Michigan. The headquarters for Isle Royale National Park during the summer is located on Mott Island, one of numerous islands associated with the Isle Royale archipelago. During the winter, the headquarters are moved to the mainland in Houghton, Michigan. Because of the brutal winters, Isle Royale's operating season only runs from April 16 to October 31, with full transportation services available from mid-June through Labor Day (reduced transportation services are available in the spring and fall). Although the park is closed from November 1 to April 15, the headquarters and visitor center in Houghton are open year-round. A $4 per person per day user fee is charged to visit the island, and a $50 season pass is available.

Lake Superior weather is cool and foggy throughout the operating season, with more sun in the summer. Heavy thunderstorms and driving rain are frequent. Weather and rough seas may delay departures to and from the island. Visitors are advised to bring plenty of warm clothing, even in August.

During the summer, visitors can reach Isle Royale via ferries departing from Houghton and Copper Harbor, Michigan, or Grand Portage, Minnesota. A seaplane service operates out of Houghton. Isle Royale can also be accessed by private boat and seaplane. On-island visitor centers are located at Rock Harbor and Windigo. Interpretive exhibits at these visitor centers and at Rock Harbor Lighthouse explore local natural and cultural history topics. Other historic landmarks accessible by sightseeing cruises include Edisen Fishery, Passage Island Lighthouse, and the Minong Copper Mine. Interpretive programs and guided walks by park rangers, park artists-in-residence, and other affiliates are offered from mid-June through Labor Day at Rock Harbor, Windigo, and Daisy Farm. Activities include nature and historical walks, evening slide programs, and campfire talks.

Rock Harbor Lodge offers reservation-required motel-style lodging on the island; it has an extensive marina with all services, general store, public showers, and laundry facilities. Windigo also offers marina services and a small general store. Isle Royale has 36 primitive campgrounds, which can get crowded during the peak summer season. Rock Harbor and Washington Creek campgrounds have drinking water. Campground use is free and includes tent sites and three-sided shelters when available; a registration permit is required to camp.

The park and the surrounding waters of Lake Superior are an angler's paradise. Pike, walleye, perch, whitefish, and trout are abundant. A Michigan license is required to fish Lake Superior, but no license is needed to fish the park's lakes.

For more information, write Isle Royale National Park, 800 East Lakeshore Drive, Houghton, MI 49931-1895, or telephone (906) 482-0984. The park's Web site is www.nps.gov/isro.

FURTHER READING

Gale, Thomas P. *Isle Royale: A Photographic History.* Houghton, MI: Isle Royale Natural History Association, 1995.

Huber, N. King. *Geologic Story of Isle Royale National Park.* Washington, DC: U.S. Geological Survey, 1975.

Peterson, Rolf O. *The Wolves of Isle Royale: A Broken Balance.* Minocqua, WI: Willow Creek, 1995.

Shelton, Napier. *Superior Wilderness: Isle Royale National Park.* Houghton, MI: Isle Royale Natural History Association, 1997.

J

JAMES A. GARFIELD NATIONAL HISTORIC SITE

Location: Mentor, Ohio
Acreage: 8
Established: December 28, 1980

Born in Cuyahoga County, Ohio, on November 19, 1831, James A. Garfield was the last of the "log-cabin" presidents. As a boy, he earned money for his education by driving canal boat teams on the Ohio and Erie Canal, and after his 1856 graduation from Williams College in Massachusetts, Garfield taught ancient languages and literature at Hiram College in Ohio. Within a year, the scholarly Garfield was appointed president at Hiram College and concurrently served in the Ohio state senate until 1861. During the Civil War, Lieutenant Colonel Garfield commanded the 42nd Regiment of the Ohio Volunteer Infantry. After proving his leadership skills in the battles of Shiloh and Chickamauga, he was promoted to Major General, a rank he held until resigning his commission in 1870. In 1862, Ohioans elected him to Congress, and he was reelected for eighteen consecutive years, becoming the leading Republican in the House of Representatives. In January 1880, Garfield was elected to the U.S. Senate for the Congressional term starting in March 1881, but on June 8, he was nominated as the Republican Party's choice for president. In the November election, Garfield claimed victory by a few thousand votes, and one month later he formally declined his Senate seat to become president of the United States. He might have been better off choosing the Senate, because, less than four months after his March 1881 inauguration, a disgruntled drifter/office-seeker named Charles Guiteau shot and wounded the nation's twentieth president. At the time, medical practice was in its infancy and attending physicians likely worsened his injuries; only two months later, on September 19, Garfield died from infections associated with his gunshot wounds and was buried in Cleveland's Lake View cemetery. He became the fourth president to die in office and the second to be assassinated.

Authorized in December 1980 and administered by the Western Reserve Historical Society, the 8-acre James A. Garfield National Historic Site preserves and protects the house he purchased in 1876 to accommodate his growing family. The home, named Lawnfield by reporters, was the site of his first successful "front porch" campaign in 1880. Four years

Arrival of visitors outside the home of President James A. Garfield in Mentor, Ohio, 1880. *(Library of Congress)*

after his assassination, the Memorial Library wing was added by Mrs. Garfield and her family, setting the precedent for presidential libraries. Located 25 miles east of Cleveland in Mentor, Ohio, the newly refurbished site is open from 10 A.M. until 5 P.M. Monday through Saturday, and from noon until 5 P.M. on Sundays. Admission is free, but tours of the main house are $6 for adults and $4 for children. The site's main visitor center is located in the 1893 carriage house, which contains interpretive exhibits, an eighteen-minute video on Garfield's life and brief presidency, and a bookstore. Park rangers offer interpretive talks and lectures; the site also has wayside exhibits that help interpret the property's buildings.

There is no food, lodging, or camping at the site, but the city of Mentor has all traveler services, and developed camping is available at Punderson State Park, 15 miles south of Mentor.

For more information, write James A. Garfield National Historic Site, 8095 Mentor Avenue, Mentor, OH 44060, or telephone (440) 255-8722. The park's Web site is www.nps.gov/jaga.

FURTHER READING

Booraem, Hendrik. *The Road to Respectability: James A. Garfield and His World, 1844–1852.* Lewisburg, PA: Bucknell University Press, 1988.

Doenecke, Justus D. *The Presidencies of James A. Garfield and Chester A. Arthur.* Lawrence: Regents Press of Kansas, 1981.

Peskin, Allan. *Garfield: A Biography.* Kent, OH: Kent State University Press, 1999.

JEAN LAFITTE NATIONAL HISTORICAL PARK AND PRESERVE

Location: New Orleans, Louisiana
Acreage: 20,005
Established: March 4, 1970

Jean Lafitte's legend looms large in western Gulf Coast lore. Around 1802, this mysterious Frenchman and his brother Pierre came to the French Louisiana colonial territory. Known as "Baratarians" after the island of Barataria on which they made their home, he and his brother were privateers and slave traders who raided ships and smuggled contraband from the Gulf of Mexico to New Orleans through the Louisiana bayous—the drowned swamplands of the lower part of the state. Lafitte attained a regional mythology; he seemed to be everywhere, a raider yet a man of the people, a pirate yet a citizen of value in the complex matrix of the new American city of New Orleans. Lafitte became an American hero during the War of 1812, when he served as a guide and adviser to the United States in the pivotal battle of New Orleans, which took place east of the city on the field of Chalmette. In part as a result of Lafitte's information, the Americans were ready and they demolished a much larger force of the British with minimal casualties of their own. After the victory in January 1815, Lafitte's status as a patriot was firmly ensconced in local lore and history—regardless of the little factual information that is known about his life.

Located in southern and western Louisiana, the 20,005-acre Jean Lafitte National Historic Park and Preserve was incorporated into a new park in 1978 to preserve the human and natural history of the Mississippi River delta region. It consists of 4 major units: New Orleans (French Quarter), Chalmette Battlefield, Barataria Preserve, and the Acadian (with its 3 Cajun cultural centers). All units are open year-round, and there are no admission fees.

In the French Market of the historic French Quarter in New Orleans is the park's visitor center, which is open daily from 9 A.M. until 5 P.M. This center interprets the history of New Orleans and the diverse cultures of the Mississippi River delta region. Rangers lead walking tours of the French Quarter, and cooking demonstrations, musical performances, and arts and crafts are regularly featured. This unit closes during Mardi Gras.

Six miles southeast of New Orleans is the Chalmette Battlefield and National Cemetery, site of the 1815 Battle of New Orleans. This unit celebrates General Andrew "Old Hickory" Jackson's victory over the British in the Battle of New Orleans, in which he lost only 13 soldiers—compared to 2,000 British casualties. A visitor center offers interpretive exhibits and programs, living-history demonstrations, and a self-guided driving tour.

The largest unit, Barataria Preserve, encompasses nearly 20,000 acres of pristine and ecologically rich delta wetlands and forests, including bayous, bald cypress swamps, freshwater marshes, and hardwood forests. Located 12 miles south of New Orleans, Barataria also contains a wide variety of mammals and birds, and twenty-two different species of snakes, including three poisonous ones: the aggressive water moccasin, copperhead, and rattlesnake. Self-guided trails lead throughout the preserve, and there is a small visitor center, which is open daily from 9 A.M. until 5 P.M. Park rangers offer guided natural history walks, canoe treks, and moonlight canoe treks.

The 3 Acadian cultural centers are located 60 to 150 miles west of New Orleans. The main Acadian Cultural Center at 501 Fisher Road in Lafayette interprets cultural resources related to the Acadian, or Cajun, people, who were relocated from Nova Scotia, Canada, to the Mississippi River delta region in the mid-eighteenth century. The Prairie Acadian Cultural Center at 250 West Park Avenue in Eunice depicts the heritage of the Prairie Acadians, a culture shaped by the region's lush grasslands, which were ideal for raising crops and grazing cattle. Artifacts, exhibits, and live demonstrations portray assorted aspects of this unique culture. The Wetlands Acadian Cultural Center is located along Bayou Lafourche, at 314 St. Mary Street, Thibodaux. The visitor center contains artifacts and exhibits that interpret a variety of cultures linked closely with the rich swamps, marshes, and coastal waters of this region.

There are no food, lodging, or camping facilities in the park, but all traveler services are available locally and there are many private campgrounds in the area.

For more information, write Jean Lafitte National Historical Park and Preserve, 365 Canal Street, Suite 2400, New Orleans, LA 70130-1142, or telephone (504) 589-3882. The park's Web site is www.nps.gov/jela.

FURTHER READING

Charnley, Mitchell V. *Jean Lafitte, Gentleman Smuggler.* New York: Viking, 1934.

Greene, Jerome A. *The Defense of New Orleans, 1718–1900, Jean Lafitte National Historical Park, Louisiana.* Denver, CO: National Park Service, 1982.

——. *Chalmette Unit, Jean Lafitte National Historical Park and Preserve.* Denver, CO: National Park Service, 1985.

Phillips, Marti. *The Last Pirate.* Lavergne, TN: Southern Star, 2000.

Ross, Nola Mae Wittler. *Jean Lafitte, Louisiana Buccaneer: A Mini-History.* Lake Charles, LA: N.M.W. Ross, 1990.

JEFFERSON NATIONAL EXPANSION MEMORIAL

Location: St. Louis, Missouri
Acreage: 91
Established: December 20, 1935

In 1803, with one stroke of his pen and a $15 million payment to France, President Thomas Jefferson doubled the size of the United States with the Louisiana Purchase. The following year, Meriwether Lewis and William Clark set out from St. Louis on an epic journey with the Corps of Discovery to explore and map this amazing piece of real estate. Their reports captured the national imagination and spawned a wave of westward migration that, in just fifty years, resulted in a continental United States that stretched from the Atlantic to the Pacific. As Americans streamed west, one location proved vital as a transportation "gateway": St. Louis. Located at the confluence of the Mississippi and Missouri rivers—important transportation corridors at the time—St. Louis became a key commercial and cultural center. There, the western fur trade had its headquarters; pioneers gathered to buy supplies before heading out West along the overland trails.

In December 1935, at the height of the Depression, Congress looked for a strange combination of projects, ones that could put lots of people to work while they imbued Americans with the valiant spirit of their history. The old waterfront in St. Louis, long decayed since its nineteenth-century heyday, fit the specifications. With input from the Park Service, energized by the availability of New Deal funding, a project for a commemoration of the fur trade was transformed into a memorial to the Louisiana Purchase. Congress designated the 91-acre Jefferson National Expansion Memorial to commemorate the territorial expansion of the United States and the pioneers that explored and settled these new western lands. In a nationwide competition, architect Eero Saarinen's inspired design for a 630-foot stainless steel arch was chosen as the perfect monument to the spirit of the western pioneers. Construction of the Gateway Arch began in 1963 and was completed two years later, for a total cost of less than $15 million. It is the tallest monument in the national park system—75 feet higher than the Washington Monument. The arch features a film called *Monument to the Dream*, which details its construction, and a new 70mm World Odyssey wide-screen theater. Visitors should also consider a tram ride to the top of the arch for a panoramic view of the St. Louis area. Separate fees are charged for tickets to see films and for the tram ride to the arch's observation tower. Since wait times for the tram can exceed two hours during the peak summer season, visitors usually buy tram tickets, then visit the museum while waiting.

Located on the riverfront in downtown St. Louis, the park also contains the Museum of Westward Expansion and St. Louis' Old Courthouse. The museum is as large as a football field and contains an extensive collection of artifacts, mounted animal specimens, an authentic American Indian tepee, and an overview of the Lewis and Clark Expedition. Both the Gateway Arch and Museum of Westward Expansion are open daily from 8 A.M. to 10 P.M. in the summer, and from 9 A.M. to 6 P.M. the remainder of the year. Entrance fees for the museum are $2 per person. Located just 2 blocks west of the Arch is the Old Courthouse, built in 1839, which is open daily from 8 A.M. to 4:30 P.M. Admission is free. It was here in 1847 and 1850 that the first two trials of the Dred Scott case were held. These trials led to the Supreme Court decision of 1857 stating that slaves and, by extension, all blacks were not citizens, and thus they did not have the legal standing to sue for freedom in federal courts. Today, the building houses a museum charting the history of St. Louis, interpretive exhibits on the Dred Scott trials, and some restored courtrooms.

There are no food, lodging, or camping facilities in the park, but St. Louis has all traveler services and private campgrounds exist in the outlying suburban areas.

For more information, write Jefferson National Expansion Memorial, 11 North 4th Street, St. Louis, MO 63102, or telephone (314) 655-1700. The park's excellent Web site is www.nps.gov/jeff.

FURTHER READING

Ambrose, Stephen E. *Undaunted Courage: Meriwether Lewis, Thomas Jefferson, and the Opening of the American West.* New York: Simon and Schuster, 1996.

Ellis, Joseph J. *American Sphinx: The Character of Thomas Jefferson.* New York: Alfred A. Knopf, 1997.

Malone, Dumas. *The Sage of Monticello.* Boston: Little, Brown, 1981.

Moulton, Gary E., ed. *The Definitive Journals of Lewis*

and Clark: Down the Columbia to Fort Clatsop. Lincoln: University of Nebraska Press, 2002.
Ronda, James P. *Lewis and Clark Among the Indians.* Lincoln: University of Nebraska Press, 1998.

JEWEL CAVE NATIONAL MONUMENT

Location: Custer, South Dakota
Acreage: 1,274
Established: February 7, 1908

In October 1900, two prospectors discovered an amazing buried treasure: the third longest cave in the world. Although their mining claim failed, Frank and Albert Michaud soon developed the cave as a crude geologic tourist attraction. In February 1908, one of those tourists—President Theodore Roosevelt—proclaimed Jewel Cave as America's thirteenth national monument. Jewel Cave is so named for the sparkling calcite crystals that glitter and shimmer on the fantastic formations in the cavern. Geologists estimate that around 60 million years ago, a massive general geologic uplift, associated with the formation of the Rocky Mountains, created the much smaller Black Hills. As water oozed into the cracked limestone, the rock dissolved and formed many caves of different sizes, among them Jewel Cave. As the water evaporated, it deposited small calcite crystals on the surface of the rock, which range in color from pale to dark green, bronze, and brown. Today, Jewel Cave National Monument preserves a 128-mile-long maze-like series of underground chambers, passageways, side galleries, and bizarre calcite crystal encrustations, and airflow within the cave suggests that much of this wonder still remains unexplored.

The park's chief feature is the cave, and tours provide outstanding opportunities for visitors to experience this pristine cave system and its wide variety of speleothems including stalactites, stalagmites, draperies, frostwork, flowstone, boxwork, and hydromagnesite balloons. Jewel Cave is also an important hibernaculum for several species of bats. Park rangers offer 3 types of tours. The popular scenic tour, which is available year-round, enters and leaves the cave via elevator in the visitor center and follows a lighted, paved, moderately strenuous trail. The historic candlelight tour commences at the log cabin Ranger Station. Because it uses an old foot trail, it is quite strenuous. Fees for these tours are $8 for adults and $4 for children ages six to sixteen. The third, and most demanding, tour is the spelunking, where experienced cavers probe and explore deep sections of the cave other tours do not cover. Reservations are required for the spelunking tour, and the fee is higher. Both the historic candlelight and the spelunking tours are only offered during the summer months. Group sizes are limited to 30 visitors per scenic tour, 20 per historic candlelight tour, and 5 per spelunking tour. The monument also has two surface trails, "Walk on the Roof" and "Canyons," which explore the surrounding Ponderosa forests and Hell and Lithograph canyons.

The visitor center is located 13 miles west of Custer, South Dakota, on Highway 16, and is open daily from 8 A.M. to 4:30 P.M., with extended hours during the summer. The center features interpretive exhibits, the Jewel Cave map (a 7.5-foot by 18-foot electronic working "document"), interactive computers, videos, the entrance for the scenic and spelunking tours, and rest rooms. In addition to leading cave tours, park rangers offer surface talks and guided hikes. Tour tickets for the scenic, historic, and spelunking tours are also available here. The park's Historic Ranger Station is located 1 mile west of the main visitor center on Highway 16, and is open daily from 8:30 A.M. until 6 P.M. from Memorial Day through Labor Day. The structure itself is listed on the National Register of Historic Structures, and the station offers a few exhibits and a small book sales outlet. Park rangers in 1930s-era uniforms lead candlelight tours through portions of the cave that have been only minimally developed. Visitation is usually highest during the summer, which can result in long waits for cave tours (though early risers will find no wait even during the peak season).

There are no food, lodging, or camping facilities at the monument, but Custer and Newcastle, Wyoming, have all traveler services. Camping is available nearby at Wind Cave National Park, at Custer State Park, and in the Black Hills National Forest.

For more information, write Jewel Cave National Monument, RR 1 Box 60 AA, Custer, SD 57730, or telephone (605) 673-2288. The park's Web site is www.nps.gov/jeca.

FURTHER READING

Conn, Herb. *The Jewel Cave Adventure: Fifty Miles of Discovery under South Dakota.* Teaneck, NJ: Zephyrus, 1977.
Gries, John Paul. *Roadside Geology of South Dakota.* Missoula, MT: Mountain, 1996.
Palmer, Art. *Jewel Cave: A Gift from the Past.* Hot Springs, SD: Black Hills Parks and Forests Association, 2000.

JIMMY CARTER NATIONAL HISTORIC SITE

Location: Plains, Georgia
Acreage: 71
Established: December 23, 1987

Few U.S. presidents have maintained such close ties with the community in which they were born and raised as the nation's thirty-ninth president. James Earl "Jimmy" Carter, Jr., was born on October 1, 1924, in Plains, Georgia, and the rural southern culture of his youth incorporated peanut farming, politics, and the Baptist faith, shaping both his character and his priorities. After graduating from the Naval Academy in 1946, Carter married Rosalynn Smith, and, in 1962, he entered Georgia state politics. By 1970 he had risen to the governor's mansion, championing

causes that included ecology, government efficiency, and racial tolerance. He was the last of a breed, a Southern Democrat who embraced the ideas of the Great Society, with its message of tolerance and fairness. Carter was well received on the national level, and in 1974, he announced his candidacy for president, promising to make government "good and honest and decent and competent," and to restore Americans' confidence in the wake of Watergate. At the Democratic Convention, Carter secured the nomination on the first ballot, and then went on to win in November, narrowly defeating incumbent President Gerald R. Ford. Despite his numerous achievements—Middle East peace accords, a national energy policy, expansion of the national park system, ratification of the Panama Canal Treaty—Carter's administration was plagued by a rocky economy characterized by rising energy costs, mounting inflation, high interest rates, and unemployment. His insistence on morally correct political behavior undermined his presidency. The seizure of the U.S. embassy staff in Iran dominated the news during Carter's last fourteen months in office and, together with continuing inflation at home, contributed to his defeat in 1980. After leaving the White House, Carter returned to Georgia, where in 1982, he founded the non-profit Carter Center in Atlanta to promote peace and human rights worldwide. In 2002, in recognition of his humanitarian efforts, Carter received the Nobel Peace Prize, becoming only the third president in American history to receive such an honor. In his acceptance speech, Carter reminded the world that "it is clear that global challenges must be met with an emphasis on peace, in harmony with others, with strong alliances and international consensus."

Established in 1987, the 71-acre Jimmy Carter National Historic Site preserves the president's residence, boyhood farm, school, and the railroad depot that served as his campaign headquarters during the 1976 election. Plains High School serves as the park's museum and visitor center, and it is open all year from 9 A.M. until 5 P.M. Admission is free. The school houses a restored and furnished classroom, principal's office, and auditorium, and other rooms feature exhibits that explain the Carters' lives in Plains, including political and business careers, education, family, religion, and postpresidency. The story of the park is told in a twenty-five-minute audiovisual presentation in the auditorium and through the site brochures. The museum also includes an audiovisual tour by Jimmy and Rosalynn Carter of their home, since the area surrounding the residence is under the protection of the Secret Service and is not open to the public.

The Plains Depot, which served as Carter's, 1976 Presidential Campaign Headquarters, contains a self-guided museum with exhibits focusing on the 1976 presidential election. During the campaign, approximately 10,000 people a day came to Plains to find out about candidate Carter. Many of the celebrations following state primary victories, as well as the presidential victory, were held in the streets around the depot. The Jimmy Carter boyhood farm, where the president lived from the age of four until he departed for college, is currently under restoration to return it to its appearance in 1937 before electricity was installed. The Park Service maintains 17 acres of the original 360-acre farm owned by Earl Carter, Jimmy's father, from 1928 until the late 1940s. Other facilities also have been restored and reconstructed, such as the barn, buggy shed, pump house, tennis court, tenant houses, and blacksmith shop.

There are no food, lodging, or camping facilities at the historic site, but Plains and Americus offer all traveler services.

For more information, write Jimmy Carter National Historic Site, 300 North Bond Street, Plains, GA 31780, or telephone (229) 824-4104. The park's Web site is www.nps.gov/jica.

FURTHER READING

Brinkley, Douglas. *The Unfinished Presidency: Jimmy Carter's Journey Beyond the White House.* New York: Viking, 1998.

Carter, Jimmy. *An Hour Before Daylight.* New York: Simon and Schuster, 2001.

Glad, Betty. *Jimmy Carter: In Search of the Great White House.* New York: W.W. Norton, 1980.

Kaufman, Burton I. *The Presidency of James Earl Carter, Jr.* Lawrence: University Press of Kansas, 1993.

Morris, Kenneth E. *Jimmy Carter: American Moralist.* Athens: University of Georgia Press, 1996.

Smith, Gaddis. *Morality, Reason, and Power: American Diplomacy in the Carter Years.* New York: Hill and Wang, 1986.

JOHN D. ROCKEFELLER, JR. MEMORIAL PARKWAY

Location: Moose, Wyoming
Acreage: 23,777
Established: August 25, 1972

> I believe that every right implies a responsibility; every opportunity, an obligation; every possession, a duty.
> *–John D. Rockefeller, Jr.*

One of America's preeminent philanthropists, John D. Rockefeller, Jr., became the leading supporter of the national parks throughout the first half of the twentieth century. Rockefeller was born in 1874, in Cleveland, Ohio, the fifth child and only son of Standard Oil tycoon John D. Rockefeller and Laura Spelman Rockefeller. After graduating from Brown University in 1897, Rockefeller, Jr., joined his father's business, where he quickly discovered that spending money was far more fulfilling than making it. After 1910 Rockefeller, Jr., devoted his life to philanthropy, creating such notable philanthropic institutions as the Rockefeller Institute for Medical Research (1901), the General Education Board (1902), and the Rockefeller Foundation (1913), as well as to sponsoring the construction of Rockefeller Center in New York City, funding of the restoration of Colonial Williamsburg, and donating land in New York

City for the United Nations complex. But in the field of conservation, Rockefeller's contributions to national parks were the most important of any individual during the three decades that followed the establishment of the Park Service in 1916. Horace M. Albright, the agency's second director and the primary mover during its first two decades, cultivated Rockefeller throughout the 1920s and 1930s. Rockefeller responded with unparalleled generosity. During his lifetime, he purchased and donated thousands of acres of land to parks using his own finances or foundation grants. Great Smoky Mountains, Acadia, Shenandoah, and Grand Teton national parks all received generous donations of land from Rockefeller, Grand Teton in essence being built around his secret acquisitions. During the 1920s, when commercial logging threatened to destroy large stands of sugar pines adjacent to Yosemite, Rockefeller provided more than $1 million to save 15,000 acres of forest. He also financed the construction of museums in Mesa Verde, Grand Canyon, and Yellowstone national parks. Rockefeller's model was passed on to his son, Laurance Rockefeller, who continued his father's tradition of giving. In 1972, Congress commemorated Rockefeller's role in the establishment of many parks, including Grand Teton, by creating the 82-mile John D. Rockefeller, Jr. Memorial Parkway, a scenic corridor of nearly 24,000 acres linking West Thumb in Yellowstone with the South Entrance of Grand Teton National Park.

For more information, write John D. Rockefeller, Jr. Memorial Parkway, P.O. Drawer 170, Moose, WY 83012, or telephone (307) 733-2880. The park's Web site is www.nps.gov/jodr.

FURTHER READING

Fosdick, Raymond B. *John D. Rockefeller, Jr., A Portrait.* New York: Harper & Brothers, 1956.
Newhall, Nancy Wynne. *Contribution to the Heritage of Every American: The Conservation Activities of John D. Rockefeller, Jr.* New York: Alfred A. Knopf, 1957.
Sontag, Bill, ed. *National Park Service: The First 75 Years.* Washington, DC: National Park Service, 2000. Available at www.cr.nps.gov/history/online_books/sontag/index.htm.
Winks, Robin. *Laurance S. Rockefeller: Catalyst for Conservation.* Washington, DC: Island, 1997.

JOHN DAY FOSSIL BEDS NATIONAL MONUMENT

Location: Kimberly, Oregon
Acreage: 13,944
Established: October 26, 1974

John Day Fossil Beds is one of the most important components of North America's paleontological past. Within the heavily eroded volcanic deposits of the John Day River basin in northcentral Oregon is a remarkably complete fossil record of plants and animals spanning more than 40 of the 65 million years of the Cenozoic Era—the "Age of Mammals and Flowering Plants."

The world-renowned John Day Fossil Beds were discovered by Thomas Condon in 1864. While fortune hunters combed the John Day River Valley for gold, Condon searched for fossils, hoping to put a definitive end to the evolution controversy that scientist Charles Darwin had begun a few years earlier. Condon named the lost world of eroded gullies and pinnacles he found "Turtle Cove" for the many fossilized tortoise shells he found.

In 1871, Othniel Marsh, America's first professor of paleontology at Yale University, launched an expedition in the area. Condon had lured Marsh out West with a box of fossils from the site. One skull, which particularly intrigued Marsh, was of a small, three-toed horse. Despite his keen interest in the horse family, Marsh only worked at the site for a week before returning to dinosaur digs in Kansas. Despite his short stay, Marsh did manage to take credit for Condon's find, however, naming the little horse Miohippus and proclaiming it the missing link of the horse family. Other collectors streamed to the fossil beds, extracting fossils and sending them back east to laboratories and universities. In 1899, John C. Merriam proposed the first University of California expedition in an effort to place the John Day fossils in their geological, chronological, and paleoecological context. To date, the biological diversity collected during these and subsequent excavations has been extraordinary—more than 2,100 species of prehistoric plants and animals have been discovered in all.

Established in October of 1974, the 13,944-acre John Day Fossil Beds National Monument is open year-round during daylight hours and admission is free. The park is divided into 3 widely separated units: the Sheep Rock Unit, Painted Hills Unit, and Clarno Unit, with the monument's main headquarters at the visitor center in the Sheep Rock Unit. The Fossil Museum and Visitor Center is open daily from 9 A.M. until 5 P.M., and until 6 P.M. from Memorial Day through Labor Day. There is also a park office located in John Day, Oregon. Park rangers offer routinely scheduled and specially arranged programs year-round, including fossil museum talks, trail hikes, and off-site presentations featuring the geologic and paleontologic story of the site. Visitors can enjoy numerous self-guided trail and auto tours, scenic roads and overlooks, and trail-side exhibits throughout the park.

There are no food, lodging, or camping facilities at the monument, but all are available locally.

For more information, write John Day Fossil Beds National Monument, HCR 82, Box 126, Kimberly, OR 97848-9701, or telephone (541) 987-2333. The park's Web site is www.nps.gov/joda.

FURTHER READING

Beckham, Stephen Dow, with Florence K. Lentz. *John Day Fossil Beds National Monument: Rocks & Hard Places: Historic Resources Study.* Seattle, WA: National Park Service, 2000.

Mark, Stephen R. *Floating in the Stream of Time: An Administrative History of John Day Fossil Beds National Monument.* Seattle, WA: Columbia-Cascades Cluster, National Park Service, 1996. Available at www.nps.gov/joda/adhi/adhi.htm.

JOHN FITZGERALD KENNEDY NATIONAL HISTORIC SITE

Location: Brookline, Massachusetts
Acreage: .09
Established: May 26, 1967

> It is time for a new generation of leadership, to cope with new problems and new opportunities. For there is a new world to be won.
>
> —*John F. Kennedy*

In July 1960, John Fitzgerald Kennedy challenged the American people to embrace the "new frontier" that he envisioned for the country; four months later, in November, the brash, handsome Massachusetts senator was on his way to the White House as the youngest man ever elected president of the United States.

Kennedy was born in Brookline, Massachusetts, on May 29, 1917. After graduating from Harvard in 1940, he entered the navy. There he earned high marks for bravery as he piloted PT-109 during World War II. Upon his return to civilian life, Kennedy entered politics as a Democratic congressman from the Boston area, advancing to the Senate in 1953. That same year he married Jacqueline Bouvier, and in 1957, Kennedy received the Pulitzer Prize in history for his book *Profiles in Courage.* After a bruising series of primaries, Kennedy gained the Democratic presidential nomination in 1960. The election featured the first-ever televised presidential debates, where Kennedy's youthful good

John Fitzgerald Kennedy National Historic Site.
(National Park Service)

looks and confident manner trumped the rumpled, unshaven appearance of the Republican candidate, Richard M. Nixon. In November, Kennedy eked out victory in the closest election since 1884, to become the first Roman Catholic president of the United States.

Kennedy's inaugural address offered the memorable injunction: "Ask not what your country can do for you; ask what you can do for your country." The president's New Frontier domestic programs included a call for new civil rights legislation, a greatly expanded space program, and economic policies that eventually ushered in the longest sustained expansion since World War II. In foreign policy, Kennedy's approach shifted from aggressive containment to careful détente. Following the frightening brinkman-

ship that emerged during the 1962 Cuban missile crisis, the president contended that both the United States and the Soviet Union had a vital interest in stopping the spread of nuclear weapons. Both sides, he said, had been "caught up in a vicious and dangerous cycle in which suspicion on one side breeds suspicion on the other, and new weapons beget counterweapons." The result was the 1963 Limited Nuclear Test-Ban Treaty that prohibited aboveground, outer space, and underwater weapons testing. Other foreign achievements included the Alliance for Progress, a ten-year, $100-billion plan to spur Latin America's economic development, and the Peace Corps. Not all of Kennedy's diplomatic and political efforts were successful. Many scholars regard the Cuban missile crisis as a result of Kennedy's inexperience; his invasion of Cuba, called the "Bay of Pigs," ended in a calamitous military and diplomatic defeat.

Whether Kennedy would have matured into a great leader will never be known. On November 22, 1963, Kennedy was assassinated as his motorcade wound through Dealey Plaza in Dallas, Texas. Although many suspect that either the Mafia or right-wing Cubans conspired to kill Kennedy, a generation of investigation has produced no one other than Lee Harvey Oswald, who worked at the Texas Schoolbook Depository from which the shots were fired, as the perpetrator of this heinous act.

Established in 1967, the John Fitzgerald Kennedy National Historic Site preserves the birthplace and boyhood home of the thirty-fifth president. The modest frame house in suburban Boston was also the first home shared by the president's father and mother, Joseph P. and Rose Fitzgerald Kennedy, and represents the social and political beginnings of one of the world's most prominent families.

The visitor center is open from April through mid-November from 10 A.M. until

4:30 P.M., Wednesday through Sunday, and features exhibits on President Kennedy's life and family. Seven historic furnished rooms of the birthplace home reflecting the 1917 period are open to visitors by guided tour only. Admission fees are $2 per adult age seventeen and older. The park periodically offers special tours of the nearby Brookline neighborhood, including the church attended by the president's family, boyhood schools, and a second family home during the visitor season, exploring some of the factors that influenced the future president between 1917 and 1931. In addition, special commemorative events celebrating President Kennedy's birthday, including tours, music, an essay program, and a public open house, are offered in late May.

There are no food, lodging, or camping facilities at the historic site, but the greater Boston area offers all traveler services.

For more information, write John Fitzgerald Kennedy National Historic Site, 83 Beals Street, Brookline, MA 02446, or telephone (617) 566-1689. The park's Web site is www.nps.gov/jofi.

FURTHER READING

Hamilton, Nigel. *JFK: Reckless Youth.* New York: Random House, 1992.
Kennedy, John F. *Profiles in Courage.* New York: Harper Perennial, 2000.
Reeve, Thomas C. *A Question of Character: A Life of John F. Kennedy.* New York: Free Press, 1991.
Salinger, Pierre. *John F. Kennedy: Commander-in-Chief.* New York: Penguin, 1997.

JOHN MUIR NATIONAL HISTORIC SITE

Location: Martinez, California
Acreage: 345
Established: August 31, 1964

In God's wildness lies the hope of the world—the great fresh unblighted, unredeemed wilderness.

–John Muir

John Muir was this country's most famous and influential naturalist and conservationist, a founder of the Sierra Club and the intellectual source for the idea of wilderness and its later emergence as a powerful political subject. He was born on April 21, 1838, in Dunbar, Scotland, and his family emigrated to the United States in 1849, settling in Wisconsin. After three years at the University of Wisconsin, Muir abruptly fled Civil War conscription and wandered throughout the northern United States and Canada, performing odd jobs to support his travels. Before this, he had established himself as a mechanical genius of some note, and he parleyed that into the management of factories. In 1867, while working at a carriage parts shop in Indianapolis, Muir suffered a blinding, though temporary, eye injury that altered his outlook forever. When he regained his sight one month later, Muir determined to appreciate the wonders of the world around him and set out on a series of adventures. To satisfy his wanderlust, Muir walked 1,000 miles from Indianapolis to the Gulf of Mexico, and sailed to Cuba, and later to Panama, where he crossed the isthmus and sailed up the West Coast, landing in San Francisco in March 1868. The Golden State captivated the imagination of this idealistic young man, who was particularly taken with California's Sierra Nevada Mountains and Yosemite. "It seemed to me the Sierra should be called not the Nevada, or Snowy Range, but the Range of Light . . . the most divinely beautiful of all the mountain chains I have ever seen."

Beginning in 1874, a series of articles by Muir entitled "Studies in the Sierra" launched his successful career as a writer, which eventually included more than 300 articles and 10 major books. In 1890, due in no small part to the efforts of Muir, an act of Congress created Yosemite National Park. Muir was also personally involved in the creation of Sequoia, Mount Rainier, Petrified Forest, and Grand Canyon national parks, earning a deserved reputation as the "Father of Our National

Naturalist and conservationist John Muir reclining in the wilderness, c. 1902. *(Library of Congress)*

Park System." In 1892, in an effort to protect his beloved Yosemite from resource interests, Muir and a number of his supporters founded the Sierra Club, in Muir's words, "to do something for wildness and make the mountains glad." Muir served as the club's president until his death in 1914. Muir's greatest heartache came out of the bitter fight to prevent the damming of Yosemite's Hetch Hetchy Valley. He lost this battle in 1913, and the valley was doomed to become a reservoir. The following year, after a short illness, John Muir—farmer, inventor, sheepherder, naturalist, explorer, writer, and conservationist—died in a Los Angeles hospital.

Authorized in 1964, the 345-acre John Muir National Historic Site preserves the 14-room mansion where the naturalist John Muir lived from 1890 until his death in 1914. The John Muir Visitor Center is open year-round from 10 A.M. until 4:30 P.M. daily, and entrance fees are $2 per person and are valid for seven days. The center features photo panels and artifacts highlighting the places and people associated with John Muir. In addition to self-guided tours of the Muir House, park rangers offer guided tours Wednesday through Sunday. The park also sponsors several special programs, including a May celebration of Muir's birthday, full-moon walks from June through September, an August Perseid Meteor Shower walk and watch, a September Ranch Day (Life on an 1880s Fruit Ranch) celebration, and a December Las Posadas and Victorian Christmas.

There are no food, lodging, or camping facilities at the historic site, but all are available in nearby Martinez. Camping is also available at the Mount Diablo State Park.

For more information, write John Muir National Historic Site, 4202 Alhambra Avenue, Martinez, CA 94553, or telephone (925) 228-8860. The park's Web site is www.nps.gov/jomu.

FURTHER READING

Cohen, Michael P. *The Pathless Way: John Muir and American Wilderness.* Madison: University of Wisconsin Press, 1984.

Ehrlich, Gretel. *John Muir: Nature's Visionary.* Washington, DC: National Geographic Society, 2000.

Fox, Stephen R. *The American Conservation Movement: John Muir and His Legacy.* Madison: University of Wisconsin Press, 1985.

Holmes, Steven J. *The Young John Muir: An Environmental Biography.* Madison: University of Wisconsin Press, 1999.

Muir, John. *Nature Writings: The Story of My Boyhood and Youth: My First Summer in the Sierra; The Mountains of California; Stickeen; Essays.* New York: Library of America, Penguin Books, 1997.

Wilkins, Thurman. *John Muir: Apostle of Nature.* Norman: University of Oklahoma Press, 1995.

JOHNSTOWN FLOOD NATIONAL MEMORIAL

Location: South Fork, Pennsylvania
Acreage: 164
Established: August 31, 1964

On Friday, May 31, 1889, disaster raged through Johnstown, Pennsylvania, when the old South Fork Dam failed and sent 20 million tons of water ripping through this steel company town of 30,000. Heavy rains had weakened the structure originally built by the Commonwealth of Pennsylvania as a reservoir for the canal basin in Johnstown. But the canal system was soon rendered obsolete by the Pennsylvania Railroad, and the property, including the rather rickety dam, was eventually sold to the South Fork Fishing and Hunting Club at a loss. In 1879, the club began repairing the dam, completing the restoration in 1881, and stocked the lake (which they called Lake Conemaugh) with 1,000 black bass. The dam held for almost ten years before bursting on that fateful May afternoon. Although the president of the South Fork Fishing and Hunting Club had sent telegraph warnings earlier that said the dam might go, the raging torrent devastated the town, killing more than 2,200 people, and injuring thousands of others. In the grim aftermath, the Red Cross, under the leadership of Clara Barton, conducted the first major disaster relief program in the United States. Today, the dam and lake no longer remain, but a short walk to one of the park's overlooks quickly conveys the size of the dam and its potential for destruction.

Authorized in August 1964, the 164-acre Johnstown Flood National Memorial preserves the remains of the South Fork Dam and portions of the former Lake Conemaugh bed, honoring those whose lives were lost during the tragedy. The park's visitor center is open all year from 9 A.M. until 5 P.M. daily, and until 6 P.M. during the summer months, and entrance fees are $2 per person, valid for seven days. The center features a thirty-five-minute motion picture re-creating the Great Flood of 1889, a fiber-optic map that describes the path of the flood, and exhibits that tell the story of the fabled South Fork Fishing and Hunting Club. Walking trails to the north and south abutments of the South Fork Dam are available for visitor enjoyment, and during the summer months, park rangers offer a variety of talks, tours, and other programs. A

The disasterous flooding of Johnstown, Pennsylvania, on May 31, 1889. *(Library of Congress)*

picnic area, located near the south abutment, is also available for public use.

There are no food, lodging, or camping facilities at the memorial, but all traveler services are available locally.

For more information, write Johnstown Flood National Memorial, 733 Lake Road, South Fork, PA 15956, or telephone (814) 495-4643. The park's Web site is www.nps.gov/jofl.

FURTHER READING

McCullough, David G. *The Johnstown Flood.* New York: Simon and Schuster, 1968.

Shappee, Nathan D. *A History of Johnstown and the Great Flood of 1889: A Study of Disaster and Rehabili-*
tation. Pittsburgh, PA, unpublished dissertation, 1940.

JOSHUA TREE NATIONAL PARK

Location: Twentynine Palms, California
Acreage: 789,745
Established: August 10, 1936

Joshua Tree National Park occupies a remarkable ecological zone encompassing 2 deserts in southeastern California. Elevation is the key factor in determining both the flora and fauna of these often stark landscapes. The Colorado desert, occupying the eastern half of the park, thrives below 3,000 feet and is dominated by the abundant creosote bush, interspersed with ocotillo and cholla cactus. The remainder of the park is defined by the higher, slightly cooler, and wetter Mojave Desert and its extensive stands of the distinctive Joshua trees, from which the park derives its name. In sharp contrast to these arid environs, the park also boasts a unique series of fan-palm oases, a third ecosystem indicating those few areas where water occurs naturally at or near the surface, meeting the special life requirements of these stately trees and desert wildlife. Aside from its ecological wonders, Joshua Tree National Park encompasses some of the most interesting geologic displays found in California's deserts, including arroyos, playas, alluvial fans, bajadas, pediments, desert varnish, granites, aplite, and gneiss.

The area's first settlers were most likely members of the hunting-and-gathering Pinto Culture, one of the Southwest's earliest inhabitants, who lived along a slow-moving river that ran through the now-dry Pinto Basin. Later, other native people traveled through this region following the harvest of pinyon nuts, mesquite beans, acorns, and cactus fruit, and leaving behind rock paintings and pottery ollas as reminders of their passing. In the late 1800s, explorers, cattlemen, and miners came to the desert, building dams to create water tanks and digging up the earth in search of gold. The remnants of their tenure include the Lost Horse and Desert Queen mines and the Desert Queen Ranch. In the 1930s, homesteaders seeking free land and the chance to start new lives ventured here as well.

The park's namesake, *Yucca brevifolia*, is found only in the American Southwest, concentrated here in the high Mojave Desert between 2,000 and 6,000 feet. Joshua trees are slow growers—less than an inch each year—

and can germinate from seed or from an underground rhizome of another Joshua tree. Determining the age of a Joshua tree can be difficult, however, since its trunk is comprised of thousands of small fibers and lacks the annual growth rings found on other trees. Its shallow root system and top-heavy branch structure make the tree rather unstable, but if it can survive the rigors of the desert, a Joshua tree can live as long as 200 years. The park is particularly lovely in spring when the creamy white blossoms of blooming Joshua trees and other desert cacti are on display.

Originally proclaimed a national monument in 1936, Joshua Tree National Park was elevated to national park status in 1994 as part of the California Desert Protection Act. This piece of legislation, long in the making, transformed the perception and management of the desert, adding not only Joshua Tree to the national park category, but Death Valley National Monument as well. In addition, millions of acres of lands were preserved in Bureau of Land Management wilderness areas and in Mojave National Preserve as a result of the act. Today, Joshua Tree National Park protects nearly 800,000 acres of desert and wilderness. Located 140 miles east of Los Angeles, the park maintains 2 visitor centers at Cottonwood Spring and Twentynine Palms. Both centers are open year-round from 8 A.M. until 4:30 P.M. (the Oasis Visitor Center in Twentynine Palms is open until 5 P.M.), and have interpretive exhibits. Park rangers offer interpretive talks and guided hikes as well as campfire programs in the spring and fall. In addition, the Black Rock Nature Center in Black Rock Canyon is open from late September to early June from 8 A.M. until 4 P.M. Entrance fees are $5 per person or $10 per vehicle, and are valid for seven days; a $25 annual pass is also available.

There are no food or lodging facilities lo-

Rock climbing in Joshua Tree National Park. *(National Park Service)*

cated in the park, but all traveler services are available in the towns of Joshua Tree, Twentynine Palms, and Yucca Valley. There are 9 campgrounds located at various elevations in Joshua Tree National Park. All are open year-round, and fees vary. Most operate on a first-come, first-served basis, but reservations are available at Indian Cove and Black Rock Canyon. There are also private campgrounds in Twentynine Palms.

For more information, write Joshua Tree National Park, 74485 National Park Drive, Twentynine Palms, CA 92277-3597, or telephone (760) 367-5500. The park's Web site is www.nps.gov/jotr.

FURTHER READING

Darlington, David. *The Mojave: A Portrait of the Definitive American Desert.* New York: Henry Holt, 1996.

Keys, Willis. *Growing Up at the Desert Queen Ranch.* Twentynine Palms, CA: Desert Moon, 1997.

Miller, A.H. *Lives of Desert Animals in Joshua Tree National Monument.* Berkeley: University of California Press, 1964.

Vuncannon, Delcie H. *Joshua Tree: The Story Behind the Scenery.* Las Vegas, NV: KC Publications, 1996.

K

KALAUPAPA NATIONAL HISTORICAL PARK

Location: Kalaupapa, Molokai, Hawaii
Acreage: 10,779
Established: December 22, 1980

On the north shore of the island of Molokai in Hawaii lies a truly remarkable component of the National Park System, which preserves a historic leper colony and rare native habitat for threatened and endangered Hawaiian plants and animals.

For nearly a millennium, native Hawaiians had called Kalaupapa home, but in 1865, King Kamehameha V implemented a policy of forced isolation for those found suffering from Hansen's disease, more commonly known as leprosy. The remoteness of the Kalaupapa Peninsula seemed an ideal destination for lepers in an age where little was known about the disease, and, over time, hundreds of people were banished to this isolated paradise.

Known as "The Place of the Living Dead," Kalaupapa's tragic history also includes the forced removal of native Hawaiians, which severed their ancient cultural ties to the 'aina (land). Without the traditional land tenants, farms began failing and conditions in this settlement devoid of hope soon deteriorated; medical services, housing, and other infrastructures were woefully inadequate.

In 1873, the arrival of Father Damien (Joseph De Veuster) brought compassion and progress to the peninsula, starting the community on the long path toward modernization. In the 1940s, new medications were discovered that eliminated concerns of contagion, and in 1969, the century-old banishment laws were abandoned. Today, the town of Kalaupapa, on the leeward side of the peninsula, is still home to many Hansen's disease survivors, while the original settlement at Kalawao, on the windward side, contains the churches of Siloama and Saint Philomena.

On the northern tip of the peninsula is the Molokai Light, which opened in 1909, and is the tallest U.S. lighthouse in the Pacific Ocean. It guides ocean vessels past Molokai and into Honolulu Harbor on Oahu.

The Hawaiian islands are the most isolated major island chain in the world–2,400 miles from the nearest continent or island group. The islands–over millions of years–were slowly colonized by plants and animals blown by the wind or carried by the sea, creating a remarkable ecosystem renowned for its ecological diversity and endemic flora and fauna. Nearly 95 percent of native Hawaiian plants and animals are found nowhere else in the world. Because they evolved without predators, however, these species are particularly vulnerable to foreign invasions. Beginning with the Polynesians, humans purposefully and accidentally imported hundreds of plants and animals that quickly displaced native flora and fauna and altered the environment. While this exotic invasion has affected even the remote Kalaupapa Peninsula, the park's relative isolation has protected some native species. Remnants of some of Hawaii's natural biological communities and native ecosystems can still be found in this area.

Established in 1980, the 10,779-acre Kalaupapa National Historical Park protects the Kalaupapa Peninsula, adjacent cliffs and valleys, a volcanic crater, a rainforest, lava tubes and caves, and submerged lands and waters a quarter mile out from the shore. There are three types of visitation possible at the park: viewing the peninsula from the overlook, touring historic Kalaupapa and Kalawao through a commercial tour, and visiting as a guest of residents. The park's visitor center is located in Kalaupapa at the Americans of Japanese Ancestry (AJA) Hall, and it has limited operating hours Monday through Saturday. The center has interpretive materials and artifact display cases. The park's cooperating association, Arizona Memorial Museum Association, maintains a small sales outlet. Wayside exhibits on the peninsula's people, history, and archeology are located throughout the Kalawao and Kalaupapa settlements, as well as at the Kalaupapa airport and at the Kalaupapa overlook at Palaau State Park.

One of the primary purposes of this unique park is the protection of the lifestyle and individual privacy of the Hansen's disease patients living here. Kalaupapa National Historical Park is administered in cooperation with several Hawaii state agencies, and all visitors must receive a permit from the Department of Health to enter the Kalaupapa settlement. Commercial tour companies arrange permits for their customers, while guests of residents have their permits arranged by their sponsor. Reservations are required for commercial tours of the settlement, mule rides on the trail, and air flights, and visitors are encouraged to make these reservations in advance. The National Park Service does not offer any regularly scheduled interpretive programs or activities because of the restricted nature of visitation to the park, and because tours are offered through a commercial service.

The park can be reached by air through commercial and charter flights from Honolulu, Oahu, and from Hoolehua, Molokai. Some visitors arrive by private boats and tie to buoys near the dock at Kalaupapa. Visitors also hike or ride mules down the steep Kalaupapa Trail, accessed off Highway 470 near Palaau State Park and the Kalaupapa overlook. At the bottom of the trail, visitors connect with the commercial tour of the settlement. There is no vehicular access to the park due to the ocean and steep cliffs.

For more information, write Kalaupapa National Historical Park, P.O. Box 2222, Kalaupapa, HI 96742, or telephone (808) 567-6802. The park's Web site is www.nps.gov/kala.

FURTHER READING
Brooker, James H. *Father Damien, the Lands of Kalaupapa, Molokai, Hawaii.* Kaunakakai, HI: Molokai Fish and Dive Corporation, 1998.
Greene, Linda W. *Exile in Paradise: The Isolation of Hawaii's Leprosy Victims and Development of Kalaupapa Settlement, 1865 to the Present.* Denver, CO: Denver Service Center, National Park Service, 1985.
Law, Anwei Skinsnes. *Kalapaupapa National Historical Park and the Legacy of Father Damien: A Pictorial History.* Honolulu, HI: Pacific Basin Enterprises, 1988.

KALOKO-HONOKOHAU NATIONAL HISTORICAL PARK
Location: Kailua-Kona, Hawaii
Acreage: 1,161
Established: November 10, 1978

Kaloko-Honokohau National Historical Park, on the Kona Coast of the island of Hawaii, is surrounded by barren and rugged lava. Native Hawaiians lived and thrived in this harsh environment for centuries, until the nineteenth-century arrival of Western culture brought an end to indigenous lifeways.

Perhaps the most striking signs left behind by these early inhabitants are the human-made Kaloko and 'Aimakapa fishponds and the 'Ai'opio fishtrap. Kaloko fishpond, with its massive seawall, provides an excellent example of the engineering skill of the ancient Hawaiians. The fishponds of Kaloko-Honokohau are also important because they are home to many kinds of waterfowl, most notably, three endangered species: the ae'o, the Hawaiian black-necked stilt, the 'alae ke'oke'o, the Hawaiian coot, and the koloa, the Hawaiian duck. Unfortunately, this unique wetland habitat has come under attack during the past decade; the invasive red mangrove, an exotic plant, has rendered the Kaloko fishpond uninhabitable for the three endangered species. In response, the Park Service has implemented an aggressive program of mangrove eradication to restore this scarce ecosystem and prevent the plant from spreading to other parts of the park.

The national significance of the Hawaiian cultural remains found at Kaloko-Honokohau was first recognized in 1962, when the Honokohau settlement was declared a national historic landmark. In 1966, the landmark was placed on the National Register of Historic Places, and in 1978, as part of one of the great omnibus national park bills, it became a national historical park. In addition to the fishponds, there are several heiau (Hawaiian temples) located in the park, the most prominent of which are Makaopi'o and Pu'uoina. Kaloko-Honokohau contains many Hawaiian grave sites, and much of the park is considered sacred. The park also protects many other sites of significance to Hawaiians, including kahua (house platforms), fishing shrines, canoe landings, ki'i pohaku (petroglyphs), a holua (a stone slide built for the recreation of Hawaiian royalty, the ali'i), and a 1-mile segment of the Mamalahoa Trail, built between 1836 and 1855 (also known as the King's Highway).

Established in 1978 for the preservation, protection, and interpretation of traditional native Hawaiian activities and culture, the 1,161-acre Kaloko-Honokohau National Historical Park encompasses portions of 4 different ahupua'a, or traditional sea-to-mountain land divisions. It is located at the base of Hualālai Volcano, along the Kona coast of the island of Hawaii, 3 miles north of Kailua-Kona, and 3 miles south of Keahole-Kona International Airport, along Highway 19 (the Queen Ka'ahumanu Highway). The Kaloko road gate is open from 8 A.M. until 3:30 P.M. daily, and though visitors are welcome in the park after 3:30 P.M., their vehicles must be out of the Kaloko area before the gate closes. Administrative headquarters for Kaloko-Honokohau is located in the Kaloko New Industrial Park along Highway 19, and admission is free. The park sponsors an annual Cultural Day and occasional special interpretive programs.

There are no food, lodging, or camping facilities in the park, but all are available locally, including a campground at Hapuna State Park.

For more information, write Kaloko-Honokohau National Historical Park, 73-4786 Kanalani Street, Suite #14, Kailua-Kona, HI 96740, or telephone (808) 329-6881. The park's Web site is www.nps.gov/kaho.

FURTHER READING

Greene, Linda Wedel. *A Cultural History of Three Traditional Hawaiian Sites on the West Coast of Hawaii Island.* Denver, CO: National Park Service, 1993. Available at www.cr.nps.gov/history/online _books/kona/history.htm.

Kay, E. Alison, ed. *A Natural History of the Hawaiian Islands: Selected Readings.* Honolulu: University Press of Hawaii, 1972.

Kirch, Patrick V. *Feathered Gods and Fishhooks: An Introduction to Hawaiian Archaeology and Prehistory.* Honolulu: University of Hawaii Press, 1985.

Stannard, David E. *Before the Horror: The Population of Hawaii on the Eve of Western Contact.* Honolulu: University of Hawaii, Social Science Research Institute, 1989.

Titcomb, Margaret. *Native Use of Fish in Hawaii.* Honolulu: University Press of Hawaii, 1972.

KATMAI NATIONAL PARK AND PRESERVE

Location: King Salmon, Alaska
Acreage: 4,093,229
Established: September 24, 1918

Katmai National Park and Preserve is truly a wilderness park—of its more than 4 million acres, most of this area is federally protected wilderness in the famed Valley of Ten Thousand Smokes. This spectacular 40-mile, 100- to 700-foot-deep, pyroclastic ash flow deposited by the 1912 explosion of Novarupta Volcano derives its name from the steam that rose from countless fumeroles in the valley. In all, at least 14 active volcanoes dot the park today, though none is currently erupting. Katmai is also famous for its brown bears and salmon. The Alaska brown bear is the world's largest carnivore, and more than 2,000 of them call Katmai "home." Each year, during the peak of the world's largest sockeye salmon run in July, and during the return of the "spawned out" salmon in September, forty to sixty bears congregate at Brooks Camp on the Brooks River, and along the Naknek Lake and Brooks Lake shorelines, to feast on the fish. Other brown bears along the 480-mile Katmai Coast satisfy their appetites with clams, crabs, and even an occasional whale carcass. Although bears have occupied this region for millennia, they have had to share the river's bounty with humans for the last four thousand years. In addition to harvesting salmon, early inhabitants sustained themselves with the great diversity of wildlife in Katmai, which includes massive, thundering herds of caribou. Today, the park's Brooks River National Historic Landmark protects North America's highest concentration of prehistoric human dwellings, which number about 900.

Originally established as a national monument in 1918, Katmai was typical of remote national monuments for the next fifty years. Katmai's relative isolation and frigid and foreboding environment protected it from the crush of tourists invading the nation's more accessible national parks. Only in 1964 did the monument receive a full-time staff member; in 1966, a superintendent was appointed for the first time. The Alaska lands question compelled an expansion of monument boundaries in 1969 and a decade later, in 1980, it was elevated to national park status as part of President Jimmy Carter's creation of almost 50 million acres of national parklands in Alaska. An additional 380,000-acre preserve was created as well.

The park maintains 3 visitor centers: Brooks Camp, King Salmon, and Three Forks. The Brooks Camp Visitor Center is open from June through mid-September, and it is located on Naknek Lake near the mouth of Brooks River, 30 air miles from King Salmon. All visitors to Brooks Camp are required to attend the Brooks Camp School of Bear Etiquette, a fifteen- to twenty-minute orientation that provides visitors with basic information to help keep them safe and the bears out of trouble. Park rangers also offer cultural walks to re-created archeological sites, guided bus tours of the Valley of Ten Thousand Smokes, and various evening programs. The King Salmon Visitor Center is open all year from 8 A.M. until 5 P.M. and is located next to the airport terminal in King Salmon. The center has exhibits on the local area as well as interpreters who can provide information on the entire Katmai region. The Three Forks Visitor Contact Station is open from June through mid-September and is located 23 miles from Brooks Camp on the only road within Katmai National Park and Preserve. Featuring exhibits on the geology and history of the Valley of Ten Thousand Smokes, the station overlooks the famous valley and is the starting point of the Ukak Falls Trail.

The primary focus of visitation at Katmai is the bear-viewing platforms along the Brooks River, where brown bears congregate to feed on sockeye salmon. In recent years, the park's world-class sportfishing and wilderness camping have led to increased use along the outer coast and elsewhere in the park interior. Katmai National Park and Preserve is located on the Alaska Peninsula, across from Kodiak Island, and park headquarters is in King Salmon, about 290 air miles southwest of Anchorage. Several commercial airlines provide daily flights into King Salmon as there is no road access. Brooks Camp, along the Brooks River approximately 30 air miles from King Salmon, is a common destination for visitors to the park and is accessible only via small floatplane or boat. Access to the coast is available by boat tours and charter air taxis from Kodiak, Homer, and Anchorage, or from many of Katmai's commercial operators and lodges.

Lodging within the park is provided by a private concessionaire, Katmailand (800-544-0551), at Brooks Lodge and 2 other lodges. These accommodations are open from June through mid-September and require advance reservations. Brooks Lodge offers meals, and the Trading Post sells many tourist supplies. Other lodges and resorts outside the park offer tour packages for Katmai and the Alaska Peninsula area as well. The Brooks Camp Campground (800-365-CAMP) is also open from June through mid-September, and like the lodges, requires advance reservations. Brooks Camp is the only Federal Fee Area within Katmai National Park and Preserve, charging a $10-per-person, per-day user fee (not entrance fee) for all persons, plus an additional $5-per-person, per-night fee for those camping at the campground.

For more information, write Katmai National Park and Preserve Headquarters, P.O. Box 7, #1 King Salmon Mall, King Salmon, AK 99613, or telephone (907) 246-3305. The park's Web site is www.nps.gov/katm.

FURTHER READING

Breiter, Matthias. *The Bears of Katmai: Alaska's Famous Brown Bears.* Portland, OR: Graphic Arts Center, 2001.

Clemens, Janet, and Frank Norris. *Building in an Ashen Land: Historic Resource Study of Katmai National Park and Preserve.* Anchorage, AK: National Park Service, 1999. Available at: www.nps.gov/katm/hrs/hrs.htm.

Norris, Frank. *Isolated Paradise: An Administrative History of the Katmai and Aniakchak NPS Units, Alaska.* Anchorage, AK: National Park Service, 1996. Available at www.nps.gov/katm/adhi/adhi.htm.

KENAI FJORDS NATIONAL PARK

Location: Seward, Alaska
Acreage: 669,983
Established: December 1, 1978

Although it is the smallest national park in Alaska, Kenai Fjords boasts one of the four major ice caps in the United States—the 300-square-mile Harding Icefield—and dramatic coastal fjords. Located on the southeastern Kenai Peninsula, the park is a pristine and rugged land supporting many natural environments and ecosystems. The Harding Icefield is a remnant of the massive ice sheet that covered much of Alaska during the Pleistocene era. Up to a mile thick in places, the Icefield feeds more than thirty glaciers that flow out of the mountains, including the park's most popular and accessible area, Exit Glacier. The park's namesake fjords are ancient, long, steep-sided, glacier-gouged valleys that are now filled with ocean waters and teeming with sea animals.

Kenai's almost-670,000 acres protect wildlife such as mountain goats, moose, bears, lynx, wolverines, marmots, and other land mammals that thrive in the fragile margin between ocean and ice. Bald eagles nest in the tops of spruce and hemlock trees, and thousands of seabirds, including puffins, kittiwakes, and murres, seasonally inhabit the steep cliffs and rocky shores of the fjords. Kayakers, anglers, and visitors on tour boats often share the park's waters with stellar sea lions, harbor seals, Dall porpoises, sea otters, and humpback, killer, and minke whales.

Originally set aside as a national monument, Kenai Fjords was redesignated a national park in 1980 as part of the Alaska Lands Act. Entrance fees valid for seven days are $2 per person or $5 per vehicle, and user fees are charged at Exit Glacier; a $15 annual pass is also available. The park's visitor center, located on Seward's small-boat harbor, is open Monday through Friday year-round, and Saturdays and Sundays from Memorial Day through Labor Day with extended hours. The center has exhibits, slide programs, maps, publications, and information, and park rangers offer tours, guided walks, and educational programs. The Exit Glacier Ranger Station, located 9 miles down Exit Glacier Road off the Seward Highway, is open daily during the summer. In addition to exhibits and information about the glacier and the Harding Icefield, park rangers offer interpretive programs and talks.

Kenai Fjords National Park lies 130 road miles south of Anchorage on the Seward Highway and is accessible by private car or public bus service (from Anchorage). During the summer months, the Alaska Railroad serves Seward from Anchorage, and the Alaska Marine Highway (ferry) System connects Seward with Homer and Seldovia via Kodiak, providing service to Valdez and Cordova. Commuter flight services also link Seward and Anchorage. Authorized commercial guides provide camping, fishing, and kayaking services in the park, and various air charters fly over the coast for flight-seeing and access to the fjords. During the summer, boat tours ply the coast, observing calving glaciers, sea birds, and marine mammals, and charter fishing expeditions give visitors the opportunity to hook halibut, lingcod, rock fish, Dolly Varden, silver and red chum, and pink salmon.

All traveler services are available locally and in Seward. In addition, Exit Glacier Campground and Back Country Cabins are open all year and feature 12 walk-in summer camping sites and 3 backcountry cabins for summer visits along the park's coastline. Located in the fjords of Holgate Arm, Aialik Bay, and North Arm, these lodging facilities are accessible by boat, kayak, or small plane. In winter, a public use cabin is available at Exit Glacier. Cabin stays are limited to three days and visitors must obtain reservations and permits in advance.

For more information, write Kenai Fjords National Park, P.O. Box 1727, Seward, AK 99664, or telephone (907) 224-3175. The park's Web site is www.nps.gov/kefj.

FURTHER READING

Cook, Linda, and Frank Norris. *A Stern and Rock-Bound Coast: Kenai Fjords National Park Historic Resource Study.* Anchorage: National Park Service, Alaska Support Office, 1998. Available at www.nps.gov/kefj/hrs/hrs.htm.

Miller, David W. *A Guide to Alaska's Kenai Fjords.* Seward, AK: Wilderness Images, 1984.

Sherwood, Morgan B. *Big Game in Alaska: A History of Wildlife and People.* New Haven, CT: Yale University Press, 1981.

KENNESAW MOUNTAIN NATIONAL BATTLEFIELD PARK

Location: Kennesaw, Georgia
Acreage: 2,884
Established: February 8, 1917

On June 27, 1864, the Union army collided with Confederate forces at Kennesaw Mountain in northwestern Georgia. In the great scheme of the Civil War, the two-day battle fought here does not evoke the emotion of Antietam, Chancellorsville, or the Wilderness. By comparison, the casualties both sides suffered were light: 3,000 Union and 1,000 Confederate at the Battle of Kennesaw Mountain; 350 Union and 1,000 Confederate at the Battle of Kolb's Farm (June 22). Yet these conflicts were significant, for they were part of a complicated Union strategy that was, ultimately, the beginning of the end of the Civil War.

In March of 1864, President Abraham Lincoln had appointed Ulysses S. Grant general of all the Union forces, and Grant soon instigated a new style of warfare—a campaign of annihilation. Hoping to inflict maximum damage on the South, Grant sent General William Tecumseh Sherman on a mission to defeat Confederate General Joe Johnston's Army of Tennessee. Sherman's Atlanta Campaign became the most famous example of this new strategy of total war. Beginning on June 9, the Union army moved east from Dallas, fighting a series of actions at Lost Mountain, Pine Mountain, Gilgal Church (or Gilgal Creek), Brushy Mountain, Noonday Creek, Ruff's Mill, Kolb's Farm, and finally, Kennesaw Mountain. For Sherman, the Battle of Kennesaw Mountain was a failure. Johnston's men repeatedly beat back Union attacks during a viciously hot and awful day of fighting. One Confederate remembered, "I never saw

so many broken down and exhausted men in my life." Yet while Johnston's victory bolstered Southern morale and increased Northern frustration, it did not stop Sherman. On September 2, the Union general captured Atlanta, which lay shattered in ruins around him. Southern diarist Mary Boykin Chesnut lamented, "Since Atlanta I have felt as if all were dead within me, forever. We are going to be wiped off the earth." From Atlanta, Sherman carved a swath of destruction across Georgia as he marched to the sea and Savannah. By December, Savannah had become an occupied city, and the South's will to fight began to disintegrate. Four months later, the Confederacy collapsed, and the war grinded to a close.

Rising 1,000 feet above the relatively flat plateau geologically known as the Central

Battle of Kennesaw Mountain, June 27, 1864. *(Library of Congress)*

Uplands, Kennesaw is the tallest mountain in a short string of peaks north and west of Atlanta. Before 1755, the area around Kennesaw Mountain was Creek land; however, after they lost the Battle of Taliwa, the land was controlled by the Cherokee. The peak itself is named for the chief of a large Cherokee village in the region, but in 1836, the Cherokees were forcibly removed from their lands by the federal government during "The Trail of Tears." The history of Kennesaw Mountain Park began in 1899, shortly after completion of the Chickamauga-Chattanooga National Military Park, when the state of Illinois purchased a small tract of land near the Dead Angle. During the 1930s, a Civilian Conservation Corps (CCC) camp was established near Pigeon Hill and workers from this camp were responsible for many of the improvements in the park, including almost all of the hiking trails. In 1933, the site was transferred to the National Park Service, and, in 1935, it was redesignated a national battlefield park.

First authorized as a national battlefield site in February 1917, the 2,884-acre Kennesaw Mountain National Battlefield Park commemorates the two battles fought here during Sherman's 1864 Atlanta Campaign. The visitor center is open daily from 8:30 A.M. until 5 P.M., and it offers an eighteen-minute orientation film, various historical exhibits, and a bookstore with Civil War merchandise. Admission is free. In addition to ranger programs, the park offers many living-history presentations and artillery demonstrations, as well as a special Battle Anniversary Weekend in late June. There are no food, lodging, or camping facilities in the park, but all traveler services are available locally.

For more information, write Kennesaw Mountain National Battlefield Park, 900 Kennesaw Mountain Drive, Kennesaw, GA 30152, or telephone (770) 427-4686. The park's Web site is www.nps.gov/kemo.

FURTHER READING
Blythe, Robert W. *Kennesaw Mountain National Battlefield Park: Historic Resource Study.* Atlanta, GA: National Park Service, Southeast Region, 1995.
Capps, Michael A. *Kennesaw Mountain National Battlefield Park: An Administrative History.* Atlanta, GA: National Park Service, Southeast Region, 1994. Available at www.cr.nps.gov/history/online _books/kemo/.
Castel, Albert E. *Decision in the West: The Atlanta Campaign of 1864.* Lawrence: University Press of Kansas, 1992.
Kelly, Dennis. *Kennesaw Mountain and the Atlanta Campaign: A Tour Guide.* Marietta, GA: Kennesaw Mountain Historical Association, 1989.

KEWEENAW NATIONAL HISTORICAL PARK
Location: Calumet, Michigan
Acreage: 1,869
Established: October 27, 1992

Keweenaw National Historical Park preserves the remarkable history of more than seven thousand years of copper mining on this Michigan peninsula. Native copper, which does not have to be smelted, occurs here as amygdule fillings in the basalt lava, and from more than 3,000 hand-dug pits, early Native Americans began mining the natural copper deposits and fashioning it into ornamental objects and knives. This oldest mining site in the Western Hemisphere was integrated into a large trade network that distributed copper items throughout archeological sites in eastern and central North America. In more recent times, Keweenaw was the site of America's first large-scale, hard-rock industrial mining operation, and the area's copper mines were critical for the industrial revolution in the United States. Indeed, Keweenaw was the only place in the world where commercially abundant quantities of elemental copper occurred. The mines, which eventually burrowed more than 9,000 feet into the earth, attracted a diverse population—a rich cultural heritage celebrated today by the park. Keweenaw itself is divided into 2 units—Quincy, home of the world's largest steam hoist, and Calumet, home of one of the world's most productive copper mines—and much of the area within it is, and will remain, in private ownership.

Established in October 1992, the 1,869-acre Keweenaw National Historical Park incorporates the Calumet and Quincy National Historic Landmarks and celebrates this legacy of human endeavor. There are presently no facilities operated by the National Park Service in the park; the Keweenaw Tourism Council serves as the park's information office. Within the park are numerous historic buildings, including the Calumet and Hecla (C&H) Mining Company's general offices, the C&H Roundhouse, the Red Jacket Town Hall and Opera House, and several notable churches, including St. Anne's and St. Paul's. The Coppertown Museum provides an overview of the company's history in the region, and during the summer months, a trackless trolley serves the Calumet unit. In the Quincy unit, there are several historically and architecturally significant residences, the most impressive of which is the Laurium Manor Inn. Cooperating sites within the park include the Quincy Mine Hoist and Underground Mine (tours available), the Houghton County Historical Museum, the Seaman Mineralogical Museum, and the Keweenaw County Historical Museum.

There are no food, lodging, or camping facilities operated by the Park Service, but all traveler services are available locally. Lodging and meals are available in Houghton, Hancock, Eagle Harbor, and Copper Harbor. In addition, McLain and Porcupine Mountains Wilderness state parks offer both cabin rentals and campgrounds, and Fort Wilkins State Park has a campground.

For more information, write Keweenaw National Historical Park, 100 Red Jacket Road, P.O. Box 471, Calumet, MI 49913, or telephone (906) 337-3168. The park's Web site is www.nps.gov/kewe.

FURTHER READING
Krause, David J. *The Making of a Mining District: Keweenaw Native Copper, 1500–1870.* Detroit, MI: Wayne State University Press, 1992.
Lankton, Larry D. *Beyond the Boundaries: Life and Landscape at the Lake Superior Copper Mines, 1840–1875.* New York: Oxford University Press, 1997.
Thurner, Arthur W. *Strangers and Sojourners: A History of Michigan's Keweenaw Peninsula.* Detroit, MI: Wayne State University Press, 1994.

KINGS MOUNTAIN NATIONAL MILITARY PARK

Location: Blacksburg, South Carolina
Acreage: 3,945
Established: March 3, 1931

By late 1780, the Revolutionary War had begun to turn against the British and their allies, the American Loyalists. The only theater where the British still found success was in the South. In South Carolina, 1780 was a rousing year for the king's forces. In May, the British captured Fort Moultrie and Charleston, South Carolina, and in August, the British crushed General Horatio Gates's soldiers at Camden, South Carolina. As a result, the British felt that the way to North Carolina, and beyond it, Virginia, was clear. Lord Cornwallis ordered Major Patrick Ferguson, a legendary sharpshooter, to collect his Loyalists and defend Cornwallis's left flank. By the time they dug in at Kings Mountain near Blacksburg, South Carolina, on October 7, 1780, Cornwallis had already taken Charlotte, North Carolina, and the Loyalists seemed on the verge of success in their invasion of North Carolina.

Although Ferguson bragged that he "was on Kings Mountain, that he was king of that mountain, and that God Almighty and all the Rebels of hell could not drive him from it," he was mistaken. The fighting began around 3 P.M. on October 17, and, after a brief skirmish, the shooting began in earnest. Using the heavily forested area at the base of the mountain for cover, American sharpshooters inflicted heavy losses on the Loyalists.

After an hour of fierce fighting, Ferguson was killed, and his second in command ordered a white flag of surrender. The fighting left 225 Loyalists dead, 163 wounded, and 716 taken prisoner. The rebels lost 28 killed and 68 wounded.

The battle at Kings Mountain changed the direction of the Revolutionary War in the South. His flank unprotected, a shaken Cornwallis retreated to South Carolina. The victory emboldened the king's opponents, and rebels, including the vaunted Swamp Fox, Francis Marion, and accelerated their raids on the British and their American allies. After Kings Mountain, the British knew they operated in a hostile territory even in the previously sympathetic South. The turning point in the battle for the South, Kings Mountain made eventual American victory a certainty.

The War Department established Kings Mountain National Military Park on March 3, 1931, but transferred it to the National Park Service with the rest of the War Department's military parks in August 1933. It is near Blacksburg, South Carolina, on South Carolina Highway 216, and operates daily from 9 A.M. to 5 P.M. and on weekends from 9 A.M. to 6 P.M. between Memorial Day and Labor Day. The park is closed on Thanksgiving Day, Christmas Day, and New Year's Day. Winters are mild with the lowest temperatures generally in the 20s. Summers are hot and humid with high temperatures in the 90s. There are no admission fees for the park, but the visitor center accepts donations.

For additional information, write Kings Mountain National Military Park, 2625 Park Road, Blacksburg, SC

Kings Mountain National Military Park. The battle of October 7, 1780, destroyed the left wing of Cornwallis's army and effectively ended Loyalist ascendance in the Carolinas. *(National Park Service)*

29702 or telephone (864) 936-7921. The park's Web site is www.nps.gov/kimo.

FURTHER READING
Battle of Kings Mountain 1780, with Fire and Sword. Washington, DC: Government Printing Office, 1991.
Messick, Hank. *King's Mountain: The Epic of the Blue Ridge "Mountain Men" in the American Revolution.* Boston: Little, Brown, 1976.

KLONDIKE GOLD RUSH NATIONAL HISTORICAL PARK

Location: Alaska and Washington
Acreage: 13,191
Established: June 30, 1976

In August 1896 when Skookum Jim Mason, Dawson Charlie, and George Washington Carmack found gold in a tributary of the Klondike River in Canada's Yukon Territory, their cries of "Gold! Gold! in the Klondike!" set off one of the greatest gold rushes in history. This last great gold rush of the nineteenth century followed so many others—the California Gold Rush most prominent among them. Yet this rush to the interior of the frozen north was different. More arduous, more dangerous, and more complicated, it created a new mythology of prospecting.

The early 1890s had been a financial disaster for many Americans, as the nation remained mired in the worst depression in its history to that point. But the possibility of striking it rich in the fabulous Klondike revived even the most pessimistic naysayers. By some estimates, more than a million people made plans to head to the great white north, although "only" about 100,000 actually made the trek. Seattle, Washington, relentlessly promoted itself as the principal "jumping-off point" to Alaska, and it even blanketed the country with a special Klondike edition of the *Seattle Post-Intelligencer.* Seattle boomed as a result, and some historians have even argued that Alaska became, for all intents and purposes, a kind of colony of this west coast city.

Certainly, Pacific Northwest merchants profited handsomely, as they mined the miners, who stocked up on everything from mules to gunny sacks, before these adventurers headed north.

The harsh realities of Alaska soon turned many of their dreams into nightmares. By 1897, of their thousands of young men had sailed toward the riches that surely awaited them. As in the California Gold Rush, towns and cities sprung up almost over night, and, in the first year, 20,000 to 30,000 stampeders swelled the populations of ramshackle settlements like Skagway and Dyea. But unlike the California experience, Alaska miners had to brave an additional 600-mile trek up and over the Chilkoot Trail out of Dyea and the White Pass Trail out of Skagway to reach the frozen goldfields. On the steep Chilkoot Trail, the men had to serve as their own pack animals, and they were heavily laden, since entry into Canada required that they bring a full complement of supplies, which they were required to show at the border. White Pass Trail, which did permit pack animals, soon earned a grisly reputation as "the animal killer," as miners pushed their overburdened mules and horses to extremes. In all, the remains of more than 3,000 animals lie at the bottom of Dead Horse Gulch.

By midsummer 1898, more than 18,000 people had arrived at "the diggings" near Dawson City. Yet, like most gold rushes, wealth remained elusive. By August, when the early Klondike winter began to set in, many headed for home with empty pockets. A few rushed to the next big find the following year in Nome, but the stampede towns of Dawson City and Skagway declined rapidly. Dyea simply disappeared, leaving behind only ghostly structures and the whispering hopes of those who had risked all for "Gold, Gold, Gold!"

First set aside as a national landmark in 1962, the 13,191-acre Klondike Gold Rush

National Historical Park celebrates the Klondike Gold Rush of 1897–1898 through 15 restored buildings within the Skagway Historic District. The park also administers the Chilkoot Trail and a small portion of the White Pass Trail, as well as a portion of the Dyea townsite at the foot of the Chilkoot Trail. Admission is free. The park's visitor center is open from 8 A.M. until 6 P.M. in May and September, and until 8 P.M. from June through August. The center features slide programs and a film on the gold rush, gold-panning demonstrations, and interpretive exhibits. Park rangers offer guided walking tours of the historic district, Dyea, and Moore House during the summer months. Visitors can also peruse local museums, explore nature on the local trails, and tour the Dyea townsite. Perhaps the best way to relive the experience of the stampeders is to hike the 33-mile Chilkoot Trail. This rugged and dif-

ficult trail begins at Taiya River bridge near the Dyea townsite and travels over Chilkoot Pass to Lake Bennett. Hikers must obtain a permit for the U.S. and Canadian portions of the Chilkoot Trail. Currently, the U.S. permit is free and the Canadian permit is $35 Canadian for adults and $17.50 Canadian for children age six to fifteen. The Seattle, Washington, unit of Klondike Gold Rush National Historical Park is open daily from 9 A.M. to 5 P.M., and it features exhibits, audiovisual programs, and ranger programs. Gold panning demonstrations, ranger programs, and a walking tour of the Pioneer Square Historical District are given daily from the middle of June to Labor Day.

Skagway, Alaska, is located 80 miles by air north of Juneau, but it can also be reached by the South Klondike Highway; it is 110 miles south of Whitehorse, Yukon Territory. There are no food or lodging facilities in the

This postcard illustrating the arduous trek to the Klondike bears this inscription: "Over Chilkoot Pass during The Gold Rush in Alaska. Thousands of Gold Seekers used This Trail." *(National Archives)*

park, but Skagway offers all traveler services. The park's Dyea Campground, open from mid-May through September and located 10 miles from Skagway near the old townsite of Dyea, has 22 rustic sites. Facilities include fire rings, picnic tables, pit toilets, a parking area, and campground host. Campgrounds are also available in Skagway.

For more information, write Klondike Gold Rush National Historical Park, Second and Broadway, P.O. Box 517, Skagway, AK 99840, or telephone (907) 983-9224. The park's Web site is www.nps.gov/klgo.

FURTHER READING

Berton, Pierre. *Klondike: The Last Great Gold Rush, 1896–1899.* Toronto: McClelland and Stewart, 1972.

Mighetto, Lisa. *Hard Drive to the Klondike: Promoting Seattle During the Gold Rush.* Seattle: University of Washington Press, 2002.

Norris, Frank B. *Legacy of the Gold Rush: An Administrative History of the Klondike Gold Rush National Historical Park.* Anchorage: National Park Service, Alaska System Support Office, 1996. Available at www.nps.gov/klgo/adhi/adhi.htm.

Schwantes, Carlos A. *The Pacific Northwest: An Interpretive History.* Lincoln: University of Nebraska Press, 1996.

Shape, William. *Faith of Fools: A Journal of the Klondike Gold Rush.* Pullman: Washington State University Press, 1998.

Wilson, Graham. *The Klondike Gold Rush: Photographs from 1896–1899.* Whitehorse, Yukon, AK: Wolf Creek Books, 1997.

KNIFE RIVER INDIAN VILLAGES NATIONAL HISTORIC SITE

Location: Stanton, North Dakota
Acreage: 1,758
Established: October 26, 1974

For nearly ten thousand years, Native Americans have lived and worked on the land surrounding Knife River Indian Villages National Historic Site. Perhaps the most well known of the region's inhabitants were the Hidatsa and Mandan tribes who developed a vast Euro-Indian trading network based upon Knife River flint. These were the Native Americans with whom the Lewis and Clark Expedition spent the winter of 1804. In both tribal groups, the village was central for political, social, and economic activities. One nineteenth-century observer described these settlements as "a cluster of molehills or muskrat cabins . . . the nearly circular huts are placed very irregularly; some so close to each other as scarcely to leave a foot-passage, others again at a distance of 20 to 30 feet apart. But about the center of each village is an open space of about four acres, around which the huts are regularly built at equal distances, fronting the open space." Today, more than 50 archeological sites and circular depressions at the 3 village sites stand as silent sentinels of the past. Permanent settlement of the region by Euro-Americans occurred in 1882, when the "wood yards" that served the river's steamship traffic evolved into the village of Stanton.

Although the primary resources of Knife River Indian Villages National Historic Site are cultural, the park encompasses significant and rare native prairie and riparian habitats, protecting them from the energy development, dam building, and agriculture that has destroyed or deteriorated similar ecosystems along the Missouri River. Authorized in October 1974, the 1,758-acre Knife River Indian Villages National Historic Site preserves the historic and archeological remnants of the culture and agricultural lifestyle of the Northern Plains Indians, and it is open year-round from 8 A.M. until 4:30 P.M. (and for extended hours during the summer). The park's visitor center, located half a mile north of Stanton, features a furnished Hidatsa earthlodge, a museum, a fifteen-minute orientation film, interpretive displays, and a bookstore. Park rangers offer educational programs and traditional cultural workshops throughout the year, and the park celebrates the Northern Plains Indian Culture Fest in late July. Visitors can also enjoy self-guided tours of the 3 historic village sites, and several paths provide bird-watching, wildlife viewing, fishing, and picnicking opportunities. In all, there are 11 miles of trails through natural areas and cultural sites, and winter activities include cross-country skiing on groomed trails.

For more information, write Knife River Indian Villages National Historic Site, P.O. Box 9, Stanton, ND 58571-0009, or telephone (701) 745-3300. The park's informative Web site is www.nps.gov/knri.

FURTHER READING

Ahler, Stanley A., Thomas D. Thiessen, and Michael K. Trimble. *People of the Willows: The Prehistory and Early History of the Hidatsa Indians.* Grand Forks: University of North Dakota Press, 1991.

Ronda, James P. *Lewis and Clark Among the Indians.* Lincoln: University of Nebraska Press, 1998.

Sullivan, Noelle, and Nicholas Peterson Vrooman. *M-è É cci Aashi Awadi: The Knife River Indian Villages.* Medora, ND: Theodore Roosevelt Nature & History Association, 1995.

L

LAKE CLARK NATIONAL PARK AND PRESERVE

Location: Port Alsworth, Alaska
Acreage: 4,030,025
Established: December 1, 1978

Lake Clark National Park and Preserve, the "alps of Alaska," includes most of the ecosystems of Alaska. Four of the five biotic communities found in Alaska–coastal, lakes/rivers/wetlands, tundra, and forest–are within the boundaries of this park and preserve. Sprawling for more than 6,000 square miles, this remarkable roadless area includes its namesake, Lake Clark, one of more than a score of glacially carved lakes that provide critical sockeye salmon habitat, the volcanic Chigmit Mountains, and a host of jagged peaks, tundra hills, and grinding glaciers. Indeed, Lake Clark is home to 2 towering stratovolcanoes, Mount Redoubt, a very alive volcano that erupted several times during the twentieth century, and Mount Iliamna, a barely dormant volcano that occasionally spews steam from fumaroles high on its flanks. This vast wilderness ecosystem rewards intrepid hikers with fine fishing and wildlife viewing, while adventurous river runners thrill to the white water of the Tlikakila, Mulchatna, and Chilikadrotna wild rivers.

After a brief period as a national monument, Lake Clark attained national park status as a result of the Alaska National Interest Land Conservation Act in 1980. Initially protected by President Jimmy Carter in 1978, the park was part of attempts to adjudicate native claims in Alaska. Carter's creation of fifteen national monuments that year pre-vented chaos; the Alaskan native Claims Settlement Act of 1971 gave the federal government seven years to select and secure legislation to protect national interest lands in Alaska. Carter's proclamation served in place of congressional legislation. The transfer to national park status happened after Carter's defeat in the 1980 election. The departing Congress made an important gift to the nation, a new national park system in Alaska. Lake Clark became an important component in that process.

Lake Clark National Park and Preserve contains fine examples of Alaska's diverse terrain, habitat, and climate and is home to an astonishing array of wildlife. Despite its sacrosanct national park status, however, the park is required to permit native subsistence hunting under the terms of ANILCA (Alaska National Interest Lands Conservation Act). Native people and other residents rely on game, especially the ever-present black bear. Brown (grizzly) bears are also common; Chinitna Bay, along the coast, supports the largest population. More than 200,000 caribou grace the park, and moose are found below the timberline throughout the park. The Chigmit Mountains are home to about 600 Dall sheep, the northernmost species of wild sheep in North America. Lake Clark is also home to animals that do not qualify as charismatic megafauna (the term for species that the public loves). Coyotes and wolves are common in the park and preserve, as are red fox and lynx. River otters, wolverines, weasels, mink, hares, and beaver also make their homes in the park. Chinitna Bay and Tuxedni Bay harbor marine mammals such as sea lions, beluga whales, harbor seals, and porpoises, and more than 125 species of birds utilize the feeding and nesting grounds in the foothills and lakes west of the Chigmit Range and on the Chulitna Flats adjacent to Lake Clark.

As do most of the Alaska parks, Lake Clark contains broad, federally protected wilderness areas–2.47 million acres–designated as part of the transfer to national park status in 1980. Alaskan wilderness is perhaps the most true wilderness in the United States, and no better example exists than Lake Clark. This enormous area is devoid of most human contact not only because the law demands it, but because of the sheer impracticability of establishing the institutions of modern society as well.

Admission to the park and preserve is free. The Port Alsworth Visitor Center is open during the summer months from 8 A.M. until 5 P.M., and from November through April upon request. The center features hands-on exhibits on the park's natural and cultural history, and slide shows and videos of the park and surrounding area are available as staffing allows. During the summer months, park rangers offer guided hikes and occasional presentations.

Summer temperatures average between 50 and 65 degrees, with considerable precipitation. Strong winds can occur at any time. Weather conditions in the region change suddenly, and proper equipment, rain and cool weather gear, extra food, and extra cooking fuel are essential for any backcountry travel. Frost and snow can occur in September and October, and even in midsummer, visitors should expect evening frost. Winter temperatures can sink to minus 40 degrees. Located 150 miles southwest of Anchorage on the west side of Cook Inlet and the north end of the Alaska Peninsula, the Lake Clark region is accessible only by small aircraft. Floatplanes land on the many lakes throughout the area, and wheeled planes land on open beaches, gravel bars, or private airstrips in or near the park. Scheduled commercial flights between Anchorage and Iliamna, 30 miles outside the park's boundary, provide another means of access, and a one- to two-hour flight from Anchorage, Kenai, or Homer provides access to most points within the park and preserve. A 2.5-mile trail to Tanalian Falls and Kontrashibuna Lake is accessible from the town of Port Alsworth. The 50-mile Telaquana Trail depicted on maps is an undeveloped historic route from Lake Clark to Telaquana Lake.

Lodging and food services are available in Port Alsworth, on Cook Inlet, and along Lake Clark. There is currently no designated camping area in Port Alsworth; however, the Park Service allows camping without a permit throughout the park (with the exception of private inholdings). Backcountry travelers must be self-sufficient, and rangers advise visitors to avoid game trails and fresh signs of bears.

For more information, write Lake Clark National Park and Preserve, Field Headquarters, 1 Park Place, Port Alsworth, AK 99653, or telephone (907) 781-2218. The park's Web site is www.nps.gov/lacl.

FURTHER READING

Branson, John B. *Bristol Bay, Alaska: From the Hinterlands to Tidewater: A Grassroots Pictorial, 1885–1965.* Anchorage, AK: National Park Service, 1998.

Catton, Theodore. *Inhabited Wilderness: Indians, Eskimos, and National Parks in Alaska.* Albuquerque: University of New Mexico Press, 1997.

Mcnab, A.J. *Lake Clark-Iliamna, Alaska, 1921: The Travel Diary of Colonel A.J. Mcnab with Related Documents.* Anchorage: Alaska Natural History Association, 1996.

Unrau, Harlan D. *Lake Clark National Park and Preserve, Alaska: Historic Resource Study.* Anchorage, AK: National Park Service, 1994.

LAKE MEAD NATIONAL RECREATION AREA

Location: Mojave Desert, Arizona and Nevada
Acreage: 1,495,664
Established: October 13, 1936

Established as a national recreation area in 1936 and made a full-fledged unit of the park system in 1964, Lake Mead National Recreation Area offers one of the most complicated national park management situations in the nation. Since establishment as an independent Park Service unit, Lake Mead National Recreation Area has undergone a transformation that parallels the urban development of the region around it. At its establishment, the area around Lake Mead was a small and idiosyncratic resort destination, far from the mainstream of U.S. society. The desert was not yet an American fashion, and the outdoor revolution, the constellation of ideas that drove the environmental revolution of the 1960s and 1970s—and the technologies to support the behaviors it encouraged—had not yet taken shape. In 1960, the population of Clark County, Nevada, the closest center of population to Lake Mead, was 127,016. By 2000, 1.5 million people lived in the area; between 2004 and 2007, the area will likely reach a population of 2 million people. Once remote from large populations, Lake Mead has become an urban park for greater Las Vegas and for vacationers from southern California and the rest of the Southwest. The enormous number of visitors, the growing demands of urban populations, the prime value placed on sites near the park or with views of the lake—in Boulder City and at nearby locations such as Lake Las Vegas—and issues such as beach and boating management and increasing crime rates illustrate the enormous changes that have taken place in the park's immediate environs.

The changing focus of national park management and the effort at inclusiveness in American society have also placed demands

Boating at Lake Mead National Recreation Area. *(National Park Service)*

on Lake Mead and its peers in the national recreation area category. The first generation of national parks offered an intellectual ideal as well as spectacular scenery: The beautiful vistas inspired Americans and reminded them of their culture's power. From their inception during the 1930s, national recreation areas were designed to offer a changing public more choices within the park system as well as to enhance the position of the National Park Service (NPS). Cynics called them examples of pork barreling and even in recent years, they have been regarded as nurturing the Park Service's affinity for tourism. Yet national recreation areas played an important role in reaching a broader public than was attracted to the conventional national parks.

From the beginning of NPS involvement at what was called Boulder Dam National Recreation Area in 1936, and even after establishment as an independent NPS unit in 1964, Lake Mead National Recreation Area operated as the prototype for a nonurban recreation unit. With the creation of Glen Canyon National Recreation Area—on precisely the model that established Lake Mead—and with the rise of the urban parks movement, the use side of the NPS mission became a primary trend in the agency as well as a way to meet its political objectives. After the establishment of Lake Mead National Recreation Area in 1964, the category rapidly multiplied and began to receive significant administrative and management attention.

After 1970, Lake Mead National Recreation Area faced a combination of the issues that confronted the newer urban parks and the more remote national recreation areas such as Lake Chelan and Glen Canyon. As Las Vegas and Clark County grew, Lake Mead National Recreation Area became an urban park, facing all the management constraints of parks such as Golden Gate and Gateway national recreation areas. Beach and boats, competing uses in limited space,

crowding, crime, search and rescue, traffic, and other urban issues replaced the questions of fish-stocking common in earlier times. Although most of the visitors and most of the issues were concentrated around Hoover Dam and a 20-mile stretch each direction, the park contained an area larger than the state of Rhode Island.

In this respect, Lake Mead National Recreation Area, the oldest and largest national recreation area in the nation, represented both sides of the bifurcated NPS mission to protect lands and to make them available to the public. In some areas, managing use dominated park policy; in others, often larger but more remote areas, preservation and resource protection became the primary obligation of park managers. With these two different responsibilities, finding balance became the challenge of managers at Lake Mead National Recreation Area (NRA).

Sturdy shoes, brimmed hats, and a good, protective sunscreen are recommended year-round. The park recommends visitors always carry water.

Lake Mead NRA is open throughout the year, twenty-four hours a day and seven days a week. The visitor center is open from 8:30 A.M. to 4:30 P.M. every day except Thanksgiving, Christmas, and New Year's Day. The park is approximately 25 miles from Las Vegas International Airport. Other communities bordering and near Lake Mead NRA have smaller airports. Nine paved roads lead into the park. There is a fee to enter. The Alan Bible Visitor Center is off U.S. Highway 93 near Boulder City, Nevada. Information stations are located on Lake Mead at Overton Beach, Echo Bay, Callville Bay, Las Vegas Bay in Nevada, and Temple Bar in Arizona. Contact stations can be found on Lake Mohave at Cottonwood Cove in Nevada, and at Katherine Landing and Willow Beach in Arizona.

For more information, write Lake Mead National Recreation Area, 601 Nevada Highway, Boulder City, NV 89005, fax 702-293-8936, or telephone visitor information (702) 293-8907, on weekends (702) 293-8990. The park's Web site is www.nps.gov/lame.

FURTHER READING

Houk, Rose. *Lake Mead National Recreation Area.* Tucson, AZ: Southwest Parks and Monuments Association, 1997.

Maxon, James C. *Lake Mead–Hoover Dam: The Story Behind the Scenery.* Las Vegas, NV: KC Publications, 1980.

Reisner, Marc. *Cadillac Desert: The American West and Its Disappearing Water.* New York: Penguin, 1993.

Rothman, Hal. *Balancing the Mandates: An Administrative History of Lake Mead National Recreation Area.* Boulder City, NV: National Park Service, 2002.

——. *Neon Metropolis: How Las Vegas Started the Twenty-First Century.* New York: Routledge, 2002.

LAKE MEREDITH NATIONAL RECREATION AREA

Location: Fritch, Texas
Acreage: 44,978
Established: March 15, 1965

In the American West, the National Park Service's recreation areas often seem like enormous mirages. They provide striking contrasts between the arid landscape and the seemingly abundant and often man-made water that is characteristic of such areas. A perfect illustration of this juxtaposition is Lake Meredith National Recreation Area, located in the Texas Panhandle. Like a jewel set in the dry and windswept High Plains, Lake Meredith is framed by scenic buttes, pinnacles, and red-brown, wind-eroded coves. The recreation area lies along the northern boundaries of a region known as the Llano Estacado, or "Staked Plains." This large expanse of nearly featureless plains encompassing western Texas and eastern New Mexico derives its name from early Spanish explorers who pounded route stakes across the region to mark their way and combat the disorienting sameness of the landscape. The lake itself was created by the Sanford Dam on the Canadian River, but the recreation area protects important stands of the nation's fragile and disappearing short- and tallgrass prairies. The mesas and hillsides support a variety of short grasses, including buffalo grass, grama, and sand dropseed, while the park's sheltered creekbeds nuture tallgrasses like Indian grass, switchgrass, and reeds as well as stands of cottonwoods, soapberry, and sandbar willows. In these environs, wildlife such as coyotes, deer, raccoons, skunks, and porcupines abound; the western diamondback and prairie rattlesnake are the only poisonous snakes in the area.

Originally set aside in March 1965, the 44,000-plus-acre Lake Meredith National Recreation Area was one of President Lyndon B. Johnson's gifts to his home state. An inveterate pork barreler, Johnson was ashamed that Texas lacked a significant national park system presence. Lake Meredith was among a number of places created to rectify that absence. Today, this national recreation area accommodates more than 1.5 million visitors each year and is one of the most popular outdoor attractions in the Texas Panhandle.

The park's headquarters is open year-round from 8 A.M. until 4:30 P.M., Monday through Friday, and a small bookstore sells a wide variety of titles covering the natural and human history of the Texas Panhandle. Admission to the recreation area is free, but there is a $4-per-day boating fee, which includes personal water craft such as jet skis and wet cycles; boaters may also purchase a three-day permit for $10, or an annual sticker for $40. The availability of the boat-launching facilities varies with the water level in Lake Meredith; typically, 3 to 7 ramps are dependably accessible, and a marina in the Sanford-Yake area provides a year-round launching ramp. The lake is the number-one walleye lake in Texas, though other favorite fish include largemouth, smallmouth, and white bass, as well as crappie, bream, and catfish.

In addition to water activities, visitors are welcome to enjoy horseback riding in Mc-Bride Canyon, Plum Creek, or other areas within the park. Off-road-vehicle use is also permitted in the recreation area within the cut banks of Blue Creek and in Rosita Flats, below a 3,000-foot elevation. Motorcycles, three- and four-wheelers, and dune buggies are prohibited in all other areas within the park, and all riders must wear eye protection and a safety helmet approved by the DOT (Department of Transportation). Below the dam are the Spring Canyon swimming area and a tract of wetlands that provide opportunities for birders. Other birding opportunities are present all year in the many canyons around the lake, where birders can identify more than 230 species, including the painted bunting, which nests in McBride Canyon. The Lake Meredith Aquatic and Wildlife Museum in Fritch provides a close-up view of local plant and animal life and contains large aquariums that display fish from Lake Meredith. The towns surrounding the lake have museums featuring the history and prehistory of the area.

There are no lodging facilities in the recreation area, but all traveler services are available in Amarillo, Borger, Dumas, Fritch, and Pampa. The marina offers food and basic supplies, and camping is available at the park's 12 designated campgrounds and at private facilities in Amarillo.

For more information, write Lake Meredith National Recreation Area, P.O. Box 1460, Fritch, TX 79036, or telephone (806) 857-3151. The park's Web site is www.nps.gov/lamr.

FURTHER READING
Brooks, Elizabeth, et al. *The Llano Estacado of the US Southern High Plains: Environmental Transformation and the Prospect for Sustainability.* New York: United Nations University Press, 2000.

Burnett, Georgellen. *We Just Toughed It Out: Women in the Llano Estacado.* El Paso: Texas Western, 1990.

The Handbook of Texas Online. Available at www.tsha.utexas.edu/handbook/online.

Morris, John Miller. *El Llano Estacado: Exploration and Imagination on the High Plains of Texas and New Mexico, 1536–1860.* Austin: Texas State Historical Association, 1997.

Parent, Laurence. *Lake Meredith National Recreation Area.* Tucson, AZ: Southwest Parks and Monuments Association, 1993.

LAKE ROOSEVELT NATIONAL RECREATION AREA
Location: Coulee Dam, Washington
Acreage: 100,390
Established: December 18, 1946

During the Great Depression, the United States began constructing what was heralded as "the biggest thing on earth"–the Grand Coulee Dam. When this engineering marvel was completed in 1941, many called it the "eighth wonder of the world." Towering 350 feet above the Columbia River in central Washington, the Grand Coulee Dam stretched nearly a mile in length, devoured nearly 12 million cubic yards of concrete, killed 77 men in the process of being built, and created the 130-mile-long reservoir named in honor of President Franklin D. Roosevelt–Lake Roosevelt. Finished just eight months before the attack on Pearl Harbor, this power-generating behemoth played a critical role in the defense industries that burgeoned in the Pacific Northwest during World War II. But if the gains it created were significant, so too were the losses.

In particular, the massive concrete dam flooded Kettle Falls, once one of the most important Native American fisheries on the Columbia River. For more than nine thousand years, the riches found at Ilthkoyape Falls–Kettle Falls–had drawn fishers and traders to the region. The staple of Columbia River people, salmon spawned up the Columbia in

A park visitor enjoys the view at Lake Roosevelt National Recreation Area. *(National Park Service)*

stunning numbers. The natural barrier of Kettle Falls proved an ideal fishing spot, where daring dipnetters braved sure death to haul in the shimmering giants that could weigh in excess of 100 pounds. All of this came to an end, however, when Lake Roosevelt began to fill.

First set aside as the Coulee Dam Recreation Area in 1946, the 100,390-acre Lake Roosevelt National Recreation Area was renamed in 1997 and offers prime water-based recreation, camping, and hiking opportunities. The visitor center, located on Highway 25, 22 miles north of Davenport, is open from mid-June through September, from 10 A.M. until 5 P.M. After the military left in 1899, Fort Spokane was converted into a boarding school for Native Americans; the museum houses special exhibits, developed in cooperation with the Colville Confederated

Tribes and the Spokane Tribe, on both historical uses of the facility. During the summer months, the park also offers historic weapons demonstrations and a living-history program every Sunday at 11 A.M. Hiking trails around the historic site have interpretive plaques about the history of the area. Admission to the park is free, but there is a $6 boat-launch fee, which is valid for seven days; a $40 annual permit is also available.

Echoes of the past can be heard along the 2-mile trail at Fort Spokane. Although quiet and peaceful now, for thousands of years the rush of the free-flowing Columbia and Spokane rivers called native peoples to the rich salmon fishery once found there. And the bugle calls that can be heard on the parade grounds today summoned soldiers to their posts one hundred years ago. For the adventurous, the trail climbs approximately 300 feet to the top of the bluff, giving a spectacular view of the fort grounds and the confluence of the rivers.

There are no lodging facilities in the recreation area, but all traveler services are available locally. The park's marinas offer food and supplies, and meals are also available at Spring Canyon Campground. There are 5 designated campgrounds in the national recreation area, which are open year-round on a first-come, first-served basis. Although the sites have no hookups, free dump stations, water for RV tanks (contingent on water levels), and comfort stations are available. Fees are $10 per night, per site, from May through September, and $5 per night, per site, from October through April. Private campgrounds are also available locally.

For more information, write Lake Roosevelt National Recreation Area, 1008 Crest Drive, Coulee Dam, WA 99116, or telephone (509) 738-6266. The park's informative Web site is www.nps.gov/laro.

FURTHER READING

Anglin, Ron, ed. *Forgotten Trails: Historical Sources of the Columbia's Big Bend Country.* Pullman: Washington State University Press, 1995.

Dietrich, William. *Northwest Passage: The Great Columbia River.* New York: Simon and Schuster, 1995.

Pitzer, Paul C. *Grand Coulee: Harnessing a Dream.* Pullman: Washington State University Press, 1994.

LASSEN VOLCANIC NATIONAL PARK

Location: Mineral, California
Acreage: 106,372
Established: May 6, 1907

First set aside as a national monument in 1907 and then promoted to national park status one week before the founding of the National Park Service, Lassen Volcanic National Park was typical of the national parks of the first two decades of the twentieth century. A collection of natural wonders in a scenic location, the 106,000-plus-acre park was small in size and confined to land that was not easily turned into dollars and cents with the technologies of the day. Its creation stemmed from the efforts of a number of groups of people with power and position in turn-of-the-century California. First proposed as a national park by California congressman John F. Raker in 1911, Lassen Volcanic National Park gained the support of leaders in nearby towns as well as the powerful conservation constituency in San Francisco. A number of women's clubs with an interest in conservation and professional geologists also offered their endorsement.

But until May 1914, when the volcanoes in the park erupted, little progress toward national park status took place. For nearly a year, the mountain spewed steam and ash in more than 150 separate eruptions before exploding on May 19, 1915, in an enormous mushroom cloud that rose 7 miles into the stratosphere. The reawakening of this volcano, which began as a vent on a larger extinct volcano known as Tehama, profoundly altered the surrounding landscape. When these volcanic explosions became national news, interest in creating the park grew, and the way to establishment was clear. Lassen Volcanic National Park was established for its volcanoes and its high mountain beauty.

The proclamation of the park inaugurated a typical transformation in the American West. A place of beauty, and in the case of the Lassen area, one that attracted national attention because of volcanic eruptions, became recognized for attributes that reflected the American nation's sense of itself. Early in the twentieth century, Americans wrestled with several intellectual and cultural dilemmas. They retained a sense of inferiority to Europe that stemmed from the lack of a comparable cultural heritage. The United States had mountain peaks and great crevasses to match the castles of Europe, and even its self-designation as "nature's nation" was not enough to quell American fears of inadequacy. Americans also grappled with a growing sense of loss that stemmed from the rapid transformation of their landscape and their social and cultural institutions in the aftermath of industrialization. Looking backward for a time in which these relationships seemed more in balance, the nation sought solace in its physical features. Lassen Volcanic National Park was a direct result of these concerns and the ways in which Progressive America sought to answer them.

Lassen Peak is the southernmost volcano in the Cascade Range, which extends from northern California into Canada. It is but one of the many volcanoes that extend around the Pacific Ocean in a great "Ring of Fire"—a zone of volcanoes that marks the edges of plates that form the earth's crust. Lassen Peak is considered the world's largest plug-dome volcano, rising 2,000 feet to an elevation of 10,457 feet. Along with the 1980 eruption of Mount Saint Helen's in Washington, Lassen is the only other Cascade volcano to erupt in the twentieth century. Today, Lassen Volcanic National Park serves as an important volcanic study area as well as a valuable laboratory for understanding the natural recovery pattern following eruptions.

In addition to its geological wonders, the Lassen area was a meeting point for at least four groups of Native American hunter-gatherers: the Atsugewi, Yana, Yahi, and Maidu. As whites flooded into the region during the mid-nineteenth century in search of gold and other valuable resources, these local tribes were devastated by both disease and warfare. Yet remarkably, in 1911, a remnant from the Yahi tribe, long thought extinct, stumbled out of the mountains and into Oroville, California. His name was Ishi, and he spent the next seven years as a living exhibit at the Anthropology Museum of the University of California in San Francisco. Before his death from tuberculosis on March 25, 1916, Ishi provided scientists and ethnologists with invaluable information about a way of life lost forever in the American West.

Another infamous individual associated with Lassen Volcanic National Park is the park's namesake, Peter Lassen, who, along with William Nobles, developed two pioneer trails that helped westward migration into California's gold fields. Notably, however, Lassen's trail took more than a month longer to complete than any other emigrant routes to the Sacramento Valley, and travelers justifiably labeled it "Lassen's Death Route." After 1850, emigrants rarely used the trail, but sections of both the Lassen and Nobles Emigrant Trail are still visible in the park today.

Originally set aside as a national monument in May 1907, Lassen attained national park status in August 1916, just as the National Park Service Organic Act approached passage. Today this park encompasses all 4 types of volcanoes found around the world and protects nearly 79,000 acres of wilderness.

Park headquarters, in the town of Mineral on State Route 36 east, is open year-round, Monday through Friday from 8 A.M. until 4:30 P.M. Entrance fees are $5 per person or $10 per vehicle and are valid for seven days; a $20 annual pass is also available. Park rangers offer several talks and guided walks, as well as evening programs and children's activities, and visitors can obtain maps, trail and road guides, and field guides at the headquarters.

The Loomis Museum at Manzanita Lake is open during the summer months from 9 A.M. until 5 P.M. It offers videos, ranger-led programs, and extensive exhibits of the artifacts and photographs illustrating the 1914–1915 eruption.

The park's Southwest Information Station is open daily from 9 A.M. until 4 P.M. from mid-June through Labor Day, and on weekends for the remainder of the summer. The station has information and park merchandise, including maps, trail and road guides, and field guides, and also children's activities, nature puppets, and ranger-led programs.

Lodging is available in the park from mid-June through mid-October at Drakesbad Guest Ranch, Manzanita Lake Camper Store, and the Lassen Chalet, which are run by California Guest Services, Inc. (530-529-1512), the park's authorized concessionaire. The park also offers 8 campgrounds, open from mid-June through mid-October; fees vary according to the available facilities. Drinks, food, and fuel are in the nearby town of Mineral and at the Manzanita Lake Camper Store at Manzanita Lake Campground.

Note that snow covers most of the park from around mid-October through approximately mid-June. The Park Road (the main road that connects Highway 89) and many attractions throughout the park are usually closed during this period.

For more information, write Lassen Volcanic National Park, P.O. Box 100, Mineral, CA 96063, or telephone (530) 595-4444. The park's Web site is www.nps.gov/lavo.

FURTHER READING

Alt, David D., and Donald W. Hyndman. *Roadside Geology of Northern and Central California*. Missoula, MT: Mountain, 2000.

Heizer, Robert F., and Theodora Kroeber. *Ishi, the Last Yahi: A Documentary History*. Berkeley: University of California Press, 1979.

Medlin, William K. *Fire Mountain: A Nation's Heritage in Jeopardy*. Santa Fe, NM: Sunstone, 1996.

Schaffer, Jeffrey P. *Lassen Volcanic National Park & Vicinity: A Natural-History Guide to Lassen Volcanic National Park, Caribou Wilderness, Thousand Lakes Wilderness, Hat Creek Valley, and McArthur–Burney Falls State Park*. Berkeley, CA: Wilderness, 1986.

LAVA BEDS NATIONAL MONUMENT

Location: Tulelake, California
Acreage: 46,560
Established: November 21, 1925

Here in northcentral California, on the north face of the largest shield volcano in the Cascade Range, lies the rugged landscape of Lava Beds National Monument. This area of the golden state has a history of volcanism, and periodic eruptions from the Medicine Lake volcano have formed an array of cinder cones, stratovolcanoes, pahoehoe (smooth and ropy) and aa (rough and clinker-like) lava flows, spatter cones, pit craters, and, perhaps the most striking feature of the monument, nearly 200 lava tube caves.

During the Modoc War of 1872–1873, the Modoc Indians used these tortuous lava flows to their advantage. Under the leadership of Captain Jack, the Modocs took refuge in this natural lava fortress, called "Captain Jack's Stronghold," and for five months, a group of fifty-three fighting men and their families held off U.S. Army forces numbering up to ten times their strength. A separate site, Petroglyph Point, contains an outstanding collection of Native American rock art.

Lava tubes are not unusual in a volcanic area, nor is their formation difficult to explain or understand. Lava that gushes from a volcano is around 1,800 degrees Fahrenheit, but its outer edges and surface begin to cool rapidly, which causes the flow to slow down and harden. This outside layer insulates the fast-moving molten lava, and then it is left behind when the eruption ends and the new "tube" drains. Many of the tubes at Lava Beds were formed about thirty thousand years ago after an eruption at Mammoth Crater on the southern boundary. Skull Cave, named for bighorn skulls found there, is one of the largest, rising nearly 80 feet above the floor. While these tubes were born in fire, a few are now ice caves. Even when temperatures outside reach 100 degrees, lava is such a good insulator that the air remains below freezing and ice formations can be found year-round.

Established in 1925, the 46,560-acre Lava Beds National Monument protects the natural fortress used by American Indians in the Modoc Indian War, as well as more than 28,000 acres of wilderness. The park's visitor center is open year-round from 8 A.M. until 5 P.M. during the winter, and until 6 P.M. during the summer. The center has interpretive exhibits, and park rangers offer various guided walks, talks, cave tours, and evening slide programs during the summer months. Entrance fees to the park are $3 per person or $5 per vehicle, and are valid for seven days; a $10 annual pass is also available.

Caving and wildlife viewing, particularly bird-watching throughout the spring and fall, are the most popular activities at Lava Beds. Many of the caves were first explored and named by J.D. Howard, a local miller, and the names he painted on the walls are still visible in most of the caves. In many of the caves, trails have been laid out and ladders installed for easier access. Mushpot Cave, an extension of the visitor center, is the only cave in which lights have been installed.

There are no food or lodging facilities in the park, but all traveler services are available in Tionesta and Tulelake, California, and Klamath and Merrill, Oregon. The Indian Well Campground at the south end of the park is open all year and has 40 campsites suitable for tents and small to medium-sized RVs. Fees are $10 per night, per site, and water and flush toilets are available. Public and private campgrounds are also available in Modoc National Forest, Tionesta, and Tulelake.

For more information, write Lava Beds National Monument, P.O. Box 867, Indian Wells Headquarters, Tulelake, CA 96134, or telephone (530) 667-2282. The park's Web site is www.nps.gov/labe.

FURTHER READING
Alt, David D. *Roadside Geology of Northern and Central California.* Missoula, MT: Mountain, 2000.
Quinn, Arthur. *Hell with the Fire Out: A History of the Modoc War.* Boston: Faber & Faber, 1997.
Riddle, Jeff C. *The Indian History of the Modoc War.* Eugene, OR: Urion, 1974.
Thompson, Erwin N. *Modoc War: Its Military History & Topography.* Sacramento, CA: Argus Books, 1971.
Waters, Aaron Clement. *Selected Caves and Lava-Tube Systems in and near Lava Beds National Monument.* Washington, DC: U.S. Geological Survey, 1990.

LINCOLN BOYHOOD NATIONAL MEMORIAL
Location: Lincoln City, Indiana
Acreage: 200
Established: February 19, 1962

The Lincoln Boyhood National Memorial protects and interprets the site of the Lincoln family farm in southern Indiana, where Abraham Lincoln, the sixteenth president of the United States, spent his formative years, from age seven to age twenty-one. The family claimed the land in December 1816, and they quickly set to work clearing the dense forest to make room for cultivation. Two years later, when young Abraham was only nine, tragedy struck when his mother, Nancy Hanks Lincoln, died at age thirty-four of an illness called "milk sick," caused by drinking milk from a cow that had eaten the poisonous white snakeroot plant. She was buried on the farm. The following year, Thomas Lincoln remarried, and Sarah Bush Johnston became Abraham's loving and capable stepmother. Over time, young Lincoln became interested in the law, and when his father sold the Indiana farm and moved the family westward to the fertile prairies of Illinois, Abraham followed. He would spend the next thirty years there, practicing law and politics, until he and his own wife, Mary Todd, moved to Washington, D.C., in 1861.

This 200-acre national memorial was authorized in February 1962 and includes the

National Park Service interpreters illustrate farm life of the 1820s at the Lincoln Boyhood National Memorial. *(National Park Service)*

Lincoln Living Historical Farm—a re-created pioneer homestead with a cabin, outbuildings, split rail fences, farm animals, vegetable and herb gardens, and field crops. National Park Service interpreters in pioneer clothing illustrate daily chores—such as cooking, splitting rails, riving shingles, breaking flax, and spinning wool—and frontier farming methods typical of the 1820 era, as part of the farm's living-history demonstrations. The farm is open every day from mid-April through September; in October it is open only on the weekends; and from November through mid-April the buildings are closed and are not staffed. However, visitors may still visit the farm and browse about the area.

The park's visitor center is open year-round, from 8 A.M. until 5 P.M., and until 6 P.M. during the summer, and features numerous exhibits, a number of Lincoln prints and images, and a movie. Admission fees are $2 per person for age seventeen and older, with a maximum charge of $4 per family. Each year the park celebrates Lincoln Day on the Sunday nearest February 12 by offering a special program in the Abraham Lincoln Hall, followed by a wreath-laying ceremony at the Nancy Hanks Lincoln grave site. The Indiana Lincoln Festival, held each June, features special demonstrations of pioneer crafts, and the Hoosier Homecoming, held on the last weekend in October, includes a candlelight walk to the Living Historical Farm.

In addition to numerous ranger-led interpretive programs, visitors can enjoy 3 established trails in the park: the Lincoln Boyhood

Trail connecting the Memorial Visitor Center and the Lincoln Living Historical Farm (this trail leads visitors past the grave site of Nancy Hanks Lincoln and the Cabin Site Memorial); the Trail of Twelve Stones, beginning at the Living Historical Farm and ending near the grave site (most visitors combine these two trails as a loop walk, since the distance is only about a mile); and the Lincoln Boyhood Nature Trail, also a circular trail approximately 1 mile in length, which winds through a natural reforested area.

The park is located on Indiana Highway 162. From I-64, exit at U.S. Highway 231 (exit 57) and travel south through Dale, continue on 231 to Gentryville, then east on Indiana Highway 162 for 2 miles. There are no food, lodging, or camping facilities in the park, but all traveler services are located nearby in Dale and Santa Claus. Camping facilities are available at Lincoln State Park, which is adjacent to Lincoln Boyhood National Memorial, and in Santa Claus.

For more information, write Lincoln Boyhood National Memorial, P.O. Box 1816, Lincoln City, IN 47552-1816, or telephone (812) 937-4541. The park's Web site is www.nps.gov/libo.

FURTHER READING

Donald, David Herbert. *Lincoln.* New York: Simon and Schuster, 1995.

HRA Gray & Pope, LLC. *The Evolution of a Sanctified Landscape: A Historic Resource Study of the Lincoln Boyhood National Memorial, Spencer County, Indiana.* Omaha, NE: National Park Service, 2002. Available at www.nps.gov/libo/hrs/hrs.htm.

Oates, Stephen B. *With Malice Toward None: A Life of Abraham Lincoln.* New York: HarperCollins, 1994.

O'Bright, Jill York. *"There I Grew Up . . .": A History of the Administration of Abraham Lincoln's Boyhood Home.* Washington, DC: National Park Service, 1987. Available at www.nps.gov/libo/adhi/adhi.htm.

Warren, Louis Austin. *Lincoln's Youth: Indiana Years, Seven to Twenty-One, 1816–1830.* Indianapolis: Indiana Historical Society, 1991.

LINCOLN HOME NATIONAL HISTORIC SITE

Location: Springfield, Illinois
Acreage: 12
Established: August 18, 1971

In the spring of 1844, a young Illinois lawyer named Abraham Lincoln bought this modest house in the heart of Springfield for his wife and son. It was the only home he ever owned. The house was originally constructed in 1839 as a single-story cottage, but the Lincolns enlarged it to a full 2 stories in 1856 to accommodate their growing family. Three of the Lincolns' four sons were born here, and one (Edward) died here in 1850 at nearly four years of age. For seventeen years, until Lincoln left for the White House, Abraham and Mary called this Greek Revival–style house home. But the Lincoln Home was also a magnet for visitors, parades, rallies, and other political festivities. Indeed, when Lincoln won the 1860 Republican presidential nomination, he received a delegation of party officials in his parlor. After winning the November election, the Lincolns held several farewell receptions before renting the home out, selling most of their furniture, and entrusting the family dog to a neighbor.

Authorized as a 12-acre historic site in August 1971, the Lincoln Home is set in the midst of a 4-block historic neighborhood that has been restored to its 1860 appearance—just as Lincoln would have remembered it. The park's visitor center, located on Seventh Street, is open year-round from 8:30 A.M. until 5 P.M., and admission is free. The center serves as a visitor service facility for both the site and the city of Springfield, providing information on Lincoln Home tours and programs, area historic sites and attractions, events, hotels, and restaurants. The lobby contains exhibits of Lincoln sculptures, as well as temporary exhibits and displays, and orientation programs are shown continuously throughout the day in the theaters.

There are no food, lodging, or camping facilities within the historic district, but all traveler services are available in Springfield.

For more information, write Lincoln Home National Historic Site, 413 South Eighth Street, Springfield, IL 62701-1905, or telephone (217) 492-4241, extension 221. The park's Web site is www.nps.gov/liho.

FURTHER READING

Donald, David. *Lincoln.* New York: Simon and Schuster, 1995.

Oates, Stephen B. *With Malice Toward None: The Life of Abraham Lincoln.* Harper Perennial Library, 1994.

Sandburg, Carl. *Abraham Lincoln: The Prairie Years.* New York: Harcourt, Brace, 1926.

LITTLE BIGHORN BATTLEFIELD NATIONAL MONUMENT

Location: Crow Agency, Montana
Acreage: 765
Established: January 29, 1879

Little Bighorn Battlefield National Monument near Crow Agency, Montana, commemorates one of America's most famous combat engagements, the Battle of the Little Bighorn. Here on June 25 and 26, 1876, two divergent cultures clashed in a struggle for control of the future. In the early 1870s, white explorers discovered gold in the Black Hills of South Dakota, land considered sacred by the Lakota (Sioux), and fortune hunters poured in. Although many Lakota had retired to reservations, others, led by Crazy Horse and Sitting Bull, left reservations and returned to their nomadic way of life. In a peculiar but strangely characteristic set of events, the military issued an order in the dead of winter declaring that all Indians who remained off the reservation would be considered hostile after March 31, 1876. There was little way to assure that this order would be communicated to off-reservation people, creating a re-

sult that some in the military desired: an all-out campaign in the summer of 1876.

During that summer, the army intended to capture a large group headed by Sitting Bull and including Crazy Horse with a three-pronged attack. The megalomaniacal Civil War hero Colonel George Armstrong Custer got ahead of the rest of his army and refused to wait. He pursued the Lakota and their Cheyenne allies, only to find his troops overmatched at Greasy Grass, the Native American name for Little Bighorn. In a short battle, Lakota and Cheyenne warriors annihilated twelve companies of Custer's Seventh Cavalry, leaving their bodies in the hot summer sun.

The Battle of the Little Bighorn has attained an almost mythic status in American history, and the story has been retold, some-

Custer's last stand at the Little Bighorn River, Montana, 1876. *(© North Wind/North Wind Picture Archives)*

Sioux veterans of the Battle of the Little Bighorn on the battleground. Photographed in 1926. *(Library of Congress)*

times inaccurately, in thousands of books, magazine articles, performances in film and theater, paintings, and other artistic expressions. The essential irony of the Battle of the Little Bighorn, however, was that the Native Americans' victory insured their defeat. "Now they will never let us rest," Sitting Bull predicted. And he was right. Custer's defeat gave Indian-haters the ammunition they needed to eradicate Plains Indian culture permanently, as the U.S. Army relentlessly tracked down the disbanded native contingents, forcing them to surrender the Black Hills and retreat to reservations.

Originally established as a national cemetery in 1879 to protect the troopers' graves, Congress redesignated the 765-acre park as Custer Battlefield National Monument in 1946 and renamed it Little Bighorn Battlefield

National Monument in 1991. The park's visitor center is open year-round from 8 A.M. until 4:30 P.M., and for extended hours during the summer months. Entrance fees are $5 per person or $10 per vehicle, but there is no charge for visiting the national cemetery. The center offers interpretive exhibits, including the Colter Ledger Drawings, as well as one of the finest collections of research materials available on the Battle of the Little Bighorn. Park rangers provide interpretive talks from Memorial Day through Labor Day, and the monument commemorates the battle anniversary each summer. Visitors can also take guided bus tours, offered through a concessionaire at Little Big Horn College, and self-guided walking tours of battle-related sites and the national cemetery. Three of the more notable walking trails are: the Reno-Benteen

Defense site, 5 miles south of the Custer field; Keogh/Crazy Horse position on battle ridge; and along Deep Ravine, west of battle ridge.

There are no food, lodging, or camping facilities in the park, but all traveler services are available in nearby Hardin.

For more information, write Little Bighorn Battlefield National Monument, P.O. Box 39, Highway 212, Crow Agency, MT 59022-0039, or telephone (406) 638-2621. The park's Web site is www.nps.gov/libi.

FURTHER READING

Ambrose, Stephen E. *Crazy Horse and Custer: The Parallel Lives of Two American Warriors.* New York: Anchor Books, 1996.

Brown, Dee. *Bury My Heart at Wounded Knee: An Indian History of the American West.* New York: Henry Holt, 2001.

Connell, Evans S. *Son of the Morning Star.* New York: Harper & Row, 1985.

Fox, Richard A. *Archaeology, History, and Custer's Last Battle: The Little Big Horn Reexamined.* Norman: University of Oklahoma Press, 1993.

Gray, John Shapley. *Custer's Last Campaign: Mitch Boyer and the Little Bighorn Reconstructed.* Lincoln: University of Nebraska Press, 1991.

LITTLE RIVER CANYON NATIONAL PRESERVE

Location: Fort Payne, Alabama
Acreage: 13,633
Established: October 24, 1992

"Mountaintop" is usually not a term used to describe a river, but Little River Canyon National Preserve is not your usual park. Instead, here in the Southern Appalachians of Alabama lies the nation's longest mountaintop river. As it winds its undammed and undeveloped course from headwaters in Georgia to its mouth at Weiss Lake near Leesburg, Alabama, the Little River also carves out of Lookout Mountain one of the Southeast's deepest canyons. It is a whitewater paradise that attracts thrill-seeking enthusiasts from across the country and around the world, proving that the American West is not the only place in the nation to test your

kayaking skills against nature. Forested uplands, waterfalls, canyon rims and bluffs, stream riffles and pools, boulders, and 600-foot sandstone cliffs offer spectacular natural settings for a variety of other recreational activities, and in keeping with the established purpose of a national preserve, the park also safeguards rare plants and animals like the blue shiner fish and the green pitcher plant.

Originally set aside in 1992, this nearly 14,000-acre preserve protects one of the cleanest and wildest waterways in all of the South, as well as the natural, recreational, and cultural resources of the Little River Canyon of northeast Alabama. There are few visitor facilities within the park, although a visitor center is planned in the future. Visitors can enjoy photography and sightseeing from overlooks located along the 23-mile scenic Canyon Rim Parkway, and a day-use area, ideal for family picnics, is located at Canyon Mouth Park. For the more adventurous tourist, the preserve offers hiking, wading, Class-3+ to Class-5 whitewater paddling (recommended only for experts), canoeing, mountain-bike riding, horseback riding (you bring the horse), and rock climbing. During the summer months, backpack camping is available at three designated primitive campsites, and the National Park Service maintains parking areas, overlooks, rest rooms, and picnic areas at key locations.

Lodging is available in the park at the DeSoto State Park Motel (800-568-8840), which offers comfortable A-frame chalets and rustic cabins surrounded by northeast Alabama's beautiful woodlands and rolling terrain. The state park also has 78 campsites with water, rest rooms, and hot showers. In addition to facilities in the preserve, all traveler services are available in nearby communities.

For more information, write Little River Canyon National Preserve, 2141 Gault Avenue North, Fort Payne,

AL 35967, or telephone (256) 845-9605. The park's Web site is www.nps.gov/liri.

LONGFELLOW NATIONAL HISTORIC SITE

Location: Cambridge, Massachusetts
Acreage: 2
Established: October 9, 1972

> Lives of great men all remind us,
> We can make our lives sublime.
> And, departing, leave behind us,
> Footprints on the sands of time.
> *—Henry Wadsworth Longfellow*

For almost half a century, from 1837 until his death in 1882, Henry Wadsworth Longfellow made his home in this elegant, red-brick, Georgian-style house. Longfellow—poet, scholar, educator—was a professor at Harvard, and his life was deeply rooted in Cambridge and Boston. He quickly rose to prominence after the publication of his first poetry collection, *Voices of the Night,* in 1839, which contained "A Psalm of Life," one of the best-loved poems of the nineteenth century:

> Life is real! Life is earnest!
> And the grave is not its goal;
> Dust thou art, to dust returnest,
> Was not spoken of the soul.

His reputation was enhanced by subsequent works such as *Evangeline* (1847), *Hiawatha* (1855), *The Courtship of Miles Standish* (1858), and *Tales of a Wayside Inn* (1863). During his lifetime, Longfellow enjoyed enormous popularity, and Longfellow House became a favorite gathering place for many celebrated philosophers and artists, including Ralph Waldo Emerson, Nathaniel Hawthorne, Julia Ward Howe, and Charles Sumner. Longfellow and his immediate and

Longfellow National Historic Site. *(National Park Service)*

extended family and friends played a central role in the intellectual and artistic life of nineteenth-century America and are credited with kindling the "American Renaissance" and shaping a uniquely American identity and culture.

In addition to housing the poet, Longfellow House also played a significant role in America's colonial history. General George Washington, commander in chief of the newly formed Continental Army, headquartered and planned the Siege of Boston here between July 1775 and April 1776.

First recognized as a National Historic Landmark in 1962, the 2-acre Longfellow National Historic Site commemorates the life and work of one of America's, and the world's, foremost poets. The park's visitor center features various interpretive exhibits, beautiful gardens, and a bookstore; admission is free. In addition to guided garden walks during the summer, park rangers offer tours of the meticulously preserved Longfellow House for $2 per adult, age seventeen and older. An outstanding example of mid-Georgian architecture, the home contains extensive museum collections, most dating from Longfellow's occupancy, which include an array of American and European decorative arts from the eighteenth and nineteenth centuries; a fine arts collection representing a broad range of important nineteenth-century painters and sculptors including Gilbert Stuart and Albert Bierstadt; Longfellow's personal library and family papers dating from the seventeenth to the twentieth centuries; and an estimated 700,000 items in manuscript/archives collections that include letters from George Washington, Thomas Jefferson, Ralph Waldo Emerson, Charles Dickens, and Abraham Lincoln. These collections possess exceptional research and aesthetic value and provide an exquisite index to nineteenth-century American culture. Longfellow and his wife, Fanny, were keenly aware of the home's historic significance, and after Longfellow's death in 1882, his family continued to carefully preserve the property until it was transferred to the National Park Service in 1972. As a result, virtually all of the furnishings are original to the house, most dating from Henry Longfellow's occupancy.

There are no food, lodging, or camping facilities at the site, but all traveler services are available locally in Cambridge and elsewhere in the Boston metropolitan area.

For more information, write Longfellow National Historic Site, 105 Brattle Street, Cambridge, MA 02138, or telephone (617) 876-4491. The park's Web site is www.nps.gov/long.

FURTHER READING

Hirsh, Edward L. *Henry Wadsworth Longfellow.* Minneapolis: University of Minnesota Press, 1964.
Johnson, Carl L. *Professor Longfellow of Harvard.* Eugene: University of Oregon, 1944.
Longfellow, Henry Wadsworth. *Selected Poems: Henry Wadsworth Longfellow.* New York: Penguin Books, 1988.

LOWELL NATIONAL HISTORICAL PARK
Location: Lowell, Massachusetts
Acreage: 141
Established: June 5, 1978

In 1810, a young Bostonian named Francis Cabot Lowell made a seemingly innocuous tour of British textile mills. But when he returned home to the United States, he carried with him sketches made from memory of the weaving machines that he had inspected. Together with a Boston mechanic, Paul Moody, Lowell created more efficient machinery for spinning cotton and invented a brand-new technology—the power loom. In 1814, with financial help from his family, Lowell opened the world's first integrated cotton mill in Waltham, near Boston. It was an instant success. A decade later, using the capital amassed in this first venture, his business partners built an entire town at the junction of the Concord and Merrimack rivers and named it "Lowell" in memory of Francis, who had died in 1817.

Between 1820 and 1860, the American economy entered a new and more complex stage of development, moving away from its reliance on agriculture as the major source of growth, and instead toward an industrial and technological future. The significant economic growth that the nation experienced during this period resulted from the reorganization of production, specifically factory production that reorganized work by breaking down the manufacture of an article into discrete steps. Further refinement led to the replacement of hand labor by power-driven machinery. Between 1820 and 1860, textile manufacturing became the country's leading industry, and mills sprang up across the New England and Middle Atlantic states. Lowell's contribution to this process was his decision to bring all the steps

of cotton cloth production together under one roof. By centralizing the manufacturing process and work force in one factory, cloth for the mass market could be produced more cheaply and more profitably.

In the 1820s and 1830s, young girls from all over New England flocked to work in Lowell, in one of the first cotton textile factories in America. By 1826, nearly 2,500 people lived here, and a decade later, the population had topped 17,000. As anticipated, most of these "mill girls" were between the ages of 15 and 29 and were unmarried, and most came from New England's middling rural families. Mill work offered them the possibility of economic independence and a chance to escape provincial rural towns for the attractions of a larger metropolitan area. Few, however, considered their decision to come to Lowell a permanent commitment. Most young women

Power looms inside the Boott Cotton Mills at Lowell National Historic Park. *(© North Wind/Nancy Carter/North Wind Picture Archives)*

came to work for a few years, might go home or to school for a few months, and then return to the mill work. Once married (and the majority of women did marry), they left the mill work force forever.

Despite the mill's attractions, the jobs were exhausting. The workday began at dawn, or even earlier, and ended about 7 P.M. in the evening; the standard schedule was twelve hours a day, six days a week, with only half an hour for breakfast and lunch. The male supervisor and two or three children roamed the aisles to survey the work and to help out, and the workrooms were noisy, poorly lit, and badly ventilated. Mill work also entailed an entirely new living situation for women workers, since the mill owners, hoping to attract "respectable women," constructed company boardinghouses where women workers had to live. Headed by a female housekeeper, the boardinghouse maintained strict rules, including a 10 o'clock curfew. Typically, four or six girls shared a small room, which contained not much more than the double beds in which they slept together and little personal privacy was possible.

Dissatisfaction with the work environment was a major reason for leaving the mills. In the 1830s and 1840s, women operatives protested against mill conditions. The owners were shocked and outraged by the strikes, considering these actions "unfeminine" and the women "ungrateful." Claiming that increased competition made wage cuts inevitable, the owners simply hired new workers—Irish immigrants, for example—to replace striking mill girls.

First authorized in June of 1978, the 141-acre historical park commemorates the history of America's industrial revolution and includes textile mills, worker housing, 5.6 miles of canals, and nineteenth-century commercial buildings. The visitor center, located on Market Street, is open year-round from 9 A.M. until 4:30 P.M., later during the summer months, and features an award-winning multi-image video program, *Lowell: The Industrial Revelation,* as well as numerous exhibits. At the Boott Cotton Mills Museum visitors can experience the roar of a 1920s weaving room with 88 operating power looms, as well as interactive exhibits and videos. The park's Working People Exhibit tells the human story of the industrial revolution by concentrating on the working people of Lowell. Canal boat tours run seven days a week from late June until Labor Day (and on a reduced schedule from Labor Day to Columbus Day), and the park hosts the Lowell Folk Festival during the last full weekend in July. Interpretive fees are charged on a per-program/tour basis. Canal tour fees: adults are $6, seniors $5, youths $4, children five and under free. Boott Cotton Mills Museum: adults $4, youths six to sixteen and students $2.

For more information, write Lowell National Historical Park, 7 Kirk Street, Lowell, MA 01852, or telephone (978) 970-5000. The park's Web site is www.nps.gov/lowe.

FURTHER READING

Blewett, Mary H. *The Last Generation: Work and Life in the Textile Mills of Lowell, Massachusetts, 1910–1960.* Amherst: University of Massachusetts Press, 1990.

Coolidge, John. *Mill and Mansion: A Study of Architecture and Society in Lowell, Massachusetts, 1820–1865.* Amherst: University of Massachusetts Press, 1992.

Dublin, Thomas. *Women at Work: The Transformation of Work and Community in Lowell, Massachusetts, 1826–1860.* New York: Columbia University Press, 1979.

Steinberg, Theodore. *Nature Incorporated: Industrialization and the Waters of New England.* New York: Cambridge University Press, 1991.

Weible, Robert, ed. *The Continuing Revolution: A History of Lowell, Massachusetts.* Lowell, MA: Lowell Historical Society, 1991.

LYNDON B. JOHNSON NATIONAL HISTORICAL PARK

Location: Johnson City, Texas
Acreage: 1,570
Established: December 2, 1969

On November 22, 1963, on board Air Force One preparing to leave Dallas, Texas, for Washington, DC, a shaken Lyndon B. Johnson stepped before his friend Judge Sarah Hughes and recited the oath of office of the presidency of the United States. Hours before, President John F. Kennedy had been assassinated in Dealey Plaza. The tragedy shocked the nation, but it was a particularly terrible moment for the vice president and Texas. Kennedy had come to Johnson's home state to restore his popularity and help heal a rift in the state Democratic Party. After the swearing-in ended, the jet whisked the now-President Johnson to the capital to commence his duties amid the collective mourning of the nation and the world.

In an instant, a transfer of power and leadership had occurred not only in the nation but on the planet as well. The suave but perplexing Kennedy—boy president, war hero, symbol of the nation's renewal, first Roman Catholic to ever hold the highest office in the land—had been replaced by a historically more common sort of president, a man of the backwoods who fashioned himself able to lead by intelligence, skill, cunning, and will. Like Andrew Jackson and Abraham Lincoln, Lyndon B. Johnson came from humble origins; like them, he fashioned a persona that brought him success in politics sometimes at the expense of personal goals and public image. A man of modest rural roots in an age of urban and military leaders in the White House, Johnson embodied a kind of empathy for ordinary people that belied his tough, manipulative, win-at-all-costs exterior.

The source of that empathy, as well as nearly everything else about the character of Lyndon B. Johnson, was the Texas Hill Country from which he came and to which he perennially sought to return. The hilly area west of Austin, called the Edwards Plateau but more commonly known as the Hill Country, had been home to his family for nearly a hundred years when he became president. The Hill Country symbolized what Johnson thought best, most meaningful, and most trying about the American experience: the ability to meet a rugged natural world on its own terms and emerge, over time and through repeated effort, equal to the task if not entirely victorious. The place is defined by its people and their values, shaped and molded by generations. Yet it is a difficult place, one of broken dreams and struggle as well as beauty. It teaches hard lessons that translate well in the rest of the world. What is real in the Hill Country is what someone can touch, decidedly not what they can dream, and that endemic pragmatism offers a strategy for success in the wider world.

But the Hill Country never releases its grip on people such as Lyndon Johnson. His home region got under his skin and stayed there, reminding him of essential truths. The Hill Country remained where Johnson most wanted to prove himself, the place where validation of his efforts had the greatest personal meaning, and the place to which he returned to look inside himself, evaluate options, and make hard choices both personal and national in character.

The Lyndon B. Johnson National Historical Park in and near Johnson City, Texas, reveals that experience and the way it shaped a president. The park encompasses two separate areas: the Johnson Settlement/Visitor Center/Boyhood Home/Park Headquarters in Johnson City and the LBJ Ranch near Stonewall. The park visitor center in Johnson City is 50 miles west of Austin and 60 miles north of San Antonio.

The Johnson City Visitor Center contains a permanent exhibit on Johnson's life and his government programs and policies. Johnson championed the little guy, and many of his Great Society programs did much to help the disadvantaged. Elsewhere in the park, the Johnson Settlement, where the president's grandfather and great-uncle established a cattle-droving headquarters in the 1860s, shows the family's regional history. Lyndon Johnson's Boyhood Home in Johnson City was his home from 1913 to 1924, when he graduated from high school.

About 14 miles away from Johnson City, the LBJ Ranch House—the famous Texas White House—was the home of president and Mrs. Johnson during his political career and the spiritual source of his energy and strength. It is also the place to which he came after the end of his term. President Johnson rebuilt the nearby Reconstructed Birthplace on the site where he was born in 1908. He is buried in the Johnson Family Cemetery at the ranch.

The park enjoys a sunny, mild climate during most of the year. April is usually the rainiest month. Winter temperatures are usually in the 50s; snow and ice are rare but possible. Summer temperatures can exceed 100 degrees in July and August, with high humidity. The park suggests lightweight clothing and sunscreen in the summer months and recommends walking shoes for those touring the Johnson Settlement.

The park is open every day except Thanksgiving, Christmas, and New Year's Day. The visitor center is open from 8:45 A.M. to 5 P.M. Park staff offer guided tours of the LBJ Boyhood Home in Johnson City seven days a week. Self-guided tours of the Johnson Settlement are available from 9 A.M. until sunset seven days a week. Rangers or costumed interpreters lead tours of the Johnson Settlement. There is no fee to visit the Johnson City District. Hours for bus tours of the LBJ Ranch near Stonewall are from 10 A.M. to 4 P.M., seven days a week. The bus tour of the LBJ Ranch costs $3 per person for persons seven years old and older. After-hours self-guided tours of a portion of the ranch are available seven days a week from 5 P.M. until dusk.

For more information, write Lyndon B. Johnson National Historical Park, P.O. Box 329, Johnson City, Texas 78636-0329, or telephone (830) 868-7128, extension 244. The park's Web site is www.nps.gov/lyjo.

FURTHER READING

Caro, Robert A. *Master of the Senate: The Years of Lyndon Johnson.* New York: Alfred A. Knopf, 2002.

Goodwin, Doris Kearns. *Lyndon Johnson and the American Dream.* New York: St. Martin's, 1991.

Rothman, Hal K. *LBJ's Texas White House: "Our Heart's Home."* College Station: Texas A&M University Press, 2001. Also available at www.nps.gov/lyjo/Ourheart%27shome/index.htm.

M

MAGGIE L. WALKER NATIONAL HISTORIC SITE

Location: Richmond, Virginia
Acreage: 1
Established: November 10, 1978

By every measure, Maggie Lena Mitchell Walker was a success, but her rise to prominence was more than just good fortune or luck. Instead, this remarkable African American woman defied the racism and discrimination of the late nineteenth to the early twentieth centuries to become an inspiration and an exemplary model of success to both women and African Americans in the postwar era. By the early twentieth century, Maggie Walker had not only proved herself as a savvy businesswoman and capable community leader, but she had also become the first woman in the United States to found a bank, as well as one of the wealthiest black women in America.

Walker could trace her humble beginnings to post–Civil War Richmond, Virginia, where she was born on July 15, 1867, daughter of Elizabeth Draper, who was a former slave. In 1883, she graduated from a normal school and began her own teaching career.

Her marriage to Armstead Walker three years later brought this phase of her life to an end, but, unlike most married women of her time, she did not resign herself to a traditional, subordinate role. Instead, Maggie Walker held surprisingly modern views of the institution of marriage. "Since marriage is an equal partnership, I believe that the woman and the man are equal in power and should by consultation and agreement, mutually decide as to the conduct of the home and the government of the children."

Maggie Walker began to channel her considerable energy and time into the local council of the Independent Order of St. Luke, which she had first joined when she was fourteen years old. This fraternal burial society, established in 1867 in Baltimore, was one of many black mutual aid societies that flourished in the postreconstruction era, by administering to the sick and aged, promoting humanitarian causes, and encouraging individual self-help and integrity. Over the years, she served in numerous capacities of increasing responsibility for the order, from that of a delegate to the biannual convention, to the top leadership position of Right Worthy Grand Secretary in 1899, a position that she held until her death. A dynamic and inspirational leader, Maggie Walker expanded the order's membership into twenty-two states. She also established its financial security; by 1924, for example, the order's funds totaled nearly $3.5 million.

In 1902, to further promote this organization, which stressed racial pride as well as charity, Walker had established *The St. Luke Herald*. From this pulpit, she urged her readers to "put our money together; let us use our money; Let us put our money out at usury among ourselves, and reap the benefit ourselves."

To this end, Walker founded the St. Luke Penny Savings Bank and served as its first president. The bank catered to black customers and was especially dedicated to assisting black families in the purchase of their own homes. When St. Luke later merged with two other Richmond banks to become The Consolidated Bank and Trust Company, Walker continued to serve as chairman of the board of directors. The Consolidated Bank and Trust Company still thrives today as the oldest continually operated African American bank in the United States, and its headquarters are currently located across the street from its original site at the corner of First and Marshall streets in Richmond.

In addition to her work for the Independent Order of St. Luke, Maggie Walker also gave her time to numerous civic groups. As an advocate of African American women's rights, she served on the board of trustees for several women's organizations, including the National Association of Colored Women (NACW) and the Virginia Industrial School for Girls. To foster race relations, she helped to organize and served locally as vice president of the National Association for the Advancement of Colored People (NAACP) and was a member of the national NAACP board. She also served as a member of the Virginia Interracial Commission. Following the tragic death of her husband in 1915, Walker's health gradually declined, and by 1928, she was using a wheelchair. Despite her physical limitations she remained actively committed to her life's work until her death on December 15, 1934.

Walker's residence at 1102 East Leigh Street was built in 1883. The address was a prime location in the heart of Jackson Ward, the center of Richmond's African American business and social life at the turn of the century. The Walkers purchased the house in 1904 and soon began making changes. Central heating and electricity were added, and with the addition of several bedrooms and enclosed porches, the home increased from 9 to 25 rooms. In 1928, an elevator was added in the rear of the house to provide Walker access to the second floor, and she lived in the home until her death. The Walker family owned the house until 1979, when the house and all of its contents were purchased by the National Park Service.

Authorized in November 1978, the 1-acre Maggie L. Walker National Historic Site commemorates the life of this progressive, determined, and talented African American woman. The park's visitor center, located at 600 North Second Street, is open year-round from 9 A.M. until 5 P.M. Monday through Saturday, and contains exhibits on the life of Maggie Walker and the Jackson Ward community, as well as an eight-minute audiovisual program on Walker's life. Park rangers also offer tours of the historic home, located at 1102 East Leigh Street, which has been fully restored to its 1930s appearance with original Walker family furnishings. Special programs include weekend activities during February, a July 15 celebration of Maggie Walker's birthday, an open house during the Second Street Festival in early October, and holiday house tours featuring period Christmas decorations.

There are no food, lodging, or camping facilities at the historic site, but all traveler services are located nearby in the Richmond area.

For more information, write Maggie L. Walker National Historic Site, 3215 East Broad Street, Richmond, VA 23223, or telephone (804) 771-2017. The park's Web site is www.nps.gov/mawa.

FURTHER READING

Hine, Darlene Clark. *A Shining Thread of Hope: The History of Black Women in America.* New York: Broadway Books, 1998.

Hine, Darlene Clark, William C. Hine, and Stanley Harrold. *The African-American Odyssey.* Upper Saddle River, NJ: Prentice-Hall, 2003.

Ross, Rosetta E. *Witnessing and Testifying: Black Women, Religion, and Civil Rights.* Minneapolis, MN: Fortress, 2003.

Sterling, Dorothy, ed. *We Are Your Black Sisters: Black Women in the Nineteenth Century.* New York: W.W. Norton, 1984.

MAMMOTH CAVE NATIONAL PARK

Location: Mammoth Cave, Kentucky
Acreage: 52,830
Established: July 1, 1941

Mammoth Cave National Park in southcentral Kentucky contains the most extensive cave system on Earth. The outer limits of this water-formed labyrinth remain unknown even today. The more than 350 miles of surveyed underground passageways make Mammoth Cave the longest known cave by a factor of three, but geologists estimate that as many as 600 miles of as-yet-undiscovered passageways may exist.

Originally authorized in May 1926, the nearly-53,000-acre park was part of the National Park Service's push at that time to acquire parklands in the eastern half of the nation. Closer to the main population centers, such areas gave the agency a national reach, which was crucial to its survival in the federal bureaucracy. Along with Shenandoah and Great Smoky Mountains, Mammoth Cave represented a new direction for the Park Service, an attempt to broaden not only its holdings but its appeal as well. With the establishment of these eastern parks, the Park Service could legitimately claim a national audience.

The eastern parks also were different from those in the West. The established western national parks were large, open areas, mostly away from people, and generally carved from public lands. Mammoth Cave had over a century of history as a tourist attraction before the National Park Service received permission to develop a new unit there. As did the other eastern parks, Mammoth Cave represented a transformation not only of the land aboveground but of the culture in the region that surrounded it. Local people found themselves faced with new choices, as well as chal-

Two boys looking at rocks piled to the ceiling at Mammoth Cave, 1892. *(Library of Congress)*

lenges, as numerous visitors came to see the natural wonder that was made nationally significant by its new designation.

Mammoth Cave reflected an intrinsic American fascination with caves. The underground world discovered here turned out to be very different from that aboveground. Visitors feared and were, at the same time, intrigued by what lurked in its depths. The mystery of Mammoth Cave drew people to it in powerful ways, making it a symbol of wild America long before it was selected for national park status. And, as speleology, the study of caves, became an increasingly widespread avocation, Mammoth Cave's importance continued to grow.

Much of the early development of Mammoth Cave National Park was a direct result of President Franklin D. Roosevelt's New Deal and its Civilian Conservation Corps (CCC). As in many other parks, CCC camps were set up, where young men, who were paid by the government, engaged in work that substantially improved park facilities. CCC crews built roads and firebreaks, cut trails, installed water systems, and constructed residences for park employees and visitor facilities. By the time the National Park Service established Mammoth Cave in 1941, the physical plant that visitors used was a direct result of CCC efforts.

Mammoth Cave itself is the product of natural forces. More than 350 million years ago, the North American continent was farther south than it is today, and a shallow sea covered the southeastern United States. These lukewarm waters supported tiny organisms with shells of calcium carbonate. As these creatures died, their shells accumulated, slowly coalescing into more than 700 feet of limestone and shale. After most of this sedimentary stone was set in place, a large river system, which emptied into the shallow sea from the north, left another 50 to 60 feet of sandstone atop the limestone and shale.

Then, 280 million years ago, the sea's water level began to fall as the continent rose, exposing the various layers of stone and inaugurating the beginning of Mammoth Cave. At first, rainwater trickled down through tiny cracks and fissures in the limestone and sandstone. Over time, more limestone gradually dissolved, and more and more water entered the system, enlarging the original microcaverns into the extensive system of caves that later people discovered and aptly called Mammoth Cave.

The caves were an attraction for humans well before the arrival of Europeans in the New World. Paleo peoples explored part of the caves more than 4,000 years ago, collecting the crystals and salts they found there. As cultural regimes changed, however, exploration of the caves came to an end, and, for the next two millennia, knowledge of the caves was lost. The American re-discovery of this cave system in 1798 initiated a new round of visitation, and, in the nineteenth century, Mammoth Cave became a popular tourist attraction. Visitors who came here first explored the site as Flatt's Cave in 1810, and, by 1816, it had become nationally known.

When Mammoth Cave was authorized as a national park in 1926, just 40 miles of passageway had been mapped. In the more than seventy-five years since, increasingly sophisticated surveying techniques have led to advances in understanding the overwhelming extent of this intricate cave system. Several caves in the park have been found to be connected, and, interestingly, the cave system is now known to extend outside the boundaries of the national park.

Mammoth Cave National Park protects the cave system, the scenic river valleys of the Green and Nolin rivers, and a section of the hill country of southcentral Kentucky. The Mammoth Cave Visitor Center is open year-round, and hours vary by season. Admission is free.

In addition to a bookstore and an information desk, the center features exhibits on cave exploration, a relief map of the park, a "video aquarium," two films—*Water and Stone* and *Voices of the Cave*—and ranger-led auditorium talks and slide presentations. A variety of cave tours are offered, ranging in cost from $3.50 to $35, and reservations can be made on-line at reservations.nps.gov. Visitors can also enjoy the surface of the park on more than 73 miles of hiking trails.

Lodging is available in the park at the Mammoth Cave Hotel (270-758-2225), and facilities include the hotel, Sunset Point Lodge, and Woodland Cottages, as well as a restaurant, coffee shop, gift shop, craft shop, and meeting rooms. Campground facilities at

Mammoth Cave include the Headquarters Campground, open from March through October, which offers 109 sites at a rate of $13 per site, per night. Twelve primitive sites on the bank of the Green River are also available at the Houchins Ferry Campground, and facilities include fresh water, portable toilets, a covered picnic shelter, and boat launch. The Maple Springs Group Campground has 4 sites for groups with horses and 3 sites for groups without horses.

Traveler services are also available nearby in Brownsville, Cave City, Horse Cave, and Park City.

For more information, write Mammoth Cave National Park, P.O. Box 7, Mammoth Cave, KY 42259, or telephone (270) 758-2251. The park's Web site is www.nps.gov/maca.

FURTHER READING

Borden, James D., and Roger W. Brucker. *Beyond Mammoth Cave: A Tale of Obsession in the World's Longest Cave.* Carbondale: Southern Illinois University Press, 2000.

Bullitt, Alexander C. *Rambles in the Mammoth Cave During the Year 1844 by a Visiter* [sic]. St. Louis, MO: Cave Books, 1985.

Burcker, Roger W., and Richard A. Watson. *The Longest Cave.* Carbondale: Southern Illinois University Press, 1976.

Palmer, Arthur N. *A Geological Guide to Mammoth Cave National Park.* Teaneck, NJ: Zephyrus, 1981.

Seymour, Randy. *Wildflowers of Mammoth Cave National Park.* Lexington: University Press of Kentucky, 1997.

Watson, Patty J., ed. *Archeology of the Mammoth Cave Area.* St. Louis, MO: Cave Books, 1997.

MANASSAS NATIONAL BATTLEFIELD PARK

Location: Manassas, Virginia
Acreage: 5,071
Established: May 10, 1940

You are green, it is true, but they are green also; you are all green alike.
                                        —Abraham Lincoln

Although the battle of First Manassas—also known as Bull Run—was indecisive, it was prophetic in terms of the devastating loss of life that would occur in the forthcoming battles of the American Civil War.

After a winter of uneasy waiting, the United States descended into civil war on April 12, 1861, when the Confederate Army began shelling Fort Sumter. Public outpourings of patriotism were common, and new recruits continually swarmed into the armies of both the North and the South. Much of the nation, including President Abraham Lincoln, believed that this conflict would be a quick, relatively bloodless affair. Indeed, Lincoln hoped for as much, knowing that the longer the war lasted, the more embittered both South and North would become, making reunion ever more difficult, if not impossible.

On a warm July 21 in 1861 in Virginia, just 25 miles outside of the nation's capital at Manassas Creek, or Bull Run, the illusion of a short war was dispelled as the two inexperienced forces clashed for the first time. A crowd of sightseers, journalists, and politicians had accompanied the Union troops, expecting an invigorating Sunday outing, but the Battle of Bull Run was no picnic. The course of the battle swayed back and forth across the field several times during the day, sending congressmen and civilians fleeing back to the safety of Washington.

Finally, the arrival of 2,300 fresh Confederate troops decided the day. The Confederate victory had also created a hero for the Confederates. This hero was General Thomas J. "Stonewall" Jackson, whose newly arrived brigade had stanched a rebel retreat. It was reported that General Bernard Bee pointed to Jackson and his men and shouted, "There stands Jackson like a stone wall! Rally behind the Virginians!"

Despite valor on both sides, soldiers were stunned by the violence and destruction of

Confederate fortifications at Manassas, Virginia. Photographed March 1862. *(Library of Congress)*

the battle that left nearly 900 young men life-less after ten hours of fighting on the fields of Matthews Hill, Henry Hill, and Chinn Ridge. As one English journalist, William Howard Russell, reported, "I saw a steady stream of men covered with mud, soaked through with rain . . . pouring irregularly, without any sem-blance of order, up Pennsylvania Avenue toward the Capitol. . . . I perceived they be-longed to different regiments . . . mingled pell-mell together. . . . Hastily [I] . . . ran down-stairs and asked an officer . . . a pale young man who looked exhausted to death and who had lost his sword . . . where the men were coming from. 'Where from? Well sir, I guess we're all coming out of Virginny as far as we can, and pretty well whipped too. . . . I

know I'm going home. I've had enough fight-ing to last my lifetime.' " But the war had only just begun, and before it was all over, the Civil War would kill more than 620,000 soldiers—one out of every four who partici-pated in it.

Like the first Battle of Bull Run, the sec-ond Battle of Bull Run was also a Confederate victory, though the men who met here again on the plains of Manassas were no longer green by August 1862. The contending forces, now made up of seasoned veterans, knew well the realities of war. The Battle of Second Manassas stretched across three torrid days in late August and brought the Confed-eracy to the peak of its power and possibility. Generals Robert E. Lee and Stonewall Jackson thoroughly routed the Union Army commanded by General John Pope, who was unaware that he was facing the entire Army of Northern Virginia. Second Manassas also produced far greater carnage than had First Manassas just thirteen months earlier. The Union lost 1,747 men killed, 8,452 wounded, and 4,263 missing or captured, while the Confederacy had endured 1,553 killed, 7,812 wounded, and 109 missing or captured. The nearly 24,000 casualties were five times greater than the figure for First Manassas, yet the battle loss did not weaken Northern resolve. In the summer of 1862, while the Confederacy's hopes were justifiably high, the war's final outcome was as yet unknown, and the sacrifices at Bull Run were only part of the much larger possible cost of Southern independence or of preserving the Union.

Manassas National Battlefield Park was established in May 1940 to preserve the scene of these two major Civil War battles, and the landscape of this 5,071-acre park still retains its wartime character. Henry Hill, focus of heavy fighting at First Manassas in July 1861, is still cleared, though now neat and lush after decades of farming, and a new farmhouse marks the site of the old. The unfinished railroad, scene of much of the fighting at Second Manassas, still runs through the woods north of the Warrenton Turnpike, while the peacefulness of the Chinn Farm, its house and outbuildings now gone, belies the violence that took place there. The Stone House—the former aid station—still stands as it has since the 1820s, overlooking the Warrenton Turnpike. In the late 1990s, the park was threatened by suburban development, but strong community support deflected plans to build a nearby mall. For the time being, the park retains its nineteenth-century character, but growth in suburban Virginia remains a constant concern.

The Henry Hill Visitor Center is open year-round, from 8:30 A.M. until 5 P.M., and features a thirteen-minute orientation slide program and a six-minute audiovisual battle-map program outlining troop movements in both First and Second Manassas. Entrance fees are $2 per person and are valid for three days; a $15 annual pass is also available. The Stuart's Hill Center and Museum, located at the intersection of State Route 29, Lee Highway, and Pageland Lane, is open daily in summer, on weekends in the spring and fall, and is closed in the winter. Visitors to the park can also enjoy ranger-guided tours and cultural programs as well as the one-hour, self-guided walking tour of the first Battle of Manassas site, and the 12-mile, self-guided driving tour of the second Battle of Manassas.

There are no food, lodging, or camping facilities in the park, but all traveler services are located nearby in Centreville, Gainsville, and Manassas.

For more information, write Manassas National Battlefield Park, 12521 Lee Highway, Manassas, VA 20109-2005, or telephone (703) 361-1339. The park's Web site is www.nps.gov/mana.

FURTHER READING

Davis, William C. *Battle at Bull Run: A History of the First Major Campaign of the Civil War.* Mechanicsburg, PA: Stackpole Books, 1995.

Hennessy, John J. *Return to Bull Run: The Battle and Campaign of Second Manassas.* Norman: University of Oklahoma Press, 1999.

McDonald, JoAnna M. *We Shall Meet Again: The First Battle of Manassas (Bull Run), July 18–21, 1861.* New York: Oxford University Press, 2000.

Russell, William Howard. *My Diary, North and South.* Philadelphia, PA: Temple University Press, 1987.

MANZANAR NATIONAL HISTORIC SITE

Location: Independence, California
Acreage: 814
Established: March 3, 1992

President Franklin D. Roosevelt called December 7, 1941, "a date which will live in infamy." On that fateful morning, the Japanese

Imperial Navy launched a devastating attack on the U.S. fleet at Pearl Harbor and propelled the nation into World War II. The attack on Pearl Harbor unleashed a powerful wave of anti-Japanese sentiment that culminated in Roosevelt's Executive Order No. 9066, issued in February 1942. The measure empowered the secretary of war to detain U.S. citizens of Japanese ancestry and Japanese resident aliens from the West Coast and confine them in internment camps. Ostensibly to protect "national security," the order caused 118,000 citizens with no more than what they could carry in two suitcases to be rounded up, routed under military guard to assembly centers, and then transported to one of ten internment camps.

One of the best preserved of the internment camps is Manzanar, at the foot of the imposing Sierra Nevada Mountains in eastern California's Owens Valley. The Manzanar War Relocation Center began as an "assembly center" for internees under U.S. Army control. Former residents of Bainbridge Island, Washington, and Terminal Island, California, quickly filled the 500-acre camp. Joining them were persons of Japanese ancestry expelled from Southern California, more than 70 percent from the Los Angeles area.

The internment camp at Manzanar consisted of 36 blocks of wooden barracks within a confined 1-square-mile area. The men, women, and children forced to live there sought to overcome the trauma of evacuation and an uncertain future by establishing some semblance of a normal life. The inhabitants beautified the barracks area with gardens and ponds, and they re-created a microcosm of an American society much like what they had been forced to leave behind.

The War Relocation Authority took control of Manzanar on June 1, 1942, and operated the camp until it closed in November 1945. In all, more than 11,400 people were processed through this facility; the camp's population peaked at 10,200 in September 1942, and by 1944 there were 6,000 residents. Manzanar was also home to 110 orphans, some as young as six months, sent to the Children's Village at Manzanar, the only camp to have such an orphanage.

Many young male internees volunteered or were drafted into the U.S. military. The 100th Battalion of the 442nd Regimental Combat Team of Japanese Americans became one of the most decorated units in the European theater. Others volunteered to serve in the Military Intelligence Service. Although they were relocated against their will, regulations allowed internees at Manzanar and the other camps to leave for jobs in other parts of the country, provided they had a sponsor. Older people and children comprised the main populace by the time the camp closed in 1945.

The family of Sadao Munemori, a nineteen-year-old boy posthumously awarded the Medal of Honor for his heroics in Italy during World War II, spent time at Manzanar, as did Toyo Miyatake, a professional photographer, who snuck a camera lens into the camp, built a camera, and became Manzanar's official photographer. Author Jeanne Wakatsuki Houston wrote about her childhood experiences in the book *Farewell to Manzanar*. When officials removed Ralph Lazo's best friends from their homes and took them to Manzanar, Lazo went too, although he was of Mexican and Irish decent, because he felt that he and his friends were all the same. His was the only documented case of a non-Asian who was not part of an Asian family who voluntarily entered the camps. Their memories recorded on film and in prose are vivid portraits of life in the camp.

Manzanar became a state historical landmark in 1972, and on February 19, 1992, on the fiftieth anniversary of the signing of Executive Order 9066, Congress passed legislation establishing Manzanar as a National

Historic Site. Today, this 814-acre park preserves the Manzanar War Relocation Center. The park is open all year during daylight hours, and admission is free. The Manzanar Interpretive Center opened in April 2004, and it is open from 8 A.M. until 6 P.M. daily.

The Eastern California Museum in Independence also has exhibits and specimens focusing on the history of Manzanar. A self-guided, walking-tour booklet is available at this museum and at the Interagency Visitor Center in Lone Pine. The tour includes the pagoda-like police post and sentry post, camp auditorium, ruins of the administrative complex, concrete foundations of many types, portions of the water systems, and the camp cemetery. There is also a 3-mile-long, self-guided auto tour of the camp with a tour description and map available at the camp entrance. Every year, on the last Saturday of April near the cemetery monument, former internees, their descendants, friends, and the general public gather together for a day of remembrance, education, and rededication of the cemetery in Christian and Buddhist ceremonies.

As part of the Save America's Treasures millennium grant, the historic perimeter barbed-wire fence that enclosed the living area of the camp was rebuilt in 2001. Other projects to be completed in the future include the reconstruction of 1 of 8 guard towers, at least 1 barracks building, and internee-built garden and ponds. These restorations, along with the visitor center exhibits, will give visitors a better sense of what Manzanar was like when it was an internment camp. A plaque at the Poston, Arizona, Relocation Center captures the spirit of Manzanar's restoration project:

> May it serve as a constant reminder of our past so that Americans in the future will never again be denied their constitutional rights and may the remembrance of that experience serve

to advance the evolution of the human spirit.

There are no food, lodging, or camping facilities at the site, but all traveler services are available nearby. The towns of Lone Pine, Independence, Olancha, Big Pine, and Bishop provide many lodging options and offer grocery stores, restaurants, gas stations, and sources for most camping and hiking supplies. During the summer, the nearby national forest campgrounds and Inyo County parks provide a number of campground facilities.

For more information, write Manzanar National Historic Site, P.O. Box 426, Independence, CA 93526-0426, or telephone (760) 878-2932. The park's Web site is www.nps.gov/manz.

FURTHER READING

Burton, Jeffery F., Mary M. Farrell, Florence B. Lord, and Richard W. Lord. *Confinement and Ethnicity: An Overview of World War II Japanese American Relocation Sites.* Seattle: University of Washington Press, 2002. Available at www.cr.nps.gov/history/online_books/anthropology74/index.htm.

Daniels, Roger. *Prisoners Without Trial: Japanese Americans in World War II.* New York: Hill and Wang, 1993.

Duus, Masayo Umezawa. *Unlikely Liberators: The Men of the 100th and 442nd.* Honolulu: University of Hawaii Press, 1987.

Garrett, Jessie A., and Ronald C. Larson, eds. *Camp and Community: Manzanar and the Owens Valley.* Fullerton: California State University, Japanese American Oral History Project, 1977.

Houston, Jeanne Wakatsuki. *Farewell to Manzanar: A True Story of Japanese American Experience During and after the World War II Internment.* Boston: Houghton Mifflin, 2002.

MARSH-BILLINGS-ROCKEFELLER NATIONAL HISTORICAL PARK

Location: Woodstock, Vermont
Acreage: 643
Established: August 26, 1992

George Perkins Marsh (1801–1882) was one of the first Americans to understand the complex and interdependent relationship between humans and their environment. In his seminal work, *Man and Nature*, published in 1864, Marsh defined the basic tenets of conservation for the first time, asserting that humanity's power to transform the natural world should entail a commensurate sense of responsibility. That it often did not, he warned, constituted a grave threat to the welfare of civilization. The old view of nature, which held that it existed to be tamed and destroyed, Marsh believed, meant that too often, humans were "a disturbing agent . . . wherever he plants his foot, the harmonies of nature are turned to discords." Marsh worried that the frenzy of consumption would lead to the impoverishment and exhaustion of the earth's natural resources unless humans preserved "what is left." His prescient writings and warnings inaugurated a national concern for conservation, and Marsh became widely known as one of the most powerful symbolic figures for the conservation movement.

In 1992, Congress created the historical park and named it the Marsh-Billings-Rockefeller National Historical Park for Marsh, who grew up on the property; Frederick Billings, an early conservationist who established a progressive dairy farm and managed and further developed the 550-acre forest on the former Marsh farm; and members of the Rockefeller family, who donated the estate and lands to the Park Service. Frederick Billings' granddaughter, Mary French Rockefeller, and her husband, conservationist Laurance S. Rockefeller, had financed and sustained Billings' practices in forestry and farming on the property throughout the latter half of the twentieth century, and in 1983, they established the Billings Farm and Museum to continue the farm's working dairy and to interpret rural Vermont life and agricultural history.

Originally set aside as a national historic landmark in 1967, the 643-acre site is the primary park in the national park system that is devoted to the history of conservation. Marsh, Billings, and the Rockefellers were major supporters of the concept of conservation, and they reflect its origins and sponsorship among the privileged classes of American society. The park preserves the Marsh home and is the first in the park system to focus on conservation history and the evolving nature of land stewardship in America.

The Carriage Barn Visitor Center is open from late May through October, from 10 A.M. until 5 P.M. It features several exhibits, including the new "Conservation Stewardship–People Taking Care of Places." From spring to fall, the 20 miles of Mount Tom carriage roads and trails are available for hiking, and in winter with snow cover, the Woodstock Ski Touring Center (802-457-6674) grooms the carriage roads for cross-country skiing and snowshoeing. The Billings Farm and Museum Visitor Center is open from May through October, from 10 A.M. until 5 P.M. The center shows *A Place in the Land,* an Academy Award–nominated film, hourly in the museum's theater. It serves as an orientation film for both the park and the Billings Farm and Museum. Park rangers offer guided tours of the Marsh-Billings-Rockefeller mansion and gardens. Admission is $6 for adults and $3 for children under sixteen. Guided tours of the Billings Farm and Museum are $8 for adults, $7 for seniors, $6 for students ages thirteen to seventeen, $4 for children five to twelve, and $1 for children three to four.

There are no food, lodging, or camping facilities at the park, but there are campsites at nearby Silver Lake State Park and other traveler services in Woodstock. The national park is off Route 12 in Woodstock.

For more information, write Marsh-Billings-Rockefeller National Historical Park, 54 Elm Street, P.O. Box 178, Woodstock, VT 05091, or telephone (802) 457-3368. The park's Web site is www.nps.gov/mabi.

FURTHER READING

Curtis, Jane. *Frederick Billings, Vermonter, Pioneer Lawyer, Business Man, Conservationist: An Illustrated Biography.* Woodstock, VT: Woodstock Foundation, 1986.

Lowenthal, David. *George Perkins Marsh: Prophet of Conservation.* Seattle: University of Washington Press, 2000.

Marsh, George Perkins. *Man and Nature, or, Physical Geography as Modified by Human Action.* Edited by David Lowenthal. Seattle: University of Washington Press, 2003.

Winks, Robin W. *Frederick Billings: A Life.* Berkeley: University of California Press, 1998.

MARTIN LUTHER KING, JR. NATIONAL HISTORIC SITE

Location: Atlanta, Georgia
Acreage: 39
Established: October 10, 1980

> I have a dream that one day on the red hills of Georgia the sons of former slaves and the sons of former slave-owners will be able to sit down together at the table of brotherhood.
>
> *—Martin Luther King, Jr.*

In his brief thirty-nine years, Martin Luther King, Jr., changed the way Americans thought about race relations and themselves. Advocating the philosophy of nonviolent civil disobedience made prominent by Mohandas K. Gandhi, King made Americans look inside themselves to confront the national disease of racial prejudice. His emphasis on faith gave the cause of civil rights standing that it had never before received, in the process, adding purpose and voice to the cause of equality during the 1950s and 1960s.

King was born on January 15, 1929, in Atlanta, Georgia, and enjoyed a middle-class upbringing as the son of a prominent Baptist minister. Named for his father, Michael Luther King, the boy was simply called "M.L." by the family. For the next twelve years, "M.L.," his parents, grandparents, siblings, aunts, uncles, and their boarders all occupied this fine 2-story Victorian home in the residential section of "Sweet Auburn," the heart of black Atlanta. Two blocks west of the home is Ebenezer Baptist Church, the pastorate of Martin's grandfather and father, and it was in these familiar surroundings of home, church, and neighborhood that "M.L." grew up and found faith, replacing his father's first name with "Martin" in honor of Martin Luther. After graduating from the prestigious Morehouse College, an all-black school, King earned a Ph.D. in theology from Boston University.

King rocketed to national prominence in December 1955, when he helped organize a boycott of the Montgomery, Alabama, bus system. On December 1, Rosa Parks, a black seamstress and well-known activist in the African American community, was arrested and jailed for refusing to give up her bus seat to a white passenger. The twenty-six-year-old King attended a hastily organized mass meeting to coordinate a citywide boycott of the transportation system. He was thrust into a position of leadership; new and without the baggage of other African American leaders, he seemed a likely figure to unite people behind this cause. No one could have anticipated what followed, as the twenty-six-year-old King became a leader of mythical proportions.

"You know, my friends, there comes a time when people get tired of being trampled over by the iron feet of oppression," he began. "And we are determined here in Montgomery to work and fight until justice runs down like water and righteousness like a mighty stream." For 381 days, Montgomery's African Americans found other means of transportation, and in November 1956, the Supreme Court ruled that bus segregation, like school segregation, was unconstitutional. Capitalizing on the momentum of the Montgomery movement, King organized the Southern Christian Leadership Conference, which called upon black people "to understand that nonviolence is not a symbol of weakness or cowardice, but as Jesus demonstrated, nonviolent resistance transforms weakness into strength and breeds courage in the face of danger." King's message translated into sit-ins, freedom rides, and voter-registration campaigns that began to eat away at decades of Jim Crow laws. Despite his adherence to nonviolence, King's activism often provoked violent response, and on April 4, 1968, he was assassinated by a lone assassin, James Earl Ray.

Established in October 1980, the 39-acre Martin Luther King, Jr. National Historic Site protects the birthplace, church, and grave of this important civil rights leader. Admission is free. The park's visitor center, at 450 Auburn Avenue, is open year-round from 9 A.M. until 5 P.M. "Courage to Lead" is the main exhibit in the visitor center. It features 6 circular pods where Dr. King's own words describe different periods of the first seventy years of the twentieth century. Each pod has a five-minute video highlighting the particular historical period. The "Children of Courage" exhibit focuses on children in the civil rights movement of the 1950s and 1960s and provides examples for today's youth on how to live positive lives. In addition to these exhibits, the center's theater shows a thirty-minute video, *A New Time, a New Voice*, about King's life and his involvement in the civil rights movement.

Park rangers offer guided tours of the King Birth Home on Auburn Avenue all year; tours limited to 15 people are filled on a first-come, first-served basis. The Ebenezer Baptist Church, at 407 Auburn Avenue, is open daily from 9 A.M. until 5 P.M., although it is closed on Sunday mornings. Park rangers offer historic talks every hour, and the church hosts the First Saturday Concert Series. Other attractions, such as Fire Station No. 6, 39 Boulevard, and Freedom Hall, 449 Auburn

Avenue, are open all year from 9 A.M. until 5 P.M. Visitors may also enjoy the Freedom Walk, an urban interpretive trail to the downtown area along Auburn Avenue. The Freedom Parkway is a vehicle parkway with a paved walking/biking path to the Carter Presidential Center. Each year the park celebrates Dr. King's birthday with the King Holiday Celebration, hosts exhibits for Black History Month (February) and Women's History Month (March), and commemorates April 4, the date of Dr. King's assassination, as Remembrance Day.

There are no food, lodging, or camping facilities at the historic site, but metropolitan Atlanta offers all traveler services.

For more information, write Martin Luther King, Jr. National Historic Site, 450 Auburn Avenue NE, Atlanta, GA 30312, or telephone (404) 331-6922. The park's Web site is www.nps.gov/malu.

FURTHER READING

Blythe, Robert W., Maureen A. Carroll, and Steven H. Moffson. *Martin Luther King, Jr., National Historic Site: Historic Resource Study.* Atlanta, GA: National Park Service, 1994. Available at www.nps.gov/malu/hrs/hrs.htm.

Branch, Taylor. *Pillar of Fire: America in the King Years, 1963–65.* New York: Simon and Schuster, 1998.

Farmer, James. *Lay Bare the Heart: An Autobiography of the Civil Rights Movement.* New York: Arbor House, 1985.

King, Martin Luther, Jr. *Stride Toward Freedom: The Montgomery Story.* New York: Harper, 1958.

Lewis, David. *King, a Critical Biography.* New York: Praeger, 1970.

Oates, Stephen B. *Let the Trumpet Sound: The Life of Martin Luther King, Jr.* New York: New American Library, 1985.

Powledge, Fred. *Free at Last? The Civil Rights Movement and the People Who Made It.* Boston: Little, Brown, 1991.

MARTIN VAN BUREN NATIONAL HISTORIC SITE

Location: Kinderhook, New York
Acreage: 40
Established: October 26, 1974

The nation's eighth president rose from humble beginnings. Martin Van Buren was born in 1782, the son of a tavern keeper and farmer, in Kinderhook, New York. As a young lawyer he became involved in New York state politics and shrewdly commandeered control of the Democratic-Republican party with an alliance of political supporters called the Bucktails. Once in office, Van Buren and the Bucktails streamlined state government and enacted nearly universal manhood suffrage. This new alignment rewarded party loyalty, rather than personal friendship or family ties, and soon became the national standard—the foundation for the Second American Party System. As the leader of the so-called Albany Regency, the effective New York political organization, Van Buren shrewdly dispensed public offices and bounty in a fashion calculated to bring votes, and in 1821 he was elected to the U.S. Senate.

Martin Van Buren, eighth president of the United States. *(National Archives)*

By 1827, Van Buren had emerged as the principal northern leader for the party's national spokesman, Andrew Jackson, and when Jackson won the presidency the next year, he rewarded Van Buren by appointing him secretary of state. Van Buren soon proved Jackson's most trusted adviser—Jackson referred to him as "a true man with no guile"—and in 1832, when Jackson won his second term, the "Little Magician" was elected vice president and became the obvious heir to the presidency.

Van Buren triumphed in the presidential election of 1836, easily outdistancing four other contenders. Unfortunately, the prosperity that had flourished during the Jackson years gave way to recession. Within three months of his inauguration, Van Buren faced a failing economy in the Panic of 1837. Jackson's destruction of the Second Bank of the United States had removed restrictions upon the inflationary practices of some state banks, and wild speculation in land, based on easy bank credit, had swept the West. To end this speculation, Jackson had issued a Specie Circular in 1836, requiring that land be purchased with hard money—gold or silver. People rushed to cash in their paper money and bonds, prompting the collapse of the banking industry. Hundreds of banks and businesses failed, and thousands lost their land. Though much of the fault lay with Jackson's policies, Van Buren took the blame, and he soon earned the nickname Martin "Van Ruin." Not surprisingly, the foundering economy cost Van Buren reelection in 1840 (he was also an unsuccessful candidate for president on the Free Soil ticket in 1848).

Van Buren purchased the Kinderhook estate in 1839 and retired there in 1841. The home, which he named Lindenwald, eventually grew to 226 acres under his direction and was a profitable working farm. Van Buren commissioned Richard Upjohn to design an Italianate addition to the 36-room Federalist mansion, and he lived in the home until his death in 1862. The mansion, which contains original wallpaper and furnishings, has been restored to the Van Buren period, while much of the cultural landscape and adjacent lands are conservation lands, which retain a very high degree of integrity to the period of President Van Buren's residence.

Authorized in October 1974, the 40-acre Martin Van Buren National Historic Site is open to the public Thursday through Monday from Memorial Day weekend to the end of October, and on Saturday and Sunday in November through the first week in December. The park's visitor center, located across the Old Post Road from the visitor parking lot, is staffed from 9 A.M. until 4:30 P.M. and offers information on tours and fees. Access to the historic house is by guided tour only. The historic site features living-history programs, concerts, and craft demonstrations, and park rangers offer interpretive talks, bike tours, and hikes.

There are no food, lodging, or camping facilities at the site, but all traveler services are available locally.

For more information, write Martin Van Buren National Historic Site, 1013 Old Post Road, Kinderhook, NY 12106, or telephone (518) 758-9689. The park's Web site is www.nps.gov/mava.

FURTHER READING
Curtis, James C. *The Fox at Bay: Martin Van Buren and the Presidency, 1837–1841.* Lexington: University Press of Kentucky, 1970.

Silbey, Joel H. *Martin Van Buren and the Emergence of American Popular Politics.* Lanham, MD: Rowman & Littlefield, 2002.

Wilson, Major L. *The Presidency of Martin Van Buren.* Lawrence: University Press of Kansas, 1984.

MARY McLEOD BETHUNE COUNCIL HOUSE NATIONAL HISTORIC SITE
Location: Washington, D.C.
Acreage: .07
Established: October 15, 1982

What does the Negro want? His answer is very simple. He wants only what all other Americans want. He wants opportunity to make real what the Declaration of Independence and the Constitution and the Bill of Rights say, what the Four Freedoms establish. While he knows these ideals are open to no man completely, he wants only his equal chance to obtain them.

—Mary McLeod Bethune

The Mary McLeod Bethune Council House National Historic Site commemorates the life of Mary McLeod Bethune—renowned educator, organizer, and national political leader—and the organization she founded, the National Council of Negro Women. The 3-story Victorian Bethune Council House was Bethune's last official Washington, D.C., residence, from 1943 until 1949, and the first headquarters of the National Council of Negro Women. Here Bethune and the council spearheaded strategies and developed programs to advance the interests of African American women and the black community. The site is also the location of the National Archives for Black Women's History, which houses the largest manuscript collection of materials solely dedicated to African American women and their organizations.

Mary McLeod Bethune's lifetime of activism provides a vital link between the social reform efforts of African Americans in the post-Reconstruction era and the vibrant civil rights protests so emblematic of the post–World War II era. On July 10, 1875, Bethune was born the fifteenth of seventeen children of former slaves. Amidst the poverty and oppression of the Reconstruction South, Bethune nevertheless prevailed, graduating from Scotia Seminary in 1894. After teaching in mission schools for several years, she became keenly aware of the importance of education in the emerging struggle for civil rights, and in 1904 she established the Daytona Educa-

Portrait of Mary McLeod Bethune, 1949. Bethune founded the National Council of Negro Women.

(Library of Congress)

tional and Industrial Institute for Training Negro Girls in Daytona Beach, Florida. As she later remembered, "the school expanded fast. In less than two years I had two hundred fifty pupils. . . . I concentrated more and more on girls, as I felt that they especially were hampered by lack of educational opportunity." Her institute later merged with the Cookman Institute, an educational facility for black boys, to become the coed Bethune-Cookman College. During the 1920s, Bethune broadened her activism to become the leader of the National Association of Colored Women, which became the National Association of Negro Women during the 1930s. The organization provided important training in organization and public speaking that would become so vital to the later civil rights movement. During the New Deal, Bethune also

enjoyed a close personal friendship with First Lady Eleanor Roosevelt. Following her appointment as director of the Division of Negro Affairs of the National Youth Administration by President Franklin D. Roosevelt, she became an important government adviser and the first African American woman to hold so high an office in the federal government. Her ideas effectively set an activist agenda for the emerging civil rights crusade. Serving as an adviser on African American affairs to four presidents, Bethune continued to be an important voice for human rights until her death in 1955 at the age of seventy-nine.

Designated in October 1982, the Mary McLeod Bethune Council House National Historic Site is an important component of the expansion of the themes of American history in the national park system. Its selection came at a time when the experiences of African Americans, women, and countless other groups were first being included in the national pageant.

The park is open Monday through Saturday from 10 A.M. until 4 P.M., and tours are available for both individuals and groups of all ages. Admission is free. The visitor center features numerous exhibits, including the Early African American Women School Founders 1861–1909 exhibit, which focuses on six African American women who founded schools in the South during the late nineteenth and early twentieth centuries. The Bethune Council House contains original furnishings and historic photographs depicting the Council House during the 1940s when it was Mary McLeod Bethune's Washington, D.C., residence and the headquarters of the National Council of Negro Women. In addition to the Bethune Birthday Celebration on July 10, the park commemorates Black History Month (February) and Women's History Month (March); it also hosts an annual open house on the first full weekend in June.

There are no food, lodging, or camping facilities at the historic site, but all traveler services are available in the metropolitan Washington, D.C., area.

For more information, write Mary McLeod Bethune Council House National Historic Site, 1318 Vermont Avenue NW, Washington, DC 20005, or telephone (202) 673-2402. The park's Web site is www.nps.gov/mamc.

FURTHER READING

Bethune, Mary McLeod. *Building a Better World: Essays and Selected Documents.* Bloomington: Indiana University Press, 1999.

Franklin, John Hope, and Alfred A. Moss, Jr. *From Slavery to Freedom: A History of African Americans.* Boston: McGraw-Hill, 2000.

Hine, Darlene Clark, William C. Hine, and Stanley Harrold. *The African-American Odyssey.* Upper Saddle River, NJ: Prentice-Hall, 2003.

MESA VERDE NATIONAL PARK

Location: Cortez, Colorado
Acreage: 52,122
Established: June 29, 1906

Mesa Verde National Park is the nation's premier archeological national park. Established in 1906 during a national burst of enthusiasm about North America's prehistoric past, the southwestern Colorado park reveals much of the story of the Anasazi, the ancient peoples of the Southwest who built the monumental masonry and stone structures that dot so many southwestern slopes. No Anasazi site captivated national attention like Mesa Verde; none were so central to the evolution of archeology as a profession in the United States.

The story of the modern discovery of Mesa Verde began with Richard Wetherill, a cowboy from a family with a history of failure across the West. Owner of a marginal ranch in the nearby Mancos, Colorado, area, Wetherill became obsessed with prehistory from the moment he, a brother, and a brother-in-law found what the Park Service now calls Cliff Palace in Mesa Verde National Park in 1889. A poor man, Wetherill simultaneously recognized the economic advantages of the prehistoric world he uncovered. He excavated the ruins and began to offer relics for sale. Soon after, he became a guide to others who wanted to excavate prehistoric ruins. No Anglo-American knew better than he the location of the most desirable ruins. Wetherill and a partner had advertised themselves as photographers, but beginning with Gustav Nordenskiöld, the twenty-three-year-old son of a Swedish baron known for his explorations of the Arctic regions, Wetherill found himself in the excavation business. Nordenskiöld had seen a collection Wetherill made in Denver and arrived at the family's ranch, bubbling with enthusiasm. At Wetherill's direction, the Swede began to excavate in what is now Mesa Verde National Park.

Wetherill built a cottage industry in the area and incurred the wrath of the nascent discipline of archeology, which was seeking to professionalize and attain status in turn-of-the-twentieth-century America. Wetherill, a mere cowboy, stood in their way, and a combination of influential scientists and their friends and government officials sought to curtail his activities. The group forced Wetherill's exile from the Mesa Verde region in the late 1890s. In an age when archeology offered much to a rapidly industrializing society, these new professionals provided momentum that led to archeological preservation. They began an effort to protect archeological ruins in the Southwest that culminated in the passage of the Antiquities Act, which allowed the president to establish a new category called "national monuments" from public lands, on June 8, 1906, and culminated with the establishment of Mesa Verde National Park just three weeks later on June 29, 1906. Within a decade of his expulsion, the area Wetherill excavated had become a national park. Seventy-three years passed before the federal government added the next piece of archeological protective leg-

The ruins of Cliff Palace, a prehistoric Anasazi dwelling, in Mesa Verde National Park. *(National Park Service)*

islation, the Archaeological Resources Protection Act of 1979.

The park preserves the remains of Anasazi culture, which flourished in the region between about 550 and the early 1300s. The period from 1100 to 1300 is considered the classic Mesa Verde period, the era during which the construction of the most impressive rock and masonry structures took place. Before that time, the Anasazi lived in small clusters of pithouses. During the classic period, the mesa's population reached several thousand, concentrated in compact villages of many rooms. They built ceremonial chambers called "kivas" inside the walls. Round towers began to appear, and the level of craftsmanship in masonry work, pottery, weaving, jewelry, and even tool making became quite sophisticated.

The people of Mesa Verde lived in their cliff dwellings for less than a hundred years. By 1300, for as yet unknown reasons, they had deserted Mesa Verde. Drought and crop failures marked the last quarter of the thirteenth century, but these people had survived earlier droughts. Maybe after hundreds of years of intense use, they had depleted the land and its resources—the soil, forests, and animals. Social and political issues may have contributed and the people looked for new opportunities elsewhere. When they left Mesa Verde, these people traveled south into New Mexico and Arizona, settling among relatives who already lived there. It is likely that today's Pueblo people, and perhaps other Native Americans, are descendants of the cliff dwellers of Mesa Verde.

The park is open daily, year-round. The Chapin Mesa Museum is open from 8 A.M. to 6:30 P.M. mid-April to mid-October; 8 A.M. to 5 P.M. the rest of the year. Far View Visitor Center is open from 8 A.M. to 5 P.M. mid-April to mid-October. Ranger-guided tours and self-guided tours are available in spring, summer, and fall. Limited services are available in winter.

Mesa Verde National Park is high in elevation and has four distinct seasons. In spring, temperatures are variable, ranging from the 30s with snow to the 70s with sun. Summer is hot; temperatures routinely reach the 90s. Afternoon thunderstorms are common in July and August. During the fall, the days are still warm and the nights, cool. The possibility of snow begins in October and continues throughout the winter. It is often below freezing at night and snow accumulates to depths of 3 to 4 feet. Snowy and icy conditions are common in winter.

Because of the altitude, Mesa Verde is difficult for people with vision, hearing, or mobility impairments. Persons with heart or respiratory ailments may have breathing problems in the thin air at altitudes up to 8,500 feet.

A vehicle is necessary to see Mesa Verde. The park entrance fee for vehicles is $10 for a seven-day pass.

For more information, write Mesa Verde National Park, P.O. Box 8, Mesa Verde National Park, CO 81330-0008, or telephone (970) 529-4465. The park's Web site is www.nps.gov/meve.

FURTHER READING

Brown, Kenneth A. *Four Corners: History, Land and People of the Desert Southwest.* New York: Harper Perennial, 1996.

McNitt, Frank. *Richard Wetherill, Anasazi.* Albuquerque: University of New Mexico Press, 1974.

Noble, David Grant. *Ancient Ruins of the Southwest: An Archaeological Guide.* Flagstaff, AZ: Northland, 2000.

Wenger, Gilbert R. *The Story of Mesa Verde National Park.* Mesa Verde National Park, CO: Mesa Verde Museum, 1991.

MINIDOKA INTERNMENT NATIONAL MONUMENT

Location: Jerome, Idaho
Acreage: 73
Established: January 17, 2001

On December 7, 1941, when the Japanese bombed Pearl Harbor in Hawaii, the United States resolved to enter World War II. But while the attack stimulated American patriotism and nationalism, it also unleashed a ferocious nativism, aimed at those of Japanese ancestry living in the United States. At the time of Pearl Harbor, about 127,000 Japanese Americans lived in the United States, the vast majority along the West Coast, a region soon seized by an anti-Japanese panic. The federal government fanned these fears, when in February 1942 President Franklin D. Roosevelt issued an executive order authorizing the removal of people of Japanese descent from the Pacific Coast "war zone" in the interest of national security. Racial fear was the real motivation. In all, more than 110,000 Japanese Americans were moved to ten guarded and barbed-wire facilities in remote interior locations throughout the West and South. More than two-thirds of those detained were Nisei, native-born American citizens. Most lost not only their liberty, but also most of their worldly possessions, including some of the best farmland in California. Finally, in 1988, Congress acknowledged the grave injustice perpetrated on its own citizens by the federal government and voted an indemnity of $1.2 billion to the estimated 60,000 survivors—about $20,000 each. As one man remembered, "It was terrible, but it was a time of war. Anything can happen. I didn't blame the United States for that." One of these relocation centers was Minidoka on the Snake River plain of southern Idaho. Most of the camp's 7,000-plus residents came from the Pacific Northwest, from Oregon, Washington, and Alaska, and were housed in 35 residential blocks. Little of the facility remains today.

Minidoka Internment National Monument was established in 2001 to protect what remains at the site, to tell the stories of what happened there, and share how this experience affected the lives of the individuals who lived this chapter of America's history. As one of the newest additions to the park system, Minidoka currently has no visitor facilities, although the park is open year-round during daylight hours. Admission is free. Visitors can walk among the remains of the entry guard station, waiting room, and rock garden; the Jerome County Museum has a relocation center display, and the Idaho Farm and Ranch Museum has a "restored" barracks. There are no food or lodging facilities available at the monument, but all traveler services can be found in nearby Twin Falls.

For more information, write Minidoka Internment National Monument, P.O. Box 570, Hagerman, ID 83332, or telephone (208) 837-4793. The park's Web site is www.nps.gov/miin.

FURTHER READING

Burton, Jeffery F., et al. *Confinement and Ethnicity: An Overview of World War II Japanese American Relocation Sites.* Seattle: University of Washington Press, 2002.

Inada, Lawson Fusao, ed. *Only What We Could Carry: The Japanese American Internment Experience.* San Francisco: California Historical Society, 2000.

Murray, Alice Yang, ed. *What Did the Internment of Japanese Americans Mean?* Boston: Bedford/St. Martin's, 2000.

Ng, Wendy L. *Japanese American Internment During World War II: A History and Reference Guide.* Westport, CT: Greenwood, 2002.

MINUTE MAN NATIONAL HISTORICAL PARK

Location: Concord, Lincoln, and Lexington, Massachusetts
Acreage: 971
Established: September 21, 1959

Listen, my children, and you shall
  hear,
Of the midnight ride of Paul Revere,
On the eighteenth of April, in
  Seventy-Five;
Hardly a man is now alive
Who remembers that famous day
  and year.
    —Henry Wadsworth Longfellow

In the fall of 1774, as tension mounted between the British Army, stationed in Boston, and American colonists, the Massachusetts House of Representatives created a Committee of Safety empowered to muster the militia. The militia was comprised of special units—the "minutemen"—who stood ready to be called at a moment's notice. Although the British general Thomas Gage worried that his forces were insufficient to suppress a rebellion, King George was convinced the time had come for war: "The New England governments are in a state of rebellion. Blows must decide whether they are to be subject to this country or independent." On the evening of April 17, 1775, under cover of darkness, Gage moved his 700 troops out of Boston to capture the store of colonial ammunition in the town of Concord. It was a fateful decision. A light in Boston's Old North Church ("one if by land, two if by sea") alerted the patriots, who quickly dispatched two men on horseback—Paul Revere and William Dawes—to forewarn the militia. By the time Gage's men reached Lexington, halfway to their destination, their cover was blown. As the troops peered through the hazy dawn, they spied some seventy, armed Minute Men assembled on the village green. In the skirmish that ensued, eight Americans were killed and ten were wounded. The British pressed on to Concord, where they were attacked and three of their soldiers were killed. Their retreat to Boston was a harrowing trek, as the entire countryside seemed riddled with enemy fire. When they finally arrived in Boston, Gage's troops had lost 73 dead and more than 200 missing; the Massachusetts Minute Men suffered 95 casualties. The events of April 18 and 19, 1775, were a turning point in the long struggle between England and her American colonies. In those few hours, months of protest and petition dissolved into revolution and a struggle for independence. This "shot heard 'round the world" would ultimately lead to the creation of a new nation, the United States of America.

First set aside in September of 1959, the 971-acre Minute Man National Historical Park preserves and protects the significant historic sites, structures, properties, and landscapes associated with the opening battles of the American Revolution. Most important, Minute Man interprets the colonial struggle for natural rights and freedoms. In addition to the park's revolutionary significance,

Minute Man National Historical Park preserves and protects the historically significant sites, structures, and landscapes associated with the opening battles of the American Revolution. *(Library of Congress)*

Minute Man preserves and interprets the nineteenth-century American literary revolution through The Wayside, home of Nathaniel Hawthorne, Louisa May Alcott, and Margaret Sidney. Admission is free.

The Minute Man Visitor Center is open year-round from 9 A.M. until 5 P.M., and features numerous exhibits, including a 40-foot battle mural, and a twenty-five-minute multimedia theater presentation detailing the events of April 18 and 19 called *The Road to Revolution.* The North Bridge Visitor Center is open year-round daily from 9 A.M. until 5 P.M., with reduced hours during the winter. The center features dioramas and costumed mannequins, as well as *April Fire,* a twelve-minute video program. Park rangers also offer a twenty-minute interpretive program called "Two Revolutions" that focuses on the area's two historical revolutions, the American Revolution of April 19, 1775, and the nineteenth-century American Literary Renaissance. The North Bridge is the site of "the shot heard 'round the world," and next to the bridge is Daniel Chester French's Minute Man Statue.

The Hartwell Tavern is open from May through October from 9:30 A.M. until 5:30 P.M. and offers several living-history programs. In "Who Were the Minute Men?" a costumed ranger gives a twenty-minute talk that includes a musket-firing demonstration; in "Life Along the Battle Road," a costumed ranger conducts a forty-minute guided walk that follows a portion of the restored Battle Road and loops back on a woodland path. Hartwell Tavern is an authentic period home, a tangible reminder of how people lived in this area at the outbreak of the American Revolution. The structure played a significant role as a landmark in the community as travelers to and from Boston stopped and shared the latest news and discussed important issues of the day.

The Wayside, Home of Authors, is open

from May through October from 9:30 A.M. until 5:30 P.M., Thursday through Tuesday. Park rangers offer a thirty-five-minute guided tour of The Wayside, but visitors must be able to climb steep stairs. Fees are $4 per person. During the Revolutionary era, The Wayside was the home of Samuel Whitney, muster master of the Concord Minute Men. During the literary renaissance of the nineteenth century, it was home to three families of authors. The young Louisa May Alcott wrote her first published work here. Extensive renovations to the house, including the vaulted tower study, were made by Nathaniel Hawthorne. Also, Harriett Lothrop, using the pen name "Margaret Sidney," wrote the "Five Little Peppers" stories at this Home of Authors. Exhibits at the home include lifelike cast figures of Louisa May Alcott, Nathaniel Hawthorne, and Margaret Sidney, and beautiful graphics, some never before on display, which illuminate the writings and lives of these Concord authors.

Visitors can also enjoy a walk along the Battle Road Trail, which connects historic sites from Meriam's Corner in Concord to the eastern boundary of the park in Lexington. The main theme of the trail is the battle of April 19, 1775, that launched the American Revolution. But the trail also interprets the broader "human story" of the people whose lives were altered by the events that took place here. Much of the trail follows original remnants of the Battle Road; other sections leave the historic road to follow the route of the Minute Men, traversing farming fields, wetlands, and forests. The entire trail is 5 miles long, and rangers offer forty-minute guided walks on Mondays, Wednesdays, and Fridays, leaving from Hartwell Tavern at 11 A.M. and 2 P.M. In addition, three- to four-hour walks or bicycle programs are presented on Sundays throughout the summer season.

There are no food, lodging, or camping facilities at the historical park, but all traveler services are available locally.

For more information, write Minute Man National Historical Park, 174 Liberty Street, Concord, MA 01742, or telephone (978) 369-6993. The park's Web site is www.nps.gov/mima.

FURTHER READING
Fischer, David Hackett. *Paul Revere's Ride.* New York: Oxford University Press, 1994.

Galvin, John R. *The Minute Men: The First Fight—Myths and Realities of the American Revolution.* Washington, DC: Pergamon-Brassey's International Defense, 1989.

Gross, Robert A. *The Minutemen and Their World.* New York: Hill and Wang, 2001.

Hallahan, William H. *The Day the Revolution Began: 19 April 1775.* New York: Avon Books, 1999.

Shaara, Jeff, *Rise to Rebellion.* New York: Ballantine Books, 2001.

Tourtellot, Arthur Bernon. *Lexington and Concord: The Beginning of the War of the American Revolution.* New York: W.W. Norton, 1963.

MISSISSIPPI NATIONAL RIVER AND RECREATION AREA

Location: Minneapolis, Minnesota
Acreage: 53,775
Established: November 18, 1988

The Mississippi National River and Recreation Area is a unique partnership park. Altogether, it encompasses 72 miles of the Mississippi River corridor extending from the north boundary at Dayton, Minnesota, through the Minneapolis/St. Paul metropolitan region and downstream to Hastings. Although the National Park Service owns only a fraction of the park's lands—35 of the recreation area's 53,775 acres—the Park Service manages the entire area in partnership with other state and local agencies. The many museums, cultural centers, and natural and historical attractions along the corridor illustrate the dynamic history of this important river.

The Mississippi River is approximately 2,300 miles in length, stretching from headwaters in Itasca State Park in Minnesota, to the river's mouth in New Orleans, Louisiana. Experts estimate a raindrop would take about ninety days to complete the journey to the Gulf of Mexico. As it winds through the nation's heartland, the Mississippi River basin drains 41 percent of the continental United States. The total size of this amazing watershed is between 1.2 and 1.8 million square miles, and this includes thirty-one states and two Canadian provinces. For nearly two hundred years, agriculture has been the primary user of the basin lands, continually altering the hydrologic cycle and energy budget of the region. The huge agribusiness industry in the Mississippi River basin produces 92 percent of the nation's agricultural exports, 78 percent of the world's exports in feed grains and soybeans, and most of the livestock and hogs produced in America. Fully 60 percent of all grain exported from the United States is shipped via the Mississippi River through the Port of New Orleans and the Port of South Louisiana. In measure of tonnage, the largest port in the world is on the Mississippi River at La Place, Louisiana. Between the two of them, the Ports of New Orleans and South Louisiana shipped more than 243 million tons of goods in 1999. Shipping at the lower end of the Mississippi is focused on petroleum, iron and steel, grain, rubber, paper and wood, coffee, coal, chemicals, and edible oils.

The Mississippi River and its floodplain are also home to a diverse population of living things, including at least 260 species of fishes—25 percent of all fish species in North America. During the spring and fall, 40 percent of the nation's migratory waterfowl use the river corridor, while 60 percent of all North American birds (326 species) use the Mississippi River basin as their migratory flyway. From Cairo, Illinois, upstream to Lake Itasca, there are 38 documented species of mussels, and on the Lower Mississippi, there may be as many as 60 separate mussel species. The upper Mississippi alone is host to

more than 50 species of mammals. At least 145 species of amphibians and reptiles inhabit the upper Mississippi River environs. The Minnesota Valley Wildlife Refuge, on the southwest boundary of the recreation area corridor in Bloomington, is open all year. The refuge maintains an interpretive center, living examples of native prairie ecosystems, and bicycle and walking trails.

Congress established the Mississippi National River and Recreation Area in November 1988. While the park headquarters are in St. Paul, the recreation area does not own land or operate a visitor center. As a result, there are no fees associated with the park itself, but some partner visitor centers and parks do charge entry fees. The Minnesota History Center, at 345 Kellogg Boulevard in St. Paul, is open all year and offers exhibits on Minnesota history and the mechanics of living in "the good old days." The center also has an extensive collection of publications and photographs chronicling Minnesota's history that are available to researchers and enthusiasts. The Science Museum of Minnesota, at 120 Kellogg Boulevard, is also open year-round, and it features the Mississippi River Gallery, a collaborative effort between the Park Service and museum. This special exhibit profiles the geologic, economic, social, and environmental impact of the Mississippi River in and near the Minneapolis/St. Paul metropolitan area. In addition, this nationally respected museum houses the omnitheater and ongoing exhibits, events, and collections that focus on anthropology, paleontology, science and design in our daily lives, the human body gallery, and a host of other topics.

The Coon Rapids Dam Visitor Center, at 9750 Egert Boulevard in Coon Rapids, is open year-round and offers indoor interpretive exhibits, including the Mississippi River Kiosk. The park has both walking trails and a bicycle trail that connect to trails honeycombing the metro area. In the summer, the visitor center rents bicycles; in the winter, it rents skis and snowshoes. The Fort Snelling State Park, at the historic confluence of the Mississippi and Minnesota rivers, is open all year and is part of the Minnesota Department of Natural Resources' state park system. Fort Snelling is the site of the Dakota Internment Camp, where the U.S. Army held many of the Sioux during the Sioux Uprising of 1862. The visitor center has exhibits on the biological communities in and near the Mississippi River, a demonstration of watershed mechanics, and an underground view of the root systems of native plants.

The St. Anthony Falls Lock and Dam, at 1 Portland Avenue in Minneapolis, is open year-round from 9 A.M. until 10 P.M., and until 9 P.M. in the winter. The U.S. Army Corps of Engineers operates the St. Anthony Falls Lock and Dam, which is the farthest upstream of the 29 locks between Lake Itasca and St. Louis. The lock has an enclosed observation deck and exhibits. Visitors can watch barges and boats "lock through" and learn how the river's natural hydraulics make it all possible. The St. Anthony Falls Heritage Trail is a 2-mile walking/bicycle loop around the Minneapolis riverfront that allows visitors to explore the historic falls and see how this part of the Mississippi helped the fledgling city of Minneapolis earn the title "milling capital of the world."

Visitors to the recreation area can also tour the Sibley House Historic Site, at 1357 Sibley Memorial Highway in Mendota. Henry Hastings Sibley came to the area in 1834 as the head of the American Fur Company Post, and he later served as a territorial representative to the U.S. Congress and as the first governor of the state. In 1839, Jean Baptiste Faribault built the house next to Sibley's, and it is part of the historic site.

There are no food, lodging, or camping facilities in the recreation area, but all traveler services are available in the Minneapolis/St. Paul metropolitan area.

For more information, write Mississippi National River and Recreation Area, 111 East Kellogg Boulevard, St. Paul, MN 55101-1256, or telephone (651) 290-4160. The park's Web site is www.nps.gov/miss.

FURTHER READING

Ambrose, Stephen E. *The Mississippi and the Making of a Nation.* Washington, DC: National Geographic, 2002.

Anfinson, John O. *The River We Have Wrought: A History of the Upper Mississippi.* Minneapolis: University of Minnesota Press, 2003.

Haites, Erik F. *Western River Transportation: The Era of Early Internal Development, 1810–1860.* Baltimore, MD: The Johns Hopkins University Press, 1975.

Kelman, Ari. *A River and Its City: The Nature of Landscape in New Orleans.* Berkeley: University of California Press, 2003.

Miles, Jim. *A River Unvexed: A History and Tour Guide to the Campaign for the Mississippi River.* Nashville, TN: Rutledge Hill, 1994.

Twain, Mark. *Mississippi Writings.* New York: Viking, 1982.

MOJAVE NATIONAL PRESERVE

Location: Barstow, California
Acreage: 1,532,426
Established: October 31, 1994

The Mojave National Preserve encompasses the eastern part of the Mojave Desert, one of the harshest terrains in the United States, but also one of the most fascinating and, in its own way, beautiful. Located in eastern California near Las Vegas, Nevada, the preserve protects more than 1.5 million acres of desert. Visitors are rewarded with stunning views of this remarkable landscape, which includes sand dunes, mountain ranges, lava fields, cinder cones, and mesas. The highest point in the park is at Teutonia Peak (at 5,643 feet) making it an ideal hiking destination. The Cinder Cones region of the park includes 32 extinct volcanoes, and hikers will appreciate the preserve's beautiful and varied plant life. Joshua trees are characteristic of this desert environment, and Cima dome, a granitic dome, is home to Joshua tree woodlands.

The preserve incorporates seven separate mountain ranges, each providing rewarding hiking opportunities as well as wildlife viewing. The New York Mountain Range contains some of the highest mountains in the park, and within this range are the Castle Peaks, with their reddish spires of volcanic rock. The Mid Hills area is home to pinyon pine and juniper trees at an elevation of 5,600 feet, while the Piute Range is where human history has converged with the natural history of the park.

Because the Piute area has the preserve's only permanent water supply, it is where human communities have formed for hundreds of years. The Fort Mojave Indians are the descendants of the earliest Native Americans to inhabit this area. The Mojave people, who were the northernmost members of the Yuman tribes, made up the largest concentration of people in the Southwest when the Spanish arrived in the sixteenth century. There were three separate groups of Mojave who lived in specific regions of the Mojave Desert. A culturally complex people, the Mojave relied on dreams and visions to guide the cosmology of their people. Farmers and traders, the Mojave were well positioned to meet the 1604 Spanish expedition that exposed them to Europeans.

Early Spanish explorers commented that the Mojave were a particularly friendly people, but the encounters between the Mojave and American mountain men such as Jedediah Smith did not reflect such positive feelings. The Mojave, offended and puzzled by

Whirlwinds in the Mojave Desert, c. 1921. *(Library of Congress)*

the Americans' disregard for the land, engaged in several decades of armed conflict with Americans and the U.S. Army during the nineteenth century. By 1865 the tribe had been split in two, those who agreed to comply with the U.S. government's demand that they move to reservations, and those who refused to do so. By the early twentieth century, many of the Mojave had been forced into boarding schools and had their names Anglicized. Nevertheless, they continue to play an important role in their homeland, which is encompassed in part by the preserve.

Established in October 1994, the Mojave National Preserve was an integral part of the California Desert Protection Act (CDPA). This legislation had been fifteen years in coming; it began with the Bureau of Land Management's 1980 California Desert Plan, an attempt to provide comprehensive protection to the eastern Mojave. Part of the impetus came from changes in federal law that demanded more thorough management planning; even more resulted from the rapid growth of population in the desert and the consequences for plants, animals, and the landscape. The CDPA created the Mojave National Preserve, added millions of acres of Bureau of Land Management (BLM) wilderness, promised the Timbisha Shoshone a homeland, and made Death Valley and Joshua Tree into national parks. The national preserve category reflected a lesser level of preservation than did conventional national park status. It allowed the extractive uses that had been characteristic of the region to continue even as it permitted higher levels of protection than had ever before existed.

Mojave National Preserve provides visitors with an excellent opportunity to explore the beautiful scenery of the Mojave Desert and the cultural heritage of the native people, who historically and presently inhabit the region. The ruins of Fort Piute, an army outpost, add Anglo-Americans to the cultural history of the area. The preserve itself is open twenty-four hours a day, year-round, and admission is free. The park maintains 2 visitor centers, which are open year-round: the Baker Desert center is open from 9 A.M. until 5 P.M., while the Needles Desert center is open from 8 A.M. until 4 P.M., and both have limited exhibits. Visitors can also utilize the Hole-in-the-Wall Ranger Station, located 20 miles north of I-40 on Essex and Black Canyon roads, on weekends as staffing permits from 10 A.M. until 2 P.M. The ranger station offers Friday evening ranger talks and Saturday morning guided hikes during the spring only.

By far, the most pleasant times of year in the desert are spring and fall, when relatively mild temperatures make hiking and sightseeing safe and enjoyable. With enough moisture, spring wildflowers carpet the desert with vivid colors from March through May, although the wildflower display varies greatly from year to year depending on rainfall. Hundreds of miles of dirt roads await the well-prepared explorer, and a detailed map is available at the Baker or Needles Desert Information Center, or on weekends at the Hole-in-the-Wall Ranger Station. Visitors can explore the dense Joshua tree forest on a 4-mile round-trip, marked trail on the way to a peak on Cima Dome. Early-morning and late-afternoon hikers will appreciate both the rosy glow of the dunes and the cooler temperatures on the 3-mile round-trip Kelso Dunes Hike.

There are no lodging facilities in the preserve, though visitors can obtain food and supplies in Cima and Nipton. Camping is available at the Hole-in-the-Wall and Mid Hills campgrounds, which are open year-round. Spaces are available on a first-come, first-served basis for $12 per site, per night. In addition, all traveler services are available in Baker, Barstow, and Needles, California, and in Laughlin and Primm, Nevada.

For more information, write Superintendent, Mojave National Preserve, 222 East Main Street, Suite 202, Barstow, CA 92311, or telephone (760) 255-8800. The park's Web site is www.nps.gov/moja.

FURTHER READING

Darlington, David. *The Mojave: A Portrait of the Definitive American Desert.* New York: Henry Holt, 1996.

Hamin, Elisabeth M. *Mojave Lands: Interpretive Planning and the National Preserve.* Baltimore, MD: Johns Hopkins University Press, 2003.

MacKay, Pam. *Mojave Desert Wildflowers: A Field Guide to the Wildflowers of the Mojave Desert, Including the Mojave National Preserve and Joshua Tree National Park.* Guilford, CT: Globe Pequot, 2003.

Nystrom, Eric, "Mojave National Preserve: An Administrative History." Unpublished, 2004.

MONOCACY NATIONAL BATTLEFIELD

Location: Frederick, Maryland
Acreage: 1,647
Established: June 21, 1934

Monocacy National Battlefield is one of the paradoxical sites of the Civil War. The site commemorates a Confederate victory on July 9, 1864, that helped the Union protect Washington, D.C., from a rebel advance. Monocacy was the culmination of the third Confederate attempt to invade the North—Antietam in 1862 and Gettysburg in 1863 put an end to the previous two raids—and became known as the "battle that saved Washington."

In June 1864, General Jubal A. Early received orders from General Robert E. Lee to move his Confederate troops to the Shenandoah Valley as a staging ground for an assault on Washington. With more than 18,000 troops, Early posed a genuine threat. Near Petersburg, Virginia, the main body of the Union forces faced Lee's outnumbered troops. Lee designed Early's advance to divert the Union forces. Their foray in early July sent shock waves through Washington. On July 2, Early reached Winchester in northwestern Virginia; a few days later, after

destroying Union military supplies at Harpers Ferry, West Virginia, his troops reached Sheperdstown, crossed into Maryland, and continued toward Fredericksburg.

General Lew Wallace, who later authored the classic *Ben-Hur,* learned from the president of the Baltimore and Ohio Railroad that a large Confederate force was advancing through Maryland. To block them, he put 5,800 soldiers, many of them newly trained recruits, in the Fredericksburg area. Wallace stationed most of them in and around two blockhouses at Monocacy Junction. The higher east bank of the Monocacy River and the blockhouses offered a strong defensive position.

When Early's troops advanced out of Fredericksburg, they encountered stiff Union resistance. The talented Early, an accomplished military leader, recognized the advantages of the Union position. Rather than attempt a direct assault, he sent General John Gordon, the tough, battle-hardened commander who had inherited Stonewall Jackson's brigade, to the east, diverting some of Wallace's men to defend the flank. Early then struck a full blow to the center of the Union lines. The battle raged the rest of the day, with the heaviest casualties in the center of the field. The Union troops eventually fell back and began to retreat toward Baltimore, leaving as many as 1,200 dead on the field. The Confederates lost between 700 and 900 killed. Although the Southerners won the battle and forced the Union troops from the field, Wallace claimed victory. He held back the Confederates for one vital day, allowing reinforcements to reach the nation's capital. When Early's men reached the outskirts of the District of Columbia on July 10, they found a powerful force of Union troops, many newly arrived reinforcements, which easily repulsed the invaders. By July 14, the advance was over. Early returned across the

Potomac to Virginia, and another Confederate advance had been blunted.

The park was one of the many New Deal–era additions of historic places to the park system. Most of the other Civil War battlefields of significance had been transferred to the Park Service by a 1933 executive order that reorganized the federal government. With the help of a cadre of historians hired through New Deal programs, the Park Service sought to add additional historic sites. Its significance to the war made Monocacy an easy choice, and the area was added in 1934.

The park can be reached from the north, east, or west on I-70. Take exit 54, Market Street, then turn south on Maryland Route 355. The Gambrill Mill Visitor Center is located one-tenth of a mile south of the Monocacy River bridge. From the south, use I-270 and take exit 26 Urbana. Turn left onto Route 80 and proceed two-tenths of a mile to the stop sign. Turn left onto Route 355 North. The Gambrill Mill Visitor Center is located 3.7 miles north on Route 355.

Gambrill Mill Visitor Center is open daily April 1 through October 31 from 8 A.M. to 4:30 P.M. and until 5:30 P.M. on weekends, Memorial Day through Labor Day. During the winter season, November 1 through March 31, it is open Wednesday through Sunday, from 8 A.M. to 4:30 P.M. The visitor center offers an electric map-orientation program, interactive-computer program, artifacts, and interpretive displays of the battle. There is currently no admission fee.

For more information, write Monocacy National Battlefield, 4801 Urbana Pike, Frederick, MD 21704-7307, or telephone (301) 662-3515. The park's Web site is www.nps.gov/mono.

FURTHER READING

Cooling, B. Franklin. *Monocacy: The Battle That Saved Washington.* Shippensburg, PA: White Mane, 2000.

Early, Jubal A. *A Memoir of the Last Year of the War for Independence in the Confederate States of America.* Columbia: University of South Carolina Press, 2001.

Gallagher, Gary W. *Jubal A. Early, the Lost Cause, and Civil War History: A Persistent Legacy.* Milwaukee, WI: Marquette University Press, 1995.

Worthington, Glenn H. *Fighting for Time.* Shippensburg, PA: White Mane, 1994.

MONTEZUMA CASTLE NATIONAL MONUMENT

Location: Camp Verde, Arizona
Acreage: 858
Established: December 8, 1906

Located in northern Arizona, Montezuma Castle National Monument is one of the finest existing examples of ancient pueblo dwellings. The pueblo is located high above the Verde Valley, under the cliffs of the Mogollon Rim in central Arizona. Its odd name does not reflect its history, since the great Aztec leader Montezuma never ventured as far north as Arizona and the ruins are clearly not a castle, in the conventional sense. Instead, the label came from the first generation of Anglo-Americans who visited the region. They had little frame of reference for the pre-Columbian world and gave the site a name they associated with New World antiquity and greatness.

Montezuma Castle National Monument protects and preserves this 5-story, 20-room dwelling built by the Sinagua Indians during the fourteenth century. The Sinagua lived in apartment-style housing, depending on the flood plain of Verde Valley to provide for the agricultural needs of the people. Like other ancient peoples of this region, the Sinagua abandoned their pueblos and migrated elsewhere, though the reasons for this move are unclear.

Montezuma Castle has been an object of interest for Anglo-Americans for more than one hundred years, and the 858-acre site was established as a national monument in 1906. Its early designation as a protected site reflected the obsession of turn-of-the-twentieth-century America with the archeological past as well as the fear that southwestern archeological sites were being vandalized. Included in the monument is a detached unit called Montezuma Well, located 11 miles from the main park off of I-17. Montezuma Well was formed by the collapse of a huge underground cavern. The large hole in the limestone is filled with water—more than 12 million gallons per day flow continuously from underground springs, creating an oasis in the desert. This amazing formation has created a unique environment that contains plant and animal life found nowhere else in the world. Ancient Hohokam and Sinaguan peoples utilized the water flowing in Montezuma Well to irrigate their fields. The well was the life-giving force that enabled them to grow corn, beans, squash, and cotton.

The park's visitor center is open year-round from 8 A.M. until 5 P.M. (extended hours during the summer) and it features numerous exhibits depicting the lifestyle of the Sinaguan Indians. Entrance fees are $2 per person and are valid for seven days. Visitors can walk to the well and view the cliff dwellings on a one-third-mile loop trail. Wayside exhibits along the self-guiding trail describe the cultural and natural history of the site. A diorama/audio program depicts the interior view of the cliff dwellings. Park rangers are available on the trail, and programs are presented when staffing permits.

There are no food, lodging, or camping facilities at the national monument, but all traveler services are available in the Camp Verde area.

For more information, write Montezuma Castle National Monument, 2800 Montezuma Castle Road, Camp Verde, AZ 86322, or telephone (928) 567-3322. The park's Web site is www.nps.gov/moca.

FURTHER READING
Bowman, Jon. *Montezuma: The Castle in the West.* Santa Fe: New Mexico Magazine, 2002.
Protas, Josh. *A Past Preserved in Stone: A History of Montezuma Castle National Monument.* Tucson, AZ: Western National Parks Association, 2002. Available at www.nps.gov/moca/protas/index.htm.

MOORES CREEK NATIONAL BATTLEFIELD
Location: Currie, North Carolina
Acreage: 88
Established: June 2, 1926

In the American South, the Revolutionary War was more complicated than in the North. Tied to the crown by their self-image as part of the English gentry, southern colonists struggled with the call for separation. In the mid-1770s, North Carolina, especially, was fiercely divided. Even as the cry of "taxation without representation" resonated, many colonists cringed at the thought of fighting the mother country.

By 1775, North Carolina had split into two groups: Patriots, about half the population, who sought independence; and Loyalists, primarily the Crown's officials, wealthy merchants, planters, and other conservatives, who did not see war as the solution to their problems with English rule. The battles of Lexington and Concord had weakened the crown's sway, however, when North Carolinians learned of them in May of 1775. Clearly, though, the British had no intention of vacating their colonies, and, in January 1776, North Carolina's exiled royal governor Josiah Martin, called upon his followers to stop what he labeled "a most daring, horrid, and unnatural Rebellion."

Martin's Loyalists planned to move along the southwest side of the Cape Fear River to the coast—crossing Moores Creek on an existing bridge—to meet up with British troops arriving by sea and initiate a reconquest of the colony. The Patriots were ready. Colonel Alexander Lillington had beaten the Loyalists to the Moores Creek bridge, arriving on February 25, and he had quickly recognized the position's defensive advantages. The dark,

Moores Creek National Battlefield commemorates the decisive February 27, 1776, victory by 1,000 Patriots over 1,600 Loyalists at the Battle of Moores Creek Bridge. *(National Park Service)*

sluggish, stream was about 35 feet wide, and it twisted and turned through swampy terrain. The bridge provided the only crossing.

Lillington built a low earthwork on a slight rise above the bridge, covering its approach from the east. Joining Lillington the next day, Colonel Richard Caswell and his men crossed the bridge and built an additional set of earthworks on the other side. By the evening of February 26, the Patriots had secured both sides of the bridge. Lillington and 150 men waited on the east side, and Caswell and his 850 men controlled the west. MacDonald's 1,600 Loyalists, with weapons for less than half their number, were only 6 miles away.

The Loyalist attack began in the middle of the night. At about 1 A.M. on February 27, seventy-five, hand-picked broadswordsmen under Captain John Campbell left their en-

campment. The route passed through thickets and swampland, and the going was difficult. During the night, Caswell had retreated across the creek. His men took the planks from the bridge, greased the posts and girders, and positioned artillery to cover the crossing. The Patriots waited in silence and darkness for the Loyalists.

As the sun rose, the Loyalists charged, swords waving high, but when they reached a distance of 30 paces from the earthworks, musket and artillery fire cut the advancing troops to shreds. The battle was over in minutes, and the Loyalists were thoroughly routed. In the end, thirty Loyalists died and forty more were wounded. Only one Patriot was killed.

Though the battle itself was small, its implications were significant. The victory revealed a vibrant Patriot force in the South, showed unexpected Patriot strength in the countryside, gave support to the idea of the Revolution, slowed Loyalists in the Carolinas, and ignited more Revolutionary fervor in the rest of the colonies. "Had the South been conquered in the first half of 1776," the historian Edward Channing concluded, "it is entirely conceivable that rebellion would never have turned into revolution. . . . At Moore's Creek and Sullivan's Island the Carolinas turned aside the one combination of circumstances that might have made British conquest possible."

Established in June 1926, the 88-acre Moores Creek National Battlefield commemorates the decisive Revolutionary engagement fought here. The park's visitor center is open year-round from 9 A.M. until 5 P.M. daily, and it offers exhibits depicting the time period as well as a twelve-minute video. In addition to park ranger talks, demonstrations, and guided walks, the park also holds an annual observance and commemoration of the battle on the last full weekend of February. The ceremony features a living-history encampment, tactical demonstrations, folk singing, and a formal commemoration program including a speaker, military band, and wreath-laying ceremony. Hikers can enjoy 2 self-guided trails at the battlefield: the 1-mile History Trail and the one-third-mile Tar Heel Trail. The History Trail explains the battle and includes the site where the Patriots and Loyalists clashed on February 27, 1776. The Tar Heel Trail explains the naval stores industry, which was the predominant industry of the area during the colonial period.

There are no food, lodging, or camping facilities at the battlefield, but all traveler services are available in the Wilmington area.

For more information, write Moores Creek National Battlefield, 40 Patriots Hall Drive, Currie, NC 28435, or telephone (910) 283-5591. The park's Web site is www.nps.gov/mocr.

FURTHER READING
Capps, Michael A., and Steven A. Davis. *Moores Creek National Battlefield: An Administrative History.* Washington, DC: National Park Service, 1999. Available at www.cr.nps.gov/history/online_books/mocr/index.htm.
Channing, Edward. *A History of the United States.* New York: Octagon Books, 1977.
Hatch, Charles E. *Moores Creek National Military Park, North Carolina: The Battle of Moores Creek Bridge.* Washington, DC: Office of History and Historic Architecture, Eastern Service Center, 1969.

MORRISTOWN NATIONAL HISTORICAL PARK

Location: Morristown, New Jersey
Acreage: 1,711
Established: March 2, 1933

During the American Revolution, the bitterly cold winters of 1777 and 1779–1780 proved crucial tests for both the Continental Army and its leader, General George Washington. In January 1777, following successive victories at Trenton and Princeton, New Jersey, the Continental Army bivouacked near Morristown. General Washington chose this area for its logistical, geographical, and topographical military advantages, and he set about rebuilding his forces in the dead of winter. Coping with harsh conditions, frequent shortages of food and clothing, and illness, the men struggled to survive. That spring, to maintain morale, Washington ordered the soldiers to build a fortification, which focused their energies and buoyed their spirits; because of the effort's nonmilitary purpose, the hill became known as Fort Nonsense. Washington returned to the site during the winter of 1779–1780 because of its proximity to New York City, which was now occupied by the British. There, he and his men would endure the worst winter of the eighteenth century. Although the soldiers had built log huts, they could not escape the driving ice and snowstorms that raked the region. Desperate for supplies, Washington appealed to the Continental Congress, but it refused to send aid. Finally, the state of New Jersey responded, and, as Washington wrote, "saved the army from dissolution or starving." Through sheer will and the inspired leadership of Washington, the Continental Army prevailed, and by 1783, the new nation achieved its independence.

First authorized in March 1933, the 1,711-acre Morristown National Historical Park preserves the encampment site of the Continental Army during the critical winters of 1777 and 1779–1780, as well as the historic Jacob Ford Mansion (General Washington's military headquarters during the winter of 1779–1780), Jockey Hollow, and Fort Nonsense. Entrance fees are $4 per person and are valid for seven days; a $15 annual pass is also available. The Jockey Hollow Visitor Center, open year-round from 9 A.M. until 5 P.M., features 5 reproduction field soldier huts in Jockey Hollow, where the men encamped, as well as living-history demonstrations and programs. Washington's headquarters and museum is open for self-guided tours from 9 A.M. until 5 P.M.; park rangers also offer hourly guided tours of the historic Ford Mansion and the eighteenth-century Wick House and Farm used by one of George Washington's officers, General Arthur St. Clair. In addition to park exhibits and tours, there are over 27 miles of foot and horse trails, which cross through the New York Brigade and New Jersey Brigade areas, located in the Jockey Hollow Unit of the park. Color-coded trail maps are available in the Jockey Hollow Visitor Center. The Jockey Hollow Unit of the park also features an automobile tour (a 2-mile loop road).

The Ford Mansion in Morristown, New Jersey, was General Washington's military headquarters during the winter of 1779–1780. *(National Park Service)*

There are no food, lodging, or camping facilities located in the historical park, but all traveler services are available nearby in Florham Park, Madison, and Morristown.

For more information, write Morristown National Historical Park, 30 Washington Place, Morristown, NJ 07960-4299, or telephone (973) 539-2085. The park's Web site is www.nps.gov/morr.

FURTHER READING

Morristown: A History and Guide, Morristown National Historical Park, New Jersey. Washington, DC: National Park Service, 1983.

Rae, John W. *Morristown, New Jersey.* Charleston, SC: Arcadia, 2002.

Weig, Melvin J. *Morristown National Historical Park: A Military Capital of the American Revolution.* Washington, DC: National Park Service, 1950.

MOUNT RAINIER NATIONAL PARK
Location: Ashford, Washington
Acreage: 235,625
Established: March 2, 1899

Mount Rainier National Park is among the first generation of national park areas. Established in 1899, it was part of the group that scholars call the "mountaintop parks." Initially, the park preserved Mount Rainier and its immediate environs. Despite being the first park created after the founding of the forest reserve system—later the national forests—Mount Rainier articulated the initial version of the idea of national parks: that they preserved spectacular scenery and not necessarily what later became ecology. At the same time, the park expressed the growing sentiment that protecting American nature was a national goal that reinforced the power, prowess, and morality of the American republic.

Its early proclamation reflected an important way for the national parks to be different than the forest reserves—later renamed national forests. Unlike Yellowstone and the three California parks that preceded it, Mount Rainier differentiated the national parks from the utilitarian movement at the

A group of men and women climbing Paradise Glacier in Mount Rainier National Park in the early twentieth century. *(Library of Congress)*

heart of Progressive conservation. The mountaintops of Mount Rainier simultaneously represented a compromise—the lands reserved in 1899 were not of practical commercial economic use at the time—and an articulation that national parks were different from other reserved lands by virtue of their scenery and the strict manner of their reservation. This melding of different ideas has haunted park managers ever since.

Mount Rainier was first reserved as part of the Pacific Forest Reserve, as were many of the early national parks. This designation in 1893 inaugurated a six-year struggle to create more comprehensive protection. A typical nineteenth-century process ensued. Local businesses and the railroads advocated the national park as a boon to economic development. This objective melded nicely with the goals of the rising northwestern preservation community. The combination proved unstoppable, and, on March 2, 1899, President William McKinley established Mount Rainier as America's fifth national park.

Proximity to Seattle, Tacoma, and the Pacific Coast played an enormous role in the development of Mount Rainier National Park. The largest and most visible constituency was day-use visitors from nearby cities. This city park function put Mount Rainier in an unusual position. A spectacular natural setting also struggled with automobiles, auto stages, early interpretive nature-guide programs, and winter use such as skiing. Urban character meant other differences. Mount Rainier was the first park to be patrolled exclusively by rangers, rather than troops from the U.S. Cavalry. In 1907, the park hired its first ranger, the first person given the title of "park ranger" in any national park. The Longmire Museum, developed in the 1920s, was one of the first museums in the national park system. The park was also on the forefront of wilderness protection decades before the passage of the 1964 Wilderness Act. In 1928, much of the northern and eastern sections of Mount Rainier National Park were set aside as "roadless areas" to remain free of roads and commercial development. In 1988, 97 percent of the park's 235,625 acres were designated as wilderness.

Mount Rainier National Park is open all year, but access is limited in winter. Entrance fees are $5 per person or $10 per vehicle, and are valid for seven days; a $20 annual pass is also available. Additional fees are charged for camping and climbing. Visitors can expect to pay a $15-per-person, per-climb fee; a $25 annual climbing pass is also available. Mount Rainier National Park maintains 3 visitor centers. The Jackson Visitor Center at Paradise is open year-round, though hours vary according to season. The center offers several audiovisual programs, including the twenty-five-minute *Rainier: The Mountain* movie, as well as exhibits on the park's natural and cultural history. Park rangers give walks and

talks on a variety of natural and cultural resource topics, as well as evening programs at the Paradise Inn in the summer. Snowshoe walks are also available from December 26 through mid-April. In addition, the Paradise Ranger Station is open from early May through September, although hours vary, and issues climbing permits for routes from Paradise.

The Ohanapecosh Visitor Center, in the southeast corner of the park, is open during the summer only, from 9 A.M. until 5 P.M. It features exhibits on old-growth forest ecology and human history. Guided walks and talks on a variety of natural and cultural resource topics are offered during the summer months, and evening programs are available at the Ohanapecosh Campground amphitheater in summer. The Sunrise Visitor Center, in the northeast part of the park, is also open only during the summer. It features exhibits on the park's natural resources as well as ranger-led walks and talks on natural and cultural resource topics and evening programs at the White River Campground. In addition, the Longmire and White River Wilderness Information Centers, open only during the summer months, issue backpacking and climbing permits.

Visitors may also wish to tour the Longmire Museum, in the Longmire Historic District in the park's southwest corner, which is open all year from 9 A.M. until 4 P.M. One of the oldest museums in the National Park Service (established in 1928), the Longmire Museum features exhibits on the natural and cultural history of Mount Rainier National Park, as well as a transportation exhibit in the historic Longmire Gas Station nearby.

Weather patterns at Mount Rainier are strongly influenced by the Pacific Ocean, elevation, and latitude. The climate is generally cool and rainy, with summer highs in the 60s and 70s. While July and August are the sunniest months, rain is possible any day, and very likely in winter, spring, and fall. As one of the snowiest places on earth, Paradise is worthy of a winter visit. From November to late May, expect to find 10 to 20 feet of snow on the ground. Approximately 630 inches of snow falls in an average winter at Paradise; in the winter of 1971–1972, Paradise established a world record with 1,122 inches. Whether hiking on its flanks, climbing its summit, snowshoeing or cross-country skiing on its slopes, camping along its glacier-fed rivers, photographing wildflower displays in subalpine meadows, or just admiring the view, nearly 2 million people come to enjoy the grandeur and beauty of Mount Rainier each year.

Mount Rainier National Park offers excellent opportunities for scenic drives, hiking, and mountain climbing. Most roads are open from late May to early October, and all provide stunning views and access to a variety of hiking trails and other sites, although parking is limited on sunny summer weekends and holidays. Visitors can explore the Longmire Historic District, and along the road from Longmire and Paradise, see Christine Falls or Narada Falls. Between Paradise and Ohanapecosh are the Reflection Lakes, Box Canyon, or the old-growth Grove of the Patriarchs forest. Sunrise is a popular destination from July to October and provides outstanding views of Mount Rainier and its glaciers, and trails through subalpine meadows.

Lodging is available in the park at the National Park Inn (360-569-2275), in the Longmire Historic District. The inn is open year-round and has 25 guest rooms, a full-service restaurant, a gift shop, and a post office. Visitors can also stay at the historic Paradise Inn, built in 1917. Open from mid-May through September, the Paradise Inn (360-569-2275) offers 117 guest rooms, a full-service restaurant, snack bar, lounge, gift shop, and post office.

Mount Rainier has 6 campgrounds, 2 of which are open year-round: Ipsut Creek and Sunshine Point. Ipsut Creek, in the northwest corner of the park, has 31 individual and 2 group sites with pit toilets. Sunshine Point, in the park's southwest corner, has 18 individual sites with drinking water and pit toilets. Three other campgrounds—Cougar Rock, Mowich Lake, and Ohanapecosh—are open from late May to mid-October, while the White River Campground is open from mid-June through September. In addition, all traveler services are available in Ashford, Elbe, Eatonville, Enumclaw, Fairfax, and Packwood.

For more information, write Mount Rainier National Park, Tahoma Woods, Star Route, Ashford, WA 98304-9751, or telephone (360) 569-2211. The park's Web site is www.nps.gov/mora.

FURTHER READING
Catton, Theodore. *Wonderland: An Administrative History of Mount Rainier National Park.* Seattle, WA: National Park Service, 1996.
Kirk, Ruth. *Sunrise to Paradise: The Story of Mount Rainier National Park.* Seattle: University of Washington Press, 1999.
Martinson, Arthur D. *Wilderness Above the Sound: The Story of Mount Rainier National Park.* Niwot, CO: Robert Rinehart, 1994.
McNulty, Tim. *Washington's Mount Rainier National Park: A Centennial Celebration.* Seattle, WA: The Mountaineer Books, 1998.
Molenaar, Dee. *The Challenge of Rainier: A Record of the Explorations and Ascents, Triumphs and Tragedies, on the Northwest's Greatest Mountain.* Seattle, WA: Mountaineers, 1979.
Sutter, Paul. *Driven Wild: How the Fight Against Automobiles Launched the Modern Wilderness Movement.* Seattle: University of Washington Press, 2002.

MOUNT RUSHMORE NATIONAL MEMORIAL
Location: Keystone, South Dakota
Acreage: 1,278
Established: March 3, 1925

Mount Rushmore is an American icon. Carved into the granite of South Dakota's

Workmen on the stone sculpture of George Washington's face, Mt. Rushmore, c. 1932. *(Library of Congress)*

Black Hills are the four faces that for many symbolize the nation's greatness: George Washington, Thomas Jefferson, Abraham Lincoln, and Theodore Roosevelt. Between 1927 and 1941, sculptor Gutzon Borglum and 400 workers hammered and chiseled these colossal 60-foot presidential visages to memorialize the birth, growth, preservation, and development of the United States. The triumphal monument originally called for only 3 heads—Washington, Jefferson, and Lincoln—but space allowed for a fourth, and Roosevelt, Progressive reformer and architect of America's "Big Stick" foreign policy, was chosen. The actual carving utilized a sophisticated measuring system known as "pointing," which allowed Borglum to expand his scaled model by twelve times (1 inch on the model to 1 foot on the mountain) to achieve a precise rendering of the figures. Former South

Dakota governor William J. Bulow marveled that "it takes a genius to figure out the proper perspective so that the carvings will look right from the point from which the human eye beholds them. Gutzon Borglum was that genius." In addition to its celebratory function, the memorial also protects many animal and plant species representative of the Black Hills ecosystem of South Dakota.

The 1,278-acre Mount Rushmore National Memorial was authorized in March 1925 to commemorate the first hundred and fifty years of the United States. Although admission is free, there is an $8 parking fee for the memorial, which is valid for the remainder of the calendar year. Visitors first enter the park via the Avenue of Flags, an outdoor display of the fifty-six state, territory, commonwealth, and district flags of the United States of America. The Lincoln Borglum Museum, located 700 feet from the parking structure via the Avenue of Flags, features interactive displays about the artist Gutzon Borglum and the workers involved in creating the sculpture; historical film footage of the carving; the original models and tools used in the making of Mount Rushmore, and a short orientation film called *The Shrine*. Other exhibits highlight the selection of the presidents, memorial dedication ceremonies, preservation of the sculpture, and Mount Rushmore in popular culture. Park rangers also offer a thirty-minute Presidential Walk that takes visitors to the base of the sculpture, and, each evening, a thirty-minute ranger presentation concludes with the illumination of the monument.

The Mount Rushmore Information Center, located at the entrance to the memorial, is open from 8 A.M. until 10 P.M. during the summer, and is closed from January through mid-April. The center features historic photos of each presidential sculpture on Mount Rushmore taken during construction. Visitors may also wish to tour the Sculptor's Studio, which is open from 9 A.M. until 6 P.M. during

Mount Rushmore National Memorial. *(National Park Service)*

the summer, and is closed for the winter. The studio is a historic structure built in 1939 as the second on-site studio for sculptor Gutzon Borglum, and it contains the Sculptor's Model, Borglum's original one-twelfth-scale model used to create the memorial; the Hall of Records Model depicting the concept of the unfinished Hall of Records; and original tools and plaster masks used by workers. Park rangers also offer a fifteen-minute presentation on the mountain carving process.

There are no lodging or camping facilities at the memorial, but all traveler services are available locally. Public campgrounds are located in the Black Hills National Forest and at Custer State Park, and private facilities are available in Custer, Hill City, Keystone, and Rapid City. Meals are available in the park only during the summer months, but food and supplies are always obtainable in nearby communities.

For more information, write Mount Rushmore National Memorial, P.O. Box 268, Keystone, SD 57751-0268, or telephone (605) 574-2523. The park's Web site is www.nps.gov/moru.

FURTHER READING

Larner, Jesse. *Mount Rushmore: An Icon Reconsidered.* New York: Thunder's Mouth/Nation Books, 2002.

Taliaferro, John. *Great White Fathers: The Story of the Obsessive Quest to Create Mount Rushmore.* New York: Public Affairs, 2002.

N

NATCHEZ NATIONAL HISTORICAL PARK

Location: Natchez, Mississippi
Acreage: 105
Established: October 7, 1988

Natchez National Historical Park preserves and interprets the rich cultural history of Natchez, Mississippi, and illustrates the crucial role the city played in the settlement of the old Southwest, the Cotton Kingdom, and the antebellum South. During the sixteenth century, this area flourished as the regional trading center for at least thirty Natchez villages. As European colonization spread throughout the New World, however, the French claimed the territory, and in 1716, they erected Fort Rosalie on the site to protect their domain. In 1798, after changing hands frequently during the eighteenth century, the Natchez area was incorporated into the Territory of Mississippi, and the community of Natchez was designated the territorial capital. Whites soon streamed into the region along the Natchez Trace—a centuries-old trail connecting the Natchez area to what is now Nashville, Tennessee—and introduced plantation agriculture and black slave labor. By the early nineteenth century, Natchez was flourishing, and wealthy plantation owners and merchants built huge Greek revival mansions with lavish gardens to publicly exhibit their fortune. These grand old homes with lush, tree-shaded grounds were spared during the Civil War and survive today as a historic remnant of the commercial, cultural, and social center of the South's "cotton belt."

Authorized in October 1988, the 105-acre Natchez National Historical Park preserves some of the significant antebellum properties in the United States. There are 3 units within the park itself: Fort Rosalie, the location of an eighteenth-century fortification built by the French and later occupied by the British, Spanish, and Americans; the William Johnson House, owned by William Johnson, a free African American businessman, whose diary tells the story of everyday life in antebellum Natchez; and Melrose, the estate of John T. McMurran, a northerner who rose from being a middle-class lawyer to a position of wealth and power in antebellum Natchez. The park's visitor reception center is open Monday through Saturday from 8 A.M. until 5 P.M., and Sunday from 9 A.M. to 4 P.M.; hours may be extended in the summer. Admission to the outbuildings, including slave quarters, and grounds is free. Park rangers offer guided tours of the Melrose estate—the only way to see the mansion—and fees are $6 per person. The park also hosts spring and fall pilgrimages (in March and October), the Natchez Literary Celebration during the first week of June, and various Christmas programs.

There are no food, lodging, or camping facilities in the historical park, but all traveler services are available in Natchez.

For more information, write Natchez National Historical Park, 640 South Canal Street, Box E, Natchez, MS 39120, or telephone (601) 446-5790. The park's Web site is www.nps.gov/natc.

FURTHER READING

Brooke, Steven. *The Majesty of Natchez.* Gretna, LA: Pelican, 1999.
Davis, Ronald L.F. *The Black Experience in Natchez, 1720–1880: Natchez, National Historical Park, Missis-*

sippi. Denver, CO: National Park Service, Denver Service Center, 1993.

Delehanty, Randolph. *Classic Natchez.* Athens: University of Georgia Press, 1996.

Gleason, David K. *The Great Houses of Natchez.* Jackson: University Press of Mississippi, 1986.

NATIONAL CAPITAL PARKS

Location: Washington, D.C.
Acreage: 6,629
Established: August 10, 1933

The National Capital Parks are a unique component of the national park system. Their origins lie in the founding of the nation's capital in July 1790, when Congress authorized not only the creation of Washington, D.C., but also the purchase or acceptance of "such quantity of land as the President shall deem proper for the use of the United States." The result was the acquisition of the original lands required to complete Pierre L'Enfant's ambitious street system and capital layout. Today, more than 300 park units derive from this pioneering vision and they celebrate the natural, cultural, and historical heritage of the United States. Their diversity is nothing short of stunning; from archeological sites to meadows and forest lands, tidal and nontidal wetlands, greenbelts, historic sites and monuments, military fortifications and cemeteries, statuary, parks and parkways, and public recreation areas, this impressive array of parks is all located within the confines of the metropolitan Washington, D.C., area.

One of the sites symbolizing the purpose of the National Capital Parks is Piscataway Park. Two hundred years ago, George Washington praised Mount Vernon by saying, "No estate in the United America is more pleasantly situated than this." In 1961, Piscataway Park was authorized to preserve Washington's tranquil view of the Maryland fields and hillsides across the Potomac River, as a pilot project in the use of easements to protect

The Lincoln Memorial is part of the National Capital Parks in Washington, D.C. *(Library of Congress)*

parklands from obtrusive urban expansion. Stretching for 6 miles, from Piscataway Creek to Marshall Hall on the Potomac River, the 4,625-acre Piscataway Park ensures that visitors today can appreciate the natural environment just as Washington did. A place of great natural beauty, it is home to bald eagles, beavers, deer, fox, osprey, and many other species. To complement the surroundings, the park has—in addition to a public fishing pier and 2 boardwalks over freshwater tidal wetlands—a variety of nature trails, meadows, and woodland areas, each with unique features.

Piscataway Park is also an active ecosystem farm, an educational demonstration area with three closely related goals: production of a sustainable harvest of high-quality vegetables that are grown in an ecologically sound manner; conduct of research to adapt sustainable practices for the unique ecosystem; and provision of educational opportunities for students, farmers, scholars, gardeners, and consumers. A trip to the ecosystem farm will introduce the visitor to an array of techniques applied to gain maximum productivity from the natural limits of the soils. The farm utilizes 2 solar panels—1 that powers an irrigation system, and another that provides power to an electric fence that keeps deer out of the fields. Throughout the entire year, the fields are covered with crops. In spring, summer, and fall, there are a number of interesting and unusual varieties of flowers, vegetables, and herbs growing there. In the winter, garlic, lettuce, spinach, and carrots grow. The farm also plants "cover crops," which are nonfood crops intended to prevent erosion, bolster soil tilth, and provide a habitat for beneficial insects. Cover crops are allowed to decompose and provide nutrients for the next crop.

The other parks administered under the National Capital Parks umbrella include the National Mall (and its memorials), East and West Potomac Parks, George Mason Memorial, National Law Enforcement Officers Memorial, National World War II Memorial, Old Post Office Tower, Anacostia Park, Baltimore-Washington Parkway, Capitol Hill Parks, Frederick Douglass National Historical Site, Greenbelt Park, Harmony Hall, Kenilworth Park and Aquatic Gardens, Mary McLeod Bethune Council House National Historic Site, Oxon Cove Park and Oxon Hill Farm, Sewall-Belmont House National Historic Site, Suitland Parkway, and Forts Dupont, Foote, and Washington. As with most sites in Washington, D.C., public transportation offers the best access to the National Capital Parks. Parking is available on city streets during non-rush-hour times (9 A.M. until 4 P.M.) during the week, but spaces are extremely scarce. There are parking lots located at the Washington Monument and Jefferson Memorial that provide two-hour parking, and

parking is available for longer periods along Ohio Drive near the Lincoln and Jefferson memorials. There are several metro train routes from the suburban areas surrounding the city, and the Smithsonian Metro stop comes out on the National Mall. Perhaps the best way to see the various memorials on the National Mall—and not have to hassle with traffic and parking—is by Tourmobile Sightseeing. Tourmobile offers narrated shuttle tours daily to 18 major sites on the National Mall and Arlington National Cemetery. One ticket allows unlimited boarding and reboarding throughout the day. There are no food, lodging, or camping facilities at the parks, but the Washington, D.C., metro area has all traveler services.

For more information, write National Capital Parks, 900 Ohio Drive, Washington, DC, 20024-2000, or telephone (202) 485-9880. The park's Web site can be found at www.nps.gov/nacc or www.nps.gov/nace.

FURTHER READING

Brown, Lenard E. *National Capital Parks: Fort Stanton, Fort Foote, and Battery Ricketts.* Washington, DC: Office of History and Historic Architecture, Eastern Service Center, 1970.

King, Marina. *Piscataway Village Rural Conservation Study: Final Report.* Upper Marlboro: Maryland-National Capital Park and Planning Commission, 1991.

Toogood, Anna Coxe. *Piscataway Park, Maryland: General Historic Background Study.* Washington, DC: U.S. Office of Archeology and Historic Preservation, 1969.

NATIONAL MALL

Location: Washington, D.C.
Acreage: 146
Established: July 16, 1790

This landscaped park extending from the Capitol to the Washington Monument defines the principle axis of Pierre L'Enfant's plan for the city of Washington, D.C. In many ways, the National Mall is also the visible soul of the United States. For here, enshrouded in

2,000 American elms and 3,000 internationally renowned Japanese cherry trees, are the shrines and memorials of the longest-lived republic in the history of the world. Amid the lush gardens and ornamental pools lie the national treasures of the Washington Monument, the Jefferson Memorial, the Lincoln Memorial, the Franklin Delano Roosevelt Memorial, the Korean War Veterans Memorial, and the Vietnam Veterans Memorial. Visitors from across the country and around the globe converge on the National Mall each year to appreciate the architectural achievements of the memorials themselves and to reflect upon their deeper meaning for both the past and the present.

While there were many "founding fathers," only one, George Washington, earned the title "Father of His Country." Indeed, many historians have argued that without Washington, there might not be a United States. His innovative and dedicated leadership of the ragtag Continental Army wrested American independence from Great Britain, and his steady guidance during the delicate deliberations that created the Constitution insured the creation of a form a government destined to endure for more than two centuries. He was unanimously elected as the first president of the United States, and his two terms in office set the precedents against which all future presidents would measure their tenure. In many ways, Washington made America what it is, and the 555-foot Washington Monument obelisk pays fitting tribute to this icon of history. The Washing-

View of the National Mall, looking west from the Grant Memorial with the Cavalry Group sculpture in the foreground. *(Library of Congress)*

ton Monument is also an excellent place to begin a tour of the National Mall, since visitors can take an elevator to the top for a commanding view of the mall and the nation's Capitol.

The third president of the United States, Thomas Jefferson, appraised his own achievements and captured the essence of his legacy, when he composed his epitaph: "Author of the Declaration of American Independence, of the Statute of Virginia for religious freedom, and Father of the University of Virginia." Jefferson's legacy, as a statesman, architect, musician, scientist, horticulturist, diplomat, inventor, and president of the United States, certainly earned him a place alongside the "founding fathers" of the United States. His political beliefs in the rights of man and a government derived from the people resulted in the founding of a two-party system; his vision of an agrarian nation led to the acquisition of the Louisiana Purchase and the notable Lewis and Clark Expedition; and his eloquent style and manner of expression captured the republican sentiments of a nation. Perhaps President John F. Kennedy put it best when he told a gathering of American Nobel Prize winners that they were the greatest assemblage of talent in the White House since Jefferson had dined there alone. Built to honor the nation's third president, the circular, colonnaded Jefferson Memorial is a classic style introduced in this country by Jefferson himself. The interior walls present inscriptions from his writings, and the heroic statue was sculpted by Rudolph Evans.

"This nation, under God, shall have a new birth of freedom; and that government of the people, by the people, for the people, shall not perish from the earth." With these words, President Abraham Lincoln consecrated the battlefield at Gettysburg in November 1863. Although he predicted that "the world will little note nor long remember what we say

here," the words and the man abide. The Lincoln Memorial is a tribute to the nation's sixteenth president, who, before an assassin's bullet tragically ended his life, signed the Emancipation Proclamation, successfully led a bitterly divided nation through a bloody Civil War (1861–1865), and signed the 13th Amendment, which outlawed slavery. "Fourscore and seven years ago," the Great Emancipator had reminded the nation, "our fathers brought forth on this continent, a new nation, conceived in Liberty, and dedicated to the proposition that all men are created equal." Because of Lincoln, the sacred bond of Union remained unbroken. The Lincoln Memorial was designed to resemble a Greek temple-like structure similar to the Parthenon, with a marble staircase leading up to its entrance, and 36 Doric columns—for the 36 states at the time of Lincoln's death—surrounding the outside. The interior of the memorial contains 3 chambers, with the central chamber containing the centerpiece of the monument, the heroic Lincoln statue, sculpted by Daniel Chester French. In the 2 flanking chambers, Lincoln's most famous speeches—the Gettysburg Address and the Second Inaugural Address—are carved on the walls.

In the history of the United States, only one man has served more than two terms in the White House, and during his twelve-year tenure, Franklin Delano Roosevelt fundamentally shaped the nation's government into its current modern form. Roosevelt's remarkable four-term legacy included guiding the nation through the dangerous shoals of the Great Depression and World War II. In 1932, he promised the nation a "New Deal" to combat the flagging economy and reminded them that "The only thing we have to fear is fear itself." After the bombing of Pearl Harbor, on December 7, 1941, Roosevelt ruminated that this would be a day that would "live in infamy" and led his country into World War II. The memorial honoring the nation's thirty-second president is a significant departure from the traditional marble-and-stature presidential monuments of Lincoln and Jefferson. Constructed of red South Dakota granite, the Franklin Delano Roosevelt Memorial is situated on 7.5 acres near the Tidal Basin in Washington, D.C.'s West Potomac Park. This walk-through, outdoor memorial unfolds like a timeline, inviting visitors to meander through and contemplate this artistic rendition of American history between 1933 and 1945. It is divided into 4 galleries—1 for each term in office—with each gallery containing bronze sculptures, inscriptions of Roosevelt's words, waterfalls and pools, and ornamental landscaping.

In addition to commemorating influential presidents, the memorials of the National Mall also pay tribute to the veterans of the Korean and Vietnam conflicts. In the aftermath of World War II, the United States and the Soviet Union engaged in a diplomatic and ideological battle known as the Cold War. As the world seemingly divided into two hostile camps, the United States embraced a foreign policy known as "containment," which endeavored to halt the spread of—thus contain—communism throughout the globe. After the perceived "loss" of China to a Communist revolution in 1949, the United States redoubled its commitment, and the stage was set for a conflict in Korea. To simplify the peace agreements at the end of World War II, Korea had been temporarily divided along the 38th Parallel—but the line became more rigid as the Cold War heated up. And when the Communist-controlled North invaded the U.S.-backed South in June 1950, President Harry S Truman did not hesitate: "If we are tough enough now . . . they won't take any next steps." Thus began a three-year engagement that, in the end, resulted in the permanent division of Korea at roughly the 38th Parallel, and the loss of 54,246 American

lives. The many parts of the Korean War Veterans Memorial form an integrated work that should be viewed as a whole. The most notable feature of the monument is the group of 19 soldiers, representing different races and branches of the military, heading uphill on patrol. Each of the men peers into the distance, trying desperately to see what cannot be seen. Along the north side of the memorial is a low stone wall, engraved with the 22 countries that comprised the UN forces in Korea. Along the south side of the memorial is the Wall of Faces. The highly polished surface of the Wall of Faces reflects all 19 soldiers, producing a total of 38 figures—representing the 38th Parallel, while the images etched on the wall itself were taken from actual photographs of soldiers, sailors, marines, airmen, and support personnel who participated in the conflict. The memorial's Pool of Remembrance invites visitors to remember those who gave their lives.

The Vietnam War also had roots in the United States' commitment to containment. When the French colonizers were thrown out of Vietnam in 1954, the region became a hotly contested battleground in the escalating Cold War. President John F. Kennedy had called Vietnam "the cornerstone of the Free World in Southeast Asia, the keystone in the arch, the finger in the dike," and in an effort to prevent the South from falling under the control of Communist Ho Chi Minh, Kennedy began sending military advisers to support South Vietnam and Ngo Dinh Diem. Following Kennedy's assassination, President Lyndon Johnson appealed to and received from Congress the Tonkin Gulf resolution, which empowered him "to take all necessary measures" to defend American forces and to protect Southeast Asia "against aggression or subversion." The result was U.S. entry into the longest and most controversial war in the nation's history, and its only loss. In February

1965, the Vietnam conflict became an American one, with the commission of ground troops. Ten years and 58,226 American lives lost later, Vietnam was reunited under a Communist government, and Saigon became Ho Chi Minh City. The Vietnam Veterans Memorial recognizes and honors the men and women who served in one of America's most divisive wars. The memorial grew out of a need to heal the nation's wounds as the United States struggled to reconcile different moral and political points of view. Today, the Vietnam Veterans Memorial serves as a meeting place where everyone, regardless of opinion, can come together and remember and honor those who served. The Memorial has 3 main elements. The Wall, the first part of the memorial to be erected, was dedicated on November 13, 1982, and is inscribed with all 58,226 names. The Wall was the inspired design of then-twenty-one-year-old Maya Ying Lin, a Chinese American, who remembered, "I thought about what death is, what a loss is. A sharp pain that lessens with time, but can never quite heal over. The idea occurred to me there on the site. I had an impulse to cut open the earth. The grass would grow back, but the cut would remain." But some initial reaction to the Wall included opinions that it did not appropriately honor the veterans of Vietnam. As a result of this debate a compromise was reached, and, in the fall of 1984, the Three Servicemen Statue, by Fredrick Hart, was placed near the Wall. The Vietnam Women's Memorial, dedicated on Veterans Day in 1993, completed the ensemble.

The memorials and monuments on the National Mall are open daily from 8 A.M. until 11:45 P.M., and admission is free. Park rangers present ten- and thirty-minute talks at each of the sites, and, during the summer months, provide two-hour walking tours that explore the history of the National Mall and other related themes. Parking is available on city streets during non-rush-hour times (9 A.M. until 4 P.M.) during the week, but spaces are extremely scarce. There are parking lots located at the Washington Monument and Jefferson Memorial that provide two-hour parking, and parking is available for longer periods along Ohio Drive near the Lincoln and Jefferson memorials. There are several metro train routes from the suburban areas surrounding the city, and the Smithsonian Metro stop comes out on the National Mall. Perhaps the best way to see the various memorials on the National Mall—and not have to hassle with traffic and parking—is by Tourmobile Sightseeing. Tourmobile offers narrated shuttle tours daily to 18 major sites on the National Mall and Arlington National Cemetery. One ticket allows unlimited boarding and reboarding throughout the day. There are no food, lodging, or camping facilities at the mall, but the Washington, D.C., metro area has all traveler services.

For more information, write National Mall, 900 Ohio Drive SW, Washington, DC 20024-2000, or telephone (202) 485-9880. The park's Web site is www.nps.gov/nama.

FURTHER READING
Allen, Thomas B. *The Washington Monument: It Stands for All.* New York: Discovery Books, 2000.

Cooper, Jason. *Korean War Memorial: Historic Landmarks.* Vero Beach, FL: Rourke Book, 2001.

Edelman, Bernard, ed. *Dear America: Letters Home from Vietnam.* New York: W.W. Norton, 1985.

Halprin, Lawrence. *The Franklin Delano Roosevelt Memorial.* San Francisco: Chronicle Books, 1997.

Jefferson Memorial: Interpretive Guide to Thomas Jefferson Memorial, District of Columbia. Washington, DC: U.S. Government Printing Office, 1998.

Palmer, Laura. *Shrapnel in the Heart: Letters and Remembrance from the Vietnam Veterans Memorial.* New York: Vintage Books, 1988.

Thomas, Christopher A. *The Lincoln Memorial and American Life.* Princeton, NJ: Princeton University Press, 2002.

Sipapu Bridge in White Canyon at Natural Bridges National Monument. *(National Archives)*

NATURAL BRIDGES NATIONAL MONUMENT

Location: Blanding, Utah
Acreage: 7,636
Established: April 16, 1908

Utah is an intriguing land with a stunning landscape, and Natural Bridges National Monument is no exception. Aided by a 1904 *National Geographic* article that introduced the beauty of the bridges to Americans, President Theodore Roosevelt designated this natural wonder as Utah's first national monument in 1908.

The region surrounding Natural Bridges has a long and vibrant human history. During part of the archaic period, from about 7000 B.C.E. to 500 C.E., native inhabitants utilized the area, and archeological sites from this period are protected by the monument. About

700 C.E., the ancestors of the modern Puebloan people moved onto the mesa tops around the Natural Bridges. Here, like other people in other parts of the Southwest, the Pueblos engaged in dry farming and hunting and gathering. By 1100 C.E., new migrants had moved into these canyons along the Colorado River and established single-family houses near the wettest and most fertile soils. Farming continued in the region until the 1300s, when the ancestral Puebloans migrated farther south. Navajo and Paiute clans occupied the area during the centuries that followed the Puebloan migration out of it.

The park's 3 bridges are named in honor of the traditions of the native peoples: Sipapu, Kachina, and Owachomo. Sipapu means "place of emergence" and is the name for the entryway through which the Hopi believe that their ancestors came into the world. Kachina was so named because there is ancient art on this bridge that resembles symbols used on Kachina dolls. And Owachomo is the Hopi word for "rock mound," which is a physical feature that marks this particular bridge. The 3 bridges also depict the three phases in a natural bridge's history: youth, maturity, and old age. Anglo-Americans became aware of the Natural Bridges' wonder when a gold prospector named Cass Hite came upon them in 1883.

Today, the 7,636-acre Natural Bridges National Monument protects the three naturally occurring rock bridges, the mesas the bridges connect, and the terrain around them. Entrance fees are $3 per person or $6 per vehicle and are valid for seven days; a $25 annual Southeast Utah Group pass is also available and covers entrance fees to Arches, Canyonlands, Hovenweep, and Natural Bridges. The park's visitor center is open from 8 A.M. until 5 P.M. year-round, and it features exhibits highlighting the natural and cultural history of the area as well as an orientation video. Park rangers offer interpretive talks, guided walks, and evening campfire programs spring through fall. The bridges and canyons can be seen from the Bridge View Drive, a one-way, 9-mile scenic loop. To truly experience the bridges, however, visitors should hike one or more of the trails that begin at various places along the drive. There are hikes of varying lengths and difficulty, any of which will allow a visitor to see the wildlife and natural beauty of the bridge area.

There are no food or lodging facilities at the monument, but all traveler services are available in Blanding, Fry Canyon, and Mexican Hat. The park has a small, 13-site campground that is open year-round. Campsites are available on a first-come, first-served basis, and they have fire grates (no wood-gathering in the monument) and picnic tables. The fee is $10 per night.

For more information, write Natural Bridges National Monument, HC 60 Box 1, Lake Powell, UT 84533-0101, or telephone (435) 692-1234. The park's Web site is www.nps.gov/nabr.

FURTHER READING

Baars, Donald L. *The Colorado Plateau: A Geologic History.* Albuquerque: University of New Mexico Press, 2000.
Chronic, Halka. *Roadside Geology of Utah.* Missoula, MT: Mountain, 1990.
Fillmore, Robert. *The Geology of the Parks, Monuments, and Wildlands of Southern Utah.* Salt Lake City: University of Utah Press, 2000.

NAVAJO NATIONAL MONUMENT
Location: Black Mesa, Arizona
Acreage: 360
Established: March 20, 1909

Navajo National Monument is anomalous among national park areas. This northeastern Arizona monument contains 3 distinct and noncontiguous sections, administered from 1 headquarters. In addition, the Navajo Reservation surrounds the 3 sections—Betatakin, Keet Seel, and Inscription House, 3 impressive prehistoric ruins. Dating from the thirteenth century, these ruins contain the primary representation of the Kayenta Anasazi within the national park system. Yet because of their location and the distance between the 3 areas, Navajo National Monument is an inholding on the Navajo reservation.

This condition has created a level of interdependence unequaled elsewhere in the park system. The park provides a range of services not otherwise available as well as significant employment opportunities for local Navajo people. Through a complex series of formal agreements and customs, local Navajos support the park and participate in its activities.

Like many other smaller southwestern national monuments, Navajo developed slowly. At its inception, the Park Service had few resources, most of which were used to improve national parks. Navajo National Monument had only a volunteer custodian from its establishment in 1909 until 1938. New Deal development bypassed the monument, and despite the construction of basic facilities, at the end of the 1950s, Navajo remained a remote place, inaccessible to most of the traveling public.

The initiation of the Mission 66 program in the 1950s and an extensive road construction program by the Navajo Nation ended the historic isolation of the monument. Mission 66 planned an extensive development for Navajo, but the plans were held in abeyance until the Park Service could acquire an adequate area of land on which to build a visitor center. A complicated series of attempts to arrange a transfer of land followed, resulting in the Memorandum of Agreement of May 1962 that allowed the Park Service to add 240 acres for development of facilities.

The land addition transformed the monument. A comprehensive capital development program began in 1962. The Park Service built the physical plant, and Navajo National Monument became a modern park area. Its ability to offer services increased dramatically, and with the completion of paved roads to the visitor center in 1965, the number of visitors increased exponentially.

Navajo National Monument had the facilities, but its resources remained limited. The transformation made the interdependence between the monument and its neighbors even more important. As the funding available to the park leveled off, the monument became more and more of an outpost. Good relations with the people of the area were crucial, and a string of superintendents worked to assure harmonious interaction. By the 1980s, the monument had become an important cog in its neighborhood, a fixture in the cultural and economic structure of the Shonto region.

The monument can be reached from Flag-staff, Arizona, by following U.S. Highway 160 to Arizona Highway 564. It is 9 miles from the turn at Black Mesa to the visitor center, which is open from 8 A.M. until 5 P.M., seven days a week throughout the year. Exhibits feature various material artifacts from Anasazi (Hisatsinom) and Navajo culture, including pots, textiles, jewelry, and a replica of a Betatakin room cluster. The auditorium offers laser-disc videos about the Betatakin cliff dwelling and the ancient Pueblo peoples, and a Navajo traditional hogan, sweat lodge, and nineteenth-century wagon are located behind the visitor center.

The park's campground is open year-round, weather permitting, and the 2 overlook trails are open year-round, weather permitting, as well. The guided hikes to Betatakin and Keet Seel, which are generally available from Memorial Day to Labor Day every year, traverse difficult terrain, with steep switchbacks, sand hills, quicksand, and other backcountry hazards that can substantially slow travel and pose potential danger. Therefore, backcountry travel requires ranger guides or permits and is recommended only for experienced and fit hikers.

Summers are warm to hot, with temperatures in the high 90s, and powerful thunderstorms in July and August bring rain, wind, and lightning. Spring and fall can be pleasant, but occasionally blustery, and winter often brings snowstorms and very cold weather.

Physically challenged visitors should know that the Sandal Trail to the Betatakin overlook is paved and accessible to wheelchairs, but its steepness means that those using manual wheelchairs will need assistance for the return trip. In addition, one site at the campground is specially paved for wheelchair access.

For more information, write Navajo National Monument, HC-71, Box 3, Tonalea, AZ 86044-9704, or telephone (520) 672-2700. The park's Web site is www. nps.gov/nava.

FURTHER READING

Iverson, Peter. *The Navajo Nation.* Westport, CT: Greenwood Press, 1981.

Rothman, Hal K. *Navajo National Monument: A Place and Its People.* Santa Fe, NM: Southwest Regional Office, National Park Service, 1991. Available at www.nps.gov/nava/adhi/adhi.htm.

White, Richard. *The Roots of Dependency: Subsistence, Environment, and Social Change Among the Choctaws, Pawnees, and Navajos.* Lincoln: University of Nebraska Press, 1984.

NEW BEDFORD WHALING NATIONAL HISTORICAL PARK

Location: New Bedford, Massachusetts
Acreage: 34
Established: November 12, 1996

Before the Civil War, New Bedford, Massachusetts, held a pivotal position in whaling, one of the United States's most important industries. This was the world the great American author Herman Melville wrote about in his classic *Moby Dick*, a world of many peoples, all chasing the holy grail of whales. The huge sea mammals provided these people with valuable necessities. The whales' great hides were stripped of skin, meat, and fat. Before kerosene, oil from whale blubber lit lamps and oiled clocks; the ambergris inside them also was an important raw ingredient in perfume and other products.

The industry had taken off in the eighteenth century, when men in small ships tracked whales along the eastern seaboard. As they depleted the local whale population, the shipmen had to travel farther and farther in search of their quarry. Soon, square-riggers scoured the globe, searching for every locale where the mammals gathered. By the 1850s, Americans had sailed from the South Seas to the Western Arctic and discovered most of the grounds of sperm, right, bowhead, humpback, and California gray whales. They created a whaling culture that brought different parts of the world closer together through travel and trade.

Whaling was a lucrative business, and New Bedford's merchants mastered the integrated industry, making the town the wealthiest in the nation. Their complex commercial network included finance, insurance, shipbuilding, barrel making, rope and sail making, and other ship supply. Commercial success bred diversity, and, as the largest whaling port in the world in the mid-1800s, New Bedford attracted sailors from all over the globe. By the end of the nineteenth century, whaling had evolved into a different kind of occupation. Its crews were almost entirely Cape Verdean, West Indian, Portuguese, and Azorean.

Nineteenth-century New Bedford also was a stop on the Underground Railroad, the loose collection of places that helped move African Americans from slavery to freedom in the North and Canada. Among those fugitives was Frederick Douglass, the nineteenth century's leading African American champion of the anti-slavery movement. Douglass lived in New Bedford for three years before becoming a well-known author and orator.

The New Bedford Whaling National Historical Park was created in 1996. It encompasses 34 acres, spread over 13 city blocks, and includes a visitor center, the New Bedford Whaling Museum, the Seamen's Bethel, the schooner *Ernestina*, and the Rotch-Jones-Duff House and Garden Museum. The park's enabling legislation also established a legislative connection with the Inupiat Heritage Center in Barrow, Alaska, to commemorate the more than 2,000 whaling voyages from New Bedford to the western Arctic.

Admission to the park is free, although several of the park's cooperating institutions charge entrance fees. The visitor center, located at 33 William Street, is open year-round from 9 A.M. until 4 P.M. and has numerous interpretive exhibits. National Park Service walking tours of historic New Bedford are offered daily during the summer months and on weekends during other times of the year.

The park and the adjacent National Register Districts embody the historical and cultural resources associated with New Bedford's role as the whaling capital of the world during the early to mid-nineteenth century. The park includes a broad array of business, residential, and institutional structures, exemplifying the Federal, Greek Revival, Italianate, and Victorian styles of architecture; museums, historical exhibits, and records convey the importance, diversity, and financial power of the whaling era. The park is located in an area of the city of New Bedford that still serves the material needs (ships chandleries and supply houses) and social needs (restaurants, clubs, and taverns) of those who make their living from the sea and supports the businesses and civic institutions that serve the broader community.

There are no food, lodging, or camping facilities in the park, but all traveler services are available in the New Bedford area.

For more information, write New Bedford Whaling National Historical Park, 33 William Street, New Bedford, MA 02740, or telephone (508) 996-4095. The park's Web site is www.nps.gov/nebe.

FURTHER READING
Allen, Everett S. *Children of the Light: The Rise and Fall of New Bedford Whaling and the Death of the Arctic Fleet.* Boston: Little, Brown, 1973.

Arato, Christine A., and Patrick L. Eleey. *Safely Moored at Last: Cultural Landscape Report for New Bedford Whaling National Historical Park.* Boston: National Park Service, 1998.

Beatty, Jerome. *From New Bedford to Siberia: A Yankee Whaleman in the Frozen North.* Garden City, NY: Doubleday, 1977.

McCabe, Marsha, and Joseph D. Thomas. *Not Just Anywhere: The Story of WHALE and the Rescue of New Bedford's Waterfront Historic District.* New Bedford, MA: Spinner, 1996.

NEW ORLEANS JAZZ NATIONAL HISTORICAL PARK

Location: New Orleans, Louisiana
Acreage: 5
Established: October 31, 1994

Jazz is, in many ways, America's music, and the New Orleans Jazz National Historical Park was established in 1994 to celebrate the origins and evolution of the nation's most widely recognized indigenous musical art form. Like the music itself, the jazz story is suffused with improvisation, innovation, controversy, and emotion, and the park provides an ideal setting for studying the cultural history of the people and places that shaped its development in New Orleans. Although jazz "came of age" during the 1920s—popularly called the "Jazz Age"—the music had deeper roots in the African American community. Talented black musicians such as trumpeter Louis Armstrong, pianist Duke Ellington, trombonist Kid Ory, and blues singer Bessie Smith helped popularize this form of protest music, which allowed African Americans to express the frustration of living in an America governed by Jim Crow. Radio brought live band performances into the homes of millions of Americans, and white bandleaders like Benny Goodman introduced the nation's youth to a new dance style—swing. During the 1940s, black artists such as Charlie Parker, Miles Davis, and Thelonius Monk transformed jazz into a sophisticated musical expression known as "bebop." Featuring more-complex rhythms and extended improvisation, it became a voice of rebellion for urban blacks.

The park protects and preserves this rich heritage through interpretive techniques designed to both educate and entertain visitors about the origins and early development of jazz in the city widely recognized as its birthplace. The French Quarter Visitor Center, located at 916 North Peters, is open from 9 A.M.

until 5 P.M. Wednesday through Sunday. It includes an orientation and information desk; indoor and outdoor stage for live performances and interpretive programs; orientation video; exhibit space; and sales area. Admission is free. A calendar of activities is published quarterly, and programs include musical performances; music demonstrations; lectures on a variety of jazz-related topics; special events; and a walking tour of significant historical jazz sites in the French Quarter. The park's headquarters is open year-round from 8 A.M. until 4:30 P.M.

There are no food, lodging, or camping facilities in the park, but all traveler services are available in the New Orleans area.

For more information, write New Orleans Jazz National Historical Park, 365 Canal Street, Suite 2400, New Orleans, LA 70130-1142, or telephone (504) 589-4841. The park's Web site is www.nps.gov/neor.

FURTHER READING
Burns, Ken. *Jazz—A Film by Ken Burns.* Walpole, NH: PBS Home Video, 2001.
Gioia, Ted. *The History of Jazz.* New York: Oxford University Press, 1997.
Kirchner, Bill, ed. *The Oxford Companion to Jazz.* New York: Oxford University Press, 2000.
Ward, Geoffrey C. *Jazz: A History of America's Music.* New York: Alfred A. Knopf, 2000.

NEZ PERCE NATIONAL HISTORICAL PARK
Location: Idaho, Montana, Oregon, and Washington
Acreage: 2,495
Established: May 15, 1965

For the Nee-Me-Poo, or Nez Perce, people, the valleys, prairies, mountains, and plateaus of the inland Northwest have been "home" for thousands of years. Their story, centered around their leader, Chief Joseph, is one of the most compelling in American history. The Nez Perce, the name given by French Canadian trappers who thought they had seen tribal members with pierced noses, had lived peacefully among the white traders and settlers for generations on the plateau where Idaho, Washington, and Oregon now meet. But the 1860 discovery of gold soon fouled these relations. Three years later, some Nez Perce leaders agreed to cede more than nine-tenths of the tribe's lands to the federal government, but the treaty was signed illegally on behalf of the entire nation. Chief Joseph, leader of the Wallowa band in Oregon, persuaded federal officials to negate the flawed treaty, but pressure from settlers and politicians reversed the decision. Chief Joseph's people set out for their assigned reservation but were soon drawn into conflict with U.S. troops, which fired on the Nez Perce truce party. The Nez Perce fought back. The conflict came just one year after the army's defeat at the Little Bighorn, and Chief Joseph knew that retaliation would be swift. He commenced an epic journey, leading about 750 Nez Perce across 1,400 miles of hostile territory, hoping to reach safety, and immunity, in Canada. His quest fell just short.

Few places in the West are as evocative of the tragic story of the Indian Wars as Big Hole National Battlefield. This 656-acre site memorializes the bravery of the Nez Perce and U.S. soldiers and volunteers who fought here during the epic flight of the Nez Perce in 1877, and it preserves the scene of one of the most famous battles of the Indian Wars. The beauty and tranquillity of the battlefield's setting in the lush Big Hole Valley in southwestern Montana add immeasurably to the solemnity of the site. "One of the great ironies associated with American battlefields is that they are often quite beautiful," cultural historian Edward Linenthal observed in his book *Sacred Ground.* Here the picturesque natural setting has changed relatively little since August 9, 1877, the day of the predawn attack on the Nez Perce encampment.

A member of the Nez Perce tribe, c. 1910. *(Library of Congress)*

Before army troops forced the Nez Perce to surrender in the Bear Paw Mountains of northern Montana, the Nez Perce fought 2,000 soldiers and 18 native auxiliary detachments, in 18 separate engagements—including the Battle of the Big Hole—over three and a half months. Promised safe return to Oregon, the Nez Perce were instead shipped to a squalid reservation in Kansas and then to Oklahoma. Finally, the federal government deported the last remnants of Chief Joseph's band under guard to the Colville Indian Reservation in Washington State, where Chief Joseph died in 1904 "of a broken heart."

Authorized in May 1965, the 2,495-acre Nez Perce National Historical Park contains 38 sites, mostly in Idaho, that follow a trail from the Wallowa Mountains of Oregon through central Idaho, Montana and Washington—1,500 miles all together. Park headquarters and the visitor center are in Spalding, Idaho, 11 miles east of Lewiston, and are open from 8 A.M. until 5:30 P.M. from June through September, and until 4:30 P.M. during the rest of the year. An additional visitor center is at Big Hole National Battlefield, 10 miles west of Wisdom, Montana. It is open from 8 A.M. until 5 P.M. Facilities are staffed year-round by personnel who can answer questions about the local area, the Nez Perce people, and the war of 1877. Movies, museum exhibits, and guided tours are available covering the Nez Perce culture and history. Although there is no visitor center at Bear Paw Battlefield in Chinook, Montana, the Blaine County Museum features a display and video on the battle. The Big Hole National Battlefield site charges a summer-only entrance fee of $2 per person or $4 per family.

Interpretive shelters at Heart of the Monster (Kamiah) and White Bird Battlefield tell the story of events at each location. The White Bird shelter presents a panoramic view of the battlefield and gives visitors an idea of how the battle occurred and how skillfully the Nez Perce used the terrain to defeat the U.S. Army. A self-guided (primitive) hiking trail is accessible via old U.S. Highway 95 north of White Bird. At Kamiah, the exhibits explain the Heart of the Monster—the Place of Beginning where the Nez Perce people sprang from the drops of blood squeezed from the monster's heart. An audio station recounts the legend. Self-guiding trails are present at the Big Hole and Bear Paw Battlefield sites, as well as a self-guided walking tour of the Spalding site.

The Nez Perce National Historic Trail also commemorates the flight of the "non-treaty" Nez Perce Indians in 1877. Beginning in northeastern Oregon, the 1,170-mile trail extends across Idaho to Montana, bisecting Yellowstone National Park in Wyoming, and ending near the Bear Paw Mountains. Congress established it in October 1986. The areas encompassed by the park display the great diversity of the American West—topography, rainfall, vegetation, and scenery, ranging from the semiarid regions of Washington, to the lush high mountain meadows of Idaho and Oregon, to the prairies of Montana.

There are no food, lodging, or camping facilities in the historical park, but all traveler services are available in Lewiston and in towns along the park's historic trail.

For more information, write Nez Perce National Historical Park, Route 1, Box 100, Highway 95 South, Spalding, ID 83540-9715, or telephone (208) 843-2261. The park's Web site is www.nps.gov/nepe.

FURTHER READING

Beal, Merrill D. *I Will Fight No More Forever: Chief Joseph and the Nez Perce War.* Seattle: University of Washington Press, 1963.

Brown, Dee. *Bury My Heart at Wounded Knee: An Indian History of the American West.* New York: Henry Holt, 2001.

Chief Joseph. *That All People May Be One People, Send Rain to Wash the Face of the Earth.* Sitka, AK: Mountain Meadow, 1995.

Greene, Jerome A. *Nez Perce Summer, 1877: The U.S. Army and the Nee-Me-Poo Crisis.* Helena: Montana Historical Society Press, 2000. Available at www. nps.gov/nepe/greene/index.htm.

Josephy, Alvin M. *The Nez Perce Indians and the Opening of the Northwest.* Boston: Houghton Mifflin, 1997.

Linenthal, Edward T. *Sacred Ground: Americans and Their Battlefields.* Urbana: University of Illinois Press, 1993.

NICODEMUS NATIONAL HISTORIC SITE

Location: Nicodemus, Kansas
Acreage: 161
Established: November 12, 1996

This fascinating park, located in Nicodemus, Kansas, preserves and interprets a powerful component of nineteenth-century U.S. history. It is the only remaining western town that was established by African Americans during and after Reconstruction. Seizing the opportunity provided by freedom from the slavery that had marked their cultural, social, and economic experience in the United States, these brave pioneers were part of a movement out of the South. Conditions for African Americans in the post–Civil War South became so bad that many picked up in the middle of the night and went west in search of economic opportunity and social liberty. Kansas, the scene of so many free-soil–pro-slavery battles during the 1850s, had the sound of freedom; it was also across the river from Missouri, which was, even after the war, hostile country for African Americans.

In September 1877, about 300 African American settlers, emigrating out of areas such as northeastern Kentucky, founded this small Kansas town. Shocked and often disappointed by the landscape, these men and women who had lived their lives in the lush southeast adjusted to the semiarid, prairie conditions of Kansas. During the early years of settlement, they often lived in dugouts because they had neither the time nor the timber to build clapboard houses.

Despite the harsh and unexpected conditions, and the personal pain of breaking generations-old familial and cultural ties with southern communities, the African Americans who moved into Nicodemus hoped to build a life free from the racial oppression and terror that increasingly marked their experiences in the South, as federal troops withdrew at the end of Reconstruction. Some white Southerners launched a reign of terror that limited the social, political, and economical opportunities of African Americans in the South; in Kansas, the settlers hoped to find freedom and a chance to fulfill their dreams. Kansas had been home to John Brown, the radical revolutionary who was hung after raiding the federal arsenal at Harpers Ferry, Virginia, to start a slave insurrection. He remained a hero to many African Americans, and the state where he had fought for freedom drew countless former slaves.

By the mid-1880s, Nicodemus was a thriving town that had three general stores, two newspapers, three churches, hotels, a school,

District No. 1 School, Nicodemus, Kansas. *(Library of Congress)*

and a bank. Growth would not last, for the railroad bypassed Nicodemus. The nearest railroad went through Bogue, which was just south of the Solomon River. Nicodemus's location north of the river doomed it to slow economic decline. By the late twentieth century, Nicodemus had countered that decline to some extent by refashioning itself as a small tourist town, with an important part to play in America's fascination with its own history.

In November 1996, Congress formally recognized the importance of Nicodemus's contribution to the nation's history by establishing the 161-acre Nicodemus National Historic Site as a unit of the National Park Service (NPS). The legislation directed the NPS to cooperate with the people of Nicodemus to preserve its 5 remaining historic structures—First Baptist Church, African Methodist Episcopal Church, St. Francis Hotel, School, and Nicodemus Township Hall—and keep alive the memory of the many roles that African Americans played throughout the American West.

Admission to this relatively new park, which is still under development, is free. A temporary visitor center offers exhibits on the history of the Nicodemus community. A Ranger Contact Station and tours are available during the summer season, and, on the last weekend in July, the park celebrates

"Homecoming," which derives from an early Nicodemus tradition called "Emancipation Day"—a celebration of the day of freedom for slaves in the West Indies, which is now a celebration of the African American spirit and legacy in the United States.

There are no food, lodging, or camping facilities at the historic site, but all traveler services are available in Hill City, Plainville, and Stockton. Camping is also available at the Webster State Recreation Area.

For more information, write Nicodemus National Historic Site, 304 Washington Avenue, Bogue, KS 67625-3015, or telephone (785) 839-4221. The park's Web site is www.nps.gov/nico.

FURTHER READING

Chu, Daniel, and Bill Shaw. *Going Home to Nicodemus: The Story of an African American Frontier Town and the Pioneers Who Settled It.* Morristown, NJ: J. Messner, 1994.

NINETY SIX NATIONAL HISTORIC SITE

Location: Ninety Six, South Carolina
Acreage: 1,022
Established: August 19, 1976

Ninety Six National Historic Site preserves the site of a small village with great historical importance for a young nation. Early traders gave the South Carolina town its unusual name because they believed, mistakenly, that it was 96 miles to the Cherokee village of Keowee located in the foothills of the Blue Ridge Mountains. Fort Ninety Six was built in 1760 to protect English settlers in the area, because relations with the surrounding native tribes were volatile and often violent. Never a large town, Ninety Six was home to about 100 settlers by 1775.

Seemingly too small to make a mark, Ninety Six became permanently part of U.S. history during the Revolutionary War. The backcountry of South Carolina was almost evenly divided between Patriots of the American cause and Loyalists to the English crown. As a result, fierce but sporadic fighting characterized the region throughout the war.

In June 1780, the British garrisoned at Ninety Six, building up its defenses and preparing to meet American General Nathanael Greene and his patriot troops. On May 22, 1781, General Greene arrived at Ninety Six and began the longest siege of the war. On June 18, 1781, the Americans, led by one of the most colorful figures in the war, Major Henry "Light Horse Harry" Lee, stormed the British stockade. The fort did not fall, and the patriot troops retreated after a thirty-day siege. The long siege and the losses incurred on both sides turned out to be for nothing. When the British commander arrived at Ninety Six, he decided that its strategic value was minimal and withdrew the British troops. The Patriots gained control of the South Carolina backcountry, but Ninety Six was burned.

Authorized in August 1976, the 1,022-acre Ninety Six National Historic Site commemorates the role the settlement played during the Revolution and preserves several historic roads and paths, the earthen British-built Star Fort, and the partially reconstructed Stockade Fort. Admission is free. The park's visitor center is open daily from 8 A.M. until 5 P.M., and it includes interpretive museum exhibits and a ten-minute video program. The site has a 1-mile-long loop trail with 7 stops that explain the fort's role in the Revolutionary War. In addition to living-history programs throughout the year, the park offers annual Autumn Candlelight Tours and military encampments.

There are no food, lodging, or camping facilities at the historic site, but all traveler services are available locally.

For more information, write Ninety Six National Historic Site, P.O. Box 496, Ninety Six, SC 29666, or telephone (864) 543-4068. The park's Web site is www. nps.gov/nisi.

FURTHER READING

Bass, Robert D. *Ninety Six, the Struggle for the South Carolina Back Country.* Lexington, SC: Sandlapper Store, 1978.

Morrill, Dan L. *Southern Campaigns of the American Revolution.* Baltimore, MD: Nautical & Aviation Publishing Company of America, 1993.

Royster, Charles. *Light-Horse Harry Lee and the Legacy of the American Revolution.* Baton Rouge: Louisiana State University Press, 1994.

Symonds, Craig L. *A Battlefield Atlas of the American Revolution.* Baltimore, MD: Nautical & Aviation Publishing Company of America, 1986.

NORTH CASCADES NATIONAL PARK

Location: Marblemount, Washington
Acreage: 504,781
Established: October 2, 1968

By the standards of the American national parks, North Cascades is small. At a little more than a half million acres, it is dwarfed by the Grand Canyon, Yellowstone, or any of the Alaskan national parks. Despite its size, it includes spectacular scenery, wildlife, and a wilderness area that stretches into two neighboring national recreation areas. In every way except its acreage, North Cascades is the quintessential national park.

What makes this park different—and so small in comparison—is the time of its establishment. A latecomer to the national park system, North Cascades was created in 1968. By then, most of the extraordinary places in the public domain had been included in federal reserves, and individual claims bisected much of the rest. While drawing the boundaries for a million-acre national park was an easy task in the open West of the late nineteenth century, by the 1960s, no such areas remained that included spectacular scenery and were devoid of mining, homesteading, logging, or other activities. As a result, national parks diminished in size. Along with

Old-growth Sitka spruce forest near Lake Chelan in North Cascades National Park. The trees are from 400 to 750 years old, and they measure 4 to 6 feet in diameter. *(National Archives)*

Guadalupe Mountains and the Redwoods, which are roughly of the same size and vintage, North Cascades is one of the last traditional national parks in the lower forty-eight states.

The unusual designation of a wilderness park in the lower forty-eight states during the 1960s is itself testimony to the unique nature of North Cascades. Beginning in the 1890s, the region's special character promoted national park efforts. These broke into three periods. Between the 1890s and the 1920s, Progressive-Era values led to an effort to create a national park. It was ultimately impaled on the rift between conservationists, who advocated wise use of resources, and preservationists, who wanted to protect them from any use. During the 1930s, the effort to establish Olympic National Park nearby led to strong opposition not only to that park but to other conservation projects, and efforts to protect North Cascades were crushed in that maelstrom. Modern environmentalism can be credited with the creation of the park. After World War II, as the nation attained new affluence, it became easier to accomplish conservation goals. Widespread support for the idea of wilderness in the 1960s finally led to the creation of the park.

The 504,781-acre North Cascades National Park Service Complex includes North Cascades National Park, and Ross Lake and Lake Chelan National Recreation Areas. Ross Lake National Recreation Area (117,575 acres) is the corridor for scenic Washington Route 20, the North Cascades Highway, and includes 3 reservoirs: 12,000-acre Ross Lake, 910-acre Diablo Lake, and 210-acre Gorge Lake—water gateways to more remote areas. Lake Chelan National Recreation Area (61,947 acres) rests in a glacially carved trough in the Cascades Range. Lake Chelan is one of the nation's deepest, reaching a depth of 1,500 feet. More than 93 percent of the park is further protected in the 634,000-acre Stephen Mather Wilderness, established in 1988, and named in honor of the National Park Service's first director.

The North Cascades Visitor Center, across the Skagit River from the North Cascades Highway (Washington State Route 20) near milepost 120 and the town of Newhalem, is open all year from 9 A.M. until 4:30 P.M. and for extended hours during the summer. The center has a relief map of the park and surrounding area and an exhibit room featuring multimedia exhibits on the park's natural and cultural history. Park rangers offer daily talks, guided hikes, and children's and other programs in summer. The park also offers special programs during Earth Week (April) and International Migra-

tory Bird Week (May). The Golden West Visitor Center, at Stehekin Landing near the north end of 50-mile-long Lake Chelan, is open from mid-March through mid-October, although hours vary. In addition to exhibits on the natural and cultural history of the area, the center features the Golden West Gallery, operated by the Arts and Humanities Council of Stehekin, which features exhibits of work by local artists and craftspeople.

The Chelan Ranger Station, in Chelan, Washington, is open all year from 7:45 A.M. until 4:30 P.M. This is an office of the Wenatchee National Forest where information can be obtained concerning Lake Chelan National Recreation Area at the other end of Lake Chelan. The North Cascades National Park Headquarters Information Station, in Sedro-Woolley, Washington, along the North Cascades Highway (Washington State Route 20) about 4 miles east of I-5, is open all year from 8 A.M. until 4:30 P.M. This station is operated jointly with the Mount Baker District of the Mount Baker–Snoqualmie National Forest, which adjoins North Cascades National Park to the west. It offers a relief map of the park and adjacent national forests. The Glacier Public Service Center, on the Mount Baker Highway just east of Glacier, Washington, is open from June through September from 8:30 A.M. until 4:30 P.M. The center has a relief map of Mount Baker and exhibits on the natural and cultural history of the Mount Baker District. Backpackers and climbers can also obtain the free Wilderness Permit required for overnight stays in the park's backcountry.

Although admission to the park is free, there are several user fees assessed within the park complex. Between May 1 and October 31, boaters must have a Dock Fee Permit to use the docks in Lake Chelan National Recreation Area. This is the same permit needed for using the docks provided by the U.S. Forest Service along other parts of the Lake Chelan shoreline. The Lake Chelan Dock Fee

Horseback riding amid the spectacular scenery of North Cascades National Park. *(National Park Service)*

Pass is $5 per day or $40 annually. The Northwest Forest Pass is required for parking anywhere along the North Cascades National Park portion of the Cascade River road or at the following trailheads in Ross Lake National Recreation Area: Thornton Lakes, Pyramid Lake, Ross Dam, East Bank, Panther Creek. The pass is also required for parking at trailheads in the adjacent national forests. The Northwest Forest Pass is $5 per day or $30 annually.

Lodging is available at North Cascades Stehekin Lodge (509-682-4494) and Ross Lake Resort (206-386-4437) in the park , and at a variety of bed and breakfasts, cabins, and lodge accommodations on private property in the Stehekin Valley within the Lake Chelan National Recreation Area. Access to Stehekin is via passenger ferry or floatplane from Chelan

or by trail. Stehekin Lodge, open all year, is a concession-operated lodge at Stehekin Landing near the head of Lake Chelan with rooms, a restaurant, a snack bar, and a small store. The Ross Lake Resort, open from June through October, has concession-operated housekeeping cabins on floats moored near the lower end of Ross Lake; the resort also rents canoes, kayaks, and outboard motor boats.

North Cascades National Park has 1 campground that is open year-round–Goodell Creek–and 2 that are open from mid-May through September–Colonial Creek and Newhalem Creek. Goodell Creek Campground is in old-growth forest on the banks of the Skagit River, and it has 21 sites, a raft/kayak launch, and a covered picnic shelter nearby. The fee is $10 per night, and potable water is available from spring into fall. Colonial Creek is also in old-growth forest on the shores of Diablo Lake. It has 62 sites, some fully accessible, a boat ramp, dump station, and potable water. The fee is $12 per night, and there are nightly amphitheater programs in summer. The Newhalem Creek Campground is just off the North Cascades Highway near milepost 120 and across the Skagit River. The fee is $12 per night, and the campground has potable water and a dump station. Park rangers present evening programs in the campground amphitheaters on weekends in the summer.

For more information, write North Cascades National Park, 2105 Washington State Route 20, Sedro-Woolley, WA 98284-9394, or telephone (360) 856-5700. The park's Web site is www.nps.gov/noca.

FURTHER READING

Alt, David D., and Donald W. Hyndman. *Roadside Geology of Washington.* Missoula, MT: Mountain, 1984.

Beckey, Fred W. *Range of Glaciers: The Exploration and Survey of the Northern Cascade Range.* Portland: Oregon Historical Society Press, 2002.

Louter, David. *Contested Terrain: North Cascades National Park Service Complex: An Administrative History.* Seattle, WA: National Park Service, 1998.

McKee, Bates. *Cascadia; the Geologic Evolution of the Pacific Northwest.* New York: McGraw-Hill, 1972.

Roe, JoAnn. *Stevens Pass: The Story of Railroading and Recreation in the North Cascades.* Caldwell, ID: Caxton, 2002.

Wassink, Jan L. *Birds of the Pacific Northwest Mountains: The Cascade Range, the Olympic Mountains, Vancouver Island, and the Coast Mountains.* Missoula, MT: Mountain, 1995.

O

OCMULGEE NATIONAL MONUMENT

Location: Macon, Georgia
Acreage: 702
Established: June 14, 1934

Known as the "Ocmulgee Old Fields," this area in central Georgia harbored one of the earliest complex civilizations to emerge among Native Americans. Human history in the Ocmulgee area began more than eleven thousand years ago, when Ice Age hunters left behind "Clovis" spears on the Macon Plateau. Pottery found in the region dates as far back as 2500 B.C.E., and archeological evidence indicates that there were villages in the area and early mounds being built during the Woodland Period, which stretched from 1000 B.C.E. to 900 C.E.

From the twelfth to the fourteenth centuries, people of the Mississippian culture, characterized by their large ceremonial centers with earthen mounds, dominated the region. Civil and religious life focused around the ceremonial center, and agriculture supported the population. By about 1350, the villages and mounds at Lamar had become more prominent than the Macon Plateau center, however, and during the Late Mississippian Period, in which the Lamar culture gained ascendancy, the Native American social and political structure became more fragmented, with smaller and more autonomous villages scattered throughout the Southeast. When the earliest Spanish explorers entered the region in 1540, it was the Lamar culture that they encountered. The Spanish noted the vibrant and complex social, political, and religious structures present in the southeastern part of North America. Yet the presence of the Spanish, even in a limited sense, led to increased social disruption among the Native Americans of the region. Disease brought by Europeans, as well as the additional strain on the natural environment caused by the Spanish and their horses, led to a gradual decline in this once powerful culture.

By 1690, both the English and the Spanish intruded on the lands of the southeastern tribes. The British established a trading post on the banks of the Ocmulgee River, which is now protected by the national monument. The British post had the effect of reorganizing the Native American social structure because many towns relocated to be near the trading center. People in the towns that sprang up near the trading post became known as the Ochese Creek Nation, which eventually became known simply as the Creek. The Creeks were not a single cultural group, but instead emerged as a political entity when various cultural and language groups came together in response to Europeans' presence in the region.

In general, the Creek were allies of the British, though conflicts such as the 1715 Yamassee War erupted over trade and utilization of natural resources. American settlers had less friendly feelings for the Creek than did the British government, because the settlers wanted access to the inland that was held by the Creek. During the Revolutionary War, the Creek Nation made an unfortunate alliance with England, which seemed a politically expedient move at the time, but ultimately resulted in the loss of much of their land to the new state of Georgia. The next fifty years of Creek history were marked by war and betrayal, leading to the removal of many native people whose ancestral homes were in Georgia. In 1839, the Creek were forcibly moved to Oklahoma territory.

Throughout the eighteenth and nineteenth centuries, non-native visitors to the Ocmulgee area noted the mounds and other artifacts of the Ocmulgee Old Fields with great interest. As American settlers moved into the area and the Creek were pushed out, the mounds became a sort of social meeting place. In 1843, a railroad was constructed through part of the Old Fields, which destroyed a portion of the Lesser Temple Mound. The old oak growth on the mounds was cut down for timber, and much of the archeological value of the region was destroyed. In 1874, part of the Funeral Mound was destroyed by another railroad. Destruction and desecration of the mounds continued until the area was designated a national monument in December 1936. Today, the 702-acre monument preserves and protects this archeologically and culturally valuable land in Georgia and commemorates the ancient cultures of the area. Despite the loss of many of the historical artifacts during the nineteenth and early twentieth centuries, Ocmulgee National Monument still offers valuable insights into early Native American history.

Admission to the monument is free. The park's visitor center is open daily from 9 A.M. to 5 P.M., and it contains artifacts, dioramas, and a seventeen-minute film called *Mysteries of the Mounds*. There are more than 6 miles of paved trails connecting the mounds, the various natural landscapes, and the historical buildings located in the park. The park also cooperates with other agencies to present the Ocmulgee Indian Celebration each year. This event allows the park to emphasize the historical and cultural significance of the Native Americans who built the mounds, as well as their descendants, who still have an important connection to the lands of Georgia.

There are no food, lodging, or camping facilities at the monument, but all traveler services are available in Forsyth, Macon, Milledgeville, and Warner Robins.

For more information, write Ocmulgee National Monument, 1207 Emery Highway, Macon, GA 31217-4399, or telephone (912) 752-8257. The park's Web site is www.nps.gov/ocmu.

FURTHER READING

Fairbanks, Charles Herron. *Archeology of the Funeral Mound, Ocmulgee National Monument, Georgia.* Tuscaloosa: University of Alabama Press, 2003.

Hally, David J., ed. *Ocmulgee Archaeology 1936–1986.* Athens: University of Georgia Press, 1994.

Marsh, Alan. *Ocmulgee National Monument: An Administrative History.* Washington, DC: National Park Service, 1986.

OKLAHOMA CITY NATIONAL MEMORIAL

Location: Oklahoma City, Oklahoma
Acreage: 6
Established: October 9, 1997

One of the most heart-wrenching and powerful memorials in the national park system, the Oklahoma City National Memorial is one of the saddest places in the United States. It enshrines the memory of the victims of the worst and most senseless terrorist attack to occur on U.S. soil until that time. On April 19, 1995, the federal building in downtown Oklahoma City was demolished by a fertilizer bomb, killing 168 people and forever impacting a nation that had considered itself immune from terrorist threat. The blast devastated Oklahoma City; the memorial is an important part of the community's healing and is special in no small part because residents have helped the Park Service design and build it.

The memorial is comprised of 3 components: the symbolic Memorial, the National

Memorial Center, and the Institute for the Prevention of Terrorism. The symbolic and powerful memorial, the first to open to the public, was designed to honor those who died in the tragedy, those who came as rescuers, and those who survived, while simultaneously reminding the nation that terrorism must be prevented. Perhaps the most striking component of the memorial is the Field of Empty Chairs; 168 empty chairs serve as a reminder of each individual who was lost that day, and of the emptiness the loss has caused in the lives of the victims' loved ones. The Reflecting Pool is dedicated more to the survivors than the victims; its shallow waters symbolize the soothing of wounds and provide visitors with a moment of peace.

The Children's Area is made up of a wall of hand-painted tiles that were sent to Oklahoma City in the months following the explosion. These tiles were hand painted by children around the country who mourned for the children who were lost that day. Chalkboards are also located in the area so that children who visit the memorial can share their emotions. The Rescuers Orchard symbolizes the generosity and wealth that flowed from people who rushed to Oklahoma City to help rescue victims, recover bodies, and rebuild a city. The fruit and flower trees in the orchard surround the Survivor's Tree, an American elm, which stands tall to represent the resilience of those who survived. The Memorial Fence, which sprang up almost instantly after the bombing, continues to be a place to which visitors come to leave all types of items, flowers, and notes dedicated to the families of the victims, the rescuers, and the survivors. Finally, the Gates of Time, which mark the entrance to the symbolic memorial, are inscribed with 9:01, the minute before the blast, and 9:03, the minute after the explosion ripped through the federal building and the heart of America.

The Institute for the Prevention of Terrorism is a component of the memorial, but it is also a research and educational institute dedicated to preventing terrorism and helping responders. The special focus of the institute is on funding and research for the responders, the men and women who first arrive on the scenes of terrorist attacks. The institute is a living memorial to those who died on April 19, 1995, and its goal is help prevent any other city from having to experience what Oklahoma City experienced, and continues to experience, as a result of a terrorist attack.

The final component of the memorial is the National Memorial Center, a large museum that tells the story of the bombing of the Murrah Federal Building in ten "chapters." The first chapter is "Chaos," and these exhibits display items from the building immediately following the bombing. Another area depicts the sixteen days of rescue when the world watched as rescuers sifted through the building for survivors and clues as to why this tragedy occurred. A particularly moving display is the "Gallery of Honor," in which hangs a picture of every victim of the bombing. The final exhibit in the National Memorial Center is "Hope," which focuses on the rebuilding, both physical and emotional, of Oklahoma City.

Established in October 1997, the 6-acre Oklahoma City National Memorial is open from 10 A.M. until 10 P.M. daily during the spring and summer (and from 8 A.M. until 8 P.M. daily for the remainder of the year), and rangers are on site to provide information and answer questions. The Symbolic Memorial is open twenty-four hours a day, every day of the year. Admission is free.

There are no food, lodging, or camping facilities at the memorial, but all traveler services are available in Oklahoma City.

For more information, write Oklahoma City National Memorial, P.O. Box 676, Oklahoma City, OK 73101-0676, or telephone (405) 235-3313. The park's Web site is www.nps.gov/okci.

FURTHER READING

Dyer, Joel. *Harvest of Rage: Why Oklahoma City Is Only the Beginning.* Boulder, CO: Westview, 1998.

Kight, Marsha, ed. *Forever Changed: Remembering Oklahoma City, April 19, 1995.* Amherst, NY: Prometheus Books, 1998.

Linenthal, Edward T. *The Unfinished Bombing: Oklahoma City in American Memory.* New York: Oxford University Press, 2001.

Michel, Lou, and Dan Herbeck. *American Terrorist: Timothy McVeigh and the Tragedy at Oklahoma City.* New York: Avon Books, 2002.

OLYMPIC NATIONAL PARK

Location: Port Angeles, Washington

Acreage: 922,651

Established: March 2, 1909

Olympic National Park brims with spectacular scenery. From its fog-shrouded coastline to the top of glacier-clad Mount Olympus, the park seems to hold landscapes worthy of several national parks. In its western reaches, booming ocean waves have sculpted a labryinth of sea stacks, arches, cliffs, and cobble-strewn beaches. Glacially carved peaks—their summits covered in snow and ice all year—dominate the interior of Olympic. Draining from these peaks toward the coast are deep, lush valleys, which nourish one of the continent's finest temperate rain forests with as many as 80 inches of rain per year.

The rich landscapes have long sustained diverse flora and fauna, and Native Americans have lived here for millenia, both along the coastlines and in the interior valleys. The land provided the native peoples with a cornucopia of resources. Salmon and shellfish served as their primary forms of subsistence, and these were supplemented with berries, roots, birds, and other animals. The area's towering cedar, spruce, and fir trees provided everything from building material to canoes and firewood. Cedar bark was fashioned into clothing and baskets, as well as woven into towels and diapers.

A European, Juan de Fuca—for whom the adjacent strait is named—may have visited the Olympic shores in 1592. Positive identification of the region, however, is credited to the sailing party of Juan Perez in 1774. Over the next several decades, English and American explorers would map the area and establish rival claims to this land for their own countries. An 1846 agreement between the United States and Great Britain resolved lingering border disputes, clearing the way for American control of the Olympic Peninsula.

The history of federal reservation of the Olympic Peninsula as parkland began in the late nineteenth century. In 1897, President Grover Cleveland created the Olympic Forest Reserve; President Theodore Roosevelt designated part of this as a national monument in 1909. At its founding, Mount Olympus was typical of national monuments established during Roosevelt's administration. Created under the auspices of the Antiquities Act, it provided largely symbolic protection. Although Mount Olympus National Monument was in no small part established to remind Congress that a president's authority extended even to the last days of his term, it also was an area that shared traits with federal game reserves. Its boundaries were linked to the needs of the Olympic or Roosevelt elk, the species the monument was ostensibly established to protect.

From 1908 until 1933, the Forest Service administered the monument as it did its other national monuments, in a manner not distinct from surrounding national forest lands. A loose parity existed, especially after the national monument was diminished by nearly half in 1915 to open up more timber acreage for the war effort. The area was designated as special, but in general, activities that were essential to the economic health of the region continued without interruption.

As part of Franklin D. Roosevelt's Executive Order 6166, the reorganization of the

Lake Crescent Lodge at Olympic National Park. *(Library of Congress)*

National Park Service signed June 10, 1933, the Park Service received Mount Olympus National Monument. The transfer gave the Park Service a stake in the region, and the Forest Service and the Park Service began an extended conflict not only over the status of the reserved area, as a national monument or park, but also concerning appropriate boundaries for both entities. In 1938, President Franklin D. Roosevelt signed legislation creating Olympic National Park. A struggle that highlighted the major difference that set Olympic National Park apart from its peers resulted. The active commercial economy that surrounded the park was a rarity in national park history. Most early parks were established on lands for which no apparent commercial economic use existed at the time. The Park Service inherited a substantial extractive history at Olympic, which was not entirely

new but was uncommon. The area that became the park had been the basis of an ongoing regional economy. The battle for Olympic National Park became the classic dispute between the Park Service and the Forest Service.

Olympic National Park required the Park Service to devise solutions to regional issues. This became the single most trying task for the Park Service, the one that caused the greatest rancor and made this park a hotspot for the agency. The combination of wilderness and extractive industry, of national conservation movement and local and regional economic engine, threatened park management principles and practices and made even basic decisions rancorous. From the 1940s until the passage of the National Environmental Policy Act (NEPA) in 1969, the Park Service faced difficult cumstances. Buffeted by national organizations with specific goals on one side and assaulted by local and regional constituencies on the other, Olympic National Park faltered numerous times as it was pulled between competing forces.

NEPA created a structure that superseded park management throughout the national park system, which both helped and hindered park management. It meant that on one level, while an enormous percentage of park resources at the local level were devoted to meeting new statutory obligations, the tension of decision-making was dampened. Even as Olympic National Park devoted more of its staff time and energy to the mass of federally mandated activities known as compliance, its managers felt the burden of addressing its public shift. After NEPA and the plethora of legislation that followed it, park managers sometimes simply relied on statute to justify decisions. Local communities could protest all they wanted, but the law was the law. This shifted management from local to national level, but oddly left the responsibility at the park level. A tense position for park leaders and their staff resulted.

By the early twenty-first century, Olympic National Park had become a bastion among American national parks. With more than 96 percent of the park in wilderness after 1988 and in a transformed regional economy in which timber had significantly diminished as a source of jobs, Olympic National Park appeared as an anchor in the region, a dependable if different source of revenue for a region in desperate need of support. It filled the role of federal facilities from prisons to military bases all across the country: it provided a stable baseline for the regional economy. The park had also emerged as an important leader in environmental management, especially in the effort to remove dams that threatened or disrupted native species.

Often referred to as "three parks in one," Olympic National Park encompasses 3 distinctly different ecosystems—rugged glacier-capped mountains, over 60 miles of wild Pacific Coast, and magnificent stands of old-growth and temperate rain forest. These diverse ecosystems are still largely pristine in character and preserve the park's biological diversity. Isolated for eons by glacial ice, the waters of Puget Sound, and the Strait of Juan de Fuca, the Olympic Peninsula has developed its own distinct array of plants and animals. Eight species of plants and five species of animals are found on the peninsula that live nowhere else in the world, including the Olympic mountain milkvetch, Olympic marmot, Olympic Mazama pocket gopher, and Olympic mud minnow.

The almost-923,000-acre Olympic National Park is open twenty-four hours a day, 365 days a year, and most roads remain open year-round, although several are subject to winter closure because of snow. Visitor centers are located in Port Angeles, Hurricane Ridge, and the Hoh Rain Forest, and each provides exhibits and visitor information. The Olympic National Park Visitor Center in Port Angeles is open and staffed year-round and serves as the park's primary information and orientation center. The Hurricane Ridge and Hoh visitor centers are open throughout the year (when road and weather conditions allow), but they may be self-service during the winter months. Exhibits are also located at Staircase, Storm King (at Lake Crescent), Ozette, and Kalaloch ranger stations. Entrance fees for the park are $5 per person or $10 per vehicle and are valid for seven days; a $20 annual pass is also available. In addition to these facilities, the park has a Wilderness Information Center, located 1 mile from Highway 101 behind the Olympic National Park Visitor Center, which is open daily from April through September. The Wilderness Information Center provides current trail reports, trip planning, safety and weather (subject to change), and Leave No Trace tips, as well as Wilderness Camping permits for any park location, and bear canisters.

To experience the park's high country and mountain vistas, many visitors drive to Hurricane Ridge. From there, a three-hour drive to the west ends at the Hoh Rain Forest, where more than 12 feet of rain per year create a stunning world of huge trees and profuse greenery. Views of the Pacific Coast and Olympic's wilderness beaches can be seen via an additional thirty- to forty-minute drive to Rialto or Ruby Beach. Visitors interested in hiking or exploring some of the park's lesser-used areas should allow at least several days to see the park, in which trails abound. Basic orientation information, as well as exhibits and an introductory slide program, are available at the Olympic National Park Visitor Center in Port Angeles.

Lodging is available in the park at Kalaloch Lodge (360-962-2271), which is open all year; Lake Crescent Lodge (360-928-3211), which is open from late April until October; Log Cabin Resort (360-928-3325), which is open for most of the year; and Sol Duc Hot Springs Resort (360-327-3583). The National Park Service also operates 16 campgrounds with a total of 910 sites. Camping fees at park campgrounds range from $8 to $12, depending on the services and amenities provided at each one. All are available on a first-come, first-served basis, and some remain open throughout the winter.

For more information, write Olympic National Park, 600 East Park Avenue, Port Angeles, WA 98362-6798, or telephone (360) 565-3130. The park's Web site is www.nps.gov/olym.

FURTHER READING

Beres, Nancy, Mitzi Chandler, and Russell Dalton, eds. *Island of Rivers: An Anthology Celebrating 50 Years of Olympic National Park.* Seattle, WA: Pacific Northwest National Parks & Forests, 1988.

Kirk, Ruth. *The Olympic Rain Forest: An Ecological Web.* Seattle: University of Washington Press, 1992.

Lien, Carsten. *Olympic Battleground: The Power Politics of Timber Preservation.* Seattle, WA: Mountaineers, 2000.

Lyman, R. Lee. *White Goats, White Lies: The Abuse of Science in Olympic National Park.* Salt Lake City: University of Utah Press, 1998.

McNulty, Tim. *Olympic National Park: A Natural History.* Seattle: University of Washington Press, 2003.

Olympic National Park: An Administrative History. Seattle, WA: National Park Service, Pacific Northwest Region, 1990.

Tabor, R.W. *Geology of Olympic National Park.* Seattle, WA: Pacific Northwest National Parks and Forests, 1987.

Twight, Ben W. *Organizational Values and Political Power: The Forest Service Versus the Olympic National Park.* University Park: Pennsylvania State University Press, 1983.

OREGON CAVES NATIONAL MONUMENT

Location: Cave Junction, Oregon
Acreage: 488
Established: July 12, 1909

The tiny Oregon Caves National Monument, originally set aside in 1909, harbors a tremendous diversity of plant and animal life as well as a beautiful three-and-a-half-mile-long marble cave carved over eons of time. Located in the Siskiyou Mountains of southwestern Oregon, the monument encompasses a remnant of one of the few remaining old-growth coniferous forests and protects an impressive array of endemic plants, including a Douglas fir tree with the widest known girth in Oregon. This lush, humid forest is home to black bears, mule deer, bobcats, gray foxes, and raccoons, as well as varied thrushes, California and mountain quail, chestnut-backed chickadees, and Lewis woodpeckers. But it is the monument's belowground features that attract most tourists. The famed Marble Halls of Oregon are an unusual feature because unlike most true caverns, which were shaped by subsurface water in limestone, Oregon Caves was formed in marble, the metamorphic equivalent of limestone. A "living" cave created over hundreds of thousands of years by natural forces such as plate tectonics and groundwater erosion by the River Styx, Oregon Caves also boasts a stunning spectacle of speleothems—mineral decorations adorning the cave's roof, floor, and walls. In addition to rather traditional formations such as stalactites, stalagmites, and columns, Oregon Caves also includes knobby deposits called "cave popcorn," draperies, flowstone, soda-straw stalactites, and helictites. Within the cave, scientists have documented one of the largest assortments of endemic cave-dwelling insects in the United States, and recent discoveries of unique Pleistocene mammal fossils of jaguars and grizzly bears have continued to enhance the monument's reputation for diversity.

One of the early national monuments, Oregon Caves National Monument is open all year for hiking, snowshoeing, and other similar outdoor activities. Access to the interior of Oregon Caves is only by guided tours, however, which are not offered during the winter. The interagency Illinois Valley Visitor Center is located in Cave Junction on Highway 46, near its intersection with Highway 199, and the Crater Lake Natural History Association operates a sales outlet there, with exhibits and information on the Oregon Caves. In addition, the Oregon Caves Information Station is open from mid-June to early September from 10 A.M. until 6 P.M. Fees for the general cave tour are $7.50 per person, although the last tour of the day (7 P.M.) is a historic candlelight tour, which costs $8 for adults and $5.50 for juniors. During summer months, special off-trail cave tours are offered at 10 A.M. every day. The tour requires crawling through narrow passageways and climbing slippery surfaces, and due to the strenuous nature of the tour, participants should be in good physical condition. The off-trail cave tour lasts four hours and costs $25 per person (minimum age is sixteen years).

Above ground at Oregon Caves, there are 5 miles of day hiking trails (4 trails total). The Big Tree Trail connects with a Siskiyou Na-

An evening campfire at Oregon Caves National Monument, 1935. *(National Archives)*

tional Forest trail to Bigelow Lakes, a popular overnight backcountry hike. The No Name Trail connects with a Siskiyou National Forest trail to reach Cave Creek Campground. The Cliff Nature Trail is a three-quarter-mile self-guided loop, which affords outstanding vistas near cliff areas, and signs along the path interpret natural features.

All traveler services are available just outside the park in Cave Junction, Grants Pass, Kerby, and O'Brien. Within the park, lodging facilities are available at the Historic Oregon Caves Chateau, a 22-room hotel operated by the Oregon Caves Company (541-592-2100; closed December, January, and February). The concession also operates a coffee shop and dining room in the chateau during the spring, summer, and fall seasons, and snacks can be purchased in the gift store. No groceries are available at the monument. There are no campgrounds within the monument, but two Forest Service and several private campgrounds and RV parks are within a short drive of the park.

For more information, write Oregon Caves National Monument, 19000 Caves Highway, Cave Junction, OR 97523, or telephone (541) 592-2100. The park's Web site is www.nps.gov/orca.

FURTHER READING

Alt, David D. *Roadside Geology of Oregon.* Missoula, MT: Mountain Press, 1978.

Gilbert, Cathy, and Marsha Tolom. *Cultural Landscape Report: Cultural Landscape Inventory of Oregon Caves National Monument.* Seattle, WA: Pacific Northwest Region, National Park Service, 1992. Available at www.nps.gov/orca/clr/clr.htm.

Kirkpatrick, Golda, Charlene Hozwarth, and Linda Mullens. *The Botanist and Her Muleskinner: Lilla Irvin Leach and John Roy Leach, Pioneer Botanists in the Siskiyou Mountains.* Portland, OR: Leach Garden Friends, 1994.

McMurry, Alex. *Oregon Caves Chateau: Oregon Caves National Monument Historic Structures Report.* Eugene: Historic Preservation Program, School of Architecture and Applied Arts, University of Oregon, 1999. Available at www.nps.gov/orca/hsr/hsr.htm.

Webber, Bert, and Margie Webber. *Awesome Caverns of Marble in the Oregon Caves National Monument: Documentary.* Medford, OR: Webb Research Group, 1998.

ORGAN PIPE CACTUS NATIONAL MONUMENT

Location: Ajo, Arizona
Acreage: 330,689
Established: April 13, 1937

Organ Pipe Cactus National Monument is a prickly place, yet even here in the Sonoran Desert of southern Arizona, life has found a way. Despite the harsh aridity—less than 8 inches of precipitation falls here each year—this wilderness ecosystem stretching from the Ajo Mountains of Arizona to the Mexican border provides a critical habitat for jackrabbits, bats, coyotes, hawks, scorpions, gila monsters, and rattlesnakes. But it is the rare succulent, which thrives in this environment of relentless sun, extreme temperatures, and infrequent rains, that gives the monument its name. The organ pipe cactus (*Stenocereus thurberi*) has adapted to the environmental challenges of the desert by perfecting its water storage capabilities in multiple trunks and colonizing south-facing slopes that enable it to withstand the cold temperatures of winter. To ensure that its flowers are not withered by the searing sun, the columnar organ pipe waits until evening to unfurl its blooms for the desert's bats and moths to pollinate. In addition to the stately and ubiquitous saguaro (*Carnegia gigantia*), the park also protects species of barrel cacti (*Ferocactus*), ocotillo (*Fouquieria splendens*), cholla (*Opuntia*), and senita (*Lophocereus schottii*), another rare, columnar cactus found nowhere else in the United States.

Originally proclaimed in April 1937, the almost-331,000-acre Organ Pipe Cactus National Monument was one of the first "representative area" national monuments: parks that were established not because of the scenic spectacularity of their attributes, but because they contained wide expanses of natural attributes. In this sense, such parks can be described as protoecological, for it is their natural essence, not their beauty, that led to establishment. Organ Pipe protects rare Sonoran Desert plants and animals found nowhere else in the United States, and it includes 312,000 acres of federally designated wilderness. The park's Twin Peaks Visitor Center, located on Highway 85, 35 miles south of Ajo, is open year-round from 8 A.M. until 5 P.M. The visitor center features a museum with a photographic exhibit and dioramas of the Sonoran Desert, as well as a fifteen-minute slide program. Park rangers offer evening programs in the amphitheater, ranger-led walks to various points of interest, and informative patio talks at the visitor center. Entrance fees are $3 per person or $5 per vehicle and are valid for seven days; a $15 annual pass is also available.

From October through April, expect sunny days with temperatures in the 60s and 70s and occasional light rains. Springtime is arguably the best time to plan a visit, with beautiful cactus blooms and warm days making for a wonderful trip. During the summer, temperatures often exceed 105 degrees, and brief, violent thunderstorms sometimes occur.

Nights are considerably cooler than days year-round.

There are no food or lodging facilities located in the park, but all traveler services are available in Ajo and Lukeville, Arizona, and Sonoyta, Mexico. Camping within the park is permitted at the Alamo and Twin Peaks campgrounds, both of which are open all year. The Alamo Campground has 4 first-come, first-served primitive sites with a pit toilet, and fees are $6 per night, per site. The Twin Peaks Campground has 208 first-come, first-served campsites with water, rest rooms, grills, tables, and a dump station for $10 per night, per site.

For more information, write Organ Pipe Cactus National Monument, Route 1, Box 100, Ajo, AZ 85321, or telephone (520) 387-6849. The park's Web site is www.nps.gov/orpi.

FURTHER READING

Bezy, John V., James T. Gutmann, and Gordon B. Haxel. *A Guide to the Geology of Organ Pipe Cactus National Monument and the Pinacate Biosphere Reserve.* Tucson: Arizona Geological Survey, 2000.

Broyles, Bill. *Organ Pipe Cactus National Monument: Where Edges Meet: A Sonoran Desert Sanctuary.* Tucson, AZ: Southwest Parks and Monuments Association, 1996.

Wilt, Richard A. *Birds of Organ Pipe Cactus National Monument.* Globe, AZ: Southwest Parks and Monuments Association, 1976.

P

PADRE ISLAND NATIONAL SEASHORE

Location: Corpus Christi, Texas
Acreage: 130,434
Established: September 28, 1962

Padre Island National Seashore, located on the southern Texas coast near Corpus Christi, encompasses 130,000-plus acres of America's vanishing barrier islands—the longest remaining undeveloped barrier island in the world. White sandy beaches, interior grasslands, ephemeral ponds, and the Laguna Madre provide habitat for coyotes, waterfowl, bats, reptiles and amphibians, nesting sea turtles, ground squirrels, and snakes. In geologic terms, Padre Island is relatively young—less than five thousand years old—and it is constantly being reshaped by wind, tides, and storms. While it provides food, water, and shelter for a multitude of diverse wildlife, the island is also a tourist mecca; from sunbathing to windsurfing to fishing, the island provides a variety of recreational opportunities for outdoor enthusiasts.

Perhaps the most important environmental contribution of Padre Island National Seashore is its leading role in the rehabilitation of threatened and endangered sea turtles. The rich waters of the Gulf of Mexico are home to leatherback, hawksbill, green, loggerhead, and Kemp's ridley sea turtles. Like many sensitive species, these marine animals were once abundant, but they have been driven to near-extinction by human development and over-hunting. While all five turtles are now classified as either threatened or endangered, the Kemp's ridley is in the greatest jeopardy. To combat this, Padre Island is in the midst of efforts to establish a second nesting area for these huge and gentle creatures, to complement their original home in Tamaulipas, Mexico. The program, begun in the late 1970s, has required patience, but in 2002, a record twenty-three nests appeared at the seashore—a hopeful sign for the future.

Authorized by Congress in September 1962, Padre Island National Seashore was part of the effort to keep much of the American coastline from becoming private property. The seashore protects a remarkable 80-mile stretch of barrier island along the Gulf Coast. The park's Malaquite Beach Visitor Center, located at 20420 Park Road 22 in Corpus Christi, is open year-round from 8:30 A.M. until 4:30 P.M., and for more extended hours during the summer. Entrance fees are $5 per person or $10 per vehicle, and are valid for seven days; a $20 annual pass is also available. The visitor center has an information desk, small museum, bookstore, concession stand, observation decks, rest rooms and showers (open twenty-four hours), a small auditorium for 20 people, and picnic tables. Information on beach conditions, weather, sea turtle releases, the latest wildlife/bird sightings, and the local area can be found here as well as information on all other aspects of the park. All exhibits are in both Spanish and English, and a three-minute video on sea turtles is available in either Spanish or English.

Educational and interpretive programs are held year-round depending on staffing and weather. Deck talks and beach walks are held almost every day. Deck talks last thirty minutes and are an in-depth discussion of objects including shells, sea beans, and man-made items to be found along the shoreline. Beach walks last forty-five minutes and are guided walks along the beach with a ranger discussing the natural history of the island and items of interest seen along the shore including shells, birds, flotsam, and plants, while touching upon environmental issues of importance to the park. Evening programs may be offered at the Malaquite Beach Campground in summer and winter. These normally last forty-five minutes and may be on a variety of topics from wildlife to history to astronomical topics such as meteor showers, comets, and the constellations. Forty-five-minute bird-watching walks may be offered at Bird Island Basin during migration. An orientation video provides insight into the wonders of the park. It is available upon request year-round at the information desk.

Padre Island's major attractions are fishing, camping, and windsurfing. The Bird Island Basin area on the Laguna Madre is one of the top spots in the nation for windsurfing because of its steady wind, warm water, and shallow depths. Bird Island Basin also has a boat-launching ramp for fishers. Personal water craft, such as jet skis and skidoos, may be launched from the boat ramp at Bird Island Basin, if they are to be used outside of the park boundaries and are taken directly there. They are not permitted in park waters in the Laguna Madre. Personal watercraft are permitted in park waters south of the 5-mile marker on the gulf side. There is only one paved road into the park, but beach driving is permitted. The gulf beach is open to conventional vehicles for the first 5 miles, and then only to four-wheel-drive vehicles beyond that point; off-road vehicles are prohibited, as is driving in the dunes.

The seashore is located southeast of the city of Corpus Christi, Texas. Visitors to Corpus Christi should head east through the city on South Padre Island Drive (Highway 358). After crossing the JFK Causeway and the bridge onto Padre Island, continue about 10 miles south on Park Road 22.

There are no food or lodging facilities in the park, but all traveler services are available locally. The park has 5 designated campgrounds—Bird Island Basin, Malaquite, North Beach, South Beach, and Yarborough Pass; open year-round, they range from primitive to semiprimitive. Fees vary accordingly.

For more information, write Padre Island National Seashore, Superintendent, P.O. Box 181300, Corpus Christi, TX 78480-1300, or telephone (361) 949-8068. The park's Web site is www.nps.gov/pais.

FURTHER READING

Pritchard, Peter Charles Howard, and Rene Marques M. Moreges. *Kemp's Ridley Turtle or Atlantic Ridley: Lepidochelys Kempi.* Gland, Switzerland: International Union for Conservation of Nature and Natural Resources, 1973.

Sheire, James W. *Padre Island National Seashore: Historic Resource Study.* Washington, DC: Office of History & Historic Architecture, 1971.

Weise, Bonnie R., and William A. White. *Padre Island National Seashore: A Guide to the Geology, Natural Environments, and History of a Texas Barrier Island.* Austin: University of Texas at Austin, 1980.

PALO ALTO BATTLEFIELD NATIONAL HISTORIC SITE

Location: Brownsville, Texas
Acreage: 3,407
Established: November 10, 1978

On May 8, 1846, troops of the United States and Mexico clashed on the prairie of Palo Alto in southern Texas in the first battle of the Mexican-American War. The battle itself pitted U.S. General Zachary Taylor's 2,300 men against 4,000 Mexican troops commanded by General Mariano Arista. Although outnumbered, the Americans scored a decisive victory, inflicting casualties estimated between 125 and 400 killed and an additional 100 to 400 injured, and forcing Arista's retreat. General Taylor became an overnight hero and eventually rode his fame to the White House in 1848. Taylor's success at Palo Alto presaged American victory in the war. In the 1848 Treaty of Guadalupe-Hidalgo, Mexico was forced to cede its northern provinces of California and New Mexico (which included present-day Arizona, Utah, Nevada, and part of Colorado) and accept the Rio Grande as the boundary of Texas. In exchange, the United States agreed to pay Mexico $15 million. As the only unit of the National Park Service with a primary focus on the Mexican-American War, Palo Alto Battlefield also interprets the entire conflict—including the details of its origins and the broad range of consequences. In an effort to turn a scene of conflict into a place of binational exchange and understanding, all research and interpretation conducted by the park reflects perspectives of both the United States and Mexico.

Authorized as a National Historic Site in November 1978, this 3,407-acre park preserves the large battlefield on which the first engagement of the war took place. The Palo Alto Battlefield Park Headquarters and Visitor Center is open year-round from 8 A.M. until 4:30 P.M. Monday through Friday, and it features exhibits on the battle of Palo Alto and the Mexican-American War, an orientation video, a book sales area of some 100 titles, and pamphlets about the park and related sites. Palo Alto Battlefield has a relatively small staff and limited visitor activity opportunities at this time. On-site facilities currently consist of a small parking area, a short (600-foot) walking trail, and several informational markers. Nevertheless, the park is entering a period of development and change, and visitors are encouraged to actively participate in this ongoing process.

General Zachary Taylor at the Battle of Palo Alto, Texas, May 8, 1846. *(Library of Congress)*

There are no food, lodging, or camping facilities at the historical site, but all traveler services are available at Brownsville, Harlingen, and South Padre Island.

For more information, write Palo Alto Battlefield National Historic Site, 1623 Central Boulevard, Room 213, Brownsville, TX 78520-8326, or telephone (956) 541-2785. The park's Web site is www.nps.gov/paal.

FURTHER READING

Griswold del Castillo, Richard. *The Treaty of Guadalupe Hidalgo: A Legacy of Conflict.* Norman: University of Oklahoma Press, 1990.

Haecker, Charles M., and Jeffrey G. Mauck. *On the Prairie of Palo Alto: Historical Archaeology of the U.S.-Mexican War Battlefield.* College Station: Texas A&M University Press, 1997.

Thompson, Jerry. *Palo Alto Battlefield National Historic Site.* Tucson, AZ: Southwest Parks and Monuments Association, 2001.

PEA RIDGE NATIONAL MILITARY PARK

Location: Pea Ridge, Arkansas
Acreage: 4,300
Established: July 20, 1956

For the Union during the Civil War, the key goal in the western theater, the area of battle that lay between the Appalachians and the Mississippi River, was the Mississippi. Control of that vital waterway not only guaranteed federal access to the interior but also divided the South in two—one of the oldest available military strategies. A key component in this larger campaign was control of the Missouri River, an important Mississippi tributary, and one way to guarantee that the slave state of Missouri would not slip into Confederate hands. In March 1862, 16,000 Confederates under the command of Major General Earl Van Dorn engaged in a fierce two-day battle against 10,250 Union soldiers under the command of Brigadier General Samuel R. Curtis. The Battle of Pea Ridge, fought in northwest Arkansas on March 7 and 8, was one of the major conflicts in the Civil

War's western theater. The battle also included about 1,000 Cherokees and Choctaw-Chickasaw Indians, who had agreed to fight for the rebels in exchange for representation in the Confederate Congress. The heaviest fighting occurred near the Elkhorn Tavern, where Curtis's artillery bombarded the men in gray and forced Van Dorn to withdraw. "The vulture and the wolf have now communion," Curtis wrote following the battle, "and the dead, friends and foes, sleep in the same lonely grave." The decisive Battle of Pea Ridge indeed saved Missouri for the Union, and the larger campaign for control of the mighty Mississippi concluded successfully the following year with Ulysses S. Grant's victory at Vicksburg on July 4.

The Pea Ridge National Military Park also includes a 2.5-mile segment of the 2,200-mile Trail of Tears National Historic Trail. The Trail of Tears commemorates two of the land and water routes used for the forced removal of more than 15,000 Cherokees from their ancestral lands in North Carolina, Tennessee, Georgia, and Alabama to the Indian Territories of Oklahoma and Arkansas. The journey stretched from June 1838 to March 1839, and 7,000 U.S. Army troops escorting the epic walk watched thousands of Native Americans (perhaps as many as 4,000, or one-quarter) die along the way.

Authorized in July 1956, the 4,300-acre Pea Ridge National Military Park preserves the site of the March 1862 battle that sealed the fate of Missouri—the state and the river—for the Union. The Park Headquarters and Visitor Center is open year-round from 8 A.M. until 5 P.M. The recently renovated visitor center includes a museum, a bookstore, and a new, thirty-minute film that provides background and orientation to the story of the battle. Entrance fees are $3 per person or $5 per vehicle and are valid for seven days; a $15 annual pass is also available. The Elk-

Battle of Pea Ridge, Arkansas, March 8, 1862. *(Library of Congress)*

horn Tavern, a reconstructed wartime structure, is open for tours from Memorial Day through the third week in October. A 7-mile, self-guided automobile tour road is open from 8 A.M. to 4:30 P.M. The drive through the battlefield and its 10 stops is designed to provide information relative to battle action and significant features in each area of the park. A separate 10-mile hiking trail takes visitors into the more natural areas of the park, although it is not designed to give significance to the battle. The military park is an excellent place for viewing wildlife, especially white-tailed deer and wild turkey, as well as spring flower and fall foliage displays. Remembrance activities are scheduled on weekends nearest the anniversary of the battle, on Memorial Day, and Veteran's Day. Currently, the park con-

ducts summer living-history programs and talks on Saturdays and Sundays throughout the summer.

There are no food, lodging, or camping facilities in the park, but all traveler services are available locally. Visitors can pick up supplies in Rogers, Pea Ridge, Garfield, or Eureka Springs, and both Rogers and Eureka Springs offer lodging accommodations. Camping is available 6 miles away at Beaver Lake, which is administered by the U.S. Army Corps of Engineers.

For more information, write Pea Ridge National Military Park, 15930 Highway 62, Garfield, AR 72732, or telephone (479) 451-8122. The park's Web site is www. nps.gov/peri.

FURTHER READING

Shea, William L. *War in the West: Pea Ridge and Prairie Grove.* Fort Worth, TX: Ryan Place, 1996.
Shea, William L., and Earl J. Hess. *Pea Ridge: Civil*

War Campaign in the West. Chapel Hill: University of North Carolina Press, 1992.

PECOS NATIONAL HISTORICAL PARK

Location: Pecos, New Mexico
Acreage: 6,670
Established: June 28, 1965

Located 25 miles east of Santa Fe, New Mexico, the Pecos National Historical Park preserves archeological remains from several cultural groups who have inhabited the Southwest during the last twelve thousand years. Northern New Mexico was the intersection where native peoples, the Spanish, the Mexicans, and the Anglo-Americans came together, at times peacefully and at times violently. The park contains a plethora of archeological sites and historical architecture, the oldest of which are the ruins of Pueblo of Pecos, which reveal the living arrangements of an ancient people who, like other southwestern natives, built shelter out of the cliffs and adobe, and worked and farmed on the mesas surrounding them. Like many other pueblos in the Southwest, the Pueblo of Pecos was abandoned, but its remains provide modern visitors with a fascinating exposure to a prehistoric culture.

Also preserved by the Pecos National Historical Park are 2 Spanish colonial missions, 1 built in the seventeenth century and the other in the eighteenth century. These missions represent one of the primary goals of Spanish presence in its northern territory in the New World. The Spanish sought to extract labor and natural resources from their territories in North America, but they also sought to convert the native inhabitants to Catholicism. To that end, Spanish priests, initially Jesuits and later Dominicans, left a trail of missions across what is now the southwestern United States.

They also inspired the enmity of Pueblo peoples, who erupted in revolt a number of times, the most successful in 1680. That year, the Pueblos drove the Spanish from New Mexico, and at Pecos, sunk a kiva, a Pueblo ceremonial chamber, inside the walls of the destroyed church. This kiva was a powerful symbol of the hatred Pueblos felt for the Spanish and an equally powerful religious statement superimposed upon the church. It suggested a reclaiming not only of land but of culture and faith.

The park is also a site along the Santa Fe Trail, which took traders, settlers, and the military from Missouri to Santa Fe in the nineteenth century. The trail served as a vital link between the new nation of Mexico and the United States, until the Mexican-American War broke out in 1846. After the United States seized full control of the area, the Santa Fe Trail became a national road and sites along it are preserved for their cultural and historical significance in the formation of this nation. The park also preserves a twentieth-century cattle ranch, the Forked Lightning Ranch, which illustrates the important cultural and economic impact of cattle ranching on the western United States.

A particularly interesting portion of the Pecos National Historical Park is the Glorieta Unit, which commemorates the site of one of the most decisive battles of the Civil War. In 1862, the Confederate Army moved west out of Texas in an effort to capture the trade routes, and ultimately Colorado's silver fields, which were in the hands of the U.S. Army. The Confederates moved steadily northwest until they were met at Glorieta Pass, where a decisive battle proved to be a victory for the United States, forcing the Confederate Army to withdraw permanently from the region.

Originally set aside as a national monument in 1965, Pecos was redesignated as a 6,670-acre national historical park in 1990. Entrance fees are $3 per person and are valid for seven days. The E.E. Fogelson Visitor Center is open daily from 8 A.M. until 5 P.M. (until 6 P.M. during the summer), and it provides a short film and various exhibits on the resources protected by the park. During the summer, the park features various cultural artists giving weekend demonstrations, and guided battlefield and ranch tours are available if arranged in advance. Visitors can also take a 13-mile, self-guided trail through Pecos pueblo and mission ruins.

There are no food, lodging, or camping facilities in the park, but all traveler services are available in Pecos and Santa Fe.

For more information, write Pecos National Historical Park, P.O. Box 418, Pecos, NM 87552-0418, or telephone (505) 757-6414. The park's Web site is www.nps.gov/peco.

FURTHER READING

Bandelier, Adolph Francis Alphonse. *Historical Introduction to Studies Among the Sedentary Indians of New Mexico; Report on the Ruins of the Pueblo of Pecos.* New York: AMS Press, 1976.

Dary, David. *The Santa Fe Trail: Its History, Legends, and Lore.* New York: Alfred A. Knopf, 2000.

Edrington, Thomas S. *The Battle of Glorieta Pass: A Gettysburg in the West, March 26–28, 1862.* Albuquerque: University of New Mexico Press, 1998.

Kessell, John L. *Kiva, Cross, and Crown: The Pecos Indians and New Mexico, 1540–1840.* Albuquerque: University of New Mexico Press, 1987.

Vestal, Stanley. *The Old Santa Fe Trail.* Lincoln: University of Nebraska Press, 1996.

PETERSBURG NATIONAL BATTLEFIELD

Location: Petersburg, Virginia
Acreage: 2,659
Established: July 3, 1926

As 1864 ended, the hopes of the Confederate states of America were fading. The army could no longer resist the Union with the intensity of earlier years, and the South's supplies were running out. An aggressive Union campaign focused on ending the war; Petersburg, Virginia, was the key to capturing Richmond, the Confederate capital, and ending the rebellion. Union General Ulysses S. Grant vowed, "I mean to end the business here." For all intents and purposes, he did. The grueling ten-month siege visited upon Petersburg remains the longest in American history, and it exemplified the kind of "total war" that Grant inflicted upon the Confederacy. The war, he believed, had to be fought both on the battlefields and in the daily lives of Southerners themselves. His campaign of annihilation used the statistical strengths of the North—population, factory and ammunition production, transportation—to wear down the resource-limited South in a frightening war of attrition that ground up men and materials at an astonishing rate. The supply lines into Petersburg were the life support of the fading Confederate Army, and both Grant and Confederate General Robert E. Lee knew it.

Beginning in June 1864, the Army of the Potomac methodically and efficiently gnawed away at the thinly stretched men of the Army of Northern Virginia defending Petersburg, encircling the city and cutting off both supply and reinforcement routes. By February 1865, Lee had only 60,000 soldiers to oppose Grant's force of 110,000 men. As Confederate numbers and odds waned, Lee finally evacuated Petersburg on the night of April 2 and headed toward Appomattox Courthouse, Pennsylvania, where he would surrender his command to Grant only a week later.

Located 25 miles south of Richmond in Petersburg, Virginia, the battlefield is comprised of 2,659 acres in 6 major units containing battlefields, earthen forts, trenches, and the Poplar Grove National Cemetery. Collectively, these sites commemorate the longest siege in American warfare and the experiences of the nearly 150,000 soldiers from both sides of the trenches.

From June through August, entrance fees

468 PETERSBURG NATIONAL BATTLEFIELD

Union soldiers in trenches at Petersburg, Virginia, December 1864. *(Library of Congress)*

at the Eastern Front Visitor Center are $5 per person or $10 per vehicle, and are valid for seven days. From September through May, entrance fees are $3 per person or $5 per vehicle, and are valid for seven days. A $15 annual pass is also available for all sites administered by the Petersburg National Battlefield. Grant's Headquarters at City Point is open year-round from 9 A.M. until 5 P.M., and admission is $1 per person. The grounds include Grant's headquarters, a plantation house with furnished rooms and outbuildings, an introductory video, a diorama, and a bookstore. The Five Forks Battlefield Ranger Station is open year-round from 9 A.M. until 5 P.M., while the Poplar Grove National Cemetery Ranger Station is open from mid-June through mid-August. Admission to both is free. The cemetery itself is open year-round. Petersburg National Battlefield is set up as a 15-stop, 26-mile driving tour with a visit to Grant's Headquarters at City Point being essential to the visit.

There are no food, lodging, or camping facilities at the battlefield, but all traveler services are available in Hopewell, Petersburg, and Prince George.

For more information, write Petersburg National Battlefield, 1539 Hickory Hill Road, Petersburg, VA 23803-4721, or telephone (804) 732-3531. The park's Web site is www.nps.gov/pete.

FURTHER READING
Long, E.B. *The Civil War Day by Day: An Almanac, 1861–1865.* New York: Da Capo, 1985.

Slotkin, Richard. *The Crater.* New York: Henry Holt, 1996.

Stevens, Joseph E. *America's National Battlefield Parks: A Guide.* Norman: University of Oklahoma Press, 1990.

PETRIFIED FOREST NATIONAL PARK

Location: Arizona
Acreage: 93,533
Established: December 8, 1906

Petrified Forest National Park appears rather suddenly out of the northeastern Arizona landscape. This national park preserves 3 fascinating features: petroglyphs carved into the stones of the region, a sea of petrified trees, and the beautiful Painted Desert. The park also contains historic structures, ancient fossils, and archeological sites.

Petrified trees litter the ground throughout parts of the park. These amazing stones are like time capsules from the ancient past, symbols of a landscape that disappeared 200 million years ago. During the Triassic Period, this region was in the equatorial region of the landmass known as Pangea. Many streams and rivers coursed through the area, and large trees grew nearly 200 feet tall. When some of these trees died, the rivers carried them into the lowlands and deposited them on the flood plains. A vast majority of the trees decomposed, but a few became petrified.

Buried for millions of years, the petrified logs returned to the surface as a result of earthquakes and the lifting of what is now the Colorado Plateau. Broken into various sized sections as they lifted, the huge chunks of stone in the shape of wood lay scattered over the land, looking as though they had been cut into sections only yesterday. The Petrified Forest is fascinating for visitors, but it is even more fascinating for geologists, who here have access to one of the most complete fossil records of the Triassic Period anywhere in the world.

The park's petroglyphs preserve a human history of the area that is much younger than the Petrified Forest. Using one of two techniques, native inhabitants of the desert Southwest carved their histories into exposed rock surfaces. One technique was to strike a direct blow to the stone with a hand-sized rock. A second, more sophisticated technique used such a rock in conjunction with a chisel. These beautiful pictures carved into rock can be viewed on trails throughout the park.

Perhaps the most awe-inspiring feature of the park, however, is the Painted Desert. Stretching for thousands of acres, these badlands are named for the colorful sedimentary layers that make up the region. About 160 miles long, the Painted Desert arcs through northern Arizona, starting north of the Grand Canyon and extending southeast almost to the New Mexico border. The multicolored layers, ranging from pinks and oranges to grays and lavenders, exist as a result of the varying mineral content of the sediment that makes up the arid badlands. The Chinle Formation, as the sediments of this region are called, is so beautiful because the colorful soil has been carved out as a result of monsoonal weather, with its harsh but sporadic rains, and the lack of protective vegetation. Each century, a foot or two of the surface material erodes, exposing the colors and creating steep hills and crevices.

First set aside as a national monument in 1906, the 93,533-acre Petrified Forest was reclassified as a national park in December 1962. Entrance fees are $5 per person or $10 per vehicle and are valid for seven days; a $20 annual pass is also available. The park's visitor center is open year-round from 8 A.M. until 5 P.M. and has exhibits and a twenty-minute video. Visitors will also enjoy the Rainbow Forest Museum's exhibits of early reptiles, dinosaurs, and petrified wood, and the Painted Desert Inn National Historic Landmark, with displays on the cultural his-

Tourist buying a piece of petrified wood near Petrified Forest National Park, Arizona, c. 1939. *(Library of Congress)*

tory of the Petrified Forest area, Fred Kabotie murals on interior walls, and the work of the Civilian Conservation Corps. Park rangers offer interpretive talks, walks, and hikes, and Native American artisans demonstrate crafts. Visitors can explore the park's natural wonders either on foot or while driving the scenic loops around the park. This landscape is stunning, but it is also extremely fragile. As a result, exploration of the park is limited to established trails for the most part; however, in the Petrified Forest Wilderness, overnight backpackers are allowed to explore with more freedom.

There are no lodging or designated camping facilities in the national park, but all traveler services are available in Holbrook. Food and supplies are available in the park at the cafeteria and store located at the north en-

trance, and also at the snack bar/soda fountain located at the south entrance.

For more information, write Petrified Forest National Park, P.O. Box 2217, Petrified Forest National Park, AZ 86028, or telephone (928) 524-6228. The park's Web site is www.nps.gov/pefo.

FURTHER READING

Bezy, John V., and Arthur S. Trevena. *Guide to Geologic Features at Petrified Forest National Park.* Tucson: Arizona Geological Survey, 2000.

Jones, Anne Trinkle. *Stalking the Past: Prehistory at Petrified Forest.* Petrified Forest National Park, AZ: Petrified Forest Museum Association, 1993.

Long, Robert A., and Rose Houk. *Dawn of the Dinosaurs: The Triassic in Petrified Forest.* Petrified Forest, AZ: Petrified Forest Museum Association, 1988.

Lubick, George M. *Petrified Forest National Park: A Wilderness Bound in Time.* Tucson: University of Arizona Press, 1996.

McCreery, Patricia. *Tapamveni: The Rock Art Galleries of Petrified Forest and Beyond.* Petrified Forest, AZ: Petrified Forest Museum Association, 1994.

PETROGLYPH NATIONAL MONUMENT

Location: Albuquerque, New Mexico
Acreage: 7,232
Established: June 27, 1990

The 7,232-acre Petroglyph National Monument preserves more than 15,000 prehistoric and historic Native American and Hispanic petroglyphs—images carved in rock—along a 17-mile stretch of the escarpment. Proclaimed in 1990, the monument on West Mesa lies on the direct line with the urban sprawl of Albuquerque, New Mexico's largest city. Its establishment was a direct response to the growth of the city and its environs. Plans for a thruway threatened the petroglyphs, and concerted effort by park advocates and an energized local population played a significant role in the preservation of these treasures of prehistory.

The petroglyphs are only the most visible dimension of the long history of human habitation along West Mesa. Since prehistory, people have traversed and inhabited the area. The Piedras Marcadas people were the most significant occupants, but the region was part of a larger zone of interaction among various people, cultures, and language groups in late-fifteenth-century and sixteenth-century pre-contact New Mexico. These include the pueblos to the west, such as Laguna, Acoma, and Zuni, as well as those to the north, including Santo Domingo, San Felipe, and Zia. Archeologists have suggested that the Petroglyph National Monument area was likely a hunting ground or a spiritual site for prehistoric peoples.

The Spanish and Mexican era, stretching from 1540 to 1846, began with the arrival of Vásquez de Coronado in 1540. It saw the slow expansion of northern New Spain and various incarnations of the Territory of New Mexico under the Mexican republic. Almost sixty years after the 1540–1542 expedition, Don Juan de Oñate came north to establish a Spanish colony. Throughout the seventeenth century, this was a tenuous endeavor, culminating in the Pueblo Revolt of 1680. Although efforts at colonization were substantial during this time, the roots such colonies sank were not deep enough to withstand the uprising of the natives that the Spanish sought to subjugate and convert.

The Spanish *entrada* into Santa Fe in 1694, which completed the *reconquista*, the process of reclaiming New Mexico after the uprising, set the stage for more permanent colonization. The founding of Albuquerque in 1706 was one piece of the slow and often unsteady development of the colony. Hampered by its great distance from sources of Spanish wealth and power in New Spain, the technological limitations of seventeenth- and eighteenth-century life and society, and a small Spanish émigré population, New Mexico remained a remote outpost.

One of the most salient characteristics of the Spanish era was the system of land grants and the patterns of use it established. In a time when land held the key to wealth, its ownership was a defining feature of the history of peripheral areas. Two primary land grants in the region, the Atrisco Land Grant of 1680 and the Town of Alameda grant of 1710, became central to the history of West Mesa. However, unirrigated land in New Mexico had little value, and even more important than land were the rights to water that accompanied it. Patterns of use, beginning with water allocation and covering agriculture, ranching, social and community relations, religious practices including those of the Penitente Brotherhood, and the development of ties through trade and transportation routes, shaped life in the region.

The patterns of the Spanish era continued after 1821, when Agustín de Iturbide, a Spanish officer, declared Mexico independent. New Mexico remained part of the new nation, but unlike most Mexican provinces, the central government granted it territorial status instead of statehood. Its governance fell under the direct control of the Mexican Congress, a kind of centralization that ran contrary to the ideal of regional autonomy so essential in the Mexican Constitution of 1824.

The arrival of the Americans in 1846 inaugurated another phase in the history of New Mexico and West Mesa. Despite the Treaty of Guadalupe Hidalgo, which guaranteed the rights and property of former Mexican citizens in the area annexed by the United States, the American legal system often failed to respect land claims and tenure dating from the Spanish and Mexican eras. It also initiated stronger trade ties with the United States, accentuated even more greatly by the coming of the railroad and the arrival of Anglo-Americans who sought to acquire land through whatever means available. U.S. property law was different, as were the practices of a nation linked by the railroad and dependent on the machined miracles of industrialization. In New Mexico, this had immediate and ever-growing importance, particularly for peripheral areas such as West Mesa. The actions alienated New Mexico lands from their traditional owners. They were used more intensively than in the past, and often overgrazing and timber-cutting upstream led to flooding along the river. The Alameda grant, now known as the community of Corrales, experienced this cause-and-effect relationship during the second half of the nineteenth century.

After statehood in 1912, the patterns begun with the arrival of the Americans continued with even greater force. Beginning in the middle of the twentieth century and accelerating greatly with the coming of World War II, Albuquerque grew in size and importance. New Mexico became a center of federal sci-

ence, initiating growth that has continued over the past fifty years. Federal agencies of all kinds gained great importance in New Mexico, and municipalities such as Albuquerque, Corrales, and Rio Rancho exerted a tremendous impact on West Mesa. The land acquisition policies of Albuquerque, the suburbanization of West Mesa and its bedroom community status, construction of highways and bridges, and other evidence of growth accentuated the need for the establishment of a national park area.

Some form of protection for these valuable cultural resources became necessary as the growth of greater Albuquerque increasingly encroached upon the petroglyphs of West Mesa, and people built homes and roads, picnicked, hiked, camped, drank, and conducted target practice. Two parks, Indian Petroglyph State Park and Volcano City Park, initiated the response to growth and development. In 1990, Congress established Petroglyph National Monument to encompass the five extinct volcanoes along the western horizon of Albuquerque, as well as the 17-mile cliff below that contains innumerable examples of prehistoric rock art.

Like the national monuments of the early twentieth century, Congress created Petroglyph National Monument to save its resources from wanton destruction. A "city park" from its inception, the monument reflected all of the problems of such areas. Preserving prehistory was only one of many management responsibilities; protecting natural and cultural resources and ambience and coordination of land acquisition and management activities with the state and the city of Albuquerque became recurring obligations.

The story of Petroglyph National Monument and its surroundings is a story often repeated in the history of New Mexico. Places once remote and inhospitable, lacking the necessities to sustain life for preindustrial people, remained protected by their isolation.

Home to a hardy few individuals with strong and deep ties, such places maintained an iconoclastic independence. Transportation technologies provided the catalyst for long-term transformation, creating new economic and social relations to accompany improved access. Over time this led to changes in patterns of land ownership and use and pressure on cultural features previously protected by their inaccessibility. In places with resources of cultural significance, national park areas often followed in the wake of such changes, responding to an increasingly urbanized environment. The historical patterns of places such as Petroglyph National Monument and West Mesa have tremendous meaning for the American public. They tell the story of the transformation of New Mexico and, in a broader sense, that of the western United States.

The park's Las Imagenes Visitor Center is open daily from 8 A.M. until 5 P.M. throughout the year and offers rotating topical exhibits and weekend cultural demonstrations from Memorial Day through Labor Day. There are no camping or lodging facilities in the park, but nearby Albuquerque offers all traveler services.

For more information, write Petroglyph National Monument, 6001 Unser Boulevard NW, Albuquerque, NM 87120-2033, or telephone (505) 899-0205. The park's Web site is www.nps.gov/petr.

FURTHER READING

Lamb, Susan. *Petroglyph National Monument.* Tucson, AZ: Southwest Parks and Monuments Association, 1993.

Welsh, Michael. *West Side Stories: Land Use and Social Change in Albuquerque's Petroglyph Area.* Sante Fe, NM: National Park Service, 1998.

PICTURED ROCKS NATIONAL LAKESHORE

Location: Munising, Michigan
Acreage: 73,236
Established: October 15, 1966

One of America's most beautiful lakeshore regions is protected by Pictured Rocks National Lakeshore in northern Michigan. Set aside in 1966, the 73,000-plus-acre Pictured Rocks, which preserves 40 miles of Lake Superior shoreline and other cultural and natural resources, significantly broadened the mission and scope of the National Park Service to include the new category of national lakeshore. Pictured Rocks National Lakeshore encompasses many of the natural landscape features that have made northern Michigan renowned for its beauty—multicolored sandstone cliffs, inland lakes, forest, waterfalls, and beaches. One early naturalist wrote that "the lake coast presents a succession of bold and rocky cliffs, with leaping streams and dunes of sand, which give many strange and wild features to the scenery of that wonderful region." Today, backcountry campgrounds allow visitors to explore the forest, to fish, and to enjoy the lake. In the spring, there is a burst of wildflowers that adds to the stunning beauty of the region. Summer is marked by perfect lake weather, with warm temperatures and lots of sunshine. In the fall, the forest takes center stage as the leaves change color, and in the winter, snowfall and ice combine with the forest and lake to create a winter wonderland of activities.

Cultural resources at the park include the Grand Marais Coast Guard Station, which protected lake goers during the mid-1930s. Converted into a museum by the National Park Service, the Grand Marais Maritime Museum portrays the maritime history of Lake Superior and presents exhibits on Lake Superior shipwrecks. The remains of 1 of these shipwrecks and a historic lighthouse can be seen near the Hurricane River Campground. The Grand Marais Museum also has exhibits concerning the U.S. Life Saving Service, a forerunner to the Coast Guard.

In addition to the museum, there are 3 visitor centers located in the park that provide

Cross-country skiing in the forest at Pictured Rocks National Lakeshore. *(National Park Service)*

information and interpretive exhibits for people who wish to explore the beauty of northern Michigan. The Grand Sable Visitor Center, located 1 mile west of Grand Marais, is open from mid-May to early September; the Munising Falls Interpretive Center is open from May through October; and the Pictured Rocks/Hiawatha Visitor Information Center in Munising is open year-round. Admission to the lakeshore is free. There are paved trails and boardwalks at Munising Falls and the Sand Point Marsh Trail, and park rangers offer guided day hike and evening campfire programs during the summer.

There are no food or lodging facilities at the lakeshore, but all traveler services are available in Grand Marais and Munising. The park maintains 3 campgrounds, and sites are available on a first-come, first-served basis with an overnight fee of $10.

For more information, write Pictured Rocks National Lakeshore, P.O. Box 40, N8391 Sand Point Road, Munising, MI 49862-0040, or telephone (906) 387-3700. The park's Web site is www.nps.gov/piro.

FURTHER READING

Anderson, Olive M. *Pictured Rocks National Lakeshore: An Illustrated Guide.* Munising, MI: Bayshore Press, 1988.

Chadde, Steve W. *Plants of Pictured Rocks National Lakeshore: A Complete Illustrated Guide to the Plants of America's First National Lakeshore.* Laurium, MI: Pocketflora Press, 1996.

Karamanski, Theodore J. *The Pictured Rocks: An Administrative History of Pictured Rocks National Lakeshore.* Omaha, NE: National Park Service, Midwest Regional Office, 1995. Available at www.nps.gov/piro/adhi/adhi.htm.

PINNACLES NATIONAL MONUMENT
Location: Paicines, California
Acreage: 17,855
Established: January 16, 1908

Looming above the chaparral-covered Gabilan Mountains, east of central California's Salinas Valley, are the crags and spires of an ancient volcano. These massive monoliths, sheer-walled canyons, and talus passages are the evidence and result of millions of years of erosion, faulting, and tectonic plate movement. The origin of Pinnacles dates back more than 30 million years, when molten lava began pouring out of a 5-mile-long rift—part of the San Andreas Rift Zone—creating a mountain that geologists estimate may have been as high as 8,000 feet above sea level—more than three times the present-day height. Over time, the earth's crust heaved and buckled, cracking the ancient lavas, and millions of years of erosion carved the park's namesake pinnacles. The monument itself is situated on the Pacific plate within the rift zone, and two faults bisect the park: the Chalone Creek Fault on the eastern side and the Pinnacles Fault on the western, with the narrow Bear Gulch gorge in between. The Pinnacles "sister rock"—the other part of the same volcanic activity—has moved nearly 200 miles to the southeast as the plates have shifted. In addition to its geologic wonders, the monument is renowned for the beauty and variety of its spring wildflowers, and a rich diversity of wildlife can be observed throughout the year.

Proclaimed as a national monument in January 1908, the park protects the rugged chaparral environment of the Gabilan Range in west-central California, as well as nearly 13,000 acres of wilderness. Entrance fees are $2 per person or $5 per vehicle and are valid for seven days; a $15 annual pass is also available. Pinnacles National Monument is divided into east and west districts that are connected by trails but not by a vehicle road. The Bear Gulch Visitor Center, located in the east district, is open year-round from 9 A.M. to 5 P.M., and features a seismograph, park topographical map, and various natural and cultural history exhibits. The Chaparral

Ranger Station, located in the west district, is open year-round from 9 A.M. to 5 P.M. (when staffing permits) and has exhibits on the park's natural and cultural history. Ranger-led walks occur every Saturday and Sunday beginning in front of the ranger station at 2 P.M. More than 30 miles of trails access geological formations, spectacular vistas, and wildland communities, while the Pinnacles' rock formations are a popular destination to challenge technical climbers. Pinnacles is a day-use park, but it occasionally offers full-moon hikes and dark-sky astronomical observations led by ranger-interpreters. The primary importance of Pinnacles National Monument is that of a natural preserve and recreational area, and the main visitor uses of the park are hiking, technical rock climbing, and as a place to study and observe the natural ecology of central California. Pinnacles has a rich flora and fauna and a complex and spectacular geology. Birding, wildflower walks, and the study of volcanic and plate tectonics are popular activities.

There are no lodging facilities at the monument, but all traveler services are available in Hollister, King City, and Soldad. The park's campground is operated on a first-come, first-served basis, and it offers bathrooms and water but no hookups or showers. The Pinnacles Campground store has food and supplies, and private campgrounds are available just outside the park.

For more information, write Pinnacles National Monument, 5000 Highway 146, Paicines, CA 95043, or telephone (831) 389-4485. The park's Web site is www. nps.gov/pinn.

FURTHER READING

Matthews, Vincent. *Pinnacles Geological Trail.* Globe, AZ: Southwest Parks and Monuments Association, 1972.

Webb, Ralph C. *A Guide to the Plants of the Pinnacles.* Globe, AZ: Southwest Parks and Monuments Association, 1971.

Webb, Ralph C., ed. *Natural History of the Pinnacles National Monument, San Benito County, California.*

Paicines, CA: Pinnacles Natural History Association, 1969.

PIPE SPRING NATIONAL MONUMENT

Location: Fredonia, Arizona
Acreage: 40
Established: May 31, 1923

Located near Fredonia, Arizona, Pipe Spring National Monument is a prime example of the strategies that the first National Park Service director, Stephen T. Mather, used to build the park system. In the early 1920s, he took Representative Louis Cramton, head of the U.S. House of Representatives Appropriations Committee and a friend of the National Park Service, on a driving tour of the Southwest. Mather wanted to enlist Cramton's support for more funding and more new parks. Pipe Spring was located about halfway between Hurricane, Utah, and the north rim of the Grand Canyon. The long dusty drive in an open 1920 automobile, Mather knew, was sure to make Pipe Spring an important attraction: Its water would be like gold after bouncing along the hot, dusty rutted roads. Mather's trick worked. Cramton enthusiastically supported the addition of Pipe Spring as a national monument, a stopping place on the auto journeys that the Park Service aggressively promoted in the 1920s.

Pipe Spring's historical importance derived from its water. The spring sustained both the Paiute people and the members of the Church of Latter Day Saints, the Mormons, who replaced them. Native American inhabitants were part of the Pueblo and Kaibab Paiute cultures, which together had almost a thousand-year history in the area watered by the spring. During the 1860s, the Mormon Church sought to expand the boundaries of its nation-state of Deseret. It sent settlers to the far reaches of its vision, among other things, initiating cattle ranching in the Arizona strip. In 1872, the Mormons

built a fort atop the springs, initiating conflict with the Paiutes who depended on it. Named "Winsor Castle," the old fort is one of the preserved historic buildings at Pipe Spring National Monument and can still be explored on ranger-guided tours.

Pipe Spring ranch was privately owned, but in 1907, it was surrounded by the Kaibab Paiute Indian Reservation. In 1923, after Mather's trip and Cramton's appropriation, the federal government bought the ranch and established it as a 40-acre national monument. An orchard, garden, corrals, complete with longhorn cattle and horses, and 2 historic cabins are preserved within the monument. Entrance fees are $3 per person (under seventeen admitted free) and are valid for seven days. The park's visitor center is open year-round from 8 A.M. until 5 P.M. (open at 7 A.M. during the summer), and offers exhibits on pioneer and Native American lifestyles, the development and use of Pipe Spring by American Indian groups and Mormon settlers, and a short introductory video. Three historic buildings are open to the public: Winsor Castle (the fort) is accessible only by ranger-guided tours offered every thirty minutes, and the East and West Cabins, which can be visited by self-guided tour along a 2-mile trail offering impressive views of the Arizona Strip. During the summer months, park rangers give daily, guided walks, talks, and demonstrations of pioneer and Native American crafts and lifeways.

Pipe Spring National Monument is located 15 miles east of Fredonia, and about 45 miles from Hurricane, on the border of Utah. Camping is available just outside the monument at the Kaibab-Paiute Tribe Campground. There is a small café next to the gift shop at the monument, and all traveler services are available in Fredonia, Arizona, and Kanab, Utah.

For more information, write Pipe Spring National Monument, HC 65, Box 5, 401 North Pipe Spring

Road, Fredonia, AZ 86022, or telephone (928) 643-7105. The park's Web site is www.nps.gov/pisp.

FURTHER READING

Lavender, David Sievert. *Pipe Spring and the Arizona Strip.* Springdale, UT: Zion Natural History Association, 1984.

McKoy, Kathleen L. *Cultures at a Crossroads: An Administrative History of Pipe Spring National Monument.* Denver, CO: National Park Service, Intermountain Region, 2000. Available at www.nsp.gov/pisp/adhi/adhi.htm.

Rothman, Hal K. *America's National Monuments: The Politics of Preservation.* Lawrence: University Press of Kansas, 1994.

PIPESTONE NATIONAL MONUMENT

Location: Pipestone, Minnesota
Acreage: 282
Established: August 25, 1937

Pipestone National Monument protects a place of vast cultural importance to the Yankton Lakota and other Plains Indian peoples. The monument preserves a quarry that has provided pipestone for Native American stone pipes for four centuries. The pipestone that comes from this quarry has been considered among the best in North America.

Pipes play an important role in the cultural traditions of Plains Indians. Each group, including the Sioux, Crow, Pawnee, and Blackfoot tribes, identifies itself with the pipestone, and Plains peoples have long associated stone pipes with significant social and cultural events. Pipes have been used for centuries as gifts, to finalize agreements between tribes and individuals, and in religious ceremonies. Archeologists have identified stone

A pipe carver at Pipestone National Monument. Although Plains Indian culture has undergone radical changes, pipe carving is not a lost art. Today, carvings are appreciated as artworks, as well as for ceremonial use. *(National Park Service)*

pipes that date back approximately two thousand years.

Native Americans began quarrying pipestone from this site in western Minnesota in the seventeenth century, and the beautiful, soft stone—ranging in color from spotted pink to brick red—quickly became the preferred material for pipestone carvers. By about 1700, the Dakota Sioux had exerted control over the area and regulated the quarrying, but, prior to this time, the sacred site was used freely by several tribes. During the mid-1800s, the Yankton established sole rights to Pipestone through treaty, in one instance enforced by U.S. cavalry that pushed Anglo-American settlers off the site. By 1928, the Yankton had been relocated to a reservation more than 100 miles away, and they sold their rights to the federal government. Designated as a national monument in August 1937, this 282-acre park is managed by the National Park Service. Active quarrying continues and is limited to people of Native American ancestry.

Entrance fees are $2 per person or $4 per family, and are valid for seven days; a $10 annual pass is also available. The park's visitor center and the Upper Mid-West Indian Cultural Center are open year-round from 8 A.M. until 5 P.M. (and for more extended hours during the summer), and these centers feature pipe and pipestone artifacts and an informative slide program. The Exhibit Quarry allows visitors to enter a former quarry and view the layers of prairie soil and Sioux quartzite overburden, as well as the pipestone layer, up close. During the summer, park rangers lead interpretive tours, and from April through October, the park sponsors Native American craft demonstrations. Pipestone National Monument also protects pristine examples of tallgrass prairie that survived the farming boom of the nineteenth century, and a three-quarter-mile Circle Trail takes visitors through native prairie to the pipestone quarries and Winnewissa Falls. During the summer, rangers along the trail provide information about the cultural traditions surrounding pipestone use, prairie plants and their medicinal use by Native Americans, and early European-American exploration.

There are no food, lodging, or camping facilities at the monument, but all traveler services are available in Pipestone, Minnesota, and Sioux Falls, South Dakota.

For more information, write Pipestone National Monument, 36 Reservation Avenue, Pipestone, MN 56164-1269, or telephone (507) 825-5464. The park's Web site is www.nps.gov/pipe.

FURTHER READING

Catlin, George. *Indian Art in Pipestone: George Catlin's Portfolio in the British Museum.* Washington, DC: Smithsonian Institution Press, 1979.

A History of Pipestone County. Pipestone, MN: Pipestone County Historical Society, 1984.

Rothman, Hal K. *Preserving the Sacred and the Secular: An Administrative History of Pipestone National Monument.* Omaha, NE: National Park Service, 1992.

POINT REYES NATIONAL SEASHORE

Location: Point Reyes, California
Acreage: 71,068
Established: September 13, 1962

The original settlers of Point Reyes were the coastal Miwok Indians, whose regional population probably reached about 10,000 by the mid-eighteenth century. The Miwoks lived in kin-based villages of large, round, earth-covered lodges, and more than 120 sites are known to exist in the park today. The first whites to venture into the area were the European explorers accompanying Sir Francis Drake, who landed in Drakes Bay in 1579. Until the 1840s, however, California would be largely the domain of the Spanish and Mexico, and not the British, and Point Reyes draws its name from this heritage, Punta de Los Reyes, or Point of the Kings. The national seashore also serves as a refuge for an astonishing number of rare plants and birds—

The biological diversity at Point Reyes National Seashore stems from a favorable location and the natural occurrence of many distinct habitats. Nearly 20 percent of California's flowering plant species are represented on the peninsula. *(National Park Service)*

23 threatened and endangered plants find sanctuary in this protected ecosystem. In all, more than 45 percent of North American bird species and nearly 20 percent of California's native flora can be found in the park. And finally, in addition to its ecological and cultural importance, Point Reyes is also a geologically significant area. This triangular-shaped peninsula was once far south of San Francisco, much closer to Los Angeles. Geologists estimate that a few million years from now, it will continue to move north and west and out to sea. The remarkable mobility of the peninsula is due to its position along the very active San Andreas Fault. On April 18, 1906, for example, Point Reyes moved 21 feet northwestward, in the earthquake that destroyed San Francisco.

Set aside by President John F. Kennedy in 1962 to protect this remarkable ecosystem, Point Reyes was part of the complicated effort to preserve the Golden Gate and its surroundings. As urban development engulfed the San Francisco Bay area, active conservation groups created the context in which Point Reyes was preserved. It became a precursor to Golden Gate National Recreation Area—in which Point Reyes was included for a number of years—an important cog in the most comprehensive urban shoreline preservation system in the nation. Point Reyes affords the modern visitor exceptional opportunities for bird-watching, especially during fall and spring migrations, as well as an excellent vantage point for viewing the annual gray whale migration, January through April. Point

Reyes maintains 3 visitor centers that are open year-round. The park's primary visitor center is Bear Valley, located in Olema, which is open from 9 A.M. until 5 P.M. Monday through Friday, and from 8 A.M. until 5 P.M. on weekends. In addition to a dramatic slide presentation on the seashore, the center offers exhibits on the natural and cultural heritage of the park as well as a weather station, seismograph, touch table, and bookstore.

The Kenneth C. Patrick Visitor Center, on Drakes Beach, is open on weekends and holidays from 10 A.M. until 5 P.M., and also during the summer months. It features exhibits on early maritime exploration as well as a 250-gallon saltwater aquarium.

The Lighthouse Visitor Center, on the Point Reyes Headlands, is open Thursday through Monday from 10 A.M. until 4:30 P.M. and features displays on whales, maritime history, and native flora and fauna. Visitors can also explore the Point Reyes Historic Lighthouse, which is open Thursday through Monday from 10 A.M. until 4:30 P.M.

The only lodging within Point Reyes National Seashore (other than backcountry camping) is the Hostelling International–Point Reyes, which offers dormitory-style accommodations, as well as one private room for parents with children five years of age or younger. The hostel is open all year and can be reached at (451) 663-8811, or see its Web site at www.norcalhostels.org/pointreyes.html.

The park also has 4 hike-in campgrounds with individual sites, which cost $12 per site and can accommodate from 1 to 6 people. Only boat-in camping is permitted on Tomales Bay. Backcountry permits are available at the Bear Valley Visitor Center or by reservation. Reservations are strongly recommended (especially for weekends and during holidays) and may be made Monday through Friday 9 A.M. to 2 P.M. by calling (415) 663-8054. Otherwise, all traveler services are available in the communities surrounding the seashore.

On weekends from late December to mid-April when the weather is good, the west end of Sir Francis Drake Boulevard is closed to vehicle traffic, and shuttle buses transport visitors to the lighthouse and Chimney Rock areas. Shuttle tickets are $4 per person over twelve years of age and may be purchased at Drakes Beach. The shuttle buses run approximately every twenty minutes and service the headlands area from Drakes Beach to the Lighthouse parking lot to Chimney Rock parking lot back to Drakes Beach. Shuttles are cancelled if weather is poor.

For more information, write Point Reyes National Seashore, Point Reyes CA 94956, or telephone (415) 464-5100. The park's Web site is www.nps.gov/pore.

FURTHER READING

Blair, Richard P. *Point Reyes Visions: Photographs and Essays, Point Reyes National Seashore and West Marin.* Inverness, CA: Color and Light Editions, 1999.

Evens, Jules G. *The Natural History of the Point Reyes Peninsula.* Point Reyes, CA: Point Reyes National Seashore Association, 1988.

Griffin, L. Martin. *Saving the Marin-Sonoma Coast: The Battles for Audubon Canyon Ranch, Point Reyes, and California's Russian River.* Healdsburg, CA: Sweetwater Springs, 1998.

Kiver, Eugene P., and David V. Harris. *Geology of U.S. Parklands.* New York: John Wiley and Sons, 1999.

Martin, Don. *Point Reyes National Seashore: A Hiking and Nature Guide.* New York: Martin, 1997.

PORT CHICAGO NAVAL MAGAZINE NATIONAL MEMORIAL

Location: Concord Naval Weapons Station, California
Acreage: not applicable
Established: October 28, 1992

On December 7, 1941, the bombing of Pearl Harbor brought the United States into World War II. In early 1942, as the demand for ammunition in the Pacific theater expanded, the United States began construction on the Port Chicago Naval Magazine, 35 miles north of

San Francisco. By 1944, the pier could simultaneously equip two ships with their volatile cargo. Most of the personnel units assigned to this dangerous work were African Americans, commanded, as was typical of the era, by white officers.

Tragedy struck on the evening of July 17, 1944, as 320 cargo handlers, crewmen, and sailors were busy loading the SS *Quinault Victory* and the SS *E.A. Bryan*. Suddenly, at 10:18 P.M., a chain-reaction explosion ripped through the facility, creating a seismic shock wave felt as far away as Boulder City, Nevada. Both ships were utterly destroyed, and all 320 men on duty were killed instantly, while another 390 were wounded. The 202 African American men killed that night accounted for 15 percent of all African American casualties in World War II, and the accident constituted the largest domestic loss of American lives during the war.

If this horror had a positive aspect, it was that the calamity and its aftermath acted as a catalyst for the United States military to begin the long journey toward racial justice and equal rights. Although African Americans had served in the ranks of the U.S. Navy since 1942, they continued to serve in segregated units commanded by white officers until the integration of the nation's armed forces in 1948.

Port Chicago Naval Magazine National Memorial is administered by the National Park Service and the U.S. Navy. It honors the memory of those who gave their lives and were injured in the explosion on July 17, 1944, recognizes those who served at the magazine, and commemorates the role of the facility during World War II. The Port Chicago Memorial, located at the Concord Naval Weapons Station, has several wayside exhibits and artifacts, but the chapel, museum, and memorial are open to the public by appointment only. A memorial ceremony is held annually in mid-July for the survivors and their

families and is open to the public by reservation only.

A substantial portion of the base has also been designated as a wildlife preserve. Deer, tule elk, golden eagles, quail, pheasants, and foxes are just some of the many animals that visitors may see in the park.

For more information, write Port Chicago Naval Magazine National Memorial, National Park Service, P.O. Box 280, Danville, CA 94526, or telephone (925) 838-0249. The park's Web site is www.nps.gov/poch.

FURTHER READING
Allen, Robert L. *The Port Chicago Mutiny.* New York: Penguin, 1993.

POVERTY POINT NATIONAL MONUMENT/STATE COMMEMORATIVE AREA

Location: Epps, Louisiana
Acreage: 911
Established: October 31, 1988

According to archeological evidence, prehistoric peoples entered the Louisiana area nearly ten thousand years ago and, over time, developed a sophisticated and far-reaching civilization in the Lower Mississippi Valley. Significantly, at Poverty Point, these ancestors of such modern tribes as the Creek, Shawnee, and Natchez left a remarkable and mysterious treasure: the largest and most elaborate earthworks in the entire western hemisphere.

In its heyday, Poverty Point was the locus of government and commercial trade in the region. Radiocarbon dating has determined that these engineering marvels were built sometime between 1730 and 1350 B.C.E., roughly the same historical era during which Britain's Stonehenge was constructed. The mounds' monumental nature indicates that the society that created them had moved beyond primitive subsistence, since construction required communal laborers to haul dirt in 50-pound-capacity baskets—an endeavor not likely in a society struggling to survive. Poverty Point Mound, itself, is a 70-foot-high, bird-shaped effigy, measuring approximately 700 feet by 640 feet at its base; to the north is the 20-foot-high Mound B.

Archeologists also have identified a number of characteristic artifacts associated with Poverty Point, including chipped and polished stone tools, and ornaments such as pendants and animal figures. Perhaps the most distinguishing hallmark of the culture are the so-called "clay balls," which were, in fact, made of silt. The prehistoric peoples heated these balls and packed them around food in a pit, which was then covered, creating an ingenious oven. Found in dozens of different styles and sizes, the balls were so common that archeologists simply referred to these artifacts as Poverty Point objects.

In 1962, Poverty Point was designated a national historic landmark by the U.S. Department of the Interior. Located in northeastern Louisiana, this 911-acre park commemorates a culture that thrived during the first and second millennia B.C.E. and preserves some of the largest prehistoric earthworks in North America. Entrance fees are $2 per person.

The monument is managed by the state of Louisiana, and there are no federal facilities. The museum has an audiovisual presentation, and numerous artifacts that were found on the site are on display. An archeological laboratory, picnic areas, an observation tower, rest rooms, and self-guided hiking trails complete the facility. The park also sponsors a number of special events, programs, and guided tours including tram tours between the Easter and Labor Day holidays.

There are no food, lodging, or camping facilities at the historic site, but all traveler services are available in nearby communities.

For more information, write Poverty Point State Historic Site, P.O. Box 276, Epps, LA 71237, or telephone (888) 926-5492. The park's Web site is www.nps.gov/popo.

FURTHER READING
Byrd, Kathleen M., ed. *The Poverty Point Culture: Local Manifestations, Subsistence Practices, and Trade Networks.* Baton Rouge: Department of Geography and Anthropology, Louisiana State University, 1991.
Gibson, Jon L. *Poverty Point: A Terminal Archaic Culture of the Lower Mississippi Valley.* Baton Rouge: Department of Culture, Recreation, and Tourism, Louisiana Archaeological Survey and Antiquities Commission, 1983. Available at www.crt.state.la.us/crt/ocd/arch/poverpoi/mapopo.htm.
Webb, Clarence H. *The Poverty Point Culture.* Baton Rouge: Louisiana State University School of Geoscience, 1982.

PRINCE WILLIAM FOREST PARK
Location: Triangle, Virginia
Acreage: 18,942
Established: November 14, 1936

In 1607, the area around Quantico Creek, originally the home of native Algonquin people, was invaded by European colonists intent on wresting wealth from the land. Their cultivation of cash crops such as tobacco depleted the soil's fertility, and their forest-clearing efforts led to the erosion and gullying of the land. Faced with diminishing returns, the region's plantation owners gradually abandoned their estates or divided their holdings into small farms, and by the turn of the twentieth century, the land had begun to recover and the forest was returning. In 1933, Congress set aside the Prince William Forest Park, about 30 miles south of the nation's capital, as the Chopawamsic Recreational Demonstration area, one of forty-six recreation demonstration projects in twenty-five states selected for rehabilitation and restoration. The Civilian Conservation Corps (CCC) began construction of five cabin camps, numerous roads and lakes, miles of trails, and utility systems, and today, the 18,942-acre park preserves a rich piedmont forest covering a major portion of the Quantico Creek watershed. The fact that the park is the largest protected greenspace in the metropolitan Washington, D.C., area, combined with its protection of one of the few remaining piedmont forest ecosystems in the national park system, make it an important national asset.

The Prince William Forest Park Visitor Center is open year-round from 8:30 A.M. until 5 P.M., and ranger-led walks and evening programs are offered throughout the year. Entrance fees are $2 per person or $4 per vehicle and are valid for three days; a $15 annual pass is also available. The park has 37 miles of hiking trails, and the Chopawamsic Backcountry area offers 400 acres of undeveloped camping experience. The Park Scenic Drive provides access to all trails and features in the park, and 4 miles of the area serve as a dedicated bike lane providing a paved, relatively flat surface ideal for beginning bicyclists. More experienced cyclists with mountain bikes have the option of off-road biking on any of the ten fire roads in the park.

Lodging is available in the park in 5 cabin camps with a capacity of 200 people, and reservations can be made by calling the park. Lodging is also available in Dumfries and Triangle, as are most traveler services. The park maintains 3 campgrounds that are open year-round. The Oak Ridge Campground is open on a first-come, first-served basis, and it has tables, fire grill (firewood provided), parking space, and room for tents or small recreational vehicles. Fees are $10 per night. The Travel Trailer Village (703-221-2474) is a private, concessionaire-operated, full-service recreational vehicle campground located on the north side of the park. The Turkey Run Ridge Campground is exclusively for group tent camping and provides picnic tables, grills, firewood, parking, and tent space. Reservations are required and fees are $30 per night.

For more information, write Prince William Forest Park, 18100 Park Headquarters Road, Triangle, VA 22172, or telephone (703) 221-7181. The park's Web site is www.nps.gov/prwi.

FURTHER READING

Ayers, Edward L., and John C. Willis, eds. *The Edge of the South: Life in Nineteenth-Century Virginia.* Charlottesville: University Press of Virginia, 1991.

Bearr, David W.C., ed. *Historic Fluvanna in the Commonwealth of Virginia: A Sketchbook of the People, Places and Events of Fluvanna County, Virginia.* Palmyra, VA: Fluvanna County Historical Society, 1998.

Joyner, Ulysses P., Jr. *The First Settlers of Orange County, Virginia: A View of the Life and Times of the European Settlers of Orange County, Virginia and Their Influence upon the Young James Madison, 1700–1776.* Baltimore, MD: Gateway Press for the Orange County Historical Society, 1987.

Koons, Kenneth E., and Warren R. Hofstra. *After the Backcountry: Rural Life in the Great Valley of Virginia, 1800–1900.* Knoxville: University of Tennessee Press, 2000.

PU'UHONUA O HONAUNAU NATIONAL HISTORICAL PARK

Location: Honaunau, Hawaii
Acreage: 420
Established: July 26, 1955

Until 1819, this sacred ground provided sanctuary to vanquished Hawaiian warriors, noncombatants, and those who broke the kapu—the ancient laws of the gods. Native Hawaiians believed that if violators of the strict rules governing daily life were not properly punished, the gods would invoke disasters such as famine, tsunamis, lava flows, or earthquakes. In this Place of Refuge, or "pu'uhonua," the offender could be absolved by a priest and avoid certain death. Defeated warriors and noncombatants could also find refuge here during times of battle. The grounds just outside the massive 10-foot-high Great Wall that encloses the pu'uhonua were home to several generations of powerful ali'i, or chiefs. Tall, carved wooden effigies called ki'i, whose fantastic grimacing faces warn against unwanted intrusions, stand guard over the refuge. In 1819, however, King Kamehameha II abolished the ancient religious system and the kapu-regulated life, stripping Pu'uhonua o Honaunau of its spiritual powers.

First authorized in July 1955, the 420-acre Pu'uhonua o Honaunau National Historical Park preserves this premier Hawaiian cultural resource, which includes the pu'uhonua and a complex of archeological sites including temple platforms, royal fishponds, sledding tracks, and some coastal village sites. The Haloe o Keawe temple and several thatched structures have been reconstructed. Entrance fees are $3 per person and are valid for seven days; a $10 annual pass is also available. The park's visitor contact station is open year-round from 7:30 A.M. until 5:30 P.M., and features interpretive exhibits, orientation talks, and a self-guided nature trail through the royal grounds and place of refuge (pu'uhonua). The park celebrates its annual Hawaiian Cultural Festival on the weekend that falls closest to July 1, and events include a royal court procession, hula, crafts, Hawaiian games, canoe rides, food tasting, and a hukilau (group fishing activity). Hikers will enjoy the historic 1871 trail—part of the King's Trail that encircled much of the island—that winds along the coast for about a mile to the park boundary, providing access to many archeological sites including temple sites (heiau), some sledding tracks (holua), old house sites, and an open lava tube on the face of a sea cliff (visitors are warned to watch their heads since ceiling is low, and flashlights are recommended).

There are no food, lodging, or camping facilities in the historical park, but all traveler services are available in Captain Cook.

For more information, write Pu'uhonua o Honaunau National Historical Park, P.O. Box 129, Honaunau, HI 96726, or telephone (808) 328-2288. The park's Web site is www.nps.gov/puho.

FURTHER READING

Greene, Linda Wedel. *A Cultural History of Three Traditional Hawaiian Sites on the West Coast of Hawaii Island.* Denver, CO: National Park Service, 1993. Available at www.cr.nps.gov/history/online _books/kona/history.htm.

Kay, E. Alison, ed. *A Natural History of the Hawaiian Islands: Selected Readings.* Honolulu: University Press of Hawaii, 1972.

Kirch, Patrick V. *Feathered Gods and Fishhooks: An Introduction to Hawaiian Archaeology and Prehistory.* Honolulu: University of Hawaii Press, 1985.

Stannard, David E. *Before the Horror: The Population of Hawai'i on the Eve of Western Contact.* Honolulu: University of Hawaii, Social Science Research Institute, 1989.

Titcomb, Margaret. *Native Use of Fish in Hawaii.* Honolulu: University Press of Hawaii, 1972.

PUUKOHOLA HEIAU NATIONAL HISTORICAL SITE

Location: Kawaihae, Hawaii
Acreage: 86
Established: August 17, 1972

The founding of the kingdom of Hawaii is directly linked to one structure in the Hawaiian Islands: Puukohola Heiau. Kamehameha I (also known as Kamehameha the Great) erected the temple (heiau), the last to be built according to ancient Hawaiian tradition, to incur the favor of the family war god Kuka'ilimoku. In the years 1790 and 1791, thousands of workers labored to construct the 100- by 224-foot temple on the summit known as Puukohola—Hill of the Whale—near Kawihae on the Big Island. The edifice symbolized Kamehameha's power, and the king soon proved his might by presenting the bodies of his chief rivals as a human sacrifice at the temple's altar. Kamehameha eventually consolidated his rule over all of the Hawaiian Islands, using western military strategy and arms he acquired from an Englishman named John Young. Young, a boatswain on a British fur-trading vessel, had been stranded on the island of Hawaii in 1790. His knowledge and weaponry attracted the king's attention, and Olohana—as the European was affectionately called by Kamehameha—was made a Hawaiian chief. Olohana taught Kamehameha's warriors how to use muskets and the cannon, and with these powerful new weapons, Kamehameha triumphed. The monarchy he established lasted for eighty-three years, from 1810 until 1893, when it was overthrown by the U.S. military.

Authorized in August 1972, the 86-acre Puukohola Heiau National Historical Site preserves the ruins of King Kamehameha the Great's "Temple on the Hill of the Whale." Admission is free, although guided tours of the site are $1 per person. The park's visitor center, open year-round from 7:30 A.M. until 4 P.M., has interpretive exhibits and self-guided trails. In addition to interpretive talks and guided tours, the park offers cultural demonstrations of traditional Hawaiian crafts each Thursday from January through September. Puukohola Heiau National Historical Site also commemorates Hawaiian Flag Day on July 31 and hosts the Hawaiian Cultural Festival on the weekend closest to August 7.

There are no food, lodging, or camping facilities in the park, but all traveler services are available locally.

For more information, write Puukohola Heiau National Historical Site, P.O. Box 44340, Kawaihae, HI 96743, or telephone (808) 882-7218. The park's Web site is www.nps.gov/puhe.

FURTHER READING

Greene, Linda Wedel. *A Cultural History of Three Traditional Hawaiian Sites on the West Coast of Hawai'i Island.* Denver, CO: National Park Service, 1993. Available at www.cr.nps.gov/history/online _books/kona/history.htm.

Kay, E. Alison, ed. *A Natural History of the Hawaiian Islands: Selected Readings.* Honolulu: University Press of Hawaii, 1972.

Kirch, Patrick V. *Feathered Gods and Fishhooks: An Introduction to Hawaiian Archaeology and Prehistory.* Honolulu: University of Hawaii Press, 1985.

Stannard, David E. *Before the Horror: The Population of Hawai'i on the Eve of Western Contact.* Honolulu: University of Hawaii, Social Science Research Institute, 1989.

Titcomb, Margaret. *Native Use of Fish in Hawaii.* Honolulu: University Press of Hawaii, 1972.

R

RAINBOW BRIDGE NATIONAL MONUMENT

Location: Rainbow Bridge National
 Monument, Utah
Acreage: 160
Established: May 30, 1910

One of the hidden beauties of the national parks system, Rainbow Bridge National Monument preserves a stunning natural formation that has important religious value for the Native American people who knew of its existence long before Anglo-Americans "discovered" it. A huge natural bridge located on the Colorado Plateau not far from Lake Powell, Rainbow Bridge rewards visitors who make the journey to see it with a spectacular view of one of the most amazing features in the desert southwest.

The rock formations that form Rainbow Bridge are hundreds of millions of years old and reflect the convergence of several natural phenomena. The base of the bridge was put in place by inland seas more than 200 million years ago, while the bridge itself is comprised of petrified sand dunes that were sculpted by wind about 200 million years ago. Six thousand feet of additional deposits created so much pressure on the sand that it hardened into rock.

Millions of years later the Colorado Plateau was formed as the earth around the "Four Corners" region—Utah, Colorado, Arizona, and New Mexico—began to rise, creating much of the beautiful landscape that the Park Service preserves in this area. At this point, however, Rainbow Bridge did not exist; it still waited to be carved out by water.

When the plateau rose, it steepened the gradient of the rivers and streams that flowed through it, giving the water more power to cut through the newly formed mountains and hills. The soft sandstone of Rainbow Bridge proved particularly vulnerable to these forces, and as water cut though the sandstone, Rainbow Bridge was formed. Because the bridge is composed of strata laid down in various times and made of different types of sediment, the rainbow phenomenon is created. The bridge is still being eroded today, and eventually, the water that created it will carry the last of it away.

Human history at the bridge has been one of wonder and reverence. Native people have considered the bridge sacred since the beginning of their cultural history. The Navajo, Hopi, Kaibab Paiute, San Juan Southern Paiute, and White Mesa Ute tribes all consider the bridge a sacred, religious site. The bridge has a central role in certain religious ceremonies, and many native people believe that it is sacrilegious to walk under it. The Park Service has consulted with these tribes in creating the management plan for Rainbow Bridge National Monument, and now it requests that visitors view the bridge but not walk on it or under it.

Anglo-Americans had heard legends about a beautiful rainbow bridge, and it is likely that during the nineteenth century some white men had come across the bridge, but it was not officially "discovered" until August 14, 1909, when two men and their Native American guides came upon it. In less than a year, on May 30, 1910, President William Howard Taft declared Rainbow Bridge a national monument. Despite this status, visitation to the bridge was limited because it was

The William B. Douglas party, including Navaho and Paiute Indians, celebrate their discovery of Rainbow Bridge, as they eat watermelon in Paiute Canyon, Utah, 1909. *(National Archives)*

extremely difficult to reach. As late as the 1950s, a trip to it required several days of rafting down the Colorado River and a hike to the bridge, requiring no less than three days. Today, visitors can access Rainbow Bridge more easily, by boat across Lake Powell, which was created when Glen Canyon Dam began filling in 1963. A dock is provided, from which visitors can hike about half a mile to the bridge. The more adventurous sort can backpack to Rainbow Bridge across Navajo lands, which requires a permit from the Navajo Nation.

Although the 160-acre Rainbow Bridge National Monument is immediately adjacent to Glen Canyon National Recreation Area, it is a separate unit of the national park system. Admission is free. There is no ranger station at the bridge, though rangers are at the location daily during the summer months and offer natural and cultural history programs. The nearest ranger station is at Dangling Rope Marina, but it is open only on an intermittent basis. Dangling Rope Marina is also the closest source of first aid, water, gas, and supplies, and it is open year-round. There are no food, lodging, or camping facilities at the monument, but all traveler services are available nearby in the Glen Canyon National Recreation Area.

For more information, write Rainbow Bridge National Monument, P.O. Box 1507, Page, AZ 86040-1507, or telephone (928) 608-6404. The park's Web site is www.nps.gov/rabr.

FURTHER READING
Babbitt, James E. *Rainbow Trails: Early-Day Adventures in Rainbow Bridge Country.* Page, AZ: Glen Canyon Natural History Association, 1990.

Hassell, Hank. *Rainbow Bridge: An Illustrated History.* Logan: Utah State University Press, 1999.

Sproul, David Kent. *A Bridge Between Cultures: An Administrative History of Rainbow Bridge National Monument.* Denver, CO: National Park Service,

Intermountain Region, 2001. Available at www. nps.gov/rabr/adhi/adhi.htm.

REDWOOD NATIONAL AND STATE PARKS

Location: Crescent City, California
Acreage: 112,512
Established: October 2, 1968

Redwood National and State Parks preserve the few remaining stands of old-growth redwood forest and the complex environment in which the mighty trees grow. Located in the north coast region, which extends from Fort Bragg, California, to Josephine County in Oregon, this unique natural environment has provided a home for the giant redwoods for millions of years. Despite the unique and spectacular nature of the trees and their environment, the growth of American industry fueled extensive logging of the trees, and by the 1960s, 90 percent of the ancient trees had been felled. Concerned citizens began lobbying for protection in the 1910s, and California responded by creating three state parks: Jedediah Smith Redwoods State Park, Del Norte Coast Redwoods State Park, and Prairie Creek Redwoods State Park. In 1968 these state parks were joined by the Redwood National Park, and in 1994 the state of California and the National Park Service consolidated the management of the four parks.

Redwood National Park is one of the last traditional national parks to be established in the continental United States. It encompasses more than 75,000 acres of coastal and inland forests, fitting the model of nineteenth-century national parks, albeit in a much-scaled-down fashion. Its scenery is spectacular, and despite having been logged more than once, the park still feels like wilderness. The park's immense, majestic old-growth redwoods simply confound the senses. These coastal giants, known scientifically as *Sequoia sempervirens*, are the world's tallest and among the longest-living organisms on the planet. Soaring as high as 367 feet, with a base width of 22 feet, the trees tower over all that exists below them. These magnificent titans, if left alone by humans, can reach an age of two thousand years old. In fact, there have been redwoods growing on this narrow section of coast for at least 20 million years, and ancestors of the redwoods existed during the time of the dinosaurs. Despite this ancient past and the obvious longevity and strength of the redwoods, they exist as part of a fragile environment that is easily unbalanced.

California's coastal redwoods are the last remnants of a global empire that, 25 million years ago, stretched across earth's northern hemisphere from the Atlantic Ocean to western Canada, from Japan to France. As the glaciers expanded southward during the Ice Age, the redwoods steadily retreated; this, coupled with the destructive power of volcanoes and the steady upward thrust of mountain ranges, helped eradicate the global redwood domain. Today, California is the only location where the last two species of redwoods exist: the coastal redwood and its physically bigger and heavier cousin, *Sequoia gigantea*, found only in the Sierra Nevada's inland areas. Quite simply, coastal redwoods can survive nowhere else in the world. Longitude, climate, and elevation combine here to create the perfect habitat. Redwoods must be continuously moist to survive, so the daily fog that rolls in from the Pacific Ocean during the summer, and the 100 inches of annual rainfall, are essential for survival. However, so much rain strips nutrients from the soil, so the redwoods are dependent on moss and mushrooms, as well as the decay of other trees, for nourishment. Redwood forests also contain a variety of other trees, such as Douglas firs, madrones, and western hemlocks. A natural recycling system exists in these forests, and this process

Dedication of Lady Bird Johnson Grove in Redwood National Park, August 27, 1969. *(National Archives)*

is essential to the continued existence of the redwood trees.

Native Americans lived for thousands of years in the lush, spectacular environment of the North Coast. These Native Americans experienced the expansion of Anglo-America somewhat differently than did many other Native American groups. First, though hundreds of villages existed along the coast and the rivers of this region, each was largely autonomous, and there was little cultural cohesion among groups. And while all of the coastal Native Americans shared a network of economic, social, and religious ties, there was no strong political entity. Living a comfortable and relatively easy existence because of the bounty provided by the natural landscape, these people reverently interacted with nature.

Anglo-Americans began pouring into the area during the 1850s as a result of the Gold Rush. Often, miners and loggers reached the area before agents of the U.S. government, and these settlers brutally massacred Native Americans in the region and disregarded their claims to the land. Formal treaties were never ratified, so Native Americans in this region lost even the very limited protection the reservation system offered. Nevertheless, their influence on the park is significant, in part because of their connection to the environment and their understanding of its fragility.

The California Gold Rush of 1849 started a chain of events that led to the redwoods' exploitation. Very attractive for commercial building purposes, the redwood trees contributed to northern California's late-nineteenth-century urban construction boom. By 1900, few old-growth redwood groves remained. Following World War I, concern over the trees' possible extinction resulted in the successful efforts by the Save-the-Redwoods League, a combination of local philanthropists and private citizens that included John Muir, to establish California's state redwood park system. One of the most avid supporters of a redwood park was Newton B. Drury, a California advertising man who later became the fourth director of the National Park Service. Some considered state protection inadequate, however, particularly after World War II, when increased logging by private firms threatened key watersheds of the last old-growth, non-state-protected groves. Conservation groups such as the Sierra Club pressured the federal government for protection of the trees, especially in 1963, when the National Geographic Society discovered the world's tallest tree, 367 feet. After a lengthy debate, the preservationists and their congressional allies succeeded. Congress authorized Redwood National Park in 1968 and expanded it ten years later to protect more key watersheds from local logging operations. The United Nations designated the park as a World Heritage Site in 1980 and an International Biosphere Reserve in 1983.

Today, this 112,512-acre park system preserves and protects this fragile habitat. Admission to the national park is free, and Jedediah Smith, Del Norte Coast, and Prairie Creek Redwoods state parks charge a nominal $2 fee. There are 5 visitor centers located in the park, which are generally open from 9 A.M. until 5 P.M., although some, such as the Hiouchi Information Center and the Jedediah Smith Visitor Center, are closed during the winter. Exhibits depict the history of coastal Native Americans and provide information about the flora and fauna of the parks. Several centers offer introductory video programs, and park rangers lead guided hikes, tours, and naturalist programs. Redwood National and State Parks is accessible all year, though rain may close roads throughout the park at times. Combined, the parks have more than 200 miles of trails from which a visitor can experience the beauty of the redwood forests and the Pacific Coast. There are several scenic drives through the old-growth forest, as well as whale-watching and tide-pool exploration points. Other wildlife, such as the Roosevelt elk, can be viewed from the meadow and prairie sites within the parks. The parks also preserve a number of historic structures, including Old Redwood Highway, ranch buildings, and a radar station dating to World War II. The Prairie Creek Fish Hatchery, near Orick, California, is one of only three remaining California hatcheries from the early twentieth century. There are extensive opportunities for visitors to hike and camp in the parks.

Lodging is available year-round in the park at the DeMartin Redwood Youth Hostel (707-482-8265) in Klamath. The national park offers four backcountry campgrounds, and each of the state parks has camping opportunities; fees and facilities vary. Food and supplies are available locally, as are other lodging and camping amenities.

For more information, write Redwood National and State Parks, 1111 Second Street, Crescent City, CA 95531, or telephone (707) 464-6101. The park's Web site is www.nps.gov/redw.

FURTHER READING

Brown, Joseph E. *Monarchs of the Mist: The Story of Redwood National Park and the Coast Redwoods.* Point Reyes, CA: Coastal Parks Association, 1982.

Moratto, Michael J. *An Archeological Overview of Redwood National Park.* Tucson, AZ: Cultural Resources Management Division, National Park Service, 1973.

RICHMOND NATIONAL BATTLEFIELD PARK

Location: Richmond, Virginia
Acreage: 2,517
Established: March 2, 1936

> As the sun rose on Richmond, such a spectacle was presented as can never be forgotten by those who witnessed it. . . . Above all this scene of terror, hung a black shroud of smoke through which the sun shone with a lurid angry glare like an immense ball of blood that emitted sullen rays of light, as if loath to shine over a scene so appalling. . . .

So Sallie Putnam voiced the lament of the South as she watched the fall of Richmond, Virginia, the Confederate capital and symbol of Southern independence, on April 3, 1865. Since the spring 1861, it had mocked the North, lying only 100 miles south of Washington, D.C. For four years, it had supplied and sustained the Army of Northern Virginia in its quest for independence.

At the beginning of April 1865, the Yankees were finally coming. It was not their first attempt. Of the seven major campaigns to capture Richmond, two had brought Union forces within sight of the city: George B. McClellan's Peninsular Campaign of 1862, which culminated in the Seven Days' Battles; and Ulysses S. Grant's devastating Overland Campaign of 1864. While the immediate outcome of both was Confederate retention of Richmond, the latter ultimately did succeed in bringing the North into this Southern capital. Had McClellan moved boldly and resolutely, Richmond might have fallen three years early. But boldness and resolution were not McClellan's strengths; President Abraham Lincoln complained bitterly that McClellan had "the slows." Grant did not. In March 1864, when he assumed command of all Union armies in the field, he attached him-

self to the Army of the Potomac and set his sights on the heart and soul of the Confederacy. His successful ten-month siege of Petersburg in 1864–1865 finally paved the way for the men in blue to enter Richmond and sent Confederate General Robert E. Lee fleeing westward toward Appomattox Court House and his final surrender on April 9, 1865.

Established in March 1936, the 2,517-acre Richmond National Battlefield Park commemorates 11 different sites associated with those campaigns, including the battlefields at Gaines' Mill, Malvern Hill, and Cold Harbor. Admission is free. The park maintains 4 visitor centers.

The Tredegar Iron Works Visitor Center, located on the Richmond Canal Walk, is open year-round from 9 A.M. until 5 P.M., and it has 3 floors of exhibits and artifacts, an orientation film, and cassettes for the Seven Days' Battles driving tour.

The Cold Harbor Battlefield Visitor Center, located 5 miles southeast of Mechanicsville on Route 156, is also open year-round from 9 A.M. until 5 P.M., and it has exhibits and artifacts on display as well as a five-minute electric map program that describes the 1864 battle of Cold Harbor. Each summer, the center commemorates the June 3–4 anniversary of the Battle of Cold Harbor.

The Fort Harrison Visitor Center, located on Battlefield Park Road off of Route 5 in Richmond, is open from June through October (hours vary). The center features exhibits on the September 29, 1864, assault on the fort and a self-guided historical walking trail. Special programs include a Memorial Day program at Fort Harrison National Cemetery, a commemoration of the battle's anniversary, and living-history demonstrations.

The Glendale/Malvern Hill Battlefields Visitor Center is open year-round from 9 A.M. until 5 P.M., although it is closed on Tuesday and Wednesday from late August until June. The center observes the June 24–25 anniversary of the Seven Days' Battles at Malvern Hill with a living-history encampment and artillery demonstrations and walking tours. In late August, the center sponsors Artillery Through the Ages at Malvern Hill, where visitors can learn about the evolution of artillery from the American Revolution to the present.

In addition, the Chimborazo Medical Museum, located at 3215 East Broad Street in Richmond, is open all year from 9 A.M. to 5 P.M. It contains exhibits on medical equipment and hospital life, including information on the men and women who staffed Chimborazo hospital.

There are no food, lodging, or camping facilities in the park, but all traveler services are available in Richmond.

For more information, write Richmond National Battlefield Park, 3215 East Broad Street, Richmond, VA 23223, or telephone (804) 226-1981. The park's Web site is www.nps.gov/rich.

FURTHER READING
Gallagher, Gary W., ed. *The Richmond Campaign of 1862: The Peninsula and the Seven Days.* Chapel Hill: University of North Carolina Press, 2000.
Miller, William J. *The Battles for Richmond, 1862.* Conshohocken, PA: Eastern National Park and Monument Association, 1996.

ROCK CREEK PARK
Location: Washington, D.C.
Acreage: 1,755
Established: September 27, 1890

An oasis in the nation's capital, Rock Creek Park was established in the late nineteenth century, prior to the creation of the National Park Service. One of the largest forested urban parks in the United States, it contains a wide array of natural, historical, and recreational amenities Congress set aside Rock Creek's wild valley to "provide for the preservation . . . of all timber, animals, or curiosities . . . and their retention in their natural condition."

Today, Rock Creek Park's entire jurisdiction encompasses 1,755 green acres, shelters historic landmarks, offers recreation and sports, and provides natural habitat for a variety of wildlife, including foxes, raccoons, squirrels, barred owls, woodpeckers, wrens, warblers, cardinals, and goldfinches. The picturesque valley of Rock Creek is especially beautiful in the spring. But all year long, this oasis of hardwood forest and meadows, within 5 miles of the White House, offers a quiet respite from the bustle of urban life for both Washingtonians and visitors to the nation's capital. The park also offers excellent opportunities for picnicking, hiking, biking, skating, horseback riding, tennis, and even golf.

The main visitor center is the Rock Creek Nature Center, which contains a planetarium and is the focal point for activities related to the park's natural history. The nature center, located at 5200 Glover Road, is open year-round from 9 A.M. until 5 P.M., Wednesday through Sunday, and features nature exhibits, nature trails, and a discovery room for younger children, as well as nature programs, planetarium shows, and a variety of educational programs.

The area's cultural history can be studied through the Old Stone House (the oldest house in Washington), Peirce Mill (a gristmill where corn and wheat were ground into flour using water power from Rock Creek), and the remains of Civil War earthen fortifications, including Fort Stevens, the site of the only battle within the District of Columbia during the Civil War. The Old Stone House, located at 3051 M Street, is open year-round, Wednesday through Sunday, from noon until 5 P.M. Peirce Mill, located at Beach and Tilden streets, is open year-round, Wednesday through Sunday, from noon until 4 P.M. The historic mill offers historical, recreational, and

Three women sitting on a scow and cooling their feet in Rock Creek in the 1920s or early 1930s. *(Library of Congress)*

natural history programs. Admission to the park is free.

There are no food, lodging, or camping facilities in the park, but all traveler services are available in the Washington, D.C., area.

For more information, write Rock Creek Park, 3545 Williamsburg Lane NW, Washington, DC 20008, or telephone (202) 426-6828. The park's Web site is www.nps.gov/rocr.

FURTHER READING

Brucksch, John P. *Old Stone House, Rock Creek Park, National Capital Region, Washington, D.C.* Harpers Ferry, WV: National Park Service, 1986.

Bushong, William. *Historic Resource Study: Rock Creek Park, District of Columbia.* Washington, DC: National Park Service, 1990.

Mackintosh, Barry. *Rock Creek Park: An Administrative History.* Washington, DC: National Park Service, 1985.

Spilsbury, Gail. *Rock Creek Park.* Baltimore, MD: Johns Hopkins University Press, 2003.

ROCKY MOUNTAIN NATIONAL PARK

Location: Estes Park, Colorado
Acreage: 265,828
Established: January 26, 1915

Rocky Mountain National Park straddled the gap between the mountaintop parks of the late nineteenth century and the larger ecological parks of the twentieth century. Established in 1915, it reflected both the ideals of beauty that underpinned the scenic monumentalism of the nineteenth century and the attempts to preserve recreational space that marked the twentieth. Encompassing over 250,000 acres, all of it above 7,800 feet, and some of it as high as 14,255 feet, Rocky Mountain National Park represented the best that Colorado had to offer the national park system.

Its establishment linked a growing recreation industry and the Progressive ideal of conservation. One man, Enos A. Mills, spearheaded the park idea at Rocky Mountain. A thirty-year resident of the mountains, Mills acquired his preservationist sentiment as he watched the mountains he loved change from human use. He had worked as a cowboy, climbed the 14,255-foot Longs Peak, and worked as a guide. By the time the park was established, Mills had spent most of two decades advocating for its protection. He wrote thousands of letters, gave dozens of lectures,

Native Americans camping beside a lake in Rocky Mountain National Park, sometime in the early twentieth century. *(Library of Congress)*

penned more than sixty newspaper and magazine articles, and circulated more than 400 photographs of the region. His energy galvanized support for the park, bringing influential people into the process of park creation. Among them was F.O. Stanley of the Stanley Steamer automobile company, who opened the Stanley Hotel in 1907. The road to park creation was clear. A combination of conservation-minded locals and wealthy and influential national elites assured its park status.

After the founding of the National Park Service in 1916, Rocky Mountain quickly became one of the most important parks in the system. Along with Yellowstone, Yosemite, and the Grand Canyon, it was central to the Park Service's aspirations as an agency. It offered the possibility of attracting large numbers of visitors and, in the 1920s, was integral to the idea of a panoramic tour of the greatest parks in the nation. Its superintendents were considered to be on the path to leadership in the agency. Among them was the agency's leading evaluator of new park proposals, Roger W. Toll, who served at Rocky Mountain from 1921 to 1929 and was headed for the director's job when he died tragically in an automobile accident in 1936. As the agency changed, however, this presumption of prerogative changed as well.

By the 1950s, Rocky Mountain faced the same onslaught of visitors that the rest of the park system encountered. It was perhaps worse at Rocky Mountain than at other parks, for proximity to urban Colorado and a long-standing resort trade increased the impact of visitors on park resources. Mission 66, the ten-year, capital-development program to refurbish the national parks by the fiftieth anniversary of the National Park Service in 1966, led to improvements in infrastructure, but the park continued to face the problems generated by more visitors than the agency could manage with the resources available.

The Ouzel fire in 1978, one of the pivotal moments in agency fire history, further illustrated the dilemmas of park management in the modern age.

The 265,828-acre Rocky Mountain National Park exhibits the massive grandeur of the Rocky Mountains. Trail Ridge Road crosses the Continental Divide and looks out over dozens of peaks that tower more than 13,000 feet high. Longs Peak, the highest peak in the park, is 14,255 feet in elevation, and the high point on Trail Ridge Road climbs to 12,183 feet. Elk, mule deer, bighorn sheep, moose, coyotes, and a great variety of smaller animals call the national park home. During the winter months snowshoeing and cross-country skiing are very popular. Hiking is available on 346 miles of trails, and almost 90 percent of the park is managed as wilderness, making it a great place to enjoy solitude and the natural beauty of the Rocky Mountains. Entrance fees are $5 per person or $15 per vehicle, and are valid for seven days; a $30 annual pass is also available.

The park maintains 6 visitor centers, 2 of which—Beaver Meadows and Kawuneeche—are open year-round. Beaver Meadows, located on U.S. Route 36, just 3 miles from the town of Estes Park, has an orientation film of the park and special Saturday evening programs, while Kawuneeche, located 1 mile north of the town of Grand Lake on U.S. Route 34, offers cultural and natural history exhibits. Visitors will also enjoy touring the Never Summer Ranch, open during the summer months, which is maintained as a 1920s dude ranch, with ranch buildings and equipment available for viewing.

There are no lodging facilities in Rocky Mountain, but the park maintains 5 campgrounds, 3 of which—Longs Peak, Moraine Park, and Timber Creek—are open year-round. Sites are available on a first-come, first-served basis, and fees are $16 per site,

per night when the water is turned on and $10 per site, per night when the water is off. Food and supplies are available in the park at the snack bar adjacent to the Alpine Visitor Center, and all traveler services are available in Estes Park and Grand Lake.

For more information, write Rocky Mountain National Park, 1000 Highway 36, Estes Park, CO 80517-8397, or telephone (970) 586-1206. The park's Web site is www.nps.gov/romo.

FURTHER READING
Buchholtz, C.W. *Rocky Mountain National Park.* Niwot: University Press of Colorado, 1983.

Elias, Scott A. *Rocky Mountains.* Washington, DC: Smithsonian Institution Press, 2002.

Emerick, John. *Rocky Mountain Natural History Handbook.* Niwot, CO: Robert Rinehart, 1994.

Geary, Michael M. *A Quick History of Grand Lake: Including Rocky Mountain National Park and the Grand Lake Lodge.* Ouray, CO: Western Reflections, 1999.

Hess, Karl. *Rocky Times in Rocky Mountain National Park: An Unnatural History.* Niwot: University Press of Colorado, 1993.

Mills, Enos A. *The Rocky Mountain Wonderland.* New York: Houghton-Mifflin, 1915.

ROGER WILLIAMS NATIONAL MEMORIAL
Location: Providence, Rhode Island
Acreage: 5
Established: October 22, 1965

The year 1629 marked the beginning of the Great Migration, the emigration of more than 20,000 dissatisfied members of the Church of England to Massachusetts. Most colonists arrived in groups from long-standing communities in eastern England, and they believed theirs was a divine mission to purify the corrupt Anglican Church in the New World. John Winthrop, governor of the colony, had reminded them, "we shall be as a city upon a hill [and] the eyes of all people are upon us." Although they had fled from religious persecution in England, the "Puritans" had little toleration for other religious points of view once they arrived in their new homeland.

Their efforts to stifle criticism and dissent soon provoked conflict, and ultimately, the founding of a new colony in America.

In 1631, clergyman Roger Williams arrived in New England to minister to the congregation in Salem. Williams firmly believed in religious toleration and the separation of church and state. He also asserted that the colonists had no absolute right to the lands of the native people, but should bargain for them as they would with any rightful owner. But Williams's ideas threatened to undermine the Puritans' utopian experiment, and he was regarded as a dangerous thinker. When efforts to quiet him proved unsuccessful, he was banished from the bay colony in 1636. With a group of loyal followers, Williams fled into Narragansett country, where he purchased land from the native people and founded the town of Providence. In 1644, he received a charter creating the colony of Rhode Island, which served as a refuge where all could come to worship as their conscience dictated without interference from the state. In 1663, a new royal charger guaranteed self-government and complete religious freedom.

Authorized in October 1965, the 5-acre Roger Williams National Memorial, a landscaped urban park located on a common lot of the original settlement of Providence, commemorates the life of the founder of Rhode Island and champion of religious freedom. The park's visitor center, located at 282 North Main, is open year-round from 9 A.M. until 4:30 P.M. and features exhibits and videos on Roger Williams, as well as his ideals and principles of religious freedom and tolerance. Wayside exhibits are located throughout the grounds of the memorial. The park also sponsors many seasonal activities and special events, including living-history demonstrations on how the early settlers in Providence established their community, played, worked, traded, and protected their interests. Admission is free.

There are no food, lodging, or camping facilities at the memorial, but all traveler services are available in Providence and other surrounding communities.

For more information, write Roger Williams National Memorial, 282 North Main Street, Providence, RI 02903, or telephone (401) 521-7266. The park's Web site is www.nps.gov/rowi.

FURTHER READING
Boyd, James P., Jr. *The Challenges of Roger Williams: Religious Liberty, Violent Persecution, and the Bible.* Macon, GA: Mercer University Press, 2002.
Gaustad, Edwin S. *Liberty of Conscience: Roger Williams in America.* Valley Forge, PA: Judson, 1999.
Hall, Timothy L. *Separating Church and State: Roger Williams and Religious Liberty.* Urbana: University of Illinois Press, 1998.

ROSIE THE RIVETER WORLD WAR II HOME FRONT NATIONAL HISTORICAL PARK
Location: Richmond, California
Acreage: 145
Established: October 25, 2000

World War II not only opened the nation's eyes to the horrors of modern warfare, including the atomic bomb, but it also revolutionized social perceptions about women and work. Overnight, as the men went off to war, "Rosie the Riveter" became a reality in America's booming defense industries. In the five years between 1940 and 1945, the numbers of employed women rose more than 50 percent, most dramatically among married women over thirty-five years of age. They also entered jobs and fields that had been exclusively male: welding, tending blast furnaces, and, of course, riveting. Yet wartime propaganda continually reinforced the notion that their status was temporary, only "for the duration." Women bus drivers, for example, were given badges for their uniforms that read, "I am taking the place of a man who went to war." The implication was clear: when that man returned, "Rosie the Riveter" was to become, once again, "Mrs. Stay-at-Home." Yet while most of their wartime employment gains were short-lived, the "Rosies" would go home to raise a generation of women who would demand far more access to and equality in the national job market.

Many of the newly employed women war workers worked "out West," where the bulk of federal war contracts went. The West's abundant natural resources combined with the cheap electricity available from the huge hydroelectric dams built during the New Deal/Depression era offered an irresistible combination. The results were striking. The population of the American West increased by 40 percent, and towns like Los Angeles and Houston became big cities seemingly overnight. Henry J. Kaiser, a California industrialist, constructed vast shipyards along the West Coast, including the one preserved here in Richmond, which slashed the time it took to build a merchant ship from one hundred and five days to two weeks. The United States defeated the Germans, in part because they could build ships faster than the U-boats could sink them.

The Rosie the Riveter World War II Home Front National Historical Park was set aside in 2000 to commemorate the remarkable transformation that World War II produced in American society and the American West, and one of its first priorities is recording the oral history experiences and stories of the people who lived and worked in Richmond during World War II. Due to the park's newness, there are limited visitor facilities, though development has begun. The renovation and development of a visitor and education center is planned as part of a mixed-use Ford Assembly Building, and even today, visitors can enjoy the Rosie the Riveter Memorial, Sheridan Observation Point, the SS *Red Oak Victory,* the Liberty Ship Memorial at Vincent Park, and Shimada Friendship Park. All sites are connected by the Bay Trail. The Rosie the Riveter Memorial in Marina Bay Park is open year round, dawn to dusk, as are the other city parks within the national park's boundaries. The *Red Oak Victory* ship is open from 10 A.M. until 4 P.M. every day except Mondays. The other sites of the park are in private ownership and are not open to the public at this time. However, their exteriors can be viewed.

For more information, write Rosie the Riveter World War II Home Front National Historical Park, 1401 Marina Way South, Suite C, Richmond, CA 94804, or telephone (510) 232-5050. The park's Web site is www.nps.gov/rori.

FURTHER READING

Bird, William L., and Harry R. Rubenstein. *Design for Victory: World War II Posters on the American Home Front.* New York: Princeton Architectural, 1998.
Gluck, Sherna Berger. *Rosie the Riveter Revisited: Women, the War, and Social Change.* New York: Penguin Books, 1988.

Rosie the Riveter, Mare Island Shipyard, California, 1942. *(Library of Congress)*

Jeffries, John W. *Wartime America: The World War II Home Front.* Chicago: I.R. Dee, 1996.

RUSSELL CAVE NATIONAL MONUMENT

Location: Bridgeport, Alabama
Acreage: 310
Established: May 11, 1961

Russell Cave, in northeastern Alabama, preserves one of the longest and most complete archeological records in the eastern United States. The treasure trove of artifacts found here demonstrates intermittent human habitation for almost ten thousand years and offers many clues about how prehistoric people in the region fed, clothed, and protected themselves.

Russell Cave itself was carved out of limestone rock that was formed over 300 million years ago at the bottom of the inland sea that covered the region. Over time, the erosionary force of water created a warren of tunnels and caverns. Russell Cave was revealed to surface dwellers about ten thousand years ago when one of the complex's cavern roofs collapsed and exposed the possible shelter to the family and kin-based native people living in the area. The geological processes of rock-fall and deposit have continued to mold and shape the cave, so that today the floor of the upper entrance is some 30 feet above the original rock fall.

Modern scientific excavation of the cave began in 1953, when the Tennessee Archeological Society discovered prehistoric relics such as bone tools, jewelry, and pottery frag-
ments. Later excavations were undertaken by the Smithsonian Institution and the National Park Service, which completed the archeological record and allowed for the establishment of an on-site museum. Originally set aside in May of 1961, the 310-acre Russell Cave National Monument preserves the almost continuous archeological record of human habitation from at least 7000 B.C.E. until 1650 C.E. Admission is free. The Gilbert H. Grosvenor Visitor Center is open all year and features a prehistoric artifacts exhibit, videos, and hiking and nature trails. Park rangers offer guided tours of the cave shelter and give prehistoric tool and weapons demonstrations. These include flint-knapping (making of arrowheads), atlatl use (the ranger demonstrates the proper way to throw a spear with an atlatl), and ancient fire building techniques. The park also sponsors a Native American festival, held the first full weekend in May.

There are no food, lodging, or camping facilities at the monument, but all traveler services are available locally.

For more information, write Russell Cave National Monument, 3729 County Road 98, Bridgeport, AL 35740, or telephone (256) 495-2672. The park's Web site is www.nps.gov/ruca.

FURTHER READING
Griffin, John W. *Investigations in Russell Cave, Russell Cave National Monument, Alabama.* Washington, DC: National Park Service, 1974.
Marsh, Dorothy. *Life at Russell Cave.* New York: Eastern Acorn, 1980.
Prentice, Guy. *Archeological Inventory and Evaluation at Russell Cave National Monument, Alabama.* Tallahassee, FL: Southeast Archeological Center, National Park Service, 1994.

S

SAGAMORE HILL NATIONAL HISTORIC SITE

Location: Oyster Bay, New York
Acreage: 83
Established: July 25, 1962

From 1886 until his death in 1919, Theodore Roosevelt, the nation's twenty-sixth president, made his home at Sagamore Hill on Long Island's Oyster Bay in New York. Roosevelt used the estate as the "Summer White House" from 1902 to 1908, and it became the focus of national attention. As a boy, Roosevelt had spent summers at the bay with his family, and the home was built in 1885 from a plan he sketched. In many ways, Theodore Roosevelt was a true renaissance man. He earned a scholarly reputation as a noted historian, biographer, essayist, editor, columnist, critic, and author of thirty-six books. He was a renowned ornithologist, an expert on and hunter of big-game animals, and along with Gifford Pinchot, a pioneer in American conservation. He was a country squire, horseman, socialite, and patron of the arts. He was a diplomat, internationalist, naval historian and strategist, combat commander of a volunteer cavalry regiment, and assistant secretary of the Navy. In his illustrious political career he not only reformed the federal civil service and the New York City Police Department, but also ran unsuccessfully for mayor in New York City, founded the national Progressive, or Bull Moose, party and finished second the 1912 presidential campaign, donned a silver star as a North Dakota deputy sheriff, and served as governor of New York and vice president of the United States. The family-centered father of six, who made sure to end his workday at 4 P.M. to play with his children, also won the Nobel Peace Prize and the Congressional Medal of Honor.

Authorized in July 1962, the 83-acre Sagamore Hill National Historic Site commemorates the life of one of America's most colorful leaders. The park's visitor center, located at 12 Sagamore Hill Drive, is open year-round from 9 A.M. until 4:30 P.M., and it features revolving exhibits of Theodore Roosevelt–related materials from the Sagamore Hill museum collection. The Theodore Roosevelt home is open year-round from 9:30 A.M. until 4 P.M. daily from Memorial Day through Labor Day, and Wednesday through Sunday the remainder of the year. A forty-five-minute guided tour is offered every thirty minutes during the summer, and hourly on the hour during the fall/winter season; fees are $5 per person, with children under sixteen admitted free. The Roosevelt home is a 23-room Queen Anne–style brick and wood shingle–sided structure furnished as it was during his lifetime, with an emphasis on the postpresidential period of 1909–1919. The Theodore Roosevelt Museum at Old Orchard is open all year from 9 A.M. until 4:45 P.M. The Museum at Old Orchard is a 1930s Georgian-style home built by President Roosevelt's eldest son, General Ted Roosevelt, Jr. (1887–1944), and the only home he owned during a lifetime of military and public service. The museum has exhibits and films on President Roosevelt's political career, his family life at Sagamore Hill, and the lives of his six children.

There are no food, lodging, or camping facilities at the historic site, but all traveler

President Theodore Roosevelt and his detectives posed on the porch with flags at Sagamore Hill, Oyster Bay, New York, 1902. *(Library of Congress)*

services are available in the Long Island vicinity.

For more information, write Sagamore Hill National Historic Site, 20 Sagamore Hill Road, Oyster Bay, NY 11771–1809, or telephone (516) 922-4788. The park's Web site is www.nps.gov/sahi.

FURTHER READING

Brands, H.W. *T.R.: The Last Romantic.* New York: Basic Books, 1997.

McCullough, David. *Mornings on Horseback: The Story of an Extraordinary Family, a Vanished Way of Life, and the Unique Child Who Became Theodore Roosevelt.* New York: Simon and Schuster, 2001.

Morris, Edmund. *Theodore Rex.* New York: Random House, 2001.

——. *The Rise of Theodore Roosevelt.* New York: Modern Library, 2001.

SAGUARO NATIONAL PARK

Location: Tucson, Arizona
Acreage: 91,440
Established: March 1, 1933

Saguaro National Park was one of the first park areas created not to protect spectacular scenery, but to preserve a plant species, the saguaro cactus. One of the monuments created by executive proclamation during the lame duck period of Herbert Hoover's administration, Saguaro represented an effort to broaden the dimension of the national park system. This strategy, a pet goal of the agency's second director, Horace M. Albright, allowed the Park Service to reach a broader audience and continue to add land to the park system. This important goal fell under the most prominent of Albright's priorities, the idea of rounding out the park system for all time. After Franklin D. Roosevelt defeated Herbert Hoover in the 1932 election, Albright, a staunch Republican, persuaded the White House to make a conservation gift to the nation. Along with Black Canyon of the Gunnison and later additions such as Joshua

Tree and Organ Pipe Cactus national monuments, the agency succeeded in creating a subcategory of "representative area" national monuments. Arguably, this effort represented the Park Service's first attempt to preserve ecology within the park system. This foreshadowed the emphasis on science that emerged in the 1960s with the "Leopold" and "Robbins" reports.

Saguaro was also an urban park, located near Tucson, Arizona. As a result, the saguaro cactus faced the threat of vandalism and destruction from the growing population in the desert. After 1945, in the aftermath of World War II, migration to Arizona grew dramatically, and Tucson ceased to be a small town and became a major city. For Saguaro National Monument, growth meant the need for a more developed protective structure. This problem was highlighted in the early 1980s, when countless vandals used guns to shoot and destroy the stately saguaro cactus. In one memorable instance, a man shot so many holes in a saguaro that it fell on him and killed him. Such organizations as the Tucson-based, radical environmental Earth First! considered this outcome poetic justice.

The growth continued, however, and the saguaro cactus needed a higher level of protection. In 1994, Saguaro attained national park status, a reflection both of the need to protect the species and of the growing national consciousness in favor of environmental preservation.

Both the Tucson Mountain and Rincon Mountain districts of the park are open daily from 7 A.M. to sunset, and visitor centers are open daily from 8:30 A.M. to 5 P.M. Admission to the Tucson Mountain District is free, but the Rincon Mountain District charges a fee of $6 per vehicle or $3 per person, which is valid for seven days. A $20 annual pass is also available. Park rangers offer a wide variety of guided programs and talks, and both visitor centers have exhibits on the cultural and natural history of the region. There are no food or lodging facilities available in the park, although the Rincon Mountain District offers permitted backcountry camping. All traveler services are available in metropolitan Tucson.

For more information, write Saguaro National Park, Headquarters and Rincon Mountain District, 3693 South Old Spanish Trail, Tucson, AZ 85730-5601, or telephone (520) 733–5153. The park's Web site is www.nps.gov/sagu.

FURTHER READING
Evans, Doris. *Saguaro National Monument.* Tucson, AZ: Southwest Parks and Monuments Association, 1993.

Hodge, Carle. *All About Saguaros.* Phoenix: Arizona Highways, 1991.

Humphreys, Anna. *Saguaro: The Desert Giant.* Tucson, AZ: Rio Nuevo, 2002.

Nabhan, Gary Paul. *Saguaro: A View of Saguaro National Monument & the Tucson Basin.* Tucson, AZ: Southwest Parks and Monuments Association, 1986.

SAINT CROIX ISLAND INTERNATIONAL HISTORIC SITE
Location: Calais, Maine
Acreage: 45
Established: June 8, 1949

Saint Croix Island International Historic Site commemorates the origins of the United States and Canada. While the Spanish were the first Europeans to conquer and settle the New World, by the late fifteenth century their successes had attracted the attention of both Great Britain and France. By the early seventeenth century, both nations were eager to lay claim to the riches of North America. Their early efforts focused on discovering the elusive Northwest Passage, a hoped-for water route through the continent. It did not exist. But these voyages of exploration laid a foundation for future colonization. By the time the English established permanent settlements at Jamestown, Virginia, in 1607 and Plymouth,

Massachusetts, in 1620, the French had already staked their claim on the continent.

In 1604, Pierre Dugua Sieur de Mons, accompanied by Samuel Champlain and seventy-seven other men, established a year-round settlement on Saint Croix Island in the territory they called La Cadie, or l'Acadie (Acadia), in today's state of Maine. It was a poor choice. A disastrous winter plagued by a scurvy epidemic led to the death of many colonists, and the following year, the leaders moved the colony to a more favorable location across the Bay of Fundy, called the Port Royal Habitation, on the shores of the present-day Annapolis Basin in Nova Scotia.

While the French presence in America would never equal the British colonial migration, they built a thriving fur trade in the New World through cooperative partnerships with Native Americans. In time, they expanded "New France" along the Great Lakes and down the Mississippi to New Orleans—effectively hemming in the British colonies along the eastern seaboard. Conflicts in Europe between these two rival powers were echoed in the Americas, as Britain and France engaged in a series of four "wars for empire" beginning in 1689. The last and most significant of these was the French and Indian War (Seven Years War), which concluded in 1763 and drove the French from North America, leaving the British in sole possession of Canada and all territory east of the Mississippi River.

Authorized as a national monument in June 1949, the 45-acre Saint Croix Island International Historic Site commemorates the founding of New France in the New World. The site is focused on establishing a quiet atmosphere of respect and contemplation, and there are no federal facilities. The park is open all year from dawn to dusk, and a short walk to the interpretive shelter affords a fine view of the estuary and Saint Croix Island. On the Canadian side of the Saint Croix

River, opposite the island, is a Parks Canada summer exhibit.

There are no food, lodging, or camping facilities at the historic site, but all traveler services are available in Calais. The historic site is on U.S. Route 1, 6 miles south of Calais, Maine, and can be reached either by Route 9 from Bangor or via U.S. Route 1, the coastal route from Portland and points south. The international historic site is best reached by private vehicle. The only visitor access to the island is by privately owned boats.

For more information, write Saint Croix Island International Historic Site, Acadia National Park, P.O. Box 177, Bar Harbor, ME 04609–0177, or telephone (207) 288–3338. The park's Web site is www.nps.gov/sacr.

FURTHER READING

Moogk, Peter N. *La Nouvelle France: The Making of French Canada: A Cultural History.* East Lansing: Michigan State University Press, 2000.
Parkman, Francis. *France and England in North America.* New York: Viking, 1983.

SAINT-GAUDENS NATIONAL HISTORIC SITE
Location: Cornish, New Hampshire
Acreage: 148
Established: August 31, 1964

Augustus Saint-Gaudens was one of the nation's most popular and talented sculptors. Born in 1848, the artist spent his most productive years at "Aspet," an eighteenth-century federal house located in western New Hampshire near Cornish; this was his summer residence from 1885 to 1897 and his permanent home from 1900 until his death in 1907.

During his lifetime, Saint-Gaudens created more than 200 works of art, including portrait reliefs, decorative projects, and public monuments, and enjoyed an international reputation and clientele. Saint-Gaudens began his long career as an apprentice cameo-cutter, which gave him the foundation he later used

Exterior of Augustus Saint-Gaudens's studio in Cornish, New Hampshire, c. 1920–1923. *(Library of Congress)*

to become one of America's great masters of relief sculpture and memorial statuary. Careful study, attention to detail, and persistent effort were the hallmarks of his success. Saint-Gaudens was best known for his six monumental bronze sculptures in honor of Civil War events: Farragut Monument, 1881, Madison Square Park, New York; Standing Abraham Lincoln, 1887, Chicago; Shaw Memorial, 1897, Boston; General Logan, 1897, Chicago; Sherman Monument, 1903, New York; and Seated Abraham Lincoln, 1907, Chicago. The first of these, the Farragut Monument, established him as a master sculptor and set him on a career path of chronicling and rendering significant American historical figures and events. Later in life, President Theodore Roosevelt commissioned him to reform American coinage and specifically to design gold coins for the nation.

In 1900, at the age of fifty-two, Saint-Gaudens was diagnosed with intestinal cancer, and he relocated full-time to Cornish, New Hampshire, where he died in 1907. Unfortunately, fire destroyed the sculptor's letters, sketchbooks, and many unfinished pieces, but after Saint-Gaudens' death, his widow Augusta and his son Homer established Aspet as a memorial to this fine and disciplined artist.

Authorized in 1964, Saint-Gaudens National Historic Site consists of 148 acres, including the home, gardens, and studios of Augustus Saint-Gaudens. The entrance fee is $4 per person, and it is valid for seven days. An excellent orientation to the site is the video presentation *Augustus Saint-Gaudens: An American Original* (twenty-eight minutes), and tours of Saint-Gaudens' home, Aspet, are conducted throughout the day. Park rangers also offer guided, hour-long walking tours of the site on most afternoons. There are 2 hiking trails that explore the park's natural areas, and a self-paced audio tour is available for rental.

There are no food, lodging, or camping facilities at the historic site, but all traveler services are available locally.

For more information, write Saint-Gaudens National Historic Site, RR 3, Box 73, Cornish, NH 03745, or telephone (603) 675-2175. The park's Web site is www.nps.gov/saga.

FURTHER READING

Greenthal, Kathryn. *Augustus Saint-Gaudens, Master Sculptor.* New York: Metropolitan Museum of Art, 1985.

Wilkinson, Burke. *Uncommon Clay: The Life and Works of Augustus Saint Gaudens.* New York: Dover, 1992.

SAINT PAUL'S CHURCH NATIONAL HISTORIC SITE

Location: Mount Vernon, New York
Acreage: 6
Established: July 5, 1943

"Shall the press be silenced that evil governors may have their way?" challenged John Peter Zenger's attorney to the colonial courts in 1735. Zenger was the editor of the new *Weekly Journal,* which had dared criticize public officials, including the governor of New York, and had advocated for freedom of speech and the press. Quickly indicted for seditious libel, Zenger responded that he had only reported information that was "notoriously" factual. "The question before the court is not the cause of a poor printer," his attor-

ney had argued, but the cause "of every free man that lives under a British government on the main of America." In a landmark trial, Zenger was acquitted, and the precedent of protecting the press from governmental interference—later enshrined in the First Amendment to the Constitution—was established.

Zenger's exposé had focused on a corrupt assemblyman election in Westchester County, New York. The Eastchester village green was the site of the "Great Election" of 1733, where local voters had thwarted a scheme by the county's sheriff to steal the election. Saint Paul's Church stood at the edge of the green, and the Great Election, and Zenger's subsequent trial, made it famous. This eighteenth-century edifice is one of New York's oldest parishes, dating from 1665, and during the important Revolutionary War battle at Pell's Point in 1776, it served as a hospital; the adjoining cemetery contains burials dating from 1665.

Originally set aside in July 1943, the 6-acre historic site was transferred from the Episcopal Diocese of New York to the National Park Service in 1980. The park opened to the public in 1984 and is operated under a cooperative agreement with the Society of the National Shrine of the Bill of Rights at Saint Paul's Church, Eastchester. Saint Paul's Church, located at 897 South Columbus Avenue in Mount Vernon, is open year-round, Monday through Friday, from 9 A.M. until 5 P.M. and offers a variety of exhibits and special programs. Park rangers conduct guided tours of the two-hundred-year-old church, which includes seeing and hearing a bell cast in 1758 at the same foundry as the Liberty Bell, and an audiovisual sample of the 1833 pipe organ, one of the oldest functioning in America. The park has a self-guided tour, Exploring Early American History at Saint Paul's, which focuses on the colonial and Revolutionary periods, as well as a self-guided walking tour on Saint Paul's Church and the Civil War, focusing on the lives and roles of the Union veterans buried in the cemetery. The Carriage House also offers permanent and rotating exhibitions on display.

There are no food, lodging, or camping facilities at the historic site, but all traveler services are available locally.

For more information, write Saint Paul's Church National Historic Site, 897 South Columbus Avenue, Mount Vernon, NY 10550, or telephone (914) 667-4116. The park's Web site is www.nps.gov/sapa.

FURTHER READING
Zenger, John Peter. *A Brief Narrative of the Case and Trial of John Peter Zenger, Printer of the New York Weekly Journal, by James Alexander.* Edited by Stanley Nider Katz. Cambridge, MA: Belknap Press of Harvard University Press, 1972.

SALEM MARITIME NATIONAL HISTORIC SITE

Location: Salem, Massachusetts
Acreage: 9
Established: March 17, 1938

No image was more important to the American colonies and indeed the United States before the Civil War than that of a man sailing to sea. Ships were the connection between the New World and the Old, the delivery system for wealth, and the means to acquire goods that marked the New World's transformation. In the New England colonies, Salem, Massachusetts, was the center of seafaring America. From its beginnings, Salem was the port of choice for much American commerce and the source of some of the most original American writing of the nineteenth century. The park comprises the center of what was once the primary waterfront in the city, containing 3 historic wharves of the more than 50 in use at the peak of the maritime economy, as well as an array of private residences, commercial structures, and historic government buildings. Among the latter is the U.S. Customs House, where author Nathaniel Hawthorne worked as a surveyor. The build-

ing inspired his most famous work, *The Scarlet Letter.*

Salem rose to prominence in the 1630s, as Puritan New England underwent the first of its many cultural and economic revolutions. Salem became one of the primary ports in a shipping triangle that included Great Britain and the West Indies. This commerce, which took New England timber and dried cod from the north seas to the West Indies, played a role in the secularization of the Puritan "City on the Hill," the new Jerusalem that the Pilgrims came to establish. Many of their children were far more attracted to commerce than religion, and Salem was the port of choice for their entrepreneurial adventures.

After the Revolutionary War and into the nineteenth century, Salem played a significant role in American commerce. New England merchants were among the most generous financial supporters of the Revolution, for British taxes, duties, and trade restraints limited their prosperity. The port became a home for American privateers, who at the behest of the Continental Congress disrupted British shipping. Salem privateers captured more than 400 ships during the war.

Salem shipowners began to travel the world after the war. At the behest of Elias Hasket Derby, who became the town's most prominent merchant, trade between Salem and China opened in 1786. Derby's ships brought silk, china, spices, and tea to New England as well as art objects. Derby was among a small cadre of merchants who became fabulously wealthy and very influential. Merchants were in the lead in supporting the ratification of the U.S. Constitution in 1787.

In 1807, when the United States embargoed trade with France and Britain, American shipping suffered a blow and Salem began a long decline. The War of 1812 devastated international shipping, and, by its end, American shipping had been reconfigured. Whaling, based out of Nantucket Island and New

The U.S. Customs House in Salem, Massachusetts. *(National Park Service)*

Bedford, Massachusetts, achieved a new prominence, leaving Salem behind.

The park preserves the largely intact historical fabric of the era of sail in the Northeast. The wharves offer the feel of waterfront life, while the warehouse sizes reveal the enormous quantities of goods shipped. The fine homes of the wealthy merchants show the fruits of success in international shipping, and the Customs House and Scale House remind visitors of the government presence and the formidable degree to which the young United States relied on tariffs and levies as its source of revenue.

The park is open daily from 9 A.M. to 5 P.M., and there is a $5-per-adult ($3 for seniors/children), per-day program fee for ranger-guided tours of *Friendship*, a full-size replica of the 1797 Salem merchant vessel, 1819 Custom House, 1762 Derby House, and

1670 Narbonne House. In all, the Salem Maritime National Historic Site encompasses an area of 9 acres. The principal resources include the 3 historic wharves—Derby, Hatch's, and Central—extending into Salem Harbor, and a row of historic government, residential, and commercial structures, including the U.S. Custom House, elegant homes of sea captains and merchants, and the more ordinary homes of craftsmen. It is the only remaining intact waterfront from America's age of sail almost two hundred years ago.

Temperatures range from hot in the summer to frigid in the winter. Dress for the season and wear sturdy walking shoes. Salem, like many New England towns, is designed for walking, and most attractions are within a reasonable walk.

Boston's Logan Airport is the closest major airport. By car, take Route 1 north off

I-93 north. Follow the signs to Salem, Massachusetts. When you reach Salem, look for signs to the Visitors' Center or Waterfront/ Pickering Wharf. The city of Salem has a few commercial parking lots downtown, close to the visitor center.

Salem is also served by the Newburyport/ Rockport commuter line from Boston's North Station, about a thirty-minute ride. Buses #455 and #450 go from the Haymarket section of Boston to the Salem rail depot. (Haymarket is on the green and orange lines of the Boston subway system.) Commercial transportation in Salem includes trolleys, pedicabs, and horse-drawn carriages.

For more information, write Salem Maritime National Historic Site, 174 Derby Street, Salem, MA 01970, or telephone (978) 740-1650 or (978) 740-1660. The park's Web site is www.nps.gov/sama.

FURTHER READING

Karlsen, Carol F. *The Devil in the Shape of a Woman: Witchcraft in Colonial New England.* New York: W.W. Norton, 1998.

National Park Service. *Salem: Maritime Salem in the Age of Sail.* Washington, DC: U.S. Department of the Interior, 1987.

Platt, John David Ronalds. *Shipping in the Revolution: Salem Maritime National Historic Site, Salem, Massachusetts; Special History Study.* Denver, CO: National Park Service, 1973.

SALINAS PUEBLO MISSIONS NATIONAL MONUMENT

Location: Mountainair, New Mexico
Acreage: 1,071
Established: November 1, 1909

The pueblos of New Mexico's Salinas Valley serve as vivid reminders of a society that thrived in this region for most of the past two millennia, and though the Pueblo people abandoned the area in the 1670s, they left a lasting mark on the region's cultural and political history. The prehistoric ancestors of the Pueblos first arrived in the region as far back as twenty thousand years ago, when nomadic tribes utilized resources in the valley. Much later, the two ancient southwestern cultures, the Anasazi and Mogollon, interacted in this valley, which means "salt" in Spanish, and formed the basis for the settlements at Abo, Gran Quivira, and Quarai.

During the late 1100s, the Anasazi culture had begun to assimilate the Mogollon tradition, and the Pueblo culture, marked by its apartment-style adobe housing, flourished in the Salinas Valley. With more than 10,000 inhabitants by the 1600s, this valley became one of the most populous in the Pueblo world, largely because of its ideal location as a center for trade. The Salinas Valley Pueblos traded food supplies with the Plains tribes to the east and the villages along the Rio Grande.

Into the midst of this thriving society came the Spanish, led initially by Juan de Oñate in 1598. The Spanish established a permanent colony but quickly realized that the harsh climate would prevent agriculture from being a profitable enterprise in the region. The Spanish crown saw the Americas as a place to carry out a mission for God, and this colony survived primarily as a missionary effort. During the 1620s, the Franciscans established at least seven missions in the region around the Salinas Valley. Missionary efforts proved difficult and dangerous for the Spanish in this area. The Pueblo had developed a complex, ritualistic religion upon which they depended for survival in this harsh land. The Christianity presented by the Franciscans could not simply replace this religion, and the result was a clash of religion and culture.

During this cultural upheaval, the Salinas Pueblos were being abandoned. Famine and disease were largely to blame. In 1672, Gran Quivira was abandoned, followed by Abo and then Quarai. Provoked in part by religious intolerance—the Spanish tried to eradicate the Kachina tradition—and in part by the slavery to which Spanish officials subjected them, the remaining Indians rebelled against the Spanish in 1680. Many of the Native Americans who had lived in the Salinas Valley retreated with the Spanish to El Paso. Although the Salinas Valley was never reinhabited by the Spanish or by native people, the ruins of four mission churches and the pueblo of Las Humanas remain as symbols of an ancient past and a violent clash of cultures.

Originally established as Gran Quivira National Monument in 1909, and then renamed in 1980, the 1,071-acre Salinas Pueblo Missions National Monument preserves ruins that reflect the vibrant culture of the Pueblo people, as well as the effects of Spanish settlement and missionary work among the Native Americans of the Southwest. Three sites, as well as surrounding areas, are protected by the national monument: Abo, Gran Quivira, and Quarai. The monument is open year-round from 9 A.M. until 5 P.M. daily (and for extended hours during the summer), and the visitor center has interpretive exhibits on the history of the region. In May, the park sponsors a Heritage Preservation Week that offers visitors and students a chance to gain hands-on experience in ruins stabilization. Occasionally, Mass and fiestas are scheduled at specific units.

There are no food, lodging, or camping facilities at the monument, but all traveler services are available in Mountainair.

For more information, write Salinas Pueblo Missions National Monument, P.O. Box 517, Mountainair, NM 87036-0517, or telephone (505) 847-2585. The park's Web site is www.nps.gov/sapu.

FURTHER READING

Ivey, James E. *"In the Midst of a Loneliness": The Architectural History of the Salinas Missions.* Santa Fe, NM: National Park Service, 1988. Available at www.nps.gov/sapu/hsr/hsr.htm.

Murphy, Dan. *Salinas Pueblo Missions National Monument.* Tucson, AZ: Southwest Parks and Monuments Association, 1993.

Noble, David Grant, ed. *Salinas: Archaeology, History, Prehistory.* Santa Fe, NM: Ancient City, 1993.

SALT RIVER BAY NATIONAL HISTORICAL PARK AND ECOLOGICAL PRESERVE

Location: Christiansted, St. Croix,
  Virgin Islands
Acreage: 978
Established: February 24, 1992

On November 14, 1493, the explorer Christopher Columbus dropped anchor in Salt River Bay in the Virgin Islands, the only known site where members of the expedition set foot on what is now U.S. territory. The island later became the focal point of European attempts to colonize the area, as Spain, France, Britain, and Holland all clashed over territorial rights. By 1650, France assumed control and ownership of the island, naming it Saint Croix, although remains of the earthen fortification known as Fort Sale from the earlier Dutch period of occupation are still visible at the park. In 1733, the Danish West Indian and Guinea Company purchased Saint Croix and turned the island into a thriving sugar colony for the next hundred and fifty years. When sugar prices collapsed at the turn of the twentieth century, causing a decline in Saint Croix's economy, the United States purchased what became the U.S. Virgin Islands in 1917. Besides its more recent history, Salt River Bay also contains traces of pre-Columbian native Caribbean settlements, including the only ceremonial prehistoric ball court ever discovered in the Lesser Antilles, village middens, and burial grounds.

Authorized in February 1992, the 978-acre Salt River Bay National Historical Park and Ecological Preserve also protects upland watersheds, mangrove forests, estuarine and marine environments, and twenty-eight federally and locally listed endangered species.

Admission is free. The park maintains a visitor center on the wharf in Christiansted, which is open daily from 8 A.M. until 5 P.M. Park rangers offer interpretive talks throughout the year on request. In addition to touring the historic and prehistoric sites, visitors can enjoy swimming and scuba diving at the park. Snorkel and diving gear are available to rent from the Anchor Dive Center in town.

There are no food, lodging, or camping facilities at the historical park, but all traveler services are available in Christiansted.

For more information, write Salt River Bay National Historical Park and Ecological Preserve, Christiansted National Historic Site, Danish Custom House, Kings Wharf, Christiansted, VI 00820-4611, or telephone (340) 773-1460. The park's Web site is www.nps.gov/sari.

FURTHER READING
Diamond, Jared M. *Guns, Germs, and Steel: The Fates of Human Societies.* New York: W.W. Norton, 1997.

SAN ANTONIO MISSIONS NATIONAL HISTORICAL PARK
Location: San Antonio, Texas
Acreage: 826
Established: November 10, 1978

Comprising 826 acres in and around San Antonio, Texas, the San Antonio Missions National Historical Park preserves the remains of the most potent symbol of Spanish presence in North America—the mission. Several missions were founded near present-day San Antonio during the Spanish colonial period, and these missions represent the comingling of two cultures: Spanish and Native American. At times this mingling was violent, at times peaceful, and the missions and the people within them experienced a new world as a result.

Spanish missions were built as walled compounds, much like medieval cities, that were far more than simple churches. Within the walls of the compound were living quarters for the priests and the Native Americans who came to learn about Christianity and to work as laborers for the Spanish, as well as a church, mill, and schools. The mission communities farmed and ranched, establishing a secular as well as a religious presence in the Southwest. Franciscans, Spanish soldiers, and Native Americans negotiated a new existence under the Spanish regime, and it was one that fundamentally altered the world that the Native Americans had built in the centuries before the Spanish arrived.

Collectively known as the Coahuiltecans, the Native Americans who were in residence at the missions around San Antonio were not a single cultural group. Rather, they were an amalgamation of many tribes who lived in or utilized the area for survival. Though the Spanish presence was oppressive, these Coahuiltecans had experienced threats from other migrating tribes in the years before the Spanish came, and they were therefore relatively accepting of Spanish religious and economic tyranny in return for protection and an assured food source.

The Spanish missionary effort extended to the San Antonio River by the early eighteenth century. Earlier missions had been located in east Texas, but difficulties along the frontier caused these missions to relocate to the San Antonio area, where two missions already existed. During the mid-eighteenth century, missions such as San Antonio de Valero (renamed the Alamo), San Jose, and Mission Nuestra Señora de la Concepción de Acuña thrived. However, secularization began to occur in the late eighteenth century as a result of increased pressure from the Apaches and Comanches, disease, and inadequate support from the Spanish seat of power in Mexico. Though the mission communities became secularized, the churches themselves survived, and many of them are active parishes even today.

The remains of these mission communities provide superb examples of Spanish colonial architecture, and these cultural and historical artifacts provide an interesting window into the past. The least restored mission, Mission Nuestra Señora de la Concepción de Acuña, was completed in 1755, and looks today much as it did two centuries ago. This mission was the home of the Father President, who was elected among the Franciscans in the region to serve as a field coordinator. San Jose, founded in 1720, was the largest mission in the area and home to approximately 300 Native Americans at its height. Known as the "Queen of the Missions," its spectacular church was completed in 1782 and became a cultural and religious center in the San Antonio area.

Established in November 1978, the San Antonio Missions National Historical Park protects not only the church, but several of the other buildings that made up the mission compound, as well as artifacts such as the Rose Window, located on the south wall of the sacristy, and a cedar panel from the sacristy door that dates back to the building of the church. Other mission sites are also protected in the park, including those of the Mission San Francisco de la Espada, and the Mission San Juan Capistrano. In addition, visitors to the park can view remains of the irrigation system that diverted water into the mission communities, granaries, living quarters, and an aqueduct at Espada. The park is largely urban today, and the major sites are connected by roads. In some places the Mission Trail has been completed, providing hiking and biking opportunities.

The park's visitor center is open year-round from 9 A.M. until 5 P.M., and it has interpretive exhibits as well as information and directions to all of the sites. There are also museums at Missions San José, San Juan, and Espada, and San José shows an award-winning, twenty-three-minute film in its auditorium. The park sponsors several special programs, including the enactment of a morality play, *Los Pastores*, at Mission San José either the last week in December or the first week in January. In November, the park's friends group, Los Compadres, sponsors "Artesanos del Pueblo," a weekend of arts and crafts demonstrations and sales, and on the first Saturday of each month there is a tour of the Spanish colonial ranch site for Mission Espada, located near Floresville, Texas.

There are no food, lodging, or camping facilities at the park, but all traveler services are available in San Antonio.

For more information, write San Antonio Missions National Historical Park, 2202 Roosevelt Avenue, San Antonio, TX 78210-4919, or telephone (210) 932-1001. The park's Web site is www.nps.gov/saan.

FURTHER READING

Almaraz, Felix D., Jr. *The San Antonio Missions and Their System of Land Tenure.* Austin: University of Texas Press, 1989.

De Zavala, Adina. *History and Legends of the Alamo and Other Missions in and Around San Antonio.* Houston, TX: Arte Publico, 1996.

Fisher, Lewis F. *The Spanish Missions of San Antonio.* San Antonio, TX: Maverick, 1998.

Torres, Luis. *San Antonio Missions.* Tucson, AZ: Southwest Parks and Monuments Association, 1993.

SAND CREEK MASSACRE NATIONAL HISTORIC SITE

Location: Kiowa County, Colorado
Acreage: 920
Established: November 7, 2000

In the 1830s, the U.S. government first adopted a formal federal policy of forcible removal and relocation of Native Americans. Most eastern tribes were sent west to "Indian Territory" in Oklahoma, while others were confined to reservations on marginal lands overlooked by westward-migrating whites. By the 1860s, this process had been extended to Plains people, who were sequestered much closer to their homes than the eastern people who moved across the continent. Once tribes, either voluntarily or by force, moved onto their reservations, they found federal support grossly lacking, particularly as successive treaties confined more and more tribes to fewer and fewer acres. Under these pressures, several Plains tribes began resisting both federal policies and white territorial expansion. The result was, predictably, a series of devastating "Indian Wars."

The event that touched off this bloody and shameful episode in American history was the Sand Creek Massacre in southeastern Colorado. The territory's governor had terminated all treaties with eastern Colorado tribes and encouraged white civilians, the Colorado Volunteers, to aid in their removal. The citizens needed little encouragement. With a long history of advocating accommodation with whites and hoping to protect his people from marauding militias, Cheyenne Chief Black Kettle brought a band of 800 settlers under a white flag to settle near the U.S. fort at Sand Creek. Having been promised

peace, Black Kettle sent most of his men out to hunt. It was the opportunity the Colorado Volunteers had been waiting for. Under the leadership of Colonel John M. Chivington, who told his men to "kill and scalp all, big and little . . . nits make lice," the volunteers swept into the unsuspecting camp early in the morning of November 29, 1864. As Black Kettle raised first an American and then a white flag, Chivington's 700 men, some of them drunk, slaughtered 105 Cheyenne women and children and 28 men. They mutilated the corpses and took scalps back to Denver as trophies. A Cheyenne woman named Iron Teeth, who survived the massacre, remembered seeing a woman "crawling along the ground, shot, scalped, crazy, but not yet dead." In the aftermath, both the Cheyenne and Arapaho tribes were forced to surrender their lands.

Sand Creek Massacre National Historic Site was authorized in 2000 to recognize the national significance of the event in American history, and its ongoing meaning for the

U.S. Cavalry charging into Black Kettle's Cheyenne village during the Sand Creek Massacre, 1864. (© North Wind/ North Wind Picture Archives)

Cheyenne and Arapaho people and the descendants of the victims. While the historic site has been authorized for over 12,000 acres and currently includes about 920 acres, it will not be open to the public until the Park Service can acquire sufficient acreage from state and private landholders.

For more information, write Sand Creek Massacre National Historic Site, P.O. Box 249, Eads, CO 81036, or telephone (719) 438-5916. The park's Web site is www.nps.gov/sand.

FURTHER READING
Brown, Dee Alexander. *Bury My Heart at Wounded Knee: An Indian History of the American West.* New York: Henry Holt, 2001.
Hoig, Stan. *The Sand Creek Massacre.* Norman: University of Oklahoma Press, 1961.
Mendoza, Patrick M. *Song of Sorrow: Massacre at Sand Creek.* Denver, CO: Willow Wind, 1993.
Ortiz, Simon J. *From Sand Creek.* Tucson: University of Arizona Press, 1999.

SAN FRANCISCO MARITIME NATIONAL HISTORICAL PARK
Location: San Francisco, California
Acreage: 50
Established: June 27, 1988

Originally set aside in 1985 as a national historic landmark and part of Golden Gate National recreation area, the 50-acre San Francisco Maritime National Historical Park was established in 1988. It includes a fleet of historic vessels at Hyde Street Pier, the Maritime Museum, and the Maritime Museum Library. This unique park, located at the west end of San Francisco's Fisherman's Wharf, offers history, music, and craft programs for all ages, and provides unique opportunities for docents, interns, and volunteers to become part of history.

Visitors are encouraged to board the park's turn-of-the-century ships—the square-rigged sailing ship *Balclutha,* the steam schooner *Wapama,* the three-masted schooner *Alma,* the steam tug *Hercules,* and the paddle-wheel tug *Eppleton Hall*—tour the museum, and learn traditional arts like boatbuilding and woodworking. The entrance fee is $6 per person (children under twelve admitted free) and is valid for seven days. The Maritime Museum is open daily from 10 A.M. until 5 P.M. Inside this ship-shaped, streamlined, modern structure—built as a Works Progress Administration project—mast sections, jutting spars, and ships' figureheads are arranged among the colorful fish and gleaming tiles of muralist Hilaire Hiler's expressionist vision of Atlantis. Displays include panels, video, oral history re-creations, models, and interactive exhibits. The Steamship Room illustrates the technological evolution of wind-to-steam power. The *Mermaid,* the one-person sailboat that transported a solo adventurer across the Pacific from Japan in ninety-four days, is displayed on the balcony, along with a statue by San Francisco sculptor Beniamino Bufano. Second-floor displays include 3 photomurals of the early San Francisco waterfront, lithographic stones, scrimshaw, and whaling guns. Visitors can participate in frequent interpretive programs such as "When Battleships Were Tricky" and "Historical Charts of San Francisco Bay." Hands-on exhibits, waysides, videos, and tours further explain the park's significance.

There are no food, lodging, or camping facilities at the park, but all traveler services are available in the San Francisco area.

For more information, write San Francisco Maritime National Historical Park, Building E, Fort Mason Center, San Francisco, CA 94123, or telephone (415) 556-3002. The park's Web site is www.nps.gov/safr.

FURTHER READING
Levingston, Steve. *Historic Ships of San Francisco: A Collective History and Guide to the Restored Historic Vessels of the National Maritime Museum.* San Francisco: Chronicle Books, 1984.
Schwendinger, Robert J. *International Port of Call: An Illustrated Maritime History of the Golden Gate.* Woodland Hills, CA: Windsor Publications, 1984.

SAN JUAN NATIONAL HISTORIC SITE

Location: San Juan, Puerto Rico
Acreage: 75
Established: February 14, 1949

On the periphery of Spain's New World Empire, the island of Puerto Rico served as a fortress that protected Spanish trade routes, while San Juan Bay served as a primary port in its plan to govern the Americas. Early in its empire building, Spain recognized the importance of San Juan Bay as a safe haven from tropical storms. It evolved into a secure base of naval operations from which to monitor all shipping entering the Caribbean from Europe. Over time, the Spanish developed Old San Juan into a fortified position that experts later acknowledged to be a "defense of the First Order." San Juan enjoyed the first municipal government in the New World, outside of Santo Domingo, as well as the first military presidio in Spanish America. By the nineteenth century, the old city had become a charming residential and commercial district.

The San Juan National Historic Site is composed of Castles San Felipe del Morro and San Cristóbal, the small Fortress of el Cañuelo, and the walls of Old San Juan. El Morro guarded the western approach and ocean entrance to the harbor while San Cristóbal loomed over the city, ready to repel land-based attacks from the east. Defenders used an elaborate system of hidden tunnels to move cannons, soldiers, and supplies from one part of San Cristóbal to the other in time of battle. Gunpowder charges set into the walls could destroy segments of the tunnels if it became necessary to block an enemy's advance. These 2 great forts, along with 5 miles of massive stone walls that surround the old city, and a small battery fort (El Cañuelo) on the western side of the harbor mouth, completed the defenses of this "gateway to the Antilles." These, together with La Fortaleza, are the largest and oldest of the fortifications constructed by the Spanish in the New World. Their importance within the framework of world history, the magnificence of their architecture, and the military engineering of their epoch make them worthy of study and preservation.

Originally set aside in February 1949, the 75-acre San Juan National Historic Site includes forts, bastions, powder houses, the wall, and El Cañuelo Fort, also called San Juan de la Cruz—defensive fortifications that once surrounded the old, colonial portion of San Juan, Puerto Rico. El Cañuelo Fort is at Isla de Cabras at the western end of the entrance to San Juan Bay. Sections of the massive sandstone walls, dating to the 1630s, remain; so, too, do the San Cristóboal and San Felipe del Morro forts. The city itself, with its institutional buildings, museums, houses, churches, plazas, and commercial buildings, is part of the San Juan Historic Zone that is administered by municipal, state, and federal agencies. Entrance fees are $2 per fort for adults, $1 per fort for youth thirteen to seventeen; children under twelve are admitted free. A $25 annual pass is also available and is valid for both forts.

There are no food, lodging, or camping facilities at the historic site, but all traveler services are available in Old San Juan, Condado, and Isla Verde. Parking in the historic district is extremely limited. Vehicles are not permitted at all on the grounds of El Morro, so visitors should plan on a five-minute, quarter-mile walk from Norzagaray Street to the drawbridge.

For more information, write San Juan National Historic Site, Fort San Cristóbal, Norzagaray Street, San Juan, PR 00901, or telephone (787) 729-6960. The park's Web site is www.nps.gov/saju.

FURTHER READING

Bearss, Edwin C. *San Juan Fortifications, 1898–1958.* Denver, CO: National Park Service, Denver Service Center, 1984.

Forts of Old San Juan: San Juan National Historic Site, Puerto Rico. Washington, DC: National Park Service, 1996.

Wilson, Patricia L. *Old San Juan, El Morro, San Cristobal.* Helena, MT: Eastern National Park and Monument Association, 1994.

SANTA FE NATIONAL HISTORIC TRAIL

Location: Colorado, Kansas, Missouri, New Mexico, and Oklahoma
Acreage: not applicable
Established: May 8, 1987

The Santa Fe National Historic Trail is unusual because it encompasses a 900-mile road and sites along it that stretch from Missouri to Santa Fe, New Mexico. Throughout the middle of the nineteenth century, the Santa Fe Trail was the embodiment of the idea of Manifest Destiny, the notion that the continent had been given to the United States and was to be developed by its people. The trail was the primary link between the United States and the southwestern portion of North America. It was an economic lifeline for Mexico and the United States, allowing the two countries to trade goods, and enabling many of the people who traversed it to become wealthy as traders.

From 1821 to 1846, the Santa Fe Trail was

It took about two months of slow travel and rough camping to cross from Missouri to Santa Fe on the Santa Fe Trail. *(© North Wind/North Wind Picture Archives)*

an international highway and trading route between Mexico and the United States. Prior to Mexican independence, Spain had discouraged contact between its settlers and the United States, but after 1821, the Santa Fe Trail saw an enthusiastic international trade. While the two countries grew richer as a result of the trade, the Plains Indians whose homelands straddled the road lost a great deal. Increased traffic affected the natural resources available to the various tribes, and increased contact with Euro-Americans brought violent conflict in many instances. The trail cut through the hunting grounds of the Comanches, Kiowas, Plains Apaches, Cheyenne, and Arapaho tribes. The Osage, Jicarilla Apache, Ute, and Pueblo people also called the land along the trail home. Sites along the trail preserve the remains of these cultures, as well as symbols of the conflict experienced by them as a result of the encroachment of Euro-Americans on their lands.

In 1846, the Mexican-American War began, and the Santa Fe Trail became the primary supply route for U.S. troops. By 1848, the United States had full control over the area encompassed by the trail, and it became a national highway, rather than an international trade route. Its importance certainly did not diminish, however, as the United States and its army sought to exert control and create an infrastructure over its new territories. By 1860, the trail enabled about $3.5 million in trade to occur. The Santa Fe Trail, which took about eight weeks to cross from Missouri to Santa Fe, maintained its important place in the history of the area until about 1880, when the railroad replaced it as the primary freight route for goods between the Southwest and the rest of the nation.

The cultural and political history of the trail is its most obvious attraction, but along this long historic trail there are many natural wonders and landscapes to be seen. On its eastern end, in Missouri, there is forest and tallgrass prairie. Farther west, the prairie becomes dominant, and then, in western Kansas, the land becomes increasingly arid. Many other national parks, national monuments, and historic sites are located along the trail, which measures a total of 1,203 miles. There are also historic buildings and archeological sites almost everywhere, and in many places, ruts from the metal wagon wheels of the nineteenth century can be easily seen.

Much of the Santa Fe Trail is owned privately, and public parts are managed by a combination of state, local, federal, and nonprofit agencies. One place of particular interest along the trail is Glorieta Pass, located within the Pecos National Historical Park. Here the movement of Confederate troops west during the Civil War was finally halted by U.S. Army troops. After this decisive battle in the war, the Union victory prohibited the Confederate Army from gaining control of the Santa Fe supply line and the silver fields of Colorado.

There are visitor centers located throughout the length of the Santa Fe Trail, in places such as Las Vegas, New Mexico, and Independence, Missouri. Many centers house museums that emphasize aspects of the trail specific to that region. The hours of the sites along the trail vary by site, however, and visitors should consult with the specific site they plan to visit. Although there is no admission fee for the trail, some museums and tourist sites charge a small entrance fee.

There are no food, lodging, or camping facilities directly affiliated with the historic trail, but all traveler services are available along its route.

For more information, write Santa Fe National Historic Trail, P.O. Box 728, Santa Fe, NM 87504-0728, or telephone (505) 988-6888. The park's Web site is www.nps.gov/safe.

FURTHER READING
Dary, David. *The Santa Fe Trail: Its History, Legends, and Lore.* New York: Alfred A. Knopf, 2000.

Vestal, Stanley. *The Old Santa Fe Trail.* Lincoln: University of Nebraska Press, 1996.

SANTA MONICA MOUNTAINS NATIONAL RECREATION AREA

Location: Thousand Oaks, California
Acreage: 154,095
Established: November 10, 1978

Known as "L.A.'s backyard," the Santa Monica Mountains provide this megalopolis of 20 million people with a stunning array of recreation opportunities, from rugged mountains, to sandy beaches, rocky shores, and chaparral-covered canyons. Creation of the world's largest urban national park was part of an effort in the 1960s and 1970s to address the burgeoning demand for outdoor amenities arising from the nation's cities. Although national recreation areas typically do not meet the more rigorous natural resource standards required of other areas included in the national park system, they do fulfill an important niche in the Park Service's goal of providing accessible recreation. For Southern California residents, the park offers immediate admission into the rarest of all the world's biomes—a Mediterranean, or broadleaf evergreen forest ecosystem. There are currently twenty-five known species native to the Santa Monica Mountains National Recreation Area that are listed as rare, threatened, or endangered—such as the steelhead trout—and another fifty candidate species for listing are also associated with the park. Amazingly, within minutes of downtown Los Angeles, mountain lions, coyotes, bobcats, and deer thrive. The park also protects more than 1,000 archeological sites associated with the region's interesting cultural history that begins with the Chumash and Gabrielino/Tongva peoples.

Established in November 1978, the 154,095-acre national recreation area features rugged mountains, a coastline with sandy beaches and rocky shores, chaparral-covered canyons, and abundant wildlife. Admission is free. The recreation area is a cooperative effort that joins federal, state, and local park agencies with private preserves and landowners to protect the natural and cultural resources of this transverse mountain range and seashore. The park's headquarters and visitor center, located at 401 West Hillcrest Drive in Thousand Oaks, is open year-round from 9 A.M. until 5 P.M.; it features orientation exhibits, interactive displays, and historical art work. The recreation area has more than 580 miles of public trails, including the newly completed, 65-mile Backbone Trail, which links the major park areas together from east to west. Visitors will also enjoy the historic Mulholland Scenic Corridor, a 55-mile scenic drive through the Santa Monica Mountains from Griffith Park to Leo Carrillo State Park.

There are no food or lodging facilities in the park, but all traveler services are available locally. Most of the campgrounds in the recreation area are California State Parks; facilities vary, and most require reservations.

For more information, write Santa Monica Mountains National Recreation Area, 401 West Hillcrest Drive, Thousand Oaks, CA 91360, or telephone (805) 370-2301. The park's Web site is www.nps.gov/samo.

FURTHER READING
Huffman, Margaret. *The Wild Heart of Los Angeles.* Niwot, CO: Robert Rinehart, 1998.
McAuley, Milt. *Wildflowers of the Santa Monica Mountains.* Canoga Park, CA: Canyon, 1985.

SARATOGA NATIONAL HISTORICAL PARK

Location: Stillwater, New York
Acreage: 3,392
Established: June 1, 1938

The stage on which the American Revolution took place was broad, and the overall war trend was generally north to south. From the "shot heard 'round the world" in Concord, Massachusetts, in 1775 through Washington's assault on Trenton in December 1776, the war was focused primarily in the north. In 1776, the British relocated their headquarters from the untenable city of Boston to the better-fortified city/harbor of New York, and thus the war's middle years, particularly 1777, witnessed the most action in the middle colonies. That same year, American victory at Saratoga, New York, caused an increasingly anxious and impatient Britain to shift its focus to a more southern theater, where the war's final years would conclude.

Saratoga, in the middle of the war, proved critical in terms of both morale and military alliance. From the outset of fighting, George Washington and his troops were outmanned, outgunned, outcommanded, and outsupplied. Despite these seemingly insurmountable odds, the Continental Army, and Washington in particular, seized upon a bold and innovative plan for achieving independence. The army was the symbol of the republican cause—as long as it survived, so too would colonial hopes of escaping monarchy. Thus, Washington used his troops carefully; he could not and would not fight traditional frontal assault battles on British terms, but instead would fight and retreat. While critics complained about his caution, Washington understood that as long as he did not lose the army, the Americans would not lose the war.

By 1777, after two years of fighting, the British grew frustrated with this annoying and costly strategy and sent in General John Burgoyne—"Gentleman Johnny"—to finish off the Americans. On September 19, three separate columns of the British Royal Army advanced on the camp in east-central New York. American General Horatio Gates and his men were ready. Fighting raged back and forth for more than three hours, before the late arrival of German reinforcements saved Burgoyne's men from defeat.

But the "victory" that day was hollow. The British were low on supplies and men—supply lines stretched across the Atlantic were simply inadequate—while the Americans drew strength daily from the surrounding countryside. In the aftermath of the first encounter, both of Burgoyne's choices were distasteful: a 200-mile retreat to Canada or an assault on the growing American ranks. Fatefully, he chose the latter. On October 7, the redcoats attacked and were quickly thrown on their heels and began to retreat northward. They got as far as Saratoga (present-day Schuylerville) before being surrounded by Gates's men and forced to surrender. On October 17, 1777, 5,800 British soldiers—all that remained of Burgoyne's command—laid down their arms and became prisoners of war. In addition to serving as the first significant American military victory during the Revolution, the battles of Saratoga also led France to recognize the independence of the United States and enter the war as a decisive military ally of the struggling colonists.

First authorized as a New York state park in 1927 on the sesquicentennial of the battles, the 3,392-acre battlefield was made part of the national park system in 1938, when Saratoga National Historical Park was authorized by the U.S. Congress. The park now comprises 3 separate units: the 4-square-mile Battlefield in Stillwater, New York, the General Philip Schuyler House 8 miles north in Schuylerville, and the Saratoga Monument in the nearby village of Victory. Entrance fees are $2 per person or $4 per vehicle and are valid for seven days; a $10 annual pass is also available. The park's visitor center, located on the north end of the battlefield, is open year-round from 9 A.M. until 5 P.M., and it has a twenty-minute introductory film, two dioramas, and a small museum containing artifacts from the time of the battles, including 5 original cannons from the defeated British army. Thematic seasonal exhibits are also offered throughout the year. Park rangers offer guided tours of Schuyler House during the summer months, as well as living-history programs and demonstrations of campfire cooking, sewing, wood carving, fire building, musket drills, music, blacksmithing, tinsmithing, and other eighteenth-century activities. During the winter and spring, the park hosts a Frost Faire, a March for Parks fund-raiser, and a Crown Forces encampment. In the summer, the battlefield offers the annual Fourth of July celebration, colonial demonstrations, military encampments, and interpretive programs on topics ranging from colonial history to the environment. In September, the park hosts an annual event to commemorate the two battles, which includes programs centered around the American, British, German, and Canadian forces encamped as they were in the fall of 1777. The 9.5-mile Battlefield Tour Road starts at the end of the visitor center parking lot and is a single-lane, one-way road that loops through the American defensive positions, then the actual battle sites, and finishes at the British defensive positions overlooking the Hudson River. There are 10 interpretive stops along the road. Saratoga battlefield's hiking trail system features the 4.2-mile Wilkinson National Historic Trail, developed and maintained in partnership with the Boy Scouts of America, through some of the most significant areas associated with the battles of Saratoga.

The Philip Schuyler Country House, located at the south end of the village of Schuylerville, approximately 7 miles north of the battlefield, is open from Memorial Day through Labor Day from 10 A.M. until 4:30 P.M. This historic home is furnished to help interpret the lives of Philip Schuyler, American Revolutionary War general and noted statesman, and his family during the period 1777–1837. Access is by guided tour only, and admission is free. The Saratoga Monument, located in the village of Victory, is an imposing 154.5-foot obelisk commemorating the battles of Saratoga and General Bur-

goyne's surrender. Begun on October 17, 1877, and eventually dedicated in 1912, the monument was built by a citizens' group and was transferred to the U.S. Department of the Interior in 1980. Three niches on the outside of the base contain life-sized statues commemorating three of the four commanders instrumental in the American victory: General Philip Schuyler, General Horatio Gates, and Colonel Daniel Morgan. A fourth niche was to house a statue of General Benedict Arnold; it stands empty, in witness to his turning traitor later in the war. The Neilson House, the only standing structure left from the time of the battles of Saratoga, also served as one of the American headquarters buildings. It is open from late May through the summer, from 10 A.M. until 4:30 P.M. It is furnished to reflect its use by the American army during their stay on Bemis Heights and is staffed by a volunteer or a park ranger in eighteenth-century-style clothing, who gives living-history demonstrations (sewing, cooking, wood carving, fire building, or other period craft).

There are no food, lodging, or camping facilities at the historical park, but all traveler services are available in Saratoga Springs, Schuylerville, and Stillwater.

For more information, write Saratoga National Historical Park, 648 Route 32, Stillwater, NY 12170, or telephone (518) 664-9821. The park's Web site is www.nps.gov/sara.

FURTHER READING

Ketchum, Richard M. *Saratoga: Turning Point of America's Revolutionary War.* New York: Henry Holt, 1997.

Mintz, Max M. *The Generals of Saratoga: John Burgoyne and Horatio Gates.* New Haven, CT: Yale University Press, 1990.

SAUGUS IRON WORKS NATIONAL HISTORIC SITE

Location: Saugus, Massachusetts
Acreage: 9
Established: April 5, 1968

In the 1640s, John Winthrop, Jr., the son of the governor of the Massachusetts Bay Colony, began to raise capital and recruit expertise to create the first iron works in the New World. In England, he found twenty-four investors willing to support the project and about sixty artisans eager to move to Massachusetts to operate the new endeavor. The younger Winthrop obtained a grant for iron ore deposits and acquired the rights to land and water, the latter to power the required mill in Saugus, 5 miles northeast of Boston on the Saugus River. In 1646, the Saugus Iron Works began operation, providing finished products such as kettles, pots, and pans as well as bulk material for other purposes.

The iron ore smelting process was one of the most complicated transformations of natural material of its day. Using gabbro, a dense rock, in place of the more traditional limestone, helped the mill eliminate impurities in the bog iron ore. The furnace required enormous amounts of charcoal, most from acres of cut hardwood trees, to maintain the heat necessary to convert the ore to a liquid form of iron. Once liquid, molders could shape the iron into any desired form.

Saugus also had one of the first company towns in the New World. Near the mill stood the town of Hammersmith, run by the company for its employees. Housing, a company farm, and other features suggest the company's power over its employees and their dependents.

In 1968, as part of a Park Service strategy to widely represent the historic and natural past of the nation, Congress authorized the 9-acre Saugus Iron Works National Historic

Saugus Iron Works National Historic Site illustrates the critical role of iron making in seventeenth-century settlement and its legacy in shaping the nation's early history. *(National Park Service)*

Site, "the forerunner of America's industrial giants," to commemorate the first integrated ironworks in North America. The site contains an open-air museum with working waterwheels, as well as the reconstructed blast furnace, forge, rolling mill, and a restored seventeenth-century house. Demonstrations, a ten-minute slide show, and living-history interpretations are offered regularly, and visitors may also tour the Iron Works House, which dates from the seventeenth century, as well as an herb garden representative of that time. A 2-mile nature trail takes visitors through a marsh and a woodland area that reveals some of the flora and fauna of the area. Admission is free.

There are no food, lodging, or camping facilities at the historic site, but all traveler services are available in the Boston area.

For more information, write Saugus Iron Works National Historic Site, 244 Central Street, Saugus, Massachusetts 01906, or telephone (781) 233-0050. The park's Web site is www.nps.gov/sair.

FURTHER READING

Carlson, Stephen P. *First Iron Works: A History of the First Iron Works Association.* Saugus, MA: Saugus Historical Society, n.d.

Hartley, E.N. *Ironworks on the Saugus: the Lynn and Braintree Ventures of the Company of Undertakers of the Ironworks in New England.* Norman: University of Oklahoma Press, 1957.

SCOTTS BLUFF NATIONAL MONUMENT

Location: Gering, Nebraska
Acreage: 3,005
Established: December 12, 1919

Today the hills of the North Platte Valley are not counted among the scenic wonders of the United States. On the Oregon Trail, to emigrants who had become bored with the flatness and drabness of the Platte scenery, and who would later be too exhausted to appreciate the grandeur of the Rocky Mountains, the landmarks along the Platte had a captivating charm. Courthouse Rock and Chimney Rock were the appetizers; Scotts Bluff was the grand climax.

Present-day Scotts Bluff is but a part of the historic "Scotts Bluffs" named for Hiram Scott, an employee of the Rocky Mountain Fur Company, whose skeleton was found in the vicinity in 1829. The first whites known to have seen Scotts Bluff were fur traders traveling from their trading post at the mouth of the Columbia River to St. Louis. Their perilous 1812 journey also blazed the route via the Upper Snake, Green, and North Platte rivers that was destined to become the

Summit observation point on the north promontory of Scotts Bluff, 1939. *(National Archives)*

Oregon Trail. By the 1840s, the transcontinental migration began in earnest, and Scotts Bluff became an important progress marker along the weary miles of the Oregon, Mormon, and California trails. In 1842, Medorem Crawford, who echoed the sentiments of many immigrants, described Scotts Bluff as "the most romantic scenery I ever saw." That same year, Lieutenant John C. Frémont led the first expedition to the Rocky Mountains, and his official report would become a standard reference. Frémont described Scotts Bluff as "an escarpment on the river of about 900 yards in length," which "forces the road to make a considerable circuit over the uplands." He found the plain between the bluffs and Chimney Rock almost entirely covered with driftwood, testifying to a recent flood.

Established in December 1919, the 3,005-acre Scotts Bluff National Monument preserves this prominent natural landmark as well as the landscape and cultural history of the vast prairie that pioneers on the overland trails traversed. The monument is open daily from 8 A.M. until 5 P.M. (and for extended hours during the summer), and the entrance fee is $5 per vehicle; a $15 annual pass is also available. The Oregon Trail Museum features exhibits on westward migration and the history and geology of the region. During the summer, the park offers living-history presentations, and park rangers give guided walks and tours. The Summit Road allows visitors to drive to the top of Scotts Bluff for a view of the valley, while the 1.6-mile Saddle Rock Trail leads hikers from the visitor center to the summit, and the half-mile Oregon Trail Pathway leads from the visitor center to the remnants of the Oregon Trail.

A special feature of Scotts Bluff National Monument is its large collection of watercolor paintings by William Henry Jackson, a frontier photographer and artist. A true American icon, Jackson lived ninety-nine years, from 1842 to 1943, bridging the nineteenth and twentieth centuries. He served in the Union Army during the Civil War, though he saw no action. In 1866, Jackson decided to go west and headed to Montana. Later, he opened a photography studio in Nebraska and was hired by the Union Pacific Railroad to photograph construction on its railroad. This work made him prominent enough that he was chosen as a photographer on the expedition to Yellowstone, and he became the first person to capture the wonders of the region on film. His work in Yellowstone was key to convincing Congress to establish it as the first national park. Scotts Bluff National Monument houses a large collection of Jackson's paintings, with 63 original watercolors.

There are no food, lodging, or camping facilities at the monument, but there are travel services in Gering and Scottsbluff.

For more information, write Scotts Bluff National Monument, P.O. Box 27, Gering, NE 69341-0027, or telephone (308) 436-4340. The park's Web site is www. nps.gov/scbl.

FURTHER READING

Brand, Donald D. *The History of Scotts Bluff Nebraska.* Berkeley, CA: National Park Service, Field Division of Education, 1934. Available at www.cr.nps. gov/history/online_books/berkeley/brand1/index. htm.

Cockrell, Ron. *Scotts Bluff National Monument, Nebraska: An Administrative History, 1960–1983.* Omaha, NE: National Park Service, Midwest Regional Office, 1983. Available at www.nps.gov/ scbl/adhi/adhi.htm.

Mattes, Merrill J. *Scotts Bluff National Monument Nebraska.* Washington, DC: National Park Service, 1958. Available at www.cr.nps.gov/history/online _books/hh/28/index.htm.

SELMA TO MONTGOMERY NATIONAL HISTORIC TRAIL AND ALL-AMERICAN ROAD

Location: Montgomery, Lowndes, and
 Dallas Counties, Alabama
Acreage: not applicable
Established: November 12, 1996

Selma-to-Montgomery marchers wave American flags in front of the Alabama State Capitol at the end of their five-day march. *(Library of Congress)*

During the first half of the 1960s, the civil rights movement captured the hearts of Americans who, when forced to confront the system of segregation that had become the national custom, found it increasingly untenable. No one contributed more to that change in sentiment than did the Reverend Dr. Martin Luther King, Jr.

A passionate and dramatic spokesman and thinker for the cause of the civil rights, King brought the techniques of nonviolence perfected by Mohandas K. Gandhi in India to the American struggle for equality. King was the most powerful moral voice in the nation in the 1960s, the one person who transcended the time and saw and clearly articulated a greater, more just nation. His strategy of ongoing passive nonviolent resis-

tance won him friends and admiration throughout the nation and the world.

By 1965, the struggle for equality under the law was nearing its end. Only the most recalcitrant of southerners remained staunch segregationists, and the list of laws that made segregation illegal had grown long. Yet resistance remained, especially to granting the right to vote to African Americans. Only in voting could anyone experience the full range of the rights of a citizen; only by denying the right to vote could segregationists retain a symbolic hold on those they sought to deny the full privileges of American citizenship.

The resistance to African Americans in the Deep South was palpable. Despite the clear shift in public opinion in favor of civil rights, African American voter registration in the South improved only marginally in the first half of the 1960s. As late as 1963, more than 80 percent of Alabama's eligible African American voters were not registered; in Dallas County, where Selma was located, only 333 of 15,000 eligible African Americans were registered. A direct-action campaign seemed the best strategy. Reverend King chose Selma as the place for the Alabama voting-rights crusade to begin.

The civil rights revolution seemed to have bypassed Selma. About 50 miles west of Alabama's capital, Montgomery, the 29,000-person town along the banks of the muddy Alabama River retained all the traits of the pre–civil rights rural South. Its population was more than 50 percent African American, but in 1964, the schools remain segregated—a full decade after the *Brown v. Board of Education* Supreme Court decision made school segregation illegal. The white community consigned African Americans to an untraveled, unpaved section of town. Despite their numbers, African Americans had few opportunities and no political clout.

On January 18, 1965, King's campaign began. Civil rights workers tested restaurants, hotels, and other facilities, and 400 marchers strode to the courthouse in search of the right to vote. The first day passed without incident, but on the second, Sheriff Jim Clark, a tough-talking, burly man who hailed from even more rural Alabama, lost his composure. He had marchers arrested, and he personally grabbed Amelia Boynton, an African American businesswoman and civil rights activist, and roughly shoved her into his car. In the following days, hundreds of marchers besieged the courthouse. Clark repeated his action with another African American woman, but she retaliated by punching him, sparking a melee in which sheriff's deputies beat her with their clubs.

The Selma-to-Montgomery march for voting rights came on the heels of the attempt to register African American voters in Selma. On "Bloody Sunday," March 7, 1965, more than 600 civil rights marchers left Selma on U.S. Route 80, led by the Reverend Hosea Williams and John Lewis, a young Student Nonviolent Coordinating Committee (SNCC) activist. When the marchers reached the Edmund Pettus Bridge 6 blocks away, George Wallace's "Storm-troopers," as civil rights workers referred to the Alabama state police, awaited them in droves. The troopers rushed forward, charging into the marchers with their clubs swinging wildly. Men and women fell to the ground in agony; a blow fractured Lewis's skull. Lewis survived the attack and went on to a long and distinguished career as a civil rights activist and political leader, later becoming a U.S. congressman from Georgia.

The attack moved the nation. ABC television interrupted the film *Judgment at Nuremberg* to show a vivid film clip of the attack; newspapers and news magazines covered the story, and throughout the nation, people marched against the violence. President Lyndon B. Johnson, perhaps the strongest supporter of civil rights ever to sit in the White House, deplored the brutality. In Detroit, more than 10,000 people joined the Republican governor of Michigan and a Democratic U.S. senator in protest. Similar demonstrations dotted the country.

On March 9, in defiance of a federal court order to desist, King led a "symbolic" march to the bridge that ended in circumstances that seemed almost biblical. The marchers reached the bridge, where a federal marshal read aloud the order that prohibited them from marching. Row after row of state troopers threatened the marchers. They asked for time to pray, which they received on the condition that they return to their church. During the prayer, one African Methodist minister from Washington, D.C., likened their quest to the exodus from Egypt and implored God to part the waters and let them pass. Immediately after, almost magically, the troopers stood to one side and left the road to Montgomery clear. The marchers did not continue; instead they returned to Selma to seek legal protection for a march to the state capital.

During the intervening days, two events changed the nature of the struggle. Segregationist thugs in Selma attacked James Reeb, a white Unitarian minister among the many clergymen who had joined King in Selma. They clubbed him in the head, and he died a few days later. Reeb's death inspired a great deal more tension than the similar death a few days earlier of Jimmie Lee Jackson, a twenty-five-year-old African American and a deacon of his church. President Johnson was so shaken by the murders that he went before Congress to introduce his Voting Rights bill, the first time in nineteen years that an American president had addressed Congress about domestic legislation. Johnson ended his speech with the anthem of the civil rights movement: "we shall overcome."

After Johnson's speech, and after the president sent military police, U.S. marshals, and other federal officials to Selma, King's planned march began. Federal District Judge Frank M. Johnson, Jr., provided legal protection. "The law is clear that the right to petition one's government for the redress of grievances may be exercised in large groups," said the judge. "And these rights may be exercised by marching, even along public highways." On Sunday, March 21, about 3,200 marchers set out for Montgomery, walking 12 miles a day. By the time they reached the capitol on March 25, they were 25,000 strong. As they marched through the streets of Montgomery, where King had begun as a pastor just a decade before, King felt that the civil rights movement had come full circle. Before the end of the year, Johnson signed the Voting Rights Act of 1965 into law, adding another layer of protection for African Americans.

In 1996, Congress created the Selma to Montgomery National Historic Trail under the National Trails System Act of 1968. Like other trails similarly designated, the Alabama trail is an original route of national significance in American history. An interagency panel recommended, and the secretary of transportation subsequently designated the trail an "All-American Road," a road that is nationally significant, cannot be duplicated, and is a destination unto itself. This designation is the highest tribute a road can receive under the Federal Highway Administration's National Scenic Byways Program.

The Selma to Montgomery National Historic Trail and All-American Road does not have visitor facilities constructed at this time; however, the driving trail from the Brown Chapel AME (African Methodist Episcopal) Church in Selma to the state capital in Montgomery is a main corridor and open for public use twenty-four hours a day, and trail markers are visible from the highway. In Selma, visitors may tour the privately owned National Voting Rights Museum, Edmund Pettus Bridge, National Voting Rights Monument, and Brown Chapel AME Church and take a historic walking tour. In Montgomery, visitors should see the Alabama State Capitol, the Civil Rights Monument, and the Dexter Avenue King Memorial Baptist Church. At press time, the Park Service had announced its plans to open a new Lowndes County Interpretive Center and a contact station in Selma sometime in early 2005.

There are no food, lodging, or camping facilities associated with the historic trail, but all traveler services are available along the trail's corridor.

For more information, write Selma to Montgomery National Historic Trail and All-American Road, 1212 Old Montgomery Road, Tuskegee, AL 36087, or telephone (334) 727-6390. The park's Web site is www.nps.gov/semo.

FURTHER READING

Branch, Taylor. *Pillar of Fire: America in the King Years, 1963–65.* New York: Simon and Schuster, 1998.

Farmer, James. *Lay Bare the Heart: An Autobiography of the Civil Rights Movement.* New York: Arbor House, 1985.

King, Martin Luther, Jr. *Stride Toward Freedom: The Montgomery Story.* New York: Harper, 1958.

Lewis, David. *King, a Critical Biography.* New York: Praeger, 1970.

Oates, Stephen B. *Let the Trumpet Sound: The Life of Martin Luther King, Jr.* New York: New American Library, 1985.

Powledge, Fred. *Free at Last? The Civil Rights Movement and the People Who Made It.* Boston: Little, Brown, 1991.

SEQUOIA AND KINGS CANYON NATIONAL PARKS

Location: Three Rivers, California
Acreage: 865,952
Established: September 25, 1890

These two adjacent parks, Sequoia and Kings Canyon National Parks, protect and preserve the majestic landscape of the Sierra foothills as they rise from central California. Sequoia, the second national park to be designated by Congress, was created just ahead of Yosemite in 1890. One week later, the small, 4-square-mile General Grant National Park was created to protect the giant sequoias that remained in the area. Both parks grew over time; in 1940, General Grant National Park was absorbed into the newly created Kings Canyon National Park, and Big Stump Basin became part of the park in 1958. In 1978, Mineral King Valley and its surrounding peaks became part of Sequoia National Park. Though designated separately, the two parks are managed as one. The U.S. Army administered the park between 1891 and 1914, providing outstanding protection but doing little to make the parks' wonders accessible to the public. As natural parks gained in popularity after 1900, roads into areas such as Grant Grove became a priority and were built during the early twentieth century.

The parks provide visitors a view of some of the most stunning, awe-inspiring natural landscape in the western United States. Primary among the visitor destinations is the Giant Forest, in which four of the five world's largest sequoias grow. These magnificent trees are estimated to be between eighteen hundred and twenty-seven hundred years old. General Sherman, the largest, is as tall as a 26-story building, with a volume of over 52,500 cubic feet. General Sherman is the largest giant sequoia now, but only because it survived the logging of the late 1800s. Walter Fry, who later became the first chief ranger and then the first civilian superintendent of the parks, was introduced to the giant sequoia on a logging team. He and his team spent five days in 1888 sawing down a giant sequoia. When it was felled, Fry counted the growth rings and discovered that he had just taken down a tree that was more than three thousand years old. This realization prompted him to change careers, and he became a vocal advocate for national park status for the area. In 1914, when the U.S. Army ceded control of the park, Fry stepped into a leadership role.

Another famous giant sequoia is General Grant, located in Grant Grove. General Grant is the third largest tree in Sequoia National Park, but its greatest distinction comes from its designation as the national Christmas tree. President Calvin Coolidge first designated it as the national Christmas tree in April 1928, and the tradition continues. Every year a ceremony that includes the placement of a wreath on the tree takes place in early December. General Grant also has the distinction of being the only living national shrine in the United States. It commemorates all Americans who have lost their lives in war.

The parks are open year-round and have

Having fun in the snow at Sequoia National Park in March 1942. *(Library of Congress)*

3 visitor centers. Foothills Visitor Center, located on the Generals Highway in Sequoia, is open from 8 A.M. until 4:30 P.M. daily, and it has exhibits focusing on the Sierra foothills ecosystem, the most biologically diverse area of these parks. The Grant Grove Visitor Center, located 3 miles east on Highway 180 from the Big Stump Entrance Station in Kings Canyon, is open from 9 A.M. until 4:30 P.M. daily; it features exhibits on the rich human and natural history of Grant Grove and its world-famous sequoia trees, as well as a slide program on the sights and sounds of Kings Canyon Park. The Lodgepole Visitor Center, located on Lodgepole Road just off the Generals Highway in Sequoia, is closed Tuesday to Thursday in winter and offers exhibits on the natural and human history of the southern Sierra Nevada, as well as a slide show about the park. Entrance fees are $5 per person or $10 per vehicle and are valid for seven days;

a $20 annual pass is also available. The 865,000-plus-acre parks also boast a fine Giant Forest Museum, housed in a historic building 16 miles from Sequoia National Park's entrance on Highway 198, with exhibits telling the story of the sequoias of Giant Forest and what has been learned here about how to protect them.

In summer, rangers lead walks and talks in the foothills, the sequoia groves, and the high country, and pack stations offer horseback riding. Come winter, cross-country skis or snowshoes can be rented to explore the sequoia groves beyond the roads, or visitors can join a ranger-guided snowshoe walk. In addition to the giant sequoias, the park contains beautiful waterfalls, caves, and other features of the foothills of the mighty Sierra Mountains. Cedar Grove, located in a glaciated valley along the Kings River, allows visitors to view waterfalls, granite cliffs, and the powerful river. The paved trail to Roaring River Falls leads visitors to a waterfall, while the Zumwalt Meadow Trail displays stunning rock formations and a view of the Kings River.

One of the most beautiful features of Sequoia and Kings Canyon is Crystal Cave. Discovered in 1918 by construction employees who were fishing on their day off, the cave is filled with stalactite and stalagmite formations. The temperature in the cave stays at a constant 48 degrees. The cave, an amazing natural wonder, can only be viewed on a guided tour, and tickets must be purchased at one of the visitor centers in Sequoia National Park. The tour is forty-five minutes long and goes from room to room in the cave on lighted pathways.

Several lodging and food options are available in the park. The Kings Canyon Park Services' Cedar Grove Lodge (559-335-5500) is open from late April to mid-November, and it offers rooms, a restaurant, market, and gift shop. Grant Grove Lodge (559-335-5500), also part of the Kings Canyon Park Services, is open year-round and has modern rooms in a lodge, rustic cabins, and housekeeping cabins in the Grant Grove area of the park. Wuksachi Village (888-252-5757), run by the Delaware North Park Services, also is open year-round and offers modern hotel rooms in several lodge buildings, with a restaurant and gift shop nearby. There are also 14 campgrounds located in the parks. Facilities and fees vary, and 4 are open year-round: Azalea in Kings Canyon, and Lodgepole, Potwisha, and South Fork in Sequoia.

For more information, write Sequoia and Kings Canyon National Parks, 47050 Generals Highway, Three Rivers, CA 93271-9651, or telephone (559) 565-3341. The park's Web site is www.nps.gov/seki.

FURTHER READING
Dilsaver, Lary M. *Challenge of the Big Trees: A Resource History of Sequoia and Kings Canyon National Parks.* Three Rivers, CA: Sequoia Natural History Association, 1990.
Jackson, Louise A. *Beulah: A Biography of the Mineral King Valley of California.* Tucson, AZ: Westernlore, 1988.
Keith, Sandra L. *Sequoia National Park: An Illustrated History.* Santa Barbara, CA: Sequoia Communications, 1989.
Orsi, Richard J., Alfred Runte, and Marlene Smith-Baranzini, eds. *Yosemite and Sequoia: A Century of California National Parks.* Berkeley: University of California Press, 1993.
Shrepfer, Susan. *The Fight to Save the Redwoods.* Madison: University of Wisconsin Press, 1983.

SHENANDOAH NATIONAL PARK
Location: Luray, Virginia
Acreage: 199,045
Established: May 22, 1926

Nestled in the Blue Ridge Mountains, the eastern portion of the Appalachian Mountains between Pennsylvania and Georgia, Shenandoah National Park represented an important expansion of the park system. Part of the National Park Service effort to become a national organization in the 1920s, Shenandoah and the two other parks authorized along with it, Mammoth Cave and Great Smoky Mountains, gave the agency a major presence in the eastern part of the nation. Along with Acadia National Park, these parks put the Park Service close to the overwhelming majority of the American population as well as the most influential congressional leaders. This presence helped push the Park Service beyond rival federal agencies such as the Forest Service and gave it a claim on congressional resources it never had before.

As did most national park efforts, the struggle to create Shenandoah began with influential local people who brought the area to the attention of the Park Service. Founded in 1916, the agency needed time to consolidate and develop a constituency before it could tackle the development of major national

Drying apples, one of the few sources of income for mountain folk in 1935, Shenandoah National Park. *(Library of Congress)*

parks in the East. The difference in strategy stemmed from the lack of public land. Most western national parks were created from the public domain, while little such land could be found in the East. As a result, the Park Service needed much more local support to create Shenandoah and its peers than it did to create similar parks in the West. The support of people such as Harry Flood, and his nephew Harry Flood Byrd, played an important role in founding the park.

Shenandoah was also the scene of a struggle about prior residents inside the park. The people who lived inside the park were reluctant to leave, and until 1934, the Park Service allowed them to stay. That year, the policy changed, and as many as 465 families were paid for their land under the power of eminent domain and removed. This controversial

action was typical of the time. It reflected a powerful sense that the public good was more important than any individual's objectives and created long-standing rancor against the park.

Shenandoah National Park is a spectacular scenic area, offering a wonderful visual experience. The Shenandoah River flows through the Shenandoah Valley to the west, where Massanutten Mountain, a 40-mile-long curvature separates the river's north and south forks. Two peaks rise above 4,000 feet, and the range of elevation, slopes and aspects, rocks and soils, precipitation, and latitude creates a mix of habitats.

The park also protects nearly 80,000 acres of wilderness, a small amount by national standards but an important component in the East. The terms of the Wilderness Act in 1964 guaranteed that most designated wilderness areas would be in the West, where public lands were abundant. The result was a stunning disparity that Congress sought to correct with the 1975 Eastern Wilderness Act. It allowed the inclusion of wild areas that showed human use but were now returning to a natural state. Shenandoah National Park had been a human landscape before its protection, and national park designation allowed a new Shenandoah, far less affected by human endeavor, to emerge. In 1976, 79,019 acres of Shenandoah National Park were added to the National Wilderness Preservation System. In 1978, an additional 560 acres were designated as wilderness, and today more than 40 percent of the park, 79,579 acres, is wilderness.

Visitors will enjoy the Skyline Drive, a 105-mile road that winds along the crest of the mountains through the length of the park, which provides vistas of the spectacular landscape to the east and west. In addition, the park has more than 500 miles of trails, including 101 miles of the Appalachian Trail, which may follow a ridge crest, lead to high places with panoramic views, or pass waterfalls in deep canyons. Many animals, including deer, black bears, and wild turkeys, flourish among the rich growth of an oak-hickory forest. In season, bushes and wildflowers bloom along the drive and trails and fill the open spaces. Apple trees, stone foundations, and cemeteries are reminders of the families who once called this place home.

The almost-200,000-acre Shenandoah National Park maintains 3 visitor contact facilities. Both the Dickey Ridge Visitor Center, at mile 4.6 on the Skyline Drive, and the Harry F. Byrd, Sr. Visitor Center, at mile 51 on the Skyline Drive, are open from mid-April through November, from 8:30 A.M. until 5 P.M. They offer exhibits, videos, sales, publications, maps, backcountry permits, and first aid. Many ranger-led programs and hikes begin here. The Loft Mountain Information Center, at mile 79.5 on the Skyline Drive, is open from late May until early November from 9 A.M. until 5 P.M., Friday through Tuesday. The information center also has an information desk, sales, publications, maps, backcountry permits, and first aid, and it offers many ranger-led programs and hikes. Entrance fees are $5 per person or $10 per vehicle, and are valid for seven days; a $20 annual pass also is available.

Lodging is available in the park at 4 locations (800-999-4714). Skyland (milepost 41.7) has 177 guest rooms, rustic cabins, multi-unit lodges, and modern suites. Big Meadows (milepost 51) has 25 rooms in the main lodge, 72 additional rooms in rustic cabins, multi-unit lodges, and modern suites. Lewis Mountain (milepost 57.5) has several rustic, furnished cabins with private baths and outdoor grill areas. The Potomac Appalachian Trail Club (703-242-0693), an authorized park concessionaire, operates 6 locked, primitive cabins in the park equipped with mattresses, blankets, and cookware. A pit toilet and spring water are nearby. Shenandoah National Park maintains 5 campgrounds, ranging from primitive to developed, and facilities and fees vary accordingly. The park itself is always open, but some portions of the Skyline Drive, the only road through Shenandoah National Park, are closed from dusk to early morning during hunting season. This road also closes in inclement weather for safety reasons. Visitor facilities and services begin operating between early April and Memorial Day and close down by late November.

For more information, write Shenandoah National Park, 3655 U.S. Highway 211 East, Luray, VA 22835-9036, or telephone (540) 999-3500. The park's Web site is www.nps.gov/shen.

FURTHER READING

Conners, John A. *Shenandoah National Park: An Interpretive Guide.* Blacksburg, VA: McDonald and Woodward, 1988.

Lambert, Darwin. *The Undying Past of Shenandoah National Park.* Boulder, CO: Roberts Rinehart, 1989.

Mitchell, Robert D. *Commercialism and Frontier: Perspectives on the Early Shenandoah Valley.* Charlottesville: University Press of Virginia, 1977.

Moore, Hullihen Williams. *Shenandoah: Views of Our National Park.* Charlottesville: University of Virginia Press, 2003.

Reeder, Carolyn, and Jack Reeder. *Shenandoah Heritage: The Story of the People Before the Park.* Washington, DC: Potomac Appalachian Trail Club, 1978.

Simpson, Marcus B. *Birds of the Blue Ridge Mountains: A Guide for the Blue Ridge Parkway, Great Smoky Mountains, Shenandoah National Park, and Neighboring Areas.* Chapel Hill: University of North Carolina, 1992.

SHILOH NATIONAL MILITARY PARK

Location: Shiloh, Tennessee
Acreage: 5,048
Established: December 27, 1894

Shiloh National Military Park commemorates the first major battle in the Civil War's western theater, a two-day bloodbath that ultimately allowed federal troops to march on and seize the Confederate railway system at Corinth, Mississippi. With nearly 24,000 Union and Confederate troops dead, missing, or wounded in its aftermath, the April 1862 Battle of Shiloh (Pittsburg Landing) was an important turning point in the war. After Shiloh, contemporaries said, the South never smiled. It was here in the western theater that Union commander Ulysses S. Grant rose to prominence. Although he had graduated toward the bottom of his class at West Point, Grant was a shrewd and modern military tactician. Yet for all of his skills and knowledge, Grant nearly lost his entire command at Shiloh. On the eve of the battle, Grant telegraphed Union General Henry W. Halleck, "I have scarcely the faintest idea of an attack . . . being made upon us." He could not have been more wrong. As Confederate troops massed early on the morning of April 6, Union soldiers blithely enjoyed their break-

fast. They were stunned by the rebel onslaught. As one private recalled, "everybody was running . . . so I ran too." But by afternoon, the federals had gathered themselves and established and held a battle line at the sunken road, known as the "Hornets Nest." When commander in chief of Confederate forces Albert Sidney Johnston was mortally wounded in the fighting, General P.G.T. Beauregard assumed command and believed that the next day would bring Confederate victory. He was unaware that during the night, General Don Buell's 20,000 men had quietly slipped in to reinforce Grant. By the morning of April 7, the Union Army outnumbered the Confederates by more than 10,000 men. After ferocious fighting, the men in blue retired and withdrew toward Corinth. Although Shiloh was recorded as a Union victory, it was a Pyrrhic one. The carnage was staggering; more men fell at the Battle of Shiloh than had fallen in the American Revolution, the War of 1812, and the Mexican War, combined. Criticism of Grant mounted in its wake, but Lincoln refused to relieve Grant of his command, saying simply, "I can't spare this man—he fights." In the battle's bloody aftermath, both the North and the South were forced to concede that this scourge of war would not pass quickly.

Established in December 1894, the 5,048-acre Shiloh National Military Park commemorates one of the bloodiest battles of the Civil War. The park's visitor center is open year-round from 8 A.M. until 5 P.M. daily, and it features museum exhibits on the battle and an introductory film. Entrance fees are $2 per person or $4 per vehicle; a $10 annual pass is also available. Living-history events are offered near the battle's anniversary, on Memorial Day weekend, and periodically during the summer months. A variety of interpretive programs, including rifle-firing demonstrations, are offered daily June through mid-August, and during fall and spring, ranger-led programs are available on weekends. The park encompasses the battlefield, Shiloh National Cemetery—the resting place for more than 3,500 Union soldiers who lost their lives during the battle—and prehistoric mounds from a much earlier age. Visitors can experience the park by taking the 10-mile, self-guided auto tour, which has 14 exhibits, or by walking through the National Cemetery and to Pittsburg Landing on the Tennessee River.

There are no food, lodging, or camping facilities at the park, but all traveler services are available in Counce, Savannah, Selmer, and Shiloh.

For more information, write Shiloh National Military Park, 1055 Pittsburg Landing Road, Shiloh, TN 38376, or telephone (731) 689-5696. The park's Web site is www.nps.gov/shil.

FURTHER READING

Daniel, Larry J. *Shiloh: The Battle That Changed the Civil War.* New York: Simon and Schuster, 1997.

Foote, Shelby. *Shiloh: A Novel.* New York: Vintage Books, 1991.

Luvaas, Jay, Stephen Bowman, and Leonard Fullenkamp, eds. *Guide to the Battle of Shiloh.* Lawrence: University Press of Kansas, 1996.

McDonough, James L. *War in Kentucky: From Shiloh to Perryville.* Knoxville: University of Tennessee Press, 1994.

SITKA NATIONAL HISTORICAL PARK

Location: Sitka, Alaska
Acreage: 113
Established: March 23, 1910

Located on Baranof Island, one of the most rugged of southeast Alaska's islands, Sitka National Historical Park celebrates the beauty and cultural diversity that characterizes Alaska. The oldest federally designated park in Alaska, Sitka National Historical Park is located at the mouth of the Indian River, adjacent to Crescent and Jamestown bays. This beautiful and harsh land was settled first by the Kiks.adi, a Tlingit clan, who were later followed by Russians and then Americans. Representing the cultural heritages of all three, Sitka National Historical Park also preserves the stunning natural landscape of the island.

Postcard of Thlinget Village in Sitka, Alaska. *(National Archives)*

Cultural resources abound at the park, though the collection of Tlingit totem poles, which depict the history of the region's oldest inhabitants, is perhaps the most compelling. Although none of the colorful totem poles is from the immediate region, Alaska's District Governor John G. Brady brought the collection to Sitka in 1905. The totem poles, many of them copies of now deteriorating originals, are displayed along a scenic coastal trail. Traditionally, the totem poles would have been in front of the houses of a Tlingit village. Totem poles served as histories of families and clans carved into cedar, and these carvings also represented the legends and folklore of the Tlingit. During the nineteenth century, Imperial Russia laid claim to the Tlingit's land, and Russian hunters and trappers began to utilize the area extensively. The Russian Bishop's House, built in 1842, is one of the very few remaining examples of Russian colonial architecture in North America. Currently, as part of Sitka National Historical Park, the Russian Bishop's House contains exhibits that portray the rich cultural heritage of Russia and its religion in the region.

Originally set aside as a federal park in 1890, Sitka was rededicated as a national monument in 1910 to commemorate the last major Tlingit Indian resistance to Russian colonization: the Battle of Sitka. In 1972, the boundaries of the national monument were expanded to include additional cultural resources, such as the Russian Bishop's House, and Sitka's designation was changed to a national historical park.

Sitka National Historical Park can only be reached by air or sea, since there are no roads from mainland Alaska. From Sitka, however, the park is only minutes from downtown. Located on a harbor on Baranof Island in southeastern Alaska, Sitka experiences a climate common to North American temperate rainforests. Most of its almost 97 inches of annual precipitation comes in the form of rain, with September through November being the wettest months. Temperatures do not vary greatly throughout the year; the average low in January is in the low 30s and the average high in July is in the mid-50s.

The visitor center and Southeast Indian Cultural Center is open daily from 8 A.M. until 5 P.M. from mid-May though September, and on weekdays for the remainder of the year. During the summer months, Tlingit artists demonstrate their skills, and park rangers lead guided walks on the flora, fauna, history, and anthropology of the park, as well as the community of Sitka. A variety of children's programs are also offered during the summer. The Russian Bishop's House is open for tours from 9 A.M. until 5 P.M. from October through mid-May (by appointment only during the remainder of the year), and it features exhibits on the Russian American Company and Russian history and orthodoxy. Two historic buildings, the Priests' Quarters and the Old School, are located on the site. Visitors can also enjoy the scenic coastal trail that winds among the totem poles and the temperate rainforest of southeastern Alaska. Jogging, walking, and wildlife viewing are the most popular outdoor activities. The entrance fee is $3 per person, which includes tours and exhibits in the Russian Bishop's House (children under twelve years are free); an annual $10 family pass is also available.

There are no food, lodging, or camping facilities in the park, but all traveler services are available in Sitka.

For more information, write Sitka National Historical Park, 103 Monastery Street, Sitka, AK 99835, or telephone (907) 747-0110. The park's Web site is www. nps.gov/sitk.

FURTHER READING

Kan, Sergei. *Memory Eternal: Tlingit Culture and Russian Orthodox Christianity Through Two Centuries.* Seattle: University of Washington Press, 1999.

Knapp, Marilyn R. *Carved History: A Totem Guide to Sitka National Historical Park.* Anchorage, AK: National Park Service, 1980.

Wharton, David. *They Don't Speak Russian in Sitka: A New Look at the History of Southern Alaska.* Menlo Park, CA: Markgraf Publications Group, 1991.

SLEEPING BEAR DUNES NATIONAL LAKESHORE

Location: Empire, Michigan
Acreage: 71,199
Established: October 21, 1970

Congress created Sleeping Bear Dunes National Lakeshore to protect the natural features of Lake Michigan's shoreline from inappropriate development from a growing tourist industry and the accompanying increase in people drawn to the area. Established in 1970, the park is on Lake Michigan slightly more than 20 miles from the established resort of Traverse City, Michigan. It lies within the loosely defined Grand Traverse Bay region, a six-county area that attracts summer and winter visitors and growing numbers of seasonal and year-round residents.

Long before the government established Sleeping Bear Dunes National Lakeshore as a national park area, Native Americans of the Great Lakes area inhabited the region. Before the coming of Europeans, they used the lake and its shores as part of their economic regime and as a source of spiritual sustenance. Ojibway people created the legend of Sleeping Bear, after whom the park and the region are named, but most of the people who lived in the region were Ottawa. French voyageurs, the *coureurs de bois* of legend, trapped the area for furs, and by 1840, they had depleted the supply. Simultaneously, changing fashion in Europe curtailed the market for beaver pelts. By the mid-nineteenth century, commercial and subsistence uses of the region became common as Americans settled the area and prized its resources. Logging the vast forests of Michigan provided the timber to support much nineteenth-century expansion of the nation and the growth of its cities and indus-

tries; beginning in the 1830s and following statehood in 1837, Michigan became a timber speculator's paradise. By 1870, Michigan led the nation in lumber production, doubling its already significant production between 1880 and 1890. By 1900, other states, especially Wisconsin, exceeded Michigan's lumber output, and the regional economy shifted away from resource extraction.

After the end of the logging era, agriculture provided a brief interlude in the Grand Traverse Bay region and within the boundaries of the future park. Elsewhere, nearer to Traverse City, cherry trees blossomed, but most agriculture in the Sleeping Bear Dunes area proved less fruitful. Soils along the shore barely sustained agriculture, and the harsh climate and short growing seasons made the region even more inhospitable. By the beginning of World War I, the Sleeping Bear Dunes region seemed to have returned to the slumber of its namesake.

The region's modern history began with the development of the automobile industry and with Henry Ford's desire to sell more of his automobiles. As the assembly line made cars affordable, the automobile industry drew workers from all over the state and the region; in return, it exported tourists, riding in the shiny black models of the Ford Motor Company. A pattern of seasonal recreational use began around Traverse City and throughout northern Michigan, supported by state activities such as the work of the Michigan Conservation Commission and the establishment of the D.H. Day State Park in the area, as well as other state parks and forests. The federal government established national forests in the area, furthering two trends, the first toward recreational use of natural resources and the second toward greater federal involvement. Tourism consistently increased, and its dramatic growth following World War II set the stage for efforts to include the Sleeping Bear Dunes region in the national park system. By 1961, the region sported as many as 1,000 summer residents, and fears of the degradation of the natural resources spurred initial efforts to preserve the Sleeping Bear Dunes region.

The late 1950s and early 1960s provided Americans a unique opportunity to expand their park system. Beginning in 1956, Mission 66, a ten-year program to upgrade park facilities and expand the system before the fiftieth anniversary of the founding of the National Park Service in 1966, received unqualified support from Congress. Development of existing parks and the addition of new ones became goals not only for the agency, but for Congress and the public as well. In this context, the Sleeping Bear Dunes area came to the attention of Park Service officials. The federal government had been lax about preserving seashores and lakeshores. The first efforts in that area began during the 1930s, more than a half century after the establishment of Yellowstone National Park. By the late 1950s, Congress has established only one area, Cape Hatteras in North Carolina. After the publication of *Our Vanishing Shoreline*, a 1955 Park Service survey that highlighted the lack of an accessible public coast, the impetus for the establishment of national seashores and lakeshores gained momentum. In 1959, U.S. Senator Richard Neuberger of Oregon, a longtime conservation advocate, proposed the authorization of ten national shoreline recreation areas, a new designation to add to the plethora of names that already existed for park areas. Among the ten was the Sleeping Bear Dunes region.

The bill kicked off a ten-year struggle to create a federally designated park in the Sleeping Bear Dunes area. U.S. Senator Philip A. Hart of Michigan played a catalytic role as the primary supporter of the park area, but local resistance slowed the process. The national press framed the issue as a battle be-

tween big government and local people who were defending their property, and a long, drawn-out, and complicated struggle ensued. Congress considered and rejected a series of bills during the early 1960s, and a three-year legislative stalemate between 1965 and 1968 further slowed the process. Hart bore the brunt of local resentment. However, as environmentalism became a primary national concern during the late 1960s, public sentiment around the nation gradually shifted to support the bill, making local resistance seem anachronistic. Hart's unyielding support of the park and the later support of the local Republican congressman, Guy Vanger Jagt, contributed to the eventual establishment of the national lakeshore, as did the growing national support for the idea of preserving the outdoors as a national rather than an individual or local legacy. The optimism and prosperity of the 1960s also played a role in creating the context for establishing the park, as Americans saw an ever-increasing bounty as their due for their participation in an expanding economy. As is the case with many park areas and a number of significant pieces of environmental legislation ranging from the Wilderness Act of 1964 to the Endangered Species Act of 1973, Congress established Sleeping Bear Dunes National Lakeshore inside of a small window of opportunity, when the values, confidence, and wealth of American society lined up in a manner that made preservation desirable—even over strident long-standing local objections.

Today, the 71,199-acre Sleeping Bear Dunes National Lakeshore encompasses a 35-mile stretch of Lake Michigan's eastern coastline, as well as North and South Manitou islands. Established primarily for its outstanding natural features, including forests, beaches, dune formations, and ancient glacial phenomena, the lakeshore also contains many cultural features, including a 1871 lighthouse, 3 former U.S. Life-Saving Service/

Coast Guard stations, and an extensive rural historic farm district. The entrance fee is $7 per vehicle, and a $15 annual pass is also available. The Philip A. Hart Visitor Center is open year-round from 9 A.M. until 4 P.M. (until 6 P.M. during the summer) and features an outstanding slide presentation, "Dreams of the Sleeping Bear," which offers a beautiful mix of photography, music, and narration, while providing an initial orientation to the park. Video and tactile exhibits explore the geological story of the Sleeping Bear Dunes area, while human history and natural history exhibits fill out the remainder of the Exhibit Room. Other visitor facilities include the Dune Center, located at the base of the Dune Climb off of M-109, which is open from mid-May through mid-October from 10 A.M. until 4 P.M.; and the Platte River Campground Ranger Station, located on Lake Michigan Road, 3 miles off M 22, which is open year-round from 8 A.M. until 8 P.M. and offers evening campfire programs during the summer. Visitors should also plan to tour the Sleeping Bear Point Maritime Museum, open from mid-June through September, which features a daily reenactment of the U.S. Life-Saving Service rescue techniques throughout the summer, and a Lyle Gun firing demonstration every Thursday afternoon. Exhibits cover the U.S. Life-Saving Service, the U.S. Coast Guard, and Great Lakes shipping history, and a room on the second floor is outfitted as a steamer wheelhouse with a panorama of the Manitou Passage shipping channel. Park and volunteer staff also give impromptu interpretive talks throughout the day. In addition, visitors can see an impressive historic boat collection at the Cannery, located in the historic village of Glen Haven, off Highway M-109/M-209. The Cannery is open from mid-June to August, and volunteer staff is available for impromptu interpretive talks.

There are no lodging facilities at the lakeshore, but camping is available at the D.H. Day Campground, open from April through November, and the Platte River Campground, open year-round. The Day Campground is in a rustic setting with 88 private sites and easy access to Lake Michigan's beach. Sites are available on a first-come, first-served basis. The Platte River Campground offers pull-in and pull-through sites for RVs, including electrical hookups, as well as tent and walk-in sites for the slightly more adventurous. Potable water and a dump station are provided, and hot showers are available. Of the 179 sites, 48 can be reserved through the national reservations system (800-365-2267). The fee is $10 per night. All traveler services can be found in Empire, Frankfort, Glen Arbor, Honor, Leland, and Traverse City.

For more information, write Sleeping Bear Dunes National Lakeshore, 9922 Front Street, Empire, MI 49630-9797, or telephone (231) 326-5134. The park's Web site is www.nps.gov/slbe.

FURTHER READING

Ashworth, William. *The Late Great Lakes: An Environmental History.* Detroit: Wayne State University Press, 1987.
Karamanski, Theodore J. *A Nationalized Lakeshore: The Creation and Administration of Sleeping Bear Dunes National Lakeshore.* Omaha, NE: National Park Service, 2000. Available at www.cr.nps.gov/history/online_books/slbe/index.htm.
Maddock, Stephen J. "An Analysis of Local Opposition to the Sleeping Bear Dunes National Lakeshore." Ph.D. diss., University of Michigan, 1971.

SPRINGFIELD ARMORY NATIONAL HISTORIC SITE

Location: Springfield, Massachusetts
Acreage: 55
Established: October 26, 1974

In 1777, the Continental Congress established the Arsenal at Springfield to manufacture cartridges and gun carriages for the American Revolution. Already the home of many skilled blacksmiths and gunsmiths,

Springfield had built a notable reputation as a firearm-manufacturing center. In addition to supplying colonial patriots with arms, the Springfield Armory also played an important role in shaping the new United States as the site of the 1787 Shays' Rebellion.

Daniel Shays, like many Massachusetts farmers, had fallen on hard times following the Revolution. Still unpaid for his military service, but with taxes and debts mounting, Shays launched a desperate bid for state assistance. Haunted by "the specter of debtor's jail," Shays and his growing group of followers had attempted to shut down western Massachusetts courts in order to block the foreclosure notices that evicted them from their farms. When this tactic failed to achieve relief, Shays led nearly 1,200 men toward the Springfield Armory, in the hope of getting federal attention. Shays' rebels were met by 4,400 Massachusetts militiamen, who panicked and opened fire, killing four and forcing Shays' men to retreat.

In the aftermath, conservative Federalists, who believed the new experiment in democracy was floundering, proposed a more centralized form of government to replace the existing Articles of Confederation, which became the Constitution. This new government's first president was George Washington, who selected Springfield as the site for one of the nation's two federal armories (the other at Harpers Ferry, Virginia). In time, Springfield became a center for invention and firearm development, and after the destruction of Harpers Ferry during the Civil War, the Springfield Armory became the only federal manufacturing point for small arms until the twentieth century. The first arms produced here were flintlock muskets, which gave way in the early twentieth century to the magazine-fed model Springfield '03, which began production in 1903. The last small arm developed by the armory was the M-14, which evolved over the years into the present-day U.S. sniping rifle—the M-21. The Springfield Armory was officially closed by the Defense Department in 1968.

Established in March 1978 to preserve the history of the first national armory from 1794–1968, the 55-acre Springfield Armory National Historic Site protects one of the most extensive and unique firearms collections in the world. The park is open year-round, Tuesday through Sunday, from 10 A.M. until 4:30 P.M., and admission is free. The central attraction is the arsenal building, constructed in the 1840s. Colonel J.G. Benton started the weapons collection housed in the main arsenal in 1870 as a technical "library" for armory personnel. It is now regarded as the nation's largest collection of small arms, second only globally to the Pattern Room of the Royal Small Arms Factory in Enfield, United Kingdom. The museum has an orientation exhibit, an eighteen-minute historical film, and site bulletins on selected Armory subjects, as well as an information desk, historical and technical books, posters, and videos. Self-guided walking tours of the historic buildings and grounds surrounding the Armory are available, and visitors are invited to browse a portion of the historic site's object and archival collections on-line.

There are no food, lodging, or camping facilities at the historic site, but all traveler services are available in the surrounding communities.

For more information, write Springfield Armory National Historic Site, One Armory Square, Springfield, MA 01105-1299, or telephone (413) 734-8551. The park's Web site is www.nps.gov/spar.

FURTHER READING

Ball, Robert W.D. *Springfield Armory Shoulder Weapons, 1795–1968.* Norfolk, VA: Antique Trader Books, 1997.

Carper, Robert L., and Richard G. Turk. *Springfield Armory National Historic Site, Massachusetts.* Denver, CO: National Park Service, 1984.

Whisker, James B. *The United States Armory at Springfield, 1795–1865.* Lewiston, NY: E. Mellen, 1997.

STATUE OF LIBERTY NATIONAL MONUMENT

Location: New York, New York
Acreage: 58
Established: October 15, 1924

A symbol of international friendship and a beacon to travelers from around the world, the Statue of Liberty National Monument is one of the United States' most recognizable monuments. The statue, which was originally named "Liberty Enlightening the World," was presented as a gift to the United States by the people of France in 1886. Initially planned as a gift to celebrate the centennial of the signing of the Declaration of Independence in July 1886, the statue arrived in New York a bit later than expected, in 1885, and it was finally dedicated on October 28, 1886, in New York harbor.

France commissioned sculptor Auguste Bartholdi to design the sculpture. Bartholdi,

Statue of Liberty National Monument, c. 1920–1950.
(Library of Congress)

together with Alexandre Gustave Eiffel, who created the Eiffel Tower, conceived the huge copper sculpture. Despite financial problems in both France and the United States, which was to build the pedestal upon which the statute would stand, the project was finished at last and the Statue of Liberty was placed upon her pedestal in the courtyard of Fort Wood.

Established as a national monument in October 1924, the 58-acre Statue of Liberty park commemorates liberty and democracy. Its placement in New York harbor destined the statue to become a physical symbol of the United States itself, and it came to embody the hopes of millions of immigrants during the late nineteenth and early twentieth centuries. The 25 windows in the statue's crown represent gemstones found on the earth. The 7 rays of the crown symbolize the 7 seas and the 7 continents of the world. The statue holds in her left hand a tablet, which is inscribed with the date July 4, 1776, written in Roman numerals.

In 1965, Ellis Island became part of the Statue of Liberty National Monument. For two hundred years, the island played an important role in American history, first as a military post and later as the inspection facility that processed the vast majority of immigrants entering the United States. Together, Ellis Island and the Statue of Liberty represent the history and culture of immigration, international friendship, and political ideals of democracy and freedom.

Liberty Island and Ellis Island are located in lower New York harbor, just over a mile from lower Manhattan. During the summer and winter, the weather in New York City can be harsh. Summer temperatures range between 80 and 95 degrees, but temperatures inside the statue itself can exceed 110 degrees. Summer visitors should drink plenty of water and wear light clothing. During the winter, temperatures can be extremely cold, and snow can make a visit difficult. Spring and autumn are the best times to visit, with mild temperatures ranging from the mid-50s to the mid-70s.

The park is open year-round from 9 A.M. until 5 P.M. (and for extended hours during the summer) and offers numerous exhibits. The Statue of Liberty exhibit, located on the second floor in the pedestal, traces the history and symbolism of the statue through museum objects, photographs, prints, videos, and oral histories. In addition to historical artifacts and descriptive text, full-scale replicas of the statue's face and foot are also on display. The Torch exhibit includes the original torch, built in 1876, and the much-altered flame in the lobby.

A visit to the crown can mean a two- to three-hour wait in line, particularly if visitation is high that day. To reach the crown, visitors must climb 354 steps, or about 22 stories. This ascent, while well worth it for the view, is not recommended for anyone with health problems. The Pedestal observation deck also provides a spectacular view of the harbor, and there is an elevator.

Free tours are available, but these cannot be reserved. Although there are no entrance fees for the Statue of Liberty or Ellis Island, access to the park is by ferry (800-600-1600) only from New York or New Jersey, and fees for the ferry are $8 per person for adults, and $3 for children.

Food and supplies are offered at cafeterias on both islands, and all traveler services can be found in the New York metropolitan area.

For more information, write Statue of Liberty National Monument, Liberty Island, New York, NY 10004, or telephone (212) 363-3200. The park's Web site is www.nps.gov/stli.

FURTHER READING

Blumberg, Barbara. *Celebrating the Immigrant: An Administrative History of the Statue of Liberty National Monument, 1952–1982.* Boston: National Park Service, 1985. Available at www.cr.nps.gov/history/online_books/stli/adhi.htm.

Dillon, Wilton S., and Neil G. Kotler, eds. *The Statue of Liberty Revisited: Making a Universal Symbol.* Washington, DC: Smithsonian Institution Press, 1994.

Holland, F. Ross. *Idealists, Scoundrels, and the Lady: An Insider's View of the Statue of Liberty–Ellis Island Project.* Urbana: University of Illinois Press, 1993.

Moreno, Barry. *The Statue of Liberty Encyclopedia.* New York: Simon and Schuster, 2000.

STEAMTOWN NATIONAL HISTORIC SITE

Location: Scranton, Pennsylvania
Acreage: 62
Established: October 30, 1986

Steamtown National Historic Site preserves the era of the steam locomotive, a dimension of American railroading that has not existed since the late nineteenth century. Railroads were the biggest of big businesses in nineteenth-century America and the transformative technology that enabled the growth of industrial America and underpinned modern American life.

The nation's first transportation "highways" had been natural waterways and human-built canal systems. The Erie Canal, completed in 1825, was the most famous of the "big ditches" American engineers created, but the "Canal Era" in history was remarkably brief. The railroads made canals obsolete.

Railroads first appeared in 1830, when the Baltimore and Ohio opened a mere 13 miles of track. Soon, however, the nation was infected with "railroad mania," and by 1860, more than 31,000 miles of track crisscrossed the country. And as the rails expanded, they brought about far-reaching social changes. The combination of direct routes, affordable rates, dependable schedules, and the creation of a national market proved irresistible. But railroads were also expensive. And the kind of men who built these big businesses became powerful enough to control, as one historian has written, "the modern ways of finance, management, labor relations, competition, and government regulation." In 1925, the railroads began to make the significant shift from coal-fired steam to diesel locomotives, but the heyday of trains was already beginning to wane. In all, the railroad era in America lasted nearly a century, but by the 1950s, railroads had themselves been replaced by new technologies such as long-haul interstate trucking and air traffic.

Congress established the 62-acre Steamtown National Historic Site in October 1986 to further public understanding and appreciation of the role steam railroading played in the development of the United States. Many people saw the park as a boondoggle, a pork barrel project for a powerful local interest, but it is the only place in the national park system that tells the story of steam railroading and the people who made it possible. The site is open daily from 9 A.M. until 5 P.M. Schedules and park orientation are provided in the visitor center. There is a 250-seat theater that shows a twenty-minute film about eastern, mainline steam railroading. The History Museum features exhibits about the people who worked on the railroad, passenger railroading, and the economics of railroading. Visitors can also tour the 1937 Roundhouse with operational steam locomotives undergoing routine maintenance, inspections, and light repairs. The Technology Museum features exhibits and models showing the development of the mechanical side of railroading, from laying track to signals. Park rangers offer Locomotive Shop Tours, "Ranger's Choice" Tours, living-history programs, and passenger railroad excursions (seasonal). Museum fees are $8 for adults, $3 for children; excursion fees are $12 for adults, $6 for children; an annual pass is also available for $45 for adults and $15 for children. In addition, the park

hosts the Coal, Steam, and Thread Celebration during the third week of April, a Memorial Day Celebration, and the Festival of Trees in late December.

There are no food, lodging, or camping facilities at the historic site, but all traveler services are available locally.

For more information, write Steamtown National Historic Site, 150 South Washington Avenue, Scranton, PA 18503-2018, or telephone (570) 340-5200. The park's Web site is www.nps.gov/stea.

FURTHER READING

Chappell, Gordon. *Steam over Scranton: The Locomotives of Steamtown: Special History Study.* Scranton, PA: National Park Service, 1991. Available at www.cr.nps.gov/history/online_books/steamtown/shs.htm.

Clemensen, A. Berle. *Historic Resource Study: Steamtown National Historic Site, Pennsylvania.* Denver, CO: National Park Service, 1988.

Westwood, J.N. *The Age of Steam: The Locomotive, the Railroads, and Their Legacy.* San Diego, CA: Thunder Bay, 2000.

STONES RIVER NATIONAL BATTLEFIELD

Location: Murfreesboro, Tennessee
Acreage: 709
Established: March 3, 1927

From December 31, 1862, through January 2, 1863, a fierce battle raged at Stones River (or Murfreesboro) in Tennessee. In the end, General Braxton Bragg's Confederates were forced to withdraw, allowing General William Rosecrans and the Union Army of the Cumberland to control middle Tennessee.

The battle began at dawn and soon appeared to be headed toward yet another Confederate victory, as Bragg's Army of Tennessee pushed the Union troops back nearly 3 miles. Rosecrans's men rallied, however, and established a new line of defense that utilized a rocky, tree-topped knoll known as the "Round Forest." From this strategic position, the Union rolled back brigade after brigade

Monument to the memory of the soldiers who fell at Stones River, Murfreesboro, Tennessee. *(Library of Congress)*

of rebels in a horrendous massacre, and the site became known to the Confederates as "Hell's Half Acre." Fighting continued for the next two days, until Union reinforcements made it prudent for Bragg to withdraw "from so unequal a contest." In just three days of battle, 23,000 soldiers had been killed, wounded, taken captive, or were missing. Although the battle was strategically inconclusive, it provided a much-needed morale boost to the North after their shattering defeat at Fredericksburg. President Abraham Lincoln later wrote to General Rosecrans, "I can never forget . . . you gave us a hard-earned victory, which had there been a defeat instead, the nation could scarcely have lived over."

Established in March 1927, the 709-acre national battlefield includes Stones River National Cemetery, established in 1865, with more than 6,000 Union graves, and the Hazen Brigade Monument, believed to be the oldest Civil War monument still standing in its original location. Portions of Fortress Rosecrans, a large earthen fort constructed after the battle, still stand and are preserved and interpreted by the National Park Service. Much of the actual battlefield, however, is in private hands.

The park's visitor center, located at 3501 Old Nashville Highway, is open year-round from 8 A.M. until 5 P.M. and features a small museum and slide program about the battle, along with an Eastern National bookstore. The battlefield can be toured by car or by foot along a loop road. The tour continues on to several sites along city and county roads, and there are short foot trails at several of the tour stops. From late May through mid-November ranger walks and talks are presented daily, and, on summer, and occasional spring and fall, weekends, the park offers living-history programs.

There are no food, lodging, or camping facilities at the battlefield, but all traveler services are available in Murfreesboro.

For more information, write Stones River National Battlefield, 3501 Old Nashville Highway, Murfreesboro, TN 37129, or telephone (615) 893-9501. The park's Web site is www.nps.gov/stri.

FURTHER READING
Cozzens, Peter. *No Better Place to Die: The Battle of Stones River.* Urbana: University of Illinois Press, 1990.
——. *The Civil War in the West: From Stones River to Chattanooga.* Urbana: University of Illinois Press, 1996.
McDonough, James Lee. *Stones River: Bloody Winter in Tennessee.* Knoxville: University of Tennessee Press, 1980.

SUNSET CRATER VOLCANO NATIONAL MONUMENT
Location: Flagstaff, Arizona
Acreage: 3,040
Established: May 26, 1930

Sunset Crater Volcano is an almost perfectly symmetrical 1,000-foot cinder cone in northern Arizona. Its name comes from the beautiful red, pink, and orange cinders that rim its crater and seem to glow as the sun goes down. Sunset Crater formed only about nine hundred years ago, making it one of the youngest, if not *the* youngest, volcano in the Southwest.

A neat bit of archeological sleuthing determined that ancient people, the Sinagua or Hisatsinom, undoubtedly witnessed the eruption. When scientists began excavating the ash, they discovered the ruined remains of native pit houses, although no valuables, indicating that the residents must have had time to evacuate. Using dendrochronology—the study of tree-ring sequences—and other evidence, scientists also determined that the volcano erupted sometime between the end of the 1064 growing season and the beginning of the 1065 growing season. When the cinder cone blew, it sprayed molten rock into the air and blanketed the region with black cinder and ash. But while this initially spelled disaster to the Sinagua, they soon discovered that the rich volcanic soil possessed excellent water-retention qualities, which enabled their agriculture to flourish for a time. Yet in the end, much of the ash was carried away by wind, and by 1225, decreased soil fertility, combined with overpopulation and drought, led to the eventual abandonment of the area.

Sunset Crater is only part of a larger 3,000-square-mile area geologists refer to as the San Francisco Peaks Volcanic Field, with Sunset Crater being the most recent of many volcanic outbursts. In addition to the looming cinder cone, the park protects spatter cones, lava drag marks, volcanic blisters, a lava tube, squeeze-ups, and hornitos. This rather stark landscape is colonized by ponderosa pines, which have even managed to survive inside the crater. In turn, the pines provide habitat for birds such as Steller's jay, nut-hatches, woodpeckers, and various migratory songbirds.

Originally set aside in May 1930, the 3,040-acre national monument is open daily from sunrise until sunset. The Sunset Crater Volcano Visitor Center is open year-round from 9 A.M. until 5 P.M. It offers numerous interpretive exhibits and special programs that include a daily forty-five-minute Lava Walk to investigate cinder cones, squeeze-ups, and more, and a one-hour evening campfire talk at Bonito Campground (during the season when the campground is open). The monument has 2 hiking trails: the Lenex Crater Cinder Cone Trail, which is a steep 1-mile round-trip hike, and the Lava Flow Trail, a 1 mile loop trail with a quarter-mile cutoff, that is a self-guided trail exploring a variety of volcanic formations. The entrance fee is $3 per person, and it is good for both Sunset Crater Volcano and Wupatki national monuments.

There are no food, lodging, or camping facilities at the national monument, but all traveler services are available in Flagstaff. The Coconino National Forest's Bonito Campground (520-526-0866) is located across from the visitor center and is generally open from late May through mid-October.

For more information, write Sunset Crater Volcano National Monument, Route 3, Box 149, Flagstaff, AZ 86002, or telephone (520) 526-0502. The park's Web site is www.nps.gov/sucr.

FURTHER READING

Houk, Rose. *Sunset Crater Volcano National Monument.* Tucson, AZ: Southwest Parks and Monuments Association, 1995.

Malotki, Ekkehart. *Earth Fire: A Hopi Legend of the Sunset Crater Eruption.* Flagstaff, AZ: Northland, 1987.

Thybony, Scott. *Fire and Stone: A Road Guide to Wupatki and Sunset Crater National Monuments.* Tucson, AZ: Southwest Parks and Monuments Association, 1987.

T

TALLGRASS PRAIRIE NATIONAL PRESERVE

Location: Cottonwood Falls, Kansas
Acreage: 10,894
Established: November 12, 1996

Outsiders have considered this prairie place barren, desolate, monotonous, a land of more nothing than almost any other place you might name.

So wrote William Least-Heat Moon in his epic of Kansas's Flint Hills, *PrairyErth*, echoing the widely held sense of the region. Yet Least-Heat Moon also saw this land's special features, the combination of nature and culture engraved on a landscape that so attracts the American eye as the twenty-first century begins. The last remaining significant expanse of tallgrass prairie in the United States, the 28-mile-wide and nearly 200-mile-long Flint Hills are a vestige of an earlier geological America. The Tallgrass Prairie National Preserve is in Chase County, Kansas, in the heart of the Flint Hills. Chase County undulates; the rise and fall of its low limestone hills create a horizon of endless serenity, at sunset and dawn, casting shadows that can stretch as much as a mile. The tranquillity masks a vigorous human history, beginning with prehistoric people and continuing to the present.

The region's unique geology, best exemplified in the Tallgrass Prairie National Preserve, defined how humans could use the resources. Distilled from the Permian Seas of the Paleozoic era, the limestone and shale hills result from erosion. More than 10,000 acres of the preserve is unplowed tallgrass prairie atop limestone and chert. Their permeability has forced most human activity to the riparian environments of the watercourses. The impact of the geology on human endeavor and habitation is one of the many stories the park tells.

Human history included much activity prior to the arrival of European-Americans. The culturally linked Osage, Kaw, Wichita, and Pawnee people all used the region, as did Native American groups that moved to Kansas during the nineteenth century, such as Ioway, Sac and Fox, Potowatamie, Delaware, Shawnee, and Kickapoo. Europeans brought their cultural values to this land, seeing it in the terms of Anglo-American commercial culture. They plotted and meted the land, measuring it in their legal terms, which often seemed strange in these mostly limestone hills.

"No other grassland system anywhere supports the biological diversity of tallgrass prairie," former U.S. Representative Dan Glickman said in 1994. "Every other ecosystem has been honored with inclusion in the national park system—mountains, seashores, desert, marshland, ancient forest—but no tallgrass prairie. A tallgrass prairie is one of the only ecosystems missing in the national park system." In 1996, the establishment of the Tallgrass Prairie National Preserve rectified that omission.

Of the 400,000 square miles of tallgrass prairie that once covered the North American continent, less than 1 percent remains today, primarily in the Flint Hills, and this almost-11,000-acre preserve protects a nationally significant example of this once-abundant ecosystem. Admission to Tallgrass Prairie is free, but a suggested entrance donation is $2 for adults and $1 for those eighteen and under.

Tallgrass Prairie was one of the first national park areas to be comanaged in public-private partnership. The National Park Trust purchased the Z-Bar ranch in 1994, and when the Department of the Interior was able to acquire 180 acres, with caveats that no future land purchase occur without the owner's consent, the legislation was passed. The National Park Trust agreed to keep the ranch in private ownership, and an "affiliate relationship" with the National Park Service (NPS) was created. This assuaged the antigovernment sentiments in the region, first manifest when a local rancher brandished a shotgun in the face of Secretary of the Interior Stewart Udall in the 1960s. The result was a public-private management structure that seemed to be an important piece of the future of the park system.

Since this is a relatively new park still under development, visitor opportunities are limited but are being expanded. Visitor information and a ten-minute orientation video are available, and a brochure and wayside exhibits provide a self-guided tour of the historic ranch headquarters area with buildings dating from the late nineteenth century; a 1-room school house; a nature trail that offers views of the Flint Hills landscape; and acres of prairie lands. Because the park is a partnership between the National Park Trust, which retains ownership of most of the acreage, and the NPS, which manages the site, visitor services are offered in partnership. Some tours are led by NPS rangers and some are led by National Park Trust guides; all offer a glimpse into the special stories represented by the natural and cultural resources of this land. On Saturdays and Sundays from mid-April through October, tours of the 1881 limestone ranch house are offered hourly from 10:30 A.M. to 3:30 P.M. In addition, a 7-mile-long Treasures of the Tallgrass guided bus tour is offered daily from mid-April through October; the fee is $5 per person ($3 for those eighteen and under), and advance reservations are recommended.

There are no food, lodging, or camping facilities in the preserve, but all visitor services are available in Cottonwood Falls, Council Grove, Emporia, and Strong City. Camping is also available at the Chase County State Park.

For more information, write Tallgrass Prairie National Preserve, P.O. Box 585, Cottonwood Falls, KS 66845, or telephone (316) 273-6034. The park's Web site is www.nps.gov/tapr.

FURTHER READING

Least Heat-Moon, William. *PrairyErth (A Deep Map): An Epic History of the Tallgrass Prairie Country.* Boston: Houghton Mifflin, 1999.
Reichman, O.J. *Konza Prairie: A Tallgrass Natural History.* Lawrence: University Press of Kansas, 1991.
Tallgrass Historians, L.C. *Tallgrass Prairie National Preserve Legislative History, 1920–1996.* Omaha, NE: National Park Service, 1998.

THADDEUS KOSCIUSZKO NATIONAL MONUMENT

Location: Philadelphia, Pennsylvania
Acreage: .02
Established: October 21, 1972

Authorized in October 1972, this monument is the smallest unit in the national park system. It serves as a memorial to the accomplishments of Thaddeus Kosciuszko (kos-choos-ko), a native of Poland who became an American patriot. Born on February 4, 1746, into a family of landed gentry who had lost their wealth, Kosciuszko studied in Paris and became a military engineer, a skill that had great applicability in the eighteenth century. He also became a leading advocate of freedom, embracing the ideals of the Enlightenment and the Age of Reason.

For many Europeans, the American Revolution was *the* model of democracy, and Kosciuszko joined the colonists just after the signing of the Declaration of Independence in

1776. Receiving a commission as colonel of engineers from the Continental Congress, serving the Army of the North, he planned forts along the Delaware River. Kosciuszko's reputation soared following the American victory at Saratoga, where his brilliant design for fortification of Bemis Heights helped compel the surrender of 6,000 troops under General John Burgoyne. The triumph was pivotal; soon after, the French entered the Revolution as allies against the British.

Kosciuszko's most important task became the fortification of West Point, overlooking the Hudson River. George Washington had called West Point "the key to America," an assessment the British understood all too well. Kosciuszko's supervised the development of intertwined artillery batteries and a 60-ton chain to block shipping and the British advance on the river. Once again, his plans succeeded. After the Revolutionary War, when

Thaddeus Kosciuszko, an advocate for freedom.
(National Archives)

West Point became the home of the U.S. Military Academy, the cadets erected the first monument there to honor Kosciuszko.

After the war, in 1784, Kosciuszko returned to Poland, where he remained a committed advocate of "liberty" in its eighteenth-century sense. Poland was being swallowed by Russia, and, in 1789, Kosciuszko was conscripted to the Polish army. When the king ordered his troops to stop fighting, Kosciuszko resigned in protest and moved to Germany, where he helped plan an insurrection. In March 1794, he again returned to Poland to lead the long-planned revolt for freedom. Kosciuszko envisioned a revolution much like the one that had succeeded in the new United States, and he mobilized the masses, including the scorned Polish peasants. His experience in America had taught him that even raw recruits with little experience could be molded into a capable fighting force, and he proved it when his 7,000, largely untrained volunteers won an unexpected victory over the Russians at Raclawice. By October, the tide had shifted. Russian and Prussian troops destroyed Kosciusko's army. Seriously wounded, he was captured and imprisoned in Moscow under Catherine the Great. Her successor, Czar Paul I, freed Kosciuszko on the condition that he never return to Poland, so he left for his adopted homeland, the United States.

Settling in Philadelphia, he renewed his friendship with Thomas Jefferson, who called him "as pure a son of liberty as I have ever known." Later in life, when Kosciuszko left America for the final time, he named Jefferson as executor of his will, which directed that his American assets be sold and the proceeds used to buy slaves and free them. After Kosciuszko's death in Switzerland in October 1817, at the age of 71, his body was returned to Poland, where it lies in a royal crypt in Cracow's Wawel Cathedral.

The house where Thaddeus Kosciuszko

resided during the winter of 1797–1798 is open Wednesday to Sunday from 9 A.M. until 5 P.M. November through May, and daily from 9 A.M. until 5 P.M. June through October. The house has exhibits, a bookstore, and a room furnished as it might have been during Kosciuszko's time. An audiovisual program describes the house and the life of Kosciuszko, and park rangers give presentations throughout the year.

There are no food, lodging, or camping facilities at the memorial, but all traveler services are available in Philadelphia.

For more information, write Thaddeus Kosciuszko National Monument, 301 Pine Street, Philadelphia, PA 19106, or telephone (215) 597-9618. The park's Web site is www.nps.gov/thko.

FURTHER READING
Greene, Meg. *Thaddeus Kosciuszko: Polish General and Patriot.* Philadelphia, PA: Chelsea House, 2002.
Kajencki, Francis C. *Thaddeus Kosciuszko: Military Engineer of the American Revolution.* El Paso, TX: Southwest Palonia, 1998.
Pula, James S. *Thaddeus Kosciuszko: The Purest Son of Liberty.* New York: Hippocrene Books, 1999.

THEODORE ROOSEVELT BIRTHPLACE NATIONAL HISTORIC SITE
Location: New York, New York
Acreage: 0.11
Established: July 25, 1962

Theodore Roosevelt, the youngest man to hold the office of president and certainly among the most original, was born into a wealthy New York family in 1858. After graduating from Harvard, he began what would be a remarkable political career as a New York State assemblyman from 1882 to 1884. Later, after Roosevelt served just two years as president of the New York Board of Police, the president of the United States, William McKinley, appointed him assistant secretary of the navy from 1897 to 1898. When the Spanish-American War broke out in 1898, Roosevelt led a group of volunteer troops, the Rough Riders, up San Juan Hill in Cuba. His heroics earned him acclaim and vaulted him into the governor's mansion in New York.

From 1889 to 1895, Roosevelt served as a member of the U.S. Civil Service Commission, and he earned a national reputation as a Progressive reformer. His growing prominence created a political problem for the Republicans, who wished to reelect President McKinley without competition from within the party. The "solution," which was proposed by Republican Party boss Thomas Platt, was to engineer Roosevelt's nomination as the Republican candidate for vice president, a position that held prestige but relatively little power. Platt's plan backfired when President McKinley was assassinated in September 1901, and Roosevelt became president.

Authorized in July 1962, the Theodore Roosevelt Birthplace National Historic Site commemorates the birthplace of America's twenty-sixth president. Roosevelt lived in the New York City brownstone home from his birth on October 27, 1858, until age fourteen. Demolished in 1916, the house was rebuilt as a memorial after his death in 1919, and furnished by the president's widow and sisters. The historic site, at 28 East 20th Street, between Broadway and Park Avenue South, is open from 9 A.M. until 5 P.M. Monday through Friday. The entrance fee is $2 per person. Park rangers offer guided tours of 5 period-furnished rooms, and visitors are free to browse the site's 2 museum galleries and small bookstore and watch the introductory video program.

There are no food or lodging facilities at the site, but all traveler services are available in the New York metropolitan area. Parking in Manhattan is limited and expensive, and use of mass transit is preferable. The Lexington Avenue #6 subway stops at the East 23rd Street station on Park Avenue South. N and R subways stop at the East 23rd Street station on Broadway; frequent service is provided twenty-four hours a day, seven days a week. Frequent bus service is provided by the M-6 and M-7 routes on Broadway; by the M-1 route on Park Avenue South; and by the M-23 route, operating cross town on 23rd Street. Service is provided twenty-four hours a day, seven days a week.

For more information, write Theodore Roosevelt Birthplace National Historic Site, 28 East 20th Street, New York, NY 10003, or telephone (212) 260-1616. The park's Web site is www.nps.gov/thrb.

FURTHER READING

McCullough, David. *Mornings on Horseback: The Story of an Extraordinary Family, a Vanished Way of Life, and the Unique Child Who Became Theodore Roosevelt.* New York: Touchstone Books, 1982.

Morris, Edmund. *The Rise of Theodore Roosevelt.* New York: Ballantine Books, 1980.

THEODORE ROOSEVELT INAUGURAL NATIONAL HISTORIC SITE

Location: Buffalo, New York
Acreage: 1
Established: November 2, 1966

On September 14, 1901, Theodore Roosevelt took the oath of office as the twenty-sixth president of the United States after the assassination of President William McKinley. Despite opposition from party stalwarts such as Mark Hanna, the political boss of Ohio, Roosevelt had been added to the McKinley ticket in 1900, partly to increase voter support for the Republicans, but partly to neutralize the growing political influence of Roosevelt. In 1901, McKinley enjoyed broad popular support, having brought the country out of the worst depression in its history to that time and having successfully ended the Spanish-American War.

That fateful September afternoon, McKinley was visiting the Pan-American Exposition in Buffalo. Unbeknownst to him, among the throng of perspiring well-wishers was Leon Czolgosz, a self-proclaimed anarchist, who shot the president twice, he claimed, in the name of the poor. McKinley did not die immediately. He lingered for nine more days before succumbing to "gangrene of both walls of the stomach and pancreas" as a result of the shooting. McKinley died at 2:15 A.M. on September 14, 1901, at the age of fifty-eight. For a stunned nation, it was the third presidential assassination in less than forty years. For Theodore Roosevelt, it meant elevation to the nation's highest office. Roosevelt had arrived in Buffalo the same day that McKinley died. That afternoon, he became the nation's twenty-sixth president, to the dismay of some Republican stalwarts. As the frustrated Hanna put it, "now look, that damned cowboy is President of the United States."

Authorized in November 1966, the 1-acre National Historic Site preserves the Ansley Wilcox estate where Roosevelt took the oath of office. Prior to becoming a National Historic Site, this outstanding example of Greek Revival architecture had a long and varied history as part of a U.S. Army barracks, a prominent Buffalo residence, and later, a popular restaurant. The historic home, located at 641 Delaware Avenue near the corner of North Street in Buffalo, is open year-round from 9 A.M. until 5 P.M. Monday through Friday, and from noon until 5 P.M. on weekends. The front portion of the house was built around 1840 as officers' quarters for the Buffalo barracks, and Wilcox enlarged the house to its present size in the 1890s. The first floor contains the visitor orientation room, 3 restored other rooms, 1 permanent exhibit room on the events of 1901, and rest rooms. The second floor has 1 restored room, a large room to rent for meetings and small get-togethers, wall space available for art shows by local artists and groups, and a gift shop. Visitors may also walk through the herb and flower gardens on-site, or enjoy a walking tour of the surrounding historic neighborhoods. House tour fees are $3 for adults, $2 for seniors, and $1 for children under fourteen.

There are no food, lodging, or camping facilities at the historic site, but all traveler services are available in the Buffalo area. Several hotels are located near the site on Delaware Avenue, and the nearest campground is located in Grand Island, New York, about 10 miles away.

For more information, write Theodore Roosevelt Inaugural National Historic Site, 641 Delaware Avenue, Buffalo, NY 14202, or telephone (716) 884-0095. The park's Web site is www.nps.gov/thri.

FURTHER READING

Brands, H.W. *T.R.: The Last Romantic.* New York: Basic Books, 1997.

Fisher, Jack C. *Stolen Glory: The McKinley Assassination.* La Jolla, CA: Alamar Books, 2001.

McCullough, David. *Mornings on Horseback: The Story of an Extraordinary Family, a Vanished Way of Life, and the Unique Child Who Became Theodore Roosevelt.* New York: Simon and Schuster, 2001.

Morris, Edmund. *The Rise of Theodore Roosevelt.* New York: Modern Library, 2001.

——. *Theodore Rex.* New York: Random House, 2001.

THEODORE ROOSEVELT NATIONAL PARK

Location: Medora, North Dakota
Acreage: 70,447
Established: April 25, 1947

> I never would have been President if it had not been for my experiences in North Dakota.
>
> —*Theodore Roosevelt*

Theodore Roosevelt, the nation's twenty-sixth president, first visited North Dakota's Badlands on a buffalo-hunting trip in September 1883. The difficult-to-traverse Badlands, which developed out of 60-million-year-old sedimentary rocks deposited at about the same time that tremendous geologic forces uplifted the Rocky Mountains and Black Hills, earned their name from the Lakota. In this rugged landscape, Roosevelt found an invigorating challenge; before returning to New York, the twenty-four-year-old bought into a cattle-raising operation on the Maltese Cross Ranch. The following year, after losing both his wife and mother, Roosevelt moved west and established the Elkhorn Ranch, where he began to develop a conservation ethic that would become a hallmark of his political career and his historical legacy to the nation. As a cattle rancher, Roosevelt fared poorly, losing most of his herd during the brutal winter of 1886–1887, but as a naturalist and observer of the alarming damage that white settlers were inflicting on the land and its wildlife, he was keen. By the time he arrived out west, most of the great herds of bison were gone, decimated by hide hunters, diminishing habitat, and diseases. Other wildlife was also suffering from the loss and alteration of natural habitats. These formative North Dakota experiences shaped the future president, and once in the White House, Roosevelt increasingly devoted his energy to conservation.

By the time he left office in 1909, he had established the first 51 bird reserves, 4 game preserves, and 150 national forests. Roosevelt had also signed the Act for the Preservation of American Antiquities, known as the Antiquities Act or the National Monuments Act, on June 8, 1906. The law, the most important piece of preservation legislation in American history, authorizes the president, at his discretion, to "declare by public proclamation historic landmarks, historic and prehistoric structures, and other objects of historic and scientific interest that are situated upon lands owned or controlled by the Government of the United States to be National Monuments." Roosevelt used the act to proclaim eighteen national monuments including the Grand Canyon, the area that became Olympic and Zion national parks, the Petrified Forest area of Arizona, Devil's Tower in Wy-

The Maltese Cross Cabin at Theodore Roosevelt National Park. *(National Park Service)*

oming, and many others. To further his goals in conservation, he established the U.S. Forest Service and signed into law five national parks—including Mesa Verde, Crater Lake, and Wind Cave. In all, Roosevelt preserved approximately 230 million acres for future generations. Today, Theodore Roosevelt National Park is also helping to restore both native flora and fauna that have been pushed to the brink of extinction, including the American bison.

Originally established in 1947 as a national memorial park, the 70,447-acre Theodore Roosevelt National Park serves as a living memorial to this colorful president and his enduring contribution to the conservation of the nation's natural resources. A seven-day entrance pass, good for both the north and south units of the park, is $5 per person or $10 per vehicle; a $20 annual pass is also available. The park maintains 3 visitor information sites. The Medora Visitor Center, in the South Unit, is open year round from 8 A.M. until 4:30 P.M. and for extended hours during the summer. Museum exhibits explore Roosevelt's life, area ranching history, and natural history, and visitors can tour Theodore Roosevelt's Maltese Cross Cabin. The North Unit Visitor Center is open year-round from 9 A.M. until 5:30 P.M. and features several natural history exhibits and a small theater for viewing park videos. Visitor information is also available at Painted Canyon, in the South Unit, from 8 A.M. until 4:30 P.M.

Park rangers offer talks, evening campfire programs, nature walks and hikes, summer cultural demonstrations, and ski tours. A major feature of the South Unit is a paved, 36-mile, scenic loop road with interpretive signs that explain some of the park's historical and natural features. A "Road Log Guide" book that explains more features is also available for sale at the visitor centers or on-line at the park bookstore. In the North Unit, visitors can enjoy the 14-mile Scenic Drive that goes from the entrance station to the Oxbow Overlook, with turnouts and interpretive signs along the way. Several self-guiding nature trails have interpretive brochures to help visitors learn more about the park. The Elkhorn Ranch Site, which was the location of Roosevelt's principal home in the Badlands, is 35 miles north of the Medora Visitor Center. The ranch buildings no longer exist, but interpretive signs explain where the house and outbuildings were.

There are no food or lodging facilities in the park, but all traveler services are available in Beach, Belfield, Dickinson, Medora, and Watford City. Year-round camping is available in the park at the 70-site Cottonwood Campground in the South Unit, on a first-come, first-served basis. Each site has a table and grill, and flush toilets and running water are available from May through September. The fee is $10 per site, per night. In the North Unit is the 50-site Juniper Campground, which is also run on a first-come, first-served basis. A dump station is available from May through September (there is no water available from October through April) and each site has a picnic table and grill. Fees are $10 per site, per night from May to September, and $5 per site, per night from October to April.

For more information, write Theodore Roosevelt National Park, Box 7, Medora, ND 58645-0007, or telephone (701) 623-4466. The park's Web site is www.nps.gov/thro.

FURTHER READING

Brands, H.W. *T.R.: The Last Romantic*. New York: Basic Books, 1997.
McCullough, David. *Mornings on Horseback: The Story of an Extraordinary Family, a Vanished Way of Life,*
and the Unique Child Who Became Theodore Roosevelt. New York: Simon and Schuster, 2001.
Morris, Edmund. *Theodore Rex*. New York: Random House, 2001.
——. *The Rise of Theodore Roosevelt*. New York: Modern Library, 2001.

THOMAS STONE NATIONAL HISTORIC SITE

Location: Port Tobacco, Maryland
Acreage: 328
Established: November 10, 1978

The men who signed the Declaration of Independence were many and varied. They came from all parts of the country and engaged in all kinds of occupations. The New Englanders were primarily merchants—engaged in trade and often shipping—or lawyers, while the southerners were often landed gentry, owners of large tracts of land and often human capital—slaves—the issue that so divided North and South. Even at the Continental Congress, the issue was a fissure as deep as the crack in the Liberty Bell itself.

Thomas Stone of Maryland was one of the many signers of the Declaration of Independence, typical of the southerners. One of four Marylanders to ink this most famous document, Stone served in the Continental Congress from 1775 to 1778 and again in 1783 and 1784. He also served on the thirteen-member committee that drafted the Articles of Confederation, the governing principles of the United States before the ratification of the U.S. Constitution in 1787.

The Thomas Stone National Historic Site was established as part of the Omnibus Act of 1978, a maneuver orchestrated by Representative Philip Burton of California. Burton was almost single-handedly responsible for exponential enlargement of the park system during the 1970s. He bundled dozens of park proposals to other kinds of legislation, typically assuring that congressional representa-

Thomas Stone, signer of the Declaration of Independence. *(Library of Congress)*

tives who opposed the primary measure could not risk voting against a park proposal—and the jobs and federal dollars it would bring—in their district. Derided as creating a "park-of-the-month" club, Burton's omnibus acts became important if sometimes controversial ways of expanding the national park system.

Stone's plantation, called Habre-de-Venture, served as Stone's home from 1743 to 1787. The mansion house, a redbrick, Georgian-style structure completed in 1771, has been furnished to match the style of the 1770s. The bedroom and the parlor include original stone artifacts along with twentieth-century reproductions of eighteenth-century furniture. Among the notable documents are the Stone family schoolbook and a desk donated by Stone family descendants, which is believed to have belonged to Thomas Stone. In addition to the mansion, the 328-acre site also contains outbuildings typical of an

eighteenth- and nineteenth-century Maryland plantation. Admission is free. The park's visitor center is open year-round from 9 A.M. until 5 P.M. and features exhibits that chronicle the life and times of Thomas Stone, future plans for the site, archeological information, and plantation life through the years. A short introductory film is also available, and park rangers provide guided tours of the historic home daily from 10 A.M. until 4 P.M. The center has a small bookstore with material focusing on colonial life, the Declaration of Independence, and the Revolutionary War, and visitors are encouraged to walk along the mowed paths to the eighteenth-century farm buildings and view the changing landscape through forests and fields, and past watersheds, ravines, and historic garden terraces.

There are no food, lodging, or camping facilities at the site, but all traveler services are available in La Plata and along U.S. Highway 301.

For more information, write Thomas Stone National Historic Site, 6655 Rosehill Road, Port Tobacco, MD 20677, or telephone (301) 934-6027. The park's Web site is www.nps.gov/thst.

FURTHER READING
Ellis, Joseph J. *Founding Brothers: The Revolutionary Generation.* New York: Alfred A. Knopf, 2000.
Shaara, Jeff, *Rise to Rebellion.* NY: Ballantine, 2001.

TIMPANOGOS CAVE NATIONAL MONUMENT
Location: American Fork, Utah
Acreage: 250
Established: October 14, 1922

Despite its name, Timpanogos Cave in north-central Utah is actually a 3-cave complex connected by human-made tunnels excavated in the 1930s. Hansen, Middle, and Timpanogos caves were carved from eroded limestone in the steep south wall of the American Fork Canyon in the Wasatch Range. Formed by faulting and uplift, the Wasatch constitutes one of the steepest mountain fronts on the planet. As water and snowmelt began the inevitable task of reducing these sheer slopes, they also created the beautiful formations in the caves, such as speleothems, flowstone, stalactites, and stalagmites. Cavers in Timpanogos will also delight in the notable displays of helictites, kinked and curved speleothems that seem to defy gravity, as well as frostwork, and anthodites, which all grow in abundance in the caves. The first white man to discover the caves was Martin Hansen in 1887. He began giving guided tours, and news of the caves' beauty spread, leading to vandalism and destruction. Timpanogos Cave was discovered in 1915 and then rediscovered in 1921. Middle Cave was the last to be seen by explorers, in 1922, and by that time, the fragile and delicate underground wonders were under the protection of the National Forest Service.

Proclaimed in October 1922, the 250-acre Timpanogos Cave National Monument preserves the 3 limestone caverns and all of their remarkably varied cave formations. The cave and cave trail are typically open from early May to early November, weather permitting. The park's visitor center is open year-round from 7 A.M. until 5:30 P.M. May through September, and from 8:30 A.M. until 5 P.M. for the remainder of the year. The center offers historic and geologic displays, a hands-on display for children, a twenty-two-minute orientation video, and a forty-five-minute actual cave tour video. The Swinging Bridge Picnic Area, a quarter mile west of the visitor center, has picnic tables, fire grills, water, and rest rooms available. Directly across from the visitor center is the Canyon Nature Trail, and brochures in English and Spanish are available for the self-guided, quarter-mile nature walk. Park rangers offer guided walks, talks, and evening programs at the visitor center and in the surrounding area, and winter programs are held every other Monday from 7 P.M. to 8 P.M. at the visitor center.

The Uinta National Forest administers American Fork Canyon, and it charges a $3-per-vehicle fee to reach Timpanogos Cave National Monument; a $10 fourteen-day pass and a $25 annual pass are also available. Fees for cave tours, ranging from forty-five to sixty minutes, are $6 for adults (age sixteen and older), $5 for juniors (ages six to fifteen), and $3 for children. The park also offers a ninety-minute introduction-to-caving tour that introduces visitors (age fourteen and up) to the sport of caving and caving ethics. Although it is not a "wild" caving experience, the tour does require bending, crawling, and passage through tight spaces. The fee is $15 per person.

There are no lodging or camping facilities in the monument, but all traveler services are available in American Fork, Orem, Provo, and Salt Lake City. There is a small snack bar in the park.

For more information, write Timpanogos Cave National Monument, RR 3, Box 200, American Fork, UT 84003-9800, or telephone (801) 756-5238. The park's Web site is www.nps.gov/tica.

FURTHER READING
Kiver, Eugene P., and David V. Harris. *Geology of U.S. Parklands.* New York: John Wiley and Sons, 1999.

Martin, George Vivian. *The Timpanogos Cave Story: The Romance of Its Exploration.* Salt Lake City, UT: Hawkes, 1973.

Trimble, Stephen. *Window into the Earth: Timpanogos Cave.* Globe, AZ: Southwest Parks and Monuments Association, 1983.

TIMUCUAN ECOLOGICAL AND HISTORIC PRESERVE

Location: Jacksonville, Florida
Acreage: 46,287
Established: February 16, 1988

The Timucuan Ecological and Historic Preserve draws its name and inspiration from the

Native Americans who lived and thrived for more than three thousand years here near the estuaries of the St. Johns and Nassau rivers. Native Timucuan people inhabited the area more than four thousand years before the arrival of the first Europeans. The area subsequently experienced more than four centuries of exploration, colonization, agriculture, and commerce under the flags of France, Spain, England, the Confederate States of America, and the United States. The Timucuan area was also part of Florida's plantation slave economy during the nineteenth century. Along the rich coastline, the production of sugar cane, indigo, and cotton thrived as enslaved Africans worked the soil at the oldest remaining Florida plantation—Kingsley Plantation. In addition to its cultural significance, this remarkable Atlantic Coast ecosystem preserves marshes, islands, tidal creeks, coastal dunes, and hardwood hammock—elements of one of the few remaining unspoiled coastal wetlands on the Atlantic seaboard.

Today the park has 2 large undeveloped upland tracts: the Theodore Roosevelt Area, which contains 600 acres of hardwood forest, wetlands, and scrub vegetation; and Cedar Point, a 400-acre spread of oak hammock, pine plantation, and scrub vegetation on the south end of Black Hammock Island. Of the 2, the Theodore Roosevelt Area is notable for its archeological sites and cultural artifacts, including oyster shell piles left by its ancient inhabitants. Trails crisscross the area and provide excellent opportunities for birding, wildlife photography, and nature study. The National Park Service acquired Cedar Point after the Theodore Roosevelt Area, and it is still under development, with limited facilities. However, a primitive boat ramp remaining from a commercial fish camp on the site forty years ago is available for use by boaters, and a network of sand trails provides access to the shoreline and to the interior.

Authorized in February 1988, the pre-serve encompasses Atlantic coastal marshes, islands, tidal creeks, and the estuaries of the St. Johns and Nassau rivers. The Timucuan Ecological and Historic Preserve Visitor Center, at 12713 Fort Caroline Road in Jacksonville, is open year-round from 9 A.M. until 5 P.M. The center has artifacts from the Timucuan and early European periods, and "Where the Waters Meet," which is a series of exhibits illustrating the ecology of the marine estuarine environment and the interaction with the environment by the peoples who have lived here for more than four thousand years. The Theodore Roosevelt and Cedar Point areas provide access to the marine estuarine environment and surrounding coastal forest for hiking, nature observation, birding, and photography, while the Kingsley Plantation, a nineteenth-century cotton plantation and the oldest remaining plantation house in Florida, offers a glimpse of plantation life. Exhibits include the planter's house, barn, slave quarters, and a small interpretive garden with crops typical of the period.

There is no food, lodging, or camping in the preserve, but all traveler services are available locally. Camping is available at Little Talbot Island State Park and Huguenot Memorial Park.

For more information, write Timucuan Ecological and Historic Preserve, 12713 Fort Caroline Road, Jacksonville, FL 32225, or telephone (904) 641-7155. The park's Web site is www.nps.gov/timu.

FURTHER READING
Milanich, Jerald T. *Archaeology of Precolumbian Florida.* Gainesville: University Press of Florida, 1994.
Worth, John E. *The Timucuan Chiefdoms of Spanish Florida.* Gainesville: University Press of Florida, 1998.

TONTO NATIONAL MONUMENT
Location: Roosevelt, Arizona
Acreage: 1,120
Established: December 19, 1907

Tonto National Monument, located in central Arizona, preserves the remains of a little-known but intriguing pre-Columbian Native American culture. The monument allows people to explore and examine the well-preserved cliff dwellings that were once occupied by the Salado people. The Salado lived in Tonto Valley in villages along the river. An agricultural people, the Salado migrated into the foothills surrounding the valley during the early thirteenth century, establishing apartment-style dwellings in the alcoves of the hills, and remained there until the early fifteenth century.

Bonding rocks with mud, the Salado created cliff dwellings in which they slept, cooked, and stored their goods. These Native Americans made the most of the natural resources available to them. A much wetter place during these centuries than it is now, the highlands offered plants and animals that kept the Salado alive. Valley dwellers grew corn, beans, pumpkins, amaranth, and cotton in irrigated fields. Some of the cliff-dwelling Salado specialized in weaving and pottery, which they traded for food and cotton from the valley. In the mid-fifteenth century the Salado, like many of the Sonoran desert people, abandoned their cliff dwellings and disappeared. Though the reasons are unclear, weather changes and increased raiding by migrating peoples, the recently arrived Athapaskan tribes who became the Navajo and the Apache, surely precipitated the abandonment of the Tonto Valley by its native inhabitants.

Very little is known of the Salado, though archeological excavation of the cliff dwellings continues to inform modern people about the lives of these early Sonoran desert dwellers. Without a written record and with no preserved chronological history of events, what is known of the Salado emerges largely from the pottery that has survived. Red clay pottery, on display at the visitor center museum at the national monument, illustrates the art and the daily life of the Salado people.

Established in 1907 in the first wave of monument proclamations, the 1,120-acre Tonto National Monument never attracted the attention that other nearby archeological areas did. Away from the main patterns of travel, it did not attract as many visitors.

Tonto Valley and the hills housing the monument are located in the Sonoran desert, so the summers are very hot. Water, hats, and sunscreen are essential during summer months. The winter is mild, with high temperatures in the 60s. This region experiences two rainy seasons each year, the first in January and February and the second from July to early September.

The park preserves the pueblos, and the artifacts within, that tell the story of the Salado Indians. The Lower Ruin consists of 16 ground-floor rooms, which were adjacent to a 12-room annex. The Upper Ruin was much larger, with 32 ground-floor rooms, and level roofs and terraces on which the Salado worked and played. The entrance fee is $3 per person. The park's visitor center is open year-round from 8 A.M. until 5 P.M. and has exhibits, a hands-on display, and an eighteen-minute video orientation program. The park hosts an Open House annually on a weekend in March (Arizona Archeology Awareness Month) and the first weekend in November. Visitors can hike the 1-mile, self-guided Lower Cliff Dwelling Trail and participate in scheduled interpretive activities and guided tours to Upper Cliff Dwelling, November through April.

There are no food, lodging, or camping facilities at the monument, but all traveler services are available in Globe, Miami, Payson, Punkin, and Roosevelt.

For more information, write Tonto National Monument, HC02 Box 4602, Roosevelt, AZ 85545, or telephone (928) 467-2241. The park's Web site is www. nps.gov/tont.

FURTHER READING

Dean, Jeffrey S., ed. *Salado*. Albuquerque: University of New Mexico Press, 2000.

Houk, Rose. *Salado*. Tucson, AZ: Southwest Parks and Monuments Association, 1992.

Nelson, Ben A., and Steven A. LeBlanc. *Short-term Sedentism in the American Southwest: The Mimbres Valley Salado*. Albuquerque: University of New Mexico Press, 1986.

TOURO SYNAGOGUE NATIONAL HISTORIC SITE

Location: Newport, Rhode Island
Acreage: .23
Established: March 5, 1946

Touro Synagogue National Historic Site celebrates the nation's oldest synagogue, and the only one that has survived from colonial times. Designated a National Historic Site in 1946, the Touro Synagogue was built and dedicated in Newport, Rhode Island, in 1762. This site represents the tradition and history of the small, but vital, Jewish population that contributed to European settlement in North America.

Touro Synagogue was built to serve a congregation whose roots went back to 1658, when descendants of the Marranos, the forcibly converted Jews who fled Spain and Portugal during the Inquisition, settled in Rhode Island for its religious freedom. By the mid-seventeenth century these people, part of the Oriental Jewish community called Sephardim, were seeking safety from religious persecution in the Caribbean. They migrated to North America hoping to find religious tolerance. Fifteen Jewish families arrived in Newport in 1658, seeking the promise of freedom of religion and liberty of conscience promised by Governor Roger Williams of Rhode Island.

The congregation relied on the concept of religious toleration and separation of church and state that had flowered in the early years of English settlement in Rhode Island in particular and in the northern colonies. For one hundred years, these families worshiped in private homes; by the mid-eighteenth century the congregation had grown such that it needed a building that could house worship and provide a place of religious instruction for the young. In 1790, George Washington visited Touro Synagogue and later wrote his famous letter "To the Hebrew Congregation in Newport, R.I.," in which he expressed his belief in religious liberty in America to the members of the congregation.

A magnificent example of eighteenth-century architecture in the English colonies, Touro Synagogue was designed by Peter Harrison. Harrison placed the building at an angle so that worshipers could stand in prayer facing east toward Jerusalem. Twelve columns, representing the twelve tribes of Israel, support the ceiling and the women's gallery. Elements of the interior architecture are in the tradition of Spanish synagogues, supporting the belief that this congregation had its earliest roots in Spain and Portugal. Still serving an active congregation, the synagogue stands as a testimony to the standard of religious freedom and civil liberty in America.

Touro Synagogue is open for public tours at specific times during each week. From November through April, there is 1 tour at 1 P.M. on Fridays. From May through June, and from September 8 through October 31, there are tours Monday through Friday from 1 to 3 P.M., and between 11 A.M. and 3 P.M. on Sunday. From July through September 7, there are tours Sunday through Friday between 10 A.M. and 5 P.M. There are no tours on Saturdays or Jewish holidays.

Rhode Island weather is subject to rapid change and is quite harsh during the winter. Temperatures during the summer range between the 70s and the 90s, and spring and fall are pleasant, ranging in temperature between the 50s and 70s.

There are no food, lodging, or camping facilities at the historic site, but all traveler services are available locally.

For more information, write Touro Synagogue, 72 Touro Street, Newport, RI 02840, or telephone (401) 847-4794. The park's Web site is www.nps.gov/tosy.

FURTHER READING

Fisher, Leonard Everett. *To Bigotry No Sanction: The Story of the Oldest Synagogue in America.* New York: Holiday House, 1999.

Gerber, Jane S. *The Jews of Spain: A History of the Sephardic Experience.* New York: Free Press, 1992.

TUMACÁCORI NATIONAL HISTORICAL PARK

Location: Tumacácori, Arizona
Acreage: 360
Established: September 15, 1908

Located in the Santa Cruz River Valley of southeastern Arizona, Tumacácori National Historical Park preserves the remains of colonial Spanish missionary work in the area. Throughout the seventeenth, eighteenth, and nineteenth centuries the Catholic Church, in conjunction with the Spanish government, sought to subdue, convert, and exploit the indigenous people of the region that is now the desert Southwest of the United States. This park protects and interprets a sophisticated complex of adobe ruins and remaining churches that reflected Spanish colonialism in the New World.

In 1687, a Jesuit missionary, Padre Eusebio Francisco Kino, traveled into the desert to convert the O'odham, or Pima, Indians. During the course of almost twenty-five years, Kino established more than two dozen mission churches in O'odham villages. In addition to proselytizing, the Spanish priest also introduced Spanish culture to the native peo-

Ruins of the San José de Tumacácori Mission Church in southern Arizona. *(National Park Service)*

ple and tried to engage them in productive labor for the Spanish government. The O'odham people lived throughout the region and were made up of several branches, each with a distinct but interrelated culture. The Sobaipuri branch lived along the Santa Cruz River when Father Kino arrived, but they soon disappeared as a result of warfare, disease, and intermarriage. The present day O'odham people who live in the river valley are the Tohono O'odham and the Akimel O'odham (Pima). Their culture descends from the O'odham people encountered by Father Kino, who themselves claimed cultural heritage from the Hohokam civilization of an earlier period.

In 1691, Father Kino visited the villages of Tumacácori and Guevavi and founded missions in both locations. In 1701, the mission at Guevavi was made mission headquarters, and a priest periodically traveled from there to Tumacácori. A priest was not permanently in residence until 1751, when Padre Joseph Garrucho began building a church he called Los Santos Angeles de Guevavi. The period in which this large adobe church was built also marked an increased tension between the Spanish and the O'odham. That year, the four-month-long Pima Rebellion exploded, during which Spanish priests were killed and symbols of Christianity destroyed. By the late 1750s, the Spanish had reasserted their control and the missionary project continued. In 1767, the Jesuits were removed from Spanish colonies and Franciscan monks took over the preexisting churches, including those in Guevavi and Tumacácori, which were near the new Spanish Presidio of Tubac. Over the course of the nineteenth century, the Tumacácori region was under Spanish, then Mexican, then U.S. control, and its churches were continually underfunded.

By 1786, only 100 native people remained at Tumacácori and the Spanish had abandoned Guevavi and nearby Tubac. Though a Franciscan monk began a new, larger church at Tumacácori in 1800, poverty and the 1828 expulsion of all Spanish priests from Mexican territory hindered the completion of the church. A series of Apache raids and an especially hard winter in 1848 led to the final abandonment of the Tumacácori mission in that year.

Established in September 1908, the 360-acre Tumacácori National Monument was among the first national monuments. It selection reflects the importance of Southwestern history in the creation of the Antiquities Act and the commitment of early-twentieth-century Americans to the preservation of this dimension of the national past.

Tumacácori park is located in southern Arizona, in what is called the Arizona Upland division of the Sonoran desert. The climate is warm and dry throughout most of the year, with the exception of monsoon season in July and August. During the monsoon, severe thunderstorms are common in the afternoons. Summer temperatures are harsh, with highs above 100 degrees during the day. Winters, however, are mild, with lows in the 30s and highs in the 60s or 70s. Winter is the peak tourist season in the region.

The monument preserves the stabilized ruins of the Franciscan church, a cemetery, and other outbuildings. There is a $3 entrance fee, good for seven days, for all individuals over age seventeen. The park and visitor center are open year-round from 8 A.M. until 5 P.M. daily, and exhibits include dioramas, santos, and other information and objects related to the Kino missions, the Spanish, and the indigenous natives, as well as a fourteen-minute introductory video. Guided tours are given daily during the winter months, and Mexican and local artisans demonstrate traditional crafts such as tortilla making, basket weaving, and pottery during the winter. With advance scheduling, living-history tours depicting life during the Franciscan period are given. The two-day Fiesta at Tumacácori is held the first weekend of every December, and it includes traditional dancers, musical groups, and crafts demonstrators. Luminarias light the grounds and mission church on Christmas Eve. Twice a year, usually in April and October, a special High Mass is given in the church. On occasion, the mission will open at night during a full moon, allowing visitors to experience Tumacácori in a different light.

There are no food, lodging, or camping facilities in the historical park, but all traveler services are available in Amado, Green Valley, Nogales, Rio Rico, Tubac, and Tumacácori.

For more information, write Tumacácori National Historical Park, P.O. Box 67, Tumacácori, AZ 85640, or telephone (520) 398-2341. The park's Web site is www.nps.gov/tuma.

FURTHER READING
Bleser, Nicholas J. *Tumacácori From Rancheria to National Monument.* Tucson, AZ: Southwest Parks and Monuments Association, 1988.
Jackson, Earl. *Tumacácori's Yesterdays.* Globe, AZ: Southwest Parks and Monuments Association, 1973.
Lamb, Susan. *Tumacácori National Historical Park.* Tucson, AZ: Southwest Parks and Monuments Association, 1993.

TUPELO NATIONAL BATTLEFIELD
Location: Tupelo, Mississippi
Acreage: 1
Established: February 21, 1929

The Battle of Tupelo (Harrisburg) in northeastern Mississippi was part of a larger strategy by Union General William Tecumseh Sherman to protect the railroad supply line for his devastating march through the South. On July 14, 1864, Confederate Lieutenant General Nathan Bedford Forrest attempted to sever that railroad link and halt the Union's push for Atlanta. Earlier, on July 5, Major General Andrew Jackson Smith and more

than 14,000 federal soldiers moved out of Tennessee to ensure that Forrest and his cavalry did not raid Sherman's railroad lifeline. Laying waste to the countryside as he advanced, Smith reached Tupelo on July 13. At 7:30 the next morning, 8,000 rebels engaged Smith in a number of uncoordinated assaults that the Yankees beat back, inflicting heavy casualties on the Southern ranks. The Confederates halted the fighting within a few hours, but Smith, short on rations, did not pursue, instead retreating to Memphis on July 15. Although criticized for not destroying Forrest's command, Smith had caused much damage and had fulfilled his mission of ensuring Sherman's supply lines. The Battle of Tupelo resulted in 1,948 casualties—648 Union, 1,300 Confederate. A granite marker commemorates the dead of both armies.

Established in February 1929, the 1-acre Tupelo National Battlefield was initially assigned to the War Department and was transferred to the Park Service as part of the reorganization of the federal government in 1933. It commemorates the last major Civil War battle fought on Mississippi soil. Admission is free. The site is within the city limits of Tupelo on Mississippi Highway 6 about 1.3 miles west of its intersection with U.S. Highway 45, and 1 mile east of the Natchez Trace Parkway. The battlefield provides a number of interpretive placards and markers, as well as a monument and period cannons.

The battlefield is also located within the much larger 52,000-acre Natchez Trace Parkway, which was originally established in May 1938 to preserve the centuries-old trail—or trace—used by American Indians and early settlers between Nashville, Tennessee, and Natchez, Mississippi. The parkway also protects several other significant historical sites such as Emerald Mound, the second largest ceremonial mound in the United States, numerous plantation sites, pioneer stands/inns, archeological sites/villages, pioneer and slave cemeteries, and a historic housing site, part of the resettlement program of Franklin D. Roosevelt's New Deal. The trace tells the story of great leaders such as Meriwether Lewis and Andrew Jackson, and outlaws such as John Murrell and Samuel Mason. Today the "Old Trace" is paralleled by the modern Natchez Trace Parkway. Designated as part of the National Scenic Byways Program, the Natchez Trace Parkway was named an All-American Road in 1995 to commemorate its beauty, landscape features, historic and intrinsic qualities. The commemorative 443-mile-long parkway represents a means by which travelers can capture a glimpse of history not easily forgotten while also enjoying a leisurely drive along a historic landscape.

The parkway's visitor center, located in Tupelo at parkway milepost 266, is open from 8 A.M. to 5 P.M. daily, and features a twelve-minute film highlighting the history and sites of the parkway. In addition to attending ranger talks and seasonal crafts festivals and demonstrations, visitors can enjoy various activities like hiking, walking, auto tours, horseback riding, bicycling, boating, swimming, fishing, and viewing various exhibits. To complement the historic parkway, the Park Service has also developed the 110-mile Natchez Trace National Scenic Trail, established in March 1983. The National Trails System Act of 1968 authorized the development of these trails in both urban and rural settings to promote enjoyment and encourage greater public access.

There are no food, lodging, or camping facilities at the battlefield, but all traveler services are available in the Tupelo area. In addition to nearby federal, state, and private campgrounds, the Natchez Trace Parkway provides 3 camping facilities for visitors at Rocky Springs (22 sites), Jeff Busby (18 sites), and Meriwether Lewis (32 sites). There are no hookups and no fees. Campsites are available on a first-come, first-served basis, and stays are limited to fifteen days during periods of heavy visitation. Individual sites have tables, grills, and a level tent site, and rest rooms and drinking water are provided; however, no hot water, showers, electrical/sanitary hookups, or dumping sites are available.

For more information, write Tupelo National Battlefield, c/o Natchez Trace Parkway, 2680 Natchez Trace Parkway, Tupelo, MS 38804, or telephone (800) 305-7417. The park's Web site is www.nps.gov/tupe.

FURTHER READING
Catton, Bruce. *The Civil War.* New York: American Heritage, 1985.
Crutchfield, James. *The Natchez Trace: A Pictorial History.* Nashville, TN: Rutledge Hill, 1985.
Davis, William C. *A Way Through the Wilderness: The Natchez Trace and the Civilization of the Southern Frontier.* New York: HarperCollins, 1995.

TUSKEGEE AIRMEN NATIONAL HISTORIC SITE
Location: Tuskegee, Alabama
Acreage: 90
Established: November 6, 1998

When the United States entered World War II, it was still a nation divided. In 1896, the Supreme Court had ruled in *Plessy v. Ferguson* that "separate but equal" was constitutional, forming the foundation for "Jim Crow," or segregation, laws throughout the country. But by the 1940s, African Americans grew increasingly dissatisfied with their second-class status, particularly in a society that drew pride from its heritage of "freedom" and democracy. Since the early twentieth century, the NAACP (National Association for the Advancement of Colored People) had been chipping away at the *Plessy* ruling in the nation's court system, while other activists had begun to directly challenge segregation in the armed forces. Black men were expected to serve their country, but in segregated service battalions often relegated to noncombat auxiliary positions in transportation and engineering corps. It was a galling double standard. As one serviceman recalled, "I saw German prisoners free to move around the camp, unlike black soldiers who were restricted. The Germans walked right into the doggone places like any white American. We were wearin' the same uniform, but we were excluded."

Anticipating the civil rights movement to come, many activists began protesting these exclusionary practices, which would finally lead to the complete desegregation of the U.S. military in 1948, after the war. During the war, however, perhaps the most visible group of black soldiers was the Tuskegee Airmen, who served in the U.S. Army Air Force. Created in 1941, the all-black unit trained at Tuskegee Army Air Field in Alabama, and unlike any other unit in the army, the Airmen were commanded by black officers. The Tuskegee Airmen earned their reputation in the North Africa campaign before supporting the mainland invasion of Italy in 1943. By the end of the war, the Airmen had flown more than 15,000 sorties and completed more than 1,500 missions. As one pilot recalled, "Once our reputation got out as to our fighting ability, we started getting special requests for our group to escort their group, the bombers. They all wanted us because we were the only fighter group in the entire air force that did not lose a bomber to action. Oh, we were much in demand."

In 1998, Congress established the Tuskegee Airmen National Historic Site at Moton Field in Tuskegee, Alabama, to pay tribute to the heroic actions of the Tuskegee Airmen during World War II. Eventually, this new addition to the park system will contain a museum and interpretive programs at the historic complex at Moton Field as well as a national center based on a public-private partnership.

There are no food, lodging, or camping facilities at the historic site, but all traveler services are available locally. Camping is available at Chewakla State Park.

For more information, write Tuskegee Airmen National Historic Site, 1212 Old Montgomery Road, Tuskegee Institute, AL 36088, or telephone (334) 727-6390. The park's Web site is www.nps.gov/tuai.

FURTHER READING

Francis, Charles E. *The Tuskegee Airmen: The Men Who Changed a Nation.* Boston: Branden, 1993.

Hine, Darlene Clark, William C. Hine, and Stanley Harrold. *The African-American Odyssey.* Upper Saddle River, NJ: Prentice-Hall, 2003.

Homan, Lynn M. *The Tuskegee Airmen.* Charleston, SC: Arcadia, 1998.

McKissack, Patricia, and Frederick McKissack. *Red-Tail Angels: The Story of the Tuskegee Airmen of World War II.* New York: Walker, 1995.

Scott, Lawrence P. *Double V: The Civil Rights Struggle of the Tuskegee Airmen.* East Lansing: Michigan State University Press, 1994.

TUSKEGEE INSTITUTE NATIONAL HISTORIC SITE

Location: Tuskegee Institute, Alabama
Acreage: 58
Established: October 26, 1974

It is difficult to separate Tuskegee Institute from its founder, Booker T. Washington, for in many ways they are like two parts of a larger whole. Washington had been born a Virginia slave in 1856. As a houseboy for a prominent white family, he had been given the unusual opportunity to learn to read and write. After the Civil War formally ended slavery in America, Washington continued to pursue his education at the Hampton Institute, one of the many all-black colleges that rose up in the aftermath of the war. In 1881, he accepted a job as principal of a newly formed black college called the Tuskegee Institute. His educational philosophy and message were simple: "No race can prosper till it learns that there is as much dignity in tilling a field as in writing a poem. It is at the bottom of life we must begin, and not at the top." At the turn of the twentieth century, this accommodationist message was welcomed by white politicians and philanthropists who were re-

Welcome address to U.S. Army Air Corps cadets at the Booker T. Washington Monument on the grounds of the Tuskegee Institute, August 19, 1941. *(National Archives)*

luctant to support racial equality, but who could and would support black economic independence earned through self-help, hard work, and a practical education. As Tuskegee grew, so too did Washington's national, and even international, reputation. And while some were intensely critical of his conservative message, Washington became one of *the* prominent leaders, black or white, in American society at the time. In 1901, President Theodore Roosevelt invited him to dine at the White House. His fund-raising skills enabled Tuskegee to flourish, and by 1906, the school had 156 faculty members and 1,590 students, and it owned 2,300 acres of land. Washington also encouraged the best and

brightest black scholars to join the Tuskegee faculty. To this end in 1896, Washington lured George Washington Carver away from Iowa State to take charge of the school's agricultural program.

In 1965, the federal government designated Tuskegee Institute a national historic landmark in recognition of its contributions and advancements in education, and Congress authorized the National Historic Site in 1974. Today, the 58-acre park includes The Oaks, Booker T. Washington's home, and the Carver Museum. Admission is free. The Carver Museum is open year-round from 9 A.M. until 5 P.M., and it features numerous exhibits and regularly scheduled, ranger-guided tours. The park celebrates Black History Month (February), the Carver Crafts Festival (May), and the Carver Sweet Potato Festival (October).

There are no food, lodging, or camping facilities at the historic site, but all traveler services are available locally. Camping is available at Chewakla State Park.

For more information, write Tuskegee Institute National Historic Site, P.O. Drawer 10, Tuskegee Institute, AL 36087, or telephone (334) 727-3200. The park's Web site is www.nps.gov/tuin.

FURTHER READING

Harlan, Louis R. *Booker T. Washington: The Making of a Black Leader, 1856–1901.* New York: Oxford University Press, 1972.

——. *Booker T. Washington: Wizard of Tuskegee, 1901–1915.* New York: Oxford University Press, 1972.

Washington, Booker T. *Working with the Hands; Being a Sequel to Up from Slavery, Covering the Author's Experiences in Industrial Training at Tuskegee.* New York: Negro Universities Press, 1969.

——. *Up from Slavery.* New York: Dover, 1995.

TUZIGOOT NATIONAL MONUMENT
Location: Clarkdale, Arizona
Acreage: 812
Established: July 25, 1939

Crowning a desert hilltop in Arizona's Verde River Valley are the ruins of an ancient Sinaguan pueblo known as Tuzigoot, an Apache word meaning "crooked water." The pueblo, first built around 1000 C.E., consisted of 110 rooms, including second- and third-story structures.

The Sinagua were agriculturalists who built irrigation systems to raise corn, beans, squash, pumpkins, and cotton. They supplemented their diet by gathering black walnuts, berries, and other plants, and by hunting deer and small animals. They also wove cotton fabrics and made red-on-buff pottery, baskets, and matting, all of which was traded across a network that spanned hundreds of miles. While this large pueblo flourished from the twelfth to the fifteenth century, archeologists estimate that the Sinagua people left the area by 1450, possibly due to drought, poor sanitation, or raids on their crops by nomadic tribes. The pueblo's stone walls eventually collapsed and buried the site, which protected it from looters and vandalism. Excavations, which began in the 1930s, have revealed an unusually fine collection of artifacts, including bowls, pots, clay figures, jewelry, and burial sites.

Proclaimed in July 1939, the 812-acre Tuzigoot National Monument preserves the ruins of this pueblo. The entrance fee is $2 per person. The Tuzigoot Visitor Center is open year-round from 8 A.M. until 5 P.M., and for extended hours during the summer. The center is one of the few museums interpreting ancient Sinaguan culture in Arizona. It features several exhibits depicting the Sinaguan lifestyle. The park also has 2 self-guided trails with wayside exhibits that describe the site's cultural and natural history. The one-third-mile Ruins Loop trail is paved, but steep, and not recommended for wheeled devices such as wheelchairs. The Tavasci Marsh Overlook trail takes the visitor to an overview of Tavasci Marsh, one of the few freshwater marshes in Arizona. Rangers are available on the trail and programs are presented when staffing permits.

There are no food, lodging, or camping facilities at the monument, but all traveler services are available in Cottonwood, Sedona, and Camp Verde.

For more information, write Tuzigoot National Monument, Tuzigoot Road, Clarkdale, AZ 86324, or telephone (520) 634-5564. The park's Web site is www. nps.gov/tuzi.

FURTHER READING

Hodge, Carle. *Ruins Along the River: Motezuma Castle, Tuzigoot, and Montezuma Well National Monuments.* Tucson, AZ: Southwest Parks and Monuments Association, 1986.

Houk, Rose. *Tuzigoot National Monument.* Tucson, AZ: Southwest Parks and Monuments Association, 1995.

U

ULYSSES S. GRANT NATIONAL HISTORIC SITE

Location: St. Louis, Missouri
Acreage: 10
Established: October 2, 1989

> "Let us have peace."
>
> *—Ulysses S. Grant*

When Ulysses S. Grant, defender of the Union, accepted the Republican nomination for president in 1868, his hope for peace in the aftermath of Civil War seemed to indicate a new era might be dawning in America. His administration was a bitter disappointment. Never able to rise above the spoils system and corruption that infested his two terms in office, Grant was destined to go down in history as the man who led the army that saved the Union, and one of the worst presidents of the United States.

Grant was born in 1822, the son of an Ohio tanner, and he reluctantly attended West Point, where he graduated in the middle of his class. During the Mexican War (1846–1848) he fought under General Zachary Taylor, and at the outbreak of the Civil War, Grant was appointed by the governor of Illinois to command an unruly volunteer regiment. His leadership ability vaulted him to the rank of brigadier general by September 1861, and he was assigned the rather daunting task of helping win control of the Mississippi Valley for the Union. By February 1862, Fort Henry had fallen, and when the Confederate commander at Fort Donelson asked for surrender terms, Grant replied, "No terms ex-

cept an unconditional and immediate surrender can be accepted." Grant got what he wanted. Recognizing Grant's leadership potential, President Abraham Lincoln promoted him to major general of volunteers, and the steely man from Ohio earned the nickname "*Unconditional Surrender*" Grant.

At Shiloh in April 1862, Grant nearly lost his command in one of the bloodiest battles in the West, but President Lincoln defended him by saying, simply, "I can't spare this man—he fights." The following summer, on July 4, Grant redeemed himself with a victory at Vicksburg, the key city on the Mississippi, whose fall cut the Confederacy in two. Grant went on to victory at Chattanooga, and Lincoln, deciding that here, at last, was the man who could win the war, appointed him general in chief of the Union Army in March 1864. Grant immediately implemented a devastating campaign against the Confederacy, directing William Tecumseh Sherman to punish the South, while with the Army of the Potomac, he wore down General Robert E. Lee's Army of Northern Virginia. Finally, on April 9, 1865, at Appomattox Court House, Lee surrendered, and the terrible war was over.

Grant's popularity easily carried him into the White House in 1868, but he was a far better general than a president. Although Grant himself was an honest man, many of his appointees were not, and by association, his reputation was tarnished. Although he easily won reelection in 1872, Grant's star quickly faded. By 1873, the country was mired in a recession, and scandal plagued his administration. After retiring from the presidency, Grant continued to struggle, especially financially. His final days were spent feverishly writing his memoirs, which he hoped would provide financial stability for his family. They did. Today, historians consider his recollections among the very finest produced concerning the Civil War. Grant died on July 25, 1885, at the age of 63.

Authorized in October 1989, the 10-acre Ulysses S. Grant National Historic Site commemorates the life, military career, and presidency of Ulysses S. Grant, as well as his wife Julia Dent Grant. The estate, also known as White Haven, consists of 5 historic structures (main house, stone building, barn, chicken house, and ice house) where Grant lived in the years prior to the Civil War. Admission is free. The park's visitor center is open year-round from 9 A.M. until 5 P.M., and it has numerous interpretive exhibits. Park rangers offer guided tours of the main house, and self-guided walking tours of the home and grounds are available year-round. Special programs are offered on the first Saturday of every month.

There are no food, lodging, or camping facilities in the park, but all traveler services are available throughout the St. Louis metropolitan area.

For more information, write Ulysses S. Grant National Historic Site, 7400 Grant Road, St. Louis, MO 63123, or telephone (314) 842-3298. The park's Web site is www.nps.gov/ulsg.

FURTHER READING

Catton, Bruce. *Grant Moves South.* Boston: Little, Brown, 1960.
——. *Grant Takes Command.* Boston: Little, Brown, 1969.
Fuller, J.F.C. *The Generalship of Ulysses S. Grant.* New York: Da Capo, 1991.
Grant, Ulysses S. *The Civil War Memoirs of Ulysses S. Grant.* New York: Forge, 2002.
Smith, Jean Edward. *Grant.* New York: Simon and Schuster, 2001.
"The White House: Ulysses S. Grant." Available at www.whitehouse.gov.history/presidents/ug18.html.

USS *ARIZONA* MEMORIAL
Location: Honolulu, Hawaii
Acreage: 11
Established: September 9, 1980

On the morning of December 7, 1941, a "date which will live in infamy," Japan suddenly and unexpectedly attacked the U.S. Pacific Fleet stationed at Pearl Harbor in Hawaii. The following day, with only one dissenting vote, Congress declared war on Japan and entered World War II. Although the United States was unprepared for the attack at Pearl Harbor, relations between the two nations had been steadily declining for more than a decade. During the 1930s, Japan's aggressive campaign of territorial expansion in the Far East had threatened American trade access as well as the region's political stability, and President Franklin D. Roosevelt hoped to use economic coercion to rein in Japanese imperialism. By embargoing critical war resources, such as aviation fuel, steel, and iron, the United States sought to assert its authority in the Far East without engaging the military. It was a delicate, balance-of-power maneuver, which Japan largely ignored. In the summer of 1941, Roosevelt added oil—the most critical resource—to the embargo, and that fall, an increasingly desperate Premier Hideki Tojo determined to attack the United States sometime after November. The United States was sure the attack would come either on Malaya or in the Philippines. They were wrong. Instead, at 7:55 A.M. on December 7, the first wave of planes hit Pearl Harbor. A second wave attacked an hour later. It was a stunning success. Most of the American planes were destroyed; eight battleships, three destroyers, and three cruisers were disabled; the *Oklahoma* and *Arizona* were completely destroyed; and 2,323 service personnel were killed. Remarkably, the fleet's aircraft carriers, which were not in port at the time, were spared in the attack, and much of Pearl

Harbor remained intact. Even more significantly, the attack galvanized American support for entry into the war and touched off a national wave of patriotism.

The USS *Arizona* Memorial is the final resting place for many of the ship's 1,177 crewmen who lost their lives on that fateful December morning. The ship exploded at approximately 8:10 A.M. and sank in less than nine minutes. The memorial grew out of a wartime desire to establish some sort of commemoration to honor those who died in the attack. According to its architect, Alfred Preis, the design of the 184-foot-long memorial, "Wherein the structure sags in the center but stands strong and vigorous at the ends, ex-

presses initial defeat and ultimate victory.... The overall effect is one of serenity. Overtones of sadness have been omitted to permit the individual to contemplate his own personal responses...his innermost feelings." The structure spans the mid-portion of the sunken battleship and consists of three main sections: the entry and assembly rooms; a central area designed for ceremonies and general observation; and the shrine room, where the names of those killed on the *Arizona* are engraved on the marble wall.

The park is open daily from 7:30 A.M. until 5 P.M. and admission is free (donations are encouraged). The interpretive program, for which visitors are given free tickets at the vis-

The USS *Arizona* burning after the Japanese attack on Pearl Harbor, December 7, 1941. *(National Archives)*

itor center, consists of a brief talk by a park ranger or a Pearl Harbor survivor, followed by a twenty-three-minute documentary film on the Pearl Harbor attack. Immediately after the film, visitors depart the theater for the boat landing, where they board a navy shuttle boat and begin their trip to the USS *Arizona* Memorial. All visitors disembark on the memorial and return to the visitor center a short time later on another shuttle boat.

There are no food, lodging, or camping facilities at the memorial, but all traveler services are available in Honolulu.

For more information, write USS *Arizona* Memorial, 1 Arizona Memorial Place, Honolulu, HI 96818, or telephone (808) 422-0561. The park's Web site is www.nps.gov/usar.

FURTHER READING

Department of Defense CD-ROM. *20th Century Complete Guide to Pearl Harbor: Encyclopedic Coverage of December 7, 1941: Remarkable Photographs, Oral Histories, Vessel Attack Reports, Casualty Lists, Japanese Force Information, Submerged Cultural Resources, USS Arizona Memorial.* Washington, DC: Progressive Management, 2002.

Jasper, Joy Waldron, James P. Delgado, and Jim Adams. *The USS* Arizona: *The Ship, the Men, the Pearl Harbor Attack, and the Symbol That Aroused America.* New York: St. Martin's, 2001.

Slackman, Michael. *Remembering Pearl Harbor: The Story of the USS Arizona Memorial.* Honolulu, HI: Arizona Memorial Museum Association, 1984.

V

VALLEY FORGE NATIONAL HISTORICAL PARK

Location: Valley Forge, Pennsylvania
Acreage: 3,466
Established: July 4, 1976

"No bread, no soldier! No bread, no soldier!" The chant of desperation grew louder and louder among the poorly fed, thinly clothed, desperately cold men huddled around campfires at Valley Forge, Pennsylvania, in January 1778. In time, Valley Forge became a symbol of endurance, of American resolve to be free from Britain and her monarchy; indeed, these were the times that tried men's souls. The 11,000 men of this ragtag Continental Army had not been paid in months. The Continental Congress, which functioned as the new nation's government through most of the American Revolution, had no money, and thus was simply unable to supply the men with food and clothing. In these dire conditions, disease spread rapidly, claiming as many as 2,500 lives that grim and gray winter. General George Washington wondered, "What is to become of this army?" His worry was real, for without the army, there was no independence movement. Yet what was forged here just 18 miles outside of Philadelphia was, as one soldier wrote, "a band of brothers." They were a "family," as Washington described them, which had encountered unspeakable hardship, endured, and prevailed. On June 19, 1778, six months after its arrival, the army marched away from Valley Forge in pursuit of the British who were moving toward New York. Although the Revolution did not come to an end for an-

other five years, the Continental Army that emerged from Valley Forge was strengthened and invigorated, and its prospects seemed considerably brighter. As one European officer who served with Washington wrote, "It is incredible that soldiers composed of men of every age, even children of fifteen, of whites and blacks, almost naked, unpaid, and rather poorly fed, can march so well and withstand fire so steadfastly."

In the late nineteenth century, the narrative of Valley Forge inspired private citizens to begin the effort to preserve the site of General Washington's soldiers' camp as a memorial. Formal recognition for the troops who wintered at Valley Forge came when the Pennsylvania legislature designated the area as a state park in 1893. Later, the 3,466-acre Valley Forge National Historical Park was designated, fittingly on July 4, 1976. Today, the mission of the National Park Service at Valley Forge is to preserve, protect, and maintain the natural and cultural resources that are associated with and commemorate the encampment of the Continental Army in 1777–1778 and to educate the American people about one of the most defining events in the nation's history. A $2-per-adult entrance fee is charged to enter Washington's headquarters from April 1 to November 30; all other park facilities at Valley Forge are available at no charge.

The park's visitor center is open year-round from 9 A.M. until 5 P.M. and features the museum exhibit "A Glimpse into Time" and the film *Valley Forge: A Winter Encampment*. Park rangers present some of their special topic programs at the Dewees' House and offer guided walking tours of the historical park. Visitors can also tour the Muhlenberg

General George Washington and a committee of Congress at Valley Forge, the winter of 1777–1778. *(National Archives)*

Brigade, open all year from 10 A.M. until 4 P.M., to learn more about the life of a soldier, as well as General Varnum's Quarters, where special programs indicate how the encampment affected civilians who lived at Valley Forge. Perhaps the highlight of the park is General Washington's headquarters, the nerve center of the encampment. Eighteen miles of trail, including 6 miles of paved multipurpose trail, wind through the park, in addition to a 10-mile, self-guided automobile tour. Cassette tapes of the tour are for sale and a free map of the tour route is available in the visitor center.

There are no lodging or camping facilities in the historical park, but all traveler services are available in Exton, King of Prussia, Philadelphia, and Reading. Food and supplies can be obtained in the park at the Kennedy-

Supplee Mansion and the snack bar at Washington Memorial Chapel.

For more information, write Valley Forge National Historical Park, P.O. Box 953, Valley Forge, PA 19482-0953, or telephone (610) 783-1077. The park's Web site is www.nps.gov/vafo.

FURTHER READING
Bodle, Wayne K. *The Valley Forge Winter: Civilians and Soldiers in War.* University Park: Pennsylvania State University Press, 2002.

Treese, Lorett. *Valley Forge: Making and Remaking a National Symbol.* University Park: Pennsylvania State University Press, 1995.

VANDERBILT MANSION NATIONAL HISTORIC SITE
Location: Hyde Park, New York
Acreage: 212
Established: December 18, 1940

In their size, scale, and substance, the ornate and sumptuous mansions of late-nineteenth-century America mimicked or exceeded the elegant chateaus and manors of Europe's wealthiest lineages. These were the splendid and luxurious homes of nouveau riche Americans who had made their fortunes in industry. And the so-called "country home" of Frederick W. Vanderbilt is a magnificent example of these great estates, where the well to do explored the outer limits of ostentation. The Vanderbilts were part of an elite cadre of captains of industry, called "Robber Barons" by their foes, who reaped fantastic wealth from the booming railroad industry of the late nineteenth century. Their gregarious and opulent lifestyle embodied what many historians have labeled the Gilded Age in American history.

Much of the family's fortune was amassed by Cornelius "Commodore" Vanderbilt, who began in the steamboat ferry business before graduating to railroads during the Civil War. By the time he died in 1877, Cornelius was the richest man in America. The bulk of his fortune was transferred to his eldest son, William Henry, who outlived his father by only eight years, but still died with his father's title of richest man in America. The mantle of money then passed largely to his son, Frederick William, who bought this Hyde Park property in 1895, described by the *New York Times* as "the finest place on the Hudson between New York and Albany."

Set aside in December 1940, the 212-acre Vanderbilt Mansion National Historic Site preserves the largely unchanged palatial estate of Frederick W. Vanderbilt as a fine example of the residential architecture of the

The Vanderbilt Mansion is perhaps the best example of the estates constructed by wealthy nineteenth-century industrialists. The 54-room mansion has breathtaking views of the Hudson River and the distant Catskill Mountains. *(National Park Service)*

elite in nineteenth-century America. The park's visitor center, located in the historic pavilion on the grounds, is open year-round from 9 A.M. until 5 P.M., and it features numerous museum exhibits related to the Vanderbilts' lifestyle and the management of the Hyde Park estate. Park rangers give talks on the Vanderbilts and their contemporaries, industrial expansion, turn-of-the-century technology, and landscape architecture. A forty-five-minute guided tour of the lavishly furnished home, including the first and second floors and a portion of basement, is also offered, and the fee is $8 per person.

There are no food, lodging, or camping facilities at the historic site, but all traveler services are available in the Hyde Park area.

For more information, write Vanderbilt Mansion National Historic Site, 4097 Albany Post Road, Hyde Park, NY 12538, or telephone (845) 229-9115. The park's Web site is www.nps.gov/vama.

FURTHER READING

Auchincloss, Louis. *The Vanderbilt Era: Profiles of a Gilded Age.* New York: Collier Books, 1990.

Gordon, John Steele. *The Scarlet Woman of Wall Street: Jay Gould, Jim Fisk, Cornelius Vanderbilt, the Erie Railway Wars, and the Birth of Wall Street.* New York: Weidenfeld and Nicolson, 1988.

Vanderbilt, Cornelius. *The Living Past of America: Pictorial Treasury of Our Historic Houses and Villages That Have Been Preserved and Restored.* New York: Crown, 1955.

VICKSBURG NATIONAL MILITARY PARK

Location: Vicksburg, Mississippi
Acreage: 1,795
Established: February 21, 1899

In the Civil War's western theater, the land that lay between the Appalachian Mountains and the Mississippi River, the Union's primary objective was the capture and control of the mighty Mississippi. The river was equally important to the Confederacy, which had established a fortress at Vicksburg, Mississippi, known as the "Gibraltar of the Confederacy," to assure that the Mississippi remained in Southern hands.

President Abraham Lincoln explained his concerns to both civil and military leaders, saying, "See what a lot of land these fellows hold, of which Vicksburg is the key! The war can never be brought to a close until that key is in our pocket. . . . We can take all the northern ports of the Confederacy, and they can defy us from Vicksburg."

The man who brought that "key" to Lincoln was Union General Ulysses S. Grant. Realizing that a direct attack was folly, Grant encircled Vicksburg in the spring and then settled in for a siege, hoping to starve out the bastion's inhabitants and defenders. "The fall of Vicksburg," Grant wrote to Lincoln, "and the capture of most of the garrison can only be a question of time." In the long run, the answer to the "question of time" was forty-seven grueling days, from May 23 to July 4, 1863. On Independence Day, the Confederate flag over Vicksburg was replaced by the Stars and Stripes. Lincoln celebrated the victory by proclaiming that "the Father of Waters again goes unvexed to the sea." When combined with the July 3 Union victory at Gettysburg, Pennsylvania, in the eastern theater, Vicksburg became an important turning point in the war.

Congress established Vicksburg National Military Park to preserve the site of this important and decisive battle and to pay tribute to the soldiers and civilians who endured the national rending known as the American Civil War. Today, the 1,795-acre battlefield includes 1,325 historic monuments and markers, 20 miles of reconstructed trenches and earthworks, a 16-mile tour road, antebellum home, 144 emplaced cannon, the restored

Entrance to the National Military Cemetery in Vicksburg, Mississippi. *(Library of Congress)*

Union gunboat, the USS *Cairo*, and the Vicksburg National Cemetery, with more than 17,000 interments, the largest number of Civil War soldiers of any national cemetery in the United States. Entrance fees are $2 per person or $4 per vehicle and are valid for seven days; a $10 annual pass is also available. The park's visitor center is open daily from 8 A.M. until 5 P.M., and it features exhibits such as Confederate Lines, Hospital Room, Union Officers Tent, Civilian Meals during the siege, Cave Life, Military Artifacts, and seasonal exhibits. Park rangers offer interpretive talks, guided battlefield tours, and living-history demonstrations. The USS *Cairo* Mu-

seum is open year-round from 8:30 A.M. until 5 P.M. (an hour later during daylight savings) and contains exhibits on Civil War river-class boats, the ironclad gunboat USS *Cairo*, and Civil War–period naval artifacts recovered from the Union vessel, as well as sailors' personal possessions, cookware, and weaponry. A six-minute video explains how the *Cairo* was sunk by a Confederate underwater mine, how it was located, and actions taken during its salvage efforts. Also included in the park are the riverfront batteries at Navy Circle, South Fort, and Louisiana Circle, and the last remaining section of Grant's Canal, where Union forces attempted to bypass Vicksburg by digging a channel through Desoto Point. Facilities include a historic state highway marker, bronze tablet, and wayside exhibits on Williams Canal, Grant's Canal, and Black Troops at Milliken's Bend. A 16-mile tour road parallels Union and Confederate siege lines, with three interconnecting roadways, 15 tour stops, wayside markers, and exhibits. Short spur trails lead to points of interest, and hikers can enjoy the primitive 12-mile Scout Compass Trail and 7- and 14-mile trails that follow the park tour road.

There are no food, lodging, or camping facilities at the park, but all traveler services are available in the Vicksburg area.

For more information, write Vicksburg National Military Park, 3201 Clay Street, Vicksburg, MS 39183, or telephone (601) 636-0583. The park's Web site is www.nps.gov/vick.

FURTHER READING
Foote, Shelby. *The Beleaguered City: The Vicksburg Campaign, December 1862–July 1863*. New York: Modern Library, 1995.
Fullenkamp, Leonard, Stephen Bowman, and Jay Luvaas, eds. *Guide to the Vicksburg Campaign.* Lawrence: University Press of Kansas, 1998.
Hoehling, A.A. *Vicksburg: 47 Days of Siege*. Mechanicsburg, PA: Stackpole Books, 1996.
Martin, David G. *The Vicksburg Campaign: April 1862–July 1863*. Conshohocken, PA: Combined Books, 1994.

VIRGIN ISLANDS NATIONAL PARK

Location: St. John, Virgin Islands
Acreage: 14,689
Established: August 2, 1956

Looking more like an idyllic movie set than a traditional national park, Virgin Islands National Park nevertheless protects the stunning and fragile coral reef gardens and marine and terrestrial life on and around St. John Island—one of nearly 100 islands that form the Virgin Islands archipelago in the Caribbean. White

sand beaches and gently swaying coconut palms give way to tropical forests, topping out at 1,277 feet above sea level at the summit of Bordeaux Mountain, and a lush second-growth forest cloaks the mountain slopes with wild mammee, banyan, mahogany, kapok, teyer palm, wild frangipani, bay rum, and soursop, while red, white, and black mangroves fringe most of the salt ponds. More than 100 species of birds inhabit this unique environment, including royal and sooty terns, mangrove cuckoos, gray kingbirds, white-crowned pigeons, and green-throated carib and Antillean crested hummingbirds.

In addition to protecting this fragile, tropical ecosystem, the park also preserves the rich cultural heritage of the island, which includes the histories of Native Americans, African slaves, and European colonizers. In prehistoric times, the islands were inhabited by Arawak Indians. The arrival of whites devastated most native Caribbean tribes, and successive waves of European colonization began in the seventeenth century. In 1718, the Danes established the first permanent settlement on St. John, and within a decade, the entrepreneurial colonists had imported African slaves and begun to establish sugar plantations. A slave revolt in 1733 marked the beginning of the end of the plantation era, and in 1848, the Danes abolished slavery, ushering in a fallow, century-long period known as the "subsistence era." In 1917, the United States recognized the strategic significance of the Virgin Islands during World War I and purchased St. John, St. Croix, St. Thomas, and approximately fifty smaller islands for $25 million.

Authorized in August 1956, the 14,689-acre Virgin Islands National Park protects approximately three-fifths of St. John Island and nearly all of Hassel Island in Charlotte Amalie harbor on St. Thomas. The park's visitor

Virgin Islands National Park is renowned throughout the world for its beauty—protected bays teeming with coral reef life, white sandy beaches, coconut palms, and tropical forests that provide a habitat for more than 800 species of plants—and visitors also can explore historic ruins. *(National Park Service)*

contact station is open year-round from 8 A.M. until 4:30 P.M. and has maps, brochures, and the latest activity schedule for the park, as well as a small bookstore with a broad selection of materials on the natural and cultural history of the area. The Trunk Bay Kiosk is open year-round and staffed by Friends of the Virgin Islands National Park volunteers. Information is also posted on bulletin boards located throughout the park.

Admission to the park is free, although a same-day use fee is collected at Annaberg and Trunk Bay ($4 per person; a $10 individual or $15 family annual pass is also available). Established in 1718, Annaberg Sugar Mill is one of St. John's best-preserved examples of the island's cultural past during the colonial and postemancipation era. Self-guided and ranger-guided tours take visitors through the sugar factory ruins. Trunk Bay is one of the Caribbean's most photographed beaches, and it features an underwater self-guided snorkeling trail. Lifeguards are on duty daily. Facilities at Trunk Bay include showers, a snack bar, a water-sports shop that rents snorkeling equipment and beach chairs, and a small gift shop. While Annaberg and Trunk Bay are the most frequently visited park sites, the park also boasts diverse beaches, coral reefs, historic ruins, and hiking trails. Visitors enjoy a variety of activities on the land and in the water, including swimming, snorkeling, scuba diving, sailing, kayaking, windsurfing, camping, hiking, and bird-watching. The Cinnamon Bay Watersports Shop rents snorkeling equipment, sea kayaks, sailboards, and small sailboats, and provides lessons. Visitors can also charter a day-sail or boat-snorkeling tour through private operators in Cruz Bay and Coral Bay.

All traveler services are available on St. Thomas. Within the park, the Cinnamon Bay Campground is the only permitted camping; backcountry and beach camping are prohibited. Accommodations at the campground include bare sites, sites prepared with tent-covered platforms, and cottages; cottages and prepared sites are equipped with cooking supplies and linens. A camp store sells food, beverages, and other supplies, and a campground restaurant serves breakfast, lunch, and dinner.

For more information, write Virgin Islands National Park, P.O. Box 710, St. John, VI 00831, or telephone (340) 776-6201. The park's Web site is www.nps.gov/viis.

FURTHER READING
Dookhan, Isaac. *History of the Virgin Islands.* Kingston, Jamaica: Canoe, 1994.
Hall, Neville A.T. *Slave Society in the Danish West Indies: St. Thomas, St. John, and St. Croix.* Baltimore, MD: Johns Hopkins University Press, 1992.
Olwig, Karen Fog. *Cultural Adaptation and Resistance on St. John: Three Centuries of Afro-Caribbean Life.* Gainesville: University of Florida Press, 1985.
Wilson, Samuel M., ed. *The Indigenous People of the Caribbean.* Gainesville: University Press of Florida, 1997.

VOYAGEURS NATIONAL PARK
Location: International Falls, Minnesota
Acreage: 218,200
Established: April 8, 1975

The establishment of Voyageurs National Park on April 8, 1975, completed a near-century-long process. Since 1891, advocates of the preservation of northeastern Minnesota had worked to protect the region in a national park area. That year, the Minnesota state legislature petitioned the U.S. Congress for a national park in the state. At this time, the birth of the conservation movement, along with rapacious cutting of forests such as those in northeastern Minnesota, stirred influential people to seek protection for trees and water. In California and elsewhere, the process often happened quickly; at Voyageurs, creation of a national park took more than eighty years.

Proposals to establish a national park began in 1891 and followed at consistent intervals. In 1899, the Minnesota Federation of Women's Clubs, the state arm of an actively conservationist national organization, offered a new proposal. Although these were stymied, they paved the way for federal protection with the creation of the Superior National Forest in 1909. With the passage of much of the region to the Forest Service, the opportunities for a national park were muted. The timber industry worked closely with the U.S. Forest Service to develop timber resources, and despite the creation of what the Forest Service called "primitive areas"—protowilderness—conventional economic development dominated the first three decades of the twentieth century.

The idea of a national park again took shape as the result of changing economic conditions. The Depression hurt the timber industry, and the National Park Service worked closely with state park agencies throughout the 1920s. With the many New Deal programs that supported park programs, the Park Service had much to offer during times of weak economic conditions.

Among the Park Service people involved in the state parks program was Conrad L. Wirth, a native of the state who was the son of the famous Minnesota park planner Theodore Wirth. Wirth rose to become director of the Park Service in 1952, adding momentum to the fight for a national park. By the early 1960s, plans for park development were under way. Reluctant state officials slowed the

Canoeing in one of the many lakes preserved by Voyageurs National Park. *(National Park Service)*

way, but in 1967, Minnesota officials stepped forward and the process gained momentum. With the support of Governor Harold Levander and U.S. Senator Walter Mondale, the battle for Voyageurs moved toward a final stage. In 1968 and 1969, bills for the new national park came before Congress; only in 1971 did authorization occur. Four years later, in 1975, the park came into existence after the federal government acquired enough land to meet the obligations of the statute.

Established in April 1975, the 218,200-acre Voyageurs National Park preserves the interconnected system of lakes and islands used by early French-Canadian fur-traders—the *voyageurs*. Admission is free. Voyageurs includes more than 30 lakes that comprise more than one-third of the park, and wildlife of all kinds is abundant. The park's surface has been scraped and shaped by glaciers, which

set the stage for the later growth of its magnificent boreal forests. Once heavily logged, the park has grown back and even former logging roads have been overtaken by dense vegetation. The park maintains 3 visitor centers. The Ash River Visitor Center, in the historic Meadwood Lodge, is open from mid-May through September from 9 A.M. until 5 P.M., and it has exhibits on the construction of this interesting log building. Several short trails leave from Ash River, including the Forest Overlook quarter-mile loop trail and the Beaver Pond Overlook—a short trail to a wildlife viewing area. The Kabetogama Overlook has an eighth-mile, fully accessible trail to a panoramic view of Kabetogama Narrows. The Kabetogama Lake Visitor Center is also open from mid-May through September from 9 A.M. until 5 P.M., and it features a bald eagle exhibit, wildlife viewing exhibit, and freshwater aquarium. Special programs include a Birds B4 Breakfast Hike, Morning Canoe Trip, Kids Explore Voyageurs, and evening campfire programs, as well as the Stargazer Cruise, Kettle Falls Cruise, Back Bays Wildlife Adventure, Sunset Wildlife Cruise, Kids' Safari Cruise, and Walleye Shorelunch Cruise. The Rainy Lake Visitor Center is open year-round from 9 A.M. until 4:30 P.M. (until 5 P.M. during the summer) and features an orientation film, a film on the fur trade, an exhibit called "River of Lakes, Roads of Ice" that explores the natural and cultural history of the park, fur trade exhibits, and a Phrenology/Touch Table exhibit. Park rangers also offer special programs including a North Canoe Voyage, Morning Canoe Adventure, Evening Canoe Adventure, Patio Talks, Wildlife Walks, and various winter programs

The historic Kettle Falls Hotel (888-534-6835), open from May through September, offers lodging within the park. Often called the "Jewel in the Wilderness," Kettle Falls is accessible by boat, floatplane, ski plane, and snowmobile. It is a concession-operated complex that includes a dining room, bar, rooms in the historic 1912 hotel, and modern housekeeping villas. Kettle Falls also offers a mechanical portage between Rainy Lake and Namakan Lake and trading post. On the four large lakes, the park has 214 individual tent-camping, houseboat, or day-use sites. Each site has been developed for a single party, with tent pads, fire ring, picnic table, privy, and bear locker. All are water-access only. The gateway communities of Ash River,

Crane Lake, Rainy Lake, and Kabetogama Lake offer a range of traveler facilities including motels, cabins, bed-and-breakfast inns, and campgrounds, and the Minnesota Department of Natural Resources operates the Woodenfrog State Forest Campground on Lake Kabetogama and the Ash River Campground on Ash River.

Voyageurs National Park is a water-based park, and access to the Kabetogama peninsula, the islands, and nearly all of the park's shoreline is by watercraft. Free public boat ramps and parking are available at the park's visitor centers and at the Kabetogama State Forest Campgrounds. Watercraft rental and water taxi service are available from private outfitters and resorts at each of the park's 4 gateway communities—Ash River, Crane Lake, International Falls, and Lake Kabetogama.

For more information, write Voyageurs National Park, 3131 Highway 53 South, International Falls, MN 56649-8904, or telephone (218) 286-5258. The park's Web site is www.nps.gov/voya.

FURTHER READING

Hafen, LeRoy R., ed. *French Fur Traders and Voyageurs in the American West.* Lincoln: University of Nebraska Press, 1997.

Nute, Grace Lee. *The Voyageur's Highway, Minnesota's Border Lake Land.* St. Paul: Minnesota Historical Society, 1965

——.*The Voyageur.* St. Paul: Minnesota Historical Society Press, 1987.

Tueuer, Robert. *Voyageur Country: A Park in the Wilderness.* Minneapolis: University of Minnesota Press, 1979.

Witzig, Fred T. *Eighty Years in the Making: A Legislative History of Voyageurs National Park.* Omaha, NE: National Park Service, 2000.

W

WALNUT CANYON NATIONAL MONUMENT

Location: Flagstaff, Arizona
Acreage: 3,579
Established: November 30, 1915

According to archeologists, the Sinagua Indians (a Spanish word meaning "without water") inhabited the high plateaus of north-central Arizona, living in pit houses and farming the open meadows, until the eruption of Sunset Crater Volcano in 1064–1065. The blast blanketed the surrounding countryside with a moisture-retaining layer of cinder and ash that attracted other agricultural peoples to the region. Feeling the pressure of rising populations, the Sinagua relocated to Walnut Canyon, just 10 miles to the south, where stream flows provided them a permanent water supply. They also took advantage of ledges in the canyon that formed natural shelters to build cliff dwellings, with three walls of Kaibab limestone masonry completing a room. A natural fortress, most cliff dwellings were built facing south and east for solar heating. The Sinagua grew squash, beans, and maize on the canyon rims and supplemented their diet with hunting and gathering. For reasons unknown, after nearly two centuries of continuous habitation, the Native Americans of Walnut Canyon abandoned their cliff dwellings toward the end of the thirteenth century. The site was subsequently looted and vandalized by pothunters and curious visitors, and many of the Sinaguan artifacts were lost. In addition to preserving these prehistoric ruins, the national monument also shelters a diversity of plant and animal species, including cacti, wild geranium, globe mallow, cliff rose, Arizona walnut trees, and mule deer, coyotes, bobcats, porcupines, foxes, cottontails, and Abert squirrels.

Proclaimed in November 1915, the 3,579-acre Walnut Canyon National Monument protects the remnant cliff dwellings of ancient Pueblo Indians in the region. A seven-day entrance pass is $3 per person. The Walnut Canyon Visitor Center is open year-round from 9 A.M. until 5 P.M., and it has numerous exhibits on the natural and cultural history of

Hiking in Walnut Canyon National Monument.
(National Park Service)

the area. Park rangers offer guided walks during June, July, and August. The Island Trail, a strenuous nine-tenths-mile round-trip, descends 85 feet into the canyon, providing access to 25 cliff-dwelling rooms; it is one of the best ways to experience the park. Backcountry hiking is not allowed in the park in order to protect fragile archeological sites.

There are no food, lodging, or camping facilities at the monument, but all traveler services are available in Flagstaff.

For more information, write Walnut Canyon National Monument, Walnut Canyon Road #3, Flagstaff, AZ 86004, or telephone (520) 526-3367. The park's Web site is www.nps.gov/waca.

FURTHER READING

Bremer, J. Michael. *Walnut Canyon Settlement and Land Use.* Phoenix: Arizona Archaeological Society, 1989.

Noble, David Grant, ed. *Wupatki and Walnut Canyon: New Perspectives on History, Prehistory, and Rock Art.* Santa Fe, NM: School of American Research, 1987.

Schroeder, Albert H. *Of Men and Volcanoes: The Sinagua of Northern Arizona.* Globe, AZ: Southwest Parks and Monuments Association, 1977.

Thybony, Scott. *Walnut Canyon.* Tucson, AZ: Southwest Parks and Monuments Association, 1996.

WAR IN THE PACIFIC NATIONAL HISTORICAL PARK

Location: Asan, Guam
Acreage: 2,037
Established: August 18, 1978

War in the Pacific National Historical Park commemorates the recapture of Guam by American forces during World War II (1941–1945). This unique national park is the only site in the system that honors those who participated in the war's Pacific Theater, regardless of their nationality or allegiance. The 7-unit park details the bloody history of the summer of 1944, when American and Japanese forces clashed on this western Pacific island in the twenty-one-day Battle of Guam, as well as the role the Mariana Islands played in helping to end the war. In addition to memorials dedicated to the Chamorro people and members of the U.S. Armed Forces, the park protects the battlefields, trenches, gun emplacements, and historic structures integral to the defense and preservation of Guam.

Authorized in August 1978, the 2,037-acre War in the Pacific National Historical Park was set aside "to commemorate the bravery and sacrifice of those participating in the campaigns of the Pacific Theater of World War II and to conserve and interpret outstanding natural, scenic, and historic values and objects on the island of Guam."

In December 2002, the park was severely damaged by a super typhoon. At press time, there was no visitor contact facility or visitor center within the park. Parts of this national historic site, however, continue to be open to visitors. There is no admission charge.

Guam also has a fringing coral reef that surrounds the island and offers excellent opportunities for snorkeling, swimming, and kayaking. The average water temperature is 78 degrees, and visibility underwater is very good. A wide variety of plants, coral, and marine life can be seen while swimming and snorkeling. Hiking is also a recommended activity, and gun emplacements, pillboxes, and military relics are easily accessible.

There are no food, lodging, or camping facilities in the park, but all traveler services are available on the island.

For more information, write War in the Pacific National Historical Park, 115 Haloda Building, Marine Drive, Asan, GU 96922, or telephone (671) 472-7240. The park's Web site is www.nps.gov/wapa.

FURTHER READING

Gailey, Harry A. *The Liberation of Guam: 21 July–10 August 1944.* Novato, CA: Presidio, 1988.

Rogers, Robert F. *Destiny's Landfall: A History of Guam.* Honolulu: University of Hawaii Press, 1995.

WASHITA BATTLEFIELD NATIONAL HISTORIC SITE

Location: Cheyenne, Oklahoma
Acreage: 315
Established: November 12, 1996

Washita Battlefield National Historic Site is a recent addition to the national park system, a part of filling out the story of the American past by including even its most reprehensible moments. Located a few miles from Cheyenne, in western Oklahoma's Roger Mills County, Washita Battlefield National Historic Site is the location of Lieutenant Colonel George Armstrong Custer's attack on Black Kettle's village early on November 27, 1868. According to army reports, as many as 100 Cheyenne men, women, and children were killed during the attack. The military lost a total of 21 men. The incident inspires great passion, and even today, more than one hundred and thirty years later, it is a source of controversy about the nature, motives, and character of westward expansion.

The Civil War framed the most important conflicts between the American nation and the tribes of the Great Plains. While the war initially took manpower away from the goals of Manifest Destiny, it trained and hardened a generation of American soldiers. With the war's end, they came west to finish the job of continental conquest that had begun earlier. The nomadic tribes of the Great Plains, made wealthy by trade, had accumulated large herds of horses, which had begun to compete with the bison on which Native Americans depended. When railroads traversed the area, the native people were threatened, and many resisted the encroachment of settlers.

The U.S. government had long sought to separate tribes and settlers from each other by establishing an Indian Territory in present-day Oklahoma. While some Plains tribes accepted life on reservations, others, including the Cheyennes, Kiowas, and Comanches, did not. They continued to hunt and live on traditional lands outside the Indian Territory, returning when compelled by soldiers or when winter drove them to the reservation commissary for supplies. At first, little conflict resulted, for there was plenty of land and few settlers. After the Civil War, however, land-hungry settlers came in droves, took over tribal hunting grounds, and made nomadic life impossible. When Plains people faced a loss of livelihood and the end of the freedom to move about, many fought rather than submit to the drudgery and degradation of reservation life.

The massacre on the Washita River was part of an era of savagery that started with the Sand Creek Massacre of 1864. On November 29, troops under the command of Colonel J.M. Chivington attacked and destroyed the Cheyenne camp of Chief Black Kettle and Chief White Antelope on Sand Creek, 40 miles from Fort Lyon, Colorado Territory. Black Kettle's people flew an American flag and a white flag, and they considered themselves at peace and under military protection. The terrible slaughter caused a massive public outcry. In response, a federal Peace Commission was created to convert Plains Indians from their nomadic way of life and settle them on reservations.

On the southern plains, the work of the commission culminated in the Medicine Lodge Treaty of October 1867. Under treaty terms, the Arapahos, Cheyennes, Comanches, Kiowas, and Plains Apaches were assigned to reservations in the Indian Territory. There they were supposed to receive perma-

Battle of Washita in the Indian Territory, an engagement between the Plains tribes and General George A. Custer's troops of the 7th U.S. Cavalry, November 27, 1868. *(Library of Congress)*

nent homes, farms, and agricultural implements, as well as annuities of food, blankets, and clothing. The treaty was doomed to failure. Many tribal officials refused to sign, and some who did sign had no real authority to compel their people to comply with such an agreement. War parties, mostly made up of young men who were violently opposed to reservation life, continued to raid white settlements in Kansas.

Major General Philip H. Sheridan, in command of the Department of the Missouri, adopted a policy that "punishment must follow crime." In retaliation for the Kansas raids,

he planned to mount a winter campaign when the Native Americans' ponies would be weak and unfit for all but limited service and their only protection was the isolation afforded by brutal weather.

In November 1868, Black Kettle and Arapaho Chief Big Mouth went to Fort Cobb to petition General William B. Hazen for peace and protection. A respected leader of the Southern Cheyenne, Black Kettle had signed the Little Arkansas Treaty in 1865 and the Medicine Lodge Treaty in 1867. Hazen told them that he could not allow them to bring their people to Fort Cobb for protection because only General Sheridan, his field commander, or Lieutenant Colonel George Custer, had that authority. Disappointed, the chiefs headed back to their people at the winter encampments on the Washita River.

Even as Black Kettle and Big Mouth parlayed with General Hazen, Custer's 7th Cavalry established a forward base of operations at Camp Supply, Indian Territory, as part of Sheridan's winter campaign strategy. Under orders from Sheridan, Custer marched south on November 23 with about 800 troopers, traveling through a foot of new snow.

After four days travel, Custer's command reached the Washita valley shortly after midnight on November 27, and silently took up a position near a native encampment their scouts had discovered at a bend in the river. Black Kettle, who had just returned from Fort Cobb a few days before, had resisted the entreaties of some of his people, including his wife, to move their camp downriver closer to the larger encampments of Cheyennes, Kiowas, and Apaches wintering there. He refused to believe that Sheridan would order an attack without first offering the Native Americans an opportunity to make peace.

Before dawn, the troopers attacked the fifty-one lodges, killing a number of men, women, and children. Custer reported about 100 killed, though Native American accounts claimed 11 warriors plus 19 women and children lost their lives. More than 50 Cheyennes were captured, mainly women and children. Custer's losses were light: 2 officers and 19 enlisted men killed. Thirteen of the military's casualties belonged to Major Joel Elliott's detachment, whose eastward foray was overrun by Cheyenne, Arapaho, and Kiowa warriors coming to Black Kettle's aid. Chief Black Kettle and his wife were killed in the attack. Following Sheridan's plan to cripple resistance, Custer ordered the slaughter of the Native

American pony and mule herd, estimated at more than 800 animals. The lodges of Black Kettle's people, with all their winter supply of food and clothing, were torched.

Realizing now that many more natives were threatening from the east, Custer feigned an attack toward their downriver camps and quickly retreated to Camp Supply with his hostages. The engagement at the Washita might have ended very differently if the larger encampments to the east had been closer to Black Kettle's camp. As it happened, the impact of losing winter supplies, plus the knowledge that cold weather no longer provided protection from attack, convinced many bands to accept reservation life.

Originally set aside in 1996 as a national historic landmark, the 315-acre Washita Battlefield National Historic Site today protects and interprets the site of one of the largest and most one-sided engagements between Plains tribes and the U.S. Army on the southern Great Plains: the Southern Cheyenne village of Chief Black Kettle, which was attacked by the 7th U.S. Cavalry under Lieutenant Colonel George A. Custer on November 27, 1868. The controversial strike was hailed at the time by the military and many civilians as a significant victory aimed at reducing raids on frontier settlements. Washita remains controversial because many Native Americans and whites labeled Custer's attack a massacre. Black Kettle is still honored as a prominent leader who never ceased striving for peace even though it cost him his life.

Admission to the site is free. The park's visitor center is housed in the Black Kettle Museum, which is open year-round from 8 A.M. until 5 P.M. Monday through Friday, 9 A.M. until 5 P.M. on Saturday, and 1 P.M. until 5 P.M. on Sunday. The center has numerous exhibits on the Cheyenne and the attack, which provide a good background on the events leading up to and surrounding Washita. A trail guide is available at the museum for the site's eight-tenths-mile trail, or visitors can go to the site overlook/trailhead and learn about what happened. The Washita Battlefield Overlook consists of a historical plaque, a monument commemorating the site, and a panel indicating the approximate route, approach, and attack of Custer, and the approximate location of the Native American village.

During the summer months (late May to mid-August), ranger-led programs are available five times a day. Afterward, visitors can also tour the Black Kettle National Grasslands, which offers hunting, boating, camping, hiking, fishing, and wildlife-watching opportunities on more than 30,000 acres of public land.

There are no food, lodging, or camping facilities at the historic site, but all traveler services are available in Cheyenne and Elk City.

For more information, write Washita Battlefield National Historic Site, P.O. Box 890, Cheyenne, OK 73628, or telephone (580) 497-2742. The park's Web site is www.nps.gov/waba.

FURTHER READING

Brill, Charles J., and Mark L Gardner. *Custer, Black Kettle, and the Fight on the Washita.* Norman: University of Oklahoma Press, 2002.

Carroll, John M., ed. *General Custer and the Battle of the Washita: The Federal View.* Norman: University of Oklahoma Press, 1978.

Hoig, Stan. *The Battle of the Washita: The Sheridan-Custer Indian Campaign of 1867–69.* Lincoln: University of Nebraska Press, 1979.

WEIR FARM NATIONAL HISTORIC SITE

Location: Ridgefield and Wilton, Connecticut
Acreage: 74
Established: August 31, 1990

Weir Farm National Historic Site was the summer home and studio of American Impressionist painter Julian Alden Weir (1852–1919). It is also the only national park area in Connecticut and the only national park dedicated to an American painter. Weir began his career in New York as an art instructor and painter of portraits and still lifes. In 1877, he had returned to the United States after studying for five years at the École des Beaux-Arts in Paris. While in Paris, Weir had visited an exhibit of the French Impressionists but found the style too unfocused and vague, although their influence on his work later became manifest. In 1882, after nearly a decade of international travel and study, he acquired the 153-acre Branchville farm in Ridgefield, Connecticut, and began to paint in earnest. The artist continued to maintain an apartment and studio in New York City, but Weir farm provided an important respite from the hectic pace of urban life.

Although the influence of the Impressionists is evident in his work, Weir's art more accurately follows the techniques of Whistler and Japanese decorative methods—an overall tone of restraint in a subdued palate. By 1890, Weir had begun to embrace plein air painting, and the farm provided inspiring subject matter for him and many of his famous artist friends, including Childe Hassam, John Twachtman, Emil Carlsen, and Albert Pinkham Ryder.

Weir twice enlarged the main farmhouse, and in 1907 acquired more land, bringing the total to 238 acres. When Weir died in 1919, his second daughter, Dorothy, an artist in her own right, inherited the Branchville farm and studio. In 1931, she married renowned sculptor Mahonri Young, grandson of Brigham Young, who was famous for his small bronzes of athletes and laborers. Young also built a studio on the site, where he completed a commissioned piece for Utah's "This Is the Place" monument, unveiled in 1947 at the mouth of Emigration Canyon, just outside of Salt Lake City, Utah.

Authorized in 1990, the 74-acre Weir Farm National Historic Site preserves the painter's home and studio as well as the landscape that inspired his work, and includes barns and outbuildings and the studio built by sculptor Mahonri Young. The park's grounds are open to the public daily from dawn until dusk, and the visitor center is open Wednesday through Sunday from 8:30 A.M. until 5 P.M. Admission is free.

The center features rotating art and history exhibitions, and park rangers offer hour-long guided studio tours. The Historic Painting Sites Trail allows visitors to actually stand where the artists did and compare paintings with the scene that inspired them; a Painting Sites Trail Guide is available for $2. During the summer, the park hosts a Visiting Artists Program and offers children's art classes, and in early September, the farm celebrates "Jazz in the Garden."

There are no food, lodging, or camping facilities at the historic site, but all traveler services are available in Ridgefield and Wilton.

For more information, write Weir Farm National Historic Site, 735 Nod Hill Road, Wilton, CT 06897, or telephone (203) 834-1896. The park's Web site is www. nps.gov/wefa.

FURTHER READING

Bolger, Doreen. *J. Alden Weir: An American Impressionist.* Newark: University of Delaware Press, 1983.

Cikovsky, Nicolai, Jr. *A Connecticut Place: Weir Farm, an American Painter's Rural Retreat.* Wilton, CT: Weir Farm Trust, 2000.

Cummings, Hildegard, Helen K. Fusscas, and Susan G. Larkin. *J. Alden Weir: A Place of His Own.* Storrs: William Benton Museum of Art, University of Connecticut, 1991.

WESTERN ARCTIC NATIONAL PARKLANDS

Created as part of the Alaska National Interest Conservation Lands Act settlement in 1978, these parks in the western Arctic were originally established by President Jimmy Carter's bold use of the Antiquities Act of 1906. As the time allotted for settlement of Alaskan native claims wound down, the federal government was faced with the difficult task of designating lands for a variety of purposes. Afraid of losing the opportunity for an enormous conservation achievement, Carter dusted off the seldom-used Antiquities Act to create an Alaskan national park system for the future of the nation. His decision was as timely as it was bold, for Carter's action more than doubled the size of the park system and guaranteed a future for countless species.

To facilitate the management of these 4 remote, lightly visited, and enormous parks, the National Park Service created a management unit called the Western Arctic National Parklands. With only one superintendent, the parks enjoy integrated preservation, wildlife management, subsistence hunting, archeological and anthropological, budgetary, and maintenance objectives and can offer coordinated ranger talks and programs.

Bering Land Bridge National Preserve

Location: Nome, Alaska
Acreage: 2,697,393
Established: December 1, 1978

A remnant of a land passage that connected Asia with North America more than thirteen thousand years ago, the Bering Land Bridge is now covered by the Chukchi and Bering seas. During the era of glaciers, this bridge was part of a migration route for people, animals, and plants when ocean levels dropped low enough to expose the land connection. Archeologists surmise that it was across this bridge, also called Beringia, that humans likely traversed the roughly 55 miles from Asia as they began to populate the Americas. For four thousand years, these early hunters trekked southward and eastward, following vegetation and game, and in time they reached the tip of South America and the eastern edge of North America. Thus, thousands of years before Columbus, people from the "old world" discovered the "new world." And archeological evidence indicates that these first peoples evolved distinct languages and lifeways in order to thrive in the varied environments that they encountered. Europeans who discovered the New World saw only homogeneous "Indians," but, over the centuries, Native Americans had become as culturally distinct and unique as the Europeans themselves.

The almost-2.7-million-acre Bering Land Bridge National Preserve is located on the Seward Peninsula in northwestern Alaska. Open year-round—yet always difficult to reach—the isolated preserve is accessible via chartered, small bush planes available at Nome or Kotzebue and boat in the summer, and by snowmobiles, dog sleds, or small planes on skis in the winter. Visitation is highest in June and July and lowest in December, January, and February.

The visitor center is located at 240 Front Street in Nome in western Alaska. There are limited federal facilities within the preserve, notably 6 shelter cabins and a bunkhouse-style cabin at Serpentine Hot Springs. Activities include camping, hiking, backpacking, exploration, nature observation, photography, and coastal boating. Winter offers excellent opportunities for snowmobiling, dog sledding, and cross-country skiing. The insects that are present during the summer are absent during the winter. Visitors can explore the remains of the gold rush era and observe

evidence of ancient Eskimo life. The preserve and its surroundings, including nearby Inupiat villages, offer opportunities to observe and learn about traditional subsistence lifestyles and historic reindeer herding.

The preserve's weather is variable. Summer temperatures on the coast are usually in the low 50s, with mid-60s to 70s, and an occasional 80 or 90 in the interior. Average January lows are minus 15 degrees on the coast and minus 50 degrees in the interior. Winds average 8 to 12 miles per hour year-round, but 57-mile-per-hour winds commonly accompany storms and produce low and dangerous wind-chill factors. Although useful, these averages cannot account for the wide variance in temperature, wind, and precipitation in the preserve. Even in the summer, snow, near-freezing temperatures, and long periods of clouds, wind, and rain are possible. Summer days are long, without darkness on the summer solstice; winter days are short, with no daylight on the winter solstice. Exposure and hypothermia are threats throughout the year. Insects are especially bad during the summer.

For more information, write Bering Land Bridge National Preserve, P.O. Box 220, Nome, AK 99762, or telephone (907) 443-2522. The park's Web site is www.nps.gov/bela.

Cape Krusenstern National Monument
Location: Kotzebue, Alaska
Acreage: 649,085
Established: December 1, 1978

Cape Krusenstern National Monument, located 26 miles above the Arctic Circle in far northwestern Alaska, is one of America's most primitive national park units. Rich archeological sites located along a succession of lateral beach ridges tell the story of six thousand years of Eskimo existence in this remote and harsh environment. Established in 1978 and totally undeveloped, this almost-650,000-

acre coastal plain speckled with sizable lagoons and framed by gently rolling limestone hills along the Chukchi Sea remains an important site for seasonal marine mammal hunting by Eskimos and local, rural residents, and park visitors must not interfere with native subsistence camps, fishnets, or other equipment.

Cape Krusenstern and nearby Kobuk Valley National Park and Noatak National Preserve are also often collectively referred to as the Northwest Alaska Areas. West to east, these parklands encompass the Brooks Range, the northernmost extension of the Rocky Mountain Range north of the Arctic Circle. Collectively, they define what geologists call the beeline, or northern limit, of tree growth as the boreal forest gives way to the tundra that stretches northward to Point Barrow on the Beaufort Sea.

During the brief summer, a beautiful display of wildflowers carpets the ridges of the beach and nearby hills. This rugged Arctic coastline is also an important nesting area for huge flocks of migratory birds. Though the monument has no facilities, campgrounds, or trails, visitors who backpack, camp, cross-county ski, and snowshoe can view a wide variety of sometimes-dangerous wildlife. Black and grizzly bears, lynx, caribou, moose, musk ox, and wolves inhabit the inland areas, while polar bears, walruses, seals, and whales may be seen on occasion in or near the ice and water.

Yet the park is a paradox. A mining road crosses the northern edge of the monument, and trucks haul zinc from an open pit mine to a tidewater port. The mine is a joint venture between NANA Regional Corporation, a Native Alaskan Corporation, and Cominco Alaska, a mining company, and was made possible by ANILCA, the Alaskan National Interest Lands Conservation Act, passed in 1980.

The park is open year-round, though visitation is highest in June and July, and, not surprisingly, lowest in January and February. Weather is typically arctic. There are high winds throughout the year. Summers are short, mild, and sunny, and on the summer solstice in June, the sun never sets. Winters are long, severe, extremely cold, and dark; on the winter solstice in December, the sun doesn't rise here at all. The monument receives about 10 to 12 inches of annual precipitation. Regardless of the season, hikers and campers should wear plenty of warm clothing, dress in layers (all of it waterproof), and wear sturdy hiking boots and waders for wet terrain. Hypothermia, giardia lamblia (an inflammatory intestinal condition caused by drinking untreated water), hungry mosquitoes, and biting flies are important concerns for even the most intrepid adventurer.

Cape Krusenstern is accessible only by chartered plane or boat from Kotzebue. At its nearest point, the monument is 10 miles from Kotzebue, which offers the most basic of traveler services. The nearby villages of Ambler, Kiana, and Noatak offer very limited services.

For more information, write Cape Krusenstern National Monument, P.O. Box 1029, Kotzebue, AK 99752, or telephone park headquarters at (907) 442-8300, or the Kotzebue Public Lands Information Center at (907) 442-3760. The monument's Web site is www.nps.gov/cakr.

Kobuk Valley National Park
Location: Kotzebue, Alaska
Acreage: 1,750,717
Established: December 1, 1978

Writer John McPhee predicted that Kobuk Valley in northwest Alaska "was, in all likelihood, the most isolated wilderness I would ever see." It is also the national park that the fewest tourists see. Embracing the central valley of the Kobuk River, the park lies encircled by the Baird and Waring mountain ranges. This remarkably diverse park protects the placid Kobuk River and the wild-and-scenic-classified Salmon River, as well as the 25-square-mile Great Kobuk Sand Dunes and the smaller Little Kobuk and Hunt River dunes. Here, too, is the northernmost extent of the boreal forest, and a rich array of arctic wildlife abounds, including caribou, grizzly and black bear, wolf, and fox. More than twelve thousand years ago, when continental glaciers formed a land bridge connecting Alaska to Asia, Kobuk Valley was ice-free, and the area attracted bison, mastodons, mammoths, and the humans who hunted them. Dunes now cover much of the southern portion of the valley. Wind and water brought in sand created by the grinding action of the ancient glaciers, and vegetation naturally stabilized the dunes.

Originally set aside as a national monument by Congress in 1978, Kobuk Valley was redesignated as a national park in 1980 as part of the massive Alaska Lands Act. Admission is free, and visitors should utilize the Kotzebue Public Lands Information Center mentioned above for park information. There are no trails or roads within the park. Visitors should expect high winds throughout the year and short, mild, cool, sunny summers. Located 26 miles above the Arctic Circle, the park experiences twenty-four hours of daylight at the summer solstice in June and a long, harsh, extremely cold winter with no daylight at all by the winter solstice in December.

There are no food, lodging, or camping facilities in the park, but all traveler services are available in Ambler, Kiana, Kotzebue, and Noatak. Commercial airlines provide service from Anchorage or Fairbanks to Nome and Kotzebue, and from either location, visitors may fly with various air taxi operators.

There are scheduled flights to villages and chartered flights to specific park areas. Summer access is by motorized and nonmotorized watercraft, aircraft, or foot, while winter access may be by snowmobile, aircraft, or foot.

For more information, write Kobuk Valley National Park, P.O. Box 1029, Kotzebue, AK 99752, or telephone (907) 442-3760. The park's Web site is www. nps.gov/kova.

Noatak National Preserve
Location: Kotzebue, Alaska
Acreage: 6,569,904
Established: December 1, 1978

The massive, almost-6.6-million-acre Noatak National Preserve protects a diverse and pristine ecosystem, ranging from river basins to mountain slopes. Almost completely encircled by the Baird and De Long mountains of the Brooks Range, the park's primary attraction is the Noatak River, designated as a National Wild and Scenic River in 1980. This gentle river originates in the Gates of the Arctic National Park and Preserve and meanders hundreds of miles westward through arctic lowlands, broad arctic valleys, and narrow canyons until it reaches the Kotzebue Sound. Access to the river is by float or wheeled plane, and fishing for arctic char, whitefish, grayling, pike, and chum salmon ranges from good to excellent. The river and its tributaries offer unparalled wilderness float-trip opportunities—from deep in the Brooks Range to the tidewaters of the Chukchi Sea—for canoeing, kayaking, and rafting. Visitors can also enjoy the 65-mile-long Grand Canyon of the Noatak, which delineates the transition between subarctic and arctic environments, and harbors an astonishing diversity of plant life.

Internationally recognized as a Biosphere Reserve, Noatak also is home to the wide-ranging, nomadic Western Arctic Caribou herd, which feeds on the tundra and low-growing vegetation of the park. With numbers approaching 300,000, the caribou herd provides a vital link in this harsh environment, supporting not only native peoples but also other large mammals such as wolves. Also inhabiting the preserve are grizzly bears, Dall sheep, red foxes, martens, lynxes, beavers, moose, and more than 130 species of birds

While there are no National Park Service facilities in the preserve, the visitor center at Kotzebue is open daily during the summer from 8 A.M. until 6 P.M. and occasionally during the winter from 3 P.M. until 5 P.M. Throughout the year programs are offered at the Kotzebue Public Lands Information Center. Park activities include primitive camping, hiking, backpacking, canoeing, kayaking, rafting, wildlife observation, and photography. Most visitors fly from Anchorage or Fairbanks to Kotzebue, and then fly to the parklands and nearby villages. During the summer, a boat charter is available, and winter access can be by snowmobiles, aircraft, or foot. There are no trails or roads within the park.

There are no food, lodging, or camping facilities in the preserve, but all traveler services are available in Ambler, Kiana, Kotzebue, and Noatak. Annual visitation is less than 4,000 people, and visitors to the park need to be self-sufficient and prepared for weather extremes. High winds are common throughout the year, and summers are short, mild, cool, and sunny. The park receives twenty-four hours of daylight at the summer solstice in June, and endures a long, severe, extremely cold winter with no daylight by the winter solstice in December. Approximately 10 to 12 inches of precipitation fall annually.

For more information, write Noatak National Preserve, National Park Service, P.O. Box 1029, Kotzebue, AK 99752, or telephone (907) 442-3760. The park's Web site is www.nps.gov/noat.

FURTHER READING

Adovasio, J.M. *The First Americans: In Pursuit of Archaeology's Greatest Mystery.* New York: Random House, 2002.

Fejes, Claire. *The Eskimo Storyteller: Folktales from Noatak, Alaska.* Anchorage: University of Alaska Press, 1999.

Jans, Nick. *The Last Light Breaking: Living Among Alaska's Inupiat Eskimos.* Anchorage: Alaska Northwest Books, 1993.

——. *A Place Beyond: Finding Home in Arctic Alaska.* Anchorage: Alaska Northwest Books, 1996.

West, Frederick Hadleigh, and Constance F. West. *American Beginnings: The Prehistory and Paleoecology of Beringia.* Chicago: University of Chicago Press, 1996.

WHISKEYTOWN NATIONAL RECREATION AREA

Location: Whiskeytown, California
Acreage: 42,503
Established: November 8, 1965

In 1849, the cry of "Eureka!" lured thousands of fortune seekers to the gold fields of California. The Whiskeytown National Recreation Area, nestled in the rugged Klamath Mountains watershed, preserves some of the history of this colorful era, while providing a wealth of water-oriented and backcountry recreation opportunities. Of the 3 parts of the Whiskeytown-Shasta-Trinity National Recreation Area, the Whiskeytown Unit is the only unit administered by the National Park Service. The other 2 are administered by the U.S. Forest Service. The Whiskeytown Unit includes the human-made 3,200-acre Whiskeytown Lake, and its clear blue waters are popular for swimming, scuba diving, water skiing, boating, fishing, and sailing; a sailing regatta is held here each Memorial Day weekend. Dedicated by President John F. Kennedy in September 1963, the Whiskeytown Dam created a lake by diverting water through tunnels and penstocks, from the Trinity River

Basin to the Sacramento River Basin. Soaring above the lake is the Shasta Bally, which rises 6,209 feet in elevation. Visitors can reach the summit by foot or by four-wheel-drive vehicle, but this area is closed in the winter. The park's mountain slopes are forested with several species of conifers, oaks, and dogwood, and this diverse environment provides a habitat for Canadian geese, bald eagles, osprey, black bears, mountain lions, and mule deer. In addition to its scenic wonders, the park also includes the Gold Rush–era Tower House Historic District, which contains the El Dorado Mine and Stamp Mill.

Authorized in November 1965, the 42,503-acre recreation area was part of the push to add recreation to the national park system. In this era, the Park Service grappled with the newly created Bureau of Outdoor Recreation to serve this important function. Parks such as Whiskeytown were designed to show the nation the Park Service's prowess. The park provides a multitude of outdoor recreation opportunities while protecting numerous historic buildings associated with the California Gold Rush. The park itself is open year-round, twenty-four hours a day, while the visitor center is open daily from 9 A.M. until 6 P.M. Memorial Day through Labor Day, and from 10 A.M. until 4 P.M. for the remainder of the year. The center has three exhibits on the California Gold Rush, an interactive computer system, and displays on the early Wintu Indians. Rangers offer guided walks, evening programs, and demonstrations and talks on the natural and cultural history of the area. Park headquarters are open daily from 8 A.M. until 4:30 P.M. The entrance fee

Whiskeytown Lake is excellent for most water-related activities, including boating, water skiing, swimming, and fishing. *(National Park Service)*

is $5 per vehicle, and a $20 annual pass is available. Visitors over age seventeen who wish to try their luck panning for gold must acquire a $1 annual permit, which is available at the visitor center and park headquarters.

The land area surrounding the lake and extending all the way to the top of Shasta Bally provides excellent opportunities for hiking, horseback riding, and mountain biking. The area's historic district dates back to the California Gold Rush era, and visitors can enjoy gold panning and touring the historic Camden House, built in the 1850s.

Lodging is available in the Whiskeytown National Recreation Area at the French Gulch Hotel (530-359-2112). This bed-and-breakfast is open all year (daily from March through December) and has eight rooms. Camping facilities in the park are located at the Brandy Creek RV Campground, which is open year-round, and sites are offered on a first-come, first-served basis. Fees are $14 per night in summer and $7 per night in winter. The Oak Bottom Campground also offers sites on a first-come, first-served basis, and fees are $18 per night during the summer and $8 per night during the winter. Primitive tent campsites, open all year, are available on a first-come, first-served basis at park headquarters, and fees are $10 per night in summer and $5 per night in winter. The Oak Bottom Marina has limited food and supplies, but all traveler services are available in Redding.

For more information, write Whiskeytown National Recreation Area, P.O. Box 188, Whiskeytown, CA 96095, or telephone (530) 246-1225. The park's Web site is www.nps.gov/whis.

FURTHER READING
Brands, H.W. *The Age of Gold: The California Gold Rush and the New American Dream.* New York: Doubleday, 2002.
Gnesios, Gregory M. *Whiskeytown National Recreation Area.* Tucson, AZ: Southwest Parks and Monuments Association, 1993.
Holliday, J.S. *Rush for Riches: Gold Fever and the Making of California.* Berkeley: University of California Press, 1999.

WHITE SANDS NATIONAL MONUMENT
Location: Alamogordo, New Mexico
Acreage: 143,733
Established: January 18, 1933

In southwestern New Mexico, in the mountain-ringed Tularosa Basin, is the largest gypsum dune field in the world. The shimmering, undulating dunes of White Sands National Monument are literally imprisoned in the basin, which is a true bolson, a desert area with internal drainage, similar to Death Valley. While the northern regions of the park contain more traditional quartz-sand dunes, it is the unique gypsum dunes that resulted in the region's Park Service protection.

A highly erodable and soluble mineral, gypsum began crystallizing in the basin during the Paleozoic era when prehistoric Lake Otero began to evaporate. Wind, rain, and temperature fluctuations began the slow erosion process of converting these crystals into sand. Today, geologists estimate that the dunes at White Sands are somewhere between twelve thousand and twenty-four thousand years old.

In addition to its stark and stunning geology, the region is also home to the White Sands Proving Ground, a military testing range for rocket technology and missile weaponry. Indeed, White Sands gained an international reputation as the location of the World War II–era, top secret Manhattan Project—the American effort to develop an atomic bomb. On July 16, 1945, at the Trinity Site, the world's first atomic bomb was successfully detonated. That same technology would be used only one month later on Hiroshima and Nagasaki, Japan, to bring an end to the war in the Pacific. The White Sands facility is still fully operational today; the missile range occasionally evacuates local ranchers and residents to test long-range missiles, and it also serves as a training ground and alternative landing site for the NASA (National Aeronautics and Space Administration) space shuttle program.

Proclaimed in January 1933, during the lame duck period of Herbert Hoover's administration, the 143,733-acre White Sands National Monument was among the first "representative area" national monuments. It was established not because of its stunning scenery, which is quite spectacular, but because of its preservation of a wide area of a natural environment typical of the environment of southcentral New Mexico. This represented a new innovation for the Park Service, a way to include more than the mountaintops that characterized the early park system and to expand the reach of the Park Service beyond that of similar federal agencies.

The entrance fee is $3 per person and is valid for seven days. The park's visitor center is open from 8 A.M. until 5 P.M., and for extended hours during the summer, and includes a museum, information desk, bookstore, and gift shop. From Memorial Day to mid-August, ranger-led activities are scheduled daily, including nature walks and evening slide programs, and free Full Moon Programs and Friday-night star talks are also available.

An 8-mile scenic drive leads from the visitor center into the heart of the dunes, and wayside exhibits at pullouts along the drive provide information about the natural history of the park. There is also a 1-mile, self-guided Big Dune Nature Trail, and a booklet available at the trailhead discusses the plants and animals that live within the dunes. The Alkali Flat Trail, which begins at the end of the Dunes Drive, is a 4.6-mile (round-trip) backcountry trail that traverses the heart of the dune field. Lake Lucero tours and Moonlight Bicycle tours are also available; Lake Lucero tours are $3 per person and Moonlight Bicycle tours are $5 per person.

There are no food or lodging facilities at the monument, but all traveler services are available in Alamogordo. Car camping is not permitted at White Sands National Monument; however, the park does have primitive backcountry campsites for backpackers wishing to enjoy a night on the white sands. The backcountry campsites, located about 1 mile from the scenic drive, are primitive with no water or toilet facilities.

For more information, write White Sands National Monument, P.O. Box 1086, Holloman AFB, NM 88330, or telephone (505) 679-2599. The park's Web site is www.nps.gov/whsa.

FURTHER READING
Atkinson, Richard. *White Sands: Wind, Sand, and Time.* Globe, AZ: Southwest Parks and Monuments Association, 1977.
Houk, Rose, and Michael Collier. *White Sands National Monument.* Tucson, AZ: Southwest Parks and Monuments Association, 1994.
Lueth, Virgil W., ed. *Geology of White Sands.* Socorro: New Mexico Geological Society, 2002.
Schneider-Hector, Dietmar. *White Sands: The History of a National Monument.* Albuquerque: University of New Mexico Press, 1993.
Welsh, Michael. *Dunes and Dreams: A History of White Sands National Monument.* Santa Fe, NM: National Park Service, 1995. Available at www.nps.gov/whsa/adhi/adhi.htm.

WHITMAN MISSION NATIONAL HISTORIC SITE
Location: Walla Walla, Washington
Acreage: 100
Established: June 29, 1936

The Whitman Mission National Historic Site commemorates an episode of cultural misunderstanding and tragedy in the early years of Anglo-American westward migration. For eleven years, beginning in 1836, the Whitman Mission, founded by Marcus Whitman in the southeastern part of what became Washington State, ministered to the Cayuse people and served as an important way station for Oregon Trail pioneers.

Marcus Whitman was born on September 4, 1802, in Federal Hollow, New York. The religious revivals that swept through the region during the early nineteenth century, as part of the Second Great Awakening, succeeded in converting to Christianity the seventeen-year-old Whitman, who announced his intent to become a minister. But his family had other ideas, and instead, Whitman became a medical doctor. An active member of the community and the Wheeler Presbyterian Church, Whitman soon attracted the attention of the American Board of Commissioners of Foreign Missions, an organization that sponsored Presbyterian missions throughout the world, including America. In 1836, he married Narcissa Prentiss and they, along with Henry and Eliza Spalding, set out for a new life as missionaries among the Cayuse Indians in the Pacific Northwest.

Life out West proved far more challenging than the Presbyterian missionaries anticipated. The primary focus of the Whitmans' missionary efforts were the Cayuse, a semi-nomadic people who followed a seasonal cycle of hunting, gathering, and fishing. In an effort to assimilate the Cayuse into more "civilized" white societal norms, the Whitman mission introduced sedentary agriculture in hopes of keeping the Cayuse closer to the mission and converting them to Christianity. The Cayuse's traditional ways of life were also being challenged by increased white migration; by the mid-1840s, the Whitman mission was a known way station along the Oregon Trail for emigrants traveling to the Willamette Valley of Oregon. The Cayuse grew increasingly suspicious of the rising tide of pioneers, and tension mounted. Finally, in 1847, the situation reached a breaking point with the measles epidemic that, within a mat-

ter of months, killed half the Cayuse tribe. When Whitman's medical expertise proved powerless on the Cayuse, they retaliated according to tribal tradition, which held that if a patient died after being treated by the medicine man, the family of the patient had the right to kill the medicine man. On November 29, 1847, eleven Cayuse took part in what is now called the "Whitman Massacre," killing Whitman, his wife, Narcissa, and eleven others in retaliation. Although the majority of the tribe was not involved in the deaths of the Whitmans and the emigrants, the entire tribe was held responsible, and five Cayuse were ultimately executed for their "crimes."

Authorized in June 1936, the 100-acre Whitman Mission National Historic Site preserves the site of Waiilatpu Mission, the Whitman's Presbyterian mission to the Cayuse Indians from 1836 to 1847, and an important way station in the early days of the Oregon Trail. The park includes the foundations of the mission buildings, the mill pond and irrigation ditch, a short segment of the Oregon Trail, and the grave where the victims are buried. Native grasses give visitors a sense of how the area looked in 1840s. Entrance fees are $3 per person or $5 per family, and a $10 annual pass is also available. The park's visitor center is open year-round from 8 A.M. until 4:30 P.M., and for extended hours during the summer. The center has a slide program and exhibits on the Whitman missionaries, Cayuse Indians, and Oregon Trail. A seven-tenths-mile-long trail provides a historical understanding of the site through numerous exhibits and the original building foundations. During the summer months, rangers offer daily programs and weekend cultural programs.

There are no food, lodging, or camping facilities at the historic site, but all traveler services are available in Walla Walla.

For more information, write Whitman Mission National Historic Site, 328 Whitman Mission Road, Walla

Walla, WA 99362-9699, or telephone (509) 522-6357. The park's Web site is www.nps.gov/whmi.

FURTHER READING

Crabtree, Jennifer. *Administrative History, Whitman Mission National Historic Site.* Seattle, WA: National Park Service, Pacific Northwest Region, 1988. Available at www.nps.gov/whmi/adhi/adhi.htm.

Drury, Clifford Merrill. *Marcus and Narcissa Whitman, and the Opening of Old Oregon.* Glendale, CA: A.H. Clark, 1973.

Jeffrey, Julie Roy. *Converting the West: A Biography of Narcissa Whitman.* Norman: University of Oklahoma Press, 1991.

Lansing, Ronald B. *Juggernaut: The Whitman Massacre Trial, 1850.* Pasadena, CA: Ninth Judicial Circuit Historical Society, 1993.

WILLIAM HOWARD TAFT NATIONAL HISTORIC SITE

Location: Cincinnati, Ohio
Acreage: 3
Established: December 2, 1969

By the end of his first and only term, it seemed William Howard Taft had failed to please anyone. This distinguished jurist and effective administrator had quietly promoted a Progressive agenda that initiated eighty antitrust suits, promoted a federal income tax and the direct election of U.S. Senators, established a postal savings system, and directed the Interstate Commerce Commission to set fair railroad rates. Yet Theodore Roosevelt's handpicked successor incited an angry Progressive onslaught against him, in no small part a result of his perceived indifference to conservation and the firing of Chief Forester Gifford Pinchot, and caused Roosevelt himself to bolt the Republican Party to form his own Progressive/Bull Moose Party and challenge for the highest office in the land.

Taft was born in 1857, the son of a distinguished judge, and graduated from Yale University. His political rise came through Republican judiciary appointments, his own competence and availability, and because, as he once wrote facetiously, he always had his "plate the right side up when offices were falling." By the age of thirty-four, he had been appointed a federal circuit judge, but his ambitious wife, Helen Herron Taft, pushed him toward the political realm. In 1900, President William McKinley sent him to the Philippines as chief civil administrator, where his empathy for the Filipinos led him to improve their economy, build roads and schools, and provide for local participation in government. In 1907, President Roosevelt made him secretary of war, a job he performed well enough that TR chose Taft to succeed him in office. Progressives were generally pleased with Taft's election in 1908 and conservatives were delighted to be rid of Roosevelt.

But Taft was not Theodore Roosevelt. A poor politician, he soon alienated many liberal Republicans by defending high tariffs and not backing Roosevelt's conservation policies. The conscientious Taft spent four uncomfortable years in the White House and was glad to be freed from the yoke of office when Woodrow Wilson won the election in 1912. Taft served as professor of law at Yale until 1921, when President Warren Harding made him chief justice of the United States, a position he held until just before his death in 1930. To Taft, this appointment was his greatest honor; he wrote: "I don't remember that I ever was President."

Authorized in December of 1969, the 3-acre William Howard Taft National Historic Site honors the only person to serve as both president and chief justice of the United States. The park is open daily from 8 A.M. until 4 P.M., and admission is free. The 1840s Greek Revival house where Taft was born and raised has been restored to its original appearance, and both ranger-led and self-guided tours of the 4 period rooms that reflect family life during Taft's boyhood are available. The home also includes second-floor exhibits highlighting Taft's life and career. The Taft Education Center, located adjacent to the birthplace, houses an orientation video, exhibits on later generations of the Taft family, and classrooms for visiting schools. The signature exhibit of the center is an animatronic figure of the president's son, Charlie Taft, telling stories about different family members.

There are no food, lodging, or camping facilities at the historic site, but all traveler services are available in Cincinnati.

For more information, write William Howard Taft National Historic Site, 2038 Auburn Avenue, Cincinnati, OH 45219, or telephone (513) 684-3262. The park's Web site is www.nps.gov/wiho.

FURTHER READING
Anderson, Donald F. *William Howard Taft: A Conservative's Conception of the Presidency.* Ithaca, NY: Cornell University Press, 1973.
Burton, David Henry. *Taft, Wilson, and World Order.* Madison, NJ: Fairleigh Dickinson University Press, 2003.
Coletta, Paolo Enrico. *The Presidency of William Howard Taft.* Lawrence: University Press of Kansas, 1973.
Scholes, Walter Vinton. *The Foreign Policies of the Taft Administration.* Columbia: University of Missouri Press, 1970.
Taft, William H. *The Collected Works of William Howard Taft: Four Aspects of Civic Duty/Present Day Problems.* Athens: Ohio University Press, 2001.
"The White House: William Howard Taft." Available at www.whitehouse.gov/history/presidents/wt27.html.

WILSON'S CREEK NATIONAL BATTLEFIELD

Location: Republic, Missouri
Acreage: 1,750
Established: April 22, 1960

The Civil War, which enveloped the nation in April 1961, deeply and bitterly divided the country. After the opening shots at Charleston, South Carolina's Fort Sumter, four border states—Virginia, Arkansas, Tennessee, and North Carolina—joined the other seven Deep South states to create the Confederate States of America. In the spring of 1861, the key challenge for President Abraham Lincoln

and the Union was to prevent the next tier of slave states—Maryland, Kentucky, and Missouri—from seceding. Of these, perhaps the most critical was Missouri, gateway to the southern portion of the Mississippi River. The fighting in the far-flung trans-Mississippi west theater was often sporadic, but in Missouri, a fierce and savage guerrilla war flourished. And Wilson's Creek, just 10 miles southwest of Springfield, became the site for the first significant Civil War engagement fought west of the Mississippi River.

The August 10, 1861, battle, known as Oak Hills to the Confederates, pitted the forces of Union General Nathaniel Lyon against the Confederates, commanded by General Benjamin McCulloch. Missouri's governor, Claiborne F. Jackson, had recently defied Lincoln's request to supply four regiments to put down the Southern insurrection, and Lyon had moved expediently to block a rumored Confederate raid on the federal arsenal in St. Louis. To secure the state for the Union, Lyon devised a bold, if audacious, plan to divide his smaller forces against McCulloch, and squeeze his rebel opponents in a deadly vise. While his plan worked to perfection, Lyon simply did not have enough men to pull off the maneuver successfully. Outnumbered nearly three to one, Lyon's soldiers fought desperately for more than five hours on "Bloody Hill." Lyon took two bullets but continued to rally his troops until a third bullet ended his life. Utterly demoralized by the loss, the remaining Federals turned and ran for the safety of Springfield. The costs of this few hours' battle were 1,222 Confederate casualties and 1,317 Union casualties.

On the heels of the Union loss at First Manassas two weeks earlier, defeat at Wilson's Creek further eroded Lincoln's and the nation's hopes for a speedy resolution to the scourge of civil war. Yet the victorious rebels failed to press their advantage here. In-

PUBLISHED BY CURRIER & IVES.   Entered according to act of Congress in the year 1861, by Currier & Ives, in the Clerk's Office of the District Court of the United States, for the Southern District of New York.   152 NASSAU ST. NEW YORK.

DEATH OF GENERAL LYON,
at the head of his troops while successfully charging the rebel forces, at the Battle of Wilsons Creek, Missouri, Aug. 10th 1861.

Nathaniel Lyon, the first Union general to be killed in combat during the Civil War, at the Battle of Wilson's Creek, Missouri, August 10, 1861. *(Library of Congress)*

stead of following up Wilson's Creek with a knockout blow that might have sent Missouri into the Confederacy, the grays allowed the blues to escape to fight again another day. When the two armies met the following year in Missouri at Pea Ridge, the outcome was instead a Union victory. Missouri never seceded, and this critical access to the mighty Mississippi River remained in federal hands throughout the war.

With the exception of the vegetation, the battlefield has changed little from its historic setting, enabling the visitor to experience the site in a near-pristine condition. Authorized in April 1960, the 1,750-acre Wilson's Creek National Battlefield commemorates the first

major engagement of the Civil War west of the Mississippi. Entrance fees are $2 per person or $4 per vehicle; a $10 annual pass is also available. The park's visitor center is open year-round from 8 A.M. until 5 P.M. and it features several battle-related exhibits and special exhibitions that vary during the year. The center also offers a thirteen-minute video presenting the historical background to the battle and a six-minute fiber-optics map program illustrating battle tactics. An excellent Civil War research library is open to visitors by appointment, although the library does not maintain an open stack or checkout policy. A 4.9-mile paved tour road provides a self-guided auto tour of the park with 8 stops at significant points of the battle. There are 5 walking trails off the tour road, varying in length from a quarter of a mile to three-quarters of a mile. A 7-mile trail system for horseback riding and hiking is accessible from the tour road.

Visitors can also tour the Ray House, dating from the 1850s, which served as a temporary field hospital for Confederate soldiers following the battle. General Nathaniel Lyon's body was brought to the house and placed in a bed for examination, and the bed is on exhibit in one of the rooms. The house is open on weekends (subject to staff and volunteer availability), Memorial Day through Labor Day. The anniversary of the battle is observed with a special program and ceremony during the morning of the anniversary date, August 10, and an annual candlelight tour is held traditionally in August. Living-history programs depicting Civil War soldier life, cavalry drills, musket firing, artillery demonstrations, Civil War medicine, and Civil War–era clothing are available on Sunday afternoons Memorial Day through Labor Day.

There are no food, lodging, or camping facilities at the battlefield, but all traveler services are available in Springfield.

For more information, write Wilson's Creek National Battlefield, 6424 West Farm Road 182, Republic, MO 65738-9514, or telephone (417) 732-2662. The park's Web site is www.nps.gov/wicr.

FURTHER READING

Bearss, Edwin C. *The Battle of Wilson's Creek.* Diamond, MO: George Washington Carver Birthplace District Association, 1975.

Brooksher, William R. *Bloody Hill: The Civil War Battle of Wilson's Creek.* Washington: Brassey's, 1995.

Piston, William Garrett, and Richard W. Hatcher III. *Wilson's Creek: The Second Battle of the Civil War and the Men Who Fought It.* Chapel Hill: University of North Carolina Press, 2000.

Stevens, Joseph E. *America's National Battlefield Parks: A Guide.* Norman: University of Oklahoma Press, 1990.

WIND CAVE NATIONAL PARK

Location: Hot Springs, South Dakota
Acreage: 28,295
Established: January 9, 1903

Wind Cave National Park in southwestern South Dakota is an anomaly among American national parks. It was the seventh national park and it dates from a time before there were clear and prevailing standards for the national park category. At this time, no federal bureau existed to manage the national parks, and they came into the system usually because someone powerful or influential sought their preservation. Wind Cave attracted attention after competing mining claims were denied. In 1898, two geologists explored the cave and pronounced it splendid. In that age, science had great social power, and the announcement of another scientific wonder in the West sufficed to alert a conservation oriented Congress that something worthy of preservation remained. Staunch conservation advocate John F. Lacey of Iowa and Senator Robert J. Gamble of South Dakota sponsored a national park bill, and in 1903 President Theodore Roosevelt signed the bill into law.

In its era, Wind Cave was unusual among national parks. It was small and not terribly scenic, and many who compared it to other national parks found it inferior. Despite such contentions, Wind Cave remained in the national park category, largely because until 1978, when Badlands became a national park, the state had no other areas in the prime category of national preservation. Despite an early history of mining, the area that included Wind Cave was in dispute in the 1890s. After claim and counterclaim, in December 1899, the Department of the Interior decided that since no mining or proper homesteading had taken place, neither party had a valid claim to the cave. In 1901, the land around the cave

In Wind Cave, 350 feet below the surface at Odd Fellows' Hall. Center in the front group are William Jennings Bryan and Governor Andrew E. Lee. Photograph by W. R. Cross, South Dakota, c. 1897. *(National Archives)*

was withdrawn from homesteading, and national park establishment followed. The park was enlarged by the addition of the Wind Cave National Game Preserve in 1935.

Today, the 28,295-acre park preserves this beautiful limestone cave set in the scenic Black Hills of South Dakota and the rare mixed-grass prairie above it. The park's visitor center is open year-round from 8 A.M. until 4:30 P.M., and for extended hours during the summer. It contains 3 exhibit rooms explaining cave exploration, cave formations, early cave history, the Civilian Conservation Corps, park wildlife, and resource management. There are 30 miles of hiking trails in the park, and 2 trails, the Rankin Ridge Trail and the Elk Mountain Trail, are self-guided

nature trails with trail booklets. Park rangers also offer guided prairie hikes, evening campfire programs, and visitor center lawn programs, in season.

The highlight of the park, of course, is the cave, and visitors can choose from 5 cave tours. The Candlelight Cave Tour lasts two hours and covers a mile of rugged terrain. Each participant carries a candle bucket that allows visitors to explore a less-developed, unlighted part of the cave. The fee is $9 per person. The Caving Experience is a four-hour tour that introduces visitors to the basics of safe caving. The fee is $20 per person. The Fairgrounds Cave Tour is a ninety-minute walk that includes some of the larger rooms found in the developed area of the cave and examples of many cave formations. The fee is $8 per person. The one-hour Garden of Eden Cave Tour visits representative features of Wind Cave, and the fee is $6 per person. The seventy-five-minute Natural Entrance Cave Tour allows visitors to walk through the middle level of the cave where boxwork is abundant. The fee is $8 per person.

There are no food or lodging facilities in the park, but all traveler services are available in Custer and Hot Springs. The 75-site Elk Mountain Campground is 1 mile from the visitor center in the park and is open from April through October. The campground has flush toilets and running water during the summer months, but there are no showers, dump stations, or electrical hookups. Campsites are available on a first-come, first-served basis, and the fee is $10 per night. Camping is also available at private and public campgrounds in Custer and Hot Springs, Custer State Park, Cold Brook Recreation Area, Angostura State Recreation Area, and the Black Hills National Forest.

For more information, write Wind Cave National Park, RR 1 Box 190, Hot Springs, SD 57747-9430, or telephone (605) 745-4600. The park's Web site is www.nps.gov/wica.

FURTHER READING

Milstein, Michael. *Badlands, Theodore Roosevelt, and Wind Cave National Parks: Wildlife Watchers Guide.* Minocqua, WI: NorthWord, 1996.

Palmer, Arthur N. *The Geology of Wind Cave, Wind Cave National Park, South Dakota.* Hot Springs, SD: Wind Cave Natural History Association, 1981.

Sanders, Peggy. *Wind Cave National Park: The First 100 Years.* Chicago: Arcadia, 2003.

Terry, Ronald A. *Wind Cave: The Story Behind the Scenery.* Las Vegas, NV: KC Publications, 1998.

WOMEN'S RIGHTS NATIONAL HISTORICAL PARK

Location: Seneca Falls, New York
Acreage: 7
Established: December 28, 1980

We hold these truths to be self-evident: that all men *and women* are created equal. . . .
—*Declaration of Sentiments*

The first women's rights convention and the Declaration of Sentiments have earned the small hamlet of Seneca Falls in upstate New York a significant place in history. The birthplace of the women's rights movement in America, Seneca Falls was a typical mid-nineteenth-century community undergoing a rough transition from agriculture to trade and commerce. Swamped by newcomers and struggling to maintain its small-town identity, the community turned to volunteer organizations to initiate reforms counteracting the effects of urbanization and industrialization. Moral reform societies intervened to keep prostitution at bay, while temperance unions strove to keep residents sober. Many of these reformers were women, and as they lobbied to change society, they began to realize their own inferior position. Women were restricted in almost every facet of public life; they could not vote, their employment opportunities were limited to "pink-collar" jobs, and married women could not own property or make contracts. Just as the later civil rights movement of the 1950s and 1960s spawned the Women's Liberation Movement, so too did the mid-nineteenth-century abolition movement give strength to the Women's Rights Movement.

Elizabeth Cady Stanton (1815–1902) was one of the founders of the nineteenth-century women's movement. This Seneca Falls housewife and mother had encountered gender discrimination in her advocacy of abolitionism, and along with Lucretia Mott, a Quaker teacher who served in a number of temperance and antislavery organizations, Stanton organized the landmark 1848 convention. Together Stanton and Mott had determined that the wrongs suffered by women should be made into rights. The Seneca Falls Conven-

Elizabeth Cady Stanton, seated, with fellow women's rights activist Susan B. Anthony. *(Library of Congress)*

tion was held at the Wesleyan Methodist Chapel on July 19 and 20, 1848. A true equal rights convention, the Seneca Falls gathering resulted in a Declaration of Sentiments, based on the language and content of the Declaration of Independence. Stating that "all men and women are created equal," the delegates demanded equal rights for women in employment and legal affairs, as well as the radical call for the right to vote. In all, more than 300 women and men attended the convention, and their Declaration would set the tone for future women's rights and suffrage activists.

Authorized in December 1980, the 7-acre Women's Rights National Historical Park was an integral part of broadening the themes of official preservation in the United States. Part of Representative Phil Burton's most comprehensive achievement, the Omnibus Bill of 1980, it was among the first generation of parks established to include dimensions of American history such as women's rights and minority experience that had long been ignored. The park commemorates the first women's rights convention and the early leaders of the women's rights movement in the United States. The entrance fee is $2 per person. The park's visitor center, located at 136 Fall Street in Seneca Falls, is open year-round from 9 A.M. until 5 P.M. and has a thirty-minute film called *Dreams of Equality* and numerous exhibits detailing the history of the women's rights movement from its beginnings to the present. The First Wave Statue exhibit portrays the planners and attendees of the first women's rights convention, while the Elizabeth Cady Stanton–An Extraordinary Woman exhibit details the life and accomplishments of Stanton. The M'Clintock House–Come Dream with Us! is an exhibit that examines the importance of the M'Clintock House and the planning session for the convention that took place in the parlor. The exhibit also explores the restoration of the house that is currently taking place.

Historic sites in the park include the 1840s Greek Revival home of Elizabeth Cady Stanton, organizer and leader of the women's rights movement; the Wesleyan Chapel, site of the first women's rights convention; Declaration Park with a 100-foot-long water wall engraved with the Declaration of Sentiments and the names of the signers of the declaration; the Hunt House, home of Jane and Richard Hunt, the site where the idea for the convention was conceived; and the M'Clintock House, home of MaryAnn and Thomas M'Clintock, site where the Declaration of Sentiments was drafted.

There are no food, lodging, or camping facilities at the historical park, but all traveler services are available in Seneca Falls and Waterloo.

For more information, write Women's Rights National Historical Park, 136 Fall Street, Seneca Falls, NY 13148, or telephone (315) 568-2991. The park's Web site is www.nps.gov/wori.

FURTHER READING

Banner, Lois W. *Elizabeth Cady Stanton: A Radical for Women's Rights.* Boston: Little, Brown, 1980.

Cott, Nancy F., ed. *No Small Courage: A History of Women in the United States.* New York: Oxford University Press, 2000.

DuBois, Ellen Carol. *Harriet Stanton Blatch and the Winning of Woman Suffrage.* New Haven, CT: Yale University Press, 1999.

Greene, Dana, ed. *Lucretia Mott: Her Complete Speeches and Sermons.* New York: E. Mellon, 1980.

Lerner, Gerda. *The Grimke Sisters from South Carolina: Pioneers for Women's Rights and Abolition.* New York: Houghton Mifflin, 1967.

Stanton, Elizabeth Cady. *Eighty Years and More: Reminiscences, 1815–1897.* New York: Schocken, 1971.

Sterling, Dorothy, ed. *We Are Your Sisters: Black Women in the Nineteenth Century.* New York: W.W. Norton, 1984.

Wheeler, Marjorie Spruill. *One Woman, One Vote: Rediscovering the Woman Suffrage Movement.* Troutdale, OR: New Sage, 1995.

WRANGELL–ST. ELIAS NATIONAL PARK AND PRESERVE

Location: Copper Center, Alaska
Acreage: 13,175,901
Established: December 1, 1978

Another of the park areas created as a result of the Alaskan Native Claims Settlement Act, Wrangell–St. Elias National Park and Preserve is the single largest unit of the national park system. Established first as a national monument in 1978, it became a national park in December 1980, when the outgoing Democratic Congress created a de facto Alaskan national park system from the wreckage of the 1980 election. Of the parks created this way, Wrangell–St. Elias is perhaps the most accessible. Less than a one-day drive east of Anchorage, it is often called the "Mountain Kingdom of North America." The Chugach, Wrangell, and St. Elias mountain ranges converge in the park, which includes the largest assemblage of glaciers and peaks above 16,000 feet in North America. Most stunning, Mount St. Elias, at 18,008 feet the second-highest peak in the United States, towers over the park.

The Park Service faced an enormous challenge at Wrangell–St. Elias. By 1985, the agency had developed plans for Wrangell–St. Elias, and the agency looked across the border to the Kluane National Park in Canada, anticipating parallel early development. Officials recognized that Wrangell–St. Elias was one of the most accessible of Alaska's national parks, which surely meant higher levels of visitation over time. The agency struggled to assess the optimum level of the park's use, finding the difficult midpoint between complete preservation and unbridled use. Such an issue always vexed the Park Service, for changing visitation and resource needs meant that the agency sought to fix a moving target.

For people who lived in the region, national park designation was not necessarily a desirable outcome. Founded as a sin city for the nearby Kennecott mine around the turn of the century, McCarthy, Alaska, had long served as a refuge for those who wanted to avoid the modern-day world. Dwindling to a few residents, the town slumbered, and gradually, after about 1960, a few people straggled in, seeking a different life. In remote Alaska, access determined all; although most travel was by air, roads were the greatest vectors of change. McCarthy was connected to the Alaskan highway system by a 60-mile, gravel road. Under the best of conditions, the 60-mile trip from Chitina took more than four hours. Even at the end of the road, the trip discouraged visitors; a hand-pulled cable-car tram was the only way across the rapid Kennicott River. Four miles from town stood the carcass of the Kennecott Copper Mine.

Climbing St. Elias, 1913. *(Library of Congress)*

The people of McCarthy still sought to keep the outside world away, but the national park changed their prospects. It served as the catalyst for change. It attracted more visitors and brought improvements, most significantly to the road. In the mid-1980s, the state widened it, graded it, and built a new Kuskulana bridge. New models replaced the old cable cars. The 60-mile trip soon averaged a little more than two hours, and the hardest part of crossing the river in the summer became waiting in line with all the visitors.

While the 5,000 or so people who visited McCarthy in 1988 seemed substantial, they were only a vanguard. The national park and the tourism it spawned brought new realities: businesses downtown and lines of visitors waiting to cross the Kennicott River on the hand-operated tram that connected it to the state road. By 1992, visitors topped 20,000, and the entire community felt the pressure. To some, the Park Service was the enemy; to

others, the sheer numbers posed a threat. This once-cohesive community, therefore, began to fracture, as some benefited from tourism while others watched it alter the sense of place they had enjoyed. Even in remote Alaskan national parks, the impact of tourism could be felt.

Of the more than 13.1 million acres managed by the National Park Service in the Wrangell–St. Elias National Park and Preserve, Congress designated 8.3 million acres as national park, and 4.8 million acres have national preserve status. Admission is free. The park's visitor center, at mile 105.5 on the Old Richardson Highway, is open year-round from 8 A.M. until 4:30 P.M. Monday through Friday, from October through May, and daily for the remainder of the year. A twelve-minute, park-orientation video is available, along with general park orientation and information. The park also maintains a visitor contact station and 3 ranger stations.

The McCarthy Kiosk Visitor Contact Station, at mile 60 on the McCarthy Road, is open from Memorial Day through Labor Day. The Chitina Ranger Station, at mile 33 on the Edgerton Highway, is also open from Memorial Day through Labor Day, from 10 A.M. until 6 p.m. daily, and has a McCarthy Road video and historic cabin. The Slana Ranger Station, at mile .5 of the Nabesna Road, is open year-round, from 8 A.M. until 5 P.M. from June through September, and by appointment for the remainder of the year. The Yakutat Ranger Station, on Mallott Avenue, is open year-round, and from 8 A.M. until 4:30 P.M. from Memorial Day through Labor Day.

All traveler services are available in Glennallen, Kenny Lake, McCarthy, and Slana. Backcountry camping is also available in the park without a permit, but registration is recommended. There are 2 gravel roads that enter the park, the McCarthy and Nabesna roads; however, some car rental companies prohibit clients from accessing these roads.

For more information, write Wrangell–St. Elias National Park and Preserve, 105.5 Old Richardson Highway, P.O. Box 439, Copper Center, AK 99573, or telephone (907) 822-5238. The park's Web site is www.nps.gov/wrst.

FURTHER READING

Decker, Robert, and Barbara Decker. *Volcanoes in America's National Parks.* New York: W.W. Norton, 2001.
Herben, George. *Picture Journeys in Alaska's Wrangell–St. Elias: America's Largest National Park.* Anchorage: Alaska Northwest Books, 1997.
Richter, Donald H. *Guide to the Volcanoes of the Western Wrangell Mountains, Alaska: Wrangell–St. Elias National Park and Preserve.* Washington, DC: GPO, 1995.

WRIGHT BROTHERS NATIONAL MEMORIAL

Location: Kill Devil Hills, North Carolina
Acreage: 428
Established: March 2, 1927

On December 17, 1903, Wilbur and Orville Wright, two bicycle-shop mechanics from Dayton, Ohio, flew into history on the Outer Banks of North Carolina. For the first time ever, a manned, heavier-than-air machine left the ground by its own power, moved forward under control without losing speed, and landed on a point as high as that from which it started. The whole momentous event lasted only twelve seconds, and the distance Orville flew was a mere 120 feet. But he had flown—of that there was no doubt. "They have done it," cried an amazed witness. "Damned if they ain't flew!" A new epoch in human history had begun.

The Wright brothers had been inseparable their entire lives, and they shared a zeal for experimentation. Born just four years apart, Wilbur in 1867, Orville in 1871, the boys earned pocket money selling home-made mechanical toys, and in 1892, they opened their own bicycle business in Dayton. Their innovative Van Cleve bicycle made the shop prosperous, but their real fascination was with flight. Stimulated by the ideas of Otto Lilienthal, whose experiments with gliders were widely celebrated, the Wright brothers began their own experiments with kites. The windy conditions near Kitty Hawk, North Carolina, proved ideal for perfecting their first glider, and by 1902, they had succeeded in controlling its movements. By the following year, they installed a 12-horsepower motor on their 750-pound flying machine, which Orville successfully piloted on that fateful December morning. Interestingly, a few hours later, Wilbur made his own flight, but an errant wind gust crashed the craft, and further flights in it became impossible.

Set aside in March 1927, the 428-acre Wright Brothers National Memorial commemorates this remarkable gravity-defying event that set the stage for a revolution in human transportation. Entrance fees are $2 per

Wilbur and Orville Wright assembling the 1903 machine in the new camp building at Kill Devil Hills, Kitty Hawk, North Carolina. *(Library of Congress)*

person or $4 per vehicle. The park's visitor center is open year-round from 9 A.M. until 5 P.M. It houses exhibits that include reproductions of the Wrights' wind tunnel, the 1902 glider, and the 1903 Flyer. Replicas of the original Wright camp buildings are a two-minute stroll from the visitor center. Adjacent to the camp buildings are granite markers that designate the lengths of the 4 successful powered flights made on December 17. The Wright Memorial Shaft crowns Big Kill Devil Hill, a 90-foot dune of once-shifting sand that has been stabilized with grass. The 60-foot pylon, constructed of gray granite from Mount Airy, North Carolina, honors the Wright brothers and marks the site of the hundreds

of glider flights that preceded the first powered flight. Park rangers offer regularly scheduled presentations each day in the Flight Room Auditorium. Each year the anniversary of the first successful flights is commemorated during special events at the park on December 17. National Aviation Day is celebrated on August 19 (Orville Wright's birthday). The 3,000-foot paved First Flight Airstrip was added to the park in 1963 to accommodate small planes. Parking at the airstrip is limited.

There are no food, lodging, or camping facilities at the memorial, but all traveler services are available in Kill Devil Hills and nearby towns.

For more information, write Wright Brothers National Memorial, 1401 National Park Drive, Manteo, NC 27954, or telephone (252) 441-7430. The park's Web site is www.nps.gov/wrbr.

FURTHER READING

Chapman, William R., and Jill K. Hanson. *Wright Brothers National Monument Historic Resource Study.* Atlanta, GA: National Park Service, 1997. Available at www.nps.gov/wrbr/hrs/hrs.htm.

Crouch, Tom D. *The Bishop's Boys: A Life of Wilbur and Orville Wright.* New York: W.W. Norton, 2003.

Crouch, Tom D., and Peter L. Jakab. *The Wright Brothers and the Invention of the Aerial Age.* Washington, DC: National Geographic Society, 2003.

Culick, Fred E., and Spencer Dunmore. *On Great White Wings: The Wright Brothers and the Race for Flight.* New York: Hyperion, 2001.

Wright, Orville. *How We Invented the Airplane: An Illustrated History.* New York: Dover Publications, 1988.

WUPATKI NATIONAL MONUMENT

Location: Flagstaff, Arizona
Acreage: 35,422
Established: December 9, 1924

From about 600 to 1300 C.E., the ancestors of the modern Hopi tribe made their home in northcentral Arizona in the geographic region known as the Colorado Plateau. The Sinagua, whose name in Spanish means "without water," lived in pit houses and practiced subsistence farming, supplemented with hunting and gathering. In 1065, the eruption of nearby Sunset Crater Volcano covered the region with fine volcanic ash. Although the Sinagua initially fled and many of their homes were buried, they subsequently discovered that the porous ash created natural mulch that enabled the soil to retain moisture, facilitating more successful agriculture in this arid region. As word spread, people of various cultures migrated into the area, including the Anasazi, Hohokam, Coconino, and Mogollon. Each brought with them their own customs and beliefs, which helps explain the many small but well-fortified pueblos found in the region.

By 1100 C.E., the Wupatki area was flourishing; extensive trade routes developed and sizable villages emerged. Wupatki Ruin, overlooking the Painted Desert to the east, was the largest pueblo in the region. Rising about 3 stories, the structure contained more than 100 rooms and had a nearby amphitheater and masonry ball court. Prosperity continued through the twelfth century, at which time the inhabitants began to leave. As the moisture-retaining soils were blown away, aridity returned, and by 1300, the region was deserted.

In addition to its prehistoric masonry pueblos and cliff dwellings, Wupatki also contains many striking geologic features, including stark black lava flows, wind-rippled cinder dunes, rusty red sandstones, and vast expanses of multihued sedimentary layers. The oldest exposed rock layers in the monument are the Kaibab and Moenkopi formations, and the monument provides a living textbook on the forces of volcanism and plate tectonics.

Proclaimed in December 1924, the 35,422-acre Wupatki National Monument was late among the first generation of archeological national monuments. Its remote location and limited travel resources contributed to its being overlooked, as did the proximity of the nearby Grand Canyon, which dominated the intellectual horizons of the day. The monument preserves the ruins of red sandstone pueblos built by farming Native Americans in about 1065. The seven-day entrance fee is $3 per person, and it also is valid for Sunset Crater Volcano National Monument. The park's visitor center is open from 8 A.M. until 5 P.M. (until 6 P.M. during the summer) and has numerous interpretive museum exhibits. Park rangers offer programs and guided hikes during the summer and occasionally in spring and fall. The Wupatki Pueblo Trail is a half-mile self-guided tour of the largest pueblo in the park. The Lomaki

Wupatki is the only known location in the Southwest where physical evidence from at least three archeologically separate ancestral Puebloan cultures is found together in a number of sites. *(National Park Service)*

Pueblo Trail is a 2-mile easy walk with access to several pueblos: Wukoki, Citadel, and Nalakihu pueblos. The 2-mile Doney Mountain Trail ascends from the picnic area to the top of the cinder cone for spectacular views of the surrounding area. Hiking in the park is restricted to established trails only to protect fragile archeological sites.

There are no food, lodging, or camping facilities at the monument, but all traveler services are available in Cameron, Flagstaff, and Gray Mountain.

For more information, write Wupatki National Monument, HC 33, Box 444A, #14, Flagstaff, AZ 86004, or telephone (520) 679-2365. The park's Web site is www.nps.gov/wupa.

FURTHER READING

Lamb, Susan. *Wupatki National Monument.* Tucson, AZ: Southwest Parks and Monuments Association, 1995.

Noble, David Grant, ed. *Wupatki and Walnut Canyon: New Perspectives on History, Prehistory, Rock Art.* Santa Fe, NM: School of American Research, 1987.

Schroeder, Albert H. *Of Men and Volcanoes—The Sinagua of Northern Arizona.* Globe, AZ: Southwest Parks and Monuments Association, 1977.

Y

YELLOWSTONE NATIONAL PARK

Location: Idaho, Montana, and
  Wyoming
Acreage: 2,219,791
Established: March 1, 1872

Yellowstone has long claimed the title of the world's first and, to its proponents, best national park and indeed, it seems to merit the claim. The first example of an area established as a park for its fantastic scenic and natural attributes, Yellowstone was also so high in elevation and so far north that it was not practical to develop its commercial and extractive assets during the late nineteenth century. As a result, after it had been revealed to the American nation as a spectacular place, it was a short step to its protection as an example of the values of the post–Civil War nation. In practical terms, no one could think of a better use for a place that was so rich in resources yet so remote that utilizing its resources seemed an impossibility.

The Yellowstone region reached the American consciousness earlier in the nineteenth century. The first Anglo-American to visit the marvels of the Yellowstone area was most likely John Colter, a soldier on the Lewis and Clark Expedition, who traveled through the region in 1808. He told of the place where steam rose from the freezing ground, only to be mocked by those who called the region "Colter's Hell." In 1829, trapper Joe Meek stumbled upon what is now known as the Norris Geyser basin area, but his stories of "fire and brimstone" were met with disbelief. These few, early accounts stirred public interest, however, and in the 1830s, mountain man Jim Bridger and others began exploring the Yellowstone region more seriously.

Tales of Yellowstone's fantastic wonders and thermal features caught the interest of the federal government, which set out to explore the park in earnest following the Civil War, particularly after the report of mine workers David E. Folsom, Charles W. Cook, and William Peterson was published in 1869. The three had visited the Grand Canyon of Yellowstone, viewed the teeming wildlife, and experienced the geysers and boiling pools. A group led by Henry D. Washburn, surveyor general of the Montana territory, was the most famous of the 1870 parties that explored the Yellowstone region. This famous Washburn party, which is credited with "discovering" Yellowstone, consisted of Nathaniel Pitt "National Park" Langford (later selected as

A jolly group enjoying the refreshing waters of Apollinalis Spring in Yellowstone National Park, 1905.
(Library of Congress)

the first park superintendent) and First Lieutenant Gustavus Doane (a veteran of the U.S.
Calvary, who headed the military escort that
accompanied the group and made an official
report to the federal government). During the
expedition, Washburn named "Old Faithful."
The following year, Congress appointed Fer-
dinand V. Hayden, head of the new U.S. Geological Survey, to lead an official exploration
into the region. He assembled a team of geologists, botanists, and zoologists as well as
artist Thomas Moran and photographer William H. Jackson to survey Yellowstone. The
party was stunned by the wonders and beauty
they saw; Moran's watercolors and Jackson's
photographs provided ample proof that the
region was unique. Hayden made a 500-page
report to Congress, and the lobbying to make
Yellowstone a national park began. One year
later, on March 1, 1872, President Ulysses S.
Grant signed into existence the world's first
national park, for "the benefit and enjoyment
of the people."

The over-2.2-million-acre park protects
Old Faithful geyser and 10,000 other hot
springs and geysers, the majority of the
earth's total. These geothermal wonders are
evidence of one of the world's largest active
volcanoes. Catastrophic volcanic eruptions
occurred in Yellowstone about 2 million
years ago, then 1.2 million years ago, and
then again six hundred thousand years ago.
The latest eruption spewed out nearly 240 cubic miles of debris, and what is now the park's
central portion collapsed, forming a 28-mile
by 47-mile caldera (or basin) that spans almost half the park. The magmatic heat pow-
ering those eruptions still fuels the park's
famous geysers, hot springs, fumaroles, and
mud pots. The spectacular Grand Canyon of
the Yellowstone River provides a glimpse of
earth's interior: its waterfalls highlight the
boundaries of lava flows and thermal areas.

This weird and wonderful wildland is also
home to threatened and endangered species

The 200-foot-high Grand Geyser in action, Upper
Basin, Yellowstone National Park. *(Library of Congress)*

such as the grizzly bear and gray wolf, as well
as free-ranging herds of bison and elk. The
park itself forms the core of the Greater Yellowstone Ecosystem, one of the largest intact
temperate zone ecosystems remaining on the
planet. Entrance fees to Yellowstone National
Park are $10 per person or $20 per vehicle
($15 for snowmobiles) and are valid for seven
days; a $40 annual pass is also available.

Yellowstone National Park maintains 5
visitor centers, 2 information centers, and 2
museums. The Albright Visitor Center, in
Mammoth Hot Springs, is open year-round.
It features museum exhibits on Native Americans, the mountain men, early exploration,
the army days, and the early National Park
Service. Visitors can tour the Moran Gallery,
where fine reproductions of watercolor
sketches by the painter and expeditionary
Thomas Moran are displayed, and the Jackson Gallery, where original photographs by
William Henry Jackson, also of the 1871 Hayden Survey, are exhibited. The center also
has film and video presentations, including

The Challenge of Yellowstone (twenty-five minutes) on the history of Yellowstone and the evolution of the national park idea, and *Thomas Yellowstone Moran* (twelve minutes) on Moran's contribution to the establishment of Yellowstone National Park. The Old Faithful Visitor Center is open from late April through early November, and from mid-December through mid-March, and offers evening ranger-led programs during the summer and winter seasons. The Canyon Visitor Center, in the Canyon Village complex, is open from late May through September and it features an exhibit on the Yellowstone bison, which explains the natural history of the animal and the bison as a symbol of wildness. The Fishing Bridge Visitor Center is a national historic landmark that is open from late May through September and has exhibits on historic bird specimens (by Carl Russell) that provide a good overview of Yellowstone's birds. Other displays include a grizzly sow and its cubs and a family of river otters. The Grant Village Visitor Center is also open from late May through September and features the movie *Yellowstone: The Unfinished Song on the 1988 Fires* (twenty minutes) and exhibits that interpret fire's role in the environment, using the fires of 1988 as the example.

The Madison Information Station, built in 1929, is a national historic landmark that is open from late May through September. The West Thumb Information Station is also open from late May through September and has park information and a small bookstore.

The Museum of the National Park Ranger, about 1 mile north of Norris Junction along the entrance road to the Norris Campground, has a small auditorium that shows a laser-disc production of the twenty-five-minute movie, *An American Legacy,* which tells the story of the development of the National Park Service (NPS). Exhibits depict the development of the park ranger profession from its roots in the military traditions through early rangers and to the present array of NPS staff-specialized duties. The historic Norris Geyser Basin Museum, a quarter mile east of Norris Junction just off the Grand Loop Road, is open from late May to early October. The museum features exhibits on geothermal geology, Norris Geyser Basin features, and life in thermal areas.

There are numerous food, lodging, and camping facilities in the park, and all traveler services are available in the surrounding area.

For more information, write Yellowstone National Park, P.O. Box 168, Yellowstone National Park, WY 82190-0168, or telephone (307) 344-7381. The park's Web site is www.nps.gov/yell.

FURTHER READING

Barringer, Mark Daniel. *Selling Yellowstone: Capitalism and the Construction of Nature.* Lawrence: University Press of Kansas, 2002.

Chittenden, Hiram. Edited and with an introduction by Richard A. Bartlett. *The Yellowstone National Park.* 1905. Reprint, Norman: University of Oklahoma Press, 1964.

Haines, Aubrey L. *Yellowstone National Park: Its Exploration and Establishment.* Washington, DC: National Park Service, 1974. Available at www.cr.nps.gov/history/online_books/haines1.

Pritchard, James A. *Preserving Yellowstone's Natural Conditions: Science and the Perception of Nature.* Lincoln: University of Nebraska Press, 1999.

Schullery, Paul D. *Searching for Yellowstone: Ecology and Wonder in the Last Wilderness.* Boston: Houghton Mifflin, 1997.

Smith, Robert B., and Lee J. Siegel. *Windows into the Earth: The Geologic Story of Yellowstone and Grand Teton National Parks.* New York: Oxford University Press, 2000.

YOSEMITE NATIONAL PARK

Location: Sierra Nevada, California
Acreage: 761,266
Established: October 1, 1890

The third American national park, Yosemite National Park, has long held a premier place in the national imagination. American conservation cut its teeth in California, and the golden state had no more prominent symbol of its desire to protect nature than the Yosemite Valley. American conservation was born in John Muir's embrace of Yosemite; its organizational structure developed through the Sierra Club, to which Yosemite was the pinnacle of American nature. Out of this milieu came the first generation of conservation leaders, including Stephen T. Mather and Horace M. Albright, the first two directors of the National Park Service. To say that Yosemite was the greatest influence on the shape of American conservation is not to exaggerate. Such a bold statement is an accurate reflection of the importance of the first park to captivate an influential regional constituency with national power.

The Yosemite Valley is a spectacular setting that has captivated Americans since pioneer artist Thomas A. Ayres first drew the region in 1855 and 1856. Visitors were entranced by the area, perceiving it as a manifestation of their desire to appreciate sublime nature. The descriptions they wrote, typified

The famous Wawona tunnel tree and stagecoach in Yosemite Valley, 1905. *(Library of Congress)*

by Samuel Bowles who observed that "no so limited space in all the known world offers such majestic and impressive beauty," created a Yosemite of the imagination that dazzled late-nineteenth-century America.

Yosemite's transformation from natural wonder to national park paralleled the changes that swept the United States in the late nineteenth century. The area's first designation came as a state park on June 30, 1864. Yosemite Valley and the Mariposa Grove of Giant Sequoias were ceded to the state of California as an inalienable public trust. As a result of inconsistent management by the Yosemite Park Commission and a hue and cry from the budding California conservation community, in 1890, Yosemite National Park was created. Because no bureau or entity in the Department of the Interior existed to manage national parks, the U.S. Cavalry was sent to manage it.

Yosemite enjoyed an iconic status by the time it became a national park in 1890. By 1890, John Muir had become "John of the Mountains," the most famous figure in early nature preservation; San Francisco had developed from a vigilante frontier town into the premier city and economic center of the West; and California had stepped to the fore in the complicated embrace of Romanticism, empiricism, and antimodernism that so strongly foreshadowed the rise of legislated conservation. For this urban society grappling with a sense of loss that stemmed from rapid growth and rampant socioeconomic inequity, Yosemite defined the value of what was lost in transition.

Yosemite also became the scene of the signature battle of early conservation, the struggle for the Hetch Hetchy Valley. Prized for its beauty, the Hetch Hetchy Valley was one of the most beautiful places inside the park. In the aftermath of the earthquake of 1906, the city of San Francisco needed a municipally owned water supply, and Hetch Hetchy

The Ahwahnee Hotel at Yosemite is a major attraction to visitors, who explore the relationship of architecture to nature, with which it has been designed to blend. *(Courtesy of DNC Parks & Resorts, Yosemite)*

provided a viable alternative. Two versions of conservation, the preservation ethic of John Muir and the utilitarian conservation of Gifford Pinchot, collided head-on. A seven-year struggle ensued, pitting the idea of "the greatest good for the greatest number in the long run" against the idea of the inviolability of national parks. By the standards of the Progressive era, the virtue of a publicly owned water supply source superseded that of a beautiful valley in a national park. After a long struggle, the dam was built.

Established in October 1890, the 761,266-acre Yosemite National Park protects the superlative landscape of the Yosemite Valley in east-central California. Entrance fees are $10

per person or $20 per vehicle and are valid for seven days; a $40 annual pass is also available. The park's visitor centers are in Yosemite Valley (open year-round) and Tuolumne Meadows (summer only), and information stations are in Wawona (spring–fall) and Big Oak Flat (spring–fall). The Yosemite Museum is open year-round from 9 A.M. until 4:30 P.M. It features displays that interpret the cultural history of Yosemite's native Miwok and Paiute people from 1850 to the present. The Indian Village of Ahwahnee is a reconstructed Miwok village, and demonstrations of basket weaving, beadwork, and/or traditional games are presented during the summer months.

The park also maintains wilderness centers and permit stations in Yosemite Valley (spring–fall; visitor center during winter) and Tuolumne Meadows (summer only). Wilderness permits are also issued at the Wawona Information Station (spring–fall), Big Oak Flat Information Station (spring–fall), and Hetch Hetchy Entrance Station (summer only). Visitors will enjoy touring the Yosemite Valley and its high cliffs and waterfalls; Wawona's history center and historic hotel; the Mariposa Grove, which contains hundreds of ancient giant sequoias; Glacier Point's (summer–fall) spectacular view of Yosemite Valley and the high country; Tuolumne Meadows (summer–fall), a large subalpine meadow surrounded by mountain peaks; and Hetch Hetchy, a reservoir in a valley considered a twin of Yosemite Valley.

A number of traveler facilities and services are available in the park. Yosemite Concession Services Corporation (559-252-4848) operates a variety of lodging units in Yosemite that range from basic cabins to high-end rooms. The concession also operates 5 High Sierra Camps (559-253-5674), which are spaced 5.7 to 10 miles apart along a loop trail in Yosemite's beautiful high country. All lodging is in canvas tent cabins that have dormitory-style steel frame beds with mattresses, pillows, woolen blankets, and comforters. Hot showers, soap, and rest room facilities are available; however, guests must provide their own sheets or sleeping bags and towels. In addition, there are 13 campgrounds in Yosemite National Park, and camping reservations for up to 7 of these campgrounds are available five months in advance. Wawona, Hodgdon Meadow, and 2 campgrounds in Yosemite Valley are open all year. Traveler services are also available in several surrounding towns and communities.

For more information, write Yosemite National Park, P.O. Box 577, Yosemite National Park, CA 95389, or telephone (209) 372-0200. The park's Web site is www. nps.gov/yose.

FURTHER READING
Cohen, Michael P. *The Pathless Way: John Muir and American Wilderness.* Madison: University of Wisconsin Press, 1999.

Ehrlich, Gretel. *John Muir: Nature's Visionary.* New York: National Geographic, 2000.

Meyerson, Harvey. *Nature's Army: When Soldiers Fought for Yosemite.* Lawrence: University Press of Kansas, 2001.

Muir, John. *John Muir: Nature Writings: The Story of My Boyhood and Youth; My First Summer in the Sierra; The Mountains of California; Stickeen; Essays.* New York: Library of America, 1997.

Runte, Alfred. *Yosemite: The Embattled Wilderness.* Lincoln: University of Nebraska Press, 1993.

YUCCA HOUSE NATIONAL MONUMENT

Location: Cortez, Colorado
Acreage: 34
Established: December 19, 1919

Finding Yucca House National Monument is one of the great adventures in the national park system. Located down a small dirt road a few miles from Cortez, Colorado, the monument has no facilities of any kind. A traveler parks on a rancher's property and walks across a stile, a device that has stairs on each side and a walkway between, over the fence, and into one of the least disturbed and most remote national park areas in the lower forty-eight states.

Originally set aside in December 1919, Yucca House National Monument preserves a large Pueblo-culture surface site in southwestern Colorado, west of Mesa Verde National Park between the towns of Towaoc and Cortez. The ancient structures are on the gently sloping base of the Sleeping Ute Mountain. The name "Yucca House" was selected for the monument because the Ute Indians called Sleeping Ute Mountain by a native name meaning yucca, because there is an abundance of the yucca plant growing on the mountainsides.

The 34-acre park is now a cluster of mounds with no sign of a wall rising above the surface. It has been managed under a policy of conservation archeology for more than a generation; in this strategy, the park's resources are to be left buried until a later date, when new technologies will offer better opportunities to assess the materials within. As a result of the large size and extent of the mounds, there is every reason to believe that, when excavated, they will prove of great archeological significance. The land upon which Yucca House resides (approximately 10 acres) was a gift from the late Henry Van Kleeck of Denver, Colorado, and the stone used to build Yucca House is mainly fossiliferous limestone that outcrops along the base of the Mesa Verde tableland a mile away.

The mounds have been known for many years and were first described by Professor William Henry Holmes, one of the leading explorers of the American West, in 1877. Holmes designated the 2 most conspicuous mounds as the "Upper House" and the "Lower House." The "Upper House" is the most prominent of all the mounds in this ancient site, rising from 15 to 20 feet above its foundation and dominating the many smaller mounds that surround it. The "Lower House" is different, and it stands isolated 100 yards from the cluster of mounds that compose and include the "Upper House."

A trip to the monument offers a glimpse into what it must have been like to visit southwestern archeological sites in the 1920s. Yucca House is remote, and there is little more than a visitor register there. Nearly a century ago, most national monuments were protected by a part-time custodian, who lived elsewhere and came to the site only when visitation was expected. A casual visitor was likely to encounter solitude and mystery, much as a visitor might at Yucca House today. This vision of the past offers another reason to brave the difficult roads to reach this distant locale.

The Park Service does not recommend travel to this monument for the casual visitor. There are currently no facilities at the monument, and the dirt road to Yucca House is impassable in wet weather. Admission is free.

There are no food, lodging, or camping facilities at the national monument, but all traveler services are available in Cortez, Durango, and Mancos.

For more information, write Yucca House National Monument, Mesa Verde National Park, P.O. Box 8, Mesa Verde, CO 81330, or telephone (970) 529-4465. The park's Web site is www.nps.gov/yuho.

FURTHER READING

Anderson, Dale. *The Anasazi Culture at Mesa Verde.* Milwaukee, WI: World Almanac Education, 2003.

Brody, J.J. *The Anasazi: Ancient Indian People of the American Southwest.* New York: Rizzoli, 1990.

YUKON-CHARLEY RIVERS NATIONAL PRESERVE

Location: Eagle, Alaska
Acreage: 2,526,512
Established: December 1, 1978

Another of the many parks created from ANILCA (Alaska National Interest Lands Conservation Act), Yukon-Charley Rivers National Preserve is one of the largest and wildest of the nation's park areas. Spanning more than 2.5-million acres along the U.S.-Canadian border, the preserve is upriver from Dawson, the center of the Klondike Gold Rush at the turn of the twentieth century. Human habitation in the region may date back eleven thousand years, but during the centuries prior to Euro-American arrival, two different Athapaskan speaking groups, the Han and Kutchakutchin, made the area home. The subsistence economy dictated that native populations remain small.

The discovery of gold on the Yukon River inaugurated a series of permanent changes. Before the Klondike Gold Rush, the Circle Mining District was filled with miners already in search of the precious metal. The Klondike discovery in 1897 sent the Circle District miners rushing downriver, draining the region of its Euro-American population. Crowded out of the best strikes in Dawson, the miners again spread out, returning to the area that is now Yukon-Charley Rivers National Preserve. In 1898, miners laid their claims on Fourth of July Creek. More followed, staking their own claims on Woodchopper Creek and Coal Creek in 1902. The remains of mining cabins and historic sites dot the preserve's landscape and recall the heyday of the gold rush.

Established in December 1978, the over-2.5-million-acre Yukon-Charley Rivers National Preserve protects 115 miles of the Yukon River and the entire 1.1-million-acre watershed of the Charley River, which itself is a National Wild River. The preserve is open year-round and admission is free. The field office in Eagle is open daily from 8 A.M. until 5 P.M. from mid-May to mid-September, and on weekdays from 8 A.M. until 5 P.M. for the remainder of the year. The center has exhibits on the area, history, and ecology of Yukon-Charley Rivers, a short video presentation on the preserve, as well as area-specific videos, and park rangers offer nature hikes, talks, and campfire programs. The Fairbanks office is open all year, Monday through Friday, from 8 A.M. until 4:30 P.M. Rafting, kayaking, and canoeing are popular on the Yukon River. Power boats are also permitted; however, personal watercraft such as jet skis are not. Many visitors start their trip in Eagle and end in Circle, arranging either to be picked up, or to be flown back to Eagle. Longer trips, from Dawson or Whitehorse to the lower Yukon or Bering Sea, are also popular ways of traveling the Yukon through the preserve. Rafting or kayaking the Charley River is also an excellent way to visit Yukon-Charley Rivers.

Yukon-Charley Rivers National Preserve is primarily a wilderness, and there are no commercial facilities of any kind located within the preserve. However, there are currently 7 public-use cabins located within the preserve. The cabins are along the Yukon River and its tributaries, located at Nation Bluff, Glenn Creek, Washington Creek, Kandik River mouth, and 3 cabins in the Coal Creek area. These cabins are available on a first-come, first-served basis. All traveler services are available in Circle and Eagle.

Although there is no road access, two highways serve towns near the preserve boundaries. The 161-mile Taylor Highway begins at Tetlin Junction on the Alaska Highway and ends at Eagle, 12 miles from the preserve. It is usually open from mid-April to mid-October and is suitable for cars. The Steese Highway is open year-round; it begins in Fairbanks and travels 162 miles to Circle, 14 miles from the preserve. In good weather it takes about five hours to drive either of these gravel roads.

For more information, write Yukon-Charley Rivers National Preserve, Eagle Ranger Station (Field Office), P.O. Box 167, Eagle, AK 99738, or telephone (907) 547-2233. The park's informative Web site is www.nps.gov/yuch.

FURTHER READING
Beckstead, Douglas. *The World Turned Upside Down: A History of Mining on Coal Creek and Woodchopper Creek, Yukon-Charley Rivers National Preserve.* Anchorage, AK: National Park Service, 2000.

Conger, Horace. *In Search of Gold: The Alaska Journals of Horace S. Conger, 1898–1899.* Anchorage: Alaska Geographic Society, 1983.

Ducker, James H. *Alaska's Upper Yukon Region: A History.* Anchorage, AK: Bureau of Land Management, 1983.

Norris, Frank. *Gold in Alaska: A Century of Mining History in Alaska's National Parks.* Anchorage, AK: National Park Service, 1997.

Z

ZION NATIONAL PARK

Location: Springdale, Utah
Acreage: 146,598
Established: July 31, 1909

Zion National Park is one of the wonders of the national park system, a place of beauty and power. One of the red rock parks and a part of the "Golden Circle" of travel that linked early national park areas, Zion has a revered place in the history of American preservation. Layer upon layer of humanity found a home in its canyons, and it has become one of the important stops on any voyage through the western national parks.

Zion's history as national park area began early in the twentieth century, during the first great burst of national park area establishment. In 1909, Mukuntuweap National Monument was established in Zion Canyon under the terms of the Antiquities Act of 1906. The new monument was largely symbolic. Few could reach it, for the roads in the area were abysmal and the closest railhead was about 100 miles away. Mukuntuweap reflected the predisposition for spectacular nature that marked the early national parks, and its economic possibilities were limited in comparison. Even before the prospect of many visitors, its reservation made considerable sense in Utah in the early 1900s.

Zion's change in status to national park followed a prevailing pattern in the early history of the national park system. Because national monuments could be created without congressional approval, the category became a storehouse for areas that awaited transfer to national park status. Even after its name change to the easily pronounceable "Zion National Monument" in 1916, national park status seemed remote.

A combination of factors quickly rectified the situation. Despite the protests of Utah Governor Simon Bamberger, who announced that he would build no more roads to rocks, the Utah State Road Commission constructed a state highway system that improved access to the southern part of the state. National Park Service Director Stephen T. Mather en-

Hiking in spectacular Zion National Park. *(National Park Service)*

visioned a "Golden Circle" of travel that included Zion, and his plans put the area on the fast track to national park status. At Mather's behest, the Union Pacific Railroad developed rail and automobile links and tourism facilities in southern Utah. By the summer of 1917, touring cars could finally reach Wylie Camp, a tent camping resort that comprised the first visitor lodging in Zion Canyon, from the rail depot at Lund, Utah, nearly 100 miles distant. Within a very few years, the Union Pacific had not only built a branch line from Lund to nearby Cedar City, but through its subsidiary, the Utah Parks Company, developed auto travel and facilities at the North Rim of the Grand Canyon, at Bryce Canyon, and in Death Valley. Zion's spectacular scenery served as the catalyst for the establishment of this park. Mather's innovative development skills and close ties to power brought the project to fruition.

Zion National Park protects a spectacular cliff-and-canyon landscape and wilderness full of the unexpected, including the world's largest arch–Kolob Arch–with a span that measures 310 feet. In addition, 75 species of mammals, 271 birds, 32 reptiles and amphibians, and 8 fish call the park "home." Commonly seen animals include mule deer, rock squirrels, lizards, and many species of birds. Rare or endangered species protected by the park include the peregrine falcon, Mexican spotted owl, Southwest willow flycatcher, desert tortoise, and the Zion snail, found nowhere else on earth. Park entrance fees are $10 per person or $20 per vehicle and are valid for seven days; a $40 annual pass is also available. The park's 2 visitor centers are open year-round and offer a variety of exhibits. The Zion Canyon Visitor Center, located 1 mile from the south entrance, is open daily from 8 A.M. until 5 P.M. and features a fifteen-minute orientation video and exhibits on the natural and cultural history of the area. Kolob Canyons Visitor Center, located off I-15 at exit 40, 45 miles north of Springdale and 17 miles south of Cedar City, is open daily from 8 A.M. until 4:30 P.M., and it has exhibits that explain the geology of the area.

Overlooks and trails abound along scenic drives through Zion, and there are ranger programs at most developed areas year-round. The variety of mountain and canyon environments makes Zion an excellent location for wildflower walks in the spring and summer and brilliant leaf color in the autumn. The Pa'rus Trail offers a paved, car-free alternative for bicyclists, pedestrians, and people with strollers or wheelchairs to visit lower Zion Canyon and access the scenic drive. During the summer, park rangers offer guided walks, short talks at the visitor centers, and evening programs at the campground amphitheaters and Zion Lodge. All programs are free.

Accommodations are available in the park at Zion Lodge (303–297-2757), located 3 miles north on the Zion Canyon Scenic Drive. Open year-round, the lodge has motel rooms, cabins, and suites available, as well as a restaurant, gift shop, and post office. Lodging is also available in Springdale, Rockville, Mount Carmel Junction, Kanab, and other nearby towns. The park also maintains 3 campgrounds: Lava Point, open from June through October; Watchman, open from April through October; and South Campground, open year-round. Fees and facilities vary.

For more information, write Zion National Park, SR 9, Springdale, UT 84767-1099, or telephone (435) 772-3256. The park's Web site is www.nps.gov/zion.

FURTHER READING

Alexander, Thomas G. *Utah: The Right Place.* Salt Lake City, UT: Gibbs Smith, 1996.

Crawford, J.L. *Zion Album: A Nostalgic History of Zion Canyon.* Springdale, UT: Zion Natural History Association, 1986.

——. *Zion National Park: Towers of Stone.* Springdale, UT: Zion Natural History Association, 1988.

Garate, Donald T. *The Zion Tunnel: From Slickrock to Switchback.* Springdale, UT: Zion Natural History Association, 1989.

Hamilton, Wayne L. *Sculpturing of Zion: Guide to the Geology of Zion.* Springdale, UT: Zion Natural History Association, 1984.

Leach, Nicky. *Zion National Park: Sanctuary in the Desert.* San Francisco: Sierra, 2000.

Stegner, Wallace Earle. *Mormon Country.* Lincoln: University of Nebraska Press, 1981.

Wauer, Roland H. *Birds of Zion National Park and Vicinity.* Logan: Utah State University, 1997.

Welsh, Stanley L. *Wildflowers of Zion National Park.* Springdale, UT: Zion Natural History Association, 1999.

BIBLIOGRAPHY

Abbey, Edward. *Desert Solitaire.* New York: Ballantine Books, 1991.

——. *The Monkey Wrench Gang.* New York: HarperPerennial, 2000.

Abbot, W.W. *The Young George Washington and His Papers.* Charlottesville: University of Virginia, 1999.

Abbott, E.C., and Helen Huntington Smith. *We Pointed Them North: Recollections of a Cowpuncher.* Norman: University of Oklahoma Press, 1978.

Adams, Edward C.L. *Tales of the Congaree.* Chapel Hill: University of North Carolina Press, 1987.

Adams, Henry. *The War of 1812.* Edited by H.A. DeWeerd. New York: Cooper Square, 1999.

Adovasio, J.M. *The First Americans: In Pursuit of Archaeology's Greatest Mystery.* New York: Random House, 2002.

Agate Fossil Beds: Agate Fossil Beds National Monument, Nebraska. Washington, DC: Government Printing Office, 1988.

Ahler, Stanley A., Thomas D. Thiessen, and Michael K. Trimble. *People of the Willows: The Prehistory and Early History of the Hidatsa Indians.* Grand Forks: University of North Dakota Press, 1991.

Albert, Richard C. *Damming the Delaware: The Rise and Fall of Tocks Island Dam.* State College: Pennsylvania State University Press, 1987.

Alberts, Robert C. *A Charming Field for an Encounter: The Story of George Washington's Fort Necessity.* Washington, DC: National Park Service, 1975.

Albright, Horace M. *Oh, Ranger!* Palo Alto, CA: Stanford University Press, 1928.

——. as told to Robert Cahn. *The Birth of the National Park Service: The Founding Years, 1913–1933.* Salt Lake City, UT: Howe Brothers, 1985.

Albright, John. *Kohrs and Bielenberg Home Ranch: Grant-Kohrs Ranch National Historic Site, Montana: Historic Resource Study and Historic Structure Report, Historical Data.* Denver, CO: Historic Preservation Division, National Park Service, 1977.

Alden, John R. *A History of the American Revolution.* New York: DaCapo, 1989.

Alderman, J. Anthony. *Wildflowers of the Blue Ridge Parkway.* Chapel Hill: University of North Carolina Press, 1997.

Alexander, Doris. *Eugene O'Neill's Creative Struggle: The Decisive Decade, 1924–1933.* University Park: Pennsylvania State University Press, 1992.

Alexander, James. *A Brief Narrative of the Case and Trial of John Peter Zenger, Printer of the New York Weekly Journal.* Edited by Stanley Nider Katz. Cambridge, MA: Belknap Press of Harvard University Press, 1972.

Alexander, Thomas G. *Utah: The Right Place.* Salt Lake City, UT: Gibbs Smith, 1996.

Allen, Everett S. *Children of the Light: The Rise and Fall of New Bedford Whaling and the Death of the Arctic Fleet.* Boston: Little, Brown, 1973.

Allen, Robert L. *The Port Chicago Mutiny.* New York: Penguin, 1993.

Allen, Thomas B. *The Washington Monument: It Stands for All.* New York: Discovery Books, 2000.

Almaraz, Felix D., Jr. *The San Antonio Missions and Their System of Land Tenure.* Austin: University of Texas Press, 1989.

Alt, David D., and Donald W. Hyndman. *Roadside Geology of Northern and Central California.* Missoula, MT: Mountain, 2000.

Ambrose, Stephen E. *Eisenhower: Soldier and President.* New York: Simon and Schuster, 1990.

——. *Crazy Horse and Custer: The Parallel Lives of Two American Warriors.* New York: Anchor Books, 1996.

——. *Undaunted Courage: Meriwether Lewis, Thomas Jefferson, and the Opening of the American West.* New York: Simon and Schuster, 1996.

——. *Nothing Like It in the World: The Men Who Built the Transcontinental Railroad, 1865–1869.* New York: Simon and Schuster, 2000.

——. *The Mississippi and the Making of a Nation.* Washington, DC: National Geographic, 2002.

Anderson, Dale. *The Anasazi Culture at Mesa Verde.* Milwaukee, WI: World Almanac Education, 2003.

Anderson, Donald F. *William Howard Taft: A Conservative's Conception of the Presidency.* Ithaca, NY: Cornell University Press, 1973.

Anderson, Olive M. *Pictured Rocks National Lakeshore: An Illustrated Guide.* Munising, MI: Bayshore Press, 1988.

Anfinson, John O. *The River We Have Wrought: A History of the Upper Mississippi.* Minneapolis: University of Minnesota Press, 2003.

Anglin, Ron, ed. *Forgotten Trails: Historical Sources of the Columbia's Big Bend Country.* Pullman: Washington State University Press, 1995.

Apostle Islands: A Guide to Apostle Islands National Lakeshore, Wisconsin. Washington, DC: National Park Service, 1988.

Arato, Christine A., and Patrick L. Eleey. *Safely Moored at Last: Cultural Landscape Report for New Bedford Whaling National Historical Park.* Boston: National Park Service, 1998.

Arnold, Morris S. *Colonial Arkansas, 1686–1804: A Social and Cultural History.* Fayetteville: University of Arkansas Press, 1991.

Arnosky, Jim. *Wild Ponies.* Washington, DC: National Geographic Society, 2002.

Aron, Stephen. *How the West Was Lost: The Transformation of Kentucky from Daniel Boone to Henry Clay.* Baltimore, MD: Johns Hopkins University Press, 1996.

Ashworth, William. *The Late Great Lakes: An Environmental History.* Detroit: Wayne State University Press, 1987.

At Home in the Smokies: A History Handbook for Great Smoky Mountains National Park, North Carolina and Tennessee. Washington, DC: National Park Service, 1984.

Atherton, Lewis. *The Cattle Kings.* Bloomington: Indiana University Press, 1971.

Atkinson, Richard. *White Sands: Wind, Sand, and Time.* Globe, AZ: Southwest Parks and Monuments Association, 1977.

Auchincloss, Louis. *The Vanderbilt Era: Profiles of a Gilded Age.* New York: Collier Books, 1990.

Averkieva, Julia. "The Tlingit Indians." In *North American Indians in Historical Perspective,* 317–42. New York: Random House, 1971.

Ayers, Edward L., and John C. Willis, eds. *The Edge of the South: Life in Nineteenth-Century Virginia.* Charlottesville: University Press of Virginia, 1991.

Baars, Donald L. *Canyonlands Country: Geology of Canyonlands and Arches National Park.* Salt Lake City: University of Utah Press, 1994.

——. *The Colorado Plateau: A Geologic History.* Albuquerque: University of New Mexico Press, 2000.

Babbitt, James E. *Rainbow Trails: Early-Day Adventures in Rainbow Bridge Country.* Page, AZ: Glen Canyon Natural History Association, 1990.

Babits, Lawrence E. *A Devil of a Whipping: The Battle of Cowpens.* Chapel Hill: University of North Carolina Press, 2001.

Badger, Curtis J. *The Barrier Islands: A Photographic History of Life on Hog, Cobb, Smith, Cedar, Parramore, Metompkin, & Assateague.* Harrisburg, PA: Stackpole Books, 1989.

Bahne, Charles. *The Complete Guide to Boston's Freedom Trail.* Cambridge, MA: Newtowne, 1993.

Bailyn, Bernard. *The Ideological Origins of the American Revolution.* Cambridge, MA: Belknap, 1992.

Bain, David Howard. *Empire Express: Building the First Transcontinental Railroad.* New York: Viking, 1999.

Baker, Thomas E. *Another Such Victory: The Story of the American Defeat at Guilford Courthouse That Helped Win the War for Independence.* New York: Eastern Acorn, 1981.

Ball, Robert W.D. *Springfield Armory Shoulder Weapons, 1795–1968.* Norfolk, VA: Antique Trader Books, 1997.

Bandelier, Adoph Francis Alphonse. *Historical Introduction to Studies Among the Sedentary Indians of New Mexico; Report on the Ruins of the Pueblo of Pecos.* New York: AMS Press, 1976.

Bandelier National Monument: An Administrative History. Santa Fe, NM: National Park Service, 1988. Available at www.nps.gov/band.

Banner, Lois W. *Elizabeth Cady Stanton: A Radical for Women's Rights.* Boston: Little, Brown, 1980.

Barbour, Barton H. *Fort Union and the Upper Missouri Fur Trade.* Norman: University of Oklahoma Press, 2001.

Barnes, F.A. *Canyonlands National Park: Early History and First Descriptions: An Illustrated Guide to the Study and Appreciation of the Early History of Canyonlands National Park.* Moab, UT: Canyon Country, 1988.

Barnes, Jay. *Florida's Hurricane History.* Chapel Hill: University of North Carolina Press, 1998.

Barringer, Mark Daniel. *Selling Yellowstone: Capitalism and the Construction of Nature.* Lawrence: University Press of Kansas, 2002.

Basler, Roy P., ed. *Abraham Lincoln: His Speeches and Writings.* New York: Da Capo, 1990.

Bass, Robert D. *Ninety Six, the Struggle for the South Carolina Back Country.* Lexington, SC: Sandlapper Store, 1978.

Bates, Daisy. *The Long Shadow of Little Rock: A Memoir.* Fayetteville: University of Arkansas Press, 1987.

Battle of Kings Mountain 1780, with Fire and Sword. Washington, DC: Government Printing Office, 1991.

Bauer, Erwin A., and Peggy Bauer. *Denali: The Wild Beauty of Denali National Park.* Seattle, WA: Sasquatch Books, 2000.

Beal, Merrill D., and Herman J. Deutsch. *I Will Fight No More Forever: Chief Joseph and the Nez Perce War.* New York: Ballantine Books, 1971.

Beals, Melba. *Warriors Don't Cry: A Searing Memoir of the Battle to Integrate Little Rock's Central High.* New York: Pocket Books, 1995.

Bearr, David W.C., ed. *Historic Fluvanna in the Commonwealth of Virginia: A Sketchbook of the People, Places and Events of Fluvanna County, Virginia.* Palmyra, VA: Fluvanna County Historical Society, 1998.

Bearss, Edwin C. *Arkansas Post National Memorial, Arkansas; Structural History Post of Arkansas, 1804–1863, and Civil War Troop Movement Maps, January, 1863.* Washington, DC: Office of History and Historic Architecture, Eastern Service Center, 1971.

——. *The Battle of Wilson's Creek.* Diamond, MO: George Washington Carver Birthplace District Association, 1975.

——. *Fort Smith, Little Gibraltar on the Arkansas.* Norman: University of Oklahoma Press, 1979.

——. *Historic Resource Study, Fort Hancock 1895–1948, Gateway National Recreation Area, New York.* Denver, CO: Denver Service Center, Historic Preservation Division, National Park Service, 1981.

——. *Fort Barrancas, Gulf Islands National Seashore, Florida.* Denver, CO: Denver Service Center, National Park Service, 1983.

——. *Fort on Ship Island (Fort Massachusetts), 1857–1935: Gulf Islands National Seashore, Harrison County, Mississippi.* Denver, CO: Denver Service Center, National Park Service, 1984.

——. *San Juan Fortifications, 1898–1958.* Denver, CO: National Park Service, Denver Service Center, 1984.

Beatty, Jerome. *From New Bedford to Siberia: A Yankee Whaleman in the Frozen North.* Garden City, NY: Doubleday, 1977.

Beck, Warren A. *New Mexico: A History of Four Centuries.* Norman: University of Oklahoma Press, 1987.

Beckey, Fred W. *Range of Glaciers: The Exploration and Survey of the Northern Cascade Range.* Portland: Oregon Historical Society Press, 2002.

Beckham, Stephen Dow, with Florence K. Lentz. *John Day Fossil Beds National Monument: Rocks & Hard Places: Historic Resources Study.* Seattle, WA: National Park Service, 2000.

Beckstead, Douglas. *The World Turned Upside Down: A History of Mining on Coal Creek and Woodchopper Creek, Yukon-Charley Rivers National Preserve.* Anchorage, AK: National Park Service, 2000.

Bedinger, M.S., et al. *The Waters of Hot Springs National Park, Arkansas—Their Nature and Origin.* Washington, DC: U.S. Government Printing Office, 1979.

Bell, James B. *In Search of Liberty: The Story of the Statue of Liberty and Ellis Island.* Garden City, NY: Doubleday, 1984.

Benedict, Michael Les. *The Impeachment and Trial of Andrew Johnson.* New York: W.W. Norton, 1999.

Benn, David W., ed. *Woodland Cultures on the Western Prairies: The Rainbow Site Investigations.* Iowa City: Office of the State Archaeologist, University of Iowa, 1990.

Bennett, Charles E. *Laudonniere and Fort Caroline: History and Documents.* Tuscaloosa: University of Alabama Press, 2001.

Benton, Lisa. *The Presidio: From Army Post to National Park.* Boston: Northeastern University Press, 1998.

Beres, Nancy, Mitzi Chandler, and Russell Dalton, eds. *Island of Rivers: An Anthology Celebrating 50 Years of Olympic National Park.* Seattle, WA: Pacific Northwest National Parks & Forests, 1988.

Berton, Pierre. *Klondike: The Last Great Gold Rush, 1896–1899.* Toronto: McClelland and Stewart, 1972.

Beschloss, Michael R. *The Conquerors: Roosevelt, Truman and the Destruction of Hitler's Germany, 1941–1945.* New York: Simon and Schuster, 2002.

Bethel, Rodman. *A Slumbering Giant of the Past: Fort Jefferson, USA in the Dry Tortugas.* Key West: Florida Flair Books, 1979.

Bethune, Mary McLeod. *Building a Better World: Essays and Selected Documents.* Bloomington: Indiana University Press, 1999.

Betts, Robert B. *Along the Ramparts of the Tetons: The Saga of Jackson Hole, Wyoming.* Boulder: University Press of Colorado, 2001.

Beus, Stanley S., and Michael Morales, eds. *Grand Canyon Geology.* New York: Oxford University Press, 2002.

Bezy, John V. *Bryce Canyon: The Story Behind the Scenery.* Las Vegas, NV: KC Publications, 1980.

Bezy, John V., and Arthur S. Trevena. *Guide to Geologic Features at Petrified Forest National Park.* Tucson: Arizona Geological Survey, 2000.

Bezy, John V., James T. Gutmann, and Gordon B. Haxel. *A Guide to the Geology of Organ Pipe Cactus National Monument and the Pinacate Biosphere Reserve.* Tucson: Arizona Geological Survey, 2000.

Bird, William L., and Harry R. Rubenstein. *Design for Victory: World War II Posters on the American Home Front.* New York: Princeton Architectural, 1998.

Black, Allida M. *Casting Her Own Shadow: Eleanor*

Roosevelt and the Shaping of Postwar Liberalism. New York: Columbia University Press, 1996.

Blair, Richard P. *Point Reyes Visions: Photographs and Essays, Point Reyes National Seashore and West Marin.* Inverness, CA: Color and Light Editions, 1999.

Blakeslee, Charles A., et al. *Wild and Beautiful Crater Lake.* Helena, MT: Farcountry Press, 2001.

Blank, Joan Gill. *Key Biscayne: A History of Miami's Tropical Island and the Cape Florida Lighthouse.* Sarasota, FL: Pineapple, 1998.

Bleser, Nicholas J. *Tumacácori From Ranchería to National Monument.* Tucson, AZ: Southwest Parks and Monuments Association, 1988.

Blewett, Mary H. *The Last Generation: Work and Life in the Textile Mills of Lowell, Massachusetts, 1910–1960.* Amherst: University of Massachusetts Press, 1990.

Blumberg, Barbara. *Celebrating the Immigrant: An Administrative History of the Statue of Liberty National Monument, 1952–1982.* Boston: National Park Service, 1985. Available at www.cr.nps.gov/history/online_books/stli/adhi.htm.

Blythe, Robert W. *Kennesaw Mountain National Battlefield Park: Historic Resource Study.* Atlanta, GA: National Park Service, Southeast Region, 1995.

Blythe, Robert W., Emily Kleine, and Steven H. Moffson. *Charles Pinckney: Historic Resource Study.* Atlanta, GA: Southeast Regional Office, National Park Service, 2000. Available at www.nps.gov/chpi/hrs/hrs.htm.

Blythe, Robert W., Maureen A. Carroll, and Steven H. Moffson. *Martin Luther King, Jr., National Historic Site: Historic Resource Study.* Atlanta, GA: National Park Service, 1994. Available at www.nps.gov/malu/hrs/hrs.htm.

Bodle, Wayne K. *The Valley Forge Winter: Civilians and Soldiers in War.* University Park: Pennsylvania State University Press, 2002.

Boehm, William D. *Glacier Bay: Old Ice, New Land.* Anchorage: Alaska Geographic Society, 1975.

Bogard, Travis. *Eugene O'Neill at Tao House.* Tucson, AZ: Southwest Parks and Monuments, 1989.

——. *From the Silence of Tao House: Essays About Eugene and Carlotta O'Neill and the Tao House Plays.* Danville, CA: Eugene O'Neill Foundation, 1993.

Bohn, Dave. *Glacier Bay: The Land and the Silence.* Anchorage: Alaska Natural History Association, 1997.

Bolger, Doreen. *J. Alden Weir: An American Impressionist.* Newark: University of Delaware Press, 1983.

Booraem, Hendrik. *The Road to Respectability: James A. Garfield and His World, 1844–1852.* Lewisburg, PA: Bucknell University Press, 1988.

Borden, James D., and Roger W. Brucker. *Beyond Mammoth Cave: A Tale of Obsession in the World's Longest Cave.* Carbondale: Southern Illinois University Press, 2000.

Bowen, Catherine Drinker. *Miracle at Philadelphia: The Story of the Constitutional Convention May to September, 1787.* New York: Book-of-the-Month Club, 1986.

Bowman, Jon. *Montezuma: The Castle in the West.* Santa Fe: New Mexico Magazine, 2002.

Boyd, James P., Jr. *The Challenges of Roger Williams: Religious Liberty, Violent Persecution, and the Bible.* Macon, GA: Mercer University Press, 2002.

Bradford, James E. *Archeological Survey: Gila Cliff Dwellings National Monument.* Santa Fe, NM: Division of Anthropology, National Park Service, 1992.

Branch, Taylor. *Pillar of Fire: America in the King Years, 1963–65.* New York: Simon and Schuster, 1998.

Brand, Donald D. *The History of Scotts Bluff Nebraska.* Berkeley, CA: National Park Service, Field Division of Education, 1934. Available at www.cr.nps.gov/history/online_books/berkeley/brand1/index.htm.

Brands, H.W. *T.R.: The Last Romantic.* New York: Basic Books, 1997.

——. *The First American: The Life and Times of Benjamin Franklin.* New York: Doubleday, 2000.

——. *The Age of Gold: The California Gold Rush and the New American Dream.* New York: Doubleday, 2002.

Bransilver, Connie. *Florida's Unsung Wilderness: The Swamps.* Englewood, CO: Westcliffe, 2000.

Branson, John B. *Bristol Bay, Alaska: From the Hinterlands to Tidewater: A Grassroots Pictorial, 1885–1965.* Anchorage, AK: National Park Service, 1998.

Brantley, W.H. *Battle of Horseshoe Bend.* Birmingham, AL: Southern University Press, 1955.

Breiter, Matthias. *The Bears of Katmai: Alaska's Famous Brown Bears.* Portland, OR: Graphic Arts Center, 2001.

Bremer, J. Michael. *Walnut Canyon Settlement and Land Use.* Phoenix: Arizona Archaeological Society, 1989.

Brill, Charles J., and Mark L Gardner. *Custer, Black Kettle, and the Fight on the Washita.* Norman: University of Oklahoma Press, 2002.

Brinkley, Douglas. *The Unfinished Presidency: Jimmy Carter's Journey Beyond the White House.* New York: Viking, 1998.

Brody, J.J. *The Anasazi: Ancient Indian People of the American Southwest.* New York: Rizzoli, 1990.

Brooke, Steven. *The Majesty of Natchez.* Gretna, LA: Pelican, 1999.

Brooker, James H. *Father Damien, the Lands of Kalaupapa, Molokai, Hawaii.* Kaunakaki, HI: Molokai Fish and Dive Corporation, 1998.

Brooks, Elizabeth, et al. *The Llano Estacado of the US Southern High Plains: Environmental Transformation and the Prospect for Sustainability.* New York: United Nations University Press, 2000.

Brooksher, William R. *Bloody Hill: The Civil War Battle of Wilson's Creek.* Washington: Brassey's, 1995.

Brown, Dee. *Bury My Heart at Wounded Knee: An Indian History of the American West.* New York: Henry Holt, 2001.

Brown, Dee Alexander. *The American Spa: Hot Springs, Arkansas.* Little Rock, AR: Rose, 1982.

Brown, Jennifer D. *Castillo de San Marcos National Monument Historic Resource Study.* Atlanta, GA: National Park Service, 1997. Available at www.nps.gov/casa/hrs/hrs.htm.

Brown, Joseph E. *Monarchs of the Mist: The Story of Redwood National Park and the Coast Redwoods.* Point Reyes, CA: Coastal Parks Association, 1982.

Brown, Kenneth A. *Four Corners: History, Land and People of the Desert Southwest.* New York: Harper Perennial, 1996.

Brown, Lenard E. *National Capital Parks: Fort Stanton, Fort Foote, and Battery Ricketts.* Washington, DC: Office of History and Historic Architecture, Eastern Service Center, 1970.

Brown, Margaret L. *The Wild East: A Biography of the Great Smoky Mountains.* Gainesville: University Press of Florida, 2000.

Broyles, Bill. *Organ Pipe Cactus National Monument: Where Edges Meet: A Sonoran Desert Sanctuary.* Tucson, AZ: Southwest Parks and Monuments Association, 1996.

Brucksch, John P. *Old Stone House, Rock Creek Park, National Capital Region, Washington, D.C.* Harpers Ferry, WV: National Park Service, 1986.

Brugge, David M. *Hubbell Trading Post: National Historic Site.* Tucson, AZ: Southwest Parks and Monuments Association, 1993.

Buchholtz, C.W. *Rocky Mountain National Park.* Niwot: University Press of Colorado, 1983.

Bullard, Mary. *Cumberland Island: A History.* Athens: University of Georgia Press, 2002.

Bullitt, Alexander C. *Rambles in the Mammoth Cave During the Year 1844 by a Visiter* [sic]. St. Louis, MO: Cave Books, 1985.

Burchard, Peter. *One Gallant Rush: Robert Gould Shaw and His Brave Black Regiment.* New York: St. Martin's, 1965.

Burcker, Roger W., and Richard A. Watson. *The Longest Cave.* Carbondale: Southern Illinois University Press, 1976.

Burnett, Georgellen. *We Just Toughed It Out: Women in the Llano Estacado.* El Paso: Texas Western, 1990.

Burns, Ken. *Jazz—A Film by Ken Burns.* Walpole, NH: PBS Home Video, 2001.

Burrows, Evan G., and Mike Wallace. *Gotham: A History of New York to 1898.* New York: Oxford University Press, 1998.

Burton, David Henry. *Taft, Wilson, and World Order.* Madison, NJ: Fairleigh Dickinson University Press, 2003.

Burton, Jeffery F., et al. *Confinement and Ethnicity: An Overview of World War II Japanese American Relocation Sites.* Seattle: University of Washington Press, 2002.

Bushong, William. *Historic Resource Study: Rock Creek Park, District of Columbia.* Washington, DC: National Park Service, 1990.

Butler, M.E. *Prophet of the Parks: The Story of William Penn Mott, Jr.* Ashburn, VA: National Recreation and Park Association, 1999.

Butler, William James. *Fort Smith, Past and Present: A Historical Summary.* Fort Smith: First National Bank of Fort Smith, Arkansas, 1972.

Byrd, Kathleen M., ed. *The Poverty Point Culture: Local Manifestations, Subsistence Practices, and Trade Networks.* Baton Rouge: Department of Geography and Anthropology, Louisiana State University, 1991.

Callahan, North. *Smoky Mountain Country.* Sevierville, TN: Smoky Mountain Historical Society, 1988.

Campbell, Carlos C. *Birth of a National Park in the Great Smoky Mountains.* Knoxville: University of Tennessee Press, 1960.

Cannon, Kelly June. *Administrative History: Fort Clatsop National Memorial.* Seattle, WA: National Park Service, Pacific Northwest Region, 1995.

Cantwell, Robert. *Alexander Wilson: Naturalist and Pioneer, a Biography.* Philadelphia, PA: Lippincott, 1961.

Cappon, Lester J., ed. *The Adams-Jefferson Letters: The Complete Correspondence Between Thomas Jefferson and Abigail and John Adams.* Chapel Hill: University of North Carolina Press, 1988.

Capps, Michael A. *Kennesaw Mountain National Battlefield Park: An Administrative History.* Atlanta, GA: National Park Service, Southeast Region, 1994. Available at www.cr.nps.gov/history/online_books/kemo/.

Capps, Michael A., and Steven A. Davis. *Moores Creek National Battlefield: An Administrative History.* Washington, DC: National Park Service, 1999. Available at www.cr.nps.gov/history/online_books/mocr/index.htm.

Carden, Marie L. *Fairsted: Home and Office of Frederick Law Olmsted: Frederick Law Olmsted National Historic Site.* Brookline, MA: Northeast Cultural Resources Center, Northeast Region National Park Service, 1998.

Carlson, Stephen P. *First Iron Works: A History of the*

First Iron Works Association. Saugus, MA: Saugus Historical Society, n.d.

Caro, Robert A. *Master of the Senate: The Years of Lyndon Johnson.* New York: Alfred A. Knopf, 2002.

Carper, Robert L., and Richard G. Turk. *Springfield Armory National Historic Site, Massachusetts.* Denver, CO: National Park Service, 1984.

Carr, Dawson. *The Cape Hatteras Lighthouse: Sentinel of the Shoals.* Chapel Hill: University of North Carolina Press, 2000.

Carr, Ethan. *Wilderness by Design: Landscape Architecture and the National Parks.* Lincoln: University of Nebraska Press, 1997.

Carroll, John M., ed. *General Custer and the Battle of the Washita: The Federal View.* Norman: University of Oklahoma Press, 1978.

Carter, Jimmy. *An Hour Before Daylight.* New York: Simon and Schuster, 2001.

Carver, George Washington. *George Washington Carver in His Own Words.* Edited by Gary R. Kremer. Columbia: University of Missouri Press, 1987.

Castel, Albert E. *Decision in the West: The Atlanta Campaign of 1864.* Lawrence: University Press of Kansas, 1992.

Catlin, George. *Indian Art in Pipestone: George Catlin's Portfolio in the British Museum.* Washington, DC: Smithsonian Institution Press, 1979.

Catton, Bruce. *Grant Moves South.* Boston: Little, Brown, 1960.

——. *Grant Takes Command.* Boston: Little, Brown, 1969.

——. *The Civil War.* New York: American Heritage, 1985.

——. *A Stillness at Appomattox.* New York: Anchor Books, 1990.

Catton, Theodore. *Land Reborn: A History of Administration and Visitor Use in Glacier Bay National Park and Preserve.* Anchorage, AK: National Park Service, 1995. Available at www.nps.gov/glba/adhi/adhi.htm.

——. *Wonderland: An Administrative History of Mount Rainier National Park.* Seattle, WA: National Park Service, 1996.

——. *Inhabited Wilderness: Indians, Eskimos, and National Parks in Alaska.* Albuquerque: University of New Mexico Press, 1997.

Catton, Theodore, and Ann Hubber. *Commemoration and Preservation: An Administrative History of Big Hole National Battlefield.* Missoula, MT: Historical Research Associates, 1999.

Cerulean, Susan, ed. *The Book of the Everglades.* Minneapolis, MN: Milkweed Editions, 2002.

Chadde, Steve W. *Plants of Pictured Rocks National Lakeshore: A Complete Illustrated Guide to the Plants of America's First National Lakeshore.* Laurium, MI: Pocketflora Press, 1996.

Channing, Edward. *A History of the United States.* New York: Octagon Books, 1977.

Chapman, William R., and Jill K. Hanson. *Wright Brothers National Monument Historic Resource Study.* Atlanta, GA: National Park Service, 1997. Available at www.nps.gov/wrbr/hrs/hrs.htm.

Chappell, Gordon. *Steam over Scranton: The Locomotives of Steamtown: Special History Study.* Scranton, PA: National Park Service, 1991. Available at www.cr.nps.gov/history/online_books/steamtown/shs.htm.

Charnley, Mitchell V. *Jean Lafitte, Gentleman Smuggler.* New York: Viking, 1934.

Chauevenet, Beatrice. *Hewett and Friends: A Biography of Santa Fe's Vibrant Era.* Santa Fe: Museum of New Mexico, 1984.

Chester, Edward W. *Fort Donelson National Battlefield: A Botanical and Historical Perspective.* Clarksville, TN: Center for Field Biology, Austin Peay State University, 1997.

Chief Joseph. *That All People May Be One People, Send Rain to Wash the Face of the Earth.* Sitka, AK: Mountain Meadow, 1995.

Childers, Frank M. *History of the Cape Canaveral Lighthouse.* Cocoa, FL: Brevard Museum of History and Natural Science, 1997.

Chittenden, Hiram. Edited and with an introduction by Richard A. Bartlett. *The Yellowstone National Park.* 1905. Reprint, Norman: University of Oklahoma Press, 1964.

Chopin, Kate. *The Awakening and Other Stories.* New York: Modern Library, 2000.

Chronic, Halka. *Pages of Stone: Geology of Western National Parks and Monuments: Sierra Nevada, Cascades, and Pacific Coast.* Seattle, WA: Mountaineers Books, 1989.

——. *Roadside Geology of Utah.* Missoula, MT: Mountain, 1990.

Chu, Daniel, and Bill Shaw. *Going Home to Nicodemus: The Story of an African American Frontier Town and the Pioneers Who Settled It.* Morristown, NJ: J. Messner, 1994.

Ciardi, John. *Saipan: The War Diary of John Ciardi.* Fayetteville: University of Arkansas Press, 1988.

Cikovsky, Nicolai, Jr. *A Connecticut Place: Weir Farm, an American Painter's Rural Retreat.* Wilton, CT: Weir Farm Trust, 2000.

Clark, Bill. *Death Valley: The Story Behind the Scenery.* Las Vegas, NV: KC Publications, 2002.

Clark, George Rogers. *The Conquest of the Illinois.* Carbondale: Southern Illinois University Press, 2001.

Clayton, Lawrence A., Vernon James Knight, Jr., and Edward C. Moore, eds. *The De Soto Chronicles: The*

Expedition of Hernando de Soto to North America in 1539–1543. Tuscaloosa: University of Alabama Press, 1993.

Clemens, Janet, and Frank Norris. *Building in an Ashen Land: Historic Resource Study of Katmai National Park and Preserve.* Anchorage, AK: National Park Service, 1999. Available at: www.nps.gov/katm/hrs/hrs.htm.

Clemensen, A. Berle. *Historic Resource Study: Steamtown National Historic Site, Pennsylvania.* Denver, CO: National Park Service, 1988.

——. *Casa Grande Ruins National Monument, Arizona: A Centennial History of the First Prehistoric Reserve, 1892–1992.* Coolidge, AZ: National Park Service, 1992.

Cloyd, Paul C. *The Two-Story Barn: Hubbell Trading Post National Historic Site, Arizona.* Denver, CO: National Park Service, 1997.

Cockrell, Ron. *Scotts Bluff National Monument, Nebraska: An Administrative History, 1960–1983.* Omaha, NE: National Park Service, Midwest Regional Office, 1983. Available at www.nps.gov/scbl/adhi/adhi.htm.

——. *Bones of Agate: An Administrative History of Agate Fossil Beds National Monument, Nebraska.* Omaha, NE: National Park Service, 1986.

——. *A Green Shrouded Miracle: An Administrative History of Cuyahoga National Recreation Area.* Omaha, NE: National Park Service, 1992.

——. *Amidst Ancient Monuments: The Administrative History of Mound City Group National Monument/Hopewell Culture National Historical Park, Ohio.* Omaha, NE: National Park Service, Midwest Support Office, 1999. Available at www.nps.gov/hocu/adhi/adhi.htm.

Cohen, Michael P. *The Pathless Way: John Muir and American Wilderness.* Madison: University of Wisconsin Press, 1984.

——. *The History of the Sierra Club, 1892–1970.* San Francisco, CA: Sierra Club Books, 1988.

Coleman, Roger E. *The Arkansas Post Story: Arkansas Post National Monument.* Santa Fe, NM: Division of History, Southwest Cultural Resources Center, Southwest Region, National Park Service 1987.

Coletta, Paolo Enrico. *The Presidency of William Howard Taft.* Lawrence: University Press of Kansas, 1973.

Comer, Douglas C. *Ritual Ground: Bent's Old Fort, World Formation, and the Annexation of the Southwest.* Berkeley: University of California Press, 1996.

Conger, Horace. *In Search of Gold: The Alaska Journals of Horace S. Conger, 1898–1899.* Anchorage: Alaska Geographic Society, 1983.

Conn, Herb. *The Jewel Cave Adventure: Fifty Miles of Discovery under South Dakota.* Teaneck, NJ: Zephyrus, 1977.

Connell, Evans S. *Son of the Morning Star.* New York: Harper & Row, 1985.

Connelly, Thomas Lawrence. *The Marble Man: Robert E. Lee and His Image in American Society.* Baton Rouge: Louisiana State University Press, 1978.

Connely, John, et al. *Appalachian Whitewater: The Northern States.* 4th ed. Birmingham, AL: Menasha Ridge, 2001.

Conners, John A. *Shenandoah National Park: An Interpretive Guide.* Blacksburg, VA: McDonald and Woodward, 1988.

Conzen, Michael P., and Kay J. Carr, eds. *The Illinois and Michigan Canal National Heritage Corridor: A Guide to Its History and Sources.* DeKalb: Northern Illinois University Press, 1988.

Cook, Joe. *River Song: A Journey Down the Chattahoochee and Apalachiocola Rivers.* Tuscaloosa: University of Alabama Press, 2000.

Cook, Linda, and Frank Norris. *A Stern and Rock-Bound Coast: Kenai Fjords National Park Historic Resource Study.* Anchorage: National Park Service, Alaska Support Office, 1998. Available at www.nps.gov/kefj/hrs/hrs.htm.

Coolidge, John. *Mill and Mansion: A Study of Architecture and Society in Lowell, Massachusetts, 1820–1865.* Amherst: University of Massachusetts Press, 1992.

Cooling, B. Franklin. *Fort Donelson's Legacy: War and Society in Kentucky and Tennessee, 1862–1863.* Knoxville: University of Tennessee Press, 1997.

——. *Monocacy: The Battle That Saved Washington.* Shippensburg, PA: White Mane, 2000.

Cooper, David J., ed. *By Fire, Storm, and Ice: Underwater Archeological Investigations in the Apostle Islands.* Madison: State Historical Society of Wisconsin, 1991.

Cooper, Jason. *Korean War Memorial: Historic Landmarks.* Vero Beach, FL: Rourke Book, 2001.

Cornog, Evan. *The Birth of Empire: DeWitt Clinton and the American Experience, 1769–1828.* New York: Oxford University Press, 1998.

Cott, Nancy F., ed. *No Small Courage: A History of Women in the United States.* New York: Oxford University Press, 2000.

Cozzens, Peter. *No Better Place to Die: The Battle of Stones River.* Urbana: University of Illinois Press, 1990.

——. *This Terrible Sound: The Battle of Chickamauga.* Urbana: University of Illinois Press, 1992.

——. *The Shipwreck of Their Hopes: The Battles for Chattanooga.* Urbana: University of Illinois Press, 1994.

——. *The Civil War in the West: From Stones River to Chattanooga.* Urbana: University of Illinois Press, 1996.

Crabtree, Jennifer. *Administrative History, Whitman Mission National Historic Site.* Seattle, WA: National Park Service, Pacific Northwest Region, 1988. Available at www.nps.gov/whmi/adhi/adhi.htm.

Craighead, Frank C., Jr. *For Everything There Is a Season: The Sequence of Natural Events in the Grand Teton–Yellowstone Area.* Helena, MT: Falcon, 1994.

Crater Lake National Park at 100: Special Issue of the Oregon Historical Quarterly, Spring 2002.

Crawford, J.L. *Zion Album: A Nostalgic History of Zion Canyon.* Springdale, UT: Zion Natural History Association, 1986.

——. *Zion National Park: Towers of Stone.* Springdale, UT: Zion Natural History Association, 1988.

Crouch, Tom D. *The Bishop's Boys: A Life of Wilbur and Orville Wright.* New York: W.W. Norton, 2003.

Crouch, Tom D., and Peter L. Jakab. *The Wright Brothers and the Invention of the Aerial Age.* Washington, DC: National Geographic Society, 2003.

Crutchfield, James. *The Natchez Trace: A Pictorial History.* Nashville, TN: Rutledge Hill, 1985.

Culick, Fred E., and Spencer Dunmore. *On Great White Wings: The Wright Brothers and the Race for Flight.* New York: Hyperion, 2001.

Cummings, Hildegard, Helen K. Fusscas, and Susan G. Larkin. *J. Alden Weir: A Place of His Own.* Storrs: William Benton Museum of Art, University of Connecticut, 1991.

Current, Richard Nelson. *Lincoln and the First Shot.* Philadelphia, PA: Lippincott, 1963.

Curtis, James C. *The Fox at Bay: Martin Van Buren and the Presidency, 1837–1841.* Lexington: University Press of Kentucky, 1970.

Curtis, Jane. *Frederick Billings, Vermonter, Pioneer Lawyer, Business Man, Conservationist: An Illustrated Biography.* Woodstock, VT: Woodstock Foundation, 1986.

Cushman, H.B. *History of the Choctaw, Chickasaw, and Natchez Indians.* Norman: University of Oklahoma Press, 1999.

Daniel, Larry J. *Shiloh: The Battle That Changed the Civil War.* New York: Simon and Schuster, 1997.

Daniels, Roger. *Prisoners Without Trial: Japanese Americans in World War II.* New York: Hill and Wang, 1993.

Daniels, Rudolph. *Trains Across the Continent: North American Railroad History.* Bloomington: Indiana University Press, 2000.

Darlington, David. *The Mojave: A Portrait of the Definitive American Desert.* New York: Henry Holt, 1996.

Dary, David. *The Santa Fe Trail: Its History, Legends, and Lore.* New York: Alfred A. Knopf, 2000.

Davidson, George E. *Red Rock Eden: The Story of Fruita.* Torrey, UT: Capitol Reef National History Association, 1986.

Davis, Anita Price. *Chimney Rock and Rutherford County.* Charleston, SC: Arcadia, 2002.

Davis, Burke. *The Cowpens-Guilford Courthouse Campaign.* Philadelphia: University of Pennsylvania Press, 2002.

Davis, Ronald L.F. *The Black Experience in Natchez, 1720–1880: Natchez, National Historical Park, Mississippi.* Denver, CO: National Park Service, Denver Service Center, 1993.

Davis, William C. *Battle at Bull Run: A History of the First Major Campaign of the Civil War.* Mechanicsburg, PA: Stackpole Books, 1995.

——. *A Way Through the Wilderness: The Natchez Trace and the Civilization of the Southern Frontier.* New York: HarperCollins, 1995.

Dean, Jeffrey S., ed. *Salado.* Albuquerque: University of New Mexico Press, 2000.

deBuys, William, ed. *Seeing Things Whole: The Essential John Wesley Powell.* Washington, DC: Island, 2001.

Decker, Robert, and Barbara Decker. *Volcanoes in America's National Parks.* New York: W.W. Norton, 2001.

Delehanty, Randolph. *Classic Natchez.* Athens: University of Georgia Press, 1996.

Department of Defense CD-ROM. *20th Century Complete Guide to Pearl Harbor: Encyclopedic Coverage of December 7, 1941: Remarkable Photographs, Oral Histories, Vessel Attack Reports, Casualty Lists, Japanese Force Information, Submerged Cultural Resources, USS Arizona Memorial.* Washington, DC: Progressive Management, 2002.

D'Este, Carlo. *Eisenhower: A Soldier's Life.* New York: Henry Holt, 2002.

De Vore, Steven Leroy. *Beads of the Bison Robe Trade: The Fort Union Trading Post Collection.* Williston, ND: Friends of Fort Union Trading Post, 1992.

De Zavala, Adina. *History and Legends of the Alamo and Other Missions in and Around San Antonio.* Houston, TX: Arte Publico, 1996.

Diamond, Jared M. *Guns, Germs, and Steel: The Fates of Human Societies.* New York: W.W. Norton, 1997.

Dietrich, William. *Northwest Passage: The Great Columbia River.* New York: Simon and Schuster, 1995.

Dillon, Wilton S., and Neil G. Kotler, eds. *The Statue of Liberty Revisited: Making a Universal Symbol.* Washington, DC: Smithsonian Institution Press, 1994.

Dilsaver, Lary M. *Challenge of the Big Trees: A Resource History of Sequoia and Kings Canyon National Parks.* Three Rivers, CA: Sequoia Natural History Association, 1990.

——. *Cumberland Island National Seashore: A History of*

Conservation Conflict. Charlottesville: University of Virginia Press, 2004.

Doenecke, Justus D. *The Presidencies of James A. Garfield and Chester A. Arthur.* Lawrence: Regents Press of Kansas, 1981.

Dolson, John. *The Black Canyon of the Gunnison: A Story in Stone: The Natural and Human History of Black Canyon of the Gunnison National Monument.* Boulder, CO: Pruett, 1982.

Donald, David Herbert. *Lincoln.* New York: Simon and Schuster, 1995.

Dookhan, Isaac. *History of the Virgin Islands.* Kingston, Jamaica: Canoe, 1994.

Douglas, Marjory Stoneman. *The Everglades: River of Grass.* Sarasota, FL: Pineapple, 1997.

Douglass, Frederick. *Frederick Douglass: Autobiographic Narrative of the Life of Frederick Douglass, an American Slave/My Bondage and My Freedom/Life and Times of Frederick Douglass.* Edited by Henry Louis Gates. New York: Library of America, 1994.

Drury, Clifford Merrill. *Marcus and Narcissa Whitman, and the Opening of Old Oregon.* Glendale, CA: A.H. Clark, 1973.

Dublin, Thomas. *Women at Work: The Transformation of Work and Community in Lowell, Massachusetts, 1826–1860.* New York: Columbia University Press, 1979.

DuBois, Ellen Carol. *Harriet Stanton Blatch and the Winning of Woman Suffrage.* New Haven, CT: Yale University Press, 1999.

Ducker, James H. *Alaska's Upper Yukon Region: A History.* Anchorage, AK: Bureau of Land Management, 1983.

Duncan, David Ewing. *Hernando de Soto: A Savage Quest in the Americas.* Norman: University of Oklahoma Press, 1997.

Duus, Masayo Umezawa. *Unlikely Liberators: The Men of the 100th and 442nd.* Honolulu: University of Hawaii Press, 1987.

Dyer, Joel. *Harvest of Rage: Why Oklahoma City Is Only the Beginning.* Boulder, CO: Westview, 1998.

Dykes, Fred W. *Jeffrey's Cutoff: Idaho's Forgotten Oregon Trail Route.* Pocatello, ID: Pocatello Copy Cat, 1989.

Early, Jubal A. *A Memoir of the Last Year of the War for Independence in the Confederate States of America.* Columbia: University of South Carolina Press, 2001.

Edelman, Bernard, ed. *Dear America: Letters Home from Vietnam.* New York: W.W. Norton, 1985.

Edgar, Walter B. *Historic Snee Farm: A Documentary Record.* Columbia: University of South Carolina Department of History, 1991.

Edrington, Thomas S. *The Battle of Glorieta Pass: A Gettysburg in the West, March 26–28, 1862.* Albuquerque: University of New Mexico Press, 1998.

Ehrlich, Gretel. *John Muir: Nature's Visionary.* Washington, DC: National Geographic Society, 2000.

Eisenhower, Dwight D. *Crusade in Europe.* Baltimore, MD: Johns Hopkins University Press, 1997.

Elias, Scott A. *Rocky Mountains.* Washington, DC: Smithsonian Institution Press, 2002.

Ellis, Joseph J. *Passionate Sage: The Character and Legacy of John Adams.* New York: Norton, 1993.

——. *American Sphinx: The Character of Thomas Jefferson.* New York: Alfred A. Knopf, 1997.

——. *Founding Brothers: The Revolutionary Generation.* New York: Alfred A. Knopf, 2000.

Ellis, William Donahue. *The Cuyahoga.* Chicago: Landfall, 1998.

Elting, John R. *Amateurs to Arms! A Military History of the War of 1812.* Chapel Hill, NC: Algonquin Books of Chapel Hill, 1991.

Elwell, Jean Nicholson. *Idaho's Silent City of Rocks: A Land of "Make-Believe."* Ogden, UT: Ramona's, 1994.

Emerick, John. *Rocky Mountain Natural History Handbook.* Niwot, CO: Robert Rinehart, 1994.

Emmel, Thomas C. *Florissant Butterflies: A Guide to the Fossil and Present-day Species of Central Colorado.* Stanford, CA: Stanford University Press, 1992.

Emmett, Chris. *Fort Union and the Winning of the Southwest.* Norman: University of Oklahoma Press, 1965.

Engel, J. Ronald. *Sacred Sands: The Struggle for Community in the Indiana Dunes.* Middletown, CT: Wesleyan University Press. Distributed by Harper & Row, 1983.

Engel, Joan G., ed. *The Indiana Dunes Story: How Nature and People Made a Park.* Michigan City, IN: Shirley Heinze Environmental Fund, 1997.

Evans, Doris. *Saguaro National Monument.* Tucson, AZ: Southwest Parks and Monuments Association, 1993.

Evens, Jules G. *The Natural History of the Point Reyes Peninsula.* Point Reyes, CA: Point Reyes National Seashore Association, 1988.

Everhart, William C. *The National Park Service.* Boulder, CO: Westview, 1983.

Ewing, Sherm. *The Ranch: A Modern History of the North American Cattle Industry.* Missoula, MT: Mountain, 1995.

Fabry, Judith K. *Guadalupe Mountains National Park: An Administrative History.* Santa Fe, NM: Southwest Cultural Resources Center, 1988. Available at www.nps.gov/gumo/adhi/adhi.htm.

Fairbanks, Charles Herron. *Archeology of the Funeral Mound, Ocmulgee National Monument, Georgia.* Tuscaloosa: University of Alabama Press, 2003.

Faragher, John Mack. *Women and Men on the Overland*

Trail. New Haven, CT: Yale University Press, 1979.

——. *Daniel Boone: The Life and Legend of an American Pioneer.* New York: Holt, 1992.

Farmer, James. *Lay Bare the Heart: An Autobiography of the Civil Rights Movement.* New York: Arbor House, 1985.

Fausold, Martin L. *The Presidency of Herbert C. Hoover.* Lawrence: University Press of Kansas, 1985.

Fein, Albert. *Frederick Law Olmsted and the American Environmental Tradition.* New York: Braziller, 1972.

Fejes, Claire. *The Eskimo Storyteller: Folktales from Noatak, Alaska.* Anchorage: University of Alaska Press, 1999.

Fillmore, Robert. *The Geology of the Parks, Monuments, and Wildlands of Southern Utah.* Salt Lake City: University of Utah Press, 2000.

Finch, Robert. *Common Ground: A Naturalist's Cape Cod.* Boston: D.R. Godine, 1981.

Finnerty, Cheryl Anne. *Lighthouses of Boston Harbor Past & Present.* Seminole, FL: Harbor Productions, 2001.

Fischer, David Hackett. *Paul Revere's Ride.* New York: Oxford University Press, 1994.

Fishbein, Seymour L. *Yellowstone Country: The Enduring Wonder.* Washington, DC: National Geographic Society, 1989.

Fisher, Irving D. *Frederick Law Olmsted and the City Planning Movement in the United States.* Ann Arbor, MI: UMI Research, 1986.

Fisher, Jack C. *Stolen Glory: The McKinley Assassination.* La Jolla, CA: Alamar Books, 2001.

Fisher, Leonard Everett. *To Bigotry No Sanction: The Story of the Oldest Synagogue in America.* New York: Holiday House, 1999.

Fisher, Lewis F. *The Spanish Missions of San Antonio.* San Antonio, TX: Maverick, 1998.

Fisher, Robin. *Vancouver's Voyage: Charting the Northwest Coast, 1791–1795.* Seattle: University of Washington Press, 1992.

——, ed. *From Maps to Metaphors: The Pacific World of George Vancouver.* Vancouver: University of British Columbia Press, 1993.

Fleming, Thomas J. *Duel: Alexander Hamilton, Aaron Burr, and the Future of America.* New York: Basic Books, 1999.

Fletcher, Colin. *The Man Who Walked Through Time.* New York: Vintage Books, 1989.

Flexner, James Thomas. *George Washington and the New Nation, 1783–1793.* Boston: Little, Brown, 1970.

——. *The Young Hamilton: A Biography.* New York: Fordham University Press, 1997.

Flint, Richard, and Shirley Cushing Flint, eds. *The Coronado Expedition to Tierra Nueva: The 1540–1542*

Route Across the Southwest. Niwot: University Press of Colorado, 1997.

Foote, Shelby. *Shiloh: A Novel.* New York: Vintage Books, 1991.

——. *Chickamauga: And Other Civil War Stories.* New York: Delta, 1993.

——. *The Beleaguered City: The Vicksburg Campaign, December 1862–July 1863.* New York: Modern Library, 1995.

Foresta, Ronald A. *America's National Parks and Their Keepers.* Washington, DC: Resources for the Future, 1984.

Fort Larned National Historic Site, Kansas: Cultural Landscape Report. Omaha, NE: Midwest Support Office, National Park Service, 1999.

Fort Necessity Memorial Association. *A Young Colonel from Virginia and the Blow He Struck for American Independence in the Year 1754, Together with Its Significance as a Feature of the Approaching Bicentennial of His Birth.* Uniontown, PA: Fort Necessity Memorial Association, 1931.

Fort Raleigh Historic Resource Study. Atlanta, GA: Southeast Regional Office, National Park Service, 1999. Available at www.nps.gov/fora/hrs/hrs.htm.

Fort Vancouver: Fort Vancouver National Historic Site, Washington. Washington, DC: National Park Service, 1981.

Forts of Old San Juan: San Juan National Historic Site, Puerto Rico. Washington, DC: National Park Service, 1996.

Fosdick, Raymond B. *John D. Rockefeller, Jr., A Portrait.* New York: Harper & Brothers, 1956.

Fox, Richard A. *Archaeology, History, and Custer's Last Battle: The Little Big Horn Reexamined.* Norman: University of Oklahoma Press, 1993.

Fox, Stephen R. *John Muir and His Legacy: The American Conservation Movement.* Boston: Little, Brown, 1981.

——. *The American Conservation Movement: John Muir and His Legacy.* Madison: University of Wisconsin Press, 1985.

Fraley, John. *A Woman's Way West: In and Around Glacier National Park, 1925–1990.* Whitefish, MT: Big Mountain, 1998.

Francis, Charles E. *The Tuskegee Airmen: The Men Who Changed a Nation.* Boston: Branden, 1993.

Franklin, John Hope, and Alfred A. Moss, Jr. *From Slavery to Freedom: A History of African Americans.* Boston: McGraw-Hill, 2000.

Franklin, Kay, and Norma Schaeffer. *Duel for the Dunes: Land Use Conflict on the Shores of Lake Michigan.* Urbana: University of Illinois Press, 1983.

Franssanito, William A. *Antietam: The Photographic Legacy of America's Bloodiest Day.* New York: Scribner, 1978.

Freeman, Douglas Southall. *R.E. Lee: A Biography.* New York: Scribner's, 1937–1940.

——. *George Washington: A Biography.* Clifton, NJ: A.M. Kelley, 1975.

Freidel, Frank. *Franklin D. Roosevelt: A Rendezvous with Destiny.* Boston: Little, Brown, 1990.

Fritz, William J. *Roadside Geology of the Yellowstone Country.* Missoula, MT: Mountain, 1985.

Frome, Michael. *Strangers in High Places: The Story of the Great Smoky Mountains.* Knoxville: University of Tennessee Press, 1994.

Fullenkamp, Leonard, Stephen Bowman, and Jay Luvaas, eds. *Guide to the Vicksburg Campaign.* Lawrence: University Press of Kansas, 1998.

Fuller, J.F.C. *The Generalship of Ulysses S. Grant.* New York: Da Capo, 1991.

Fuson, Robert Henderson. *Juan Ponce de Leon and the Spanish Discovery of Puerto Rico and Florida.* Granville, OH: McDonald & Woodward, 2000.

Futch, Ovid. *History of Andersonville Prison.* Gainesville: University of Florida Press, 1968.

Gailey, Harry A. *The Liberation of Guam: 21 July–10 August 1944.* Novato, CA: Presidio, 1988.

Gale, Thomas P. *Isle Royale: A Photographic History.* Houghton, MI: Isle Royale Natural History Association, 1995.

Gallagher, Gary W. *Jubal A. Early, the Lost Cause, and Civil War History: A Persistent Legacy.* Milwaukee, WI: Marquette University Press, 1995.

——, ed. *The Richmond Campaign of 1862: The Peninsula and the Seven Days.* Chapel Hill: University of North Carolina Press, 2000.

Galvin, John R. *The Minute Men: The First Fight—Myths and Realities of the American Revolution.* Washington, DC: Pergamon-Brassey's International Defense, 1989.

Garate, Donald T. *The Zion Tunnel: From Slickrock to Switchback.* Springdale, UT: Zion Natural History Association, 1989.

Garfield, Brian. *The Thousand-Mile War: World War II in Alaska and the Aleutians.* Fairbanks: University of Alaska Press, 1995.

Garrett, Jessie A., and Ronald C. Larson, eds. *Camp and Community: Manzanar and the Owens Valley.* Fullerton: California State University, Japanese American Oral History Project, 1977.

Gaustad, Edwin S. *Liberty of Conscience: Roger Williams in America.* Valley Forge, PA: Judson, 1999.

Geary, Michael M. *A Quick History of Grand Lake: Including Rocky Mountain National Park and the Grand Lake Lodge.* Ouray, CO: Western Reflections, 1999.

Geluso, Kenneth N., Ronal C. Kerbo, and J. Scott Altenbach. *Bats of Carlsbad Caverns National Park.* Carlsbad, NM: Carlsbad Caverns Natural History Association, 1996.

Gerber, Jane S. *The Jews of Spain: A History of the Sephardic Experience.* New York: Free Press, 1992.

Gibson, Arrell Morgan. *The Chickasaws.* Norman: University of Oklahoma Press, 1971.

Gibson, Jon L. *Poverty Point: A Terminal Archaic Culture of the Lower Mississippi Valley.* Baton Rouge: Department of Culture, Recreation, and Tourism, Louisiana Archaeological Survey and Antiquities Commission, 1983. Available at www.crt.state.la.us/crt/ocd/arch/poverpoi/mapopo.htm.

Gieck, Jack. *A Photo Album of Ohio's Canal Era, 1825–1913.* Kent, OH: Kent State University Press, 1992.

Gienapp, William E. *Abraham Lincoln and Civil War America.* New York: Oxford University Press, 2002.

Gilbert, Cathy. *Cultural Landscape Report: Fruita Rural Historic District, Capitol Reef National Park.* Denver, CO: National Park Service, Intermountain Region, 1997.

Gilbert, Dave. *Waterpower: Mills, Factories, Machines and Floods at Harpers Ferry, West Virginia, 1762–1991.* Harpers Ferry, WV: Harpers Ferry Historical Association, 1999.

Gilliam, Harold, and Ann Gilliam. *Marin Headlands: Portals of Time.* San Francisco: Golden Gate National Park Association, 1993.

Gilman, Carolyn. *The Grand Portage Story.* St. Paul: Minnesota Historical Society, 1992.

Gioia, Ted. *The History of Jazz.* New York: Oxford University Press, 1997.

Glad, Betty. *Jimmy Carter: In Search of the Great White House.* New York: W.W. Norton, 1980.

Gleason, David K. *The Great Houses of Natchez.* Jackson: University Press of Mississippi, 1986.

Glover, James M. *A Wilderness Original: The Life of Bob Marshall.* Seattle, WA: Mountaineers Books, 1986.

Gluck, Sherna Berger. *Rosie the Riveter Revisited: Women, the War, and Social Change.* New York: Penguin Books, 1988.

Gnesios, Gregory M. *Whiskeytown National Recreation Area.* Tucson, AZ: Southwest Parks and Monuments Association, 1993.

Goetzmann, William H. *Exploration and Empire: The Explorer and the Scientist in the Winning of the American West.* New York: Norton, 1978.

Goodrich, Thomas. *War to the Knife: Bleeding Kansas, 1854–1861.* Mechanicsburg, PA: Stackpole Books, 1998.

Goodwin, Doris Kearns. *Lyndon Johnson and the American Dream.* New York: St. Martin's, 1991.

Gordon, John Steele. *The Scarlet Woman of Wall Street:*

Jay Gould, Jim Fisk, Cornelius Vanderbilt, the Erie Railway Wars, and the Birth of Wall Street. New York: Weidenfeld and Nicolson, 1988.

Gordon, Robert B. *American Iron, 1607–1900.* Baltimore, MD: Johns Hopkins University Press, 1996.

Gould, Philip. *Natchitoches and Louisiana's Timeless Cane River.* Baton Rouge: Louisiana State University Press, 2002.

Grant, Campbell. *Canyon de Chelly: Its People and Rock Art.* Albuquerque: University of New Mexico Press, 1978.

Grant, Ulysses S. *The Civil War Memoirs of Ulysses S. Grant.* New York: Forge, 2002.

Grassick, Mary K. *Fort Point: Fort Point National Historic Site, Presidio of San Francisco, California.* Harpers Ferry, WV: Division of Historic Furnishings, Harpers Ferry Center, National Park Service, 1994.

Gray, John Shapley. *Custer's Last Campaign: Mitch Boyer and the Little Bighorn Reconstructed.* Lincoln: University of Nebraska Press, 1991.

Greber, N'omi. *The Hopewell Site: A Contemporary Analysis Based on the Work of Charles C. Willoughby.* Boulder, CO: Westview, 1989.

Greene, Dana, ed. *Lucretia Mott: Her Complete Speeches and Sermons.* New York: E. Mellon, 1980.

Greene, Jerome A. *The Historic Pool, El Morro National Monument, New Mexico.* Denver, CO: Denver Service Center, National Park Service, 1978.

——. *The Defense of New Orleans, 1718–1900, Jean Lafitte National Historical Park, Louisiana.* Denver, CO: National Park Service, 1982.

——. *Chalmette Unit, Jean Lafitte National Historical Park and Preserve.* Denver, CO: National Park Service, 1985.

——. *Historic Resource Study: Fort Davis National Historic Site.* Denver, CO: National Park Service, 1986.

——. *Fort Christiansvaern: Christiansted National Historic Site, Christiansted Virgin Islands.* Harpers Ferry, WV: Harpers Ferry Center, National Park Service, 1988.

——. *Nez Perce Summer, 1877: The U.S. Army and the Nee-Me-Poo Crisis.* Helena: Montana Historical Society Press, 2000. Available at www.nps.gov/nepe/greene/index.htm.

Greene, Linda Wedel. *Exile in Paradise: The Isolation of Hawaii's Leprosy Victims and Development of Kalaupapa Settlement, 1865 to the Present.* Denver, CO: Denver Service Center, National Park Service, 1985.

——. *A Cultural History of Three Traditional Hawaiian Sites on the West Coast of Hawai'i Island.* Denver, CO: National Park Service, 1993. Available at www.cr.nps.gov/history/online_books/kona/history.htm.

Greene, Meg. *Thaddeus Kosciuszko: Polish General and Patriot.* Philadelphia, PA: Chelsea House, 2002.

Greenthal, Kathryn. *Augustus Saint-Gaudens, Master Sculptor.* New York: Metropolitan Museum of Art, 1985.

Gries, John Paul. *Roadside Geology of South Dakota.* Missoula, MT: Mountain, 1996.

Griffin, John W. *Investigations in Russell Cave, Russell Cave National Monument, Alabama.* Washington, DC: National Park Service, 1974.

——. *Archaeology of the Everglades.* Gainesville: University Press of Florida, 2002.

Griffin, L. Martin. *Saving the Marin-Sonoma Coast: The Battles for Audubon Canyon Ranch, Point Reyes, and California's Russian River.* Healdsburg, CA: Sweetwater Springs, 1998.

Griffith, Samuel B. *The War for American Independence: From 1760 to the Surrender at Yorktown in 1781.* Urbana: University of Illinois Press, 2002.

Griswold del Castillo, Richard. *The Treaty of Guadalupe Hidalgo: A Legacy of Conflict.* Norman: University of Oklahoma Press, 1992.

Gross, Mathew Barrett, ed. *The Glen Canyon Reader.* Tucson: University of Arizona Press, 2003.

Gross, Robert A. *The Minutemen and Their World.* New York: Hill and Wang, 2001.

Gunderson, Mary Alice. *Devils Tower: Stories in Stone.* Glendo, WY: High Plains, 1988.

Gunter, Pete A.Y. *The Big Thicket: A Challenge for Conservation.* New York: Viking, 1972.

——. *The Big Thicket: An Ecological Reevaluation.* Denton: University of North Texas Press, 1993.

Haecker, Charles M., and Jeffrey G. Mauck. *On the Prairie of Palo Alto: Historical Archaeology of the U.S.-Mexican War Battlefield.* College Station: Texas A&M University Press, 1997.

Hafen, Le Roy Reuben. *Fort Laramie and the Pageant of the West, 1834–1890.* Lincoln: University of Nebraska Press, 1984.

——, ed. *French Fur Traders and Voyageurs in the American West.* Lincoln: University of Nebraska Press, 1997.

Hagood, Allen. *Dinosaur: The Story Behind the Scenery.* Las Vegas, NV: KC Publications, 1990.

Haines, Aubrey L. *Yellowstone National Park: Its Exploration and Establishment.* Washington, DC: National Park Service, 1974. Available at www.cr.nps.gov/history/online_books/haines1.

Haites, Erik F. *Western River Transportation: The Era of Early Internal Development, 1810–1860.* Baltimore, MD: The Johns Hopkins University Press, 1975.

Hall, Neville A.T. *Slave Society in the Danish West Indies: St. Thomas, St. John, and St. Croix.* Baltimore, MD: Johns Hopkins University Press, 1992.

Hall, Philip S. *Reflections of the Badlands.* Vermillion: University of South Dakota Press, 1993.

Hall, Timothy L. *Separating Church and State: Roger Williams and Religious Liberty.* Urbana: University of Illinois Press, 1998.

Hallahan, William H. *The Day the Revolution Began: 19 April 1775.* New York: Avon Books, 1999.

Haller, Stephen A. *Post and Park: A Brief Illustrated History of the Presidio.* San Francisco: Golden Gate National Parks Association, 1997.

Hally, David J., ed. *Ocmulgee Archaeology 1936–1986.* Athens: University of Georgia Press, 1994.

Halprin, Lawrence. *The Franklin Delano Roosevelt Memorial.* San Francisco: Chronicle Books, 1997.

Hamby, Alonzo L. *Man of the People: A Life of Harry S Truman.* New York: Oxford University Press, 1995.

Hamilton, Alexander, James Madison, and John Jay. *The Federalist Papers.* Edited by Clinton Rossiter. New York: Mentor Books, 1999.

Hamilton, Nigel. *JFK: Reckless Youth.* New York: Random House, 1992.

Hamilton, Wayne L. *Sculpturing of Zion: Guide to the Geology of Zion.* Springdale, UT: Zion Natural History Association, 1984.

Hamin, Elisabeth M. *Mojave Lands: Interpretive Planning and the National Preserve.* Baltimore, MD: Johns Hopkins University Press, 2003.

Hampton, Bruce. *Children of Grace: The Nez Perce War of 1877.* Lincoln, NE: Bison Books, 2002.

The Handbook of Texas Online. Available at www.tsha.utexas.edu/handbook/online.

Hanna, Warren L. *Montana's Many Splendored Glacierland: All You've Ever Wanted to Know About Glacier Park.* Seattle, WA: Superior, 1976.

——. *Stars over Montana: Men Who Made Glacier National Park History.* West Glacier, MT: Glacier Natural History Association, 1988.

Hannibal, Joseph T. *Geology Along the Towpath: Stones of the Ohio & Erie and Miami & Erie Canals.* Columbus: State of Ohio, 1998.

Hanor, Jeffrey S. *Fire in Folded Rocks.* Hot Springs, AR: Hot Springs National Park, 1980.

Harlan, Louis R. *Booker T. Washington: The Making of a Black Leader, 1856–1901.* New York: Oxford University Press, 1972.

——. *Booker T. Washington: The Wizard of Tuskegee, 1901–1915.* New York: Oxford University Press, 1983.

Harmon, Rick. *Crater Lake National Park: A History.* Corvallis: Oregon State University Press, 2002.

Harris, Burton. *John Colter: His Years in the Rockies.* Lincoln: University of Nebraska Press, 1993.

Harrison, Lowell Hayes. *George Rogers Clark and the War in the West.* Lexington: University Press of Kentucky, 2001.

Hartley, E.N. *Ironworks on the Saugus: the Lynn and Braintree Ventures of the Company of Undertakers of the Ironworks in New England.* Norman: University of Oklahoma Press, 1957.

Hartzog, George B., Jr. *Battling for the National Parks.* Mt. Kisco, NY: Moyer Bell Limited, 1988.

Harvey, Mark W.T. *A Symbol of Wilderness: Echo Park and the American Conservation Movement.* Seattle: University of Washington Press, 2000.

Hassell, Hank. *Rainbow Bridge: An Illustrated History.* Logan: Utah State University Press, 1999.

Hatch, Charles E. *Moores Creek National Military Park, North Carolina: The Battle of Moores Creek Bridge.* Washington, DC: Office of History and Historic Architecture, Eastern Service Center, 1969.

Hauk, Joy Keve. *Badlands: Its Life and Landscape; The Natural History Story of Badlands National Monument.* Interior, ND: Badlands Natural History Association, 1969.

Hayes, Alden C. *A Portal to Paradise: 11,537 Years, More or Less, on the Northeast Slope of the Chiricahua Mountains: Being a Fairly Accurate and Occasionally Anecdotal History of That Part of Cochise County, Arizona, and the Country Immediately Adjacent, Replete with Tales of Glory and Greed, Heroism and Depravity, and Plain Hard Work.* Tucson: University of Arizona Press, 1999.

Hayle, Buchanan. *Wildflowers of Southwestern Utah: A Field Guide to Bryce Canyon, Cedar Breaks and Surrounding Plant Communities.* Helena, MT: Distributed by Falcon, 1992.

Hedren, Paul L. *Fort Laramie in 1876: Chronicle of a Frontier Post at War.* Lincoln: University of Nebraska Press, 1988.

——. *Fort Laramie and the Great Sioux War.* Norman: University of Oklahoma Press, 1998.

Heizer, Robert F., and Theodora Kroeber. *Ishi, the Last Yahi: A Documentary History.* Berkeley: University of California Press, 1979.

Hennessy, John J. *Return to Bull Run: The Battle and Campaign of Second Manassas.* Norman: University of Oklahoma Press, 1999.

Henry, Marguerite. *Misty of Chincoteague.* New York: Simon & Schuster Books for Young Readers, 2000.

Herben, George. *Picture Journeys in Alaska's Wrangell–St. Elias: America's Largest National Park.* Anchorage: Alaska Northwest Books, 1997.

Hess, Earl. *Pickett's Charge: The Last Confederate Attack at Gettysburg.* Chapel Hill: University of North Carolina Press, 2001.

Hess, Karl. *Rocky Times in Rocky Mountain National*

Park: An Unnatural History. Niwot: University Press of Colorado, 1993.

Higginbotham, Don. *George Washington and the American Military Tradition.* Athens: University of Georgia Press, 1985.

Hill, Carol A. *Geology of Carlsbad Cavern and Other Caves in the Guadalupe Mountains, New Mexico and Texas.* Socorro: New Mexico Bureau of Mines & Mineral Resources, 1987.

Hill, Ruth Ann. *Discovering Old Bar Harbor and Acadia National Park: An Unconventional History and Guide.* Camden, ME: Down East Books, 1996.

Hine, Darlene Clark. *A Shining Thread of Hope: The History of Black Women in America.* New York: Broadway Books, 1998.

Hine, Darlene Clark, William C. Hine, and Stanley Harrold. *The African-American Odyssey.* Upper Saddle River, NJ: Prentice-Hall, 2003.

Hirsh, Edward L. *Henry Wadsworth Longfellow.* Minneapolis: University of Minnesota Press, 1964.

A History of Pipestone County. Pipestone, MN: Pipestone County Historical Society, 1984.

Hobbs-Olson, Laurie. *Discovering Acadia: An Introduction to the Park & Its Environment.* Charlottesville, VA: Elan, 2001.

Hodge, Carle. *Ruins Along the River: Motezuma Castle, Tuzigoot, and Montezuma Well National Monuments.* Tucson, AZ: Southwest Parks and Monuments Association, 1986.

——. *All About Saguaros.* Phoenix: Arizona Highways, 1991.

Hoehling, A.A. *Vicksburg: 47 Days of Siege.* Mechanicsburg, PA: Stackpole Books, 1996.

Hoffman, Carl. *Saipan: The Beginning of the End.* Reprint. Nashville, TN: Battery, 1987.

Hoff-Wilson, Joan, and Marjorie Lightman, eds. *Without Precedent: The Life and Career of Eleanor Roosevelt.* Bloomington: Indiana University Press, 1984.

Hoig, Stan. *The Sand Creek Massacre.* Norman: University of Oklahoma Press, 1961.

——. *The Battle of the Washita: The Sheridan-Custer Indian Campaign of 1867–69.* Lincoln: University of Nebraska Press, 1979.

Holdman, Annette. *Window to the Channel: A Guide to the Resources of the Channel Islands National Marine Sanctuary.* Santa Barbara, CA: Channel Islands National Marine Sanctuary, Santa Barbara Museum of Natural History, 1990.

Holland, F. Ross. *Idealists, Scoundrels, and the Lady: An Insider's View of the Statue of Liberty–Ellis Island Project.* Urbana: University of Illinois Press, 1993.

Holliday, J.S. *Rush for Riches: Gold Fever and the Making of California.* Berkeley: University of California Press, 1999.

Holmes, Steven J. *The Young John Muir: An Environmental Biography.* Madison: University of Wisconsin Press, 1999.

Homan, Lynn M. *The Tuskegee Airmen.* Charleston, SC: Arcadia, 1998.

Homestead National Monument of America, Beatrice, Nebraska: Cultural Landscape Report. Omaha, NE: National Park Service, Midwest Systems Support Office, 2000.

Horton, James O. "An Interview with Robert Stanton." *OAH Newsletter,* May 1999.

Houk, Rose. *Going-to-the-Sun: The Story of the Highway Across Glacier National Park.* DelMar, MT: Glacier Natural History Association, 1984.

——. *Black Canyon of the Gunnison.* Tucson, AZ: Southwest Parks and Monuments, 1991.

——. *Curecanti National Recreation Area.* Tucson, AZ: Southwest Parks and Monuments, 1991.

——. *Salado.* Tucson, AZ: Southwest Parks and Monuments Association, 1992.

——. *Great Smoky Mountains National Park: A Natural History Guide.* Boston: Houghton Mifflin, 1993.

——. *Sunset Crater Volcano National Monument.* Tucson, AZ: Southwest Parks and Monuments Association, 1995.

——. *Tuzigoot National Monument.* Tucson, AZ: Southwest Parks and Monuments Association, 1995.

——. *Casa Grande Ruins National Monument.* Tucson, AZ: Southwest Parks and Monuments Association, 1996.

——. *Lake Mead National Recreation Area.* Tucson, AZ: Southwest Parks and Monuments Association, 1997.

Houk, Rose, and Michael Collier. *White Sands National Monument.* Tucson, AZ: Southwest Parks and Monuments Association, 1994.

Houston, Jeanne Wakatsuki. *Farewell to Manzanar: A True Story of Japanese American Experience During and after the World War II Internment.* Boston: Houghton Mifflin, 2002.

Howard, John. *The Shifting Wind: The Supreme Court and Civil Rights from Reconstruction to Brown.* Albany: State University of New York Press, 1999.

Howorth, Peter. *Channel Islands.* Las Vegas, NV: KC Publications, 1982.

Hoxie, Frederick. *Parading Through History: The Making of the Crow Nation in America, 1805–1935.* New York: Cambridge University Press, 1997.

HRA Gray & Pope, LLC. *The Evolution of a Sanctified Landscape: A Historic Resource Study of the Lincoln Boyhood National Memorial, Spencer County, Indiana.* Omaha, NE: National Park Service, 2002. Available at www.nps.gov/libo/hrs/hrs.htm.

Hubbard, Bernard R. "A World Inside a Mountain: Aniakchak, the New Volcano Wonderland of the

Alaska Peninsula, Is Explored." *National Geographic Magazine* 60 (September 1931): 319–46.

Huber, N. King. *Geologic Story of Isle Royale National Park.* Washington, DC: U.S. Geological Survey, 1975.

Hudson, Charles. *Knights of Spain, Warriors of the Sun: Hernando de Soto and the South's Ancient Chiefdoms.* Athens: University of Georgia Press, 1997.

Huffman, Margaret. *The Wild Heart of Los Angeles.* Niwot, CO: Robert Rinehart, 1998.

Humphreys, Anna. *Saguaro: The Desert Giant.* Tucson, AZ: Rio Nuevo, 2002.

Humphries, George. *Along the Blue Ridge Parkway.* Englewood, NJ: Westcliffe, 1997.

Hurst, Jack. *Nathan Bedford Forrest: A Biography.* New York: Alfred A. Knopf, 1993.

Inada, Lawson Fusao, ed. *Only What We Could Carry: The Japanese American Internment Experience.* San Francisco: California Historical Society, 2000.

Ise, John. *Our National Park Policy: A Critical History.* Baltimore, MD: Johns Hopkins University Press, 1961.

Israel, Paul. *Edison: A Life of Invention.* New York: John Wiley and Sons, 1998.

Iverson, Peter. *The Navajo Nation.* Westport, CT: Greenwood Press, 1981.

Ivey, James E. *"In the Midst of a Loneliness": The Architectural History of the Salinas Missions.* Santa Fe, NM: National Park Service, 1988. Available at www.nps.gov/sapu/hsr/hsr.htm.

Jackson, Earl. *Tumacácori's Yesterdays.* Globe, AZ: Southwest Parks and Monuments Association, 1973.

Jackson, Frances O. *National Parks in Hawaii: 50 Years, 1916–1966: A Short History of Hawaii Volcanoes National Park.* Honolulu: Hawaii Natural History Association, 1966.

——. *An Administrative History of Hawaii Volcanoes National Park, Haleakala National Park.* Honolulu, HI: National Park Service, 1972.

Jackson, John C. *Shadow on the Tetons: David E. Jackson and the Claiming of the American West.* Missoula, MT: Mountain, 1993.

Jackson, Louise A. *Beulah: A Biography of the Mineral King Valley of California.* Tucson, AZ: Westernlore, 1988.

Jacoway, Elizabeth, and C. Fred Williams, eds. *Understanding the Little Rock Crisis: An Exercise in Remembrance and Reconciliation.* Fayetteville: University of Arkansas Press, 1999.

Jans, Nick. *The Last Light Breaking: Living Among Alaska's Inupiat Eskimos.* Anchorage: Alaska Northwest Books, 1993.

——. *A Place Beyond: Finding Home in Arctic Alaska.* Anchorage: Alaska Northwest Books, 1996.

Jasper, Joy Waldron, James P. Delgado, and Jim Adams. *The USS* Arizona: *The Ship, the Men, the Pearl Harbor Attack, and the Symbol That Aroused America.* New York: St. Martin's, 2001.

Jefferson Memorial: Interpretive Guide to Thomas Jefferson Memorial, District of Columbia. Washington, DC: U.S. Government Printing Office, 1998.

Jeffrey, Julie Roy. *Converting the West: A Biography of Narcissa Whitman.* Norman: University of Oklahoma Press, 1991.

Jeffries, John W. *Wartime America: The World War II Home Front.* Chicago: I.R. Dee, 1996.

Jennings, Jesse David. *Glen Canyon: An Archaeological Summary.* Salt Lake City: University of Utah Press, 1998.

Jensen, Merrill. *The Articles of Confederation: An Interpretation of the Social-Constitutional History of the American Revolution, 1774–1781.* Madison: University of Wisconsin Press, 1970.

Jochelson, Waldemar. *History, Ethnology, and Anthropology of the Aleut.* Salt Lake City: University of Utah Press, 2002.

Johnson, Carl L. *Professor Longfellow of Harvard.* Eugene: University of Oregon, 1944.

Johnson, Madeleine C. *Fire Island, 1650s–1980s.* Mountainside, NJ: Shoreland, 1983.

Johnson, Ross B. "The Great Sand Dunes of Southern Colorado." *Mountain Geologist* (1968): 23–29.

Jolley, Harley E. *Blue Ridge Parkway: The First 50 Years.* Boone, NC: Appalachian Consortium, 1985.

Jones, Anne Trinkle. *Stalking the Past: Prehistory at Petrified Forest.* Petrified Forest National Park, AZ: Petrified Forest Museum Association, 1993.

Josephy, Alvin M. *The Indian Heritage of America.* Boston: Houghton Mifflin, 1991.

——. *The Nez Perce Indians and the Opening of the Northwest.* Boston: Houghton Mifflin, 1997.

Joyner, Ulysses P., Jr. *The First Settlers of Orange County, Virginia: A View of the Life and Times of the European Settlers of Orange County, Virginia and Their Influence upon the Young James Madison, 1700–1776.* Baltimore, MD: Gateway Press for the Orange County Historical Society, 1987.

Kajencki, Francis C. *Thaddeus Kosciuszko: Military Engineer of the American Revolution.* El Paso, TX: Southwest Palonia, 1998.

——. *Casimir Pulaski, Cavalry Commander of the American Revolution.* El Paso, TX: Southwest Polonia, 2001.

Kan, Sergei. *Memory Eternal: Tlingit Culture and Russian Orthodox Christianity Through Two Centuries.* Seattle: University of Washington Press, 1999.

Kania, Alan. *John Otto: Trials and Trails.* Niwot: University Press of Colorado, 1996.

Kantor, MacKinlay. *Andersonville.* New York: Plume, 1993.

Kaplanoff, Mark D. "Charles Pinckney and the American Republican Tradition." In *Intellectual Life in Antebellum Charleston.* Edited by Michael O'Brien and David Moltke-Hansen. Knoxville: University of Tennessee Press, 1986.

Karamanski, Theodore J. *The Pictured Rocks: An Administrative History of Pictured Rocks National Lakeshore.* Omaha, NE: National Park Service, Midwest Regional Office, 1995. Available at www.nps.gov/piro/adhi/adhi.htm.

——. *A Nationalized Lakeshore: The Creation and Administration of Sleeping Bear Dunes National Lakeshore.* Omaha, NE: National Park Service, 2000. Available at www.cr.nps.gov/history/online_books/slbe/index.htm.

Karlsen, Carol F. *The Devil in the Shape of a Woman: Witchcraft in Colonial New England.* New York: W.W. Norton, 1998.

Kasler, Ben. *Priceless Heritage: History and Lore of Estate St. George, Home of the St. George Village Botanical Garden of St. Croix.* St. Croix, U.S. Virgin Islands: privately published, 1980.

Kaufman, Burton I. *The Presidency of James Earl Carter, Jr.* Lawrence: University Press of Kansas, 1993.

Kay, E. Alison, ed. *A Natural History of the Hawaiian Islands: Selected Readings.* Honolulu: University Press of Hawaii, 1972.

Kein, Sybil, ed. *Creole: The History and Legacy of Louisiana's Free People of Color.* Baton Rouge: Louisiana State University Press, 2000.

Keith, Sandra L. *Sequoia National Park: An Illustrated History.* Santa Barbara, CA: Sequoia Communications, 1989.

Kellogg, George Albert. *A History of Whidbey Island.* Coupeville, WA: The Island County Historical Society, 1968.

Kelly, Dennis. *Kennesaw Mountain and the Atlanta Campaign: A Tour Guide.* Marietta, GA: Kennesaw Mountain Historical Association, 1989.

Kelman, Ari. *A River and Its City: The Nature of Landscape in New Orleans.* Berkeley: University of California Press, 2003.

Kelsey, Harry. *Juan Rodriguez Cabrillo.* San Marino, CA: Huntington Library, 1986.

Kennedy, John F. *Profiles in Courage.* New York: Harper Perennial, 2000.

Kessell, John L. *Kiva, Cross, and Crown: The Pecos Indians and New Mexico, 1540–1840.* Albuquerque: University of New Mexico Press, 1987.

Ketchum, Richard M. *Saratoga: Turning Point of America's Revolutionary War.* New York: Henry Holt, 1997.

Keys, Willis. *Growing Up at the Desert Queen Ranch.* Twentynine Palms, CA: Desert Moon, 1997.

Kight, Marsha, ed. *Forever Changed: Remembering Oklahoma City, April 19, 1995.* Amherst, NY: Prometheus Books, 1998.

King, Marina. *Piscataway Village Rural Conservation Study: Final Report.* Upper Marlboro: Maryland-National Capital Park and Planning Commission, 1991.

King, Martin Luther, Jr. *Stride Toward Freedom: The Montgomery Story.* New York: Harper, 1958.

Kirch, Patrick V. *Feathered Gods and Fishhooks: An Introduction to Hawaiian Archaeology and Prehistory.* Honolulu: University of Hawaii Press, 1985.

Kirchner, Bill, ed. *The Oxford Companion to Jazz.* New York: Oxford University Press, 2000.

Kirk, Ruth. *The Olympic Rain Forest: An Ecological Web.* Seattle: University of Washington Press, 1992.

——. *Sunrise to Paradise: The Story of Mount Rainier National Park.* Seattle: University of Washington Press, 1999.

Kirkland, Thomas J. *Historic Camden.* Camden, SC: Kershaw County Historical Society, 1994.

Kirkpatrick, Golda, Charlene Hozwarth, and Linda Mullens. *The Botanist and Her Muleskinner: Lilla Irvin Leach and John Roy Leach, Pioneer Botanists in the Siskiyou Mountains.* Portland, OR: Leach Garden Friends, 1994.

Kiver, Eugene P., and David V. Harris. *Geology of U.S. Parklands.* New York: John Wiley and Sons, 1999.

Kluger, Richard. *Simple Justice.* New York: Alfred A. Knopf, 1975.

Knapp, Marilyn R. *Carved History: A Totem Guide to Sitka National Historical Park.* Anchorage, AK: National Park Service, 1980.

Knight, Dennis. *Vegetation Ecology in the Bighorn Canyon National Recreation Area.* Laramie: University of Wyoming, 1987.

Knott, Stephen F. *Alexander Hamilton and the Persistence of Myth.* Lawrence: University Press of Kansas, 2002.

Koogler, C.V., and Virginia Koogler Whitney. *Aztec: A Story of Old Aztec from the Anasazi to Statehood.* Fort Worth, TX: American Reference, 1972.

Koons, Kenneth E., and Warren R. Hofstra. *After the Backcountry: Rural Life in the Great Valley of Virginia, 1800–1900.* Knoxville: University of Tennessee Press, 2000.

Korp, Maureen. *The Sacred Geography of the American Mound Builders.* Lewiston, NY: E. Mellen, 1990.

Kraft, Herbert C. *The Dutch, the Indians and the Quest for Copper: Pahaquarry and the Old Mine Road.* Union, NJ: Lenape Books, 1996.

Krako, Jere L. *Administrative History of Castillo de San Marcos National Monument and Fort Matanzas National Monument.* Washington, DC: National Park Service, 1986.

Krause, David J. *The Making of a Mining District: Keweenaw Native Copper, 1500–1870*. Detroit, MI: Wayne State University Press, 1992.

Krick, Robert K. *Stonewall Jackson at Cedar Mountain*. Chapel Hill: University of North Carolina Press, 1990.

Kugel, Rebecca. *To Be the Main Leaders of Our People: A History of Minnesota Ojibwe Politics, 1825–1898*. East Lansing: Michigan State University Press, 1998.

Kunhardt, Philip B., Jr. *A New Birth of Freedom, Lincoln at Gettysburg*. Boston: Little, Brown, 1983.

Kuppenheimer, L.B. *Albert Gallatin's Vision of Democratic Stability: An Interpretive Profile*. Westport, CT: Praeger, 1996.

Kupperman, Karen Ordahl. *Roanoke: The Abandoned Colony*. Totowa, NJ: Rowman & Allanheld, 1984.

Kurtz, Rick S. *Glacier Bay National Park and Preserve: Historic Resources Study*. Anchorage: National Park Service, Alaska System Support Office, 1995.

Lacey, Robert. *Sir Walter Raleigh*. London: Phoenix, 2000.

Lageson, David R., Stephen G. Peters, and Mary M. Lahren, eds. *Great Basin and Sierra Nevada*. Boulder, CO: Geological Society of America, 2000.

Lamb, Susan. *Petroglyph National Monument*. Tucson, AZ: Southwest Parks and Monuments Association, 1993.

——. *Tumacácori National Historical Park*. Tucson, AZ: Southwest Parks and Monuments Association, 1993.

——. *Wupatki National Monument*. Tucson, AZ: Southwest Parks and Monuments Association, 1995.

——. *Channel Islands National Park*. Tucson, AZ: Southwest Parks and Monuments Association, 2000.

Lambert, Darwin. *The Undying Past of Shenandoah National Park*. Boulder, CO: Roberts Rinehart, 1989.

Lamberton, Ken. *Chiricahua Mountains: Bridging the Borders of Wildness*. Tucson: University of Arizona Press, 2003.

Lamborn, Alan C., and Stephen P. Mumme. *Statecraft, Domestic Politics, and Foreign Policy Making: The El Chamizal Dispute*. Boulder, CO: Westview, 1988.

Lampe, Gregory P. *Frederick Douglass: Freedom's Voice, 1818–1845*. East Lansing: Michigan State University Press, 1998.

Landrum, Wayne L. *Biscayne: The Story Behind the Scenery*. Las Vegas, NV: KC Publications, 2001.

Lange, Charles H., and Carroll L. Riley. *Bandelier: The Life and Adventures of Adolph Bandelier*. Salt Lake City: University of Utah Press, 1996.

Lankton, Larry D. *Beyond the Boundaries: Life and Landscape at the Lake Superior Copper Mines, 1840–1875*. New York: Oxford University Press, 1997.

Lansing, Ronald B. *Juggernaut: The Whitman Massacre Trial, 1850*. Pasadena, CA: Ninth Judicial Circuit Historical Society, 1993.

Larner, Jesse. *Mount Rushmore: An Icon Reconsidered*. New York: Thunder's Mouth/Nation Books, 2002.

Lavender, David Sievert. *Fort Laramie and the Changing Frontier: Fort Laramie National Historic Site, Wyoming*. Washington, DC: National Park Service, 1983.

——. *Pipe Spring and the Arizona Strip*. Springdale, UT: Zion Natural History Association, 1984.

——. *Desoto, Coronado, Cabrillo: Explorers of the Northern Mystery*. Washington, DC: Government Printing Office, 1992.

Law, Anwei Skinsnes. *Kalapaupapa National Historical Park and the Legacy of Father Damien: A Pictorial History*. Honolulu, HI: Pacific Basin Enterprises, 1988.

Layton, Stanford J. *To No Privileged Class: The Rationalization of Homesteading and Rural Life in the Early Twentieth-Century American West*. Salt Lake City, UT: Signature Books, 1988.

Leach, Nicky. *Cedar Breaks National Monument*. Springdale, UT: Zion Natural History, 1994.

——. *Zion National Park: Sanctuary in the Desert*. San Francisco: Sierra, 2000.

Least Heat-Moon, William. *PrairyErth (A Deep Map): An Epic History of the Tallgrass Prairie Country*. Boston: Houghton Mifflin, 1999.

Leavitt, Sarah. *Slater Mill*. Dover, NH: Arcadia, 1997.

Lee, Lawrence Bacon. *Kansas and the Homestead Act, 1862–1905*. New York: Arno, 1979.

Lepore, Jill. *The Name of War: King Philip's War and the Origins of American Identity*. New York: Alfred A. Knopf, 1998.

Lerner, Gerda. *The Grimke Sisters from South Carolina: Pioneers for Women's Rights and Abolition*. New York: Houghton Mifflin, 1967.

Leuchtenburg, William E. *Franklin D. Roosevelt and the New Deal, 1932–1940*. New York: Harper and Row, 1963.

Leveillee, Alan. *An Old Place, Safe and Quiet: A Blackstone River Valley Cremation Burial Site*. Westport, CT: Bergin & Garvey, 2002.

Levering, Dale. *An Illustrated Flora of the Boston Harbor Islands*. Boston: Northeastern University Press, 1978.

Levingston, Steve. *Historic Ships of San Francisco: A Collective History and Guide to the Restored Historic Vessels of the National Maritime Museum*. San Francisco: Chronicle Books, 1984.

Lewie, Chris J. *Two Generations on the Allegheny Portage*

Railroad: The First Railroad to Cross the Allegheny Mountains. Shippensburg, PA: Burd Street, 2001.

Lewis, David. *King, a Critical Biography.* New York: Praeger, 1970.

Lewis, Thomas A. *For King and Country: George Washington: The Early Years.* New York: John Wiley and Sons, 1995.

Lien, Carsten. *Olympic Battleground: The Power Politics of Timber Preservation.* Seattle, WA: Mountaineers, 2000.

Lindquist, Robert C. *The Geology of Bryce Canyon National Park.* Bryce Canyon, UT: Bryce Canyon Natural History Association, 1977.

Linenthal, Edward T. *Sacred Ground: Americans and Their Battlefields.* Urbana: University of Illinois Press, 1993.

——. *The Unfinished Bombing: Oklahoma City in American Memory.* New York: Oxford University Press, 2001.

Lingenfelter, Richard. *Death Valley and the Amargosa: Land of Illusion.* Berkeley: University of California Press, 1986.

Lister, Robert H., and Florence C. Lister. *Aztec Ruins on the Animas. Excavated, Preserved, and Interpreted.* Albuquerque: University of New Mexico Press, 1987.

——. *Aztec Ruins National Monument: Administrative History of an Archeological Preserve.* Santa Fe, NM: National Park Service, Division of History, Southwest Cultural Resources Center, 1990. Available at www.nps.gov/azru/adhi/adhi.htm.

Lodge, Thomas E. *The Everglades Handbook: Understanding the Ecosystem.* Boca Raton, FL: St. Lucie, 1998.

Lohman, Stanley William. *The Geologic Story of Colorado National Monument.* Gunnison: Colorado and Black Canyon Natural History Association, 1965.

Long, E.B. *The Civil War Day by Day: An Almanac, 1861–1865.* New York: Da Capo, 1985.

Long, Robert A., and Rose Houk. *Dawn of the Dinosaurs: The Triassic in Petrified Forest.* Petrified Forest, AZ: Petrified Forest Museum Association, 1988.

Longfellow, Henry Wadsworth. *Selected Poems: Henry Wadsworth Longfellow.* New York: Penguin Books, 1988.

Louter, David. *Administrative History: Craters of the Moon National Monument, Idaho.* Seattle, WA: Cultural Resources Division, Pacific Northwest Region, 1992. Available at www.nps.gov/crmo/adhi.htm.

——. *Contested Terrain: North Cascades National Park Service Complex: An Administrative History.* Seattle, WA: National Park Service, 1998.

Lowenthal, David. *George Perkins Marsh: Prophet of Conservation.* Seattle: University of Washington Press, 2000.

Lowenthal, Larry, ed. *Days of Siege: A Journal of the Siege of Fort Stanwix in 1777.* New York: Eastern Acorn, 1983.

Lubick, George M. *Petrified Forest National Park: A Wilderness Bound in Time.* Tucson: University of Arizona Press, 1996.

Lueth, Virgil W., ed. *Geology of White Sands.* Socorro: New Mexico Geological Society, 2002.

Luvaas, Jay, and Harold W. Nelson. *U.S. Army War College Guide to the Battle of Antietam: The Maryland Campaign of 1862.* New York: Perennial Library, 1988.

Luvaas, Jay, Stephen Bowman, and Leonard Fullenkamp, eds. *Guide to the Battle of Shiloh.* Lawrence: University Press of Kansas, 1996.

Luzader, John F. *The Construction and Military History of Fort Stanwix.* Washington, DC: U.S. Office of Archeology and Historic Preservation, Division of History, 1969.

Lyman, R. Lee. *White Goats, White Lies: The Abuse of Science in Olympic National Park.* Salt Lake City: University of Utah Press, 1998.

MacDonald, Gordon A. *Volcanoes in the Sea: The Geology of Hawaii.* Honolulu: University of Hawaii Press, 1983.

MacDonald, Gordon A., and Douglas H. Hubbard. *Volcanoes of the National Parks in Hawaii.* Hawaii Volcanoes National Park: Hawaii Natural History Association in cooperation with the National Park Service, 1982.

Mack, Jim. *Haleakala: The Story Behind the Scenery.* Las Vegas, NV: KC Publications, 1993.

MacKay, Pam. *Mojave Desert Wildflowers: A Field Guide to the Wildflowers of the Mojave Desert, Including the Mojave National Preserve and Joshua Tree National Park.* Guilford, CT: Globe Pequot, 2003.

Mackintosh, Barry. *Rock Creek Park: An Administrative History.* Washington, DC: National Park Service, 1985.

Maddock, Stephen J. "An Analysis of Local Opposition to the Sleeping Bear Dunes National Lakeshore." Ph.D. diss., University of Michigan, 1971.

Mallory, Kenneth. *Boston Harbor Islands: National Park Area.* Camden, ME: Down East Books, 2003.

Malone, Dumas. *The Sage of Monticello.* Boston: Little, Brown, 1981.

Malotki, Ekkehart. *Earth Fire: A Hopi Legend of the Sunset Crater Eruption.* Flagstaff, AZ: Northland, 1987.

Manchester, Albert, and Ann Manchester. *Hubbell Trading Post National Historic Site: An Administrative History.* Santa Fe, NM: Southwest Cultural Resources Center, National Park Service, 1993. Available at www.nps.gov/hutr/adhi/adhi.htm.

Mangum, Neil C. *In the Land of Frozen Fires: A History of Occupation in El Malpais Country.* Santa Fe, NM: National Park Service, 1990. Available at www.nps.gov/elma/hist/hist.htm.

Manning, Russ. *The Historic Cumberland Plateau: An Explorer's Guide.* Knoxville: University of Tennessee Press, 1999.

Mapes, Ruth B. *Old Fort Smith: Cultural Center on the Southwestern Frontier.* Little Rock, AR: Pioneer, 1965.

Mark, Stephen R. *Floating in the Stream of Time: An Administrative History of John Day Fossil Beds National Monument.* Seattle, WA: Columbia-Cascades Cluster, National Park Service, 1996. Available at www.nps.gov/joda/adhi/adhi.htm.

Marsh, Alan. *Ocmulgee National Monument: An Administrative History.* Washington, DC: National Park Service, 1986.

Marsh, Dorothy. *Life at Russell Cave.* New York: Eastern Acorn, 1980.

Marsh, George Perkins. *Man and Nature, or, Physical Geography as Modified by Human Action.* Edited by David Lowenthal. Seattle. University of Washington Press, 2003.

Martin, David G. *The Vicksburg Campaign: April 1862–July 1863.* Conshohocken, PA: Combined Books, 1994.

Martin, Don. *Point Reyes National Seashore: A Hiking and Nature Guide.* New York: Martin, 1997.

Martin, George Vivian. *The Timpanogos Cave Story: The Romance of Its Exploration.* Salt Lake City, UT: Hawkes, 1973.

Martin, Waldo. *The Brown Decision: A Brief History with Documents.* Boston: Bedford Books, 1998.

Martini, John A. *Fort Point: Sentry at the Golden Gate.* San Francisco: Golden Gate National Park Association, 1991.

Martinson, Arthur D. *Wilderness Above the Sound: The Story of Mount Rainier National Park.* Niwot, CO: Robert Rinehart, 1994.

Marvel, William. *Andersonville: The Last Depot.* Chapel Hill: University of North Carolina Press, 1994.

Mathien, Frances Joan, ed. *Environment and Subsistence of Chaco Canyon, New Mexico.* Albuquerque, NM: National Park Service, 1985.

Matter, William D. *If It Takes All Summer: The Battle of Spotsylvania.* Chapel Hill: University of North Carolina Press, 1988.

Mattes, Merrill J. *Scotts Bluff National Monument Nebraska.* Washington, DC: National Park Service, 1958. Available at www.cr.nps.gov/history/online_books/hh/28/index.htm.

——. *Fort Laramie Park History, 1834–1977.* Washington, DC: National Park Service, 1980. Also available at www.nps.gov/fola/history/index.htm.

Matthews, Vincent. *Pinnacles Geological Trail.* Globe, AZ: Southwest Parks and Monuments Association, 1972.

Mattison, Ray H. *History of Devils Tower.* Gillette, WY: Devils Tower Natural History Association, 2001.

Mattson, Thomas. *Small Town: Reflections of People, History, Religion and Nature in Central New England.* Grafton, MA: Northfield, 1992.

Maxon, James C. *Lake Mead–Hoover Dam: The Story Behind the Scenery.* Las Vegas, NV: KC Publications, 1980.

Maxwell, Ross A. *The Big Bend of the Rio Grande: A Guide to the Rocks, Landscape, Geologic History, and Settlers of the Area of Big Bend National Park.* Austin: University of Texas, 1990.

McAuley, Milt. *Wildflowers of the Santa Monica Mountains.* Canoga Park, CA: Canyon, 1985.

McCabe, Marsha, and Joseph D. Thomas. *Not Just Anywhere: The Story of WHALE and the Rescue of New Bedford's Waterfront Historic District.* New Bedford, MA: Spinner, 1996.

McCally, David. *The Everglades: An Environmental History.* Gainesville: University Press of Florida, 1999.

McChristian, Douglas C. *Ranchers to Rangers: An Administrative History of Grant-Kohrs Ranch National Historic Site.* Washington, DC: National Park Service, 1977. Available at www.nps.gov/grko/adhi/adhi.htm.

McClellan, Robert J. *The Delaware Canal: A Picture Story.* New Brunswick, NJ: Rutgers University Press, 1967.

McCreery, Patricia. *Tapamveni: The Rock Art Galleries of Petrified Forest and Beyond.* Petrified Forest, AZ: Petrified Forest Museum Association, 1994.

McCullough, David. *The Johnstown Flood.* New York: Simon and Schuster, 1968.

——. *Truman.* New York: Simon and Schuster, 1992.

——. *John Adams.* New York: Simon and Schuster, 2001.

——. *Mornings on Horseback. The Story of an Extraordinary Family, a Vanished Way of Life, and the Unique Child Who Became Theodore Roosevelt.* New York: Simon and Schuster, 2001.

McDonald, H.G. "More Than Just Horses: Hagerman Fossils Beds." *Rocks and Minerals* 68 (1993): 322–26.

McDonald, JoAnna M. *We Shall Meet Again: The First Battle of Manassas (Bull Run), July 18–21, 1861.* New York: Oxford University Press, 2000.

McDonough, James Lee. *Stones River: Bloody Winter in Tennessee.* Knoxville: University of Tennessee Press, 1980.

——. *War in Kentucky: From Shiloh to Perryville.* Knoxville: University of Tennessee Press, 1994.

McGrath, John T. *The French in Early Florida.* Gainesville: University Press of Florida, 2000.

McGregor, Roberta. *Prehistoric Basketry of the Lower Pecos, Texas.* Madison, WI: Prehistory, 1992.

McGrew, Paul Orman, and Michael Casilliano. *The Geological History of Fossil Butte National Monument and Fossil Basin.* Washington, DC: National Park Service, 1975.

McKain, James D. *Index to Historic Camden, Colonial and Revolutionary and Nineteenth Century.* Columbia: The South Carolina Magazine of Ancestral Research, 1995.

McKee, Bates. *Cascadia; the Geologic Evolution of the Pacific Northwest.* New York: McGraw-Hill, 1972.

McKissack, Patricia, and Frederick McKissack. *Red-Tail Angels: The Story of the Tuskegee Airmen of World War II.* New York: Walker, 1995.

McKitrick, Eric L. *Andrew Johnson and Reconstruction.* New York: Oxford University Press, 1988.

McKoy, Kathleen L. *Cultures at a Crossroads: An Administrative History of Pipe Spring National Monument.* Denver, CO: National Park Service, Intermountain Region, 2000. Available at www.nsp.gov/pisp/adhi/adhi.htm.

McMurry, Alex. *Oregon Caves Chateau: Oregon Caves National Monument Historic Structures Report.* Eugene: Historic Preservation Program, School of Architecture and Applied Arts, University of Oregon, 1999. Available at www.nps.gov/orca/hsr/hsr.htm.

McMurry, Linda O. *George Washington Carver, Scientist and Symbol.* New York: Oxford University Press, 1982.

Mcnab, A.J. *Lake Clark-Iliamna, Alaska, 1921: The Travel Diary of Colonel A.J. Mcnab with Related Documents.* Anchorage: Alaska Natural History Association, 1996.

McNitt, Frank. *Richard Wetherill, Anasazi.* Albuquerque: University of New Mexico Press, 1974.

McNulty, Tim. *Washington's Mount Rainier National Park: A Centennial Celebration.* Seattle, WA: Mountaineer Books, 1998.

——. *Olympic National Park: A Natural History.* Seattle: University of Washington Press, 2003.

McPherson, James M. *Battle Cry of Freedom: The Civil War Era.* New York: Oxford University Press, 1988.

——. *Crossroads of Freedom: Antietam.* New York: Oxford University Press, 2002.

Meanley, Brooke. *Bird Life at Chincoteague and the Virginia Barrier Islands.* Centreville, MD: Tidewater, 1981.

Medlin, William K. *Fire Mountain: A Nation's Heritage in Jeopardy.* Santa Fe, NM: Sunstone, 1996.

Meikle, Lyndel, ed. *Very Close to Trouble: The Johnny Grant Memoir.* Pullman: Washington State University Press, 1996.

Melosi, Martin V. *Thomas A. Edison and the Modernization of America.* New York: Longman, 1990.

Mendoza, Patrick M. *Song of Sorrow: Massacre at Sand Creek.* Denver, CO: Willow Wind, 1993.

Merkel, Jim. *Majestic Lights: The Apostle Island Lighthouses.* St. Louis, MO: JCM Press, 2001.

Merritt Island National Wildlife Refuge. *Protecting Endangered Species.* New York: Time Life, 1996.

Merritt, Jane T. *The Administrative History of Fort Vancouver National Historic Site.* Seattle, WA: National Park Service, Pacific Northwest Region, 1993.

Messick, Hank. *King's Mountain: The Epic of the Blue Ridge "Mountain Men" in the American Revolution.* Boston: Little, Brown, 1976.

Meyer, Herbert W. *The Fossils of Florissant.* Washington, DC: Smithsonian Institution, 2003.

Meyerson, Harvey. *Nature's Army: When Soldiers Fought for Yosemite.* Lawrence: University Press of Kansas, 2001.

Michel, Lou, and Dan Herbeck. *American Terrorist: Timothy McVeigh and the Tragedy at Oklahoma City.* New York: Avon Books, 2002.

Michie, James L. *An Archeological Survey of Congaree Swamp: Cultural Resources Inventory and Assessment of a Bottomland Environment in Central South Carolina.* Columbia: Institute of Archeology and Anthropology, University of South Carolina, 1980.

Mighetto, Lisa. *Hard Drive to the Klondike: Promoting Seattle During the Gold Rush.* Seattle: University of Washington Press, 2002.

Milanich, Jerald T. *Archaeology of Precolumbian Florida.* Gainesville: University Press of Florida, 1994.

——. *The Timucua.* Cambridge, MA: Blackwell, 1996.

Miles, Jim. *A River Unvexed: A History and Tour Guide to the Campaign for the Mississippi River.* Nashville, TN: Rutledge Hill, 1994.

Miller, A.H. *Lives of Desert Animals in Joshua Tree National Monument.* Berkeley: University of California Press, 1964.

Miller, David W. *A Guide to Alaska's Kenai Fjords.* Seward, AK: Wilderness Images, 1984.

Miller, John C. *The Origins of the American Revolution.* Boston: Little, Brown, 1943.

Miller, Lee. *Roanoke: Solving the Mystery of the Lost Colony.* New York: Arcade, 2001.

Miller, Martin G., and Lauren Wright. *Geology of Death Valley National Park: Landforms, Crustal Extension, Geologic History.* Dubuque, IA: Kendall/Hunt, 2001.

Miller, William J. *The Battles for Richmond, 1862.* Conshohocken, PA: Eastern National Park and Monument Association, 1996.

Mills, Enos A. *The Rocky Mountain Wonderland*. New York: Houghton-Mifflin, 1915.

Mills, Gary B. *The Forgotten People: Cane River's Creoles of Color*. Baton Rouge: Louisiana State University Press, 1977.

Milstein, Michael. *Badlands, Theodore Roosevelt, and Wind Cave National Parks: Wildlife Watchers Guide*. Minocqua, WI: NorthWord, 1996.

Minge, Ward A. *Acoma: Pueblo in the Sky*. Albuquerque: University of New Mexico Press, 1976.

Mintz, Max M. *The Generals of Saratoga: John Burgoyne and Horatio Gates*. New Haven, CT: Yale University Press, 1990.

Mitchell, Robert D. *Commercialism and Frontier: Perspectives on the Early Shenandoah Valley*. Charlottesville: University Press of Virginia, 1977.

Molenaar, Dee. *The Challenge of Rainier: A Record of the Explorations and Ascents, Triumphs and Tragedies, on the Northwest's Greatest Mountain*. Seattle, WA: Mountaineers, 1979.

Molotsky, Irvin. *The Flag, the Poet and the Song: The Story of the Star-Spangled Banner*. New York: Dutton, 2001.

Monjo, F.N. *Slater's Mill*. New York: Simon and Schuster, 1972.

Moogk, Peter N. *La Nouvelle France: The Making of French Canada: A Cultural History*. East Lansing: Michigan State University Press, 2000.

Moore, Harry L. *A Roadside Guide to the Geology of the Great Smoky Mountains National Park*. Knoxville: University of Tennessee Press, 1988.

Moore, Hullihen Williams. *Shenandoah: Views of Our National Park*. Charlottesville: University of Virginia Press, 2003.

Moore, Jackson W., Jr. *Bent's Old Fort: An Archeological Study*. Denver: State History Society of Colorado, 1973.

Moratto, Michael J. *An Archeological Overview of Redwood National Park*. Tucson, AZ: Cultural Resources Management Division, National Park Service, 1973.

Moreno, Barry. *The Statue of Liberty Encyclopedia*. New York: Simon and Schuster, 2000.

Morgan, Edmund S. *Benjamin Franklin*. New Haven, CT: Yale University Press, 2002.

Morison, Samuel Eliot. *History of United States Naval Operations in World War II*. Urbana: University of Illinois Press, 2001.

——. *New Guinea and the Marianas: March 1944–August 1944*. Vol. 8, *History of United States Naval Operations in World War II*. Urbana: University of Illinois Press, 2001–2002.

Morrill, Dan L. *Southern Campaigns of the American Revolution*. Baltimore, MD: Nautical & Aviation Publishing Company of America, 1993.

Morris, Edmund. *The Rise of Theodore Roosevelt*. New York: Modern Library, 2001.

——. *Theodore Rex*. New York: Random House, 2001.

Morris, John Miller. *El Llano Estacado: Exploration and Imagination on the High Plains of Texas and New Mexico, 1536–1860*. Austin: Texas State Historical Association, 1997.

Morris, Kenneth E. *Jimmy Carter: American Moralist*. Athens: University of Georgia Press, 1996.

Morristown: A History and Guide, Morristown National Historical Park, New Jersey. Washington, DC: National Park Service, 1983.

Morseth, Michele. *Puyulek Pu'irtuq!: The People of the Volcanoes: Aniakchak National Monument and Preserve Ethnographic Overview and Assessment*. Anchorage, AK: National Park Service, 1998.

Moulton, Gary E., ed. *The Definitive Journals of Lewis and Clark: Down the Columbia to Fort Clatsop*. Lincoln: University of Nebraska Press, 2002.

Mozier, Jeanne. *Way Out in West Virginia: A Must Have Guide to the Oddities and Wonders of the Mountain State*. Charleston, WV: Quarrier, 1999.

Mudd, Nettie, ed. *The Life of Dr. Samuel A. Mudd, Containing His Letters from Fort Jefferson, Dry Tortugas Island, Where He Was Imprisoned Four Years for Alleged Complicity in the Assassination of Abraham Lincoln*. R.D. Mudd, privately published, 1962.

Mueller, Jerry E. *Restless River: International Law and the Behavior of the Rio Grande*. El Paso: Texas Western University Press, 1975.

Muir, John. *John Muir: Nature Writings: The Story of My Boyhood and Youth; My First Summer in the Sierra; The Mountains of California; Stickeen; Essays*. New York: Library of America, 1997.

——. *My First Summer in the Sierra*. New York: Penguin Books, 1997.

Mumey, Nolie. *John Williams Gunnison (1812–1853), The Last of the Western Explorers: A History of the Survey Through Colorado and Utah, with a Biography and Details of His Massacre*. Denver, CO: Artcraft, 1955.

Murfin, James V. *The Gleam of Bayonets: the Battle of Antietam and the Maryland Campaign of 1862*. New York: T. Yoseloff, 1965.

Murie, Adolph. *The Wolves of Mount McKinley*. Seattle: University of Washington Press, 1985.

——. *The Grizzlies of Mount McKinley*. Seattle: University of Washington Press, 2000.

Murphy, Dan. *El Morro National Monument*. Tucson, AZ: Southwest Parks and Monuments Association, 1989.

——. *Salinas Pueblo Missions National Monument*. Tucson, AZ: Southwest Parks and Monuments Association, 1993.

Murray, Alice Yang, ed. *What Did the Internment of*

Japanese Americans Mean? Boston: Bedford/St. Martin's, 2000.

Nabhan, Gary Paul. *Saguaro: A View of Saguaro National Monument & the Tucson Basin.* Tucson, AZ: Southwest Parks and Monuments Association, 1986.

Nadeau, Remi A. *Fort Laramie and the Sioux.* Lincoln: University of Nebraska Press, 1982.

Nagel, Paul C. *The Adams Women: Abigail and Louisa Adams, Their Sisters and Daughters.* New York: Oxford University Press, 1987.

Nash, George H. *Life of Herbert Hoover: The Humanitarian, 1914–1917.* New York: W.W. Norton, 1996.

National Park Service. *Hopewell Furnace: A Guide to Hopewell Village National Historic Site, Pennsylvania.* Washington, DC: National Park Service, 1983.

——. *Salem: Maritime Salem in the Age of Sail.* Washington, DC: U.S. Department of the Interior, 1987.

——. *Historic Resources Study: City of Rocks National Reserve, Southcentral Idaho.* Washington, DC: National Park Service, 1996.

National Park Trust. "NPT Interview with NEW NPS Director Fran Mainella." *Legacy News,* Spring 2002.

The Nature Conservancy. *Uncommon Wealth: Essays on Virginia's Wild Places.* Missoula, MT: Falcon, 1999.

The Nature of the Towpath. Cuyahoga, OH: Cuyahoga Valley Trails Council, 1999.

Nauman, James D. *An Account of the Voyage of Juan Rodriguez Cabrillo.* San Diego, CA: Cabrillo National Monument Foundation, 1999.

Nelson, Ben A., and Steven A. LeBlanc. *Short-term Sedentism in the American Southwest: The Mimbres Valley Salado.* Albuquerque: University of New Mexico Press, 1986.

Nelson, W. Dale. *The President Is at Camp David.* Syracuse, NY: Syracuse University Press, 1995.

Newhall, Nancy Wynne. *Contribution to the Heritage of Every American: The Conservation Activities of John D. Rockefeller, Jr.* New York: Alfred A. Knopf, 1957.

Ng, Wendy L. *Japanese American Internment During World War II: A History and Reference Guide.* Westport, CT: Greenwood, 2002.

Niven, Penelope. *Carl Sandburg: A Biography.* New York: Scribner's Sons, 1991.

Noble, David Grant. *Understanding the Anasazi of Mesa Verde and Hovenweep.* Santa Fe, NM: Ancient City, 1985.

——. ed. *Wupatki and Walnut Canyon: New Perspectives on History, Prehistory, and Rock Art.* Santa Fe, NM: School of American Research, 1987.

——. ed. *Houses Beneath the Rock: The Anasazi of Canyon de Chelly and Navajo National Monument.* Santa Fe, NM: Ancient City, 1992.

——. *Zuni and El Morro Past and Present.* Santa Fe, NM: Ancient City Press, 1993.

——. *Ancient Ruins of the Southwest: An Archaeological Guide.* Flagstaff, AZ: Northland, 2000.

——. *Salinas: Archaeology, History, Prehistory.* Santa Fe, NM: Ancient City, 1993.

Norrell, Robert J. *Reaping the Whirlwind: The Civil Rights Movement in Tuskegee.* New York: Knopf, 1985.

Norris, Frank. *Isolated Paradise: An Administrative History of the Katmai and Aniakchak NPS Units.* Anchorage, AK: National Park Service, 1996. Available at www.nps.gov/katm/adhi/adhi.htm.

——. *Legacy of the Gold Rush: An Administrative History of the Klondike Gold Rush National Historical Park.* Anchorage: National Park Service, Alaska System Support Office, 1996. Available at www.nps.gov/klgo/adhi/adhi.htm.

——. *Gold in Alaska: A Century of Mining History in Alaska's National Parks.* Anchorage, AK: National Park Service, 1997.

Norton, Stephen L. *Devils Tower: The Story Behind the Scenery.* Las Vegas, NV: KC Publications, 1992.

Nute, Grace Lee. *The Voyageur's Highway, Minnesota's Border Lake Land.* St. Paul: Minnesota Historical Society, 1965.

——. *The Voyageur.* St. Paul: Minnesota Historical Society Press, 1987.

Nymeyer, Robert, and William R. Halliday. *Carlsbad Cavern: The Early Years.* Carlsbad, NM: Carlsbad Caverns, Guadalupe Mountains Association, 1991.

Nystrom, Eric, "Mojave National Preserve: An Administrative History." Unpublished, 2004.

Oates, Stephen B. *To Purge This Land with Blood: A Biography of John Brown.* Amherst: University of Massachusetts Press, 1984.

——. *Let the Trumpet Sound: The Life of Martin Luther King, Jr.* New York: New American Library, 1985.

——. *With Malice Toward None: A Life of Abraham Lincoln.* New York: HarperPerennial, 1994.

——. *A Woman of Valor: Clara Barton and the Civil War.* New York: Free Press, 1994.

O'Bright, Jill York. *"There I Grew Up . . .": A History of the Administration of Abraham Lincoln's Boyhood Home.* Washington, DC: National Park Service, 1987. Available at www.nps.gov/libo/adhi/adhi.htm.

——. *The Perpetual March: An Administrative History of Effigy Mounds National Monument.* Omaha, NE: National Park Service, 1989.

Oliva, Leo E. *Fort Larned on the Santa Fe Trail.* Topeka: Kansas State Historical Society, 1982.

——. *Fort Union and the Frontier Army in the Southwest.* Santa Fe, NM: Division of History, National Park Service, 1993.

——. *Fort Scott: Courage and Conflict on the Border.* Topeka: Kansas State Historical Society, 1996.

——. *Fort Larned: Guardian of the Santa Fe Trail.* Topeka: Kansas State Historical Society, 1997.

Olsen, Nancy H. *Hovenweep Rock Art: An Anasazi Visual Communication System.* Los Angeles: Institute of Archaeology, University of California, Los Angeles, 1985.

Olson, Sarah. *Portsmouth Village, Cape Lookout National Seashore, North Carolina.* Denver, CO: National Park Service, 1982.

Olwig, Karen Fog. *Cultural Adaptation and Resistance on St. John: Three Centuries of Afro-Caribbean Life.* Gainesville: University of Florida Press, 1985.

Olympic National Park: An Administrative History. Seattle, WA: National Park Service, Pacific Northwest Region, 1990.

O'Neill, Eugene. *Eugene O'Neill.* Broomall, PA: Chelsea House, 2000.

Onuf, Peter S. *Statehood and Union: A History of the Northwest Ordinance.* Bloomington: Indiana University Press, 1987.

Opler, Morris Edward. *An Apache Life-Way: The Economic, Social, and Religious Institutions of the Chiricahua Indians.* Lincoln: University of Nebraska Press, 1996.

O'Reilly, Francis Augustin. *The Fredericksburg Campaign: Winter War on the Rappahannock.* Baton Rouge: Louisiana State University Press, 2003.

Orsi, Richard J., Alfred Runte, and Marlene Smith-Baranzini, eds. *Yosemite and Sequoia: A Century of California National Parks.* Berkeley: University of California Press, 1993.

Ortiz, Simon J. *From Sand Creek.* Tucson: University of Arizona Press, 1999.

Overland, Orm. *Immigrant Minds, American Identities: Making the United States Home, 1870–1930.* Urbana: University of Illinois Press, 2000.

Palmer, Art. *Jewel Cave: A Gift from the Past.* Hot Springs, SD: Black Hills Parks and Forests Association, 2000.

Palmer, Arthur N. *A Geological Guide to Mammoth Cave National Park.* Teaneck, NJ: Zephyrus, 1981.

—— *The Geology of Wind Cave, Wind Cave National Park, South Dakota.* Hot Springs, SD: Wind Cave Natural History Association, 1981.

Palmer, Laura. *Shrapnel in the Heart: Letters and Remembrance from the Vietnam Veterans Memorial.* New York: Vintage Books, 1988.

Parent, Laurence. *Capulin Volcano National Monument.* Tucson, AZ: Southwest Parks and Monuments Association, 1991.

——. *Gila Cliff Dwellings National Monument.* Tucson, AZ: Southwest Parks and Monuments Association, 1992.

——. *Lake Meredith National Recreation Area.* Tucson, AZ: Southwest Parks and Monuments Association, 1993.

Parkman, Francis. *France and England in North America.* New York: Viking, 1983.

Patterson, Patricia. *Queen, New Mexico: A Historical Perspective on the Settlement in the Guadalupe Mountains, 1865–1975.* Roswell, NM: Hall-Poorbaugh, 1985.

Perkins, Jack. *Acadia: Visions and Verse.* Camden, ME: Down East Books, 1999.

Perkins, William D. *Chestnuts, Galls, and Dandelion Wine: Useful Wild Plants of the Boston Harbor Islands.* Halifax, MA: Plant, 1982.

Perry, John. *Unshakable Faith: Booker T. Washington and George Washington Carver.* Sisters, OR: Multnomah, 1999.

Peskin, Allan. *Garfield: A Biography.* Kent, OH: Kent State University Press, 1999.

Peterson, Charles E. *Notes on Hampton Mansion.* College Park: National Trust for Historic Preservation Library Collection of the University of Maryland Libraries, 2000.

Peterson, Charles S. *Hubbell Trading Post National Historic Site, Arizona.* Tucson, AZ: Southwest Parks and Monuments Association, 1983.

Peterson, Lynelle A. *The 1987 Investigations at Fort Union Trading Post: Archeology and Architecture.* Lincoln, NE: National Park Service, Midwest Archeological Center, 1990.

Peterson, Rolf O. *The Wolves of Isle Royale: A Broken Balance.* Minocqua, WI: Willow Creek, 1995.

Petty, Bruce M. *Saipan: Oral Histories of the Pacific War.* Jefferson, NC: McFarland, 2001.

Phillips, Marcus. *Indian Folklore Atlas of Hot Springs National Park.* Hot Springs, AR: Garland County Historical Society, 1994.

Phillips, Marti. *The Last Pirate.* Lavergne, TN: Southern Star, 2000.

Pierce, Daniel S. *The Great Smokies: From Natural Habitat to National Park.* Knoxville: University of Tennessee Press, 2000.

Piston, William Garrett, and Richard W. Hatcher III. *Wilson's Creek: The Second Battle of the Civil War and the Men Who Fought It.* Chapel Hill: University of North Carolina Press, 2000.

Pitzer, Paul C. *Grand Coulee: Harnessing a Dream.* Pullman: Washington State University Press, 1994.

Platt, John David Ronalds. *Shipping in the Revolution: Salem Maritime National Historic Site, Salem, Massachusetts; Special History Study.* Denver, CO: National Park Service, 1973.

Poe, Edgar Allan. *Complete Stories and Poems of Edgar Allan Poe.* Garden City, NY: Doubleday, 1966.

Porcher, Richard D. *A Guide to the Wildflowers of*

South Carolina. Columbia: University of South Carolina Press, 2001.

Porter, Eliot. *The Place No One Knew: Glen Canyon on the Colorado*. San Francisco: Sierra Club, 1963.

Potter County Historical Survey Committee. *Alibates Flint Quarries: A National Monument*. Canyon, TX: Potter County Historical Survey Committee, 1963.

Powledge, Fred. *Free at Last? The Civil Rights Movement and the People Who Made It*. Boston: Little, Brown, 1991.

Prentice, Guy. *Archeological Inventory and Evaluation at Russell Cave National Monument, Alabama*. Tallahassee, FL: Southeast Archeological Center, National Park Service, 1994.

Preston, Douglas J. *Cities of Gold: A Journey Across the American Southwest*. Albuquerque: University of New Mexico Press, 1999.

Pritchard, James A. *Preserving Yellowstone's Natural Conditions: Science and the Perception of Nature*. Lincoln: University of Nebraska Press, 1999.

Pritchard, Peter Charles Howard, and Rene Marques M. Moreges. *Kemp's Ridley Turtle or Atlantic Ridley: Lepidochelys Kempi*. Gland, Switzerland: International Union for Conservation of Nature and Natural Resources, 1973.

Protas, Josh. *A Past Preserved in Stone: A History of Montezuma Castle National Monument*. Tucson, AZ: Western National Parks Association, 2002. Available at www.nps.gov/moca/protas/index.htm.

Pryor, Elizabeth Brown. *Clara Barton: Professional Angel*. Philadelphia: University of Pennsylvania Press, 1987.

Pula, James S. *Thaddeus Kosciuszko: The Purest Son of Liberty*. New York: Hippocrene Books, 1999.

Purcell, Sarah J. *The Life and Work of Eleanor Roosevelt*. Indianapolis: Alpha, 2002.

Pyne, Stephen J. *How the Canyon Became Grand: A Short History*. New York: Penguin, 1999.

Quinn, Arthur. *Hell with the Fire Out: A History of the Modoc War*. Boston: Faber & Faber, 1997.

Rae, John W. *Morristown, New Jersey*. Charleston, SC: Arcadia, 2002.

Rankin, Hugh F. *The Pirates of Colonial North Carolina*. Raleigh, NC: State Department of Archives and History, 1965.

———. *Greene and Cornwallis: The Campaign in the Carolinas*. Raleigh, NC: Department of Cultural Resources, Division of Archives and History, 1976.

Ranney, Edward. *Prairie Passage: The Illinois and Michigan Canal Corridor*. Urbana: University of Illinois Press, 1998.

Ransom, John. *John Ransom's Andersonville Diary/Life Inside the Civil War's Most Infamous Prison*. New York: Berkley Books, 1994.

Rau, William Herman. *Traveling the Pennsylvania Railroad: The Photographs of William H. Rau*. Philadelphia: University of Pennsylvania Press, 2002.

Redd, Jim. *The Illinois and Michigan Canal: A Contemporary Perspective in Essays and Photographs*. Carbondale: Southern Illinois University Press, 1993.

Reeder, Carolyn, and Jack Reeder. *Shenandoah Heritage: The Story of the People Before the Park*. Washington, DC: Potomac Appalachian Trail Club, 1978.

Reeve, Thomas C. *A Question of Character: A Life of John F. Kennedy*. New York: Free Press, 1991.

Reichman, O.J. *Konza Prairie: A Tallgrass Natural History*. Lawrence: University Press of Kansas, 1991.

Reisner, Marc. *Cadillac Desert: The American West and Its Disappearing Water*. New York: Penguin, 1993.

Renehan, Edward J. *The Secret Six: The True Tale of the Men Who Conspired with John Brown*. Columbia: University of South Carolina, 1996.

Reupsch, Carl F., ed. *The Cabrillo Era and His Voyage of Discovery*. San Diego, CA: Cabrillo Historical Association, 1982.

Rice, Otis K., and Stephen W. Brown. *West Virginia: A History*. Lexington: University Press of Kentucky, 1993.

Richter, Donald H. *Guide to the Volcanoes of the Western Wrangell Mountains, Alaska: Wrangell–St. Elias National Park and Preserve*. Washington, DC: GPO, 1995.

Riddle, Jeff C. *The Indian History of the Modoc War*. Eugene, OR: Urion, 1974.

Righter, Robert W. *Crucible for Conservation: The Struggle for Grand Teton National Park*. Boulder: Colorado Association University Press, 1982.

Ripple, Jeff. *Big Cypress Swamp and the Ten Thousand Islands: Eastern America's Last Great Wilderness*. Columbia: University of South Carolina Press, 1992.

Roak, John Craig. *A Brief Historical Sketch of Gloria Dei Church (Old Swedes'), Philadelphia: Oldest Church in Pennsylvania*. Philadelphia, PA: n.p., 1938.

Roberts, Anne Rockefeller. *Mr. Rockefeller's Roads: The Untold Story of Acadia's Carriage Roads and Their Creator*. Camden, ME: Down East Books, 1990.

Robertson, James I., Jr. *Stonewall Jackson: The Man, the Soldier, the Legend*. New York: Macmillan, 1997.

Roe, JoAnn. *Stevens Pass: The Story of Railroading and Recreation in the North Cascades*. Caldwell, ID: Caxton, 2002.

Rogers, Robert F. *Destiny's Landfall: A History of Guam*. Honolulu: University of Hawaii Press, 1995.

Rohrbough, Malcolm J. *The Trans-Appalachian Frontier: People, Societies, and Institutions, 1775–1850*. Belmont, CA: Wadsworth, 1990.

Romain, William F. *Mysteries of the Hopewell: Astronomers, Geometers, and Magicians of the Eastern Wood-*

lands. Akron, OH: University of Akron Press, 2000.

Ronda, James P. *Lewis and Clark Among the Indians.* Lincoln: University of Nebraska Press, 2002.

Ross, Nola Mae Wittler. *Jean Lafitte, Louisiana Buccaneer: A Mini-History.* Lake Charles, LA: N.M.W. Ross, 1990.

Ross, Rosetta E. *Witnessing and Testifying: Black Women, Religion, and Civil Rights.* Minneapolis, MN: Fortress, 2003.

Rothman, Hal K. "Shaping the Nature of a Controversy: The Park Service, the Forest Service and the Cedar Breaks National Monument." *Utah Historical Quarterly,* Summer 1987.

———. *Preserving Different Pasts: The American National Monuments.* Urbana: University of Illinois Press, 1989.

———. *Navajo National Monument: A Place and Its People.* Santa Fe, NM: Southwest Regional Office, National Park Service, 1991. Available at www.nps.gov/nava/adhi/adhi.htm.

———. *On Rims and Ridges: The Los Alamos Area Since 1880.* Lincoln: University of Nebraska Press, 1992.

———. *Preserving the Sacred and the Secular: An Administrative History of Pipestone National Monument.* Omaha, NE: National Park Service, 1992.

———. *America's National Monuments: The Politics of Preservation.* Lawrence: University Press of Kansas, 1994.

———. *Maintaining a Legacy: An Administrative History of George Rogers Clark National Historical Park.* Omaha, NE: National Park Service, 1994.

———. *On Rims and Ridges: The Los Alamos Area Since 1880.* Lincoln: University of Nebraska Press, 1997.

———. "Promise Beheld and the Limits of Place: A Historic Resource Study of Carlsbad Caverns and Guadalupe Mountains National Parks and the Surrounding Areas." Washington, DC: National Park Service, 1998.

———. *LBJ's Texas White House: "Our Heart's Home."* College Station: Texas A&M University Press, 2001. Also available at: www.nps.gov/lyjo/Ourheart%27shome/index.htm.

———. *Balancing the Mandates: An Administrative History of Lake Mead National Recreation Area.* Boulder City, NV: National Park Service, 2002.

———. *Neon Metropolis: How Las Vegas Started the Twenty-First Century.* New York: Routledge, 2002.

———. *The Park That Makes Its Own Weather: An Administrative History of Golden Gate National Recreation Area.* San Francisco: National Park Service, 2002.

———. *The New Urban Park: Golden Gate National Recreation Area and Civic Environmentalism.* Lawrence: University Press of Kansas, 2003.

Rountree, Helen C. *Before and After Jamestown: Virginia's Powhatans and Their Predecessors.* Gainesville: University Press of Florida, 2002.

Royster, Charles. *A Revolutionary People at War: The Continental Army and American Character, 1775–1783.* Charlottesville: University of Virginia Press, 1979.

———. *Light-Horse Harry Lee and the Legacy of the American Revolution.* Baton Rouge: Louisiana State University Press, 1994.

Runte, Alfred. *National Parks: The American Experience.* Lincoln: University of Nebraska Press, 1987.

———. *Yosemite: The Embattled Wilderness.* Lincoln: University of Nebraska Press, 1993.

Russell, Peter. *Gila Cliff Dwellings National Monument: An Administrative History.* Santa Fe, NM: Southwest Region, Division of History, National Park Service, 1992. Available at www.nps.gov/gicl/adhi/adhi.htm.

Russell, William Howard. *My Diary, North and South.* Philadelphia, PA: Temple University Press, 1987.

Ryser, Fred A. *Birds of the Great Basin: A Natural History.* Reno: University of Nevada Press, 1985.

Salinger, Pierre. *John F. Kennedy: Commander-in-Chief.* New York: Penguin, 1997.

Sandburg, Carl. *The Complete Poems of Carl Sandburg.* New York: Harcourt Brace Jovanovich, 1970.

———. *Abraham Lincoln: The Prairie Years and the War Years.* San Diego, CA: Harcourt, Brace, Jovanovich, 1982.

Sandburg, H., and G. Crile. *Above and Below: A Journey Through Our National Underwater Parks.* New York: McGraw-Hill, 1969.

Sandburg, Helga. *A Great and Glorious Romance: The Story of Carl Sandburg and Lilian Steichen.* New York: Harcourt Brace Jovanovich, 1978.

Sanders, Peggy. *Wind Cave National Park: The First 100 Years.* Chicago: Arcadia, 2003.

Saunt, Claudio. *A New Order of Things: Property, Power, and the Transformation of the Creek Indians, 1733–1816.* Cambridge, UK, and New York: Cambridge University Press, 1999.

Saylor, Roger B. *The Railroads of Pennsylvania.* University Park: Pennsylvania State University, 1964.

Schaffer, Jeffrey P. *Lassen Volcanic National Park & Vicinity: A Natural-History Guide to Lassen Volcanic National Park, Caribou Wilderness, Thousand Lakes Wilderness, Hat Creek Valley, and McArthur–Burney Falls State Park.* Berkeley, CA: Wilderness, 1986.

Schiller, Herbert M. *Sumter Is Avenged! The Siege and Reduction of Fort Pulaski.* Shippensburg, PA: White Mane, 1995.

———. *Fort Pulaski and the Defense of Savannah.* Conshohocken, PA: Eastern National Park and Monument Association, 1997.

Schlesinger, Arthur M., Jr. *The Coming of the New Deal.* Boston: Houghton Mifflin, 1988.

———. *The Crisis of the Old Order, 1919–1933.* Boston: Houghton Mifflin, 1988.

———. *The Politics of Upheaval.* Boston: Houghton Mifflin, 1988.

Schneider, Mark L. *Boston Confronts Jim Crow, 1890–1920.* Boston: Northeastern University Press, 1997.

Schneider, Paul. *The Enduring Shore: A History of Cape Cod, Martha's Vineyard, and Nantucket.* New York: Henry Holt, 2000.

Schneider-Hector, Dietmar. *White Sands: The History of a National Monument.* Albuquerque: University of New Mexico Press, 1993.

Schock-Roberts, Lisa. *A Classic Western Quarrel: A History of the Road Controversy at Colorado National Monument.* Denver, CO: National Park Service, 1997.

Scholes, Walter Vinton. *The Foreign Policies of the Taft Administration.* Columbia: University of Missouri Press, 1970.

Schrepfer, Susan. *The Fight to Save the Redwoods: A History of Environmental Reform 1971–1978.* Madison: University of Wisconsin Press, 1983.

Schroeder, Albert H. *Of Men and Volcanoes: The Sinagua of Northern Arizona.* Globe, AZ: Southwest Parks and Monuments Association, 1977.

Schullery, Paul D. *Searching for Yellowstone: Ecology and Wonder in the Last Wilderness.* Boston: Houghton Mifflin, 1997.

Schulte, Steven C. *Wayne Aspinall and the Shaping of the American West.* Niwot: University Press of Colorado, 2002.

Schwantes, Carlos. *In Mountain Shadows: A History of Idaho.* Lincoln: University of Nebraska Press, 1990.

———. *The Pacific Northwest: An Interpretive History.* Lincoln: University of Nebraska Press, 1996.

Schwendinger, Robert J. *International Port of Call: An Illustrated Maritime History of the Golden Gate.* Woodland Hills, CA: Windsor Publications, 1984.

Scott, Lawrence P. *Double V: The Civil Rights Struggle of the Tuskegee Airmen.* East Lansing: Michigan State University Press, 1994.

Seabrook, Charles. *Cumberland Island: Strong Women, Wild Horses.* Winston-Salem, NC: John F. Blair, 2002.

Sears, Stephen W. *Landscape Turned Red.* Norwalk, CT: Easton, 1983.

———. *Chancellorsville.* Boston: Houghton Mifflin, 1996.

Sebastian, Lynne. *The Chaco Anasazi: Sociopolitical Evolution in the Prehistoric Southwest.* New York: Cambridge University Press, 1992.

Seitz, Frederick. *The Cosmic Inventor: Reginald Aubrey Fessenden (1866–1932).* Philadelphia, PA: American Philosophical Society, 1999.

Sellars, Richard. *Natural Resource Management in the National Parks: A History.* New Haven, CT: Yale University Press, 1997.

———. *Preserving Nature in the National Parks: A History.* New Haven, CT: Yale University Press, 1997.

Seymour, Randy. *Wildflowers of Mammoth Cave National Park.* Lexington: University Press of Kentucky, 1997.

Shaara, Jeff. *Rise to Rebellion.* New York: Ballantine Books, 2001.

Shaara, Michael. *The Killer Angels.* New York: Ballantine Books, 1993.

Shafer, Harry J. *Ancient Texans: Rock Art and Lifeways Along the Lower Pecos.* Houston, TX: Gulf, 1992.

Shaffer, Marguerite. *See America First: Tourism and National Identity, 1880–1940.* Washington, DC: Smithsonian Institution, 2001.

Shallat, Todd A., and Kathryn Ann Baxter. *Secrets of the Magic Valley and Hagerman's Remarkable Horse.* Boise, ID: Black Canyon Communications, 2002.

Shankland, Robert. *Steve Mather of the National Parks.* New York: Alfred A. Knopf, 1953; 3rd ed. 1970.

Shape, William. *Faith of Fools: A Journal of the Klondike Gold Rush.* Pullman: Washington State University Press, 1998.

Shaw, Edward R. *Legends of Fire Island Beach and the South Side.* Port Washington, NY: I.J. Friedman, 1969.

Shaw, Ronald E. *Erie Water West: A History of the Erie Canal, 1792–1854.* Lexington: University Press of Kentucky, 1990.

———. *Canals for a Nation: The Canal Era in the United States, 1790–1860.* Lexington: University Press of Kentucky, 1993.

Shea, William L. *War in the West: Pea Ridge and Prairie Grove.* Fort Worth, TX: Ryan Place, 1996.

Shea, William L., and Earl J. Hess. *Pea Ridge: Civil War Campaign in the West.* Chapel Hill: University of North Carolina Press, 1992.

Sheads, Scott, and Merle T. Cole. *Fort McHenry and Baltimore's Harbor Defenses.* Charleston, SC: Arcadia, 2001.

Sheire, James W. *Padre Island National Seashore: Historic Resource Study.* Washington, DC: Office of History & Historic Architecture, 1971.

Shelton, Napier. *Superior Wilderness: Isle Royale National Park.* Houghton, MI: Isle Royale Natural History Association, 1997.

Sherman, William T. *Memoirs of W.T. Sherman.* New York: Library of America, 1990.

Sherwood, Morgan B. *Big Game in Alaska: A History of Wildlife and People.* New Haven, CT: Yale University Press, 1981.

Shoemaker, Earl Arthur. *The Permanent Indian Frontier: The Reason for the Construction and Abandonment of*

Fort Scott, Kansas, During the Dragoon Era: A Special History Study. Washington, DC: National Park Service, 1986.

Shrepfer, Susan. *The Fight to Save the Redwoods.* Madison: University of Wisconsin Press, 1983.

Siebert, Diane. *Rhyolite: The True Story of a Ghost Town.* New York: Clarion Books, 2003.

Siebert, Wilbur Henry. *The Underground Railroad from Slavery to Freedom.* 1898. Reprint, New York: Arno, 1968.

Silbey, Joel H. *Martin Van Buren and the Emergence of American Popular Politics.* Lanham, MD: Rowman & Littlefield, 2002.

Silverman, Kenneth. *Edgar A. Poe: Mournful and Never-ending Remembrance.* New York: HarperCollins, 1991.

Simmons, Glen. *Gladesmen: Gator Hunters, Moonshiners, and Skiffers.* Gainesville: University Press of Florida, 1998.

Simonelli, Jeanne M. *Crossing Between Worlds: The Navajos of Canyon de Chelly.* Santa Fe, NM: School of American Research, 1997.

Simpson, Marcus B. *Birds of the Blue Ridge Mountains: A Guide for the Blue Ridge Parkway, Great Smoky Mountains, Shenandoah National Park, and Neighboring Areas.* Chapel Hill: University of North Carolina, 1992.

Sinden, Frank W., Robert H. Socolow, and Harold A. Feiveson, eds. *Boundaries of Analysis: An Inquiry into the Tocks Island Dam Controversy.* Boston: Ballinger, 1976.

Sites, George Lytrelle. *Boater's Guide to Biscayne Bay: Miami to Jewfish Creek.* Coral Gables, FL: University of Miami Press, 1971.

Sitton, Thad. *Backwoodsmen: Stockmen and Hunters Along a Big Thicket River Valley.* Norman: University of Oklahoma Press, 1995.

Skinner, Woodward B. *The Apache Rock Crumbles: The Captivity of Geronimo's People.* Pensacola, FL: Skinner, 1987.

Slackman, Michael. *Remembering Pearl Harbor: The Story of the USS Arizona Memorial.* Honolulu, HI: Arizona Memorial Museum Association, 1984.

Slater, John M. *El Morro, Inscription Rock, New Mexico: The Rock Itself, the Inscriptions Thereon, and the Travelers Who Made Them.* Los Angeles: Plantin, 1961.

Slotkin, Richard. *The Crater.* New York: Henry Holt, 1996.

Smith, Gaddis. *Morality, Reason, and Power: American Diplomacy in the Carter Years.* New York: Hill and Wang, 1986.

Smith, Jean Edward. *Grant.* New York: Simon and Schuster, 2001.

Smith, Robert B., and Lee J. Siegel. *Windows into the Earth: The Geologic Story of Yellowstone and Grand Teton National Parks.* New York: Oxford University Press, 2000.

Smith, Walter R. *Aniakchak Crater, Alaska Peninsula.* Washington, DC: Government Printing Office, 1925.

Snow, Edward Rowe. *The Islands of Boston Harbor, 1630–1971.* New York: Dodd, Mead, 1971.

Sontag, Bill, ed. *National Park Service: The First 75 Years.* Washington, DC: National Park Service, 2000. Available at www.cr.nps.gov/history/online_books/sontag/index.htm.

Souza, Donna J. *The Persistence of Sail in the Age of Steam: Underwater Archaeological Evidence from the Dry Tortugas.* Boston: Plenum, 1998.

Spalding, Phinizy. *Oglethorpe in America.* Athens: University of Georgia Press, 1984.

Spalding, Phinizy, and Harvey H. Jackson, eds. *Oglethorpe in Perspective: Georgia's Founder after Two Hundred Years.* Tuscaloosa: University of Alabama Press, 1989.

Spilsbury, Gail. *Rock Creek Park.* Baltimore, MD: Johns Hopkins University Press, 2003.

Sproul, David Kent. *A Bridge Between Cultures: An Administrative History of Rainbow Bridge National Monument.* Denver, CO: National Park Service, Intermountain Region, 2001. Available at www.nps.gov/rabr/adhi/adhi.htm.

Stampp, Kenneth M. *And the War Came: The North and the Secession Crisis, 1860–1861.* Westport, CT: Greenwood, 1980.

Stannard, David E. *Before the Horror: The Population of Hawai'i on the Eve of Western Contact.* Honolulu: University of Hawaii, Social Science Research Institute, 1989.

Stanton, Elizabeth Cady. *Eighty Years and More: Reminiscences, 1815–1897.* New York: Schocken, 1971.

Steele, D. Gentry. *Land of the Desert Sun: Texas' Big Bend Country.* College Station: Texas A&M University Press, 1998.

Steers, Edward, Jr. *Blood on the Moon: The Assassination of Abraham Lincoln.* Lexington: University Press of Kentucky, 2001.

Stegner, Wallace Earle. *Mormon Country.* Lincoln: University of Nebraska Press, 1981.

——, ed. *This Is Dinosaur: Echo Park Country and Its Magic Rivers.* New York: Roberts Rinehart, 1985.

——. *Beyond the Hundredth Meridian: John Wesley Powell and the Second Opening of the West.* New York: Penguin, 1992.

Steinberg, Theodore. *Nature Incorporated: Industrialization and the Waters of New England.* New York: Cambridge University Press, 1991.

Sterling, Dorothy. *Freedom Train: The Story of Harriet Tubman.* Garden City, NY: Doubleday, 1954.

——, ed. *We Are Your Black Sisters: Black Women in the Nineteenth Century.* New York: W.W. Norton, 1984.

Stevens, Joseph E. *America's National Battlefield Parks: A Guide.* Norman: University of Oklahoma Press, 1990.

Stewart, John. *Secret of the Bats: The Exploration of Carlsbad Caverns.* Philadelphia, PA: Westminster, 1972.

Stone, Charles P. *Hawaii's Plants and Animals: Biological Sketches of Hawaii Volcanoes National Park.* Honolulu: Hawaii Natural History Association, 1994.

Strain, Paula M. *The Blue Hills of Maryland: History Along the Appalachian Trail on South Mountain and the Catoctins.* Vienna, VA: Potomac Appalachian Trail Club, 1993.

Strutin, Michal. *Chaco: A Cultural Legacy.* Tucson, AZ: Southwest Parks and Monuments Association, 1994.

Sturgeon, Stephen C. *The Politics of Western Water: The Congressional Career of Wayne Aspinall.* Tucson: University of Arizona Press, 2002.

Sullivan, Noelle, and Nicholas Peterson Vrooman. *M-ē É cci Aashi Awadi: The Knife River Indian Villages.* Medora, ND: Theodore Roosevelt Nature & History Association, 1995.

Sutter, Paul. *Driven Wild: How the Fight Against Automobiles Launched the Modern Wilderness Movement.* Seattle: University of Washington Press, 2002.

Svejda, George J. *History of the Star-Spangled Banner from 1814 to the Present.* Washington, DC: Division of History, Office of Archeology and Historic Preservation, 1969.

Svensson, Ole, ed. *Three Towns: Conservation and Renewal of Charlotte Amalia, Christiansted, and Frederiksted of the U.S. Virgin Islands.* Copenhagen: Danish West Indian Society, 1980.

Swain, Donald C. *Wilderness Defender: Horace M. Albright and Conservation.* Chicago: University of Chicago Press, 1970.

Swanberg, W.A. *First Blood: The Story of Fort Sumter.* New York: Scribner, 1957.

Swanson, James L., and Daniel R. Weinberg. *Lincoln's Assassins: Their Trial and Execution.* Santa Fe, NM: Arena Editions, 2001.

Sweeney, Edwin R. *Cochise: Chiricahua Apache Chief.* Norman: University of Oklahoma Press, 1991.

——. *Mangas Coloradas: Chief of the Chiricahua Apaches.* Norman: University of Oklahoma Press, 1998.

Symonds, Craig L. *A Battlefield Atlas of the American Revolution.* Baltimore, MD: Nautical & Aviation Publishing Company of America, 1986.

Taber, Thomas Townsend. *Railroads of Pennsylvania: Encyclopedia and Atlas.* T.T. Taber, 1987.

Tabor, R.W. *Geology of Olympic National Park.* Seattle, WA: Pacific Northwest National Parks and Forests, 1987.

Taft, William H. *The Collected Works of William Howard Taft: Four Aspects of Civic Duty/Present Day Problems.* Athens: Ohio University Press, 2001.

Taliaferro, John. *Great White Fathers: The Story of the Obsessive Quest to Create Mount Rushmore.* New York: Public Affairs, 2002.

Tallgrass Historians, L.C. *Tallgrass Prairie National Preserve Legislative History, 1920–1996.* Omaha, NE: National Park Service, 1998.

Taylor, Terri A., and Patricia C. Erigero. *Cultural Landscape Report: Fort Vancouver National Historic Site, Vancouver, Washington.* Seattle, WA: National Park Service, Pacific Northwest Region, 1992.

Tennant, Alan, and Michael Allender. *The Guadalupe Mountains of Texas.* Austin: University of Texas Press, 1980.

Terry, Ronald A. *Wind Cave: The Story Behind the Scenery.* Las Vegas, NV: KC Publications, 1998.

Thomas, Christopher A. *The Lincoln Memorial and American Life.* Princeton, NJ: Princeton University Press, 2002.

Thompson, Erwin N. *Grand Portage: A History of the Sites, People, and Fur Trade.* Washington, DC: U.S. Office of Archeology and Historic Preservation, Division of History, 1969.

——. *Modoc War: Its Military History & Topography.* Sacramento, CA: Argus Books, 1971.

Thompson, Ian. *The Towers of Hovenweep.* Mesa Verde National Park, CO: Mesa Verde Museum Association, 1993.

Thompson, Jerry. *Palo Alto Battlefield National Historic Site.* Tucson, AZ: Southwest Parks and Monuments Association, 2001.

Thorsett, Peter E. "Reorganizing the U.S. National Park Service." Unpublished paper, University of Tennessee, Knoxville, 1998.

Thurner, Arthur W. *Strangers and Sojourners: A History of Michigan's Keweenaw Peninsula.* Detroit, MI: Wayne State University Press, 1994.

Thybony, Scott. *Fire and Stone: A Road Guide to Wupatki and Sunset Crater National Monuments.* Tucson, AZ: Southwest Parks and Monuments Association, 1987.

——. *Fort Davis: The Men of Troop H.* Tucson, AZ: Southwest Parks and Monuments Association, 1990.

——. *Fort Davis National Historic Site.* Tucson, AZ: Southwest Parks and Monuments Association, 1990.

——. *Walnut Canyon.* Tucson, AZ: Southwest Parks and Monuments Association, 1996.

Titcomb, Margaret. *Native Use of Fish in Hawaii.* Honolulu: University Press of Hawaii, 1972.

Toogood, Anna Coxe. *Piscataway Park, Maryland: General Historic Background Study.* Washington, DC: U.S. Office of Archeology and Historic Preservation, 1969.

Torres, Louis. *Historic Resource Study of Cape Hatteras National Seashore.* Denver, CO: National Park Service, 1985.

——. *San Antonio Missions.* Tucson, AZ: Southwest Parks and Monuments Association, 1993.

Tourtellot, Arthur Bernon. *Lexington and Concord: The Beginning of the War of the American Revolution.* New York: W.W. Norton, 1963.

Treese, Lorett. *Valley Forge: Making and Remaking a National Symbol.* University Park: Pennsylvania State University Press, 1995.

Trefousse, Hans Louis. *Andrew Johnson: A Biography.* New York: W.W. Norton, 1997.

Trimble, Stephen. *Window into the Earth: Timpanogos Cave.* Globe, AZ: Southwest Parks and Monuments Association, 1983.

——. *The Sagebrush Ocean: A Natural History of the Great Basin.* Reno: University of Nevada Press, 1999.

——. *Great Sand Dunes National Monument: The Shape of the Wind.* Tucson, AZ: Southwest Parks and Monuments Association, 2000.

Trudeau, Noah A. *Like Men of War: Black Troops in the Civil War, 1862–1865.* Boston: Little Brown, 1998.

Truman, Harry, and Margaret Truman, ed. *Where the Buck Stops: The Personal and Private Writings of Harry S Truman.* New York: Warner Books, 1989.

Tueuer, Robert. *Voyageur Country: A Park in the Wilderness.* Minneapolis: University of Minnesota Press, 1979.

Tushnet, Mark. *Making Civil Rights Law: Thurgood Marshall and the Supreme Court, 1936–1961.* New York: Oxford University Press, 1994.

Twain, Mark. *Mississippi Writings.* New York: Viking, 1982.

Twight, Ben W. *Organizational Values and Political Power: The Forest Service Versus the Olympic National Park.* University Park: Pennsylvania State University Press, 1983.

Tyler, Ronnie C. *The Big Bend: A History of the Last Texas Frontier.* College Station: Texas A&M University Press, 1996.

Unrau, Harlan D. *Basin and Range: A History of Great Basin National Park, Nevada.* Denver, CO: National Park Service, 1990.

——. *Lake Clark National Park and Preserve, Alaska: Historic Resource Study.* Anchorage, AK: National Park Service, 1994.

Unrau, John D., Jr. *The Plains Across: The Overland Emigrants and the Trans-Mississippi West, 1840–1860.* Urbana: University of Illinois Press, 1979.

Utley, Robert Marshall. *Fort Davis National Historic Site, Texas.* Washington, DC: National Park Service, 1965.

——. *A Clash of Cultures: Fort Bowie and the Chiricahua Apaches.* Washington, DC: Office of Publications, National Park Service, 1977.

——. *Fort Union National Monument.* Washington, DC: National Park Service, 1984.

——. *Fort Union and the Santa Fe Trail.* El Paso: Texas Western, 1989.

——. *Fort Larned National Historic Site.* Tucson, AZ: Southwest Parks and Monuments Association, 1993.

Vanderbilt, Cornelius. *The Living Past of America: Pictorial Treasury of Our Historic Houses and Villages That Have Been Preserved and Restored.* New York: Crown, 1955.

Vestal, Stanley. *The Old Santa Fe Trail.* Lincoln: University of Nebraska Press, 1996.

Vivian, R. Gwinn. *Chaco Canyon.* New York: Oxford University Press, 2002.

Vuncannon, Delcie H. *Joshua Tree: The Story Behind the Scenery.* Las Vegas, NV: KC Publications, 1996.

Walker, Joseph E. *Hopewell Village: A Social and Economic History of an Iron-making Community.* Philadelphia: University of Pennsylvania Press, 1966.

Wallace, David H. *Little Kinnakeet Life-Saving Station (1874–1915)/Coast Guard Station (1915–1954), Cape Hatteras National Seashore, North Carolina.* Harpers Ferry, WV: National Park Service, 1991.

Walters, R. *Albert Gallatin: Jefferson Financier and Diplomat.* New York: Macmillan, 1957.

Ward, Geoffrey C. *Jazz: A History of America's Music.* New York: Alfred A. Knopf, 2000.

Warren, Louis Austin. *Lincoln's Youth: Indiana Years, Seven to Twenty-One, 1816–1830.* Indianapolis: Indiana Historical Society, 1991.

Warren, William W. *History of the Ojibway People.* St. Paul: Minnesota Historical Society, 1984.

Washington, Booker T. *Education of the Negro.* Albany, NY: J.B. Lyon, 1904.

——. *Working with the Hands; Being a Sequel to Up from Slavery, Covering the Author's Experiences in Industrial Training at Tuskegee.* New York: Negro Universities Press, 1969.

——. *Up from Slavery.* Edited by William L. Andrews. New York: W.W. Norton, 1995.

Wassink, Jan L. *Birds of the Pacific Northwest Mountains: The Cascade Range, the Olympic Mountains, Vancouver Island, and the Coast Mountains.* Missoula, MT: Mountain, 1995.

Waterbury, Jean Parker, ed. *Defenses and Defenders at*

St. Augustine. St. Augustine, FL: St. Augustine Historical Society, 1999.

Waters, Aaron Clement. *Selected Caves and Lava-Tube Systems in and near Lava Beds National Monument.* Washington, DC: U.S. Geological Survey, 1990.

Watson, Patty J., ed. *Archeology of the Mammoth Cave Area.* St. Louis, MO: Cave Books, 1997.

Wauer, Roland H. *Birds of Zion National Park and Vicinity.* Logan: Utah State University, 1997.

Webb, Clarence H. *The Poverty Point Culture.* Baton Rouge: Louisiana State University School of Geoscience, 1982.

Webb, Ralph C., ed., *Natural History of the Pinnacles National Monument, San Benito County, California.* Paicines, CA: Pinnacles Natural History Association, 1969.

——. *A Guide to the Plants of the Pinnacles.* Globe, AZ: Southwest Parks and Monuments Association, 1971.

Webber, Bert, and Margie Webber. *Awesome Caverns of Marble in the Oregon Caves National Monument: Documentary.* Medford, OR: Webb Research Group, 1998.

Weible, Robert, ed. *The Continuing Revolution: A History of Lowell, Massachusetts.* Lowell, MA: Lowell Historical Society, 1991.

Weig, Melvin J. *Morristown National Historical Park: A Military Capital of the American Revolution.* Washington, DC: National Park Service, 1950.

Weise, Bonnie R., and William A. White. *Padre Island National Seashore: A Guide to the Geology, Natural Environments, and History of a Texas Barrier Island.* Austin: University of Texas at Austin, 1980.

Welsh, Michael. *Dunes and Dreams: A History of White Sands National Monument.* Santa Fe, NM: National Park Service, 1995. Available at www.nps.gov/whsa/adhi/adhi.htm.

——. *A Special Place, a Sacred Trust: Preserving the Fort Davis Story.* Santa Fe, NM: Intermountain Cultural Resources Center, National Park Service, 1996. Available at www.nps.gov/foda/adhi/adhi.htm.

——. *West Side Stories: Land Use and Social Change in Albuquerque's Petroglyph Area.* Sante Fe, NM: National Park Service, 1998.

Welsh, Stanley L. *Wildflowers of Zion National Park.* Springdale, UT: Zion Natural History Association, 1999.

Wenger, Gilbert R. *The Story of Mesa Verde National Park.* Mesa Verde National Park, CO: Mesa Verde Museum, 1991.

Weslager, C.A. *The Stamp Act Congress: With an Exact Copy of the Complete Journal.* Newark: University of Delaware Press, 1976.

West, Frederick Hadleigh, and Constance F. West. *American Beginnings: The Prehistory and Paleoecology of*

Beringia. Chicago: University of Chicago Press, 1996.

Westwood, J.N. *The Age of Steam: The Locomotive, the Railroads, and Their Legacy.* San Diego, CA: Thunder Bay, 2000.

Wharton, David. *They Don't Speak Russian in Sitka: A New Look at the History of Southern Alaska.* Menlo Park, CA: Markgraf Publications Group, 1991.

Wheeler, Marjorie Spruill. *One Woman, One Vote: Rediscovering the Woman Suffrage Movement.* Troutdale, OR: New Sage, 1995.

Whisker, James B. *The United States Armory at Springfield, 1795–1865.* Lewiston, NY: E. Mellen, 1997.

"The White House: Ulysses S. Grant." Available at www.whitehouse.gov.history/presidents/ug18.html.

"The White House: William Howard Taft." Available at www.whitehouse.gov/history/presidents/wt27.html.

White, J.A. "The Hagerman Zebra and Other Wildlife." *Idaho Yesterdays* 11:1 (1967): 20–21.

White, Richard. *Land Use, Environment, and Social Change: The Shaping of Island County, Washington.* Seattle: University of Washington Press, 1980.

——. *The Roots of Dependency: Subsistence, Environment, and Social Change Among the Choctaws, Pawnees, and Navajos.* Lincoln: University of Nebraska Press, 1984.

Wilkins, Thurman. *John Muir: Apostle of Nature.* Norman: University of Oklahoma Press, 1995.

Wilkinson, Burke. *Uncommon Clay: The Life and Works of Augustus Saint Gaudens.* New York: Dover, 1992.

Williams, Frederick D., ed. *The Northwest Ordinance: Essays on Its Formulation, Provisions, and Legacy.* East Lansing: Michigan State University Press, 1989.

Williams, Michael Ann. *Great Smoky Mountains Folklife.* Jackson: University Press of Mississippi, 1995.

Willoughby, Lynn. *Fair to Middlin': The Antebellum Cotton Trade on the Apalachicola/Chattahoochee River Valley.* Tuscaloosa: University of Alabama Press, 1993.

——. *Flowing Through Time: A History of the Lower Chattahoochee River.* Tuscaloosa: University of Alabama Press, 1999.

Wills, Brian Steel. *A Battle from the Start: The Life of Nathan Bedford Forrest.* New York: HarperCollins, 1992.

Wills, Gary. *Lincoln at Gettysburg, the Words That Remade America.* New York: Simon and Schuster, 1992.

Wilson, Alexander. *The Life and Letters of Alexander Wilson.* Philadelphia, PA: American Philosophical Society, 1983.

Wilson, Graham. *The Klondike Gold Rush: Photographs from 1896–1899.* Whitehorse, Yukon, AK: Wolf Creek Books, 1997.

Wilson, Joan Hoff. *Herbert Hoover: Forgotten Progressive.* Boston: Little, Brown, 1975.

Wilson, Major L. *The Presidency of Martin Van Buren.* Lawrence: University Press of Kansas, 1984.

Wilson, Patricia L. *Old San Juan, El Morro, San Cristobal.* Helena, MT: Eastern National Park and Monument Association, 1994.

Wilson, Samuel M., ed. *The Indigenous People of the Caribbean.* Gainesville: University Press of Florida, 1997.

Wilt, Richard A. *Birds of Organ Pipe Cactus National Monument.* Globe, AZ: Southwest Parks and Monuments Association, 1976.

Winik, Jay. *April 1865: The Month That Saved America.* New York: HarperCollins, 2001.

Winks, Robin W. *Laurance S. Rockefeller: Catalyst for Conservation.* Washington, DC: Island, 1997.

——. *Frederick Billings: A Life.* Berkeley: University of California Press, 1998.

Wirth, Conrad L. *Parks, Politics, and the People.* Norman: University of Oklahoma Press, 1961; 1980.

Withey, Lynne. *Dearest Friend: A Life of Abigail Adams.* New York: Simon & Schuster, 2001.

Witzig, Fred T. *Eighty Years in the Making: A Legislative History of Voyageurs National Park.* Omaha, NE: National Park Service, 2000.

Wood, Gordon S. *The Creation of the American Republic, 1776–1787.* Chapel Hill: University of North Carolina Press, 1998.

Woodworth, Steven E. *Chickamauga: A Battlefield Guide with a Section on Chattanooga.* Lincoln: University of Nebraska Press, 1999.

Wooster, Robert. *Fort Davis: Outpost on the Texas Frontier.* Austin: Texas State Historical Association, 1994.

Worster, Donald. *A River Running West: The Life of John Wesley Powell.* New York: Oxford University Press, 2001.

Worth, John E. *The Timucuan Chiefdoms of Spanish Florida.* Gainesville: University Press of Florida, 1998.

Worthington, Glenn H. *Fighting for Time.* Shippensburg, PA: White Mane, 1994.

Wright, Bill. *Portraits from the Desert: Bill Wright's Big Bend.* Austin: University of Texas Press, 1998.

Wright, Orville. *How We Invented the Airplane: An Illustrated History.* Mineola, NY: Dover, 1989.

Yancey, Franklin D. *The Mammals of Lake Meredith National Recreation Area and Adjacent Areas, Hutchinson, Moore, and Potter Counties, Texas.* Lubbock: Museum of Texas Tech University, 1998.

Yans-McLaughlin, Virginia, and Margorie Lightman. *Ellis Island and the Peopling of America.* New York: New Press, 1997.

Yoder, Clayton P. *Delaware Canal Journal: A Definitive History of the Canal and the River Valley Through Which It Flows.* Bethlehem, PA: Canal, 1972.

Zenger, John Peter. *A Brief Narrative of the Case and Trial of John Peter Zenger, Printer of the New York Weekly Journal, by James Alexander.* Edited by Stanley Nider Katz. Cambridge, MA: Belknap Press of Harvard University Press, 1972.

Zhu, Liping. *Fort Union National Monument: An Administrative History.* Santa Fe, NM: Southwest Cultural Resources Center, National Park Service, 1992. Available at www.nps.gov/foun/adhi/adhi.htm.

INDEX